**A very warm welcome to the** [...] **otball League Review.**

This book is now commonly refe [...] ors of the media and is undoubtedly th [...] from the League's point of view, Scotti [...] ion is greatly appreciated. Sponsorshi[ ...] elop-ment of the game in this country, [...] ficial to the sponsor and I am sure tha [...] their association with this prestigious publication.

Season 1994/95 is indeed a watershed in our national game with many dramatic changes taking place both on and off the field of play. On the playing side, we witness the start of a new set-up of four divisions of ten clubs with each club playing 36 matches; two new clubs, namely Caledonian Thistle and Ross County; a new points system with three points now being awarded for a win; automatic promotion and relegation between the First and Second Divisions and Second and Third Divisions on a two up two down basis; a two leg play-off system being introduced between the ninth club in the Premier Division and the second top club in the First Division to finally decide the composition of the Premier and First Divisions for season 1995/96 and two new sponsors, Bell's and Coca-Cola, who will sponsor the League Championship and the League Cup competitions respectively and which will be renamed the Bell's League Championship and the Coca-Cola Cup.

Off the field, fans attending matches from Dingwall in the north to Stranraer in the south will notice the dramatic and indeed welcome changes taking place at many of our stadiums with clubs now requiring to comply with the Taylor Report. With major refurbishment and rebuilding work taking place at grounds particularly in the Premier Division, fans will be able to enjoy watching their football in much more comfortable and safer surroundings. As I write this article, work is carrying on at many grounds and will continue to do so throughout the course of this season and beyond, which can only be of tremendous long term benefit in encouraging fans and indeed families to attend matches in Scotland.

This book continues to grow in both content and quality and involves a tremendous amount of time and effort and I would like to extend my sincere thanks to the following:

David C. Thomson (Editor); all other staff at The Scottish Football League; the 40 member clubs; Alan Elliott; many sectors of the Scottish media for their kind assistance in providing photographs; our sponsors and contributors; Programme Publications Limited and in particular, Bill Cotton; Inglis Allen and in particular Bert Brown, Ali McLaren, Les Lovell and Jackie Hay.

In conclusion, as I have already mentioned, the next few months will witness many changes taking place both on and off the park and I am confident that the new structure will provide a fresh and exciting challenge to all clubs, officials and players with meaningful and competitive matches being sustained throughout the course of the whole season, thereby stimulating interest for fans right through until next May.

> **Scottish Football League Management Committee, Season 1994/95**
> J. Y. Craig, J.P., C.A. (President), D. B. Smith (Vice-President),
> D. McK. MacIntyre (Treasurer), I. R. Donald, J. K. Kelly, R. C. Ogilvie,
> D. W. M. Cromb, G. J. Fulston, G. S. Brown, J. W. Baxter, J. L. Smith,
> J. McGoogan, LL.B.

**HAVE AN ENJOYABLE SEASON**

*YULE CRAIG,*

*President,*

*The Scottish Football League*

---

## A WORD FROM OUR SPONSORS

For over 30 years, ale drinkers throughout the UK have been enjoying Younger's Tartan Special. Since 1749, when William Younger first started brewing in Leith, near Edinburgh, the range of Younger's ales have spread worldwide and today are easily identified by the "Father William" trademark.

As Tartan grew to become Scotland's favourite ale, so too did its commitment to supporting sport at all levels across the country. For many years, Tartan Special Football Awards were bestowed monthly upon players and managers as recognition of their contribution to Scottish football. At Junior level, Tartan sponsored the League Cup of the Scottish Junior Football Association's Central Division for several seasons.

Other popular sports such as golf, boxing and bowling have also benefited from sponsorship by Tartan Special. In 1994, the Tartan Special Indoor Bowling Classic attracted top bowlers from all over Scotland. The St. Andrew's Sporting Club in Glasgow, under the banner of Tartan Special, has brought quality boxing to thousands of enthusiasts. In more recent years, Younger's Tartan Special teamed up with the Scottish Professional Golf Championship to attract a field of top golfers to compete in a four day tournament at Dalmahoy Golf, Hotel and Country Club.

**Continuing to support Scotland's national game, Tartan Special is delighted to sponsor the 1994/95 Scottish Football League Review, an essential reference book for all football enthusiasts.**

*Collin Wood, Managing Director, Scottish Brewers*

*Lord Macfarlane of Bearsden, Chairman of United Distillers, launches the Bell's sponsorship of the new four divisional League Championships.*

# Bell's ring in new deal

*Never before, in the 104 year history of The Scottish Football League, have supporters in each division of the new League structure, had so much innovation and novelty to look forward to.*

If the critics, who have said that the domestic game was becoming staid and predictable are correct, then they cannot continue to talk down a fresh start that has radical change as the thread through a fundamental revision.

The new sponsorship of The Scottish Football League Championship by Bell's Whisky, involving a massive £6 million over the next four years, will have a dramatic effect on club finances from the top of the Premier Division to the foot of the Third Division.

Not only is the cash input to the game vital but there is a significant signpost for the sport in Scotland, with the return of the very first company to sponsor the Scottish League Cup, back to our national game.

Bell's have for some years enjoyed a fruitful link with golf's Scottish Open, and whatever the background to the termination of that support, the company's choice of football as an alternative is the clearest indication that football is alive and vibrant. But Bell's

have not been the only company to see the promotional potential at Ibrox, East End Park, Broadwood and Victoria Park, just to take a random selection through the forty venues in the new League set-up.

For one of the globe's biggest companies, Coca-Cola, have picked up where Skol left off and are the new sponsors of the Scottish League Cup, a competition that has seen an increase in goals, tight, dramatic finishes and

increased attendances as its compelling selling points.

When the support from Tartan Special for this publication and the £110,000 from B & Q, for the immensely popular B & Q Cup are added in, it is clear that this summer has been the most lucrative ever for The Scottish Football League.

And the vast income for the domestic game comes at a time when even politicians at their most optimistic, are

being rather coy when it comes to quantifying the degree by which the country is coming out of the most severe recession ever.

But it is not only in off field activity that the winds of change have blown through the game, for there are new elements to the sport, that entitle fans to approach the new season with appetites restored for the new season.

Perhaps the most interesting feature, is the change to three points for a victory, that has not only been a feature of the game in England, but was also introduced to the World Cup for the first time ever at the Finals in the U.S.A. during the summer.

And the experience in the United States during June and July, with most countries putting the emphasis firmly on attacking and entertaining football, suggest that in the Bell's Scottish League Championship there will be more adventure, more goals and less negative play to savour.

And the new incentive is coming forward at a time when the much discussed "fear factor" has been substantially reduced in the Bell's Premier Division, by the re-introduction of automatic promotion and relegation on a one-up, one down basis, with additional excitement created by a two leg Play-Off between the second bottom club in the Premier Division and the second top club in the First Division.

Although everyone inside and outside the game has their opinion as to what is the best formula to pursue, previous experience has shown two things that are a matter of record and are not in dispute.

The old extended two division Scottish League Championship set-up had outlived its usefulness when the Premier Division was introduced in 1975. Turnstile returns clearly indicated that fans would no longer pay to watch the top half dozen teams in Division One play the bottom clubs.

Further to that, even with two clubs relegated from the Premier Division's ten team compliment . . . talk about fear factor . . . attendances through the first decade of the new reconstructed League

*Sergei Baltacha, Caledonian Thistle manager, and Ross County boss, Bobby Wilson, launch the incentives package for the 1994/95 Coca-Cola Cup.*

*The B & Q Cup Trophy.*

set-up rose, season after season.

So although some experienced and respected judges from within the sport's structure still have their objections to the new slimmer divisions, history has told us, in the loudest language possible, that of crisp pound notes, that the fans like the competitive nature of a ten team Premier Division, and their opinion has to matter. And when the fans, hopefully as in last season, increase in numbers and file through the turnstiles at the opening of this new and invigorating campaign, there will be an appreciation of the bright new surroundings that many will confront.

At Tynecastle for instance, there will be the sight of the brand new Wheatfield Stand, opposite the existing Main Stand, which will rise as a monument to a summer of feverish activity that has seen Hearts get to grips

with the Taylor Report. Hibs, too, will have seats installed at Easter Road, although their efforts have been curtailed in order to give the Board time to consider what the long term best option will be to fall in line with the all seated rules.

Dundee United, too, have been busy, perhaps busier than ever, and visiting fans will be seated in a new stand to the right of the George Fox Stand and completion of the brand new two-tier East Stand at the opposite end will result in a well planned and executed development.

Aberdeen, who were at the forefront of providing comfort for fans, by being the first all seated stadium in Britain, saw the completion of the new Richard Donald Stand last season at a cost of over £4m,

*The new Wheatfield Stand being constructed at Tynecastle Park.*

*Pittodrie Stadium with the impressive Richard Donald Stand to the left.*

while St. Johnstone's McDiarmid Park, has been the role model for many clubs to use as a benchmark for spectator comfort and of course Stirling Albion's new Forthbank Stadium became the second new ground to be built in recent years.

three new purpose built stands being erected and which will all be completed at various stages during the course of this season.

Fans visiting Partick Thistle's Firhill Stadium will enjoy the

comforts of the new 6,000 East Stand opposite the Main Stand, which will be ready in October, 1994 at a cost of £2m. St. Mirren have not been left behind either, with construction of a new 3,000 seater West Stand costing £1.4m, and which will include multi-functional facilities that can be used by the Paisley public during the week, including an indoor football pitch. And of course, Celtic are now engaged in a £22m development to rebuild Celtic Park during the course of the next twelve months and during this period, have been permitted by the football authorities to play its home matches at the National Stadium, Hampden Park, which of course, has already witnessed the completion of Phase One with the building of the new North and East Stands, with Phase Two anticipated to begin within the next few months.

*Clyde's new Broadwood Stadium.*

*Partick Thistle's new East Stand under construction.*

Clyde's new stadium at Broadwood is already in use and Airdrie will be their house guests in the short term, while the Lanarkshire club watch their new stadium being constructed after Broomfield had been consigned, with affection, to the history books.

At Motherwell, the next phase of their refurbishment programme will take the Fir Park club a significant step closer to completion, with the construction of the new North Stand which will be available in January, 1995 while at Ibrox, work continues to further embellish an already magnificent stadium and edge the capacity of the Champion's ground ever higher.

Down at Rugby Park, Kilmarnock have embarked on a very ambitious project with

*Fir Park, Motherwell.*

The finance that has had to be found, and other works are going ahead at virtually every ground in the country, has had a strangling effect on the very ambitious playing staff plane of many clubs but remarkably, most have made a major impact in complying with the Taylor Report and still allocated funds to frustrated managers. The comfort of the next generation of supporters will be the justification.

In the three other divisions of the Bell's Scottish League Championship, the set-up should also increase the competitive nature, with the resultant effect being that a greater number of

meaningful fixtures should see an increase in the number of spectators attending in each division and equally important, the new set-up will place many more teams much closer to a major prize for their season's work. There will be four Champions instead of three as well as more second place promotion spots available, and with the B & Q Cup to play for, life in the lower reaches of the game, will be much more exciting, not least of all in the Highlands, where two new teams will represent that fertile part of the Scottish football map.

Caledonian and Inverness Thistle will represent that city, which has been the scene of so much Scottish Cup grief over the decades for League clubs, as Caledonian Thistle, while Ross County, also Scottish Cup shock experts, will join them in the Bell's Scottish League Third Division.

As previously mentioned, there will even be the introduction of the play-off system that has aroused so much interest in England at the end of the season, at the foot of the Premier Division and the top of the First Division. The ninth team in the top division will be required to play the second top team in the First Division, over two legs, home and away, to finally decide the make up of the two top divisions for season 1995/96.

Many will say that is virtually a return to two teams being relegated from the Premier Division and some will argue that it offers another chance to one of the many ambitious clubs striving to compete at the highest level. As always in football, once the legislators and administrators as well as the sponsors have done their bit, it will be down to two sets of players, a football, and a pitch.

So it's welcome to Bell's Whisky and Coca-Cola and hello again B & Q and Tartan Special. There will be few guarantees from this great game, which uniquely in this small country touches virtually every man, woman and child in the population. But one pledge can be given with impunity . . . it won't be dull.

**Ray Hepburn**
**(Freelance)**

*An aerial view of the impressive Ibrox Stadium.*

# Six in a row – just!

*A politician once said there is little or nothing to choose between facts, statistics and lies.*

This may be true in the world of politics where everything is twisted to suit. However in football, statistics certainly don't lie.

And on the evidence of last season's stats, the Premier Division is undoubtedly becoming more competitive if somewhat predictable. Rangers retained the title for the sixth season in succession. However, the Light Blues' winning margin of three points over closest challengers Aberdeen was their narrowest for three years.

Dundee, who were bottom of the table all season, finished 29 points behind Rangers. This also closed the gap considerably when you recall bottom club Airdrieonians ended up 44 points behind Rangers the previous season.

Without wishing to detract anything from the marvellous achievement of Rangers, the high drama of the season was reserved for the fight against the third relegation spot. Rangers eventually clinched the title on the same evening they lost to Hibernian at

Easter Road as Motherwell lost at home to Dundee United. By this time, both Aberdeen and Motherwell had run out of games in which to close the gap.

With the League set-up switching to four divisions of ten for season 1994/95, three teams had to be relegated from the Premier Division to accommodate the new set-up. While Dundee and Raith Rovers were detached for quite some time, there was a monumental struggle to avoid the third relegation spot which ensued right until the very last kick of the season.

Eventually, St Johnstone drew the short straw, going down by the narrowest margin possible, on goal difference by one goal. This, despite equalling their highest ever Premier points total of 40 and a total good enough for them to occupy sixth place the previous term.

To add insult to their agony, Saints actually won their last game of the season against Motherwell at Fir Park. However, even this praiseworthy victory wasn't enough to save Paul Sturrock's side, with Kilmarnock drawing against Hibs at Easter

Road and Hearts winning at Firhill against Partick Thistle. However, as the McDiarmid Park boss, who replaced John McClelland half way through the season, bravely admitted: "The season lasted 44 games, not just one."

Although Rangers topped the table on goal difference after their opening day victory over Hearts at Ibrox, they never opened up a substantial gap. In fact, they didn't always top the table.

With no fewer than 11 Ibrox first team pool members requiring surgery during the season, it wasn't surprising the fluency of previous seasons was missing. However, in the Scottish Football Writers'

*Walter Smith holds aloft the Premier Division trophy.*

Player of the Year, Mark Hateley, Rangers had a man for all seasons. Not only did he finish top scorer with 24 League goals from 40 appearances, the former England International striker also played comfortably at centre half against Kilmarnock at Rugby Park as the Ibrox injury list refused to go away.

Second placed Aberdeen blew hot and cold. Many reckoned this was the Dons' best chance to topple injury ravaged Rangers. However, Willie Miller's side struggled to string a run of results together, three wins in a row being their best spell.

This happened only once, not nearly often enough to put the Champions under pressure. Although the Dons had the best defensive record, losing just 35 goals, lack of goals cost them dearly. If success can be measured without trophies, Motherwell were certainly successful. Their third place finish with 54 points was a double first for the Fir Park team. Considering they just escaped relegation the previous season, this marked a massive improvement of 19 points from the same number of games.

This was achieved without the spending power of Rangers, particularly as most of Motherwell's available finances at the present time are being spent on ground reconstruction. What little manager Tommy McLean had for new players was certainly spent wisely. Look no further than Tommy Coyne, Paul Lambert and Rab Shannon. Three outstanding buys. Unfortunately, McLean and his fellow directors didn't see eye to eye over this policy and the manager resigned during the summer.

As a consequence of finishing second and third respectively, both Aberdeen and Motherwell will represent Scotland in the U.E.F.A. Cup this season.

Although Celtic closed the gap on Rangers from 13 points to eight over the year, it was still a disappointing season for the Parkhead club. With big

Tommy Coyne celebrates scoring for Motherwell in this season's preliminary round of the U.E.F.A. Cup.

Dons top scorer Duncan Shearer.

changes in the Board Room, manager's office and dressing room during the last 12 months, it may take some time yet before Celtic mount a serious challenge again.

They used four different managers, if you count interim bosses Joe Jordan and Frank Connor between Liam Brady and Lou Macari, who have both departed. Add this to using 28 different players and you'll see Celtic have a long way to go to find the required stability.

Hibs, who also lost the League Cup Final to Rangers, finished a disappointing fifth, especially after the start they got off to following the injection of new blood in the form of Jim Leighton, Kevin McAllister and Michael O'Neill.

Dundee United, at long last, won the Tennents Scottish Cup but new manager, Ivan Golac, found consistency in the League far more difficult to achieve. Amazingly United only won 11 of their 44 games with just five of these victories recorded at Tannadice. However, the ability of record £650,000 signing, Gordan Petric, from Partizan Belgrade suggests better things to come.

Hearts tied with United on 42 points, just two outside the relegation slot. However, this was not enough to keep Sandy Clark in a job. After Wallace Mercer sold 51 per cent of his shares to Chris Robinson, Clark was sacked.

Partick Thistle and Kilmarnock finished on the same total as St. Johnstone but escaped the drop by their fractionally better goal difference.

Killie in particular did well to stay up in their first season back with the big boys. Manager Tommy Burns was rightly praised for his enterprising tactics.

Thistle, too, did well given their restricted resources and crowds. Raith Rovers won many friends by their refusal to play cautiously and their 46 goal tally was the sixth best return as manager Jimmy Nicholl's refreshing style paid dividends of a kind.

Dundee never got out of the bit. Simon Stainrod didn't survive long in the hot seat before being replaced by Jim Duffy. To the Dark Blues' credit, they never resorted to defensive football and, in fact, they were a far more attractive team to watch than their position indicated.

At the end of the day however, it must be stated that fear of relegation ruined too many games.

It also resulted in a very high managerial casualty rate in the Premier Division. For one reason or another Liam Brady, Lou Macari, Simon Stainrod, Sandy Clark, Tommy McLean and John McClelland all fell by the wayside.

With three points now rewarded for a win, let us hope the new set-up leads to more expressive football this time round.

**BILL McFARLANE
(Sunday Post)**

# ABERDEEN

Pittodrie Stadium, Pittodrie Street,
Aberdeen AB2 1QH

**CHAIRMAN**
Ian R. Donald

**VICE-CHAIRMAN**
Denis J. Miller

**DIRECTORS**
Gordon A. Buchan & Stewart Milne

**SECRETARY**
Ian J. Taggart

**MANAGER**
William Miller M.B.E.

**ASSISTANT MANAGERS**
Roy Aitken & Drew Jarvie

**PLAYER/COACH**
Neil Cooper

**TRAINER**
Teddy Scott

**CLUB DOCTOR**
Dr. Derek Gray

**PHYSIOTHERAPISTS**
David Wylie & Eric Ferguson

**S.F.A. COMMUNITY COACH**
Chic McLelland

**CHIEF SCOUT**
Jimmy Carswell

**GROUNDSMAN**
Jim Warrender

**COMMERCIAL EXECUTIVE**
David Johnston
(0224) 630944

**TELEPHONES**
Ground/Ticket Office
(0224) 632328
Fax (0224) 644173
Donsline (0898) 121551

**CLUB SHOP**
c/o Crombie Sports, 23 Bridge Street,
Aberdeen, Tel (0224) 593866
and Ticket Office, c/o Aberdeen F.C.,
Pittodrie Stadium, Aberdeen

**OFFICIAL SUPPORTERS CLUB**
Association Secretary
Mrs. Susan Scott, 32 Earns Heugh
Crescent, Cove, Aberdeen AB1 4RU

**TEAM CAPTAIN**
Stewart McKimmie

**SHIRT SPONSOR**
Northsound Radio

## LIST OF PLAYERS 1994-95

| SURNAME | FIRST NAME | MIDDLE NAME | DATE OF BIRTH | PLACE OF BIRTH | DATE OF SIGNING | HEIGHT FT INS | WEIGHT ST LBS | PREVIOUS CLUB |
|---|---|---|---|---|---|---|---|---|
| Adams | Derek | | 25/06/75 | Glasgow | 05/09/91 | 5 10.0 | 10 12 | Deeside B.C. |
| Aitken | Robert | Sime | 24/11/58 | Irvine | 27/06/92 | 6 0.0 | 13 0 | St. Mirren |
| Booth | Scott | | 16/12/71 | Aberdeen | 28/07/88 | 5 9.0 | 11 10 | Deeside B.C. |
| Cooper | Neil | | 12/08/58 | Aberdeen | 23/09/91 | 5 11.0 | 12 7 | Hibernian |
| Dodds | William | | 05/02/69 | New Cumnock | 25/07/94 | 5 8.0 | 10 10 | St. Johnstone |
| Gilbert | Kenneth | | 08/03/75 | Aberdeen | 07/06/91 | 5 6.5 | 11 4 | East End "A" |
| Grant | Brian | | 19/06/64 | Bannockburn | 15/08/84 | 5 9.0 | 11 2 | Stirling Albion |
| Hetherston | Peter | | 06/11/64 | Bellshill | 04/07/94 | 5 9.0 | 10 7 | Raith Rovers |
| Irvine | Brian | Alexander | 24/05/65 | Bellshill | 19/07/85 | 6 2.5 | 13 7 | Falkirk |
| Jess | Eoin | | 13/12/70 | Aberdeen | 13/11/87 | 5 9.5 | 11 6 | Rangers |
| Kane | Paul | James | 20/06/65 | Edinburgh | 22/11/91 | 5 9.5 | 11 0 | Oldham United |
| McKimmie | Stewart | | 27/10/62 | Aberdeen | 12/12/83 | 5 8.0 | 11 4 | Dundee |
| McKinnon | Raymond | | 05/08/70 | Dundee | 07/02/94 | 5 8.0 | 9 11 | Nottingham Forest |
| Miller | Joseph | | 08/12/67 | Glasgow | 30/07/93 | 5 8.0 | 9 12 | Celtic |
| Reeley | Derek | | 26/12/74 | Glasgow | 08/08/91 | 5 8.0 | 10 7 | "S" Form |
| Robertson | Hugh | Scott | 19/03/75 | Aberdeen | 24/08/93 | 5 9.0 | 12 7 | Lewis United |
| Shearer | Duncan | | 28/08/62 | Fort William | 09/07/92 | 6 0.0 | 13 8 | Blackburn Rovers |
| Smith | Gary | | 25/03/71 | Glasgow | 06/08/91 | 6 0.0 | 11 10 | Falkirk |
| Snelders | Theodorus | G.A. | 07/12/63 | Westervoort | 22/07/88 | 6 2.0 | 14 12 | F.C. Twente |
| Stillie | Derek | | 03/12/73 | Irvine | 03/05/91 | 6 0.0 | 11 10 | Notts County |
| Thomson | Scott | Munro | 29/01/72 | Aberdeen | 05/11/91 | 5 10.0 | 11 10 | Brechin City |
| Watt | Michael | | 27/11/70 | Aberdeen | 02/07/87 | 6 1.0 | 12 6 | Cove Rangers "A" |
| Winnie | David | | 26/10/66 | Glasgow | 22/11/90 | 6 1.0 | 12 7 | St. Mirren |
| Woodthorpe | Colin | | 13/01/69 | Liverpool | 19/07/94 | 6 1.0 | 12 4 | Norwich City |
| Wright | Stephen | | 27/08/71 | Bellshill | 28/11/87 | 5 10.5 | 11 2 | Eastercraigs |

## MILESTONES

**YEAR OF FORMATION**: 1903
**MOST CAPPED PLAYER**: Alex McLeish
**NO. OF CAPS**: 77
**MOST LEAGUE POINTS IN A SEASON**: 64 (Premier Division - Season 1992/93) (44 games)
**MOST LEAGUE GOALS SCORED BY A PLAYER IN A SEASON**: Benny Yorston (Season 1929/30)
**NO. OF GOALS SCORED**: 38
**RECORD ATTENDANCE**: 45,061 (-v- Heart of Midlothian – 13.3.1954)
**RECORD VICTORY**: 13-0 (-v- Peterhead – Scottish Cup 9.2.1923)
**RECORD DEFEAT**: 0-8 (-v- Celtic – Division 1, 30.1.65)

## SEASON TICKET INFORMATION

### Seated
Main Stand Centre Adult ........................................ £225
Wing Stand Adult .................................................... £210
South Stand Adult .................................................. £160
Merkland Stand Parent & Juvenile .......................... £200
Merkland Stand Juvenile/OAP ................................. £60
Richard Donald Stand ............................. £210/185/160

## LEAGUE ADMISSION PRICES

### Seated
Main Stand Centre Adult ......................................... £15
Main Stand Wing Adult ......................................... £13.50
South Stand Home Support ....................................... £9
South Stand East (Visitors) Adult ........................... £9.50
                        Juvenile/OAP .................... £4
Merkland Stand Adult .............................................. £8
                    Juvenile/OAP .............................. £3.50
Richard Donald Stand ............................................... £9

REGISTERED STRIP: Shirt – Red with Dark Blue Multi Pattern on Right Hand Side and Left Sleeve. Dark Blue Trim on Collar
Shorts - Red with Dark Blue Multi Pattern on Right Hand Side
Stockings – Red with Dark Blue Diamonds and Two Horizontal White Stripes at Top

CHANGE STRIP: Shirt – Navy with Gold Stripes, Shorts – Navy with Gold Trim, Stockings – Navy with Gold Trim

# CLUB FACTFILE 1993/94 . . RESULTS . . APPEARANCES . . SCORERS

## The DONS

| Date | Venue | Opponents | Result | Snelders T. | McKimmie S. | Connor R. | Grant B. | Irvine B. | Smith G. | Richardson L. | Bett J. | Booth S. | Jess E. | Paatelainen M-M. | Shearer D. | Kane P. | McLeish A. | Miller J. | Wright S. | Aitken R. | Ten Caat T. | Winnie D. | Gibson A. | Watt M. | Roddie A. | Stillie D. | Robertson H. | Burridge J. | McKinnon R. | Thomson S. |
|---|---|---|---|---|---|---|---|---|---|---|---|---|---|---|---|---|---|---|---|---|---|---|---|---|---|---|---|---|---|---|
| Aug 7 | A | Dundee United | 1-1 | 1 | 2 | 3 | 4 | 5 | 6 | 7 | 8 | 9[1] | 10 | 11 | 12 | | | | | | | | | | | | | | | |
| 14 | H | Kilmarnock | 1-0 | 1 | 2 | 3 | | | 6 | 7 | 8 | 9 | 14 | 11 | 10 | 4[1] | 5 | 12 | | | | | | | | | | | | |
| 21 | A | Dundee | 1-1 | 1 | 2 | 14 | | | 6 | 7 | | | 9 | 11 | 10[1] | 4 | 5 | 8 | 3 | 12 | | | | | | | | | | |
| 28 | H | St. Johnstone | 0-0 | 1 | 2 | | | 6 | 3 | 8 | | 9 | 7 | 12 | 10 | 4 | 5 | 14 | | | 11 | | | | | | | | | |
| Sep 4 | A | Celtic | 1-0 | 1 | 2 | 3 | | 6 | | 7 | 8 | 9 | 14 | 12[1] | 10 | 4 | 5 | 11 | | | | | | | | | | | | |
| 11 | A | Hibernian | 1-2 | 1 | 2 | 3 | | 6 | | | 8 | | 9 | 11 | 10[1] | 4 | 5 | 7 | | | | 12 | 14 | | | | | | | |
| 18 | H | Rangers | †2-0 | 1 | 2 | 11 | | 6 | | 8 | | 14 | 9 | 12 | 10[1] | 4 | 5 | 7 | 3 | | | | | | | | | | | |
| 25 | H | Raith Rovers | 4-1 | 1 | 2 | 11 | | 6 | | 8[2] | | | 9[1] | 14 | 10[1] | 4 | 5 | 7 | 3 | | 12 | | | | | | | | | |
| Oct 2 | A | Motherwell | 0-0 | 1 | 2 | 11 | | 6 | 14 | 8 | | | 9 | 12 | 10 | 4 | 5 | 7 | 3 | | | | | | | | | | | |
| 5 | H | Heart of Midlothian | 0-0 | 1 | 2 | 11 | | 6 | | 8 | | | | 14 | 10 | 4 | 5 | 7 | 3 | | 12 | | 9 | | | | | | | |
| 9 | A | Partick Thistle | 2-3 | | 2 | 12 | | 6 | 14 | | 8 | | 9 | 11[1] | 10[1] | 4 | 5 | 7 | 3 | | | | | 1 | | | | | | |
| 14 | A | Kilmarnock | 1-1 | 1 | 2 | 12 | 8 | 6 | 3 | 7 | | 14 | 9 | 11[1] | 10 | 4 | 5 | | | | | | | | | | | | | |
| 23 | H | Dundee United | 2-0 | 1 | 2 | | 8 | 6 | 3 | 7 | | | 9 | 11[1] | 10[1] | 4 | 5 | 12 | 14 | | | | | | | | | | | |
| 30 | H | Dundee | 1-0 | 1 | 2 | 12 | 8 | 6 | 3 | 7 | | 14 | 9 | 11 | 10[1] | 4 | 5 | | | | | | | | | | | | | |
| Nov 6 | A | St. Johnstone | 1-1 | 1 | 2 | 3 | 8 | 6 | | 7 | | 14[1] | 9 | 11 | 10 | 4 | 5 | | 12 | | | | | | | | | | | |
| 9 | H | Celtic | †1-1 | 1 | 2 | 3 | 8 | 6 | | 7 | | 9 | 10 | | 12 | 4 | | 11 | 5 | | | 14 | | | | | | | | |
| 13 | H | Motherwell | 1-1 | | 2 | 3 | 8 | 6 | | 7 | | 9[1] | | 11 | 14 | 4 | | 10 | 5 | | | | | 1 | | | | | | |
| 27 | H | Hibernian | 4-0 | 1 | 2 | 11[1] | 8[1] | 6 | | | | | 9 | | 10[1] | 4[1] | 5 | 7 | 3 | | | | | | | | | | | |
| Dec 1 | A | Rangers | 0-2 | | 2 | 11 | 8 | 6 | | 14 | | | 9 | 12 | 10 | 4 | 5 | 7 | 3 | | | | | 1 | | | | | | |
| 4 | A | Heart of Midlothian | 1-1 | 1 | | 11 | 8 | 6 | 3 | 14 | | | 10 | 9 | 12[1] | 4 | 5 | 7 | 2 | | | | | | | | | | | |
| 7 | A | Raith Rovers | 1-1 | 1 | | 3 | 8 | 6 | | 11 | | 9 | 14 | 12 | 10 | 4 | 5 | 7[1] | 2 | | | | | | | | | | | |
| 14 | H | Partick Thistle | 2-1 | 1 | | 11 | 8 | 6[1] | 3 | | | 14 | 9 | 12 | 10[1] | 4 | 5 | 7 | 2 | | | | | | | | | | | |
| 18 | H | Kilmarnock | 3-1 | 1 | | 11 | | 6 | 3 | 8[1] | | 14 | 9 | 12 | 10[1] | 4 | 5 | 7[1] | 2 | | | | | | | | | | | |
| 27 | A | Dundee United | 1-0 | 1 | 2 | 11 | | 6 | | | | 14 | 9[1] | 12 | 10 | 4 | 5 | 7 | 3 | | | 8 | | | | | | | | |
| Jan 8 | H | St. Johnstone | 1-1 | 1 | 2 | 11 | 12 | 6 | | | | 14 | 9 | | 10[1] | 4 | 5 | 7 | 3 | | | 8 | | | | | | | | |
| 11 | A | Dundee | 1-0 | 1 | 2 | 11 | 8 | 6[1] | | | | 9 | 7 | | 10 | 4 | 5 | | 3 | | | 12 | | | 14 | | | | | |
| 19 | A | Celtic | 2-2 | | 2 | | 8 | 6[1] | | 11 | | 14 | 9[1] | | 10 | 4 | 5 | 7 | 3 | | | 12 | | 1 | | | | | | |
| 22 | H | Rangers | 0-0 | 1 | 2 | | 8 | 6 | | 11 | | 14 | 9 | 12 | 10 | 4 | 5 | 7 | 3 | | | | | | | | | | | |
| Feb 5 | A | Hibernian | 1-3 | 1 | 2 | 11 | 4 | 6 | | 8[1] | | 9 | 7 | 14 | 10 | | 5 | | 3 | | | | | | | | | | | |
| 12 | H | Raith Rovers | 4-0 | 1 | 2 | | 4 | 6 | | | 8 | 14[1] | 7 | 11[2] | 10[1] | 9 | 5 | | 3 | | | | | | | | | | | |
| Mar 5 | H | Heart of Midlothian | 0-1 | 1 | 2 | | 4 | 6 | | 8 | | 9 | | 12 | 10 | 11 | 5 | 7 | 3 | | | | | | | ` 13 | | | | |
| 8 | A | Motherwell | 1-1 | | 2 | | 12 | 6 | 4 | 8 | | 9 | 7 | 14 | 10[1] | 11 | 5 | | 3 | | | | | | | 1 | | | | |
| 19 | A | Kilmarnock | 3-2 | | 2 | | | 6 | 4 | 8 | | | 7[1] | 14 | 10[1] | 11 | 5 | 9[1] | 3 | | | | | | | 1 | | | | |
| 26 | H | Dundee United | 1-0 | | 2 | | 12 | 6 | | 8 | | | 7 | 14 | 10[1] | 4 | 5 | 9 | 3 | | | | | | | 1 | 11 | | | |
| 29 | H | Hibernian | 2-3 | | 2 | | | 6 | | 8 | | | 7[1] | 14 | 10 | 4 | 5 | 9[1] | 3 | | | | | | | 1 | 11 | | | |
| Apr 2 | A | Rangers | 1-1 | | 2 | | 11 | 6 | | 8 | | | 7 | 12 | 10 | 4[1] | 5 | | 3 | | | | | | | | | 1 | 9 | |
| 5 | A | Partick Thistle | †1-1 | | 2 | | 11 | 6 | | 8 | | | 7 | 10 | | 4 | 5 | | | | | | | | | | 3 | 1 | 9 | 14 |
| 16 | H | Motherwell | 0-0 | 1 | 2 | | 12 | 6 | 3 | 8 | | 9 | 7 | | 10 | 4 | 5 | | 11 | | | | | | | | | | | |
| 23 | H | Partick Thistle | 2-0 | 1 | 2 | | 8[1] | 6 | 5 | 14 | | 9 | 7[1] | 12 | 10 | 4 | | | 3 | | | | | | | | | | 11 | |
| 27 | A | Heart of Midlothian | 1-1 | 1 | 2 | | 8 | 6[1] | 5 | | | 9 | 7 | 12 | 10 | | | | 3 | | | | | | 14 | | 11 | | 4 | |
| 30 | H | Dundee | 1-1 | 1 | 2 | | 4 | 6[1] | 5 | 8 | | | 7 | 11 | 10 | | | | 3 | | | | | | 12 | | 9 | | | 14 |
| May 3 | A | Raith Rovers | 2-0 | 1 | 2 | | 4 | 6 | 5 | 8 | | | 7 | 12 | 10[1] | | | | 3 | | | | | | 11[1] | | 9 | | | 14 |
| 7 | A | St. Johnstone | 1-0 | 1 | 2 | | 4 | 6[1] | 5 | 12 | | | 7 | | 10 | 8 | | | 3 | | | | | | 11 | | 14 | | 9 | |
| 14 | H | Celtic | 1-1 | | 2 | | 4 | 6[1] | 5 | 8 | | | 7 | | 10 | 9 | | | 3 | | | | | | 11 | | 14 | 1 | | |
| TOTAL FULL APPEARANCES | | | | 33 | 40 | 21 | 26 | 42 | 19 | 31 | 6 | 14 | 38 | 14 | 39 | 39 | 35 | 24 | 34 | | 1 | 2 | 1 | 4 | 3 | 4 | 6 | 3 | 5 | |
| TOTAL SUB APPEARANCES | | | | | | (4) | (4) | | (2) | (4) | | (11) | (3) | (22) | (4) | | | (3) | (2) | (1) | (2) | (4) | (1) | | (3) | (1) | (2) | | | (3) |
| TOTAL GOALS SCORED | | | | | | 1 | 2 | 7 | | 4 | | 4 | 6 | 6 | 17 | 3 | | 4 | | | | | | | 1 | | | | | |

*Small bold figures denote goalscorers. † denotes opponent's own goal.*

## PITTODRIE STADIUM

**CAPACITY:** 21,634 (All seated)

**PITCH DIMENSIONS:** 109 yds x 72 yds

**FACILITIES FOR DISABLED SUPPORTERS:** Wheelchair section in front of Merkland Stand and in front row of Richard Donald Stand and also front row of Main Stand Section F. (Please telephone Ticket Office and reserve place(s) in advance).

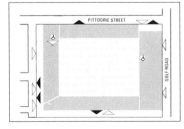

## HOW TO GET THERE

**You can reach Pittodrie Stadium by these routes:**

**BUSES:** The following buses all depart from the city centre to within a hundred yards of the ground. Nos. 1, 2, 3 and 11.

**TRAINS:** The main Aberdeen station is in the centre of the city and the above buses will then take fans to the ground.

**CARS:** Motor Vehicles coming from the city centre should travel along Union Street, then turn into King Street and the park will be on your right, about half a mile further on.

Parking on Beach Boulevard, King Street and Golf Road.

# CELTIC

**LIST OF PLAYERS 1994-95**

| SURNAME | FIRST NAME | MIDDLE NAME | DATE OF BIRTH | PLACE OF BIRTH | DATE OF SIGNING | HEIGHT FT INS | WEIGHT ST LBS | PREVIOUS CLUB |
|---------|-----------|-------------|---------------|----------------|-----------------|---------------|---------------|---------------|
| Bonner | Patrick | Joseph | 24/05/60 | Donegal | 06/08/94 | 6 2.0 | 13 1 | Keadue Rovers |
| Boyd | Thomas | | 24/11/65 | Glasgow | 06/02/92 | 5 11.0 | 11 4 | Chelsea |
| Byrne | Paul | Peter | 13/06/72 | Dublin | 26/05/93 | 5 11.0 | 13 0 | Bangor |
| Carberry | Garrett | | 01/11/75 | Glasgow | 27/05/93 | 5 11.0 | 10 7 | Celtic B.C. |
| Collins | John | Angus P. | 31/01/68 | Galashiels | 13/07/90 | 5 7.0 | 10 10 | Hibernian |
| Donnelly | Simon | | 01/12/74 | Glasgow | 27/05/93 | 5 9.0 | 10 12 | Celtic B.C. |
| Falconer | William | Henry | 05/04/66 | Aberdeen | 10/02/94 | 6 1.0 | 13 0 | Sheffield United |
| Galloway | Michael | | 30/05/65 | Oswestry | 16/06/89 | 6 0.0 | 13 0 | Heart of Midlothian |
| Gillespie | Gary | Thomson | 05/07/60 | Bonnybridge | 15/08/91 | 6 3.0 | 13 0 | Liverpool |
| Grant | Peter | | 30/08/65 | Bellshill | 27/07/82 | 5 9.0 | 10 3 | Celtic B.C. |
| Gray | Stuart | | 18/12/73 | Harrogate | 07/07/92 | 5 11.0 | 11 0 | Giffnock North A.F.C. |
| Hay | Christopher | Drummond | 28/08/74 | Glasgow | 27/05/93 | 5 11.0 | 11 7 | Giffnock North A.F.C. |
| Kerr | Stewart | | 13/11/74 | Bellshill | 27/05/93 | 6 2.0 | 13 0 | Celtic B.C. |
| Mackay | Malcolm | George | 19/02/72 | Bellshill | 06/08/93 | 6 1.0 | 11 7 | Queen's Park |
| Marshall | Gordon | George B. | 19/04/64 | Edinburgh | 12/08/91 | 6 2.0 | 12 0 | Falkirk |
| Martin | Lee | Andrew | 05/02/68 | Hyde | 19/01/94 | 5 11.0 | 12 8 | Manchester United |
| McAdam | Thomas | Ian | 09/04/54 | Glasgow | 13/07/93 | 6 0.0 | 12 9 | Airdrieonians |
| McGinlay | Patrick | David | 30/05/67 | Glasgow | 30/07/93 | 5 10.0 | 11 10 | Hibernian |
| McLaughlin | Brian | | 14/05/74 | Bellshill | 07/07/92 | 5 4.0 | 8 7 | Giffnock North A.F.C. |
| McNally | Mark | | 10/03/71 | Motherwell | 15/05/87 | 5 9.0 | 10 7 | Celtic B.C. |
| McQuilken | James | | 03/10/74 | Glasgow | 31/03/93 | 5 9.0 | 10 7 | Giffnock North B.C. |
| McStay | Paul | Michael L. | 22/10/64 | Hamilton | 20/02/81 | 5 10.0 | 10 7 | Celtic B.C. |
| McStay | Raymond | | 16/05/70 | Hamilton | 15/05/87 | 5 11.0 | 11 0 | Celtic B.C. |
| Moran | James | | 09/10/75 | Glasgow | 07/12/93 | 5 10.0 | 10 7 | Possilpark Y.M.C.A. |
| Mowbray | Anthony | Mark | 22/11/63 | Saltburn | 08/11/91 | 6 1.0 | 13 2 | Middlesbrough |
| Nicholas | Charles | | 30/12/61 | Glasgow | 04/08/94 | 5 9.0 | 11 0 | Aberdeen |
| O'Neil | Brian | | 06/09/72 | Paisley | 10/07/91 | 6 1.0 | 12 4 | Porirua Viard United |
| O'Neill | John | Joseph | 03/01/74 | Glasgow | 16/05/94 | 5 10.0 | 10 4 | Queen's Park |
| Paterson | Alistair | James | 02/08/75 | Dundee | 08/06/94 | 5 8.5 | 9 6 | Unattached |
| Slavin | James | | 18/01/75 | Lanark | 24/12/92 | 6 2.0 | 14 0 | Giffnock North A.F.C. |
| Smith | Barry | Martin | 19/02/74 | Paisley | 21/06/91 | 5 10.0 | 12 0 | Giffnock North A.F.C. |
| Vata | Rudi | | 13/02/69 | Schroder | 18/08/92 | 6 1.0 | 12 5 | Dinamo Tirana |
| Walker | Andrew | | 06/04/65 | Glasgow | 01/07/94 | 5 8.0 | 10 7 | Bolton Wanderers |
| White | Gerald | | 10/07/76 | Bellshill | 08/06/94 | 5 11.5 | 13 5 | Celtic B.C. |

## MILESTONES

**YEAR OF FORMATION:** 1888
**MOST CAPPED PLAYER:** Paul McStay
**NO. OF CAPS:** 69
**MOST LEAGUE POINTS IN A SEASON:** 72 (Premier Division – Season 1987/88)
**MOST LEAGUE GOALS SCORED BY A PLAYER IN A SEASON:** Jimmy McGrory (Season 1935/36)
**NO. OF GOALS SCORED:** 50
**RECORD ATTENDANCE:** 92,000 (-v- Rangers 1.1.1938)
**RECORD VICTORY:** 11-0 (-v- Dundee – Division 1, 26.10.1895)
**RECORD DEFEAT:** 0-8 (-v- Motherwell – Division 1, 30.4.1937)

## SEASON TICKET INFORMATION

| | | |
|---|---|---|
| North Stand | Adult | £295 |
| | Child/OAP | £200 |
| Outer Wing East | Adult | £225 |
| | Child/OAP | £150 |
| Outer Wing West **(Family Section)** | | |
| | Adult & Child | £330 |
| | Child/OAP | £150 |
| East/West Stands | Adult | £160 |
| | Child/OAP | £95 |

## LEAGUE ADMISSION PRICES

| | | |
|---|---|---|
| North Stand | Adult | £16 |
| | Child | £9 |
| Front Stand | Adult | £12 |
| | Child | £7 |
| Outer Wing East | Adult | £11 |
| | Child | £6 |
| Outer Wing West **(Family Section)** | | |
| | Adult | £10 |
| | Child | £6 |
| East/West Stands | Adult | £8 |
| | Child | £5 |

Celtic Park, 95 Kerrydale Street,
Glasgow G40 3RE
PLEASE NOTE THAT OWING TO THE REBUILDING OF
CELTIC PARK, ALL HOME MATCHES WILL BE PLAYED AT
HAMPDEN PARK DURING SEASON 1994/95

**CHAIRMAN**
J. Kevin Kelly

**DIRECTORS**
Fergus McCann (Managing Director);
Dominic W. Keane;
James M. Farrell M.A, LL.B.

**SECRETARY**
Dominic W. Keane

**MANAGER**
Thomas Burns

**ASSISTANT MANAGER**
William Stark

**RESERVE TEAM MANAGER**
Frank Connor

**CHIEF SCOUT**
David Hay

**RESERVE TEAM COACH**
Tom McAdam

**YOUTH TEAM COACH**
William McStay

**CLUB DOCTOR**
Jack Mulhearn

**PHYSIOTHERAPIST**
Brian Scott

**RESERVE TEAM PHYSIOTHERAPIST**
Gerry McElhill

**GROUNDSMAN**
John Hayes

**MARKETING DIRECTOR**
Patrick Ferrell

**PUBLIC RELATIONS MANAGER**
Peter McLean

**MANAGING DIRECTOR CELTIC POOLS**
John McGuire

**TELEPHONES**
Ground 041-556 2611
Matchdays Only 041-632 1275
Fax 041-551 8106
Telex 931 2100437 BW
Ticket Office 041-551 8654

**CLUB SHOPS**
18/20 Kerrydale Street,
Glasgow G40 3RE
Tel 041-554 4231 (9.00 a.m. to
5.00 p.m. Mon-Sat) and
40 Dundas Street, Glasgow G1 2AQ
Tel 041-332 2727
(9.00 a.m. to 5.00 p.m. Mon-Sat)

**OFFICIAL SUPPORTERS CLUB**
Celtic Supporters Association,
1524 London Road, Glasgow G40 3RJ

**TEAM CAPTAIN**
Paul McStay

**SHIRT SPONSOR**
C.R. Smith

**REGISTERED STRIP:** Shirt – Green and White Hoops, Shorts – White Stockings – White with Green Trim

**CHANGE STRIP:** Shirt – Black With Green and White Striped Panel on Chest Shorts – Black with Green Side Panels and Black and White Striped Trim, Stockings – Black with White and Green Patterned Turnover

# CLUB FACTFILE 1993/94 .. RESULTS .. APPEARANCES .. SCORERS

## The BHOYS

Small bold figures (shown here in [brackets]) denote goalscorers. † denotes opponent's own goal.

| Date | Venue | Opponents | Result | Bonner P. | Boyd T. | Wdowczyk D. | Grant P. | McNally M. | Galloway M. | Slater S. | McStay P. | McAvennie F. | Creaney G. | Collins J. | Nicholas C. | McGinlay P. | Payton A. | O'Neil B. | Vata R. | Mowbray A. | Smith B. | Gillespie G. | Byrne P. | Marshall G. | McLaughlin B. | Biggins W. | Martin L. | Muggleton C. | Falconer W. | Donnelly S. | Hay C. |
|---|---|---|---|---|---|---|---|---|---|---|---|---|---|---|---|---|---|---|---|---|---|---|---|---|---|---|---|---|---|---|---|
| Aug 7 | A | Motherwell | 2-2 | 1 | 2 | 3 | 4 | 5 | 6 | 7[1] | 8 | 9[1] | 10 | 11 | 12 | 14 | | | | | | | | | | | | | | | |
| 14 | H | Hibernian | 1-1 | 1 | 2 | 3 | 4 | 5 | 6 | | 8 | 9 | | 11 | 10[1] | 7 | 12 | 13 | | | | | | | | | | | | | |
| 21 | H | Rangers | 0-0 | 1 | 2 | 3 | 4 | 5 | 6 | | 8 | 9 | | 11 | 10 | 7 | 12 | | | | | | | | | | | | | | |
| 28 | A | Partick Thistle | 1-0 | 1 | 2 | 3 | 4 | 5[1] | 6 | | 8 | 9 | | 11 | 10 | 7 | 12 | | | | | | | | | | | | | | |
| Sep 4 | A | Aberdeen | 0-1 | 1 | 2 | 3 | 4 | 5 | 6 | 14 | | 9 | | 11 | 10 | 7 | 12 | 8 | | | | | | | | | | | | | |
| 11 | A | Raith Rovers | 4-1 | 1 | 2 | 3 | 4 | | 6 | 14 | | 9 | | 11 | 10[2] | 7 | 12[2] | 8 | 5 | | | | | | | | | | | | |
| 18 | H | Dundee United | 1-1 | 1 | 2 | 3 | 4 | 5 | 6 | 11 | 8 | 9[1] | | | 10 | 7 | 12 | | | | | | | | | | | | | | |
| 25 | A | Heart of Midlothian | 0-1 | 1 | 2 | 3 | 4 | | 6 | 11 | 8 | 9 | 10 | | | 7 | 12 | | 5 | 14 | | | | | | | | | | | |
| Oct 2 | H | Kilmarnock | 0-0 | 1 | | 3 | 14 | | 5 | 6 | 8 | | 10 | | 12 | 7 | 9 | | | 11 | 2 | | | | | | | | | | |
| 6 | A | St. Johnstone | 1-2 | 1 | | 3 | | | 4 | 6 | 8 | | 9[1] | | 10 | 7 | | | 5 | 11 | 2 | | 12 | | | | | | | | |
| 9 | H | Dundee | 2-1 | 1 | | 3 | | | 4 | 5 | 6 | 8 | 10 | 9[1] | 11 | 12[1] | 13 | | | | 2 | | 7 | 1 | | | | | | | |
| 16 | A | Hibernian | 1-1 | 1 | | 3 | | 4 | | | 8 | 9[1] | 10 | 11 | | 6 | | | 5 | | 2 | | 7 | | | | | | | | |
| 30 | A | Rangers | 2-1 | 1 | | 3 | | 4 | | | 8 | 9 | 10 | 11[1] | | 6 | 14 | 12[1] | 5 | | 2 | | 7 | | | | | | | | |
| Nov 6 | H | Partick Thistle | 3-0 | 1 | 2 | 3 | 4 | | | | 8 | 9 | | | 10[1] | 6[2] | | | 5 | 11 | | 12 | 7 | | 14 | | | | | | |
| 9 | A | Aberdeen | 1-1 | 1 | | 3 | 4 | 5 | | | 8 | 9 | | 11 | 10[1] | 14 | | 12 | | | 2 | | 7 | | | | | | | | |
| 13 | A | Kilmarnock | 2-2 | 1 | 2 | 3 | 4 | 5 | 9 | | 8 | | | 12 | 10[1] | 6[1] | | | | 11 | | | 7 | | | | | | | | |
| 20 | H | Heart of Midlothian | 0-0 | 1 | | 3 | 4 | 5 | | | 8 | 9 | | 11 | 10 | 6 | | | | | 2 | | 7 | | | | | | | | |
| 24 | H | Motherwell | 2-0 | 1 | | 3 | 4 | 5 | | | 8 | | | 11 | 10 | 7 | | 6[2] | | | 2 | 9 | | | | 14 | | | | | |
| 27 | H | Raith Rovers | 2-0 | 1 | | 3 | 4 | 5 | | | 8 | 9 | | 11[2] | 10 | 7 | | 12 | | | 2 | | | | | 14 | | | | | |
| 30 | A | Dundee United | 0-1 | 1 | | 3 | 4 | 5 | | 14 | 8 | 9 | | 11 | 10 | 6 | | 7 | | | 2 | | | | | 12 | | | | | |
| Dec 4 | H | St. Johnstone | 1-0 | 1 | | 3 | 4 | 5 | | | 8 | 14 | 7 | 11 | | 6[1] | | | | | 2 | 9 | | | | 10 | | | | | |
| 11 | A | Dundee | 1-1 | 1 | | 3 | 4 | 5 | | | 8 | 14 | 7[1] | 11 | | 6 | | | | | 2 | 9 | | | | 10 | | | | | |
| 18 | H | Hibernian | 0-1 | 1 | | 3 | 4 | 5 | | | 8[1] | 14 | | 11 | 12 | 6 | | | | | 2 | 9 | 7 | | | 10 | | | | | |
| Jan 1 | A | Rangers | 2-4 | 1 | | 3 | 4 | 5 | 12 | | 8 | | | 11[1] | 10[1] | 6 | | | | | 2 | 9 | 7 | | | 14 | | | | | |
| 8 | A | Partick Thistle | 0-1 | 1 | | 3 | | 4 | 5 | 6 | 8 | | 9 | 11 | | | 14 | | | 12 | 2 | | 7 | | | | | | | | |
| 11 | A | Motherwell | 1-2 | 1 | | 3 | | 4 | 6[1] | 12 | 8 | 14 | 10 | 9 | | 11 | | | 5 | | 2 | | 7 | | | | | | | | |
| 19 | H | Aberdeen | 2-2 | 1 | | | 6 | 14 | | | 8[1] | | | 11 | 10 | 4 | 12 | | 5 | | 2 | 7[1] | | | 9 | 3 | | | | | |
| 22 | A | Dundee United | 0-0 | | | 3 | | | 6 | | 8 | | | 11 | 10 | 9 | 12 | | 5 | | 2 | 7 | | | 4 | 1 | | | | | |
| Feb 5 | A | Raith Rovers | 0-0 | | | 3 | | | 6 | | 8 | 9 | | 11 | 4 | 10 | | | 5 | | 12 | 7 | | 14 | 2 | 1 | | | | | |
| 12 | A | Heart of Midlothian | 2-0 | | | 3 | | | 4 | | 8 | | | 11 | 9[2] | 6 | 12 | 14 | 5 | | 2 | 7 | | | | 1 | 10 | | | | |
| Mar 1 | H | Kilmarnock | 1-0 | | | 3 | | | 6 | | | | | 11[1] | 9 | 7 | 8 | | 5 | | 2 | 12 | | | 4 | 1 | 10 | | | | |
| 5 | A | St. Johnstone | 1-0 | | | 3 | | | 2 | 14 | 8 | | | 11 | 9 | 6 | | | 5 | | 12 | 7[1] | | | 4 | 1 | 10 | | 14 | | |
| 19 | A | Hibernian | 0-0 | | | 3 | | | 4 | | 8 | | | 11 | 9 | 6 | | | 5 | | | 7 | | | 2 | 1 | 10 | | | | |
| 26 | H | Motherwell | 0-1 | | | 3 | | | 4 | | 8 | | | 11 | 9 | 6 | 14 | | 5 | | 2 | 7 | | | | 1 | 10 | | 12 | | |
| 30 | H | Raith Rovers | 2-1 | | | 3 | | | | | 4 | 8 | | 11 | | 6 | 14 | | 5 | | | 7 | | | 12 | | 10 | | 1 | 9[2] | |
| Apr 2 | A | Dundee United | 3-1 | | | 3 | | | 8 | 4 | | | | 11[1] | | 6 | 14 | 7 | 5[1] | | | 12 | | | | | 10[1] | | 1 | 9 | |
| 6 | H | Dundee | 1-1 | | | 3 | | | 4 | 10 | 8 | | | 11 | | 6 | | 7 | | | | 5 | | | 12 | | 10 | | 1 | 9[1] | |
| 9 | H | Heart of Midlothian | 2-2 | | | 3 | | | 4 | 14 | 8 | | | 11[1] | 6 | | | 7[1] | | | | 5 | | | | | 10 | | 1 | 9 | |
| 16 | A | Kilmarnock | 0-2 | | | 3 | | | 4 | 2 | 8 | | | 11 | 12 | 6 | | 7 | | | | 5 | | | | 14 | 10 | | 1 | 9 | |
| 23 | A | Dundee | 2-0 | 1 | | | 5 | | 4 | 2 | | | | 11 | 8 | 6[2] | | | | | | 3 | | | | | 7 | | 10 | 9 | |
| 27 | H | St. Johnstone | 1-1 | 1 | | | 5 | | 4 | 2 | | | | 11 | 8 | 6 | 14 | | | | | 3 | | | 12 | 14 | 3 | | 10 | 9 | |
| 30 | H | Rangers | 1-1 | 1 | | | 7 | 4 | 6 | | | | | 11[1] | 8 | | | | 5 | | 2 | 12 | 14 | | | | 3 | | 10 | 9 | |
| May 7 | H | Partick Thistle | 1-1 | 1 | | | 6 | 12 | 4 | | | | | 11 | 8[1] | | | | 5 | | 2 | | 13 | | | | 3 | | 10 | 9 | 7 |
| 14 | A | Aberdeen | 1-1 | 1 | | | 4 | 12 | | | | | | 11 | 8 | | | | 5 | | 2 | 6 | 14 | | | | 3 | | 10 | 9[1] | 7 |
| **TOTAL FULL APPEARANCES** | | | | 31 | 38 | 24 | 27 | 30 | 16 | 3 | 35 | 8 | 17 | 38 | 30 | 39 | 1 | 14 | 6 | 20 | 6 | 25 | 18 | 1 | | 4 | 15 | 12 | 14 | 10 | 2 |
| **TOTAL SUB APPEARANCES** | | | | | (1) | (1) | (2) | (6) | (2) | | (3) | (1) | | (5) | (2) | (6) | (13) | (4) | (2) | (1) | (2) | (4) | | | (8) | (5) | | | (2) | |
| **TOTAL GOALS SCORED** | | | | | | | 2 | | | | 1 | 2 | 1 | 5 | 8 | 8 | 10 | | 2 | 2 | | 1 | 1 | | | 2 | | 1 | 5 | |

Small bold figures denote goalscorers. † denotes opponent's own goal.

---

## HAMPDEN PARK

**CAPACITY:** 38,113 (All Seated)

**PITCH DIMENSIONS:** 115 yds x 75 yds

**FACILITIES FOR DISABLED SUPPORTERS:** Capacity 222 – Weelchair 54, Ambulant Seated 48, Ambulant Standing 120 (Hampden Park).

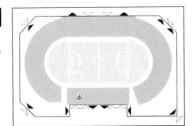

## HOW TO GET THERE

The following routes may be used to reach Hampden Park:

**TRAINS:** There are two stations within five minutes walk of the ground. Mount Florida Station, on the Cathcart Circle and King's Park Station. A 15 minute service runs from Glasgow Central.

**BUSES:** Services to approach Mount Florida end of Stadium: From City Centre: 5, 5A, 5B, M5, M14, 31, 37, 66, 66A, 66B, 66C; From Govan Cross: 34; From Drumchapel: 96,97; Circular Service: 89,90; G.C.T. Service: 1. Services to approach King's Park end of Stadium: From City Centre: 12, 12A, 74; Circular Service: 89, 90; G.C.T. Service: 19.

**CARS:** Car parking facilities are available in the car park at the front of the Stadium, which is capable of holding 1,200 vehicles. Side streets can also be used on major occasions.

# DUNDEE UNITED

## LIST OF PLAYERS 1994-95

Tannadice Park, Tannadice Street,
Dundee DD3 7JW

**CHAIRMAN/MANAGING
DIRECTOR**
James Y. McLean

**VICE-CHAIRMAN**
Douglas B. Smith

**DIRECTORS**
Alistair B. Robertson
William M. Littlejohn
John H. McConnachie

**SECRETARY**
Miss Priti Trivedi

**MANAGER**
Ivan Golac

**COACHING STAFF**
Gordon Wallace, Paul Hegarty,
Maurice Malpas, Kenny Cameron,
Ian Campbell, Graeme Liveston

**CLUB DOCTOR**
Dr. Derek J. McCormack

**PHYSIOTHERAPIST**
David Rankine

**CHIEF SCOUT**
Kenny Cameron

**S.F.A. COMMUNITY OFFICER**
Atholl Henderson

**COMMERCIAL MANAGER**
Mark Walker
(0382) 833166

**TELEPHONES**
Ground (0382) 833166
Fax (0382) 89398

**CLUB SHOP**
The United Shop, Unit 2,
5/15 Victoria Road, Dundee
Tel (0382) 204066 – Open 9.00 a.m.
to 5.30 p.m. Mon-Sat
Souvenir shops are also situated
within the ground and are open
on match days

**TEAM CAPTAIN**
Maurice Malpas

**SHIRT SPONSOR**
Rover

| SURNAME | FIRST NAME | MIDDLE NAME | DATE OF BIRTH | PLACE OF BIRTH | DATE OF SIGNING | HEIGHT FT INS | WEIGHT ST LBS | PREVIOUS CLUB |
|---|---|---|---|---|---|---|---|---|
| Agnew | Steven | | 07/10/75 | Irvine | 02/10/92 | 5 7.0 | 10 5 | Hamilton Thistle |
| Benvie | Gregor | William | 22/08/72 | Dundee | 20/06/89 | 5 9.0 | 11 4 | Sporting Club '85 |
| Black | Paul | Alexander | 30/10/77 | Aberdeen | 27/07/94 | 5 9.5 | 10 9 | Dundee United B.C. |
| Bollan | Gary | | 24/03/73 | Dundee | 20/06/89 | 5 11.0 | 12 12 | Fairmuir B.C. |
| Bowman | David | | 10/03/64 | Turnbridge Wells | 21/05/86 | 5 10.0 | 11 6 | Coventry City |
| Brewster | Craig | James | 13/12/66 | Dundee | 05/08/93 | 6 1.0 | 12 9 | Raith Rovers |
| Burns | Thomas | B. | 06/08/77 | Bellshill | 17/08/94 | 5 11.5 | 11 2 | Dundee United B.C. |
| Canning | Stephen | | 31/10/77 | Motherwell | 27/07/94 | 5 7.0 | 9 6 | Dundee United B.C. |
| Cargill | Andrew | | 02/09/75 | Dundee | 25/03/93 | 5 6.5 | 10 8 | Downfield Juniors |
| Cleland | Alexander | | 10/12/70 | Glasgow | 18/06/87 | 5 8.5 | 11 7 | "S" Form |
| Connolly | Patrick | | 25/06/70 | Glasgow | 02/08/86 | 5 9.5 | 10 11 | "S" Form |
| Crabbe | Scott | | 12/08/68 | Edinburgh | 03/10/92 | 5 8.0 | 11 4 | Heart of Midlothian |
| Craig | David | William | 11/06/69 | Glasgow | 09/06/94 | 6 1.0 | 11 7 | East Stirlingshire |
| Dailly | Christian | Eduard | 23/10/73 | Dundee | 02/08/90 | 6 0.5 | 12 10 | "S" Form |
| Garden | Stuart | Robertson | 10/02/72 | Dundee | 01/03/93 | 5 11.5 | 12 3 | Dundee North End |
| Gilmour | Stuart | John | 17/08/77 | Broxburn | 27/07/94 | 5 7.0 | 9 9 | Dundee United B.C. |
| Gray | Dale | Ronald J. | 15/02/78 | Edinburgh | 27/07/94 | 6 0.0 | 9 8 | Dundee United B.C. |
| Hannah | David | | 04/08/74 | Coatbridge | 04/09/91 | 5 11.0 | 11 8 | Hamilton Thistle |
| Hegarty | Ryan | Michael | 08/03/76 | Edinburgh | 27/07/94 | 5 11.0 | 9 7 | Dundee United B.C. |
| Honeyman | Ben | | 14/02/77 | Adelaide | 27/07/94 | 5 9.0 | 9 5 | Dundee United B.C. |
| Hughes | John | Paul | 03/10/76 | Bellshill | 27/07/94 | 5 10.0 | 10 2 | Dundee United B.C. |
| Johnson | Ian | Grant | 24/03/72 | Dundee | 07/09/90 | 5 11.0 | 11 2 | Broughty Ferry |
| Jorgensen | Henrik | | 16/02/66 | Fredericia | 12/08/94 | 6 1.0 | 13 4 | Viborg |
| Kennedy | Grahame | David | 07/07/77 | Dundee | 27/07/94 | 6 0.0 | 9 9 | Dundee United B.C. |
| Lamb | John | | 12/08/77 | Bellshill | 27/07/94 | 5 9.5 | 10 5 | Dundee United B.C. |
| Main | Alan | David | 05/12/67 | Elgin | 25/11/86 | 5 11.5 | 13 0 | Elgin City |
| Malpas | Maurice | Daniel R. | 03/08/62 | Dunfermline | 14/08/79 | 5 8.0 | 11 6 | "S" Form |
| McBain | Roy | Adam | 07/11/74 | Aberdeen | 14/04/92 | 5 11.0 | 11 5 | Dyce B.C. |
| McInally | James | Edward | 19/02/64 | Glasgow | 21/05/86 | 5 8.5 | 11 9 | Coventry City |
| McKinlay | William | | 22/04/69 | Glasgow | 24/06/85 | 5 8.0 | 11 7 | Hamilton Thistle |
| McLaren | Andrew | | 05/06/73 | Glasgow | 20/06/89 | 5 10.5 | 11 7 | Rangers B.C. |
| Mitchell | David | | 24/09/76 | Irvine | 27/07/94 | 5 11.5 | 11 8 | Dundee United B.C. |
| Moule | Andrew | Gareth | 16/04/77 | Neath | 29/05/94 | 5 11.5 | 10 8 | Dyce Juniors |
| Myers | Chris | | 01/04/69 | Yeovil | 05/08/93 | 5 10.0 | 12 2 | Torquay United |
| Nixon | Jerren | Kendall | 25/06/73 | Trinidad | 31/12/93 | 6 0.0 | 11 11 | E.C.M. Motown |
| Perry | Mark | George | 07/02/71 | Aberdeen | 09/08/88 | 6 1.0 | 12 11 | Cove Rangers |
| Petric | Gordan | | 30/07/69 | Belgrade | 19/11/93 | 6 2.5 | 13 9 | Partizan Belgrade |
| Prior | Peter | | 07/10/73 | Glasgow | 04/09/91 | 5 7.5 | 11 3 | Clydebank B.C. |
| Ristic | Dragutin | | 05/08/64 | Pula | 13/07/94 | 6 0.0 | 12 7 | Falkirk |
| Ross | Leo | Kenneth | 29/08/77 | Newcastle-Upon-Tyne | 27/07/94 | 5 11.0 | 11 8 | Burnside B.C. |
| Stirling | Anthony | | 07/09/76 | Glasgow | 27/07/94 | 6 0.0 | 11 8 | Dundee United B.C. |
| Van De Kamp | Guido | | 08/02/64 | Den Bosch | 27/07/91 | 6 2.5 | 12 12 | BVV Den Bosch |
| Walker | Paul | | 20/08/77 | Kilwinning | 27/07/94 | 5 5.5 | 8 8 | Dundee United B.C. |
| Welsh | Brian | | 23/02/69 | Edinburgh | 24/06/85 | 6 2.0 | 13 8 | Tynecastle B.C. |
| Winters | Robert | | 04/11/74 | East Kilbride | 11/01/92 | 5 10.0 | 11 6 | Muirend Amateurs |

## MILESTONES

**YEAR OF FORMATION:** 1923 (1909 as Dundee Hibs)
**MOST CAPPED PLAYER:** Maurice Malpas
**NO. OF CAPS:** 55
**MOST LEAGUE POINTS IN A SEASON:** 60 (Premier Division – Season 1986/87)
**MOST LEAGUE GOALS SCORED BY A PLAYER IN A SEASON:** John Coyle (Season 1955/56).
**NO. OF GOALS SCORED:** 41
**RECORD ATTENDANCE:** 28,000 (-v- Barcelona – 16.11.1966)
**RECORD VICTORY:** 14-0 (-v- Nithsdale Wanderers – Scottish Cup 17.1.1931)
**RECORD DEFEAT:** 1-12 (-v- Motherwell – Division 2. 23.1.1954)

## SEASON TICKET INFORMATION

**George Fox Stand**
Top Tier
Adult .................................. £190
Juvenile/OAP ..................... £100
Middle Tier
Adult .................................. £250
Juvenile/OAP ..................... £150
Lower Tier
Adult .................................. £144
Juvenile/OAP ..................... £ 75

**East Stand**
Top Tier
Adult .................................. £190
Juvenile/OAP ..................... £100
Lower Tier
Adult .................................. £144
Juvenile/OAP ..................... £75
Family Section
1 Adult & 1 Juvenile .......... £180

## LEAGUE ADMISSION PRICES

**George Fox Stand**
Top Tier
Adult ............. £10     Juvenile/OAP ..... £6
Lower Tier
Adult ............. £8     Juvenile/OAP ..... £4
**East Stand**
Top Tier
Adult ............. £10     Juvenile/OAP ..... £6
Lower Tier
Adult ............. £8     Juvenile/OAP ..... £4
Family Section
1 Adult & 1 Juvenile .......................... £12
Each Additional Juvenile ...................... £4

**South Stand**
(Away Supporters)
Adult .................................................. £10
Juvenile/OAP ...................................... £6
**West Stand**
(Away Supporters)
Adult .................................................. £8
Juvenile/OAP ...................................... £4

REGISTERED STRIP: Shirt – Tangerine with Black and White Vertical Stripes, Shorts – Black with Tangerine and White Trim, Stockings – Tangerine with Black and White Hoops at Top

CHANGE STRIP: Shirt – White with Two Black Hoops and Purple and Black Collar and Cuffs Shorts – White with Purple and Black Trim Stockings – White with Black and Purple Hoops at Top

# CLUB FACTFILE 1993/94 . . RESULTS . . APPEARANCES . . SCORERS

## The TERRORS

| Date | Venue | Opponents | Result | Main A. | Van Der Hoorn F. | Malpas M. | Cleland A. | Welsh B. | Narey D. | Bowman D. | McKinlay W. | Connolly P. | Dailly C. | Brewster C. | Bollan G. | Clark J. | Myers C. | McLaren A. | McInally J. | McBain R. | O'Neil J. | Crabbe S. | Perry M. | Johnson I.G. | Van De Kamp G. | Petric G. | Nixon J. | Hannah D. | Files B. |
|---|---|---|---|---|---|---|---|---|---|---|---|---|---|---|---|---|---|---|---|---|---|---|---|---|---|---|---|---|---|
| Aug 7 | H | Aberdeen | 1-1 | 1 | 2 | 3 | 4 | 5 | 6 | 7 | $8^1$ | 9 | 10 | 11 | 12 | | | | | | | | | | | | | | |
| 14 | A | Partick Thistle | 2-1 | 1 | 2 | | | 5 | 6 | 7 | 8 | 9 | $10^2$ | | 3 | 4 | | 11 | 12 | 14 | | | | | | | | | |
| 21 | A | St. Johnstone | 1-1 | 1 | | | | 5 | 6 | 7 | $8^1$ | 9 | 10 | | 3 | 2 | | 11 | 4 | 12 | 14 | | | | | | | | |
| 28 | H | Heart of Midlothian | 0-0 | 1 | 6 | | | 5 | | 7 | | 9 | 10 | | 3 | 2 | 11 | 8 | 4 | | 12 | 14 | | | | | | | |
| Sep 4 | A | Raith Rovers | 1-1 | 1 | 6 | | | 5 | | 7 | $8^1$ | | 10 | 12 | 3 | 2 | 11 | 9 | 4 | | | | 14 | | | | | | |
| 11 | H | Dundee | 1-0 | 1 | 6 | | | 5 | | 7 | 8 | | 10 | | 3 | 2 | | $9^1$ | | | | 11 | 4 | 14 | | | | | |
| 18 | A | Celtic | 1-1 | 1 | 11 | | 2 | 5 | 6 | | $8^1$ | | 10 | | 3 | | | 9 | | | | | 4 | 7 | | | | | |
| 25 | H | Motherwell | 0-0 | 1 | 2 | 6 | 3 | 5 | | | 8 | | 10 | | 12 | | | 9 | | | 7 | 14 | 4 | 11 | | | | | |
| Oct 2 | A | Hibernian | 0-2 | 1 | 2 | 3 | 6 | 5 | | | 8 | 10 | 14 | | 9 | | | 12 | | | 11 | 4 | 7 | | | | | | |
| 5 | A | Kilmarnock | 1-1 | 1 | 2 | 3 | | | | | $8^1$ | 10 | 14 | 12 | 5 | | | 9 | 6 | | 11 | 4 | 7 | | | | | | |
| 9 | H | Rangers | 1-3 | 1 | 2 | 3 | | $5^1$ | | 7 | 8 | 14 | 10 | | 4 | | | 9 | 6 | | 12 | | 11 | | | | | | |
| 16 | H | Partick Thistle | 2-2 | 1 | | 3 | 6 | 5 | | 7 | 8 | 14 | 10 | $11^1$ | 2 | | | 9 | | | $12^1$ | 4 | | | | | | | |
| 23 | A | Aberdeen | 0-2 | 1 | 4 | 3 | 6 | 5 | | | 8 | | 10 | | 2 | | | 9 | | | 11 | 12 | | 7 | | | | | |
| 30 | A | St. Johnstone | 2-0 | 1 | 4 | | 3 | 5 | | | $8^1$ | | 10 | $7^1$ | 2 | | | 9 | | | 11 | 12 | | 6 | | | | | |
| Nov 6 | A | Heart of Midlothian | 1-1 | 1 | 4 | | 3 | 6 | 5 | 7 | 8 | | 10 | 11 | 2 | | | 9 | | | $14^1$ | | | | | | | | |
| 9 | H | Raith Rovers | 2-2 | 1 | 4 | 3 | | 5 | | $7^1$ | 8 | | 10 | 11 | 2 | | | $9^1$ | | | 6 | | | | | | | | |
| 13 | H | Hibernian | 2-2 | 1 | 4 | 3 | 2 | 5 | | 7 | $8^1$ | 14 | 10 | $11^1$ | | | | 9 | | | 6 | | | | | | | | |
| 20 | A | Motherwell | 0-2 | | 2 | 3 | 8 | 6 | | 7 | | | 10 | 14 | | | | 9 | 4 | | 11 | 12 | | | 1 | 5 | | | |
| 30 | H | Celtic | 1-0 | | 2 | 3 | 11 | 6 | | 7 | 8 | $9^1$ | | 10 | | | | 4 | | | 12 | | | | 1 | 5 | | | |
| Dec 4 | H | Kilmarnock | 0-0 | | 2 | 3 | 11 | 6 | | 7 | 8 | 9 | | 10 | | | | 4 | | | 14 | 12 | | | 1 | 5 | | | |
| 7 | A | Dundee | 2-1 | | 2 | 3 | 11 | 6 | | 7 | 8 | $9^1$ | 14 | $10^1$ | | | | 4 | | | | | | | 1 | 5 | | | |
| 11 | A | Rangers | 3-0 | | 2 | 3 | 11 | 6 | | $7^1$ | 8 | $9^1$ | 14 | $10^1$ | | | | 4 | | | 12 | | | | 1 | 5 | | | |
| 18 | A | Partick Thistle | 0-1 | | 2 | 3 | 11 | 6 | | 7 | 8 | 9 | 14 | 10 | | | | 4 | | | 12 | | | | 1 | 5 | | | |
| 27 | H | Aberdeen | 0-1 | | 2 | 3 | | 6 | | 7 | 8 | 9 | 11 | 10 | | | 14 | 4 | | | | | | | 1 | 5 | | | |
| Jan 8 | H | Heart of Midlothian | 3-0 | | 2 | 3 | 12 | 6 | | 7 | 8 | $9^1$ | | $10^1$ | | | | 4 | | | $11^1$ | | | | 1 | 5 | 14 | | |
| 15 | A | Raith Rovers | 2-0 | | 2 | 3 | 8 | 6 | | 7 | | 9 | $10^2$ | | | | | 4 | | | 11 | | | | 1 | 5 | 12 | 14 | |
| 22 | A | Celtic | 0-0 | | 2 | 3 | 8 | 6 | | 7 | | 9 | 14 | 10 | | | | 4 | | | 11 | | | | 1 | 5 | 12 | | |
| 25 | A | St. Johnstone | 1-1 | | 2 | 3 | 6 | | | 7 | 8 | 9 | 14 | 10 | | | | 4 | | | 11 | | | | 1 | 5 | 12 | | |
| Feb 5 | H | Dundee | 1-1 | | 2 | 3 | | 6 | | 7 | 8 | $9^1$ | | 10 | | | | 4 | | | 11 | | | | 1 | 5 | 12 | | |
| 12 | H | Motherwell | 1-2 | | 2 | 3 | | 6 | | 7 | 8 | 9 | 14 | $10^1$ | | | | 4 | | | 11 | | | | 1 | 5 | 12 | | |
| 26 | A | Hibernian | 1-0 | | | 3 | 2 | 6 | | | 8 | 14 | 7 | 10 | | | | 4 | | | 11 | | | | 1 | 5 | $9^1$ | 12 | |
| Mar 5 | A | Kilmarnock | †1-1 | | | 3 | 2 | 6 | | | 8 | | 7 | 10 | | | | 4 | 11 | | | | | | | 5 | 9 | 14 | 1 |
| 19 | H | Partick Thistle | 2-2 | | | 3 | $2^1$ | 6 | | 7 | 8 | 9 | | $10^1$ | | | 14 | 4 | | | 11 | | | | | 5 | 9 | | |
| 26 | A | Aberdeen | 0-1 | | | 3 | 2 | | 6 | 7 | 8 | | 9 | 10 | | | 14 | 4 | | | | 11 | | 1 | | 5 | | | |
| 29 | A | Dundee | 1-1 | | | 3 | 2 | 6 | | 7 | 8 | 9 | 11 | $10^1$ | | | | 4 | | | | | | | 1 | 5 | | | |
| Apr 2 | H | Celtic | 1-3 | | | 3 | 11 | 6 | 2 | 7 | 8 | 9 | | $10^1$ | | | 14 | 4 | | | | | | | 1 | 5 | | | |
| 5 | H | Rangers | 0-0 | | | 3 | 2 | 6 | | | 8 | 12 | 10 | 11 | | | 9 | 4 | | | | | | | 1 | 5 | 14 | 7 | |
| 16 | H | Hibernian | 3-0 | | | 2 | | | | 7 | $8^1$ | 14 | 3 | $10^1$ | | | 9 | 4 | | | 6 | 12 | | 1 | $5^1$ | | 11 | |
| 23 | A | Rangers | 1-2 | | | 3 | 2 | 6 | | 7 | | $10^1$ | | 8 | | | 9 | 4 | | | | | | 1 | 5 | 14 | 11 | |
| 26 | H | Kilmarnock | 1-3 | 1 | | 3 | 2 | 6 | | 7 | 8 | 11 | 10 | | 4 | | | 14 | | | | | | | 5 | 9 | $12^1$ | |
| 30 | H | St. Johnstone | 0-0 | | | 3 | 2 | | | 7 | 8 | | 6 | 10 | | | 14 | 4 | | | | | | 1 | 5 | 9 | 11 | |
| May 3 | H | Motherwell | 2-1 | | | 3 | 2 | 6 | | 7 | $8^1$ | 11 | $10^1$ | | | | 14 | 4 | | | 12 | | | 1 | 5 | 9 | | |
| 7 | A | Heart of Midlothian | 0-2 | | | 2 | | | | 7 | 8 | 14 | 11 | 10 | 3 | 12 | | 6 | | | | | | 1 | 5 | 9 | 4 | |
| 14 | H | Raith Rovers | 2-3 | | | 3 | 2 | | | 7 | 8 | 14 | 11 | $10^1$ | 12 | | | 4 | | | | | | 1 | 5 | 9 | $6^1$ | |
| **TOTAL FULL APPEARANCES** | | | | 18 | 28 | 35 | 32 | 37 | 6 | 35 | 39 | 21 | 29 | 30 | 10 | 13 | 4 | 18 | 29 | 8 | 10 | 8 | 8 | 25 | 27 | 7 | 6 | 1 | |
| **TOTAL SUB APPEARANCES** | | | | | | (1) | | | | (7) | (9) | (3) | (2) | (1) | (1) | (9) | (2) | (1) | (4) | (11) | (1) | (2) | | | (8) | (4) | | |
| **TOTAL GOALS SCORED** | | | | | | 1 | 1 | | | 2 | 9 | 5 | 3 | 16 | | | | 2 | | | 1 | 2 | | | 1 | 1 | 2 | |

*Small bold figures denote goalscorers.   † denotes opponent's own goal.*

---

## TANNADICE PARK

**CAPACITY:** 12,616 (All seated)

**PITCH DIMENSIONS:** 110 yds x 72 yds

**FACILITIES FOR DISABLED SUPPORTERS:** Lower Tier – George Fox Stand – Cover for home supporters only on request.

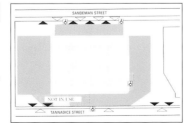

## HOW TO GET THERE

**Tannadice Park can be reached by the following routes:**

**BUSES:** The following buses leave from the city centre at frequent intervals. Nos. 18, 19 and 21 from Commercial Street and No. 20 from Reform Street.

**TRAINS:** Trains from all over the country pass through the main Dundee station and fans can then proceed to the ground by the above bus services from stops situated within walking distance of the station.

**CARS:** There is parking in the streets adjacent to the ground.

# FALKIRK

Brockville Park, Hope Street,
Falkirk FK1 5AX

**CHAIRMAN**
George J. Fulston

**DIRECTOR**
Alexander D. Moffat

**SECRETARY**
Alexander D. Moffat

**MANAGER**
James Jefferies

**ASSISTANT MANAGER/
RESERVE TEAM COACH**
Billy Brown

**COACH**
Willie Wilson

**CLUB DOCTOR**
Dr. Alan N. Dick M.B.Ch.B.

**PHYSIOTHERAPIST**
John Sharp L.V.M.C. (Mem) S.T.S.

**CHIEF SCOUT**
John Murray

**S.F.A. COMMUNITY COACH**
Peter Houston

**GROUNDSMAN**
Allan Wright

**COMMERCIAL DIRECTOR**
George Miller
(0324) 624121

**STADIUM MANAGER**
James Hendry
(0324) 624121

**TELEPHONES**
Ground/Ticket Office/Information
Service (0324) 624121/632487
Fax (0324) 612418

**CLUB SHOP**
Brockville Park
(Situated behind Main Stand)

**TEAM CAPTAIN**
John Hughes

**SHIRT SPONSOR**
Beazer Homes

## LIST OF PLAYERS 1994-95

| SURNAME | FIRST NAME | MIDDLE NAME | DATE OF BIRTH | PLACE OF BIRTH | DATE OF SIGNING | HEIGHT FT INS | WEIGHT ST LBS | PREVIOUS CLUB |
|---|---|---|---|---|---|---|---|---|
| Cadette | Richard | Ray | 21/03/65 | Hammersmith | 10/01/92 | 5 8.0 | 11 4 | Brentford |
| Cameron | David | Anthony | 24/08/75 | Bangor | 16/08/94 | 6 0.0 | 11 7 | Carse Thistle |
| Fulton | Stephen | | 10/08/70 | Greenock | 12/08/94 | 5 10.0 | 11 0 | Bolton Wanderers |
| Hamilton | Graeme | John | 22/01/74 | Stirling | 19/06/91 | 5 10.0 | 10 10 | Gairdoch United |
| Henderson | Nicholas | Sinclair | 08/02/69 | Edinburgh | 04/03/94 | 5 10.0 | 11 1 | Cowdenbeath |
| Hughes | John | | 09/09/64 | Edinburgh | 22/08/90 | 6 0.0 | 13 7 | Swansea City |
| James | Kevin | Francis | 03/12/75 | Edinburgh | 17/11/93 | 6 0.0 | 12 0 | Musselburgh Athletic |
| Johnston | Forbes | Duthie S. | 03/08/71 | Aberdeen | 08/09/90 | 5 10.0 | 9 12 | Musselburgh Athletic |
| Lamont | William | Fleming | 24/07/66 | Falkirk | 11/03/94 | 5 11.5 | 13 12 | Whitburn Juniors |
| MacKenzie | Scott | | 07/07/70 | Glasgow | 08/09/90 | 5 9.0 | 10 5 | Musselburgh Athletic |
| May | Edward | | 30/08/67 | Edinburgh | 02/03/91 | 5 7.5 | 10 3 | Brentford |
| McCall | Ian | Holland | 30/09/65 | Dumfries | 31/07/92 | 5 9.0 | 11 7 | Dundee |
| McDonald | Colin | | 10/04/74 | Edinburgh | 08/07/93 | 5 7.0 | 10 8 | Hibernian |
| McGlynn | David | John | 26/06/75 | Edinburgh | 04/02/94 | 6 0.0 | 11 3 | Musselburgh Athletic |
| McGowan | Jamie | | 05/12/70 | Morecambe | 02/03/94 | 6 0.0 | 11 1 | Dundee |
| McLaughlin | Joseph | | 02/06/60 | Greenock | 12/09/92 | 6 1.0 | 12 0 | Watford |
| McQueen | Thomas | Feeney | 01/04/63 | Glasgow | 06/10/90 | 5 9.0 | 11 7 | West Ham United |
| McStay | John | | 24/12/65 | Larkhall | 19/08/94 | 5 9.5 | 10 12 | Raith Rovers |
| Oliver | Neil | | 11/04/67 | Berwick-Upon-Tweed | 07/08/91 | 5 11.0 | 11 10 | Blackburn Rovers |
| Parks | Anthony | | 28/01/63 | Hackney | 23/10/92 | 5 10.0 | 13 2 | Rotherham United |
| Rice | Brian | | 11/10/63 | Bellshill | 09/08/91 | 6 1.0 | 11 7 | Nottingham Forest |
| Shaw | Gregory | | 15/02/70 | Dumfries | 31/12/92 | 6 0.0 | 10 12 | Ayr United |
| Weir | David | Gillespie | 10/05/70 | Falkirk | 01/08/92 | 6 2.0 | 13 7 | Celtic B.C. |

## MILESTONES

**YEAR OF FORMATION:** 1876
**MOST CAPPED PLAYER:** Alex H. Parker
**NO. OF CAPS:** 14
**MOST LEAGUE POINTS IN A SEASON:** 59 (Division 2 – Season 1935/36)
**MOST LEAGUE GOALS SCORED BY A PLAYER IN A SEASON:** E. Morrison (Season 1928/29)
**NO. OF GOALS SCORED:** 43
**RECORD ATTENDANCE:** 23,100 (-v- Celtic 21.2.1953)
**RECORD VICTORY:** 21-1 (-v- Laurieston – Scottish Cup 23.3.1893)
**RECORD DEFEAT:** 1-11 (-v- Airdrieonians – Division 1 28.4.1951)

## SEASON TICKET INFORMATION

**Seated**
Adult ............................................................. £175/£160
Juvenile/O.A.P. ...................................... £130/£100
Husband and Wife .................................................. £330
**Standing**
South Enclosure    Adult ................................... £140
                            Juvenile/O.A.P. ........................ £90
Ground                  Adult ................................... £130
                            Juvenile/O.A.P. ........................ £85

## LEAGUE ADMISSION PRICES

**Seated**
Adult ................................................................ £10 and £9
Juvenile/OAP ........................................ £6 (Wing Stand)
**Standing**
Enclosure    Adult ....................................... £8.50
Ground        Adult ............................................ £8
                    Juvenile/O.A.P. ............................ £5

EST. 1876

| | |
|---|---|
| **REGISTERED STRIP:** | Shirt – Navy with Navy Collar with Red under Placket Shorts – White with Navy/White/Navy Hoops on Leg, Stockings – Navy |
| **CHANGE STRIP:** | Shirt – Gold with Navy Collar with White Band and Navy Sleeve with Gold and White Print, Shorts – Navy with Navy/Gold/Navy Hoops on Legs Stockings – Gold |

# CLUB FACTFILE 1993/94 .. RESULTS .. APPEARANCES .. SCORERS

## The BAIRNS

*Small bold figures denote goalscorers.   † denotes opponent's own goal.*

| Date | Venue | Opponents | Result | Parks A. | Duffy C. | Johnston F. | Weir D. | Hughes J. | Rice B. | Sloan S. | May E. | Cadette R. | McCall I. | Shaw G. | Young K. | McQueen T. | Oliver N. | McLaughlin J. | MacKenzie S. | Taggart C. | McDonald C. | Drinkell K. | Burley G. | Westwater I. | Hamilton G. | McLaren C. | Ristic D. | McGowan J. | Henderson N. | Gallacher J. |
|---|---|---|---|---|---|---|---|---|---|---|---|---|---|---|---|---|---|---|---|---|---|---|---|---|---|---|---|---|---|---|
| Aug 7 | H | Dunfermline Athletic | 3-2 | 1 | 2 | 3[1] | 4 | 5[1] | 6[1] | 7 | 8 | 9 | 10 | 11 | 14 | | | | | | | | | | | | | | | |
| 14 | A | Greenock Morton | 5-1 | 1 | 2[2] | 6 | | | | 7 | | 9[1] | 10 | 11[1] | | 3 | 4 | 5 | | | | 8 | | | 14[1] | | | | | |
| 21 | H | Stirling Albion | 2-0 | 1 | 6[1] | 2 | | 5 | | 7 | | 9[1] | 10 | 11 | | 3 | 4 | | | | | 8 | | | 14 | 12 | | | | |
| 28 | A | Hamilton Academical | 1-1 | 1 | 6 | 2 | | 5 | | 7 | | 9 | 10 | 11[1] | | 3 | 4 | | | | | 8 | | | | | | | | |
| Sep 4 | H | Clydebank | 0-4 | 1 | 6 | 2 | | 5 | | 7 | | 9 | 10 | 11 | | 3 | 4 | | | | | 8 | | | 14 | 12 | | | | |
| 11 | H | Airdrieonians | 2-1 | 1 | 6[1] | 3 | 4 | | | 7 | | 9 | 10 | | | 2 | 5 | | 11 | | | 8[1] | | | | | | | | |
| 14 | A | Ayr United | 3-0 | 1 | 6 | | 4 | | | 7[1] | 14 | 9[1] | 10 | 12 | | 2 | 5[1] | | 11 | 3 | | 8 | | | | | | | | |
| 18 | A | Dumbarton | 1-0 | 1 | | | 4 | | 6 | 7 | | 9 | 10 | | | 3 | 2 | 5[1] | 11 | 14 | | 8 | | | | | | | | |
| 25 | H | St. Mirren | 2-0 | 1 | | | 4 | | 6 | 7 | | 9 | 10 | | | 3 | 2 | 5 | 11 | | | 8[2] | | | | | | | | |
| 29 | H | Clyde | 0-1 | 1 | | | 4 | | 6 | 7 | | 9 | 10 | 12 | | 3 | 2 | 5 | 11 | 14 | | 8 | | | | | | | | |
| Oct 2 | A | Brechin City | 0-0 | 1 | | | 4 | | 6 | 14 | | 7 | 9 | 10 | 12 | 3 | 2 | 5 | 11 | | | 8 | | | | | | | | |
| 9 | A | Dunfermline Athletic | 0-1 | 1 | 10 | | 4 | | 6 | 14 | | 7 | 9 | 12 | | 3 | 2 | 5 | | 11 | | 8 | | | | | | | | |
| 16 | H | Ayr United | 2-0 | 1 | 11 | | 4 | 12 | 6 | | | 7[1] | 9[1] | 10 | | 3 | 2 | 5 | | | | 8 | | | | | | | | |
| 23 | A | Airdrieonians | 1-1 | 1 | 11[1] | | 4 | 6 | 10 | | | 7 | 9 | | | 3 | 2 | 5 | | | 14 | 8 | | | | | | | | |
| 30 | A | Stirling Albion | 4-3 | 1 | 11 | | 4[1] | 5 | 6 | 10[1] | | 7 | 9[1] | | | 3 | 2 | | | 14 | 12 | 8[1] | | | | | | | | |
| Nov 6 | H | Hamilton Academical | 3-3 | 1 | 2 | | 4 | 5 | 6 | 11 | | 9[2] | 10 | 14 | | 3 | | 7 | | | 12 | 8[1] | | | | | | | | |
| 9 | A | Clydebank | 1-1 | 1 | 2[1] | | 4 | 6 | 10 | 11 | | 7 | 9 | 14 | | 3 | | 5 | | | 12 | 8 | | | | | | | | |
| 13 | H | Brechin City | 2-0 | 1 | 2[1] | | 4 | 6 | 10 | 11 | | 7 | 9 | 14 | | 3 | | 5 | | | 12[1] | 8 | | | | | | | | |
| 23 | H | Clyde | 2-0 | 1 | 2[2] | | 4 | 6 | 10 | 11 | | 7 | 9 | | | 3 | | 5 | | | 12 | 8 | | | | | | | | |
| Dec 4 | H | Dumbarton | 1-1 | 1 | 2 | | 4 | 6[1] | 10 | 11 | | 7 | 9 | 14 | | 3 | | 5 | | | | 8 | | | | | | | | |
| 18 | A | Ayr United | 3-0 | 1 | 2 | | 4[1] | 6 | 11 | 14 | | 7 | 9[1] | 10 | | 3 | 12 | 5 | | | | 8[1] | | | | | | | | |
| Jan 3 | A | St. Mirren | †1-3 | 1 | 2 | | | | 6 | 10 | 11 | 12 | 9 | | | 3 | 4 | 5 | | 7 | | 8 | | | | | | | | |
| 8 | A | Hamilton Academical | 1-1 | 1 | | | 4 | 6 | 12 | 8 | | 9[1] | 10 | | | 3 | | 5 | | 7 | 11 | 14 | 2 | | | | | | | |
| 11 | H | Greenock Morton | 5-1 | 1 | 2 | | 4 | 6 | 10[1] | | | 8[1] | 9[1] | 11[2] | | 3 | 12 | 5 | | 14 | 7 | | | | | | | | | |
| 15 | H | Clydebank | 0-0 | | 2 | | 4 | 6 | 10 | | | 8 | 9 | 14 | 11 | 3 | | 5 | | 12 | 7 | | | 1 | | | | | | |
| 18 | H | Dunfermline Athletic | 2-0 | | 2 | 14 | 4 | 6 | 10 | | | 7[1] | 9[1] | 11 | | 3 | | 5 | | 8 | | 12 | | 1 | | | | | | |
| 22 | A | Greenock Morton | †1-1 | | | 3 | 2 | 6 | 10 | | | 7 | 9 | 11 | | | 5 | 4 | | | 12 | 8 | | 1 | | | | | | |
| Feb 5 | A | Airdrieonians | 0-0 | 1 | 11 | 3 | 4 | | 6 | | | 9 | 10 | | | | 5 | | 8 | 7 | | | | | 2 | | | | 14 | |
| 12 | A | Brechin City | 2-0 | 1 | | 3 | 4 | 6 | 11 | | | 9[2] | 10 | 8 | | | 5 | | 12 | 14 | 7 | | | | 2 | | | | | |
| 15 | H | Stirling Albion | 3-1 | 1 | 8[1] | 7 | 4 | 6 | | | | 9 | 10[1] | 11[1] | | | 3 | 5 | | | 12 | | | | 2 | | | | 14 | |
| Mar 1 | H | Clyde | 2-0 | 1 | | 7 | 2[1] | 4 | 6 | | | 14 | 9 | 10 | 11[1] | | 3 | 5 | | | | | | | | | | 8 | | |
| 5 | A | Dumbarton | 1-0 | 1 | | 2 | 4 | 6 | | | | 14 | 9[1] | 10 | 11 | 3 | | 5 | | | | | | | | | 7 | 8 | | |
| 12 | A | St. Mirren | 4-0 | 1 | | 2 | 4 | 6 | | | | 9[1] | 10 | 11[1] | | 3 | 8 | 5 | | 14 | | | | | | | 7[2] | | | |
| 19 | H | Ayr United | 2-0 | 1 | | 2 | 4 | 6 | | | | 9 | 10 | 11[1] | | 3 | 8[1] | 5 | 12 | | | | | | | | 7 | | 14 | |
| 26 | A | Dunfermline Athletic | 1-1 | 1 | | 2 | 4 | 6 | | | 14 | 9 | 10 | 11[1] | | 3 | 8 | 5 | | | | | | | | | 7 | | | 12 |
| 29 | H | Greenock Morton | 1-0 | 1 | | 2 | 4 | 6 | | | | 9[1] | 10 | 11 | | 3 | 8 | 5 | | 14 | | | | | | | 7 | | 12 | |
| Apr 2 | A | Airdrieonians | 0-0 | 1 | | 2 | 4 | 6 | | | | 9 | 10 | 11 | | 3 | | 5 | | | 8 | | | | | | 7 | | | |
| 9 | H | Brechin City | 4-2 | 1 | 3 | | | | 6[1] | | | 11 | 9[1] | 10 | 12 | 4[1] | 5 | | | | 2 | | | | | 7 | 8 | 14[1] | | |
| 16 | A | Clyde | 1-1 | 1 | 3 | | | | 6 | | | 11 | 9 | 10[1] | 12 | 4 | 5 | | | | 2 | | | | | 7 | 8 | 14 | | |
| 23 | H | Dumbarton | 4-0 | 1 | 3 | | | | 6 | | | 11[2] | 9[1] | 10 | | 4 | 5 | | | | 2 | | | | | 7[1] | 14 | 8 | 12 | |
| 26 | A | St. Mirren | 3-0 | 1 | | | | | 6 | | | 9[1] | 10 | | | 4 | 5 | 12 | 14 | | 2 | | | | | 7[1] | 3[1] | 8 | 11 | |
| 30 | A | Stirling Albion | 1-0 | 1 | 2 | | 4 | | 6 | | | 9 | 10 | 14 | | 3 | 5 | | | | | | | | | 7 | 12[1] | 8 | 11 | |
| May 7 | H | Hamilton Academical | 3-0 | 1 | 2 | | 4[1] | | 6 | | | 9[1] | 10 | 12[1] | | 3 | 5 | | | 14 | | | | | | 7 | 8 | 11 | | |
| 14 | A | Clydebank | 1-1 | 1 | 2 | | 4 | | 6 | | | 11 | 9 | 10 | | | 5 | | 14 | | | | | | 7 | 3 | 8[1] | | | |
| **TOTAL FULL APPEARANCES** | | | | 41 | 23 | 14 | 37 | 28 | 36 | 8 | 34 | 39 | 32 | 18 | | 26 | 31 | 37 | 14 | 4 | 5 | 18 | 1 | 3 | 7 | | 12 | 6 | 8 | 2 |
| **TOTAL SUB APPEARANCES** | | | | | (1) | (1) | (1) | (4) | (4) | | (3) | | (10) | (1) | | | (2) | | (5) | (9) | (12) | (2) | | | (2) | | (3) | (2) | (4) |
| **TOTAL GOALS SCORED** | | | | | 10 | 1 | 3 | 3 | 3 | 1 | 9 | 17 | 2 | 10 | | 2 | 2 | | 1 | 1 | 6 | | | | | 4 | 2 | 2 | |

---

## BROCKVILLE PARK

**CAPACITY:** 12,800; Seated 2,661, Standing 10,139

**PITCH DIMENSIONS:** 110 yds x 72 yds

**FACILITIES FOR DISABLED SUPPORTERS:** Viewing area behind each goal.

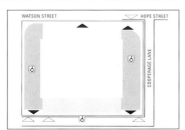

WATSON STREET · HOPE STREET · COOPERAGE LANE

## HOW TO GET THERE

Brockville Park can be reached by the following routes:

**TRAINS:** The main Edinburgh-Glasgow railway line passes by the ground and passengers can alight at Grahamston Station. They will then have a walk of 100 yards to the ground.

**BUSES:** All buses departing from the city centre pass by Brockville.

**CARS:** Car parking facilities are available in the Meeks Road car park for coaches and cars and also in a local shopping car park which can hold 500 cars. Supporters coaches and cars will be directed to the appropriate parking area by the police on duty.

YOUNGER'S
**TARTAN SPECIAL**

# HEART OF MIDLOTHIAN

**LIST OF PLAYERS 1994-95**

Heart of Midlothian F.C. PLC.,
Tynecastle Park, Gorgie Road,
Edinburgh EH11 2NL

**CHAIRMAN**
Christopher P. Robinson

**VICE-CHAIRMAN**
Leslie G. Deans

**DIRECTORS**
Fraser S. Jackson & Colin G. Wilson

**SECRETARY**
Leslie W. Porteous

**MANAGER**
Thomas McLean

**COACHES**
Eamonn Bannon, Thomas Forsyth
& Walter Kidd

**YOUTH COACH**
Brian Whittaker

**CLUB DOCTOR**
Dr. Melvin

**PHYSIOTHERAPIST**
Alan Rae

**S.F.A. COMMUNITY OFFICER**
Bobby Jenks

**CHIEF SCOUT**
Douglas Dalgleish

**GROUNDSMAN**
Ronnie Blair

**COMMERCIAL MANAGER**
Charles Burnett
Tel 031-337 9011
Fax 031-346 8974

**TELEPHONES**
Ground 031-337 6132
Fax 031-346 0699
Telex 72694
Ticket Office 031-337 9011
Information Service 031-346 8556

**CLUB SHOP**
Heart of Midlothian Sport & Leisure,
Tynecastle Park, McLeod Street,
Edinburgh. Tel 031-346 8511.
Open 9.30 a.m. – 5.30 p.m.
Mon. to Sat. and match days.

**OFFICIAL SUPPORTERS CLUB**
Heart of Midlothian Federation,
Alex Jones, 9 George Crescent,
Loanhead

**TEAM CAPTAIN**
Alan McLaren

**SHIRT SPONSOR**
Strongbow

| SURNAME | FIRST NAME | MIDDLE NAME | DATE OF BIRTH | PLACE OF BIRTH | DATE OF SIGNING | HEIGHT FT INS | WEIGHT ST LBS | PREVIOUS CLUB |
|---|---|---|---|---|---|---|---|---|
| Barnes | Derek | | 20/09/77 | Glasgow | 19/08/94 | 6 0.0 | 11 0 | Rangers B.C. |
| Barr | Anthony | | 11/09/77 | Bellshill | 20/07/94 | 5 9.0 | 10 1 | Yett Farm B.C. |
| Berry | Neil | | 06/04/63 | Edinburgh | 05/12/84 | 6 0.0 | 12 7 | Bolton Wanderers |
| Bradley | Mark | | 10/08/76 | Glasgow | 31/07/92 | 5 6.0 | 9 7 | Highbury B.C. |
| Burns | John | Paul | 11/03/78 | Kirkcaldy | 20/07/94 | 5 6.0 | 10 9 | Yett Farm B.C. |
| Callaghan | Stuart | | 20/07/76 | Calderbank | 03/08/92 | 5 8.0 | 10 3 | Blantyre B.C. |
| Colquhoun | John | Mark | 14/07/63 | Stirling | 27/07/93 | 5 8.0 | 11 2 | Sunderland |
| Duncan | Grant | | 04/04/77 | Edinburgh | 25/08/93 | 5 7.0 | 10 7 | Hutchison Vale B.C. |
| Foster | Wayne | Paul | 11/09/63 | Tyldesley | 11/08/86 | 5 10.0 | 12 3 | Preston North End |
| Frail | Stephen | Charles | 10/08/69 | Glasgow | 31/03/94 | 6 0.0 | 11 13 | Dundee |
| Harrison | Thomas | Edward | 22/01/74 | Edinburgh | 25/04/90 | 5 9.0 | 11 8 | Salvesen B.C. |
| Hogg | Graeme | James | 17/06/64 | Aberdeen | 23/08/91 | 6 2.0 | 13 5 | Portsmouth |
| Horn | Robert | | 03/08/77 | Edinburgh | 20/07/94 | 5 9.0 | 11 0 | Yett Farm B.C. |
| Johnston | Allan | | 14/12/73 | Glasgow | 23/06/90 | 5 11.0 | 11 0 | Tynecastle Boys Club |
| Johnston | Maurice | Thomas | 13/04/63 | Glasgow | 20/10/93 | 5 9.0 | 11 4 | Everton |
| Kidd | Walter | Joseph | 10/03/58 | Edinburgh | 12/08/94 | 5 11.0 | 12 3 | Airdrieonians |
| Leitch | Donald | Scott | 06/10/69 | Motherwell | 06/08/93 | 5 9.0 | 11 8 | Dunfermline Athletic |
| Levein | Craig | William | 22/10/64 | Dunfermline | 25/11/83 | 6 2.0 | 13 0 | Cowdenbeath |
| Locke | Gary | | 16/06/75 | Edinburgh | 31/07/92 | 5 10.0 | 11 8 | Whitehill Welfare |
| Mackay | Gary | | 23/01/64 | Edinburgh | 16/06/80 | 5 9.0 | 11 8 | Salvesen B.C. |
| Mathieson | Peter | David | 18/10/77 | Edinburgh | 19/08/94 | 5 3.0 | 8 8 | Yett Farm B.C. |
| McKinlay | Thomas | Valley | 03/12/64 | Glasgow | 07/12/88 | 5 10.0 | 11 9 | Dundee |
| McLaren | Alan | James | 04/01/71 | Edinburgh | 04/07/87 | 6 0.0 | 13 0 | Cavalry Park |
| McManus | Allan | William | 17/11/74 | Paisley | 03/08/92 | 6 0.0 | 12 0 | Links United |
| McNicol | Grant | | 07/09/77 | Edinburgh | 20/07/94 | 5 9.0 | 10 1 | Yett Farm B.C. |
| Millar | John | | 08/12/66 | Bellshill | 26/07/91 | 5 10.0 | 11 10 | Blackburn Rovers |
| Murie | David | | 02/08/76 | Edinburgh | 31/07/92 | 5 8.0 | 10 4 | Tynecastle B.C. |
| Murray | Grant | Robert | 29/08/75 | Edinburgh | 31/07/92 | 5 10.0 | 12 0 | Hutchison Vale B.C. |
| O'Connor | Gary | | 07/04/74 | Newtongrange | 23/02/94 | 6 2.0 | 12 4 | Berwick Rangers |
| Petrucci | Massimo | | 16/05/78 | Edinburgh | 20/07/94 | 5 7.0 | 10 9 | Yett Farm B.C. |
| Queen | Kevin | | 16/08/78 | Glasgow | 26/08/94 | 5 11.0 | 10 10 | Yett Farm B.C. |
| Ritchie | Paul | Simon | 21/08/75 | Kirkcaldy | 31/07/92 | 5 11.0 | 12 0 | Links United |
| Robertson | John | Grant | 02/10/64 | Edinburgh | 09/12/88 | 5 6.0 | 11 4 | Newcastle United |
| Smith | Henry | George | 10/03/56 | Lanark | 05/08/81 | 6 2.0 | 13 2 | Leeds United |
| Storrar | Andrew | David | 06/10/77 | Stirling | 20/07/94 | 5 5.0 | 10 6 | Yett Farm B.C. |
| Thomas | Kevin | Roderick | 25/04/75 | Edinburgh | 31/07/92 | 5 11.0 | 12 5 | Links United |
| Walker | Joseph | Nicol | 29/09/62 | Aberdeen | 23/08/89 | 6 2.0 | 12 7 | Rangers |
| Weir | James | McIntosh | 15/06/69 | Motherwell | 15/08/93 | 6 1.0 | 12 5 | Hamilton Academical |
| Wright | George | | 22/12/69 | South Africa | 04/07/87 | 5 9.0 | 11 4 | Hutchison Vale B.C. |

## MILESTONES

**YEAR OF FORMATION:** 1874
**MOST CAPPED PLAYER:** Bobby Walker
**NO. OF CAPS:** 29
**MOST LEAGUE POINTS IN A SEASON:** 63 (Premier Division – Season 1991/92)
**MOST LEAGUE GOALS SCORED BY A PLAYER IN A SEASON:** Barney Battles (Season 1930/31)
**NO. OF GOALS SCORED:** 44
**RECORD ATTENDANCE:** 53,496 (-v- Rangers 13.2.1932)
**RECORD VICTORY:** 18-0 (-v- Vale of Lothian – Edinburgh Shield 17.9.1887)
**RECORD DEFEAT:** 1-8 (-v- Vale of Leven – Scottish Cup 1883)

## SEASON TICKET INFORMATION

**Seated**
**Main Stand**
| | | | |
|---|---|---|---|
| Old Centre Stand | Adult .......... £203 | | |
| Old North Stand | Adult .......... £183 | OAP ............. £140 | |
| North Enclosure | Adult .......... £170 | Juvenile/OAP ... £90 | |

**Wheatfield Stand**
| | | |
|---|---|---|
| New Centre Stand – Club Room Facilities | Adult ............. £325 | |
| New Centre Stand | Adult ............. £235 | |
| New Centre Stand Inner Section | Adult ............. £220 | |
| New Centre Stand Outer Section | Adult ............. £200 | |
| Family Section | Adult .......... £155 | Juvenile .......... £75 |

## LEAGUE ADMISSION PRICES

**Seated**
**Main Stand**
| | | Cat A Matches | Cat B Matches |
|---|---|---|---|
| Old Centre Stand | | £11 | £10 |
| Old North Stand | | £10 | £9 |
| North Enclosure | Adult | £9.50 | £8.50 |
| | Juvenile/OAP | – | £5 |

**Wheatfield Stand**
| | | | |
|---|---|---|---|
| New Centre Stand | | £13 | £12 |
| New Centre Stand Inner Section | | £12 | £11 |
| New Centre Stand Outer Section | | £11 | £10 |
| Family Section | Adult | £9 | £8 |
| | Juvenile/OAP | £4 | £4 |

**REGISTERED STRIP:** Shirt – Maroon with White Trim, Shorts – White with Maroon Trim, Stockings – Maroon with White Trim
**CHANGE STRIP:** Shirt – White with a Maroon Candy Stripe, Shorts – Maroon with White Trim, Stockings – White with Maroon Trim

## CLUB FACTFILE 1993/94 .. RESULTS .. APPEARANCES .. SCORERS

### The JAM TARTS

| Date | Venue | Opponents | Result | Smith H. | Locke G. | McKinlay T. | Levein C. | Berry N. | Van De Ven P. | Colquhoun J. | Mackay G. | Fashanu J. | Wright G. | Robertson J. | Ferguson I. | Johnston A. | Thomas K. | Weir J. | Hogg G. | Leitch S. | McLaren A. | Walker J.N. | Harrison T. | Johnston M. | Millar J. | Foster W. | Frail S. |
|---|---|---|---|---|---|---|---|---|---|---|---|---|---|---|---|---|---|---|---|---|---|---|---|---|---|---|---|
| Aug 7 | A | Rangers | 1-2 | 1 | 2 | 3 | 4 | 5 | 6 | 7 | 8 | 9 | 10 | 11 | $12^1$ | 14 | | | | | | | | | | | |
| 14 | H | Raith Rovers | 1-0 | 1 | 2 | 3 | 4 | 5 | 6 | 7 | 8 | 9 | 10 | $11^1$ | 12 | 14 | | | | | | | | | | | |
| 21 | H | Hibernian | 1-0 | 1 | 2 | 3 | 4 | 5 | | 7 | 8 | 9 | 10 | 11 | $12^1$ | 14 | 6 | | | | | | | | | | |
| 28 | A | Dundee United | 0-0 | 1 | 2 | 3 | 4 | | | 7 | 8 | 9 | 10 | 12 | 11 | | 6 | 5 | 14 | | | | | | | | |
| Sep 4 | H | Partick Thistle | 2-1 | 1 | 2 | 3 | $4^1$ | | 6 | 7 | 8 | $9^1$ | 10 | 12 | 11 | | | 5 | 14 | | | | | | | | |
| 11 | A | Motherwell | 0-2 | 1 | 2 | 3 | 4 | | | 7 | 8 | 9 | 10 | 11 | 12 | | | 14 | 6 | | | | | | | | |
| 18 | A | Kilmarnock | 0-1 | 1 | 2 | 3 | 4 | | | 7 | 8 | | | 11 | 9 | 14 | | 5 | 12 | 10 | 6 | | | | | | |
| 25 | H | Celtic | 1-0 | 1 | 2 | 3 | 4 | | | 7 | 8 | 9 | | $11^1$ | 14 | | | 12 | 5 | 10 | 6 | | | | | | |
| Oct 2 | A | Dundee | 0-2 | | 2 | 3 | | 4 | | 7 | | 9 | | 11 | 12 | 14 | | 8 | 5 | 10 | 6 | 1 | | | | | |
| 5 | A | Aberdeen | 0-0 | | 2 | 3 | | 6 | | 12 | 8 | 9 | | 11 | | | | 7 | 5 | 10 | 4 | 1 | | | | | |
| 9 | A | St. Johnstone | 1-1 | | 2 | 3 | | 6 | | 8 | 9 | | | $11^1$ | 7 | 14 | | 5 | 10 | 4 | 1 | | | | | | |
| 16 | A | Raith Rovers | 0-1 | | 2 | 3 | | | | 12 | 8 | 9 | | 11 | 7 | 14 | | 6 | 5 | 4 | 1 | 10 | | | | | |
| 23 | A | Partick Thistle | 0-0 | | | 3 | 4 | | | 9 | 7 | | | 11 | | | | 6 | 5 | 8 | 2 | 1 | 10 | | | | |
| 30 | H | Hibernian | 2-0 | | 8 | 3 | 4 | | | $9^2$ | | | | 11 | 14 | | | 2 | 5 | 7 | 6 | 1 | 10 | | | | |
| Nov 3 | A | Rangers | 2-2 | | 7 | | 4 | | | $9^1$ | $14^1$ | | 3 | 11 | 12 | | | 2 | 5 | 8 | 6 | 1 | 10 | | | | |
| 6 | H | Dundee United | 1-1 | | 2 | 3 | | | | 9 | 8 | | 4 | 11 | 12 | | | 5 | 7 | 6 | 1 | $10^1$ | | | | | |
| 13 | H | Dundee | †1-2 | | 2 | 3 | | | | 9 | 8 | | 4 | 11 | 12 | 14 | | 5 | 7 | 6 | 1 | 10 | | | | | |
| 20 | A | Celtic | 0-0 | | 8 | 3 | | 6 | | 9 | | | | 11 | | | | 2 | 5 | 7 | 4 | 1 | 10 | 14 | | | |
| 30 | A | Kilmarnock | 0-0 | | 8 | 3 | | | | 7 | 11 | | | 9 | | 12 | 14 | 2 | 5 | 6 | 4 | 1 | 10 | | | | |
| Dec 4 | H | Aberdeen | 1-1 | | | 3 | | 5 | | $7^1$ | 8 | | | 11 | 14 | 9 | 2 | | 6 | 4 | 1 | 10 | | | | | |
| 11 | H | St. Johnstone | 0-2 | | 14 | 3 | | 5 | | 7 | 8 | 12 | | 11 | | 9 | 2 | | 6 | 4 | 1 | 10 | | | | | |
| 15 | H | Motherwell | 2-3 | | 10 | 3 | | 5 | | 7 | 11 | | | | 9 | 2 | | | $6^1$ | 4 | 1 | $8^1$ | 14 | 12 | | | |
| 18 | H | Raith Rovers | 0-1 | | 11 | 3 | | 5 | | 7 | 8 | | | 12 | 9 | 2 | | | 6 | 4 | 1 | 10 | | 14 | | | |
| 27 | A | Rangers | 2-2 | | 6 | 3 | | 2 | | 9 | | 14 | $12^1$ | 7 | | 5 | | | 4 | 1 | 8 | $10^1$ | 11 | | | | |
| Jan 8 | A | Dundee United | 0-3 | | 6 | 3 | | 2 | | 9 | 12 | | | 14 | 7 | | 5 | | 8 | 4 | 1 | 10 | 11 | | | | |
| 12 | H | Hibernian | 1-1 | 1 | 2 | 3 | 4 | 5 | | 12 | 8 | | | 11 | | | | 7 | 6 | | 10 | $14^1$ | 9 | | | | |
| 15 | H | Partick Thistle | 1-0 | 1 | 14 | 3 | 4 | 5 | | 7 | 8 | | | 11 | | | | 9 | 2 | | 10 | $6^1$ | | | | | |
| 22 | H | Kilmarnock | 1-1 | 1 | 2 | 3 | 4 | 5 | | 7 | 8 | | | $11^1$ | 14 | | | 9 | 6 | | 10 | | 12 | | | | |
| Feb 5 | A | Motherwell | 1-1 | 1 | 2 | 3 | 4 | 5 | | | 8 | | 12 | $11^1$ | | | | 7 | 6 | | 10 | | 9 | | | | |
| 12 | H | Celtic | 0-2 | 1 | 2 | 3 | 4 | | | | 8 | | | 11 | 14 | | | 5 | 7 | 6 | 10 | | 9 | | | | |
| Mar 1 | A | Dundee | 2-0 | 1 | | 3 | 4 | 5 | | 7 | 8 | | | 2 | | | | | 14 | 6 | $10^2$ | 11 | 9 | | | | |
| 5 | A | Aberdeen | 1-0 | 1 | | 14 | 3 | 4 | 5 | 7 | | | | 12 | | | | 2 | | $8^1$ | 6 | 10 | 11 | 9 | | | |
| 19 | A | Raith Rovers | 2-2 | 1 | | 14 | 3 | $4^1$ | | $7^1$ | | | | 12 | | | | 2 | 5 | 8 | 6 | 10 | 11 | 9 | | | |
| 26 | A | Rangers | 1-2 | 1 | | 6 | 3 | 4 | | 7 | | | | 9 | 12 | | | 2 | 5 | | | 10 | 11 | $14^1$ | | | |
| 30 | H | Motherwell | 0-0 | 1 | | | 3 | 4 | 5 | 7 | 8 | | 2 | 9 | 14 | | | | | | 6 | 10 | 11 | 12 | | | |
| Apr 2 | A | Kilmarnock | 1-0 | 1 | | | 3 | 4 | 5 | 7 | 8 | | | 9 | | | | | | | 6 | 10 | $11^1$ | 12 | 2 | | |
| 6 | H | St. Johnstone | †2-2 | 1 | | | 3 | 4 | 5 | 7 | 8 | | | $9^1$ | 14 | | | | | | 6 | 10 | 11 | 2 | | | |
| 9 | A | Celtic | 2-2 | 1 | | | 3 | 4 | 5 | $7^1$ | 8 | | | 9 | 14 | | | | | | 6 | 10 | 11 | 12 | $2^1$ | | |
| 16 | H | Dundee | 0-2 | 1 | | | 3 | 4 | 5 | 7 | 8 | | | 9 | 12 | 6 | | | | | | 10 | 11 | 14 | 2 | | |
| 23 | A | St. Johnstone | 0-0 | 1 | | | 3 | 4 | 5 | 7 | 8 | | | 9 | | 6 | | | | | | 10 | 11 | | 2 | | |
| 27 | H | Aberdeen | 1-1 | 1 | | | 3 | 4 | 5 | 7 | 8 | | | $9^1$ | | | | | | | 6 | 10 | 11 | | 2 | | |
| 30 | A | Hibernian | 0-0 | 1 | | | 3 | 4 | 5 | 7 | 8 | | | 9 | | | | | | | 6 | 10 | 11 | 12 | 2 | | |
| May 7 | H | Dundee United | 2-0 | 1 | 8 | | 3 | $4^1$ | 5 | 7 | | | | 9 | | | | | | | 6 | 10 | 11 | 12 | $2^1$ | | |
| 14 | A | Partick Thistle | 1-0 | 1 | 11 | | 3 | 4 | | 7 | 8 | | | 9 | | | | | 5 | | $6^1$ | 10 | 14 | | 2 | | |
| **TOTAL FULL APPEARANCES** | | | | 27 | 29 | 43 | 30 | 30 | 2 | 38 | 34 | 10 | 10 | 32 | 3 | 5 | 7 | 25 | 16 | 24 | 37 | 17 | 1 | 31 | 16 | 8 | 9 |
| **TOTAL SUB APPEARANCES** | | | | | (4) | | | | | (3) | (2) | (1) | (2) | | (4) | (3) | (23) | (5) | (1) | (1) | (4) | | | (4) | (10) | | |
| **TOTAL GOALS SCORED** | | | | | | 3 | | | | 6 | 1 | 1 | | 8 | 1 | 1 | | | | | 2 | 1 | | 4 | 4 | 1 | 2 |

*Small bold figures denote goalscorers.   † denotes opponent's own goal.*

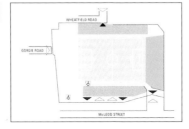

### TYNECASTLE PARK

**CAPACITY:** 17,000 (All Seated)
PLEASE NOTE: CAPACITY MAY ALTER DURING THE COURSE OF THE SEASON OWING TO RE-BUILDING WORK TAKING PLACE AT STADIUM

**PITCH DIMENSIONS:** 108 yds x 73 yds

**FACILITIES FOR DISABLED SUPPORTERS:** Ten spaces (must be pre-booked) at South end of the Enclosure.

### HOW TO GET THERE

Tynecastle Park can be reached by the following routes:

**BUSES:** A frequent service of buses leaves from the city centre, Nos. 1, 2, 3, 4, 33, 34, 35 and 44 all pass the ground.

**TRAINS:** Haymarket Station is about half a mile from the ground.

**CARS:** Car Parking facilities exist in the adjacent side streets in Robertson Avenue and also the Westfield area.

# HIBERNIAN

## LIST OF PLAYERS 1994-95

| SURNAME | FIRST NAME | MIDDLE NAME | DATE OF BIRTH | PLACE OF BIRTH | DATE OF SIGNING | HEIGHT FT INS | WEIGHT ST LBS | PREVIOUS CLUB |
|---|---|---|---|---|---|---|---|---|
| Balmain | Kenneth | John A. | 08/11/73 | Bellshill | 14/05/91 | 5 9.0 | 12 0 | Eastercraigs B.C. |
| Beaumont | David | | 10/12/63 | Edinburgh | 17/10/91 | 6 0.0 | 12 9 | Luton Town |
| Brown | Stewart | Anderson | 08/10/75 | Bangour | 03/08/92 | 5 9.0 | 11 7 | Hutchison Vale B.C. |
| Dallas | Stephen | | 02/11/74 | Glasgow | 03/08/92 | 5 7.0 | 10 4 | Duntocher B.C. |
| Dods | Darren | | 07/06/75 | Edinburgh | 03/08/92 | 6 1.0 | 12 13 | Hutchison Vale B.C. |
| Donald | Graeme | Still | 14/04/74 | Stirling | 12/06/91 | 6 0.0 | 12 1 | Gairdoch United |
| Evans | Gareth | John | 14/01/67 | Coventry | 06/02/88 | 5 7.5 | 11 0 | Rotherham United |
| Farrell | David | | 29/10/69 | Glasgow | 12/08/88 | 5 9.0 | 11 4 | Oxford United |
| Findlay | William | McCall | 29/08/70 | Kilmarnock | 13/06/87 | 5 10.0 | 12 13 | Kilmarnock B.C. |
| Gardiner | Jason | Stanley | 30/10/73 | Edinburgh | 14/05/91 | 6 0.0 | 13 3 | Salvesen B.C. |
| Hamilton | Brian | | 05/08/67 | Paisley | 18/07/89 | 6 0.0 | 12 6 | St. Mirren |
| Harper | Kevin | Patrick | 15/01/76 | Oldham | 03/08/92 | 5 6.0 | 10 13 | Hutchison Vale B.C. |
| Hunter | Gordon | | 03/05/67 | Wallyford | 10/08/83 | 5 10.0 | 12 3 | Musselburgh Windsor |
| Jackson | Christopher | | 29/10/73 | Edinburgh | 14/05/91 | 5 7.0 | 10 11 | Salvesen B.C. |
| Jackson | Darren | | 25/07/66 | Edinburgh | 14/07/92 | 5 10.0 | 11 0 | Dundee United |
| Laidlaw | Douglas | | 17/01/76 | Edinburgh | 03/08/92 | 5 10.0 | 11 4 | Hutchison Vale B.C. |
| Leighton | James | | 24/07/58 | Johnstone | 14/07/93 | 6 0.0 | 13 6 | Dundee |
| Lockhart | Darren | Derek | 06/09/77 | Edinburgh | 03/06/94 | 5 10.0 | 10 1 | Hutchison Vale B.C. |
| Love | Graeme | | 07/12/73 | Bathgate | 14/05/91 | 5 10.0 | 12 0 | Salvesen B.C. |
| McAllister | Kevin | | 08/11/62 | Falkirk | 29/07/93 | 5 5.0 | 11 0 | Falkirk |
| McDonald | Ian | | 07/03/78 | Newcastle | 19/07/94 | 6 0.0 | 12 3 | Salvesen B.C. |
| McGraw | Mark | Robertson | 05/01/71 | Rutherglen | 14/02/90 | 5 11.5 | 11 2 | Greenock Morton |
| Miller | Graeme | | 21/02/73 | Glasgow | 11/06/90 | 5 7.0 | 10 3 | Tynecastle B.C. |
| Miller | Greg | | 01/04/76 | Glasgow | 29/07/94 | 5 7.5 | 9 6 | Hutchison Vale B.C |
| Miller | William | | 01/11/69 | Edinburgh | 14/03/87 | 5 8.0 | 11 2 | Edina Hibs B.C. |
| Mitchell | Graham | | 02/11/62 | Glasgow | 31/12/86 | 5 10.0 | 11 12 | Hamilton Academical |
| Mitchell | Scott | Cameron | 18/04/76 | Paisley | 29/04/93 | 5 11.0 | 11 9 | Duntocher B.C. |
| O'Neill | Michael | Andrew M. | 05/07/69 | Portadown | 20/08/93 | 5 11.5 | 11 3 | Dundee United |
| Orr | Alan | John | 05/01/77 | Vale of Leven | 20/07/93 | 5 9.0 | 10 5 | "S" Form |
| Paton | Eric | John | 01/08/78 | Glasgow | 19/07/94 | 5 8.5 | 10 4 | Hutchison Vale B.C. |
| Reid | Christopher | Thomas | 04/11/71 | Edinburgh | 20/06/88 | 5 11.0 | 13 7 | Hutchison Vale B.C. |
| Renwick | Michael | | 29/02/76 | Edinburgh | 03/08/92 | 5 9.0 | 11 0 | Hutchison Vale B.C. |
| Riley | Paul | | 07/08/75 | Edinburgh | 03/08/92 | 5 7.0 | 9 11 | Hutchison Vale B.C. |
| Tortolano | Joseph | | 06/04/66 | Stirling | 29/08/85 | 5 8.0 | 11 6 | West Bromwich Albion |
| Tweed | Steven | | 08/08/72 | Edinburgh | 25/08/90 | 6 3.0 | 15 0 | Hutchison Vale B.C. |
| Weir | Michael | Graham | 16/01/66 | Edinburgh | 14/01/88 | 5 4.0 | 10 3 | Luton Town |
| Wight | Craig | MacDonald | 24/07/78 | Glasgow | 19/07/94 | 5 11.0 | 10 4 | Salvesen B.C. |
| Wright | Keith | | 17/05/65 | Edinburgh | 01/08/91 | 5 11.0 | 12 6 | Dundee |

### Easter Road Stadium, 64 Albion Road, Edinburgh EH7 5QG

**CHAIRMAN**
Douglas W. M. Cromb

**DIRECTORS**
Robert Huthersall
Allan Munro
Thomas J. O'Malley
Kenneth McLean
Ian Brennan

**SECRETARY**
Cecil F. Graham, F.F.A.

**MANAGER**
Alexander Miller

**COACH**
Donald Park & Jocky Scott

**CLUB DOCTOR**
James Ledingham

**PHYSIOTHERAPIST**
Stuart Collie

**S.F.A. COMMUNITY COACH**
John Ritchie

**COMMERCIAL MANAGER**
Ian Erskine
031-661 2159

**TELEPHONES**
Ground 031-661 2159
Fax 031-659-6488
Ticket Office 031-652 0630
Information Service
(0891) 121189

**CLUB SHOP**
178A Easter Road, Edinburgh

**OFFICIAL SUPPORTERS CLUB**
11 Sunnyside Lane, Off Easter Road,
Edinburgh EH7

**TEAM CAPTAIN**
Gordon Hunter

**SHIRT SPONSOR**
Calor Gas (Scotland)

## MILESTONES

**YEAR OF FORMATION:** 1875
**MOST CAPPED PLAYER:** Lawrie Reilly
**NO. OF CAPS:** 38
**MOST LEAGUE POINTS IN A SEASON:** 57 (First Division – Season 1980/81)
**MOST LEAGUE GOALS SCORED BY A PLAYER IN A SEASON:** Joe Baker (Season 1959/60)
**NO. OF GOALS SCORED:** 42
**RECORD ATTENDANCE:** 65,860 (-v- Heart of Midlothian – 2.1.1950)
**RECORD VICTORY:** 22-1 (-v- 42nd Highlanders 3.9.1881)
**RECORD DEFEAT:** 0-10 (-v- Rangers 24.12.1898)

## SEASON TICKET INFORMATION

**Seated**

| | | |
|---|---|---|
| Centre Stand | Adult | £195 |
| | Juvenile/OAP | £150 |
| Wing Stand | Adult | £165 |
| | Juvenile/OAP | £120 |
| Seated Enclosure | Adult | £140 |
| | OAP | £75 |
| | Juvenile | £50 |
| Family Enclosure | Adult | £130 |
| | First Child | £50 |
| | Second Child | £40 |
| East Seated Terrace | Adult | £140 |
| | Juvenile/OAP | £75 |

## LEAGUE ADMISSION PRICES

**Seated**

| | | |
|---|---|---|
| Centre Stand | Adult | £11 |
| Wing Stand North | Adult | £9.50 |
| Wing Stand South | Adult | £10 |
| Seated Enclosure | Adult | £8 |
| | Juvenile/OAP | £4 |
| Family Enclosure | Adult | £8 |
| | Juvenile | £4 |
| Seated Terrace | Adult | £8 |
| | Juvenile/OAP | £4 |
| South Enclosure | Adult | £9 |

Please note: No concessions in all ticket games -v- Celtic, Hearts and Rangers (No Juvenile/OAP gates)

REGISTERED STRIP: Shirt – Green with Green and White Striped Sleeves, White Collar
Shorts – White with Green Trim, Stockings – Green with White Tops

CHANGE STRIP: Shirt – Purple and Green Stripes with Green Collar
Shorts – Purple with Green Trim, Stockings – Purple with Green Tops

## CLUB FACTFILE 1993/94 .. RESULTS .. APPEARANCES .. SCORERS

### The HIBEES

| Date | Venue | Opponents | Result | Leighton J. | Miller W. | Tortolano J. | McIntyre T. | Tweed S. | Hunter G. | McAllister K. | Hamilton B. | Wright K. | Jackson D. | Findlay W. | Lennon D. | McGraw M. | Beaumont D. | Donald G. | Farrell D. | O'Neill M. | Evans G. | Mitchell G. | Jackson C. | Harper K. | Love G. | Bannon E. | Miller G. |
|---|---|---|---|---|---|---|---|---|---|---|---|---|---|---|---|---|---|---|---|---|---|---|---|---|---|---|---|
| Aug 7 | H | Partick Thistle | 0-0 | 1 | 2 | 3 | 4 | 5 | 6 | 7 | 8 | 9 | 10 | 11 | 12 | 14 | | | | | | | | | | | |
| 14 | A | Celtic | 1-1 | 1 | 2 | | 4 | 5[1] | 6 | 7 | 8 | 9 | 10 | 14 | | | 3 | | | 11 | 12 | | | | | | |
| 21 | A | Heart of Midlothian | 0-1 | 1 | 2 | | 4 | | 6 | 7 | 8 | 9 | 10 | | 14 | | 3 | | 5 | 11 | 12 | | | | | | |
| 28 | H | Dundee | 2-0 | 1 | 2 | | 4 | | 6 | 7[1] | 14 | 9 | 12 | | | 8 | 3[1] | | 5 | 11 | 10 | | | | | | |
| Sep 4 | A | Kilmarnock | 1-1 | 1 | 2 | | 4 | 3 | 6 | 7 | 5 | 12 | 10 | 8 | | | | | | 14 | 11 | 9[1] | | | | | |
| 11 | A | Aberdeen | 2-1 | 1 | 2 | | | 5 | 6 | 7[1] | 14 | 9[1] | 10 | 8 | | | | | 4 | 11 | 12 | 3 | | | | | |
| 18 | H | St. Johnstone | 3-1 | 1 | 2 | | | 5 | 6 | 7[1] | | 9[1] | | 8 | | | | | 4 | 11[1] | 10 | 3 | 12 | 14 | | | |
| 25 | A | Rangers | 1-2 | 1 | 2 | | | 5 | 6 | 7 | 4 | 9 | 10 | | | | | | 14 | 11 | 8[1] | 3 | | | | | |
| Oct 2 | H | Dundee United | 2-0 | 1 | 2 | 14 | | 5 | | 7 | 8 | 9 | 10[2] | | | | 6 | | 4 | 11 | 12 | 3 | | | | | |
| 5 | H | Raith Rovers | 3-2 | 1 | 2 | | | 5 | | 7[1] | 8 | 9 | 10[1] | | | | 6 | | 4 | 11[1] | 12 | 3 | | | | | |
| 9 | A | Motherwell | 2-0 | 1 | 2 | | | 5 | | 7 | 8 | 9[1] | 10[1] | | | | 6 | | 4 | 11 | 12 | 3 | | | | | |
| 16 | H | Celtic | 1-1 | 1 | 2 | 14 | | | 6 | 7 | 8 | 9 | | | | | 5 | | 4 | 11 | 10[1] | 3 | | | | | |
| 30 | H | Heart of Midlothian | 0-2 | 1 | 2 | | | 5 | 6 | 7 | 8 | 9 | 10 | | | | | | 4 | 11 | 12 | 3 | | | | | |
| Nov 2 | A | Partick Thistle | 0-0 | 1 | 2 | 12 | | 5 | 6 | 7 | 8 | 9 | 14 | | | | | | | 11 | 10 | 3 | 4 | | | | |
| 6 | A | Dundee | †2-3 | 1 | 2 | | | 5 | 6 | 7 | 8 | 9[1] | 10 | | | | | | 12 | | | 3 | 4 | 11 | | | |
| 9 | H | Kilmarnock | 2-1 | 1 | 2 | | | 5[1] | 6[1] | 7 | 8 | 9 | 10 | | | | | | 14 | 11 | 12 | 3 | 4 | | | | |
| 13 | A | Dundee United | 2-2 | 1 | 2 | 14 | | 5 | 6 | | 8[1] | 9 | 10[1] | | | | 7 | | | 12 | 11 | 3 | 4 | | | | |
| 20 | H | Rangers | 0-1 | 1 | 2 | 3 | | 5 | 6 | | 8 | 9 | 10 | 14 | | | | | 4 | 11 | 7 | | | | | | |
| 27 | A | Aberdeen | 0-4 | 1 | 2 | 7 | | 5 | 6 | | 8 | | 10 | | | | 12 | | 4 | 11 | 9 | 3 | | | | | |
| 30 | H | St. Johnstone | 0-0 | 1 | 2 | 12 | | 5 | 6 | | 8 | 9 | 10 | 14 | | | | | | 11 | 7 | 3 | 4 | | | | |
| Dec 4 | A | Raith Rovers | 2-1 | 1 | 2 | 7 | | 5 | 6 | | 8 | 9[1] | 10 | 4[1] | | | | | | 11 | 14 | 3 | 12 | | | | |
| 11 | H | Motherwell | 3-2 | 1 | 2 | 7 | | 5 | 6 | | 8 | 9[1] | 10 | 4[1] | | | | | | 14 | 11 | 12 | 3[1] | | | | |
| 18 | A | Celtic | 0-1 | 1 | 2 | 11 | | | 6 | 7 | 8 | 9 | 10 | 4 | | | 5 | | | 14 | 12 | 3 | | | | | |
| 27 | H | Partick Thistle | 5-1 | 1 | 2 | 11 | | 14 | 6 | 7[1] | 8[1] | 9[1] | 10[1] | | | | 5 | | 4[1] | | 12 | 3 | | | | | |
| Jan 8 | H | Dundee | 2-0 | 1 | 2 | 11[1] | | 5 | | 7[1] | 8 | 9 | 10 | 14 | | | 6 | | 4 | | 12 | 3 | | | | | |
| 12 | A | Heart of Midlothian | 1-1 | 1 | 2 | 11 | | | 6 | 7 | 8 | 9[1] | 12 | | | | 5 | | 4 | | 10 | 3 | | | | | |
| 15 | A | Kilmarnock | 3-0 | 1 | 2 | 14 | | | 6 | 7 | 8 | 9 | | | | | 5[1] | | 4[1] | 11 | 10[1] | 3 | | | | | |
| 22 | A | St. Johnstone | 2-2 | 1 | 2 | 11 | | | | 7 | 8 | 9 | 12[1] | | | | 5 | | 4 | 6[1] | 10 | 3 | | | | | |
| Feb 5 | H | Aberdeen | 3-1 | 1 | 2 | | | | 6 | 7 | | 9[2] | | 8[1] | | | 5 | | 4 | 11 | 10 | 3 | | | | | |
| 12 | A | Rangers | 0-2 | 1 | 2 | | | 5 | 6 | 7 | | 9 | | | | | 14 | 12 | 4 | 11 | 10 | 3 | | | | | |
| 26 | H | Dundee United | 0-1 | 1 | | | | 5 | | 7 | 8 | 9 | 10 | | | 6 | 2 | | 4 | 11 | 12 | 3 | | | | | |
| Mar 5 | H | Raith Rovers | 3-0 | 1 | 2 | | 2 | 5 | | 7 | 8 | 9[2] | 12 | 4[1] | | | 6 | | | 11 | 10 | 3 | 14 | | | | |
| 12 | A | Motherwell | 0-0 | 1 | | | | 5 | 6 | 7 | 8 | 9 | 12 | 4 | | | 2 | | | 14 | 11 | 10 | 3 | | | | |
| 19 | A | Celtic | 0-0 | 1 | | | | | 6 | 7 | 8 | 9 | 12 | 4 | | | 5 | | | 2 | 11 | 10 | 3 | | | | |
| 26 | A | Partick Thistle | 0-1 | 1 | | | | | 14 | 6 | 7 | 8 | 9 | 10 | 4 | | 5 | | 12 | 2 | 11 | 3 | | | | | |
| 29 | A | Aberdeen | 3-2 | 1 | | | | 5[1] | 6 | 7 | 8 | 9[2] | 12 | | | | | | 2 | 11 | 10 | 3 | 4 | | | | |
| Apr 2 | H | St. Johnstone | 0-0 | 1 | | | | 5 | | 7 | 8 | 9 | 12 | 14 | | | 4 | | 2 | 11 | 10 | 3 | 6 | | | | |
| 16 | A | Dundee United | 0-3 | 1 | 2 | 3 | | | 6 | 7 | 8 | 9 | 12 | | | | 5 | | 4 | 11 | 10 | | 14 | | | | |
| 23 | A | Motherwell | 0-2 | 1 | 2 | 3 | | | | 7 | 8 | 9 | 10 | | | | 5 | | 4 | 11 | 12 | 3 | | | 6 | | |
| 26 | A | Raith Rovers | 1-1 | 1 | 2 | | | 5 | | 8 | 9[1] | 10 | 7 | | | | | | 4 | 11 | 12 | 3 | 14 | | 6 | | |
| 30 | H | Heart of Midlothian | 0-0 | 1 | 2 | | | 5 | | 8 | 9 | 10 | 7 | | | | | | 4 | 11 | 12 | 3 | | | 6 | | |
| May 3 | H | Rangers | 1-0 | 1 | 2 | | | 5 | | 7 | 8 | 9[1] | 10 | 12 | | | 4 | | | 6 | 11 | 3 | | | | | |
| 7 | A | Dundee | 0-4 | 1 | 2 | | | 5 | | 7 | 8 | 9 | 10 | 6 | | | 4 | | 14 | 12 | 11 | 3 | | | | | |
| 14 | H | Kilmarnock | 0-0 | 1 | 2 | | | 5 | | 7 | 8 | 9 | 10 | | | | 12 | | | 11 | 3 | 4 | | | 6 | | 14 |
| **TOTAL FULL APPEARANCES** | | | | 44 | 37 | 12 | 11 | 27 | 29 | 36 | 40 | 41 | 29 | 15 | 3 | | 24 | 2 | 26 | 36 | 23 | 36 | 8 | 1 | 3 | 1 | |
| **TOTAL SUB APPEARANCES** | | | | | | (6) | | (2) | | (2) | | (1) | (10) | (5) | (2) | (2) | (2) | | (4) | (9) | | (17) | (4) | (1) | (1) | | (1) |
| **TOTAL GOALS SCORED** | | | | | | 1 | | 3 | 1 | 6 | 2 | 16 | 7 | 3 | 1 | | 2 | | | 2 | 3 | 4 | 1 | | | | |

*Small bold figures denote goalscorers.  † denotes opponent's own goal.*

---

## EASTER ROAD

**CAPACITY:** 13,709 (All seated)

**PITCH DIMENSIONS:** 112 yds x 74 yds

**FACILITIES FOR DISABLED SUPPORTERS:** Area in South Seated Enclosure.

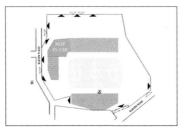

## HOW TO GET THERE

Easter Road Stadium can be reached by the following routes:

**BUSES:** The main bus station in the city is served by buses from all over the country and the following local buses departing from Princes Street all stop near the ground. Nos. 4, 15, 42 and 44.

**TRAINS:** Edinburgh Waverley Station is served by trains from all parts of the country and the above buses all stop near the ground.

# KILMARNOCK

## LIST OF PLAYERS 1994-95

| SURNAME | FIRST NAME | MIDDLE NAME | DATE OF BIRTH | PLACE OF BIRTH | DATE OF SIGNING | HEIGHT FT INS | WEIGHT ST LBS | PREVIOUS CLUB |
|---|---|---|---|---|---|---|---|---|
| Adams | Charles | Stuart S. | 21/03/76 | Irvine | 20/07/94 | 5 10.0 | 11 5 | Kilmarnock B.C. |
| Anderson | Derek | Christopher | 15/05/72 | Paisley | 04/11/93 | 6 0.0 | 11 0 | Kilwinning Rangers |
| Black | Thomas | | 11/10/62 | Lanark | 08/11/91 | 5 8.0 | 10 12 | St. Mirren |
| Brown | Thomas | | 01/04/68 | Glasgow | 27/08/93 | 5 7.0 | 10 0 | Glenafton Athletic |
| Burns * | Thomas | | 16/12/56 | Glasgow | 09/12/89 | 5 11.0 | 11 3 | Celtic |
| Connor | Robert | | 04/08/60 | Kilmarnock | 11/08/94 | 5 11.0 | 11 4 | Aberdeen |
| Crainie | Daniel | | 24/05/62 | Kilsyth | 07/11/92 | 5 8.0 | 10 11 | Airdrieonians |
| Doig | Kevin | | 06/11/75 | Glasgow | 01/06/94 | 5 11.5 | 12 4 | Kilmarnock B.C. |
| Geddes | Alexander | Robert | 12/08/60 | Inverness | 25/05/90 | 6 0.0 | 11 4 | Dundee |
| Hamilton | Steven | James | 19/03/75 | Baillieston | 16/08/94 | 5 9.0 | 11 9 | Troon Juniors |
| Henry | John | | 31/12/71 | Vale of Leven | 15/08/94 | 5 9.0 | 10 0 | Clydebank |
| Jack | Alan | | 11/11/76 | Glasgow | 20/07/94 | 5 6.0 | 10 8 | Kilmarnock B.C. |
| Lauchlan | James | Harley | 02/02/77 | Glasgow | 20/07/94 | 5 11.0 | 10 13 | Kilmarnock B.C. |
| MacPherson | Angus | Ian | 11/10/68 | Glasgow | 10/06/86 | 5 11.0 | 10 4 | Rangers |
| Maskrey | Stephen | William | 16/08/62 | Edinburgh | 11/08/94 | 5 6.0 | 10 0 | St. Johnstone |
| McCarrison | Dugald | | 22/12/69 | Lanark | 26/02/93 | 5 11.0 | 10 7 | Celtic |
| McCloy | Steven | | 28/04/75 | Girvan | 30/09/93 | 5 9.0 | 11 9 | Craigmark Juniors |
| McCluskey | George | McKinlay | 19/09/57 | Hamilton | 25/07/92 | 5 10.5 | 12 6 | Hamilton Academical |
| McSkimming | Shaun | Peter | 29/05/70 | Stranraer | 13/07/91 | 5 11.0 | 10 8 | Dundee |
| Meldrum | Colin | George | 26/11/75 | Kilmarnock | 03/09/93 | 5 10.5 | 13 4 | Kilwinning Rangers |
| Millen | Andrew | Frank | 10/06/65 | Glasgow | 04/08/93 | 5 11.0 | 11 2 | Hamilton Academical |
| Mitchell | Alistair | Robert | 03/12/68 | Kirkcaldy | 05/07/91 | 5 7.0 | 11 0 | East Fife |
| Montgomerie | Samuel | Raymond | 17/04/61 | Irvine | 12/08/88 | 5 8.0 | 11 7 | Dumbarton |
| Napier | Craig | Cameron | 14/11/65 | East Kilbride | 01/02/94 | 5 9.0 | 12 0 | Hamilton Academical |
| Paterson | Craig | Stewart | 02/10/59 | South Queensferry | 29/10/91 | 6 2.5 | 12 12 | Motherwell |
| Reilly | Mark | | 30/03/69 | Bellshill | 05/07/91 | 5 8.0 | 10 0 | Motherwell |
| Roberts | Mark | Kingsley | 29/10/75 | Irvine | 07/02/92 | 5 9.5 | 9 10 | Bellfield B.C. |
| Skilling | Mark | James | 06/10/72 | Irvine | 01/10/91 | 5 9.5 | 10 13 | Saltcoats Victoria |
| Stark ** | William | | 01/12/56 | Glasgow | 03/08/92 | 6 1.0 | 11 11 | Hamilton Academical |
| Williamson | Robert | | 13/08/61 | Glasgow | 15/11/90 | 5 7.5 | 12 9 | Rotherham United |

* Appointed Manager of Celtic F.C.
** Appointed Assistant Manager of Celtic F.C.

## MILESTONES

**YEAR OF FORMATION:** 1869
**MOST CAPPED PLAYER:** Joe Nibloe; **NO. OF CAPS:** 11
**MOST LEAGUE POINTS IN A SEASON:** 58 (Division 2 – Season 1973/74)
**MOST LEAGUE GOALS SCORED BY A PLAYER IN A SEASON:** Harry "Peerie" Cunningham (Season 1927/28) and Andy Kerr (Season 1960/61)
**NO. OF GOALS SCORED:** 34
**RECORD ATTENDANCE:** 34,246 (-v- Rangers – August, 1963)
**RECORD VICTORY:** 13-2 (-v- Saltcoats – Scottish Cup 12.9.1896)
**RECORD DEFEAT:** 0-8 (-v- Rangers and Hibernian – Division 1)

## SEASON TICKET INFORMATION

**Seated**
**West**
Adult ........................................ £175
Juvenile/O.A.P. .......................... £85
**East**
Adult ........................................ £155
Juvenile/O.A.P. .......................... £85
**Family Enclosure**
Adult £140, Juvenile £35 plus £20 for each additional Juvenile Season Ticket.

## LEAGUE ADMISSION PRICES

**Seated**
**West**
Adult ........................... £10
O.A.P. ........................... £5
**Family Enclosure (Moffat Stand South)**
Adult £8, Juvenile £4 (Juvenile must be accompanied by an Adult)
**East**
Adult ........................... £9
Juvenile/OAP .................. £5
**\*Standing – North (Visitors)** Adult ........................... £9
Juvenile/OAP .................. £5

\*PLEASE NOTE THAT DURING THE COURSE OF THE SEASON, THE NORTH TERRACING WILL BE DEMOLISHED AND THE NEW CHADWICK STAND BUILT

Rugby Park, Rugby Road,
Kilmarnock KA1 2DP

**CHAIRMAN**
Robert Fleeting

**VICE-CHAIRMAN**
James H. Moffat

**DIRECTORS**
Mrs. Laurel J. Chadwick
John Paton
Ronald D. Hamilton

**SECRETARY**
Kevin D. Collins

**MANAGER**
Alexander Totten

**ASSISTANT MANAGER**
Kenneth Thomson

**GOALKEEPING COACH**
Jim Stewart

**YOUTH COACHES**
Stuart McLean & Alan Robertson

**HON. MEDICAL OFFICER**
Dr. Robin Magee

**PHYSIOTHERAPIST**
Hugh Allan

**S.F.A. COMMUNITY OFFICER**
Jim Clark

**CHIEF SCOUT**
Kenneth McAlpine

**GROUNDSMAN**
Angus Hollas

**COMMERCIAL MANAGER**
Denny Martin
(0563) 25184

**TELEPHONES**
Ground (0563) 25184
Fax (0563) 22181
Matchday/Ticket Information
(0563) 42999

**CLUB SHOP**
Killie Sports, 36 Bank Street,
Kilmarnock. Tel (0563) 34210.
Open Mon to Sat 9.00 a.m. –
5.00 p.m. Also portacabin at
ground on match days.

**OFFICIAL SUPPORTERS CLUB**
c/o Rugby Park, Kilmarnock KA1 2DP

**TEAM CAPTAIN**
Raymond Montgomerie

**SHIRT SPONSOR**
A.T. Mays, Travel Agents

REGISTERED STRIP: Shirt – Blue and White Stripes, Shorts: White, Stockings: White
CHANGE STRIP: Shirt – White with Blue Trim, Shorts: Blue, Stockings: Blue

# CLUB FACTFILE 1993/94 .. RESULTS .. APPEARANCES .. SCORERS

## KILLIE

| Date | Venue | Opponents | Result | Geddes R. | MacPherson A. | Black T. | Montgomerie R. | Skilling M. | Millen A. | Mitchell A. | Reilly M. | Brown T. | McCluskey G. | McSkimming S. | Crainie D. | Williamson R. | Roberts M. | Campbell C. | Porteous I. | Paterson C. | Stark W. | Burns T. | Lauchlan J. | McInally A. | Napier C. | McCloy S. |
|---|---|---|---|---|---|---|---|---|---|---|---|---|---|---|---|---|---|---|---|---|---|---|---|---|---|---|
| Aug 7 | H | Dundee | 1-0 | 1 | 2 | 3 | 4 | 5 | 6 | 7 | 8 | 9[1] | 10 | 11 | 12 | | | | | | | | | | | |
| 14 | A | Aberdeen | 0-1 | 1 | 2 | 3 | 4 | 5 | 6 | 7 | 8 | | 10 | 11 | 12 | 9 | 14 | | | | | | | | | |
| 21 | H | Motherwell | 0-1 | 1 | 2 | 3 | 4 | 5 | 6 | 7 | 8 | | 10 | 11 | 12 | 9 | | 14 | | | | | | | | |
| 28 | A | Rangers | 2-1 | 1 | 2 | 3 | 4 | 5 | 6 | 7 | | | 14 | 10 | 11 | 9[1] | 8[1] | 12 | | | | | | | | |
| Sep 4 | H | Hibernian | 1-1 | 1 | 2 | 3 | 4 | 5 | 6 | 7 | | | 14 | 10[1] | 11 | 9 | 8 | | | | | | | | | |
| 11 | H | St. Johnstone | 0-0 | 1 | 2 | 3 | 4 | 5 | 6 | 7 | | | 10 | 11 | | 9 | 8 | 12 | 14 | | | | | | | |
| 18 | A | Heart of Midlothian | 1-0 | 1 | 2 | 3 | 4 | 5[1] | 6 | 7 | 8 | | 10 | 11 | | 9 | | 12 | | | | | | | | |
| 25 | H | Partick Thistle | 3-1 | 1 | 2 | 3[1] | 4 | 5 | 6 | 7 | 8 | | 10[1] | 11 | | 9[1] | 14 | 12 | | | | | | | | |
| Oct 2 | A | Celtic | 0-0 | 1 | 2 | 3 | 4 | 5 | 6 | 7 | 8 | | 10 | 11 | | 9 | 14 | | | | | | | | | |
| 5 | H | Dundee United | 1-1 | 1 | 2 | 3 | 4 | 5 | 6 | 7 | 8 | | | 11 | | 9 | 10[1] | | | | | | | | | |
| 9 | A | Raith Rovers | 2-2 | 1 | 2 | 3 | 4 | 5 | 6 | 7[1] | 8 | | | 11 | | 9[1] | 10 | | | | | | | | | |
| 16 | H | Aberdeen | 1-1 | 1 | 2 | 3 | 4 | 5 | 6 | 7[1] | 8 | | 10 | 14 | 11 | 9 | | | | | | | | | | |
| 23 | A | Dundee | 0-1 | 1 | 2 | 3 | | 5 | 6 | 7 | 8 | | 10 | 14 | 11 | 9 | | | | 4 | | | | | | |
| 30 | A | Motherwell | 2-2 | 1 | 2 | 3 | 4 | 5 | 6 | 7[1] | 8 | | 12 | 11 | | 9 | | | 10[1] | | | | | | | |
| Nov 6 | H | Rangers | 0-2 | 1 | 2 | 3 | 4 | 5 | 6 | | 8 | 7 | | 11 | | 9 | 12 | | 10 | | | | | | | |
| 9 | A | Hibernian | 1-2 | 1 | 2 | 3 | 4 | 5 | 6 | | 8 | 7[1] | | 11 | | 9 | 12 | | 10 | | | | | | | |
| 13 | H | Celtic | 2-2 | 1 | 2 | 3 | 4 | 5[1] | 6 | | 8 | 7 | | 11 | | 9[1] | 10 | | 12 | | | | | | | |
| 20 | H | Partick Thistle | 1-0 | 1 | 2 | 3 | 4 | 5 | 6 | | 8 | | | 11 | 12[1] | 9 | 7 | | 10 | | | | | | | |
| 27 | A | St. Johnstone | 1-0 | 1 | 2 | 3 | 4 | 5 | 6 | | 8 | 12 | | 11 | 14 | 9[1] | 7 | | 10 | | | | | | | |
| 30 | H | Heart of Midlothian | 0-0 | 1 | 2 | 3 | 4 | 5 | 6 | | 8 | 7 | | 11 | | 9 | | 14 | 10 | | | | | | | |
| Dec 4 | A | Dundee United | 0-0 | 1 | 2 | 3 | 4 | 5 | 6 | | 8 | 7 | | 11 | 12 | 9 | | | 10 | | | | | | | |
| 11 | H | Raith Rovers | 1-0 | 1 | 2 | 3 | 4 | 5 | 6 | | 8 | 7[1] | | | 14 | 9 | | | | | | 10 | 11 | | | |
| 18 | A | Aberdeen | 1-3 | 1 | 2 | 3 | 4 | 5[1] | 6 | 10 | 8 | 7 | | 11 | | 9 | | | | | | | | | | |
| Jan 1 | H | Motherwell | 0-0 | 1 | 2 | 3 | 4 | | 6 | 9 | | 8 | | 11 | | 7 | 14 | | 10 | | 5 | | | | | |
| 4 | H | Dundee | 1-0 | 1 | 2 | 3 | 4 | | 6 | 9 | 8 | | 10 | 11[1] | | 7 | 14 | | 12 | | 5 | | | | | |
| 8 | A | Rangers | 0-3 | 1 | 2 | 3 | 4 | | 6 | 9 | 8 | | 10 | 11 | | 7 | | | | | 5 | | | | | |
| 15 | H | Hibernian | 0-3 | 1 | 2 | 3 | 4 | | 6 | 7 | 8 | | 10 | 11 | 12 | 9 | | | | | 5 | 14 | | | | |
| 22 | A | Heart of Midlothian | 1-1 | 1 | 2[1] | 3 | | | 6 | 7 | 8 | | 10 | 11 | | 9 | | | | 4 | 5 | | | | | |
| Feb 5 | H | St. Johnstone | 0-0 | 1 | 2 | 3 | 4 | | 6 | 7 | 8 | | | 11 | | 9 | | | | | 5 | 14 | | 10 | 12 | |
| 12 | H | Partick Thistle | 1-2 | 1 | 2 | 3 | 4 | | 6 | 7[1] | 8 | | | 11 | | 9 | | | | | 5 | 14 | | 10 | 12 | |
| Mar 1 | A | Celtic | 0-1 | 1 | 2 | 3 | 4 | | 6 | 7 | 8 | | | | | 9 | | | | | 5 | | | 10 | 14 | 11 |
| 5 | H | Dundee United | 1-1 | 1 | 2 | 3 | 4 | | 6 | 7 | 8[1] | | 10 | | | 9 | | | | | | 5 | | 12 | 11 | 14 |
| 15 | A | Raith Rovers | 2-3 | 1 | 2 | 3 | 4 | | 6 | 7[1] | 8 | | | | | 9 | | | 11[1] | | | 10 | | | 5 | 14 |
| 19 | H | Aberdeen | 2-3 | 1 | 2 | 3[1] | 4 | | 6 | | 8 | | | | | 9 | | | 10 | 11 | 12 | 5 | | 7 | 14[1] | |
| 26 | A | Dundee | 0-3 | 1 | | 3 | | | 6 | 7 | | | | | | 9 | | | 11 | | 5 | 10 | | 12 | 2 | 8 |
| 30 | A | St. Johnstone | 1-0 | 1 | 2[1] | 3 | 4 | | 6 | 7 | | | 5 | | | 10 | | | 11 | | | 9 | | 8 | 14 | |
| Apr 2 | H | Heart of Midlothian | 0-1 | 1 | 2 | 3 | 4 | | 6 | 7 | | | 5 | | | 14 | | 10 | | | | 9 | | 8 | 12 | |
| 16 | H | Celtic | 2-0 | 1 | 2 | 3[1] | 4 | | 6 | 7 | 8 | | 10[1] | 14 | 11 | 9 | | | | 5 | | | | 12 | | |
| 19 | A | Partick Thistle | 0-1 | 1 | 2 | 3 | 4 | | 6 | 7 | 8 | | 10 | 14 | 11 | 9 | | | | 5 | | | | 12 | | |
| 23 | H | Raith Rovers | 0-0 | 1 | 2 | 3 | 4 | | 6 | 7 | 8 | | 10 | 9 | 11 | 12 | | | | | | | 14 | | 5 | |
| 26 | A | Dundee United | 3-1 | 1 | 2 | 3 | 4 | | 6 | 7 | 14 | | 10 | 11[1] | | 9[2] | | | | | | 5 | | 12 | 8 | |
| 30 | A | Motherwell | 0-1 | 1 | 2 | 3 | 4 | | 6 | 7 | | | 10 | 11 | | 9 | | | | | 12 | 5 | | 14 | 8 | |
| May 7 | H | Rangers | 1-0 | 1 | 2 | 3[1] | 4 | | 6 | | 8 | 12 | 10 | 11 | | 9 | | | | | | 7 | | 5 | | |
| 14 | A | Hibernian | 0-0 | 1 | 2 | 3 | 4 | | 6 | 7 | 8 | | 9 | 10 | 11 | | | | | | 5 | | | | 12 | |
| **TOTAL FULL APPEARANCES** | | | | 44 | 43 | 44 | 42 | 23 | 44 | 34 | 37 | 26 | 16 | 40 | 6 | 36 | 7 | | 7 | 4 | 6 | 12 | | 2 | 10 | 1 |
| **TOTAL SUB APPEARANCES** | | | | | | | | | | (1) | (5) | (7) | (8) | | (2) | (6) | | (1) | (6) | (2) | (2) | | (1) | (6) | (5) | (5) |
| **TOTAL GOALS SCORED** | | | | | 2 | 4 | | 3 | | 5 | 5 | 2 | 3 | 1 | | 7 | 2 | | 1 | | | | | | 1 | |

*Small bold figures denote goalscorers.   † denotes opponent's own goal.*

---

## RUGBY PARK

**CAPACITY**: 12,246; Seated 9,246, Standing 3,000
PLEASE NOTE: CAPACITY WILL ALTER DURING THE COURSE OF THE SEASON

**PITCH DIMENSIONS**: 112 yds x 72 yds

**FACILITIES FOR DISABLED SUPPORTERS**:
By prior arrangement with the Secretary.

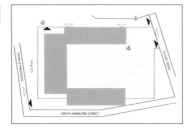

## HOW TO GET THERE

Rugby Park can be reached by the following routes:

**BUSES:** The main bus station, which is served by services from all over the country, is ten minutes walk from the ground, but there are three local services which run from here to within a two minute walk of the park. These are the Kilmarnock-Saltcoats, Kilmarnock-Ardrossan and Kilmarnock-Largs.

**TRAINS:** Kilmarnock station is well served by trains from Glasgow and the West Coast, and the station is only a 15 minute walk from the ground.

**CARS:** Car parking is available in the club car park. Entry ONLY from Dundonald Road. Visiting supporters enter ONLY from Dundonald Road Entrance.

# MOTHERWELL

Motherwell Football & Athletic Club Ltd., Fir Park, Firpark Street, Motherwell ML1 2QN

**CHAIRMAN**
John C. Chapman O.B.E. A.R.A.gS.

**VICE-CHAIRMAN**
William H. Dickie, R.I.B.A.

**SECRETARY**
Alan C. Dick

**PLAYER/MANAGER**
Alexander McLeish

**ASSISTANT MANAGER**
Andrew Watson

**COACH**
Cameron Murray

**HON. MEDICAL OFFICERS**
Mr. Ian Kerr & Dr. Robert Liddle

**PHYSIOTHERAPIST**
John Porteous

**S.F.A. COMMUNITY OFFICER**
William McLean

**YOUTH DEVELOPMENT OFFICER/ CHIEF SCOUT**
John Park

**GROUNDSMAN**
Andrew Russell

**COMMERCIAL MANAGER**
John Swinburne
(0698) 261437

**TELEPHONES:**
Ground (0698) 261437
Fax (0698) 276333
Ticket Office (0698) 261437
Information Service (0891) 121553

**CLUB SHOP**
Motherwell Football & Athletic Club, Firpark Street, Motherwell ML1 2QN Tel (0698) 261437. Open 9.00 a.m. – 4.30 p.m. Mon. to Fri. (Open Saturdays from 10.00 a.m. to 5.00 p.m. on first team home match days only)

**OFFICIAL SUPPORTERS CLUB**
c/o Fir Park, Firpark Street, Motherwell ML1 2QN.

**TEAM CAPTAIN**
Chris McCart

**SHIRT SPONSOR**
Motorola

## LIST OF PLAYERS 1994-95

| SURNAME | FIRST NAME | MIDDLE NAME | DATE OF BIRTH | PLACE OF BIRTH | DATE OF SIGNING | HEIGHT FT INS | WEIGHT ST LBS | PREVIOUS CLUB |
|---|---|---|---|---|---|---|---|---|
| Allan | Raymond | George K. | 05/05/55 | Cowdenbeath | 29/07/94 | 6 0.0 | 11 7 | Brechin City |
| Arnott | Douglas | | 05/08/61 | Lanark | 29/10/86 | 5 7.0 | 10 7 | Pollok Juniors |
| Burns | Alexander | | 04/08/73 | Bellshill | 06/08/91 | 5 8.0 | 10 0 | Shotts Bon-Accord |
| Coyne | Thomas | | 14/11/62 | Glasgow | 30/11/93 | 6 0.0 | 10 7 | Tranmere Rovers |
| Davies | William | McIntosh | 31/05/64 | Glasgow | 12/03/94 | 5 6.0 | 10 9 | Dunfermline Athletic |
| Denham | Greig | Paterson | 05/10/76 | Glasgow | 19/08/93 | 6 0.0 | 12 2 | Cumbernauld United |
| Dolan | James | | 22/02/69 | Salsburgh | 13/06/87 | 5 9.0 | 10 7 | Motherwell B.C. |
| Ferguson | Paul | | 12/03/75 | Dechmont | 25/08/93 | 5 7.0 | 9 12 | Stoneyburn United |
| Gow | Garry | | 24/06/77 | Glasgow | 23/11/93 | 5 11.0 | 11 12 | Yoker Athletic |
| Griffin | James | | 01/01/67 | Hamilton | 24/06/85 | 5 8.0 | 11 4 | Fir Park B.C. |
| Kirk | Stephen | David | 03/01/63 | Kirkcaldy | 23/05/86 | 5 11.0 | 11 4 | East Fife |
| Krivokapic | Miodrag | | 06/09/59 | Niksic Crna Gora | 10/07/93 | 6 1.0 | 12 6 | Dundee United |
| Lambert | Paul | | 07/08/69 | Glasgow | 07/09/93 | 5 11.0 | 9 10 | St. Mirren |
| Martin | Brian | | 24/02/63 | Bellshill | 14/11/91 | 6 0.0 | 13 0 | St. Mirren |
| McCart | Christopher | | 17/04/67 | Motherwell | 19/12/84 | 6 1.0 | 12 10 | Fir Park B.C. |
| McCulloch | Lee | | 14/05/78 | Bellshill | 18/08/94 | 6 0.0 | 12 5 | Carluke Rovers |
| McGrillen | Paul | | 19/08/71 | Glasgow | 14/04/90 | 5 8.0 | 10 5 | Motherwell B.C. |
| McKinnon | Robert | | 31/07/66 | Glasgow | 08/01/92 | 5 10.0 | 11 12 | Hartlepool United |
| McLeish | Alexander | | 21/01/59 | Glasgow | 15/07/94 | 6 1.5 | 13 4 | Aberdeen |
| McMillan | John | David | 09/08/76 | Irvine | 22/03/94 | 5 8.0 | 10 12 | Carluke Rovers |
| McMillan | Stephen | | 19/01/76 | Edinburgh | 19/08/93 | 5 10.0 | 11 0 | Troon |
| O'Donnell | Philip | | 25/03/72 | Bellshill | 30/06/94 | 5 10.0 | 10 5 | Motherwell B.C. |
| Philliben | John | | 14/03/64 | Stirling | 05/09/86 | 5 11.5 | 12 7 | Doncaster Rovers |
| Ritchie | Innes | | 24/08/73 | Edinburgh | 14/08/93 | 6 0.0 | 12 7 | Bathgate Thistle |
| Roddie | Andrew | Robert | 04/11/71 | Glasgow | 20/08/94 | 5 10.5 | 11 6 | Aberdeen |
| Ross | Ian | | 27/08/74 | Broxburn | 14/08/93 | 5 10.0 | 10 7 | Bathgate Thistle |
| Shannon | Robert | | 20/04/66 | Bellshill | 21/07/93 | 5 11.0 | 11 8 | Dunfermline Athletic |
| Woods | Stephen | Gerard | 23/02/70 | Glasgow | 22/07/94 | 6 2.0 | 12 0 | Preston North End |

## MILESTONES

**YEAR OF FORMATION:** 1886
**MOST CAPPED PLAYER:** George Stevenson
**NO. OF CAPS:** 12
**MOST LEAGUE POINTS IN A SEASON:** 66 (Division 1 – Season 1931/32)
**MOST LEAGUE GOALS SCORED BY A PLAYER IN A SEASON:** William McFadyen (Season 1931/32)
**NO. OF GOALS SCORED:** 52
**RECORD ATTENDANCE:** 35,632 (-v- Rangers – Scottish Cup 12.3.1952)
**RECORD VICTORY:** 12-1 (-v- Dundee United – Division 2, 23.1.1954)
**RECORD DEFEAT:** 0-8 (-v- Aberdeen – Premier Division 26.3.1979)

## SEASON TICKET INFORMATION

**Seated**
Main Stand (Members)   Adult ........................... £165
                       Juvenile/OAP ............. £100
East Stand             Adult ........................... £132
                       Juvenile/O.A.P. ............ £66
**Family Section**
Parent & Juvenile £185 plus an additional £20 for every additional Juvenile.

## LEAGUE ADMISSION PRICES

**Seated**
Main Stand (Members)   Adult ........................... £10
                       Juvenile/OAP ................ £6
East Stand             Adult ........................... £8
                       Juvenile/OAP ................ £4
North Stand            Adult ........................... £9
                       Juvenile/OAP ................ £5
                       (from January, 1995)
South Stand (Visiting Support) Adult ........... £9
                       Juvenile/OAP ................ £5
**Family Section**
Parent & Juvenile £11 plus an additional £1 for every additional Juvenile.

| REGISTERED STRIP: | Shirt – Amber with Claret Chestband and Trimmings |
| | Shorts – Claret, Stockings – Amber |
| CHANGE STRIP: | Shirt – Claret with half inch Amber Stripes |
| | Shorts – White, Stockings – Claret |

## CLUB FACTFILE 1993/94 .. RESULTS .. APPEARANCES .. SCORERS

### The WELL

| Date | Venue | Opponents | Result | Dykstra S. | Shannon R. | McKinnon R. | Krivokapic M. | Martin B. | McCart C. | Kirk S. | Angus I. | Arnott D. | O'Donnell P. | Burns A. | McGrillen P. | Philliben J. | Graham A. | Cooper D. | Dolan J. | Ferguson I. | Lambert P. | Griffin J. | Coyne T. | Burley G. | Davies W. | McMillan S. |
|---|---|---|---|---|---|---|---|---|---|---|---|---|---|---|---|---|---|---|---|---|---|---|---|---|---|---|
| Aug 7 | H | Celtic | 2-2 | 1 | 2 | 3 | 4 | 5 | 6 | 7 | 8 | 9¹ | 10 | 11¹ | 12 | 14 | | | | | | | | | | |
| 14 | A | Dundee | 2-1 | 1 | 2 | 3¹ | 4 | 5 | 6 | 12 | 8 | 9 | 10 | 7 | 11¹ | 14 | | | | | | | | | | |
| 21 | A | Kilmarnock | 1-0 | 1 | 2 | 3 | 4 | 5 | 6 | 7 | 8 | 9 | 10 | | 11¹ | | 12 | 14 | | | | | | | | |
| 28 | H | Raith Rovers | †4-1 | 1 | 2 | 3¹ | 4 | 5 | 6 | 14¹ | 8 | 9 | 10 | | 11¹ | | 12 | 7 | | | | | | | | |
| Sep 4 | A | St. Johnstone | 0-3 | 1 | 2 | 3 | 4 | 5 | 6 | 12 | | | 10 | | 11 | | 14 | 7 | 8 | 9 | | | | | | |
| 11 | H | Heart of Midlothian | 2-0 | 1 | 2 | 3 | 4 | 5 | 6 | 14 | | | 10¹ | | 11¹ | | 9 | 12 | 8 | | 7 | | | | | |
| 18 | A | Partick Thistle | 0-1 | 1 | 2 | 3 | 4 | 5 | 6 | 14 | | | 10 | | 11 | | 9 | 12 | 8 | | 7 | | | | | |
| 25 | A | Dundee United | 0-0 | 1 | 2 | 3 | 4 | 5 | 6 | 9 | | | 10 | | 11 | | | | 8 | | 7 | | | | | |
| Oct 2 | H | Aberdeen | 0-0 | 1 | 2 | 3 | 4 | 5 | 6 | 10 | 14 | 9 | | | 11 | | | | 12 | | 8 | 7 | | | | |
| 6 | A | Rangers | 2-1 | 1 | 2 | 3 | 4 | 5 | 6 | 9 | 10 | 12² | | | 11 | 14 | | | | | 7 | | | | | |
| 9 | A | Hibernian | 0-2 | 1 | 2 | 3 | 4 | 5 | 6 | 8 | 12 | 9 | 10 | | 11 | | | | | | 7 | | | | | |
| 16 | H | Dundee | 1-0 | 1 | 2 | 3 | 4 | 5 | 6 | 11 | 9¹ | 10 | | | 12 | | | 14 | 8 | | 7 | | | | | |
| 30 | H | Kilmarnock | 2-2 | 1 | 2 | 3 | 4 | 5¹ | 6 | 11¹ | 9 | 10 | | | 12 | | | 14 | 8 | | 7 | | | | | |
| Nov 6 | A | Raith Rovers | 3-0 | 1 | 2 | 3 | 4 | 5 | 6 | 8 | 9² | 10¹ | | | 11 | | | 12 | | | 7 | 14 | | | | |
| 9 | H | St. Johnstone | 1-0 | 1 | 2 | 3 | 4 | 5 | 8 | 9 | 10 | | | | 12 | 6 | | 11 | | | 7¹ | 14 | | | | |
| 13 | A | Aberdeen | 1-1 | 1 | 12 | 3 | 4 | 5 | 6 | 8¹ | 9 | 10 | | | 14 | 2 | | 11 | | | 7 | | | | | |
| 20 | H | Dundee United | 2-0 | 1 | 2 | 3 | 4 | 5 | 6 | 8¹ | 9¹ | | | | 11 | 12 | | 14 | 10 | | 7 | | | | | |
| 24 | A | Celtic | 0-2 | 1 | 2 | 3 | 4 | 5 | 6 | 8 | 11 | | 10 | | 9 | 12 | | 14 | | | | | | | | |
| 30 | H | Partick Thistle | 1-0 | 1 | 2 | 3 | 4 | 5 | 6 | 7 | | 9 | 10¹ | | 14 | | | | 8 | | 12 | | 11 | | | |
| Dec 4 | H | Rangers | 0-2 | 1 | 2 | | 4 | 5 | 6 | 12 | | 9 | 10 | | 14 | | | | 8 | | 7 | 3 | 11 | | | |
| 11 | A | Hibernian | 2-3 | 1 | 2 | 3 | 4 | 5 | 6 | 9 | | | 10 | | | 14 | | | 8 | | 7 | | 11² | | | |
| 15 | A | Heart of Midlothian | 3-2 | 1 | 2 | 3¹ | | 5 | 6 | 12 | | | 10 | | 9 | 4 | | | 8 | | 7 | | 11² | | | |
| 18 | A | Dundee | 3-1 | 1 | 2 | 3 | 4 | 5 | 6 | 9 | 14 | 10² | | | | 8 | | | 12 | | 7 | | 11¹ | | | |
| Jan 1 | A | Kilmarnock | 0-0 | 1 | 2 | 3 | 4 | 5 | 6 | 9 | 12 | 10 | | | | | | | 8 | | 7 | | 11 | | | |
| 11 | H | Celtic | 2-1 | 1 | 2 | 3 | 4 | 5 | 6 | 12 | | 9 | 10² | | 14 | 8 | | | | | 7 | | 11 | | | |
| 22 | A | Partick Thistle | 0-0 | 1 | 2 | 3 | 4 | 5 | 6 | 9 | | | 10 | | 12 | 8 | | 14 | | | 7 | | 11 | | | |
| 25 | H | Raith Rovers | 3-1 | 1 | 2 | 3 | 4 | 5 | 6 | 9¹ | | 7 | 10 | | 12¹ | | | | 8 | | 14 | | 11¹ | | | |
| Feb 5 | H | Heart of Midlothian | †1-1 | 1 | 2 | 3 | 4 | 5 | 6 | 7 | 14 | 9 | | | 12 | 10 | | | 8 | | | | 11 | | | |
| 8 | A | St. Johnstone | 1-2 | 1 | 2 | 3 | 4 | 5 | | 7 | 10 | 12 | | | 9 | 6 | | | 14 | | | | 11¹ | 8 | | |
| 12 | A | Dundee United | ††2-1 | 1 | 2 | 3 | 4 | 5 | 6 | 9 | | | 10 | | 12 | 8 | | | 7 | | | | 11 | 14 | | |
| Mar 5 | A | Rangers | 1-2 | 1 | | 3 | 4 | 5 | 6 | | | 9 | 10 | 12 | | 2 | | | 8 | | 7¹ | | 11 | 14 | | |
| 8 | H | Aberdeen | †1-1 | 1 | 12 | 3 | 4 | 5 | 6 | | | 9 | 10 | | 14 | 2 | | | 8 | | 7 | | 11 | | | |
| 12 | H | Hibernian | 0-0 | 1 | 2 | 3 | 4 | 5 | 6 | | | 9 | 10 | | 14 | 12 | | | 8 | | | | 11 | 7 | | |
| 19 | H | Dundee | †3-1 | 1 | 2 | 3 | 4 | 5¹ | 6 | | | 7 | 10 | | 11 | 12 | | | 8 | | | | 9¹ | 14 | | |
| 26 | A | Celtic | 1-0 | 1 | 2 | 3 | 4 | 5 | 6 | | | 9¹ | 10 | | 12 | 14 | | | 8 | | | | 11 | 7 | | |
| 30 | A | Heart of Midlothian | 0-0 | 1 | 2 | 3 | 4 | 5 | 6 | | | | 10 | | 11 | | | | 8 | | 7 | | 9 | 12 | | |
| Apr 2 | H | Partick Thistle | 2-2 | 1 | 2 | 3 | 4 | | 6 | | | 9 | 10 | | 14 | 5¹ | | | 8 | | 7 | | 11¹ | | | |
| 16 | A | Aberdeen | 0-0 | 1 | 2 | 3 | 4 | 5 | | | | 9 | 10 | | 12 | 6 | | | 8 | | | | 11 | 3 | 7 | |
| 23 | A | Hibernian | 2-0 | 1 | 2 | 3 | 4¹ | 5 | 6 | 14 | | | | | 11 | 12 | | | 8 | | 7 | | 9¹ | | 10 | |
| 26 | H | Rangers | 2-1 | 1 | 2 | 3 | 4 | 5 | | 14 | | | 10 | | 11 | 6¹ | | | 8 | | 7 | | 9¹ | | 12 | |
| 30 | H | Kilmarnock | 1-0 | 1 | 2 | 3 | 4 | 5 | | 11 | | | 10 | | 14 | 6 | | | 8 | | 7 | | 9¹ | | 12 | |
| May 3 | H | Dundee United | 1-2 | 1 | 2 | 3 | 4 | 5 | | | | 8¹ | 11 | | 12 | 6 | | | 7 | | | | 9 | | 10 | |
| 7 | A | Raith Rovers | 3-3 | 1 | 2 | 3¹ | 4 | 5 | | 12¹ | | | | | 14 | 11 | 6 | | 8 | | 7¹ | | 9 | | 10 | |
| 14 | H | St. Johnstone | 0-1 | 1 | 2 | 3 | | 5 | | 10 | 11 | | | | 12 | 6 | | | 8 | | 7 | | 9 | 4 | | 14 |
| **TOTAL FULL APPEARANCES** | | | | 44 | 41 | 42 | 42 | 43 | 36 | 25 | 8 | 25 | 35 | 2 | 20 | 18 | 2 | 2 | 32 | 1 | 30 | 1 | 26 | 3 | 6 | |
| **TOTAL SUB APPEARANCES** | | | | | (2) | | | | | (11) | (3) | (4) | | (2) | (20) | (10) | (3) | (8) | (4) | | (2) | (2) | | (2) | (4) | (1) |
| **TOTAL GOALS SCORED** | | | | | | 4 | 1 | | 2 | | | 7 | | | 8 | 7 | 1 | 5 | 2 | | 3 | | 12 | | | |

*Small bold figures denote goalscorers.  † denotes opponent's own goal.*

---

## FIR PARK

**CAPACITY:** 14,069 (All seated)
(Between August 1994-January 1995:
Capacity 11,369)

**PITCH DIMENSIONS:** 110 yds x 75 yds

**FACILITIES FOR DISABLED
SUPPORTERS:** Area in front of South
West Enclosure. Prior arrangement must
be made with the Secretary.

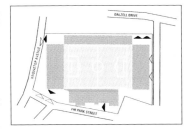

## HOW TO GET THERE

**The following routes can be used to reach Fir Park:**

**BUSES:** Fir Park is less than a quarter of a mile from the main thoroughfare through the town and numerous buses serving Lanarkshire and Glasgow all pass along this road. De-bus at the Civic Centre.

**TRAINS:** Motherwell Station is a main-line station on the Glasgow-London (Euston) route, and the station is particularly well served by trains running from numerous points throughout the Strathclyde Region. Motherwell station is a twenty minute walk from Fir Park, while the new station at Airbles is only fifteen minutes away.

**CARS:** Car Parking is only available in the many side streets around the ground. There is no major parking area close to Fir Park.

# PARTICK THISTLE

**LIST OF PLAYERS 1994-95**

Firhill Stadium, 80 Firhill Road,
Glasgow G20 7BA.

**CHAIRMAN**
James Oliver

**VICE-CHAIRMAN**
T. Brown McMaster

**DIRECTORS**
Angus MacSween
Harry F. Scott
John Lambie
Robert G. S. McCamley

**PRESIDENT**
James R. Aitken

**SECRETARY**
Robert W. Reid

**MANAGER**
John Lambie

**GENERAL MANAGER**
Jez Moxey
041-945 4811

**ASSISTANT MANAGER**
Gerry Collins

**COACH**
Robert McCulley

**CLUB DOCTOR**
Alan W. Robertson

**PHYSIOTHERAPIST**
Frank Ness

**S.F.A. COMMUNITY COACH**
Gordon Chisholm

**CHIEF SCOUT**
Robert Dinnie

**GROUNDSMAN**
David Lyle

**TELEPHONES**
Ground/Ticket Office 041-945 4811
Fax 041-945 1525

**CLUB SHOP**
c/o 90 Firhill Road
Glasgow G20 7AL
Tel 041-945 4811
Open Tues-Thurs 12.30-5.30 p.m.
and Fri 12.30-5.00 p.m. and
match days/evenings

**OFFICIAL SUPPORTERS CLUB**
Ms. Morag McHaffie
99 Somerville Drive
Glasgow G42 9BH
Tel 041-632 3604

**TEAM CAPTAIN**
Willie Jamieson

**SHIRT SPONSOR**
Texstyle World

| SURNAME | FIRST NAME | MIDDLE NAME | DATE OF BIRTH | PLACE OF BIRTH | DATE OF SIGNING | HEIGHT FT INS | WEIGHT ST LBS | PREVIOUS CLUB |
|---|---|---|---|---|---|---|---|---|
| Archibald | Alan | Maxwell | 13/12/77 | Glasgow | 13/06/94 | 5 9.0 | 11 7 | Possilpark Y.M.C.A. |
| Ayton | Stuart | | 19/10/75 | Glasgow | 01/07/94 | 5 8.0 | 10 12 | Rangers |
| Budinauckas | Kevin | | 16/09/74 | Bellshill | 10/08/92 | 5 10.0 | 11 0 | Armadale Thistle |
| Byrne | David | Stuart | 05/03/61 | London | 10/07/93 | 5 9.0 | 10 9 | St. Johnstone |
| Cameron | Ian | | 24/08/66 | Glasgow | 30/07/92 | 5 9.0 | 10 4 | Aberdeen |
| Charnley | James | Callaghan | 11/06/63 | Glasgow | 19/11/93 | 5 9.0 | 11 12 | Djurgarden |
| Chisholm | Donald | | 08/11/75 | Glasgow | 01/07/94 | 6 1.0 | 11 8 | Rangers |
| Clarke | Cortez | | 03/04/76 | Glasgow | 29/04/94 | 5 10.0 | 11 7 | Ayr United |
| Craig | Albert | Hughes | 03/01/62 | Glasgow | 28/08/92 | 5 8.0 | 11 5 | Dundee |
| Diamond | Neal | | 21/06/71 | Glasgow | 18/02/94 | 5 10.0 | 12 7 | Benburb Juniors |
| Docherty | Stephen | | 18/02/76 | Glasgow | 25/08/93 | 5 8.0 | 10 10 | Pollok Juniors |
| English | Isaac | | 12/11/71 | Paisley | 28/06/89 | 5 8.0 | 10 5 | St. Mirren |
| Gibson | Andrew | | 02/02/69 | Dechmont | 18/12/93 | 5 9.5 | 11 10 | Aberdeen |
| Glancy | Martin | Paul | 24/03/76 | Glasgow | 16/08/94 | 5 6.0 | 10 0 | Clydebank |
| Gormill | Steven | David | 16/02/78 | Lanark | 01/07/94 | 5 6.0 | 9 9 | Possilpark Y.M.C.A. |
| Grant | Roderick | John | 16/09/66 | Gloucester | 14/07/93 | 5 11.0 | 11 0 | Dunfermline Athletic |
| Henderson | Brian | Martin | 24/05/76 | Glasgow | 09/02/94 | 5 8.0 | 10 11 | Aston Villa |
| Jamieson | William | George | 27/04/63 | Barnsley | 21/09/92 | 5 11.0 | 12 0 | Dundee |
| Law | Robert | | 24/12/65 | Bellshill | 08/10/84 | 5 9.5 | 11 12 | Stonehouse Violet |
| McLachlan | James | | 10/04/77 | Paisley | 31/03/94 | 5 9.0 | 11 0 | St. Mirren |
| McWilliams | Derek | | 16/01/66 | Broxburn | 02/08/94 | 5 10.0 | 12 0 | Dunfermline Athletic |
| Miller | Derek | | 28/10/77 | Vale of Leven | 13/06/94 | 5 8.0 | 10 11 | Possilpark Y.M.C.A. |
| Milne | Callum | | 27/08/65 | Edinburgh | 04/09/93 | 5 8.5 | 10 7 | Hibernian |
| Murdoch | Andrew | Gerard | 20/07/68 | Greenock | 15/02/91 | 6 1.0 | 12 0 | Celtic |
| Nelson | Craig | Robert | 28/05/71 | Coatbridge | 11/04/91 | 6 1.0 | 12 3 | Cork City |
| Ramsay | Scott | McKenna | 02/10/75 | Glasgow | 01/07/94 | 5 7.0 | 11 5 | Possilpark Y.M.C.A. |
| Sharkey | Andrew | Michael | 30/11/76 | Vale of Leven | 13/07/93 | 5 11.0 | 10 2 | Celtic |
| Smith | Thomas | William | 12/10/73 | Glasgow | 27/11/92 | 5 8.5 | 11 7 | Cork City |
| Stirling | Jered | | 13/10/76 | Stirling | 29/09/93 | 6 0.0 | 11 6 | St. Rochs |
| Taylor | Alexander | | 13/06/62 | Baillieston | 02/07/93 | 5 9.5 | 11 7 | Falkirk |
| Tierney | Peter | Grant | 11/10/61 | Falkirk | 17/07/90 | 6 0.5 | 13 13 | Dunfermline Athletic |
| Watson | Gregg | | 21/09/70 | Glasgow | 14/08/93 | 5 9.5 | 10 9 | Aberdeen |
| West | Joseph | | 02/08/78 | Glasgow | 02/08/94 | 5 5.0 | 9 0 | Wolves B.C. |
| Wood | David | Wilson | 30/12/75 | Broxburn | 15/11/93 | 5 9.5 | 11 2 | Brighton & Hove Albion |

## MILESTONES

**YEAR OF FORMATION:** 1876
**MOST CAPPED PLAYER:** Alan Rough
**NO. OF CAPS:** 53
**MOST LEAGUE POINTS IN A SEASON:** 57 (First Division – Season 1991/92)
**MOST LEAGUE GOALS SCORED BY A PLAYER IN A SEASON:** Alec Hair (Season 1926/27)
**NO. OF GOALS SCORED:** 41
**RECORD ATTENDANCE:** 49,838 (-v- Rangers – 18.2.1922)
**RECORD VICTORY:** 16-0 (-v- Royal Albert – Scottish Cup 17.1.1931)
**RECORD DEFEAT:** 0-10 (-v- Queen's Park – Scottish Cup 3.12.1881)

## SEASON TICKET INFORMATION

**Seated**
Adult ................................................£180
OAP ................................................£100
Juvenile ................................................£90
**Standing**
Adult ................................................£120
Juvenile/OAP ................................................£70

## LEAGUE ADMISSION PRICES

**Seated**
Adult ................................................£10
Juvenile/OAP ................................................£5
**Standing**
Adult ................................................£8
Juvenile/OAP ................................................£4

| REGISTERED STRIP: | Shirt – Red and Yellow Vertical Stripes with Black Shadings between the Lines |
|---|---|
| | Shorts – Black with Red and Yellow Trim, Stockings – Black with Yellow Tops |
| CHANGE STRIP: | Shirt – Navy Blue with Red and Yellow Collar |
| | Shorts – Navy Blue with Red and Yellow Trim |
| | Stockings – Navy Blue with Red Tops |

# CLUB FACTFILE 1993/94 .. RESULTS .. APPEARANCES .. SCORERS

### The JAGS

Player columns (left to right): Nelson C., McKilligan N., Law R., Jamieson W., Tierney P. G., Clark M., Byrne D., Craig A., Britton G., Cameron I., English I., McKee K., Watson G., Kinnaird P., Grant R., Farningham R., Shaw G., McClashan C., Milne C., Taylor A., Murdoch A., Smith T., Charnley J., Gibson A., Barnes D.

| Date | Venue | Opponents | Result | Nelson C. | McKilligan N. | Law R. | Jamieson W. | Tierney P.G. | Clark M. | Byrne D. | Craig A. | Britton G. | Cameron I. | English I. | McKee K. | Watson G. | Kinnaird P. | Grant R. | Farningham R. | Shaw G. | McClashan C. | Milne C. | Taylor A. | Murdoch A. | Smith T. | Charnley J. | Gibson A. | Barnes D. |
|---|---|---|---|---|---|---|---|---|---|---|---|---|---|---|---|---|---|---|---|---|---|---|---|---|---|---|---|---|
| Aug 7 | A | Hibernian | 0-0 | 1 | 2 | 3 | 4 | 5 | 6 | 7 | 8 | 9 | 10 | 11 | | | | | | | | | | | | | | |
| 14 | H | Dundee United | 1-2 | 1 | | | 4 | 5 | | 7 | 8$^1$ | 9 | 10 | 6 | 2 | 3 | | 11 | 14 | | | | | | | | | |
| 21 | A | Raith Rovers | 2-2 | 1 | | | 4 | 5 | | 6 | | 9$^1$ | 10 | | 2 | 3 | | 11 | 7$^1$ | 8 | 12 | 14 | | | | | | |
| 28 | H | Celtic | 0-1 | 1 | 14 | 3 | 5 | | 6 | 7 | 8 | 9 | 11 | 12 | 2 | | | 10 | 4 | | | | | | | | | |
| Sep 4 | A | Heart of Midlothian | 1-2 | 1 | 14 | | 4 | 5 | 6 | | 8 | 9$^1$ | 10 | | 2 | | | 11 | | 12 | | 3 | 7 | | | | | |
| 11 | A | Rangers | 1-1 | 1 | | | 4 | 5 | 6 | 7 | 8 | 9 | 12 | 10 | 2 | | | 11$^1$ | | | 3 | 14 | 1 | | | | | |
| 18 | H | Motherwell | 1-0 | 1 | | | 4 | 5 | 6 | 14 | 8$^1$ | 9 | | 10 | 2 | | | 11 | | | 3 | 7 | 1 | | | | | |
| 25 | A | Kilmarnock | 1-3 | 1 | | | 4 | 5 | 6 | | 8$^1$ | 9 | 12 | 10 | 2 | | 14 | 11 | | | 3 | 7 | 1 | | | | | |
| Oct 2 | H | St. Johnstone | 4-1 | 1 | | 2 | 5 | | 6 | 8 | | | 10 | 11 | | 4 | | 9$^3$ | | 7 | | 3 | 12$^1$ | | 14 | | | |
| 5 | A | Dundee | 2-2 | 1 | | 2 | 5 | | | 6 | 8 | 12 | 10 | 11 | | 4 | | 9 | | 7$^1$ | | 3 | 14$^1$ | | | | | |
| 9 | H | Aberdeen | 3-2 | 1 | | 2 | 5 | 12 | | 8$^1$ | 10 | 11 | | | 4 | | 9$^1$ | | 7 | | 3 | 6$^1$ | | 14 | | | | |
| 16 | A | Dundee United | 2-2 | 1 | | 2 | 5 | | | 8 | 10 | 11 | | | 4 | | 9$^1$ | | 7 | | 3$^1$ | 6 | | | | | | |
| 23 | A | Heart of Midlothian | 0-0 | 1 | | 2 | 5 | | | 8 | 10 | 11 | 12 | | 4 | | 9 | | 7 | | 3 | 6 | | | | | | |
| 30 | H | Raith Rovers | 1-1 | 1 | | 2 | 5 | | | 8$^1$ | 10 | 11 | 14 | 12 | | 4 | | 9 | | 7 | | 3 | 6 | | | | | |
| Nov 2 | H | Hibernian | 0-0 | 1 | | | 5 | | | 7 | 8 | 10 | 11 | 12 | 2 | 4 | | 9 | | | 3 | 6 | | | | | | |
| 6 | A | Celtic | 0-3 | 1 | | | 5 | | 12 | 6 | 8 | 10 | 11 | | 2 | 4 | | 9 | | 7 | | 3 | | 14 | | | | |
| 13 | A | St. Johnstone | 3-1 | 1 | | | 5 | | | 8$^1$ | 10$^1$ | 11 | 11 | 12 | 2 | 4 | | 9$^1$ | | 7 | | 3 | 6 | | | | | |
| 20 | A | Kilmarnock | 0-1 | 1 | | | 5 | | | 9 | 10 | 12 | 4 | 8 | | 7 | | 3 | 6 | | | 14 | 11 | | | | | |
| 27 | H | Rangers | 1-1 | 1 | | | | 5 | 6 | | 9 | 8 | 10$^1$ | 2 | 4 | | | 14 | | 3 | 7 | | 11 | | | | | |
| 30 | A | Motherwell | 0-1 | 1 | | | 12 | 5 | 6 | | 9 | 11 | 10 | 2 | 4 | | 14 | | 7 | 3 | 8 | | | | | | | |
| Dec 4 | H | Dundee | 3-2 | 1 | | | 5 | | 6 | 12$^2$ | | 10 | 9 | 2 | 4 | | 7 | | 3 | 8$^1$ | | 11 | | | | | | |
| 14 | A | Aberdeen | 1-2 | 1 | | | 5 | | 11 | 8$^1$ | 14 | 10 | 9 | 2 | 4 | | 7 | | 3 | 6 | | 12 | | | | | | |
| 18 | H | Dundee United | 1-0 | 1 | | 3 | 5 | | | 8$^1$ | 9 | 6 | | 2 | 4 | | 14 | | 10 | | | 11 | 7 | | | | | |
| 27 | A | Hibernian | 1-5 | 1 | | 3 | 5 | 4$^1$ | | 8 | 9 | 6 | 12 | 2 | | | | 10 | 16 | | | 11 | 7 | | | | | |
| Jan 8 | H | Celtic | 1-0 | 1 | | | 6 | 5 | 3 | 8 | | 12 | 2 | 4 | | 7$^1$ | | 10 | | | 11 | 9 | | | | | | |
| 12 | A | Raith Rovers | 1-0 | 1 | | | 6 | 5 | 3 | 8 | | 12 | 2 | 4 | | 9$^1$ | | 10 | | | 11 | 7 | | | | | | |
| 15 | A | Heart of Midlothian | 0-1 | 1 | | | 6 | 5 | 3 | 8 | | 14 | 12 | 4 | | 9 | | 10 | | | 11 | 7 | | | | | | |
| 22 | H | Motherwell | 0-0 | 1 | | 2 | 5 | | | 8 | | 6 | 9 | 4 | | 7 | | 3 | | | 11 | 10 | | | | | | |
| Feb 5 | A | Rangers | 1-5 | 1 | | 2 | 5 | 12 | | 8 | | 14$^1$ | 9 | 4 | | 7 | | 3 | 6 | | 10 | | 11 | | | | | |
| 12 | A | Kilmarnock | 2-1 | 1 | | | 5 | | | 8$^1$ | | 11 | 14 | 2 | 6 | 9$^1$ | | 3 | 4 | | 10 | | | 7 | | | | |
| Mar 5 | A | Dundee | 0-1 | 1 | | | 5 | 14 | | | 11 | | | 2 | 6 | 9 | | 3 | 4 | | 8 | 10 | 12 | 7 | | | | |
| 19 | A | Dundee United | 2-2 | 1 | | 2 | 5 | 5$^1$ | | | 10 | 8 | | 4 | | 9 | | 3 | 6 | | 7 | 11$^1$ | 12 | | | | | |
| 22 | H | St. Johnstone | 0-0 | 1 | | 2 | 5 | | | 6 | 11 | 8 | | 4 | | 9 | | 3 | 7 | | 10 | | | | | | | |
| 26 | H | Hibernian | 1-0 | 1 | | 3 | 6 | 5 | | 2 | 7 | 8 | 10 | 4 | | 9$^1$ | | 11 | | | | | | | | | | |
| 29 | H | Rangers | 1-2 | 1 | | 3 | 6 | 5 | | 2 | 7 | 8 | 10$^1$ | 4 | | 9 | | 11 | 14 | | | | | | | | | |
| Apr 2 | A | Motherwell | 2-2 | 1 | | 2 | 6 | 5 | | | 8 | 7 | 10$^1$ | 4 | | 9$^1$ | | 3 | 14 | | 11 | | 12 | | | | | |
| 5 | A | Aberdeen | 1-1 | 1 | | 3 | 6 | 5 | | 2 | 8 | 7 | 10 | 4 | | 9$^1$ | | 11 | | | | | | | | | | |
| 16 | A | St. Johnstone | 0-1 | 1 | | 3 | 6 | 5 | | 2 | 8 | 7 | 10 | 4 | | 9 | | 12 | | | 11 | 14 | | | | | | |
| 19 | H | Kilmarnock | 1-0 | 1 | | 2 | 5 | | | 3 | 8$^1$ | 7 | 10 | 4 | | 9 | | 12 | 6 | | 11 | 14 | | | | | | |
| 23 | A | Aberdeen | 0-2 | 1 | | 2 | 5 | | | 3 | 8 | 7 | 10 | 4 | | 9 | | 14 | 6 | | 11 | | | | | | | |
| 26 | H | Dundee | 1-0 | 1 | | 2 | 5 | | | 3 | 8$^1$ | 7 | 10 | 4 | | 9 | | 6 | | | 11 | 14 | | | | | | |
| 30 | H | Raith Rovers | 2-2 | 1 | | 2 | 5 | | | 3 | 8$^1$ | 7 | 10$^1$ | 4 | | 9 | | 6 | | | 11 | 12 | | | | | | |
| May 7 | A | Celtic | 1-1 | | | 2 | 5 | | | 12 | 8 | 7 | 10 | 4 | | 9 | | 3 | 6 | 1 | 14$^1$ | 11 | | | | | | |
| 14 | H | Heart of Midlothian | 0-1 | | | 2 | 5 | 14 | | 3 | 8 | 7 | | 4 | | 9 | | 6 | | 1 | 11 | 10 | 12 | | | | | |
| **TOTAL FULL APPEARANCES** | | | | 39 | 1 | 25 | 42 | 18 | 10 | 21 | 37 | 20 | 37 | 25 | 22 | 37 | 2 | 35 | 2 | 13 | 29 | 27 | 5 | 3 | 25 | 6 | 3 | |
| **TOTAL SUB APPEARANCES** | | | | | (2) | | (1) | (4) | (1) | (2) | (1) | (2) | (4) | (11) | (1) | | (1) | (2) | | (4) | (1) | (2) | (5) | (1) | (5) | (1) | (5) | (4) |
| **TOTAL GOALS SCORED** | | | | | | | 1 | 1 | | | 14 | 3 | 1 | 4 | | | | 13 | | 2 | | 1 | | 4 | | 1 | 1 | |

Small bold figures denote goalscorers.  † denotes opponent's own goal.

---

## FIRHILL STADIUM

**CAPACITY:** 14,403; Seated 2,813, Standing 11,590

PLEASE NOTE: CAPACITY WILL INCREASE TO 20,653 IN OCTOBER, 1994 ON COMPLETION OF NEW EAST STAND GIVING A TOTAL SEATED CAPACITY OF 9,063

**PITCH DIMENSIONS:** 110 yds x 74 yds

**FACILITIES FOR DISABLED SUPPORTERS:** Covered places available in North Enclosure. 10 Weelchair spectators, 10 attendants, 10 ambulant disabled. Telephone call in advance to Office Secretary for arrangements.

FIRHILL ROAD

## HOW TO GET THERE

The following routes may be used to reach Firhill Stadium:

**TRAINS:** The nearest railway stations are Glasgow Queen Street and Glasgow Central and buses from the centre of the city pass within 100 yards of the ground.

**BUSES:** The following buses from the city centre all pass by the park. Nos. 1, 8, 18, 21, 21A, 57, 60, 61, 61B, 89, and 90 and the frequency of buses is just over 12 minutes.

**UNDERGROUND:** The nearest GGPTE Underground station is St. George's Cross and supporters walking from here should pass through Cromwell Street into Maryhill Road and then walk up this road as far as Firhill Street. The ground is then on the right. The Kelvinbridge Underground Station is also not far from the park and supporters from here should walk along Great Western Road as far as Napiershill Street and then follow this into Maryhill Road.

**CARS:** Car Parking is available at the north end of the ground.

# RANGERS

Ibrox Stadium, Glasgow G51 2XD

**CHAIRMAN**
David E. Murray

**VICE-CHAIRMAN**
Donald R. Findlay Q.C., LL.B.

**DIRECTORS**
Hugh R. W. Adam, Jack Gillespie,
R. Campbell Ogilvie,
Ian Skelly, Walter Smith

**SECRETARY**
R. Campbell Ogilvie

**MANAGER**
Walter Smith

**ASSISTANT MANAGER**
Archie Knox

**FIRST TEAM COACH**
Davie Dodds

**RESERVE COACHES**
John McGregor & Billy Kirkwood

**YOUTH COACH**
John Chalmers

**S.F.A. COMMUNITY OFFICER**
Ewan Chester

**PUBLIC RELATIONS EXECUTIVE**
John Greig M.B.E.

**FINANCIAL CONTROLLER**
Douglas Odam

**OPERATIONS EXECUTIVE**
Alistair Hood Q.P.M.

**RANGERS CATERING MANAGER**
Peter Kingstone

**MANAGER, MARKETING &
PUBLICATIONS DEPARTMENT**
Brian Main

**COMMERCIAL SALES EXECUTIVE**
John Lawson

**STADIUM ACCESS ADMINISTRATOR**
Ian Hosie

**PITCH SUPERINTENDENT**
Alan Ferguson

**COMMERCIAL MANAGER**
Bob Reilly 041-427 8822

**TELEPHONES**
Ground 041-427 8500
Fax 041-427 2676
Stadium Access Administration
(Tickets) 041-427 8800
Public Relations Department
041-427 8500

**CLUB SHOPS**
The Rangers Shop, 150 Copland Road,
Glasgow G51. Open 10.00 a.m. –
5.00 p.m. Mon to Sat
The Rangers Shop, 103 St. Vincent
Street, Glasgow, G2. Open
10.00 a.m. – 5.30 p.m. Mon to Sat

**OFFICIAL SUPPORTERS CLUB**
Rangers F.C. Supporters Association,
250 Edmiston Drive, Glasgow G51 1YU

**TEAM CAPTAIN**
Richard Gough

**SHIRT SPONSOR**
McEwan's Lager

## LIST OF PLAYERS 1994-95

| SURNAME | FIRST NAME | MIDDLE NAME | DATE OF BIRTH | PLACE OF BIRTH | DATE OF SIGNING | HEIGHT FT INS | WEIGHT ST LBS | PREVIOUS CLUB |
|---|---|---|---|---|---|---|---|---|
| Boli | Basile | | 02/01/67 | Adjame, Ivory Coast | 05/07/94 | 5 11.0 | 13 2 | Olympique de Marseille |
| Boyack | Steven | | 04/09/76 | Edinburgh | 01/07/93 | 5 10.0 | 10 7 | Rangers B.C. |
| Brown | John | | 26/01/62 | Stirling | 15/01/88 | 5 11.0 | 11 2 | Dundee |
| Caldwell | Neil | | 25/09/75 | Glasgow | 02/07/92 | 5 6.0 | 10 2 | Rangers B.C. |
| Dair | Lee | | 28/05/77 | Dunfermline | 01/07/93 | 5 10.0 | 11 10 | Rangers B.C. |
| Davidson | William | | 09/07/78 | Glasgow | 06/07/94 | 5 8.0 | 9 7 | Rangers S.A.B.C. |
| Douglas | John | | 05/09/77 | Belfast | 06/07/94 | 5 8.0 | 11 7 | Rangers S.A.B.C. |
| Durie | Gordon | Scott | 06/12/65 | Paisley | 24/11/93 | 5 10.0 | 13 1 | Tottenham Hotspur |
| Durrant | Ian | | 29/10/66 | Glasgow | 27/07/84 | 5 8.0 | 9 7 | Glasgow United |
| Ferguson | Barry | | 02/02/78 | Glasgow | 06/07/94 | 5 7.0 | 9 2 | Rangers S.A.B.C. |
| Ferguson | Duncan | | 27/12/71 | Stirling | 20/07/93 | 6 3.0 | 13 3 | Dundee United |
| Ferguson | Ian | | 15/03/67 | Glasgow | 15/02/88 | 5 10.0 | 10 11 | St. Mirren |
| Fotheringham | Kevin | George | 13/08/75 | Dunfermline | 06/05/92 | 5 10.0 | 11 4 | Rangers B.C. |
| Galloway | Andrew | | 12/03/77 | Glasgow | 01/07/93 | 5 10.0 | 11 5 | Rangers B.C. |
| Goram | Andrew | Lewis | 13/04/64 | Bury | 27/06/91 | 5 11.0 | 12 13 | Hibernian |
| Gough | Charles | Richard | 05/04/62 | Stockholm | 02/10/87 | 6 0.0 | 11 12 | Tottenham Hotspur |
| Hagen | David | | 05/05/73 | Edinburgh | 23/08/89 | 5 11.0 | 13 0 | Grahamston B.C. |
| Hateley | Mark | | 07/11/61 | Wallasey | 19/07/90 | 6 2.5 | 13 0 | A.S. Monaco |
| Huistra | Pieter | | 18/01/67 | Goenga | 10/08/90 | 5 11.0 | 11 4 | F.C. Twente Enschede |
| Inglis | Neil | David | 10/09/74 | Glasgow | 02/07/91 | 6 1.0 | 12 2 | Rangers B.C. |
| Juttla | Jaswinder | Singh | 02/08/77 | Glasgow | 06/07/94 | 5 6.0 | 9 12 | Rangers S.A.B.C. |
| Kerr | Roddy | | 04/05/77 | Bellshill | 09/07/93 | 5 8.0 | 9 7 | "S" Form |
| Laudrup | Brian | | 22/02/69 | Vienna | 21/07/94 | 6 0.0 | 13 2 | Fiorentina AC |
| Mathieson | Ross | | 15/11/77 | Greenock | 06/07/94 | 5 6.0 | 9 1 | Rangers S.A.B.C. |
| Maxwell | Alastair | Espie | 16/02/65 | Hamilton | 12/04/92 | 5 10.0 | 10 12 | Motherwell |
| McCall | Stuart | | 10/06/64 | Leeds | 15/08/91 | 5 8.0 | 11 12 | Everton |
| McCoist | Alistair | | 24/09/62 | Bellshill | 09/06/83 | 5 10.0 | 12 0 | Sunderland |
| McCulloch | Scott | Anderson J. | 29/11/75 | Irvine | 02/07/92 | 5 11.0 | 11 12 | Rangers B.C. |
| McGinty | Brian | | 10/12/76 | East Kilbride | 01/07/93 | 6 1.0 | 11 4 | Rangers B.C. |
| McKnight | Paul | | 08/02/77 | Belfast | 05/08/93 | 5 7.0 | 11 4 | St. Andrews B.C. |
| McPherson | David | | 28/01/64 | Paisley | 04/06/92 | 6 3.0 | 11 11 | Heart of Midlothian |
| McShane | Paul | | 13/04/78 | Alexandria | 06/07/94 | 5 8.0 | 10 4 | Rangers S.A.B.C. |
| Mikhailitchenko | Alexei | | 30/03/63 | Kiev | 05/07/91 | 6 2.5 | 13 3 | UC Sampdoria SpA |
| Miller | Charles | | 18/03/76 | Glasgow | 02/07/92 | 5 9.0 | 10 8 | Rangers B.C. |
| Moore | Craig | Andrew | 12/12/75 | Canterbury, Aus. | 16/09/93 | 6 1.0 | 12 0 | Australian Institute |
| Morrow | John | | 20/11/71 | Belfast | 29/07/88 | 5 7.0 | 10 0 | Linfield |
| Murray | Neil | | 21/02/73 | Bellshill | 23/08/89 | 5 9.0 | 10 10 | Rangers Amateurs F.C |
| Nicoll | Mark | Charles | 20/11/77 | Dumfries | 06/07/94 | 5 7.0 | 10 1 | Rangers S.A.B.C. |
| Nicolson | Iain | | 13/10/76 | Glasgow | 04/06/93 | 5 10.0 | 10 4 | Rangers B.C. |
| Pollock | Christopher | | 06/11/77 | Kilwinning | 06/07/94 | 5 8.0 | 10 11 | Rangers S.A.B.C. |
| Pressley | Steven | | 11/10/73 | Elgin | 02/08/90 | 6 0.0 | 11 0 | Inverkeithing B.C. |
| Rae | Michael | | 24/11/76 | Inverness | 06/07/94 | 5 10.0 | 12 0 | Mayburgh A.F.C. |
| Redpath | James | | 03/03/77 | Belfast | 05/08/93 | 5 10.0 | 12 3 | St. Andrew's B.C. |
| Reid | Brian | Robertson | 15/06/70 | Paisley | 25/03/91 | 6 2.0 | 11 12 | Greenock Morton |
| Robertson | David | | 17/10/68 | Aberdeen | 02/07/91 | 5 11.0 | 11 0 | Aberdeen |
| Robertson | Lee | | 25/08/73 | Edinburgh | 23/06/90 | 5 7.0 | 9 6 | Salvesen B.C. |
| Scott | Colin | | 19/05/70 | Glasgow | 21/08/87 | 6 1.0 | 12 4 | Dalry Thistle |
| Shields | Greg | | 21/08/76 | Falkirk | 01/07/93 | 5 9.0 | 10 10 | Rangers B.C. |
| Steven | Trevor | | 21/09/63 | Berwick Upon Tweed | 29/07/92 | 5 9.0 | 10 12 | Olympique de Marseille |
| Stevens | Michael | Gary | 27/03/63 | Barrow-In Furness | 19/07/88 | 5 11.0 | 12 7 | Everton |
| Thomson | William | Marshall | 10/02/58 | Linwood | 27/07/94 | 6 2.0 | 12 3 | Motherwell |
| Wilson | Scott | | 19/03/77 | Edinburgh | 01/07/93 | 6 1.0 | 11 4 | Rangers B.C. |
| Wishart | Fraser | | 01/03/65 | Johnstone | 27/07/93 | 5 8.0 | 10 0 | Falkirk |

## MILESTONES

**YEAR OF FORMATION:** 1873
**MOST CAPPED PLAYER:** George Young
**NO. OF CAPS:** 53
**MOST LEAGUE POINTS IN A SEASON:** 76 (Division 1 – Season 1920/21)
**MOST LEAGUE GOALS SCORED BY A PLAYER IN A SEASON:** Sam English (Season 1931/32)
**NO. OF GOALS SCORED:** 44
**RECORD ATTENDANCE:** 118,567 (-v- Celtic – 2.1.1939)
**RECORD VICTORY:** 14-2 (-v- Blairgowrie – Scottish Cup 20.1.1934)
**RECORD DEFEAT:** 2-10 (-v- Airdrieonians – 1886)

## SEASON TICKET INFORMATION

| PREMIER CLUB | Adults | Concession | Child |
|---|---|---|---|
| Red/Brown Sections | £280 | £140 | £120 |
| Yellow/Orange Sections | £310 | £155 | £120 |
| Blue Section | £340 | £170 | £120 |
| | Adults | Concession | Child |
| Govan Stand Front | £220 | £110 | £100 |
| Copland Stand Front | £194 | £100 | £100 |
| Copland Stand Rear | £206 | £100 | £100 |
| Seated Enclosure | £220 | £100 | £100 |
| Main Stand Section A | £180 | £110 | £100 |
| Main Stand Section B | £180 | £100 | £100 |
| Main Stand Sections C & D | £206 | £100 | £100 |
| Main Stand Section E | £240 | £120 | £100 |
| Main Stand Sections F & G | £180 | £100 | £100 |
| Main Stand Section H | £360 | £180 | £100 |
| Main Stand Sections J,K,M & N | £240 | £120 | £100 |
| Main Stand Sections O & P (Family Section) | £180 | £100 | £100 |
| Main Stand Sections Q & R | £206 | £100 | £100 |
| Main Stand Sections S & T | £180 | £100 | £100 |

## LEAGUE ADMISSION PRICES

Broomloan Rear, Copland Rear & Govan Front ........................................ (Adult) £11
............................................................................................................... (Juvenile) £6
............................................................................................................... (OAP) £8
Broomloan Front, Copland Front & Main Stand Rear ........................... (Adult) £10
............................................................................................................... (Juvenile) £6
............................................................................................................... (OAP) £8
Seated Enclosure ................................................................................... (Adult) £11
............................................................................................................... (Juvenile) (£6
............................................................................................................... (OAP) £8
Main Stand Front & Govan Rear ........................................................... (Adult) £15
............................................................................................................... (Juvenile) £6
............................................................................................................... (OAP) £8
Club Deck .............................................................................................. (Adult) £18
............................................................................................................... (Juvenile) £9
............................................................................................................... (OAP) £12

| | |
|---|---|
| REGISTERED STRIP: | Shirt – Royal Blue with Three White Bands on Sleeves<br>Shorts – White with Three Royal Blue Bands, Stockings – Black with Red Tops |
| CHANGE STRIP: | Shirt – Red with Black Candy Stripes, Shorts – Black with Red and White Trim<br>Stockings – Red with Black and White Tops |

# CLUB FACTFILE 1993/94 .. RESULTS .. APPEARANCES .. SCORERS

## The GERS

*Small bold figures (shown as [n]) denote goalscorers. † denotes opponent's own goal.*

| Date | Venue | Opponents | Result | Maxwell A. | McCall S. | Wishart F. | Gough R. | Pressley S. | Brown J. | Murray N. | Ferguson I. | Hateley M. | Hagen D. | Mikhailitchenko A. | Durrant I | Huistra P. | Steven T. | Vinnicombe C. | McPherson D. | Ferguson D. | Stevens G. | Robertson D. | Kouznetsov O. | Morrow J. | Miller C. | McCoist A. | Scott C. | Durie G. | Goram A. | Moore C. |
|---|---|---|---|---|---|---|---|---|---|---|---|---|---|---|---|---|---|---|---|---|---|---|---|---|---|---|---|---|---|---|
| Aug 7 | H | Heart of Midlothian | 2-1 | 1 | 2 | 3 | 4 | 5 | 6 | 7 | 8 | 9[1] | 10[1] | 11 | 12 | | 14 | | | | | | | | | | | | | |
| 14 | A | St. Johnstone | 2-1 | 1 | | 3 | 4[1] | 5 | 6 | 2 | 8[1] | | | | 9 | 12 | 10 | 11 | 7 | 14 | | | | | | | | | | |
| 21 | A | Celtic | 0-0 | 1 | | 3 | 4 | 2 | 6 | | 8 | 10 | 14 | | 12 | 11 | 7 | | 5 | 9 | | | | | | | | | | |
| 28 | H | Kilmarnock | 1-2 | 1 | | | 4 | 5[1] | 6 | | 8 | 10 | | 11 | 12 | | 7 | | 9 | | 2 | 3 | | | | | | | | |
| Sep 4 | H | Dundee | 1-1 | 1 | | | 4 | 5 | | | 8 | 10 | | | 12 | 11 | 7 | | | | 9 | 2 | | | | 3 | | 6 | | |
| 11 | H | Partick Thistle | 1-1 | 1 | | | 4 | | | | 8 | 10[1] | | | 12 | | 7 | 6 | 5 | | 9 | 2 | | | | 3 | | 11 | | |
| 18 | A | Aberdeen | 0-2 | 1 | 4 | | | | 6 | | 8 | 10 | | | | | 7 | | 11 | 5 | 12 | 2 | 3 | | | 9 | | | | |
| 25 | H | Hibernian | 2-1 | 1 | | 6 | 4 | | | | 14 | 8 | 10[1] | 9 | 11 | | 7[1] | | 5 | | 2 | 3 | | | | | | | | |
| Oct 2 | A | Raith Rovers | †1-1 | 1 | | | 4 | 5 | | 3 | 8 | 10 | | | | | 7 | | | | 2 | | | | | 9 | 15 | | | |
| 6 | H | Motherwell | 1-2 | 1 | | | 4 | 5 | | 3 | 8[1] | 10 | | 9 | 14 | 6 | 12 | | | | 2 | | | | | | 11 | | 1 | |
| 9 | A | Dundee United | 3-1 | 1 | | 6 | 4 | 12 | | | 8 | 10[1] | | | 7 | 9 | 11[2] | | 5 | | 2 | 3 | | | | 14 | | | | |
| 16 | H | St. Johnstone | 2-0 | 1 | | | 4 | | | | 8 | 10[1] | | 6 | 12 | 11[1] | 7 | | 5 | | 2 | 3 | | | | 9 | | | | |
| 30 | H | Celtic | 1-2 | 1 | | 6 | 4 | 14 | | | 8 | 10 | | 12 | 11 | | 7 | | 5 | | 2 | 3 | | | | 9[1] | | | | |
| Nov 3 | A | Heart of Midlothian | 2-2 | 1 | 2 | | 4 | 14 | 6 | | 8 | 10[2] | | 7 | | | 11 | | 5 | | | 3 | | | | 9 | | | | |
| 6 | A | Kilmarnock | 2-0 | 1 | 2 | | 4 | 14 | 6 | | 8[1] | 10 | | | 7 | 11 | 12[1] | | 5 | | | 3 | | | | 9 | | | | |
| 10 | H | Dundee | 3-1 | 1 | | | 4 | | 6 | | 8[1] | 10 | | | 11 | 14 | 7 | | 5 | | 2 | 3 | | | | 9[2] | | | | |
| 13 | H | Raith Rovers | 2-2 | 1 | 5 | | 4 | | 6 | | 8 | 10[2] | | | 7 | 9 | 11 | | | | 2 | 3 | | | | 14 | | | | |
| 20 | A | Hibernian | 1-0 | 1 | 7 | | 4[1] | | 6 | 2 | 8 | 10 | | 11 | 9 | | | | 5 | | | 3 | | | | | | | | |
| 27 | A | Partick Thistle | 1-1 | 1 | 2 | | 4 | | 6 | | 8 | 10 | | 9 | | 14[1] | | | 5 | 12 | | 3 | | | | | | 7 | | |
| Dec 1 | H | Aberdeen | 2-0 | 1 | 2 | | 4 | 14 | 6 | 11 | 8 | 10[2] | | | 12 | | 7 | | | | | 3 | | | | | | 9 | | |
| 4 | A | Motherwell | 2-0 | 1 | | | 4 | | 6 | 11 | 8 | 10 | | | 12 | | 7 | | | | 5 | 2 | 3 | | | | | 9[2] | | |
| 11 | H | Dundee United | 0-3 | 1 | | 6 | 4 | 14 | | 11 | 8 | 10 | | | 12 | | 7 | | | | 5 | 2 | 3 | | | | | 9 | | |
| 18 | A | St. Johnstone | 4-0 | 1 | | | 4 | | | 5 | 8 | 10[2] | | | 11 | | 7[1] | | 3 | | 2 | | 6 | | | | | 9[1] | | |
| 27 | H | Heart of Midlothian | 2-2 | 1 | | | 4 | 5 | | 6 | 8 | 10[2] | | | 11 | | 12 | | 7 | 14 | 2 | | 8 | | | | | 9 | | |
| Jan 1 | A | Celtic | 4-2 | 1 | 8 | | 4 | 5 | 6 | 3 | | 10[1] | | 11[2] | 12 | | 7 | | | | 2 | | | | | 14[1] | | | | |
| 8 | H | Kilmarnock | 3-0 | 1 | 8 | | 4 | | 6 | 5 | | 10[2] | | 11 | 12[1] | | 7 | | | | 2 | 3 | | | | | | 9 | | |
| 15 | A | Dundee | 1-1 | 1 | 8 | | | 5 | 6 | 4 | | 10 | | 11 | 12 | | 7 | | | | 2 | 3 | 14 | | | | | 9[1] | | |
| 22 | A | Aberdeen | 0-0 | 1 | 8 | | 4 | | 6 | 5 | | 10 | | 11 | 12 | | 7 | | | | 2 | 3 | | | | | | 9 | | |
| Feb 5 | H | Partick Thistle | 5-1 | 1 | 8[1] | | 4 | | 6 | | | 10 | | 11[1] | | | 7[1] | | | | 2 | 3 | | | | | | 9[2] | | |
| 12 | H | Hibernian | 2-0 | | 5 | | 4 | | 6 | | 8 | 10 | | 11 | | | 7[1] | | | | 2 | 3 | | | | | 14 | 9[1] | | 1 |
| 26 | A | Raith Rovers | 2-1 | | 4 | | | | 6 | | 8[1] | 10 | | 14 | | | 7 | | 5 | | | 3 | | | | 9 | | 11[1] | | 1 |
| Mar 5 | H | Motherwell | 2-1 | | 5 | | 4 | | 6 | | 8 | 10[1] | | 11 | | | 7 | | | 12 | 2 | 3 | | | | 14 | | 9[1] | | 1 |
| 19 | H | St. Johnstone | 4-0 | | 2[1] | | 4 | | 6 | | 8 | 10[1] | | | | | 7 | | 5[1] | | | 3 | | | | 9 | | 11[1] | | 1 |
| 26 | A | Heart of Midlothian | 2-1 | | 3 | | 4 | | 6 | | 8 | 10[1] | | 12 | | | 7 | | 5 | | 2 | | | | | 9[1] | | 11 | | |
| 29 | A | Partick Thistle | 2-1 | | 3 | | 4[1] | | 6 | | 8 | 10 | | 11 | | | 7 | | 5 | 14 | 2 | | | | | 9[1] | | 12 | | |
| Apr 2 | H | Aberdeen | 1-1 | | 7[1] | | 4 | | 6 | 3 | 8 | 10 | | 12 | | | | | 5 | | 2 | | | | | 9 | | 11 | | |
| 5 | A | Dundee United | 0-0 | 15 | 7 | | 4 | 6 | | 3 | | 12 | | | 11 | | 8 | | 5 | 10 | | | | | | 9 | | | 1 | 2 |
| 16 | H | Raith Rovers | 4-0 | 1 | 2 | | 4 | | 6 | | 8 | 12 | | 14[1] | 7 | | | | 5 | 10[1] | | 3[1] | | | | 9[1] | | 11 | | |
| 23 | H | Dundee United | 2-1 | 1 | 2 | | 4 | | 6 | | 8 | 10 | | | | | 7 | | 5 | | | 3 | | | | 9 | | 11[2] | | |
| 26 | A | Motherwell | 1-2 | 1 | 2 | | 4 | | 6 | | 8 | | | 12 | | | 7 | | 5 | 10 | | 3 | | | | 9[1] | | 11 | | |
| 30 | H | Celtic | 1-1 | | 2 | | 4 | | 6 | | 8 | 10 | | 12[1] | | | 7 | | 5 | | | 14 | | | | 3 | | 9 | 1 | 11 |
| May 3 | A | Hibernian | 0-1 | | 2 | | 4 | | 6 | 14 | 8 | 10 | | 11 | 9 | | 7 | | | | | 3 | | | | | | 12 | 1 | |
| 7 | A | Kilmarnock | 0-1 | | | 2 | 4 | 5 | | | | 10 | | 12 | 11 | 7 | 14 | | | | 3 | 6 | | | | 8 | 9 | | 1 | |
| 14 | H | Dundee | 0-0 | | | 6 | 4 | | | | 8 | 10 | | 12 | 11 | | 7 | | | | 5 | 2 | 3 | | | 14 | | 1 | | 9 |
| **TOTAL FULL APPEARANCES** | | | | 31 | 34 | 5 | 37 | 17 | 24 | 20 | 35 | 40 | 4 | 24 | 14 | 10 | 32 | 2 | 27 | 7 | 28 | 32 | 4 | 2 | 2 | 16 | 5 | 23 | 8 | 1 |
| **TOTAL SUB APPEARANCES** | | | | | (1) | | | (6) | | (2) | | (2) | | (2) | (10) | (9) | (11) | | | (2) | | (1) | (3) | (1) | | (2) | (1) | (5) | (1) | (1) |
| **TOTAL GOALS SCORED** | | | | | | | 3 | 3 | | 1 | 5 | 22 | 1 | 5 | 6 | 4 | 1 | | 1 | | 1 | 1 | | | | 7 | | 12 | | |

---

## IBROX STADIUM

**CAPACITY:** 46,836 (All seated)

**PITCH DIMENSIONS:** 115 yds x 78 yds

**FACILITIES FOR DISABLED SUPPORTERS:**
Special area within stadium and also special toilet facilities provided. We also have a Rangers Disabled Supporters' Club. Contact: D. Currie, Secretary, Disabled Supporters' Club, c/o Ibrox Stadium, Glasgow G51 2XD.

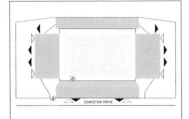

EDMISTON DRIVE

## HOW TO GET THERE

You can reach Ibrox Stadium by these routes:

**BUSES:** The following buses all pass within 300 yards of the Stadium and can be boarded from the Glasgow City centre. Nos. 4, 9A, 23, 23A, 52, 53, 53A, 54A, 54B, 65, 89 and 91.

**UNDERGROUND:** GGPTE Underground station is Ibrox, which is two minutes walk from the Stadium.

**CARS:** Motor Vehicles can head for the Stadium from the city centre by joining the M8 Motorway from Waterloo Street. Take the B768 turn-off for Govan. This will then take you to the ground. There are parking facilities available at the Albion car park.

(Photo: courtesy of the Falkirk Herald)

# No middle road

It was never going to be a season where teams could take their feet off the accelerator and settle for mid-table mediocrity. For there was no such thing as a mid-table in the First Division last term – clubs were either hoping to chase the single promotion spot up for grabs or were going to find themselves embroiled in a desperate battle to avoid the FIVE relegation places that had been set aside to facilitate the new League set-up that is in place this season.

And while the clubs involved might not have enjoyed the cut-throat nature of the new competition, the fans were not complaining as just about every game was of crucial importance.

A two horse race developed for the Championship between eventual victors, Falkirk and front-runners, Dunfermline, who won more matches (30) and scored more goals (93) but lost out by a single point. The fact that both clubs regard each other as local rivals, despite being separated by the River Forth, only added to the jagged edge of tension that was felt by everyone associated with the Bairns and Pars in the last few weeks of the season.

With two Saturdays left, Dunfermline led on goal difference but were faced with a trip to Airdrie, where the Diamonds were celebrating their last match at Broomfield. In truth, it was the last place Bert Paton's men would have wanted to visit on such an occasion. The kick-off was delayed for ten minutes to allow the big crowd – and a parachutist who was supposed to drop into the centre circle – to arrive.

Airdrie were desperate to sign off with a victory and in goalkeeper, John Martin, had a player in inspired form. Dunfermline striker, Stewart Petrie, was denied on countless occasions by his brilliance – but even a draw would have suited the Fifers who had a vastly superior goal difference over Falkirk, should both have finished level on points. It wasn't to be, however. Neale Cooper, so often the cornerstone of the Dunfermline defence, deflected a cross into his own net. The Fifers had lost.

On the same day, Falkirk were playing their last home game of the season, knowing they could not afford to drop even a single point against Hamilton. They kept their nerve

superbly to win 3-0 and set up a tale of two matches on the final day of the season. Falkirk, now in front by a point, had to go to Kilbowie Park and avoid defeat, where they had never won under Jim Jefferies. They were up against a Clydebank team that had already whipped them 4-0 at Brockville, earlier in the season, and who had shown their capabilities by getting off to a flying start in the League, winning their first seven matches before being hammered by injuries and gradually sliding out of contention. Dunfermline, meanwhile, were at home to already relegated Clyde. They had to win and pray for the right result at Clydebank.

By half-time at East End Park, they were obviously going to keep their end of the bargain – they were 4-0 up and eventually added another in the second half.

If the atmosphere was tense at Dunfermline, it was unbearable at Kilbowie. An early goal by Falkirk's Nicky Henderson should have eased the pressure but the Bankies hit back before the break and equalised through John Henry. For 45 minutes, Falkirk were one mistake away from

*A jubilant Nicky Henderson after scoring the promotion-clinching goal against Clydebank.*

undoing an entire season's work – but they held out to the delight and relief of their 5000 travelling fans.

"I've never experienced an afternoon like it," admitted Jefferies.

"It was not very pleasant. In fact, if I'm ever faced with that kind of situation again, I'm resigning on the Friday night!"

The Bairns boss believes that they should have been joined in the Premier Division by the team that pushed them all the way.

"Dunfermline deserved to go up with us," he added. "They must be heartbroken to have put so much effort into the season and come away with nothing. The truth is that both teams were a class above the rest of the division and it is unfortunate that we both could not have been rewarded."

Falkirk's League Championship win followed hot on the heels of their B & Q Cup victory and their second string won the Reserve League East title to cap a memorable season.

Striker, Richard Cadette's 27 goals in all competitions won him the Player of the Year accolade from his fellow pros and the general feeling among Bairns fans was that if Falkirk had entered the Grand National and Wimbledon last season, they would probably have won them both as well!

They will certainly be a valuable addition to the Premier Division next season.

But while they succeeded in getting out of the First Division, spare a thought for the five who lost the fight to stay in it.

Only Brechin City were cast adrift early on but the others involved in the relegation issue, Clyde, Greenock Morton, Stirling Albion and Dumbarton are all part-time and perhaps it is no coincidence that they succumbed, while Ayr United, the other team involved in the battle for most of the season, had a nucleus of full-time professionals who saw them through.

Despite their part-time status, however, the relegated clubs showed enough ambition to suggest that they can bounce straight back. Stirling and Clyde have moved into their superb purpose-built stadia at Forthbank and Broadwood respectively. Attendances at both clubs improved substantially as a result. They also have big name managers in Kevin Drinkell at Stirling, and Alex Smith at Clyde, men who are used to success and will be determined to enjoy more at their clubs.

Dumbarton are another club with a fine young manager in Murdo MacLeod, and he won't be satisfied until the Sons return to the First Division.

Of the remaining teams, St. Mirren and Hamilton Accies were frustrated by their own inconsistencies. Occasionally, they threatened to mount a title challenge, but then a couple of defeats from teams at the other end of the table would set them back.

*Nicky Henderson celebrates with the Bairns' fans.*

Saints reached the Final of the B & Q Cup and have a superb set of young players, whom Jimmy Bone could forge into a potent Championship chasing squad in the coming months.

Airdrie, who scuppered Dunfermline's chances, fell away after a bright start, but they too will be there or thereabouts this term, as will Clydebank.

But all of these teams will have to conjure up something special to match the drama that the First Division produced last season.

**David McCarthy
(Evening News)**

*Last season's First Division Player of the Year, Richard Cadette, in action against Clydebank.*

# AIRDRIEONIANS

Broadwood Stadium,
Cumbernauld G68 9NE
ALL CORRRESPONDENCE SHOULD BE
ADDRESSED TO:
32 Stirling Street, Airdrie ML6 0AH

**CHAIRMAN**
George W. Peat, C.A.

**VICE-CHAIRMAN**
David W. Smith, C.Eng., M.I.C.E.

**DIRECTORS**
Joseph M. Rowan
Alexander P. Bryce
Alexander MacDonald

**SECRETARY**
George W. Peat, C.A.

**MANAGER**
Alexander MacDonald

**ASSISTANT MANAGER**
John McVeigh

**COACH**
John Binnie

**CLUB DOCTOR**
Brian Dunn, M.B.,C.L.B.,M.R.C.P.(UK)

**PHYSIOTHERAPIST**
Ian Constable

**S.F.A. COMMUNITY COACH**
Jim Chapman

**YOUTH DEVELOPMENT OFFICER**
Roy Tomnay

**TELEPHONES**
Ground
(0236) 451511 (Match Days Only)
Office (0236) 762067
Fax (0236) 760698
Ticket Office (0236) 747255
Information Service (0236) 762067

**CLUB SHOP**
93 Graham Street, Airdrie, ML6 6DE.
Tel (0236) 747255. Open Mon-Fri.
10.00 a.m. till 1.00 p.m. and 2.00 p.m.
till 4.00 p.m. (Closed Wednesday)
Sat 9.00 a.m. – 3.00 p.m.

**OFFICIAL SUPPORTERS CLUB**
c/o David Johnstone,
16 Deveron Street, Coatbridge
Tel (0236) 423812

**TEAM CAPTAIN**
James Sandison

**SHIRT SPONSOR**
John C. Dalziel (Airdrie) Limited

## LIST OF PLAYERS 1994-95

| SURNAME | FIRST NAME | MIDDLE NAME | DATE OF BIRTH | PLACE OF BIRTH | DATE OF SIGNING | HEIGHT FT INS | WEIGHT ST LBS | PREVIOUS CLUB |
|---|---|---|---|---|---|---|---|---|
| Balfour | Evan | William | 09/09/65 | Edinburgh | 12/05/89 | 5  11.0 | 12  6 | Whitburn Juniors |
| Black | Kenneth | George | 29/11/63 | Stenhousemuir | 12/09/91 | 5  9.0 | 11 10 | Portsmouth |
| Boyle | James | | 19/02/67 | Glasgow | 11/08/89 | 5  6.0 | 11  2 | Queen's Park |
| Ferguson | Iain | John H. | 04/08/62 | Newharthill | 14/09/93 | 5  9.0 | 10  7 | Motherwell |
| Harvey | Paul | Edward | 28/08/68 | Glasgow | 25/01/94 | 5  8.0 | 10  7 | Clydebank |
| Hay | Graham | Stuart | 27/11/65 | Falkirk | 25/01/94 | 6  0.0 | 12  7 | Clydebank |
| Honor | Christian | Robert | 05/06/68 | Bristol | 10/08/91 | 5 10.5 | 12  2 | Bristol City |
| Jack | Paul | Dunn | 15/05/65 | Malaya | 05/08/89 | 5 10.0 | 11  7 | Arbroath |
| Lawrence | Alan | | 19/08/62 | Edinburgh | 31/03/89 | 5  7.0 | 10  0 | Dundee |
| Martin | John | Galloway K. | 27/10/58 | Edinburgh | 30/04/80 | 6  1.0 | 12  0 | Tranent Juniors |
| McCulloch | William | | 02/04/73 | Baillieston | 11/09/92 | 6  6.0 | 12  6 | Rutherglen Glencairn |
| McIntyre | James | | 24/05/72 | Alexandria | 23/09/93 | 5  11.0 | 11  5 | Bristol City |
| McIntyre | Thomas | | 26/12/63 | Bellshill | 29/07/94 | 6  0.0 | 12  5 | Hibernian |
| Reid | Wesley | | 10/09/68 | London | 20/03/92 | 5  9.0 | 11  4 | Bradford City |
| Sandison | James | William | 22/06/65 | Edinburgh | 27/07/91 | 5 10.5 | 10 10 | Heart of Midlothian |
| Smith | Andrew | Mark | 22/11/68 | Aberdeen | 09/08/90 | 6  1.0 | 12  7 | Peterhead |
| Smith | Anthony | | 28/10/73 | Bellshill | 02/06/93 | 5  8.0 | 9  7 | Heart of Midlothian |
| Stewart | Alexander | | 14/10/65 | Bellshill | 14/10/89 | 5  8.0 | 11  0 | Kilmarnock |
| Wilson | Marvyn | | 01/12/73 | Bellshill | 22/07/92 | 5  7.5 | 10  0 | Heart of Midlothian |

## MILESTONES

**YEAR OF FORMATION:** 1878
**MOST CAPPED PLAYER:** Jimmy Crapnell
**NO. OF CAPS:** 9
**MOST LEAGUE POINTS IN A SEASON:** 60 (Division 2 – Season 1973/74)
**MOST LEAGUE GOALS SCORED BY A PLAYER IN A SEASON:** Hugh Baird (Season 1954/55)
**NO. OF GOALS SCORED:** 53
**RECORD ATTENDANCE:** 24,000 (-v- Heart of Midlothian 8.3.1952)
**RECORD VICTORY:** 15-1 (-v- Dundee Wanderers – Division 2. 1.12.1894)
**RECORD DEFEAT:** 1-11 (-v- Hibernian – Division 1, 24.10.1959)

## SEASON TICKET INFORMATION

Seated
Adult ............................................................ £125
Juvenile/OAP ................................................ £65

## LEAGUE ADMISSION PRICES

Seated
Adult ................................................................ £8
Juvenile/OAP .................................................... £4

**REGISTERED STRIP:** Shirt – White with Red Diamond, Shorts – Red, Stockings – Red
**CHANGE STRIP:** Shirt – Red with Black Collar, Shorts – Black, Stockings – Black

## CLUB FACTFILE 1993/94 .. RESULTS .. APPEARANCES .. SCORERS

### The DIAMONDS

| Date | Venue | Opponents | Result | Martin J. | Stewart A. | Kirkwood D. | Sandison J. | Caesar G. | Reid W. | Boyle J. | Balfour E. | Davenport P. | Lawrence A. | Smith Andrew | Conn S. | Abercromby M. | McVicar D. | Black K. | Honor C. | Jack P. | Ferguson I. | McIntyre J. | Wilson M. | Tommay D. | Smith Anthony | Hay G. | Harvey P. | McCulloch W. | Connelly G. |
|---|---|---|---|---|---|---|---|---|---|---|---|---|---|---|---|---|---|---|---|---|---|---|---|---|---|---|---|---|---|
| Aug 7 | A | St. Mirren | 1-0 | 1 | 2 | 3 | 4 | 5 | 6$^1$ | 7 | 8 | 9 | 10 | 11 | 12 | 14 | | | | | | | | | | | | | |
| 14 | H | Brechin City | 1-0 | 1 | 2 | 7 | 4 | 5 | | 8 | | 9$^1$ | | 11 | | 14 | 10 | 3 | 6 | | | | | | | | | | |
| 21 | H | Hamilton Academical | 4-0 | 1 | 2 | 7$^1$ | 4 | 5 | | 8 | 12 | 9$^2$ | | 11$^1$ | 14 | | 3 | 6 | 10 | | | | | | | | | | |
| 28 | A | Dunfermline Athletic | 2-3 | 1 | 2 | 7$^2$ | 4 | 5 | 12 | 8 | | 9 | 11 | 10 | | 14 | 6 | 3 | | | | | | | | | | | |
| Sept 4 | H | Greenock Morton | †2-0 | 1 | | 7 | 4 | 5 | 14 | 8 | | 9$^1$ | 11 | 10 | 12 | | 6 | 2 | 3 | | | | | | | | | | |
| 11 | A | Falkirk | 1-2 | 1 | | 7 | 4 | 5 | 14 12 | 8 | | | 11$^1$ | 9 | | 3 | 6 | 10 | 2 | | | | | | | | | | |
| 14 | H | Clyde | 2-1 | 1 | | 7 | 4 | 5 | | 8 | | 9 | | 11$^1$ | 14 | 3 | 6 | 2 | 12 | 10$^1$ | | | | | | | | | |
| 18 | H | Stirling Albion | †3-2 | 1 | | | 4 | 5 | 14 | 8 | | 9$^1$ | 11 | 12 | | 3 | 6$^1$ | 2 | 7 | 10 | | | | | | | | | |
| 25 | A | Clydebank | 2-1 | 1 | | 7 | | 5 | 14 | 8 | | 9 | 12$^1$ | 11 | | 3 | 6 | 2 | 4 | 10$^1$ | | | | | | | | | |
| 28 | A | Dumbarton | 1-0 | 1 | | 7 | | 5 | 14 12 | 8 | | 9 | 11 | 10$^1$ | | 3 | 6 | 2 | 4 | | | | | | | | | | |
| Oct 2 | H | Ayr United | 1-1 | 1 | | 7$^1$ | | 5 | | 12 | | 8 | 9 | 14 | 10 | 3 | 6 | 2 | 4 | 11 | | | | | | | | | |
| 9 | H | St. Mirren | 1-1 | 1 | 2 | 7$^1$ | | 5 | 14 | 8 | | 9 | 11 | 10 | | 3 | 6 | | 4 | 12 | | | | | | | | | |
| 16 | A | Clyde | 2-0 | 1 | 2 | 7 | | 5 | | 8 | | 9 | 14 | 11$^1$ | | 3 | 6 | 12 | 4 | 10$^1$ | | | | | | | | | |
| 23 | A | Falkirk | 1-1 | 1 | 2 | 7 | | 5 | | 8 | | 9 | | 10$^1$ | | 3 | 6 | 12 | 4 | 11 | | | | | | | | | |
| 30 | A | Hamilton Academical | 2-3 | 1 | 2 | 7 | | | 14 | 8 | | 9 | 12$^1$ | 11 | | 3 | 6 | 5$^1$ | 4 | 10 | | | | | | | | | |
| Nov 6 | H | Dunfermline Athletic | 1-1 | 1 | 2 | 12$^1$ | | | | 7 | 8 | 9 | 10 | 14 | | 3 | 6 | 5 | 4 | | | 11 | | | | | | | |
| 9 | A | Greenock Morton | 0-0 | 1 | 2 | 8 | | | | 7 | | 9 | 14 | 10 | 12 | 3 | | 5 | 4 | 11 | | 6 | | | | | | | |
| 13 | A | Ayr United | 2-1 | 1 | 3 | 7 | | | | 10 | 2 | 9$^2$ | | 11 | | | 5 | | 8 | | 4 | 6 | 14 | | | | | | |
| 20 | A | Dumbarton | 0-1 | 1 | 2 | | | | | 8 | 7 | 9 | | 11 | | 3 | 6 | 5 | | 10 | 14 | 4 | | | | | | | |
| 30 | H | Clydebank | 2-1 | 1 | 2 | 10$^2$ | | | | 8 | 7 | 14 | 9 | | 12 | 3 | 6 | 5 | 4 | | | 11 | | | | | | | |
| Dec 4 | A | Stirling Albion | †4-0 | 1 | 2 | 7$^1$ | | 5$^1$ | 8 | | 12 | 9 | | 10 | | | 6 | 3 | | 4 | 14$^1$ | 11 | | | | | | | |
| 11 | A | Brechin City | 2-0 | 1 | 2 | 7 | | 5 | | 8$^1$ | | 14 | | 10 | 12 | 3 | 6 | | | 4 | 9$^1$ | 11 | | | | | | | |
| 18 | H | Clyde | 3-2 | 1 | 2 | 7$^1$ | | 5 | | 8 | | 12 | 14$^1$ | 10 | | 3 | 6 | | | 4 | 9$^1$ | 11 | | | | | | | |
| Jan 11 | A | St. Mirren | 0-3 | 1 | 3 | 7 | | | 5 | 8 | 2 | 14 | 10 | 12 | 9 | | 6 | | | 4 | 11 | | | | | | | | |
| 18 | H | Hamilton Academical | 0-1 | 1 | 2 | 3 | 5 | | | 7 | 8 | 9 | 11 | 14 | | | 6 | | | 4 | 10 | 12 | | | | | | | |
| 22 | H | Brechin City | 0-1 | 1 | 2 | 7 | 4 | 5 | 14 | | | 10 | 12 | | | 6 | | 3 | 9 | 11 | 8 | | | | | | | | |
| 25 | A | Dunfermline Athletic | 0-0 | 1 | 2 | 7 | 4 | | | 12 | 9 | | 14 | | 3 | 6 | 8 | | 10 | | | | | | 5 | 11 | | | |
| Feb 1 | H | Greenock Morton | 2-2 | 1 | | 7 | 4 | | | 2 | 9 | 11 | 14$^1$ | | | 3 | 6 | 8$^1$ | 5 | | | | | | | 10 | 16 | | |
| 5 | A | Falkirk | 0-0 | 1 | 2 | 7 | | 5 | | | 8 | 12 | 11 | 9 | | 14 | 6 | 4 | 3 | | | | | | | 10 | | | |
| 12 | H | Ayr United | 0-0 | 1 | 2 | 7 | 4 | | | 14 | | 8 | 12 | 9 | | | 6 | 3 | | 11 | | | | | | 5 | 10 | | |
| Mar 1 | A | Dumbarton | 0-0 | 1 | 2 | 7 | 4 | 5 | | | | 11 | 12 | | | 6 | 8 | 14 | 9 | | | | | | | 3 | 10 | | |
| 5 | H | Stirling Albion | 3-0 | 1 | 2 | | 4 | 5 | 8 | 7$^1$ | | 9 | | | | | 3 | 11$^1$ | | | | | | | | 6 | 10$^1$ | | |
| 19 | A | Clyde | 1-0 | 1 | 2 | | 4 | | 8 | 7 | | 10 | | 9 | | 12 | 6 | 3 | | | | | | | | 5$^1$ | | | |
| 22 | A | Clydebank | 1-2 | 1 | 2 | | 4 | | 8 | 7 | | 9 | | 12 | | 6 | 3 | 14$^1$ | 11 | | | | | | | 5 | 10 | | |
| 26 | H | St. Mirren | 0-2 | 1 | 3 | | 4 | | 8 | 7 | | 9 | 10 | | | 14 | 6 | 5 | 2 | | 11 | | | | | | 12 | | |
| 29 | A | Brechin City | 2-0 | 1 | 2 | | 4 | | | 14 | | 9 | | | | 6 | 5 | 3 | 10$^1$ | 12 | 7 | | 11$^1$ | | | 8 | | | |
| Apr 2 | H | Falkirk | 0-0 | 1 | 2 | | 4 | | | 7 | | 10 | 9 | | | 6 | 8 | 3 | 11 | 14 | | | | | | 5 | 12 | | |
| 9 | H | Ayr United | 3-2 | 1 | 2$^1$ | | 4 | | | 7 | | 10$^1$ | 9$^1$ | | | 6 | 11 | 3 | | 14 | | | | | | 5 | | 8 | |
| 16 | H | Dumbarton | 1-1 | 1 | 2 | | 4 | | | | 10 | 9$^1$ | 14 | | | 6 | | 3 | | 8 | 11 | 5 | | | | | | 7 | |
| 23 | A | Stirling Albion | 1-1 | 1 | 2 | | 4 | | | | 11 | 9$^1$ | | | | 6 | 8 | 3 | | 10 | | 5 | | | | | | 7 | |
| 26 | H | Clydebank | 0-0 | 1 | 2 | | 4 | | | | 14 | 9 | | | | 6 | 8 | 3 | 7 | 11 | 10 | | | | | 5 | 12 | | |
| 30 | H | Hamilton Academical | 0-1 | 1 | 2 | | 4 | | | 5 | 11 | 9 | | | | 6 | 7 | 3 | | | 8 | 12 | | | | | 10 | | 14 |
| May 7 | H | Dunfermline Athletic | †1-0 | 1 | 2 | | 4 | | | 7 | | 9 | | | | 6 | 5 | 3 | 10 | | | 8 | 11 | | | | | | |
| 14 | A | Greenock Morton | 3-1 | 1 | 2$^1$ | | 4 | | | 7 | | 9 | | | | 6 | 5 | 3 | 10$^1$ | | 8$^1$ | | 11 | | | | 12 | 14 | |
| **TOTAL FULL APPEARANCES** | | | | 44 | 36 | 28 | 33 | 16 | 14 | 17 | 18 | 35 | 20 | 25 | 1 | 20 | 40 | 32 | 32 | 26 | 8 | 11 | 1 | 4 | 11 | 9 | 3 | | |
| **TOTAL SUB APPEARANCES** | | | | | (1) | | (4) | (10) | (7) | | (3) | | (7) | (13) | (2) | (6) | (1) | | | (2) | (3) | (2) | (5) | | (2) | | (4) | (1) | (2) |
| **TOTAL GOALS SCORED** | | | | | 2 | 10 | | | | 1 | 2 | 1 | | | | 9 | 5 | 7 | | | 1 | 2 | 1 | 9 | | 1 | 1 | 1 | |

*Small bold figures denote goalscorers.  † denotes opponent's own goal.*

---

## BROADWOOD STADIUM

**CAPACITY:** 6,203 (All Seated)

**PITCH DIMENSIONS:** 112 yds x 76 yds

**FACILITIES FOR DISABLED SUPPORTERS:** Facilities available in both Home and Away Stands.

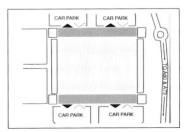

## HOW TO GET THERE

Broadwood Stadium can be reached by the following routes:

**BUSES:** From Buchanan Street Bus Station, Glasgow Bus No. 36A (Glasgow to Westfield).

**TRAINS:** From Queen Street Station, Glasgow to Croy Station. The Stadium is a 15 minute walk from here.

**CARS:** From Glasgow City Centre via Stepps By Pass joining A80 towards Stirling. Take Broadwood turn-off to Stadium.

# AYR UNITED

Somerset Park, Tryfield Place,
Ayr KA8 9NB

**CHAIRMAN**
Donald McK. MacIntyre

**VICE-CHAIRMAN**
Donald R. Cameron

**DIRECTORS**
David McKee
George H. Smith
William J. Barr

**SECRETARY**
John A. Eyley B.A., A.C.M.A.

**ASSISTANT SECRETARY**
Mrs Helen Nelson

**PLAYER/MANAGER**
Simon Stainrod

**PLAYER/ASSISTANT MANAGER**
Samuel McGivern

**CLUB DOCTORS**
Dr. Faith Gardner, M.B.B.S., D.R.C.O.G.
Dip. Sports Medicine
(London Edinburgh)
Dr. Marion McNaught, M.B., Ch.B.

**CROWD DOCTOR**
Dr. Robert Paterson M.B.,Ch.B.

**GROUNDSMAN**
David Harkness

**COMMERCIAL MANAGER**
Sandy Kerr
(0292) 280095

**TELEPHONES**
Ground/Ticket Office (0292) 263435
Fax (0292) 281314

**CLUB SHOP**
Ayr United Enterprises, Tryfield Place,
Ayr, KA8 9NB. Tel (0292) 280095.
Open 9.00 a.m. – 3.30 p.m. Mon-Fri
and 1.00 p.m.-3.00 p.m. on all first
team match days.

**OFFICIAL SUPPORTERS CLUB**
c/o Ayr United F.C., Somerset Park,
Ayr KA8 9NB

**TEAM CAPTAIN**
Hugh Burns

**SHIRT SPONSOR**
What Everyone Wants

## LIST OF PLAYERS 1994-95

| SURNAME | FIRST NAME | MIDDLE NAME | DATE OF BIRTH | PLACE OF BIRTH | DATE OF SIGNING | HEIGHT FT INS | WEIGHT ST LBS | PREVIOUS CLUB |
|---|---|---|---|---|---|---|---|---|
| Biggart | Kevin | | 10/11/73 | Kilmarnock | 13/01/94 | 5 8.5 | 11 1 | Dundee United |
| Bilsland | Brian | | 06/08/71 | Glasgow | 11/02/94 | 5 10.0 | 10 0 | Hunter Clark A.F.C. |
| Burns | Hugh | | 13/12/65 | Lanark | 20/06/93 | 6 0.0 | 11 7 | Kilmarnock |
| Connie | Cameron | | 03/01/71 | Paisley | 17/02/94 | 5 10.0 | 12 0 | Kilbirnie Ladeside |
| Coyle | Thomas | | 06/08/77 | Glasgow | 27/05/94 | 5 10.0 | 10 9 | Pollok B.C. |
| Duncan | Cameron | | 04/08/65 | Coatbridge | 23/03/91 | 6 1.0 | 12 4 | Partick Thistle |
| George | Duncan | Henry | 04/12/67 | Paisley | 29/03/91 | 5 10.0 | 10 7 | Stranraer |
| Gilzean | Ian | | 10/12/69 | London | 21/07/94 | 6 1.0 | 12 10 | Northampton Town |
| Gribben | Kevin | | 30/08/75 | Irvine | 02/05/94 | 5 6.0 | 10 0 | Aberdeen |
| Hood | Gregg | | 29/05/74 | Bellshill | 01/07/91 | 6 0.0 | 12 7 | Ayr United B.C. |
| Jackson | Justin | | 10/12/74 | Nottingham | 21/07/94 | 5 10.0 | 11 0 | Lancaster |
| MacFarlane | Colin | | 03/07/70 | Bellshill | 15/07/94 | 6 3.0 | 12 3 | Baillieston Juniors |
| McConnell | Kevin | | 09/01/78 | Irvine | 02/05/94 | 5 5.0 | 8 10 | Ayr Boswell B.C. |
| McGivern | Samuel | | 09/10/63 | Kilwinning | 01/01/93 | 5 8.0 | 10 10 | Falkirk |
| McIntosh | Stuart | | 06/02/74 | Ayr | 16/08/94 | 5 11.0 | 11 12 | Maybole Juniors |
| McKilligan | Neil | | 02/01/74 | Falkirk | 31/03/94 | 5 10.0 | 11 0 | Partick Thistle |
| McVicar | Don | Frederick | 06/11/62 | Perth | 25/03/94 | 5 9.0 | 11 12 | Airdrieonians |
| Moore | Vincent | | 21/08/64 | Scunthorpe | 28/09/93 | 5 11.0 | 12 0 | Stirling Albion |
| Paterson | Garry | | 10/11/69 | Dunfermline | 21/07/94 | 6 4.0 | 13 10 | Dundee |
| Rolling | Frank | | 23/08/68 | Colnar | 08/08/94 | 6 2.0 | 13 6 | F.C. Pau |
| Sharples | John | Benjamin | 26/01/73 | Bury | 13/07/94 | 6 1.0 | 12 8 | Heart of Midlothian |
| Spence | William | Waddell | 20/07/66 | Glasgow | 07/09/92 | 6 2.0 | 13 7 | Clydebank |
| Stainrod | Simon | Allan | 01/02/59 | Sheffield | 26/12/93 | 6 0.0 | 13 0 | Dundee |
| Thomson | Andrew | | 27/11/75 | Glasgow | 02/05/94 | 5 10.0 | 10 0 | Ayr United B.C. |
| Traynor | John | Francis C. | 10/12/66 | Glasgow | 07/11/91 | 5 10.0 | 11 0 | Clydebank |
| Woods | Thomas | | 17/04/71 | Glasgow | 11/02/94 | 5 9.0 | 10 7 | Baillieston Juniors |

## MILESTONES

**YEAR OF FORMATION:** 1910
**MOST CAPPED PLAYER:** Jim Nisbett
**NO. OF CAPS:** 3
**MOST LEAGUE POINTS IN A SEASON:** 61 (Second Division – Season 1987/88)
**MOST LEAGUE GOALS SCORED BY A PLAYER IN A SEASON:** Jimmy Smith (Season 1927/28)
**NO. OF GOALS SCORED:** 66
**RECORD ATTENDANCE:** 25,225 (-v- Rangers – 13.9.1969)
**RECORD VICTORY:** 11-1 (-v- Dumbarton – League Cup 13.8.1952)
**RECORD DEFEAT:** 0-9 (-v- Rangers, Heart of Midlothian, Third Lanark – Division 1)

## SEASON TICKET INFORMATION

| Seated | | |
|---|---|---|
| Centre Stand | Adult | £150 |
| | OAP | £125 |
| Wing Stand | Adult | £130 |
| | Juvenile/OAP | £110 |
| Family Stand | Adult/Juvenile | £130 |
| **Standing** | | |
| Ground/Enclosure | Adult | £100 |
| | Juvenile/OAP | £50 |

## LEAGUE ADMISSION PRICES

| Seated | | |
|---|---|---|
| Main Stand | Adult | £10 (Centre) |
| | Adult | £9 (Wing) |
| Family Stand | Adult/Juvenile | £8 |
| | (Plus £2.00 for each additional Juvenile) | |
| **Standing** | | |
| Enclosure | Adult | £6.50 |
| Ground | Adult | £6 |
| | Juvenile/OAP | £3 |

| | |
|---|---|
| REGISTERED: | Shirt – White with Two Black Vertical Stripes, Black Sleeves |
| | Shorts – Black with White Trim, Stockings – White with Black Top |
| CHANGE STRIP: | Shirt – Gold with Navy Blue Collar and Cuffs |
| | Shorts – Navy Blue with Gold Side Patches |
| | Stockings – Gold with Navy Blue Band |

## CLUB FACTFILE 1993/94 . . RESULTS . . APPEARANCES . . SCORERS

### THE HONEST MEN

Player columns (left to right): Duncan C., Burley G., Robertson G., Shotton M., Traynor J., George D., Mair G., Bryce S., McGivern S., McNab N., Scott B., Kennedy D., McQuilter R., Howard N., Burns H., Walker T., Beattie J., McGlashan C., Moore V., Lennox G., Jack R., Hood G., Grierson G., Spence W., Albiston A., Stainrod S., Biggart K., Woods T., Bisland B., Connie C., Donaldson D., McVicar D., McKilligan N., Williams R.

| Date | Venue | Opponents | Result | Team / shirt numbers (as printed) |
|---|---|---|---|---|
| Aug 7 | A | Clydebank | 0-1 | 1 2 3 4 5 6 7 8 9 10 11 |
| 14 | H | Stirling Albion | † 2-1 | 1 2 10 8 9 6 11¹ 3 4 5 7 12 |
| 21 | A | Clyde | 1-0 | 1 2 3 4 10 8¹ 9 6 11 14 5 7 |
| 28 | H | Dumbarton | 0-1 | 1 2 4 10 7 8 9 6 11 5 12 3 |
| Sept 4 | A | St. Mirren | 1-0 | 1 3 4 6 7 9¹ 11 5 10 8 |
| 11 | A | Brechin City | 2-0 | 1 14 2 5 6 7 9 11 4¹10 3 8¹ |
| 14 | H | Falkirk | 0-3 | 1 2 3 5 6 7 11 14 4 10 9 8 |
| 18 | A | Hamilton Academical | 1-2 | 1 2 7 6 12 9¹ 11 5 4 10 3 8 |
| 25 | H | Dunfermline Athletic | 1-1 | 1 2 4 7¹ 3 12 9 11 6 5 10 8 |
| 28 | H | Greenock Morton | † 2-2 | 1 2 4 5 3 12 9 11 6 10 8 7¹ |
| Oct 2 | A | Airdrieonians | 1-1 | 1 2 7 4 5 3 11 9 10 8¹ 6 |
| 9 | H | Clydebank | 1-1 | 1 2 4 5 6 3 11 10¹ 8 7 9 |
| 16 | A | Falkirk | 0-2 | 1 2 14 4 5 6 3 11 9 8 10 7 12 |
| 23 | H | Brechin City | 1-0 | 1 3 4 5 6 11 9¹ 2 10 8 7 14 |
| 30 | H | Clyde | 1-0 | 1 3 4 6 11 9¹ 2 10 8 7 5 |
| Nov 6 | A | Dumbarton | 1-1 | 1 2 3 4 10 6 11¹ 9 8 7 12 5 |
| 9 | H | St. Mirren | 0-1 | 1 4 2 6 9 3 10 8 7 11 5 |
| 13 | H | Airdrieonians | 1-2 | 1 2 3 4 6 9¹ 12 10 8 7 11 5 |
| 20 | A | Greenock Morton | 1-0 | 1 2 3 4¹ 14 9 6 10 8 7 11 5 |
| Dec 4 | H | Hamilton Academical | 1-1 | 1 2 3 4 6 11 12 9¹ 10 8 7 5 |
| 11 | A | Stirling Albion | 0-0 | 1 3 4 2 6 11 14 10 8 7 12 5 |
| 14 | A | Dunfermline Athletic | 1-6 | 1 2 3 4 5 6 11 9¹ 14 10 8 7 17 |
| 18 | A | Falkirk | 0-3 | 4 6 9 2 8 10 7 11 5 1 3 |
| Jan 4 | A | Clydebank | 2-0 | 4 12 6 3 11 2 10¹8 7 9 5¹ 1 14 |
| 8 | A | Dumbarton | 1-1 | 4 12 6 3 14 11 2 10 8 7 9 5¹ 1 |
| 11 | A | Clyde | 0-0 | 4 12 6 3 14 11 2 10 8 7 9 5 1 |
| 22 | H | Stirling Albion | 3-1 | 4 12 6 3 9¹ 2 14 8 7¹10 5¹ 1 11 |
| 25 | A | St. Mirren | 1-3 | 4 12 6 3 9 2 14 8¹7 10 5 1 11 |
| Feb 5 | A | Brechin City | 4-1 | 4 8²6 3 9 14 2 11 7 10 5 1 12² |
| 12 | A | Airdrieonians | 0-0 | 4 2 3 8 9 11 6 10 5 1 7 12 14 |
| Mar 1 | H | Greenock Morton | 2-1 | 4¹2 3 9 11 8 6 10 5 1 7 12 14¹ |
| 5 | A | Hamilton Academical | 1-2 | 4 2 3 9¹ 11 8 6 12 5 1 7 10 14 |
| 12 | H | Dunfermline Athletic | 0-4 | 1 6 3 9 2 11 7 5 14 12 8 10 4 |
| 19 | A | Falkirk | 0-2 | 1 4 2 3 9 11 8 6 10 5 12 7 14 |
| 26 | H | Clydebank | 0-0 | 4 6 9 2 11 8 5 1 10 7 14 12 3 |
| 29 | A | Stirling Albion | 3-1 | 4 6 9² 2¹ 11 8 5 1 10 7 14 12 3 |
| Apr 2 | H | Brechin City | 0-0 | 4 6 9 2 11 8 1 10 7 14 3 5 |
| 9 | H | Airdrieonians | 2-3 | 1 4 6 9 2 11 5 10²7 12 14 3 8 |
| 16 | A | Greenock Morton | 1-0 | 1 4 6 11 9 2 5 10 7 12 14¹ 3 8 |
| 23 | H | Hamilton Academical | 1-0 | 1 4 6 9¹ 2 11 5 7 12 10 14 3 8 |
| 26 | A | Dunfermline Athletic | 0-1 | 1 4 14 9 2 11 8 5 7 12 10 3 6 |
| 30 | H | Clyde | 1-1 | 1 4 12 9 2 11 8 10 7 14 3 6¹ |
| May 7 | A | Dumbarton | 1-1 | 1 4 12 14 2 5 10 7 9¹11 3 6 |
| 14 | H | St. Mirren | 0-1 | 1 4 5 9 2 10 7 11 12 8 3 6 14 |

**TOTAL FULL APPEARANCES:** 31 12 20 38 34 18 25 12 38 4 12 6 7 5 35 2 3 34 19 23 14 26 13 1 7 16 3 5 2 1 10 8

**TOTAL SUB APPEARANCES:** (1) (1) (8) (1) (5)(2)' (2)(3)(1) (2) (2) (4)(1)(1) (3)(2)(8)(8)(4) (1)

**TOTAL GOALS SCORED:** 2 3 2 12 1 1 2 3 2 1 3 2 2 1 2 1

*Small bold figures denote goalscorers.   † denotes opponent's own goal.*

---

## SOMERSET PARK

**CAPACITY:** 13,918; Seated 1,498, Standing 12,420

**PITCH DIMENSIONS:** 110 yds x 72 yds

**FACILITIES FOR DISABLED SUPPORTERS:** Enclosure and toilet facilities for wheelchairs. Match commentary available for blind persons at all first team matches.

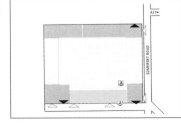

## HOW TO GET THERE

Somerset Park can be reached by the following routes:

**TRAINS:** There is a half hourly train service from Glasgow to either Ayr or Newton-on-Ayr. The ground is a ten minute walk from both stations.

**BUSES:** There are several buses from the town centre with a frequency approximately every five minutes. Fans should board buses bound for Dalmilling, Whitletts or any bus passing Ayr Racecourse. The ground is only a ten minute walk from the town centre.

**CARS:** Car parking facilities are available at Craigie Park and at Ayr Racecourse.

# CLYDEBANK

Kilbowie Park, Arran Place,
Clydebank G81 2PB

**CHAIRMAN**
Charles A. Steedman

**DIRECTORS**
William Howat
Ian C. Steedman, C.A.
Colin L. Steedman, B.Acc., C.A.
C. Graham Steedman
James H. Heggie

**MANAGING DIRECTOR**
John S. Steedman C.B.E.

**SECRETARY**
Ian C. Steedman, C.A.

**COACH**
Brian Wright

**ASSISTANT COACHES**
Ken Eadie & Davie Cooper

**CLUB DOCTOR**
Stuart Hillis

**PHYSIOTHERAPIST**
Peter Anderson

**S.F.A. COMMUNITY COACH**
Tony Gervaise

**CHIEF SCOUT**
Robert Gallie

**GROUNDSMAN**
George Furze

**COMMERCIAL MANAGER**
David Curwood
041-952 2887

**TELEPHONES**
Ground 041-952 2887
Fax 041-952 6948

**OFFICIAL SUPPORTERS CLUB**
c/o Bankies Club, Kilbowie Park,
Clydebank

**TEAM CAPTAIN**
Sean Sweeney

**SHIRT SPONSOR**
Wet Wet Wet

## LIST OF PLAYERS 1994-95

| SURNAME | FIRST NAME | MIDDLE NAME | DATE OF BIRTH | PLACE OF BIRTH | DATE OF SIGNING | HEIGHT FT INS | WEIGHT ST LBS | PREVIOUS CLUB |
|---|---|---|---|---|---|---|---|---|
| Agnew | Paul | | 28/06/72 | Coatbridge | 14/06/94 | 5 7.0 | 10 10 | Arthurlie Juniors |
| Bowman | Gary | | 12/08/74 | Glasgow | 30/03/94 | 5 11.0 | 11 4 | Knightswood Juveniles |
| Conville | Edward | | 02/04/73 | Carnwath | 06/08/94 | 6 0.5 | 12 5 | Dundee United |
| Cooper | David | | 25/02/56 | Hamilton | 27/12/93 | 5 8.5 | 12 5 | Motherwell |
| Crawford | Derek | | 18/06/74 | Glasgow | 05/07/93 | 5 8.0 | 10 0 | Rangers |
| Currie | Thomas | | 06/11/70 | Vale of Leven | 29/08/92 | 6 1.0 | 12 7 | Shettleston Juniors |
| Eadie | Kenneth | William | 26/02/61 | Paisley | 16/01/88 | 5 10.0 | 11 8 | Falkirk |
| Ferguson | Graeme | | 03/03/71 | Stirling | 05/11/93 | 5 10.0 | 11 10 | Aberdeen |
| Flannigan | Craig | | 11/02/73 | Dumfries | 13/03/92 | 5 6.0 | 10 2 | Rangers |
| Grady | James | | 14/03/71 | Paisley | 14/06/94 | 5 7.0 | 10 0 | Arthurlie Juniors |
| Harris | Colin | | 22/02/61 | Sanquhar | 25/11/93 | 6 0.0 | 12 2 | Cowdenbeath |
| Jack | Stephen | J. | 27/03/71 | Bellshill | 28/05/92 | 5 11.0 | 10 0 | Queen's Park |
| Kerrigan | Steven | John | 09/10/72 | Bellshill | 11/02/94 | 6 0.0 | 11 8 | Albion Rovers |
| Lansdowne | Alan | | 08/04/70 | Glasgow | 13/06/89 | 5 11.0 | 11 4 | Drumchapel Amateurs |
| Matthews | Gary | | 15/03/70 | Paisley | 21/03/94 | 6 3.5 | 16 2 | Kilmarnock |
| McQueen | James | | 10/06/61 | Edinburgh | 18/10/93 | 6 3.0 | 12 5 | Meadowbank Thistle |
| Monaghan | Allan | | 06/10/72 | Glasgow | 10/08/93 | 6 0.0 | 12 7 | Rutherglen Glencairn |
| Murdoch | Scott | McKenzie | 27/02/69 | Glasgow | 22/10/92 | 5 7.0 | 10 7 | St. Rochs |
| Smith | Shaun | | 13/04/71 | Bangour | 06/08/93 | 6 0.0 | 12 2 | Alloa |
| Sutherland | Colin | | 15/03/75 | Glasgow | 04/03/94 | 5 11.0 | 11 10 | Kilpatrick Juveniles |
| Sweeney | Sean | Brian | 17/08/69 | Glasgow | 04/09/85 | 6 0.0 | 11 0 | Clydebank B.C. |
| Thomson | Ian | | 24/09/65 | Coatbridge | 23/10/93 | 6 0.0 | 11 7 | Raith Rovers |
| Walker | John | | 12/12/73 | Glasgow | 31/07/93 | 5 9.0 | 11 6 | Rangers |
| Wright | Brian | Vincent | 05/10/58 | Glasgow | 29/05/94 | 5 11.0 | 11 3 | Queen of the South |

## MILESTONES

**YEAR OF FORMATION**: 1965
**MOST LEAGUE POINTS IN A SEASON**: 58 (Division 1 – Season 1976/77)
**MOST LEAGUE GOALS SCORED BY A PLAYER IN A SEASON**: Ken Eadie (Season 1990/91)
**NO. OF GOALS SCORED**: 29
**RECORD ATTENDANCE**: 14,900 (-v- Hibernian – 10.2.1965)
**RECORD VICTORY**: 8-1 (-v- Arbroath – Division 1, 3.1.1977)
**RECORD DEFEAT**: 1-9 (-v- Gala Fairydean – Scottish Cup 15.9.1965)

## SEASON TICKET INFORMATION

**Seated**
Adult .......................................................... £95 and £80
Juvenile/OAP ............................................... £45 and £40

## LEAGUE ADMISSION PRICES

**Seated**
Adult ..................................................... £7.00 and £6.00
Juvenile/OAP ........................................ £3.50 and £3.00

REGISTERED: Shirt – White with Black Collar and Red and Black Shoulder Flashings
Shorts – White with Red/Black Trim
Stockings – White with Red/Black Stripes

CHANGE STRIP: Shirt – Purple with White Trim, Shorts – Purple with White Trim
Stockings – Purple with White Trim

# CLUB FACTFILE 1993/94 .. RESULTS .. APPEARANCES .. SCORERS

## The BANKIES

| Date | Venue | Opponents | Result | Woods S. | Treanor M. | Hay G. | Maher J. | Sweeney S. | McIntosh M. | Harvey P. | Henry J. | Eadie K. | Flannigan C. | Lansdowne A. | Crawford D. | Murdoch S. | Smith S. | Jack S. | Nelson M. | Currie T. | Crawford J. | Lee K. | Monaghan A. | McQueen J. | Thomson I. | Ferguson G. | Sutherland C. | Walker J. | Harris C. | Cooper D. | Quigg S. | Eliot D. | Kerrigan S. | Matthews G. | Bowman G. |
|---|---|---|---|---|---|---|---|---|---|---|---|---|---|---|---|---|---|---|---|---|---|---|---|---|---|---|---|---|---|---|---|---|---|---|
| Aug 7 | H | Ayr United | 1-0 | 1 | 2 | 3 | 4 | 5 | 6 | 7 | 8 | 9 | $10^1$ | 11 | | | | | | | | | | | | | | | | | | | | | |
| 14 | A | Dunfermline Athletic | 2-0 | 1 | 2 | 6 | | 5 | 14 | $7^1$ | 12 | 9 | $10^1$ | | 3 | 4 | 8 | 11 | | | | | | | | | | | | | | | | | |
| 21 | A | Dumbarton | † 4-2 | 1 | 2 | | | 5 | $6^1$ | 7 | 12 | $9^1$ | 10 | | 3 | 4 | 11 | $8^1$ | | | | | | | | | | | | | | | | | |
| 28 | H | Clyde | 2-1 | 1 | $2^1$ | 6 | | 5 | 12 | 7 | 8 | $9^1$ | 10 | | 3 | 4 | 11 | 14 | | | | | | | | | | | | | | | | | |
| Sept 4 | A | Falkirk | 4-0 | 1 | $2^1$ | 6 | | 5 | | $7^1$ | 8 | 9 | $10^2$ | | 3 | 4 | 12 | 11 | 14 | | | | | | | | | | | | | | | | |
| 11 | H | Greenock Morton | 3-0 | 1 | 2 | 6 | | 5 | | 7 | $8^1$ | $9^1$ | $10^1$ | | 3 | 4 | 12 | 11 | 14 | | | | | | | | | | | | | | | | |
| 15 | A | Hamilton Academical | 3-2 | 1 | 2 | 6 | | 5 | | 7 | $8^1$ | $9^1$ | $10^1$ | | 3 | 4 | 12 | 11 | 14 | | | | | | | | | | | | | | | | |
| 18 | A | Brechin City | 0-1 | 1 | 2 | 6 | | 5 | | 7 | 8 | | 10 | 12 | 3 | 4 | 9 | 11 | 14 | | | | | | | | | | | | | | | | |
| 25 | A | Airdrieonians | 1-2 | 1 | 2 | 6 | | 5 | | 7 | 8 | | $9^1$ | 10 | 3 | 4 | 12 | 11 | 14 | | | | | | | | | | | | | | | | |
| 28 | A | Stirling Albion | 3-0 | 1 | 2 | 6 | | 5 | | 7 | 8 | $9^2$ | 10 | | 4 | | $11^1$ | | | 3 | 12 | | | | | | | | | | | | | | |
| Oct 2 | H | St. Mirren | 1-1 | | 2 | 6 | | 5 | | 7 | 8 | 9 | $10^1$ | | 4 | | 11 | | | 3 | | 1 | | | | | | | | | | | | | |
| 9 | A | Ayr United | 1-1 | | | | | 5 | | 7 | 8 | 9 | 10 | | 4 | | $11^1$ | 14 | | 6 | 3 | 2 | 1 | | | | | | | | | | | | |
| 16 | A | Hamilton Academical | 2-2 | | | | | 5 | | $7^1$ | 8 | 9 | | 14 | 4 | | $10^1$ | 11 | | 6 | 3 | 2 | 1 | | | | | | | | | | | | |
| 23 | A | Greenock Morton | 0-0 | | | | | 5 | | 7 | 8 | | 10 | 14 | 3 | 4 | 9 | 2 | | 6 | 12 | | | 1 | 11 | | | | | | | | | | |
| 30 | H | Dumbarton | 2-1 | | | | | 5 | | $7^1$ | | | 8 | 3 | 4 | 9 | 11 | | | 6 | 12 | 2 | | 1 | $10^1$ | | | | | | | | | | |
| Nov 6 | A | Clyde | 1-1 | | | 6 | | | | 7 | 8 | | | 14 | 3 | 4 | | 10 | | 5 | $9^1$ | 12 | | 1 | 11 | 2 | | | | | | | | | |
| 9 | H | Falkirk | 1-1 | | | 6 | | | | 7 | 8 | | 10 | 12 | 4 | | $11^1$ | | | 5 | 9 | | | 1 | 3 | 2 | 14 | | | | | | | | |
| 13 | A | St. Mirren | 0-1 | | | 6 | | | | 7 | 8 | | 12 | | 4 | 9 | 10 | | | 5 | 3 | | | 1 | 11 | 2 | | 14 | | | | | | | |
| 20 | H | Stirling Albion | 2-1 | | | | | | | 7 | 8 | | $11^1$ | | 4 | $9^1$ | 10 | | | 5 | 6 | | | 1 | 3 | 2 | | | | | | | | | |
| 30 | A | Airdrieonians | 1-2 | | | 6 | | | | 7 | 8 | | 11 | | 4 | 9 | $10^1$ | | | | 1 | 3 | 2 | | | | 5 | | | | | | | | |
| Dec 4 | H | Brechin City | 3-2 | | | 5 | | | | | 7 | $12^2$ | 8 | 14 | 4 | 9 | 10 | | | 3 | | | | 1 | 11 | 2 | | $6^1$ | | | | | | | |
| 11 | H | Dunfermline Athletic | 0-3 | | | 6 | | | | 7 | 8 | 12 | 11 | | 4 | 9 | 2 | | | 5 | 3 | | | 1 | | | | 10 | | | | | | | |
| 18 | A | Hamilton Academical | 0-1 | | | 6 | | | | 7 | 8 | 10 | 11 | | 9 | 2 | | | | 5 | 3 | | | 1 | 14 | | | 4 | | | | | | | |
| Jan 4 | A | Ayr United | 0-2 | | | 6 | | | | 8 | 10 | | 9 | | 4 | 14 | 11 | | | 5 | | | | 1 | 3 | 2 | | 12 | 7 | | | | | | |
| 8 | H | Clyde | 0-2 | | | 3 | | | | 11 | 8 | 9 | | | | 6 | | | | 5 | 12 | | | 1 | 2 | | | 4 | 7 | 10 | | | | | |
| 15 | A | Falkirk | 0-0 | | | 6 | | 5 | | 11 | 8 | 10 | | 3 | 4 | | 2 | | | | 1 | | | 14 | 12 | | | 9 | 7 | | | | | | |
| 18 | H | Dumbarton | 2-2 | | | 6 | | 5 | | 11 | 8 | $10^1$ | | 3 | | | 9 | | | | 1 | | | $12^1$ | 2 | | | 4 | 7 | 14 | | | | | |
| 22 | A | Dunfermline Athletic | 0-2 | | | 6 | | 5 | | 11 | 8 | 10 | | 3 | | | | | | | 1 | 9 | 2 | 12 | | | | 4 | 7 | | | | | | |
| Feb 5 | H | Greenock Morton | 0-0 | | | 5 | | | | 8 | | 10 | 14 | 3 | 4 | | 2 | | | 6 | 9 | | | 1 | 11 | | | 12 | 7 | | | | | | |
| 12 | H | St. Mirren | 0-3 | | | 5 | | | | 8 | | 14 | | 3 | 4 | 10 | 2 | | | 6 | | | | 1 | 11 | | | 12 | 7 | | 9 | | | | |
| 26 | A | Stirling Albion | 2-1 | | | 5 | | | | $8^1$ | 10 | | | | 12 | | | | | $2^1$ | 3 | | | 1 | 11 | | | 6 | 4 | 7 | 9 | | | | |
| Mar 5 | H | Brechin City | 1-0 | | | 5 | | | | 8 | 10 | | | | 3 | $14^1$ | | | | 2 | | | | 1 | 11 | | | 6 | 7 | 4 | 12 | 9 | | | |
| 19 | A | Hamilton Academical | 3-2 | | | 5 | | | | 8 | $12^3$ | 10 | | | 3 | | 7 | | | 2 | | | | 1 | 11 | | | 6 | 4 | 14 | | 9 | | | |
| 22 | H | Airdrieonians | 2-1 | | | 5 | | | | $8^1$ | 9 | | | | 4 | | 11 | | | 2 | 3 | | | 1 | 14 | $6^1$ | | | 7 | 12 | | 10 | | | |
| 26 | A | Ayr United | 0-0 | | | 5 | | | | 8 | 9 | 10 | | | | | 11 | | | 2 | | | | 1 | 3 | 6 | | | 4 | 7 | | 12 | | | |
| 29 | H | Dunfermline Athletic | 0-1 | | | 5 | | | | 8 | 9 | 10 | | | 2 | 7 | | | | | 1 | | | 3 | 6 | | | 4 | 11 | | | 12 | | | |
| Apr 2 | A | Greenock Morton | 1-1 | | | 5 | | | | 8 | 9 | 10 | | | | 7 | $11^1$ | | | 2 | | | | 1 | 3 | 6 | | 4 | 15 | | | 12 | | | |
| 9 | A | St. Mirren | 0-2 | | 2 | 5 | | | | 8 | 12 | 10 | | | 4 | | 11 | | | | 3 | | | | 14 | 6 | | 7 | | | | 9 | 1 | | |
| 16 | H | Stirling Albion | 2-1 | | | 5 | | | | 8 | $9^1$ | $10^1$ | 7 | 3 | 4 | 14 | 11 | | | 6 | | | | | 2 | | | | | | | 12 | 1 | | |
| 23 | H | Brechin City | 2-1 | | | 5 | | | | $8^1$ | 9 | 10 | 7 | 3 | 4 | | | | | 5 | | | | | 11 | 2 | | $6^1$ | | | | 12 | 1 | 14 | |
| 26 | A | Airdrieonians | 0-0 | | | 5 | | | | 8 | 9 | 10 | 14 | 3 | 4 | | 11 | | | 5 | | | | | 2 | 6 | | | 7 | | | 12 | 1 | | |
| 30 | H | Dumbarton | 2-0 | | | 5 | | | | 8 | | 10 | 12 | 3 | 4 | | 14 | | | 5 | | | | | $2^2$ | 6 | 11 | | | 7 | | 9 | 1 | | |
| May 7 | A | Clyde | 1-1 | | 2 | 5 | | | | 8 | | 10 | 3 | | 4 | 12 | 14 | | | | | | | | | 6 | $11^1$ | | 7 | | | 9 | 1 | | |
| 14 | H | Falkirk | 1-1 | | 2 | 5 | | | | $8^1$ | | 10 | 3 | | 4 | | 11 | | | | | | | | 6 | 12 | 14 | 7 | | | | 9 | 1 | | |
| **TOTAL FULL APPEARANCES** | | | | 10 | 14 | 22 | 1 | 31 | 2 | 26 | 42 | 19 | 34 | 11 | 22 | 34 | 16 | 33 | | 26 | 15 | 3 | 15 | 12 | 19 | 14 | 12 | 4 | 16 | 14 | 1 | | 9 | 7 | |
| **TOTAL SUB APPEARANCES** | | | | | | | (2) | | (2) | (2) | (2)(10) | (1) | | (10) | (1) | (3) | (4) | (3) | (2) | | | | | (4) | (2) | (2) | (2) | (4) | (4) | | (1) | (6) | | (1) | |
| **TOTAL GOALS SCORED** | | | | | 2 | | | 1 | 3 | 7 | 11 | 11 | 1 | | | 3 | 6 | | | 1 | 1 | | | 2 | 2 | | 1 | 2 | 1 | | | | | |

*Small bold figures denote goalscorers.   † denotes opponent's own goal.*

---

## KILBOWIE PARK

**CAPACITY:** 9,950 (All Seated)

**PITCH DIMENSIONS:** 110 yds x 68 yds

**FACILITIES FOR DISABLED SUPPORTERS:** Accommodation for about eight Wheelchairs by prior arrangement with Club Secretary.

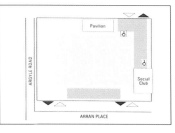

## HOW TO GET THERE

The following routes may be used to reach Kilbowie Park:

**TRAINS:** The train service from Glasgow Queen Street and Glasgow Central Low Level both pass through Singer Station, which is a two minute walk from the ground.

**BUSES:** A number of SMT buses pass down Kilbowie Road, which is two minutes walk from the ground. The buses are bound for Faifley, Duntocher and Parkhall and passengers should alight at Singer Station.

**CARS:** Car Parking is available in side streets adjacent to the park. The private car park in front of Kilbowie is reserved on match days for Directors, Players, Officials, Referee and certain Social Club members.

# DUNDEE

## LIST OF PLAYERS 1994-95

Dens Park Stadium,
Sandeman Street,
Dundee DD3 7JY

**CHAIRMAN**
Ronald N. Dixon

**VICE-CHAIRMAN**
Malcolm Reid

**DIRECTORS**
Robert W. Hynd
John F. Black
Nigel R. Squire

**PLAYER/MANAGER**
James Duffy

**SECRETARY**
Andrew P. Drummond
LL.B. (Hons) Dip., L.P., N.P.

**ASSISTANT MANAGER/COACH**
John McCormack

**CLUB DOCTOR**
Dr. Phyllis Windsor

**PHYSIOTHERAPIST**
James Crosbie

**GROUNDSMAN**
Brian Robertson

**COMMERCIAL MANAGER**
George Reid
(0382) 826104

**TELEPHONES**
Ground/Ticket Office
(0382) 826104
Fax (0382) 832284

**CLUB SHOP**
Dundee F.C. Shop, Unit 71,
Forum Centre, Dundee
Tel (0382) 823422. Open Mon. to
Sat. 9.00 a.m. – 5.30 p.m.

**OFFICIAL SUPPORTERS CLUB**
The Dee Club, Taylor Street,
Lochee, Dundee

**TEAM CAPTAIN**
Dusan Vrto

**SHIRT SPONSOR**
Auto Windscreens

| SURNAME | FIRST NAME | MIDDLE NAME | DATE OF BIRTH | PLACE OF BIRTH | DATE OF SIGNING | HEIGHT FT INS | WEIGHT ST LBS | PREVIOUS CLUB |
|---|---|---|---|---|---|---|---|---|
| Anderson | Iain | | 23/07/77 | Glasgow | 10/08/94 | 5 8.0 | 9 7 | "X" Form |
| Bain | Kevin | | 19/09/72 | Kirkcaldy | 28/06/89 | 6 0.0 | 11 9 | Abbey Star |
| Blake | Noel | Lloyd G. | 12/01/62 | Kingston | 10/12/93 | 6 1.0 | 13 10 | Bradford City |
| Britton | Gerard | Joseph | 20/10/70 | Glasgow | 11/01/94 | 6 1.0 | 11 0 | Partick Thistle |
| Czachowski | Piotr | | 07/11/66 | Warsaw | 22/09/93 | 5 10.0 | 11 9 | Legia Warsaw |
| Dailly | Marcus | Graham | 01/10/75 | Dundee | 06/07/94 | 5 9.0 | 11 6 | Dundee United |
| Dinnie | Alan | | 14/05/63 | Glasgow | 10/11/89 | 5 10.0 | 11 5 | Partick Thistle |
| Duffy | Cornelius | | 05/06/67 | Glasgow | 01/03/94 | 6 1.0 | 11 13 | Falkirk |
| Duffy | James | | 27/04/59 | Glasgow | 03/06/94 | 5 10.0 | 11 11 | Partick Thistle |
| Farningham | Raymond | Paul | 10/04/61 | Dundee | 06/06/94 | 5 8.0 | 11 5 | Partick Thistle |
| Hamilton | James | | 09/02/76 | Aberdeen | 31/01/94 | 6 0.0 | 10 10 | Keith |
| Mathers | Paul | | 17/01/70 | Aberdeen | 06/10/86 | 5 11.0 | 11 6 | Sunnybank "A" |
| McCann | Neil | Docherty | 11/08/74 | Greenock | 14/05/92 | 5 10.0 | 10 0 | Greenock Morton B.C. |
| McDonald | Donald | Byrne | 03/04/77 | Vale of Leven | 08/08/94 | 5 11.0 | 12 0 | Duntocher B.C. |
| McKeown | Gary | | 19/10/70 | Oxford | 31/07/94 | 5 10.5 | 11 8 | Arsenal |
| McQuillan | John | | 20/07/70 | Stranraer | 18/08/87 | 5 10.0 | 11 7 | Stranraer |
| Pageaud | Michel | | 30/08/66 | Paris | 26/02/94 | 6 0.0 | 12 9 | Valenciennes |
| Pittman | Stephen | Lee | 18/07/67 | Wilson, North Carolina | 06/11/92 | 5 10.0 | 12 0 | Fort Lauderdale Strikers |
| Ritchie | Paul | Michael | 25/01/69 | St. Andrews | 29/02/92 | 5 11.0 | 12 0 | Brechin City |
| Shaw | George | | 10/02/69 | Glasgow | 11/01/94 | 5 7.0 | 10 9 | Partick Thistle |
| Tannock | Gordon | | 11/06/74 | Kilmarnock | 14/05/92 | 5 11.0 | 10 10 | Bellfield B.C. |
| Teasdale | Michael | Joseph | 28/07/69 | Elgin | 11/01/94 | 6 0.0 | 13 0 | Elgin City |
| Thompson | Barry | Crawford | 12/07/75 | Glasgow | 13/08/93 | 6 1.0 | 12 5 | Aviemore Thistle |
| Tosh | Paul | James | 18/10/73 | Arbroath | 04/08/93 | 6 0.0 | 11 10 | Arbroath |
| Tully | Craig | | 07/01/76 | Stirling | 18/04/94 | 5 11.0 | 11 0 | Victoria Juveniles |
| Vrto | Dusan | | 29/10/65 | Banksa Stiavnica | 07/08/92 | 6 0.0 | 10 12 | Banik Ostrava |
| Wieghorst | Morten | | 25/02/71 | Glostrup | 02/12/92 | 6 3.0 | 14 0 | Lyngby |

## MILESTONES

**YEAR OF FORMATION:** 1893
**MOST CAPPED PLAYER:** Alex Hamilton
**NO. OF CAPS:** 24
**MOST LEAGUE GOALS SCORED BY A PLAYER IN A SEASON:** Alan Gilzean (Season 1963/64)
**NO. OF GOALS SCORED:** 52
**RECORD ATTENDANCE:** 43,024 (-v- Rangers – 1953)
**RECORD VICTORY:** 10-0 (-v- Fraserburgh, 1931; -v- Alloa, 1947; -v- Dunfermline Athletic, 1947;
-v- Queen of the South, 1962)
**RECORD DEFEAT:** 0-11 (-v- Celtic – Division 1. 26.10.1895)

## SEASON TICKET INFORMATION

**Seated**
| Centre Stand | Adult | £160 |
| | Juvenile/OAP | £100 |
| South Enclosure | Adult | £120 |
| | Juvenile/OAP | £60 |

## LEAGUE ADMISSION PRICES

**Seated**
| Stand | Adult | £8 |
| | Juvenile/OAP | £5 |
| South Enclosure | Adult | £6 |
| | Juvenile/OAP | £3 |
| West Enclosure | Adult | £6 |
| | Juvenile/OAP | £3 |

**REGISTERED STRIP:** Shirt – Navy Blue with Red Pinstripes, Shorts – Navy Blue with White Pockets, Stockings – Navy Blue with Red Tops

**CHANGE STRIP:** Shirt – Rivtera Blue with White Stripe, Shorts – White, Stockings – White

# CLUB FACTFILE 1993/94 .. RESULTS .. APPEARANCES .. SCORERS

## The DARK BLUES

Player columns (in order):
Mathers P., Frail S., Pittman S., Wieghorst M., David L., McGowan J., McMartin G., Vrto D., Ritchie P., Tosh P., Christie M., Paterson G., McQuillan J., McKeown G., Stainrod S., Dodds W., Adamczuk D., Duffy J., Armstrong L., Farningham R., Ristic D., Czachowski P., McCann M., Mobilio D., Bain K., Blake N., Dinnie A., Shaw G., Britton G., Pageaud M., Duffy C., Teasdale M., Tully C., Hamilton J., Anderson I.

*Small bold figures denote goalscorers. † denotes opponent's own goal. (Superscript shown below as [n].)*

| Date | Venue | Opponents | Result | Line-up (shirt numbers used) |
|---|---|---|---|---|
| Aug 7 | A | Kilmarnock | 0-1 | 1 2 3 4 5 6 7 8 9 10 11 12 14 |
| 14 | H | Motherwell | 1-2 | 1 14 3 4 6 8 12 11 5 2 7[1] 9 10 |
| 21 | H | Aberdeen | 1-1 | 1 12 3 4 6 8 9 5 2 11 10[1] 7 |
| 28 | A | Hibernian | 0-2 | 1 2 3 4 7 12 9 6 11 10 8 5 14 |
| Sept 4 | H | Rangers | 1-1 | 1 2 3 4 7 8 9 6[1] 11 10 5 14 |
| 11 | A | Dundee United | 0-1 | 1 2 3 7 8 9 6 11 10 12 5 4 |
| 18 | H | Raith Rovers | 0-1 | 1 2 3 14 8 9 12 6 11 10 7 5 4 |
| 25 | A | St. Johnstone | 1-2 | 1 2 3 8 9 6 14 7 12 5 4 10[1] 11 |
| Oct 2 | A | Heart of Midlothian | 2-0 | 1 2 3 8 5[1] 4 7 10 14 6 9[1] 11 12 |
| 5 | H | Partick Thistle | 2-2 | 1 2 3[1] 8 5 4 7 10[1] 12 9 6 11 14 |
| 9 | A | Celtic | 1-2 | 1 2 3 4 8 5 7 10[1] 12 6 9 11 14 |
| 16 | A | Motherwell | 0-1 | 1 2 3 14 8 12 7 10 6 5 4 9 11 |
| 23 | H | Kilmarnock | 1-0 | 1 3 14 8 12 5 2 10 7[1] 6 4 9 11 |
| 30 | A | Aberdeen | 0-1 | 1 2 8 7 5 12 10 3 6 4 9 11 |
| Nov 6 | H | Hibernian | 3-2 | 1 2 3[1] 8 7[1] 14 5 12 10 4 6 9[1] 11 |
| 10 | A | Rangers | 1-3 | 1 2 3 8 14 7 12 5 4 10[1] 6 9 11 |
| 13 | H | Heart of Midlothian | 2-1 | 1 2 3 8 7[1] 14 5 12 4 10 6 9 11[1] |
| 20 | A | St. Johnstone | 0-1 | 1 2 12 8 7 14 5 3 4 10 6 9 11 |
| Dec 1 | H | Raith Rovers | 1-2 | 1 2 4[1] 14 8 12 3 7 10 6 9 11 5 |
| 4 | A | Partick Thistle | 2-3 | 1 2 3 12 6 8 7[1] 5 10[1] 4 9 11 14 |
| 7 | H | Dundee United | 1-2 | 1 2 3 4 8 7 10 6 9[1] 12 11 5 |
| 11 | H | Celtic | 1-1 | 1 2 14 7 8 10 6 4 9[1] 11 3 5 |
| 18 | H | Motherwell | 1-3 | 1 2 3 7 8 4 10 6 14 9[1] 11 5 |
| Jan 4 | A | Kilmarnock | 0-1 | 1 2 14 8 7 12 6 10 3 4 9 11 5 |
| 8 | A | Hibernian | 0-2 | 1 2 8 7 9 10 6 14 3 4 5 11 |
| 11 | H | Aberdeen | 0-1 | 1 2 3 8 12 4 6 11 5 10 7 9 |
| 15 | H | Rangers | 1-1 | 1 2 3 4[1] 8 14 12 6 11 5 10 7 9 |
| 22 | H | Raith Rovers | 2-2 | 1 2 3 4 8 6 11 5[1] 10 7[1] 9 |
| Feb 5 | H | Dundee United | 1-1 | 1 2 3 10 8 9 4 6 12 14[1] 11 5 7 |
| 12 | A | St. Johnstone | 1-1 | 1 3 10 8 2 6 11[1] 5 4 7 9 |
| Mar 1 | H | Heart of Midlothian | 0-2 | 2 3 10 12 8 11 14 5 4 7 9 1 6 |
| 5 | H | Partick Thistle | 1-0 | 12 3 8 14 2 10 11 5 4 7[1] 9 1 6 |
| 19 | A | Motherwell | 1-3 | 1 4 3 10 8 7 2[1] 12 11 5 9 6 14 |
| 26 | H | Kilmarnock | 3-0 | 12 3 10 8 14 2 6 11[1] 5[1] 7 9[1] 1 4 |
| 29 | H | Dundee United | 1-1 | 3 10 8 2 6 11 5 7 9 1 4[1] |
| Apr 2 | H | Raith Rovers | 1-1 | 3 10 8 12 2 6 11 14 5 7[1] 9 1 4 |
| 6 | H | Celtic | †1-1 | 3 8 11 2 6 4 12 5 7 9 10 |
| 9 | H | St. Johnstone | 0-1 | 1 3 8 7 2 6 4 11 5 9 10 14 |
| 16 | H | Heart of Midlothian | 2-0 | 3 8 11 12 2 6 4 10 5 7[2] 9 1 |
| 23 | H | Celtic | 0-2 | 8 12 14 6 2 11 10 5 7 9 1 4 3 |
| 26 | A | Partick Thistle | 0-1 | 8 12 14 10 3 4 11 5 7 9 1 6 2 |
| 30 | A | Aberdeen | 1-1 | 8 9 2 10 3 11 5 7 14 6[1] 12 |
| May 7 | H | Hibernian | 4-0 | 3[1] 9 8 2 10[1] 4 11 5 7[1] 1 6 12 14[1] |
| 14 | A | Rangers | 0-0 | 3 9 8 2 10 6 11 7 12 1 4 |

**TOTAL FULL APPEARANCES:** 33 28 35 21 1 11 1 38 10 14 1 17 27 18 1 23 7 32 20 16 18 20 4 23 7 17 15 11 12 2 1

**TOTAL SUB APPEARANCES:** (4) (1) (3) (3) (2) (7)(11) (3) (7) (1) (1) (4) (1) (5) (2) (2) (2) (3) (2) (3) (1) (1)

**TOTAL GOALS SCORED:** 3 2 2 1 2 1 2 5 1 2 6 1 1 2 6 1 2 1

*Small bold figures denote goalscorers.  † denotes opponent's own goal.*

---

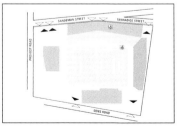

## DENS PARK

**CAPACITY:** 15,181; Seated 10,581, Standing 4,600

**PITCH DIMENSIONS:** 110 yds x 72 yds

**FACILITIES FOR DISABLED SUPPORTERS:** East End of Stand Enclosure.

## HOW TO GET THERE

You can reach Dens Park by the following routes:

**BUSES:** There is a frequent service of buses from the city centre. Nos. 1A and 1B leave from Albert Square and Nos. 18, 19 and 21 leave from Commercial Street.

**TRAINS:** Trains from all over the country pass through the mainline Dundee station and fans can then proceed to the ground by the above buses from stops situated close to the station.

**CARS:** Cars may be parked in the car park and local streets adjacent to the ground.

# DUNFERMLINE ATHLETIC

East End Park, Halbeath Road,
Dunfermline, Fife, KYI2 7RB

**CHAIRMAN**
C. Robert Woodrow

**VICE-CHAIRMAN**
W. Blair F. Morgan, LL.B., N.P.

**DIRECTORS**
William M. Rennie
Gavin G. Masterton F.I.B. (Scot)
Joseph B. Malcolm B.Sc.Eng.
Andrew T. Gillies

**SECRETARY**
Paul A. M. D'Mello

**MANAGER**
Robert Paton

**ASSISTANT MANAGER**
Richard Campbell

**COACHING STAFF**
Joe Nelson

**CLUB DOCTOR**
Hugh Whyte

**PHYSIOTHERAPIST**
Philip Yeates, M.C.S.P.

**S.F.A. COMMUNITY COACH**
Graeme Robertson

**YOUTH DEVELOPMENT MANAGER**
David McParland

**SAFETY/SECURITY ADVISOR**
William Nellies

**COMMERCIAL MANAGER**
Mrs. Audrey M. Kelly
(0383) 724295

**TELEPHONES**
Ground/Ticket Office
(0383) 724295/721749
Fax (0383) 723468

**CLUB SHOP**
Intersport, Kingsgate, Dunfermline
Open 9.00 a.m. – 5.00 p.m.
Mon to Sat

**OFFICIAL SUPPORTERS CLUB**
c/o Mrs. J. Malcolm, Secretary,
Dunfermline Athletic Supporters Club,
15 Meadowfield, Leuchatsbeath,
Cowdenbeath, KY4 9BF

**TEAM CAPTAIN**
Norman McCathie

**SHIRT SPONSOR**
Landmark Home Furnishing

## LIST OF PLAYERS 1994-95

| SURNAME | FIRST NAME | MIDDLE NAME | DATE OF BIRTH | PLACE OF BIRTH | DATE OF SIGNING | HEIGHT FT INS | WEIGHT ST LBS | PREVIOUS CLUB |
|---------|-----------|-------------|---------------|----------------|-----------------|---------------|---------------|----------------|
| Bowes | Mark | John | 17/02/73 | Bangour | 26/02/91 | 5 8.0 | 10 10 | Gairdoch United |
| Cooper | Neale | James | 24/11/63 | Darjeeling | 29/11/91 | 6 0.0 | 12 7 | Reading |
| Den Bieman | Ivo | Johannes | 04/02/67 | Wamel | 05/08/93 | 6 2.0 | 12 10 | Dundee |
| French | Hamish | Mackie | 07/02/64 | Aberdeen | 23/10/91 | 5 10.5 | 11 7 | Dundee United |
| Hawkins | Andrew | | 12/10/75 | Cambridge | 13/08/94 | 5 9.0 | 10 4 | "X" Form |
| Higgins | Gary | | 15/09/72 | Stirling | 10/06/94 | 5 11.0 | 11 5 | Rosyth Recreation |
| Laing | Derek | James | 11/11/73 | Haddington | 17/07/90 | 5 10.0 | 11 7 | Salvesen B.C. |
| McCathie | Norman | | 23/03/61 | Edinburgh | 17/08/81 | 6 0.0 | 12 10 | Cowdenbeath |
| McCulloch | Mark | Ross | 19/05/75 | Inverness | 02/08/94 | 5 11.0 | 12 0 | Inverness Clachnacuddin |
| McNamara | Jackie | | 24/10/73 | Glasgow | 17/09/91 | 5 8.0 | 9 7 | Gairdoch United |
| Moore | Allan | | 25/12/64 | Glasgow | 26/03/94 | 5 7.0 | 10 0 | St. Johnstone |
| Petrie | Stewart | James J. | 27/02/70 | Dundee | 27/08/93 | 5 10.0 | 11 11 | Forfar Athletic |
| Robertson | Craig | Peter | 22/04/63 | Dunfermline | 30/08/91 | 5 10.0 | 12 0 | Aberdeen |
| Sharp | Raymond | | 16/11/69 | Stirling | 18/08/86 | 5 11.0 | 12 5 | Gairdoch United |
| Sinclair | Christopher | | 11/11/70 | Sheffield | 10/03/89 | 5 9.0 | 10 10 | Sauchie Athletic |
| Smart | Craig | William | 23/03/75 | Dunfermline | 14/07/93 | 6 0.0 | 10 3 | Hutchison Vale B.C. |
| Smith | Paul | McKinnon | 02/11/62 | Edinburgh | 06/01/93 | 5 11.0 | 12 0 | Falkirk |
| Tod | Andrew | | 04/11/71 | Dunfermline | 04/11/93 | 6 3.0 | 12 0 | Kelty Hearts |
| Ward | Kenneth | | 16/06/63 | Blairhall | 05/08/94 | 5 7.0 | 11 4 | Hamilton Academical |
| Westwater | Ian | | 08/11/63 | Loughborough | 30/03/94 | 6 2.0 | 14 8 | Dundee |
| Will | James | | 07/10/72 | Turriff | 04/07/94 | 6 1.0 | 14 7 | Arsenal |

## MILESTONES

**YEAR OF FORMATION**: 1885
**MOST CAPPED PLAYER**: Istvan Kozma
**NO. OF CAPS**: Hungary 29 – (13 whilst with Dunfermline Athletic)
**MOST LEAGUE POINTS IN A SEASON**: 65 (First Division – Season 1993/94)
**MOST LEAGUE GOALS SCORED BY A PLAYER IN A SEASON**: Bobby Skinner (Season 1925/26)
**NO. OF GOALS SCORED**: 53
**RECORD ATTENDANCE**: 27,816 (-v- Celtic – 30.4.1968)
**RECORD VICTORY**: 11-2 (-v- Stenhousemuir – Division 2. 27.9.1930)
**RECORD DEFEAT**: 0-10 (-v- Dundee – Division 2. 22.3.1947)

## SEASON TICKET INFORMATION

**Seated**
Centre Stand
Adult ............................ £140
Juvenile/OAP .................... £70
West Enclosure
Adult ............................ £105
Juvenile/OAP .................... £53
Family West Wing Stand Parent & Child ................ £176
Extra Parent ................ £123
Extra Child ................ £60
OAP & Child .................. £120

**Standing**
Adult .................................................. £105
Juvenile/OAP ........................................ £53

## LEAGUE ADMISSION PRICES

**Seated**
Stand
Adult .................................. £8
Juvenile/OAP .................... £4
West Enclosure
Adult .................................. £6
Juvenile/OAP .................... £3

**Standing**
Ground
Adult .................................. £6
Juvenile/OAP .................... £3

REGISTERED STRIP: Shirt – White with Black Vertical Stripes, Shorts – Black with Red and White Band at Bottom of Shorts, Stockings – Black with Red and White Band at Top

CHANGE STRIP: Shirt – Purple and Lime Green Vertical Stripes with a Thin White Stripe through the Purple Stripe, Shorts: Purple with a Purple and White Band at Bottom of Shorts, Stockings: Purple with a Purple and White Band at Top

# CLUB FACTFILE 1993/94 .. RESULTS .. APPEARANCES .. SCORERS

## The PARS

Small bold figures denote goalscorers. † denotes opponent's own goal.

| Date | Venue | Opponents | Result | Hamilton L. | Bowes M. | Cunnington E. | McCathie N. | Moyes D. | Davies W. | Den Bieman I. | Smith P. | French H. | Robertson C. | Preston A. | Laing D. | McWilliams D. | Sharp R. | Baillie W.A. | O'Boyle G. | Petrie S. | McNamara J. | Sinclair C. | Hillcoat J. | Cooper N. | Tod A. | Moore A. | Westwater I. |
|---|---|---|---|---|---|---|---|---|---|---|---|---|---|---|---|---|---|---|---|---|---|---|---|---|---|---|---|
| Aug 7 | A | Falkirk | 2-3 | 1 | 2 | 3 | 4 | 5 | 6 | 7$^1$ | 8 | 9$^1$ | 10 | 11 | 12 | 14 | | | | | | | | | | | |
| 14 | H | Clydebank | 0-2 | 1 | 2 | | 4 | | 6 | 7 | 8 | 9 | | 11 | 12 | 14 | 3 | 5 | 10 | | | | | | | | |
| 21 | A | Brechin City | 0-1 | 1 | 2 | | 4 | | 6 | 7 | 8 | 9 | 10 | 11 | 12 | | 3 | 5 | | | | | | | | | |
| 28 | A | Airdrieonians | 3-2 | 1 | 2 | | 4 | | 6 | 7 | 8$^1$ | | | 11$^1$ | 12 | 14 | 3 | 5 | 10$^1$ | 9 | | | | | | | |
| Sept 4 | A | Clyde | 2-0 | 1 | 2 | | 4 | | 6 | 7 | 8$^1$ | | | 11 | 12 | 14 | 3 | 5 | 10$^1$ | 9 | | | | | | | |
| 11 | A | Stirling Albion | 0-2 | 1 | 2 | | 4 | | 6 | 7 | 8 | 9 | 10 | 11 | 12 | 14 | 3 | 5 | | | | | | | | | |
| 14 | H | St. Mirren | 3-4 | | 2 | 3 | 4 | | 6 | 7 | 8$^1$ | 9 | 10 | 11$^1$ | | | | 5$^1$ | | | | | | | | | 1 |
| 18 | H | Greenock Morton | 4-0 | | 2 | 3 | 4$^1$ | | 6 | 7 | 8 | 9$^2$ | 10 | 11$^1$ | 12 | 14 | | 5 | | | | | | | | | 1 |
| 25 | A | Ayr United | 1-1 | | 2 | 3 | 4 | | 6 | 7 | 8 | 9 | 10$^1$ | 11 | | 14 | | 5 | | | | | | | | | 1 |
| 29 | A | Hamilton Academical | 2-0 | | 2 | 3 | 4 | | 6 | 7 | 8 | 9 | 10 | 11$^2$ | 12 | 14 | | 5 | | | | | | | | | 1 |
| Oct 2 | H | Dumbarton | 4-1 | | 2 | 3 | 4$^1$ | | 6$^1$ | 7 | 8 | 9 | 10$^1$ | 11 | 12 | 14$^1$ | | 5 | | | | | | | | | 1 |
| 9 | H | Falkirk | 1-0 | | 2 | 3 | 4 | | 6 | 7 | 8 | 9 | 10 | 11 | 12$^1$ | | | 5 | | | | | | | | | 1 |
| 16 | A | St. Mirren | 2-1 | | 2 | 3 | 4 | | 6$^1$ | 7$^1$ | 8 | 9 | 10 | 11 | 12 | | | 5 | | | | | | | | | 1 |
| 23 | H | Stirling Albion | 3-0 | | 2 | 3 | 4 | | 6 | 7 | 8$^1$ | 9 | 10$^2$ | 11 | 12 | 14 | | 5 | | | | | | | | | 1 |
| 30 | H | Brechin City | 4-0 | 1 | 2 | 3 | 4$^1$ | | 6$^1$ | 7 | 8 | 9$^1$ | 10 | 11$^1$ | 12 | 14 | | 5 | | | | | | | | | |
| Nov 6 | A | Airdrieonians | 1-1 | 1 | 2 | 3 | 4 | | 6$^1$ | 7 | 8 | 9 | 10 | 11 | 12 | | | 5 | | | | | | | | | |
| 9 | H | Clyde | 4-0 | 1 | 2 | 3 | 4$^1$ | | 6$^1$ | 7$^1$ | 8 | 9 | 10$^1$ | 11 | 12 | 14 | | 5 | | | | | | | | | |
| 13 | A | Dumbarton | 5-1 | 1 | 2 | 3 | 4 | | 6 | 7$^3$ | 8 | 9$^2$ | 10 | 11 | 12 | 14 | | 5 | | | | | | | | | |
| Dec 4 | A | Greenock Morton | 0-0 | 1 | 2 | 3 | 4 | | 6 | 7 | 8 | 9 | 10 | 11 | 12 | 14 | | 5 | | | | | | | | | |
| 7 | H | Hamilton Academical | 4-0 | 1 | 2 | 3 | 4 | | 6$^1$ | 7 | 8 | 9$^2$ | 10 | 11 | 12 | 14$^1$ | | 5 | | | | | | | | | |
| 11 | A | Clydebank | 3-0 | 1 | 2 | 3 | 4$^1$ | | 6 | 7 | 8 | 9$^1$ | 10 | 11 | 12$^1$ | | | 5 | | | | | | | | | |
| 14 | H | Ayr United | 6-1 | 1 | 2 | 3$^1$ | 4$^1$ | | 6$^1$ | 7$^1$ | 8 | 9 | 10 | 11 | 12$^1$ | 14 | | 5 | | | | | | | | | |
| 18 | H | St. Mirren | 4-2 | 1 | 2 | 3 | 4 | | 6 | 7$^3$ | 8 | 9 | 10 | 11 | 12$^1$ | 14 | | 5 | | | | | | | | | |
| Jan 4 | A | Brechin City | 1-0 | 1 | 2 | 3 | 4 | | 6 | 7 | 8 | 9 | 10 | 11 | 12 | 14 | | 5$^1$ | | | | | | | | | |
| 18 | A | Falkirk | 0-2 | 1 | 2 | 3 | 4 | | 6 | 7 | 8 | 9 | 10 | 11 | 12 | 14 | | 5 | | | | | | | | | |
| 22 | H | Clydebank † | 2-0 | 1 | 2 | 3 | 4 | | 6 | 7 | 8 | 9$^1$ | 10 | 11 | 12 | 14 | | 5 | | | | | | | | | |
| 25 | A | Airdrieonians | 0-0 | 1 | 2 | 3 | 4 | | 6 | 7 | 8 | 9 | 10 | 11 | 12 | 14 | | 5 | | | | | | | | | |
| Feb 5 | A | Stirling Albion | 0-1 | 1 | 2 | 3 | 4 | | 6 | 7 | 8 | 9 | 10 | 11 | 12 | 14 | | 5 | | | | | | | | | |
| 12 | H | Dumbarton | 3-2 | 1 | 2 | 3 | 4 | | 6 | 7 | 8 | 9$^1$ | 10$^2$ | 11 | 12 | 14 | | 5 | | | | | | | | | |
| 19 | A | Clyde | 1-0 | 1 | 2 | 3 | 4 | | 6 | 7 | 8 | 9 | 10$^1$ | 11 | | 14 | | 5 | | | | | | | | | |
| Mar 2 | A | Hamilton Academical | 1-1 | 1 | 2 | 3 | 4$^1$ | | 6 | 7 | 8 | 9 | 10 | 11 | 12 | 14 | | 5 | | | | | | | | | |
| 5 | A | Greenock Morton | 3-0 | 1 | 2 | 3 | 4 | | 6 | 7 | 8 | 9 | 10 | 11 | 12 | 14$^1$ | | 5 | 10$^2$ | | | | | | | | |
| 12 | A | Ayr United | 4-0 | 1 | 2 | 3 | 4 | | 6$^1$ | 7$^1$ | 8 | 9$^2$ | 10 | 11 | 12 | 14 | | 5 | | | | | | | | | |
| 19 | A | St. Mirren | 2-0 | 1 | 2 | 3 | 4 | | 6 | 7 | 8 | 9 | 10$^1$ | 11$^1$ | 12 | 14 | | 5 | | | | | | | | | |
| 26 | H | Falkirk | 1-1 | 1 | 2 | 3 | 4 | | 6 | 7 | 8 | 9 | 10$^1$ | 11 | 12 | 14 | | 5 | | | | | | | | | |
| 29 | A | Clydebank | 1-0 | 1 | 2 | 3 | 4 | | 6 | 7 | 8 | 9 | 10$^1$ | 11 | 12 | 14 | | 5 | | | | | | | | | 1 |
| Apr 2 | H | Stirling Albion | 2-1 | | 2 | 3 | 4 | | 6$^1$ | 7 | 8 | 9 | 10$^1$ | 11 | | | | 5 | | | | | | | | | 1 |
| 12 | A | Dumbarton | 2-0 | | 2 | 3 | 4 | | 6 | 7 | 8$^1$ | 9 | 10 | 11 | 12 | 14$^1$ | | 5 | | | | | | | | | 1 |
| 16 | H | Hamilton Academical | 2-1 | | 2 | 3 | 4 | | 6 | 7 | 8 | 9 | 10$^1$ | 11$^1$ | 12 | 14 | | 5 | | | | | | | | | 1 |
| 23 | A | Greenock Morton | 2-2 | | 2 | 3 | 4$^1$ | | 6 | 7 | 8 | 9 | 10 | 11$^1$ | 12 | 14 | | 5 | | | | | | | | | 1 |
| 26 | A | Ayr United | 1-0 | | 2 | 3 | 4 | | 6 | 7 | 8 | 9$^1$ | 10 | 11 | 12 | | | 5 | | | | | | | | | 1 |
| 30 | H | Brechin City | 2-1 | | 2 | 3 | 4 | | 6 | 7 | 8 | 9 | 10 | 11$^1$ | 12 | 14$^1$ | | 5 | | | | | | | | | 1 |
| May 7 | A | Airdrieonians | 0-1 | | 2 | 3 | 4 | | 6 | 7 | 8 | 9 | 10 | 11 | | 14 | | 5 | | | | | | | | | 1 |
| 14 | H | Clyde | 5-0 | | 2 | 3 | 4 | | 6 | 7 | 8 | 9 | 10$^4$ | 11$^1$ | 12 | 14 | | 5 | | | | | | | | | 1 |
| **TOTAL FULL APPEARANCES** | | | | 27 | 4 | 7 | 43 | 1 | 3 | 33 | 43 | 31 | 40 | 20 | 11 | 12 | 30 | 14 | 28 | 30 | 38 | 1 | 8 | 30 | 19 | 2 | 9 |
| **TOTAL SUB APPEARANCES** | | | | | (2) | (2) | | | (1) | (8) | (1) | (5) | | (6) | (16) | (8) | | (1) | (4) | (7) | (1) | (5) | | (3) | (6) | |
| **TOTAL GOALS SCORED** | | | | | | | 8 | | | 3 | 9 | 15 | 3 | 5 | 8 | 3 | 1 | | 17 | 6 | | | 1 | 2 | 11 | | |

---

## EAST END PARK

**CAPACITY**: 18,328; Seated 4,008, Standing 14,320

**PITCH DIMENSIONS**: 115yds x 68yds

**FACILITIES FOR DISABLED SUPPORTERS**: Special ramped area in West Enclosure.

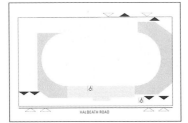

HALBEATH ROAD

## HOW TO GET THERE

East End Park may be reached by the following routes:

**TRAINS:** Dunfermline Station is served by trains from both Glasgow and Edinburgh and the ground is a 15 minute walk from here.

**BUSES:** Buses destined for Kelty, Perth, St. Andrews and Kirkcaldy all pass close to East End Park.

**CARS:** Car Parking is available in a large car park adjoining the East End of the ground and there are also facilities in various side streets. Multi-storey car parking approximately 10 minutes walk from ground.

# HAMILTON ACADEMICAL

## LIST OF PLAYERS 1994-95

| SURNAME | FIRST NAME | MIDDLE NAME | DATE OF BIRTH | PLACE OF BIRTH | DATE OF SIGNING | HEIGHT FT INS | WEIGHT ST LBS | PREVIOUS CLUB |
|---|---|---|---|---|---|---|---|---|
| Baptie | Crawford | Bowie | 24/02/59 | Glasgow | 08/07/93 | 6 1.0 | 11 7 | Falkirk |
| Campbell | Duncan | Matthew | 11/09/70 | Paisley | 24/09/93 | 5 8.0 | 11 5 | St. Andrews (Malta) |
| Chalmers | Paul | | 31/10/63 | Glasgow | 07/07/93 | 5 10.0 | 11 4 | Dunfermline Athletic |
| Clark | Gary | | 13/09/64 | Glasgow | 25/06/91 | 5 10.0 | 11 10 | Clyde |
| Clark | Patrick | John | 13/03/74 | Hamilton | 07/02/94 | 5 11.0 | 11 1 | Dundee United |
| Cormack | David | | 29/11/70 | Lanark | 01/11/93 | 6 2.0 | 13 7 | Vale of Clyde |
| Duffield | Peter | | 04/02/69 | Middlesbrough | 24/09/93 | 5 6.0 | 10 4 | Sheffield United |
| Ferguson | Allan | Thomas | 21/03/69 | Lanark | 31/12/87 | 5 10.5 | 12 6 | Netherdale Com A.F.C |
| Hillcoat | Christopher | Patrick | 03/10/69 | Glasgow | 19/05/87 | 5 10.0 | 11 3 | St. Bridget's B.G. |
| Lorimer | David | James | 26/01/74 | Bellshill | 04/08/93 | 5 9.5 | 11 0 | Hamilton Accies B.C. |
| McCormick | Steven | | 10/11/75 | Bellshill | 02/06/94 | 5 6.0 | 9 10 | Mill United |
| McEntegart | Sean | David | 01/03/70 | Dublin | 24/07/92 | 6 0.0 | 11 7 | Queen's Park |
| McGill | Derek | | 14/10/75 | Lanark | 28/06/93 | 5 11.5 | 11 4 | Dunfermline Athletic |
| McIntosh | Martin | Wylie | 19/03/71 | East Kilbride | 01/02/94 | 6 2.0 | 12 4 | Clydebank |
| McInulty | Stephen | James | 22/09/71 | Bellshill | 30/01/93 | 5 11.0 | 11 0 | Larkhall Thistle |
| McKenzie | Paul | Vincent | 22/09/64 | Glasgow | 30/01/91 | 5 11.0 | 12 4 | Dumbarton |
| McLean | Charles | Crossan N. | 08/11/73 | Glasgow | 08/07/93 | 5 10.0 | 10 8 | Celtic |
| McQuade | John | | 08/07/70 | Glasgow | 31/08/93 | 5 9.0 | 10 4 | Dumbarton |
| Nicholls | David | Clarkson | 05/04/72 | Bellshill | 01/03/94 | 5 10.0 | 11 5 | Coleraine |
| Renicks | Steven | John | 28/11/75 | Bellshill | 01/06/94 | 5 7.0 | 10 4 | Hamilton Accies B.C. |
| Sherry | James | Cunningham | 09/09/73 | Glasgow | 19/05/92 | 5 8.0 | 11 9 | Hamilton Accies B.C. |
| Tennant | Gary | | 16/08/75 | Bellshill | 07/05/94 | 6 1.0 | 12 0 | Bellshill B.C. |
| Waters | Michael | Joseph | 28/09/72 | Stirling | 27/10/92 | 5 8.0 | 12 10 | Kilsyth Rangers |

## MILESTONES

**YEAR OF FORMATION:** 1874
**MOST CAPPED PLAYER:** Colin Miller (Canada)
**NO. OF CAPS:** 29
**MOST LEAGUE POINTS IN A SEASON:** 57 (First Division – Season 1991/92)
**MOST LEAGUE GOALS SCORED BY A PLAYER IN A SEASON:** David Wilson (Season 1936/37)
**NO. OF GOALS SCORED:** 34
**RECORD ATTENDANCE:** 28,690 (-v- Heart of Midlothian – Scottish Cup 3.3.1937)
**RECORD VICTORY:** l0-2 (-v- Cowdenbeath – Division 1, 15.10.1932)
**RECORD DEFEAT:** l-ll (-v- Hibernian – Division 1, 6.11.1965)

## SEASON TICKET INFORMATION

**Seated**
Adult ................................................................ £120
Juvenile/OAP ................................................... £70

## LEAGUE ADMISSION PRICES

**Seated**
Adult ................................................................ £7
Juvenile/OAP ................................................... £4

Douglas Park, Douglas Park Lane,
Hamilton ML3 ODF

**GROUND ADDRESS**
Firhill Stadium, 80 Firhill Road,
Glasgow G20 7BA

**CHAIRMAN**
James W. Watson C.A.

**DIRECTORS**
William P. Davidson
Alistair R. Duguid
Robert D. Gibb

**SECRETARY**
Scott A. Struthers B.A.

**HON. LIFE PRESIDENTS**
Jan W. Stepek
Dr. Alexander A. Wilson

**MANAGER**
Iain Munro

**PLAYER/COACH**
Crawford Baptie

**HON. MEDICAL OFFICER**
Dr. Brian Lynas

**HON. ORTHOPAEDIC SURGEON**
Mr. S. K. Mukherjee

**PHYSIOTHERAPISTS**
Alistair McPhee
Tim Williamson

**SFA COMMUNITY COACH**
Phil Bonnyman

**COMMERCIAL MANAGER**
Frank Layton
(0698) 286103

**TELEPHONES**
Office (0698) 286103
Ground 041-945 4811 (Matchdays Only)
Fax (0698) 285422
Information Service (0891) 666492

**CLUB SHOP**
"The Acciesshop", c/o Douglas Park,
Douglas Park Lane,
Hamilton ML3 ODF.

**OFFICIAL SUPPORTERS CLUB**
The Stand Club, c/o Douglas Park,
Douglas Park Lane,
Hamilton ML3 ODF

**TEAM CAPTAIN**
Crawford Baptie

**SHIRT SPONSOR**
Wilson Homes

| | |
|---|---|
| REGISTERED STRIP: | Shirt – Red and White Oscilloscope Hoops, with Red Collar and Navy Blue Trim<br>Shorts – White with Red and White Hoop on Leg<br>Stockings – Red with Navy Blue Turnover |
| CHANGE STRIP: | Shirt – White with Navy Blue Horizontal Matchsticks with Navy Blue Collar and<br>Red and White Trim, Shorts – Navy Blue with Red and White Hoop on Leg<br>Stockings – Navy Blue with Red Turnover |

# CLUB FACTFILE 1993/94 .. RESULTS .. APPEARANCES .. SCORERS

## The ACCIES

Players: Ferguson A., McKenzie P., Napier C., Reid W., Weir J., McInulty S., Clark G., Baptie C., Chalmers P., Ward K., Lorimer D., McEntegart S., McLean C., Hilcoat C., Miller C., Moyes D., Walsh D., McQuade I., McGill D., Fitzpatrick P., Duffield P., Campbell D., McIntosh M., Clark P., Sherry J., Powell L., Cormack D., Nicholls D.

| Date | Venue | Opponents | Result | Appearances / Scorers |
|---|---|---|---|---|
| Aug 7 | A | Brechin City | 2-1 | 1 2 3 4 5 6 7 8 9¹ 10¹ 11 |
| 14 | H | St. Mirren | 0-0 | 1 2 3 8 5 6 7 — 10 11 9 4 |
| 21 | A | Airdrieonians | 0-4 | 1 2 3 8 6 7 9 10 11 12 4 5 14 |
| 28 | H | Falkirk | 1-1 | 1 2 3 8 6 7 9 11 10 12¹ 4 5 |
| Sept 4 | A | Dumbarton | 0-0 | 1 2 3 8 6 10 9 14 12 4 5 7 11 |
| 11 | A | Clyde | 0-2 | 1 2 8 6 10 9 11 14 3 5 7 4 |
| 15 | H | Clydebank | 2-3 | 1 2 11¹ 8 6 10 9 12 14¹ 3 5 7 4 |
| 18 | H | Ayr United | 2-1 | 1 2 11 8 10¹ 5 6 12 9¹ 3 7 4 |
| 25 | A | Stirling Albion | 1-3 | 1 14 2 8 10 5 6¹ 12 3 7 4 9 11 |
| 29 | H | Dunfermline Athletic | 0-2 | 1 2 11 8 12 5 6 3 7 4 9 10 |
| Oct 2 | A | Greenock Morton | 2-1 | 1 2 6 14 10¹ 5 12¹ 11 3 7 4 9 8 |
| 9 | H | Brechin City | 5-0 | 1 2 8 6 10¹ 5 11¹ 14 3 12 4¹ 9¹ 7¹ |
| 16 | H | Clydebank | 2-2 | 1 5 2 8 6 10 11¹ 14 3 12 4 9¹ 7 |
| 23 | H | Clyde | 2-0 | 1 5 2 8 6 10¹ 7 11 14 3 12 4 9¹ |
| 30 | H | Airdrieonians | 3-2 | 1 5 2 8 6 10² 7 11¹ 3 14 4 9 |
| Nov 6 | A | Falkirk | 3-3 | 1 5 2¹ 8 7 10 12 3 6 4 9¹ 11¹ |
| 10 | H | Dumbarton | 2-0 | 1 5 2 8 14 12 7 10 3 6 4 9² 11 |
| 13 | H | Greenock Morton | 4-1 | 1 5 2 8 3 14 11 12 10 3 6 4 9² 7² |
| 30 | A | St. Mirren | 0-1 | 1 5 2 8 12 11 14 10 3 6 4 9 7 |
| Dec 4 | A | Ayr United | 1-1 | 1 5 2 8 14 12 11 10 3 6 4 9 7¹ |
| 7 | A | Dunfermline Athletic | 0-4 | 1 5 2 8 14 12 11 10 3 6 4 9 7 |
| 18 | H | Clydebank | † 1-0 | 1 5 2 8 6 10 5 14 12 3 7 4 9 11 |
| Jan 8 | H | Falkirk | 1-1 | 1 2 8 6 10 5 11¹ 3 4 12 9 7 |
| 11 | A | Brechin City | 0-0 | 1 2 8 6 10 5 11 3 4 12 9 7 |
| 15 | A | Dumbarton | 1-0 | 1 2 8 6 10¹ 5 4 14 3 7 11 9 12 |
| 18 | A | Airdrieonians | 1-0 | 1 14 2 8 6 10 5 4 3 12 11 9¹ 7 |
| 22 | A | St. Mirren | 0-0 | 1 2 8 6 10 5 4 3 12 11 9 7 |
| Feb 2 | H | Stirling Albion | 0-1 | 1 14 8 3 10 5 4 2 7 9 12 11 6 |
| 5 | A | Clyde | 2-0 | 1 2 8 10 5 11 4 3 12 9 14¹ 7¹ 6 |
| 12 | A | Greenock Morton | 2-2 | 1 2 8 5¹ 11 4 3 12 9¹ 14 7 6 10 |
| Mar 2 | H | Dunfermline Athletic | 1-1 | 1 2 11 5 12 7 8 3 14 9¹ 10 6 4 |
| 5 | H | Ayr United | 2-1 | 1 2 14 5 12 7 8 3 9¹ 10¹ 11 6 4 |
| 12 | A | Stirling Albion | 1-1 | 1 2 5 14 12 11 8 3 7 9 10¹ 6 4 |
| 19 | A | Clydebank | 2-3 | 1 2 11 5 9 14 8¹ 3 12 10 6 4 7¹ |
| 26 | H | Brechin City | 9-1 | 1 2 3 11¹ 5¹ 9 7¹ 14 4 8¹ 10⁴ 6¹ 12 |
| 29 | H | St. Mirren | 2-0 | 1 2 3 11¹ 5 9¹ 7 4 8 10 6 12 |
| Apr 2 | A | Clyde | 2-1 | 1 2 3 11 5 9 7 4 8¹ 10¹ 6 12 |
| 13 | H | Greenock Morton | 3-2 | 1 2 3 11 5 9¹ 7¹ 4 8¹ 10 6 12 |
| 16 | H | Dunfermline Athletic | 1-2 | 1 2 3 5 4 8 14 9 10 6¹ 11 7 12 |
| 23 | A | Ayr United | 0-1 | 1 2 3 5 9 12 14 4 8 11 10 6 7 |
| 27 | H | Stirling Albion | 0-1 | 2 3 11 5 12 14 4 9 10 8 7 1 6 |
| 30 | H | Airdrieonians | 1-0 | 2 3 11 5 9¹ 4 8 10 7 1 6 |
| May 7 | A | Falkirk | 0-3 | 2 3 11 5 9 8 4 14 10 7 12 1 6 |
| 14 | H | Dumbarton | 2-1 | 2 3 5 12 11 4 7 8 10² 9 14 1 6 |
| TOTAL FULL APPEARANCES | | | | 40 33 27 30 2 31 29 33 14 24 9 27 9 1 31 5 21 13 17 33 21 13 6 5 2 4 4 |
| TOTAL SUB APPEARANCES | | | | (3) (3) (3) (3) (6) (6) (9) (2) (9) (1)(10) (3) (1) (3) (1) (4) (3) |
| TOTAL GOALS SCORED | | | | 2 9 2 5 8 7 3 1 19 6 2 1 |

*Small bold figures denote goalscorers.  † denotes opponent's own goal.*

## FIRHILL STADIUM

**CAPACITY:** 14,403 Seated 2,183, Standing 11,590

PLEASE NOTE: CAPACITY WILL INCREASE TO 20,653 IN OCTOBER, 1994 ON COMPLETION OF NEW EAST STAND GIVING A TOTAL SEATED CAPACITY OF 9,063

**PITCH DIMENSIONS:** 110 yds x 74 yds

**FACILITIES FOR DISABLED SUPPORTERS:** Covered places available in North Enclosure. 10 Weelchair spectators, 10 attendants, 10 ambulant disabled. Telephone in advance to Club Secretary for arrangements.

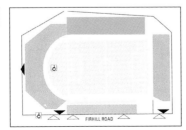

FIRHILL ROAD

## HOW TO GET THERE

The following routes may be used to reach Firhill Stadium:

**TRAINS:** The nearest railway stations are Glasgow Queen Street and Glasgow Central and buses from the centre of the city pass within 100 yards of the ground.

**BUSES:** The following buses from the city centre all pass by the park. Nos. 1, 8, 18, 21, 21A, 57, 60, 61, 61B, 89, and 90 and the frequency of buses is just over 12 minutes.

**UNDERGROUND:** The nearest GGPTE Underground station is St. George's Cross and supporters walking from here should pass through Cromwell Street into Maryhill Road and then walk up this road as far as Firhill Street. The ground is then on the right. The Kelvinbridge Underground Station is also not far from the park and supporters from here should walk along Great Western Road as far as Napiershill Street and then follow this into Maryhill Road.

**CARS:** Car Parking is available at the north end of the ground.

**YOUNGER'S TARTAN SPECIAL**

# RAITH ROVERS

Stark's Park, Pratt Street,
Kirkcaldy, Fife KY1 1SA

**CHAIRMAN**
Alexander A. Penman

**VICE-CHAIRMAN**
William Shedden

**DIRECTORS**
John Litster
Charles A. Cant
James M. Nicholl

**SECRETARY**
Mrs. Susan Boehm

**PLAYER/MANAGER**
James M. Nicholl

**ASSISTANT MANAGER**
Martin Harvey

**CHIEF SCOUT/YOUTH COACH**
Derek Smith

**CLUB DOCTOR**
Dr. G. K. M. Hall

**PHYSIOTHERAPIST**
Gerry Docherty

**GROUNDSMAN**
Andy Leigh

**COMMERCIAL MANAGER**
Alex Kilgour
(0592) 263514

**TELEPHONES**
Ground (0592) 263514
Fax (0592) 263514
Ticket Office (0592) 263514
Club Call (0891) 884479

**CLUB SHOP**
Stark's Park, Pratt Street, Kirkcaldy
Tel (0592) 263514. Open during
home match days, and 9.00 a.m. to
4.00 p.m. Mon. to Fri.

**OFFICIAL SUPPORTERS CLUB**
c/o Fraser Hamilton,
22 Tower Terrace, Kirkcaldy, Fife

**TEAM CAPTAIN**
Daniel Lennon

**SHIRT SPONSOR**
Jackie O's

## LIST OF PLAYERS 1994-95

| SURNAME | FIRST NAME | MIDDLE NAME | DATE OF BIRTH | PLACE OF BIRTH | DATE OF SIGNING | HEIGHT FT INS | WEIGHT ST LBS | PREVIOUS CLUB |
|---|---|---|---|---|---|---|---|---|
| Broddle | Julian | | 01/11/64 | Sheffield | 14/07/93 | 5 9.0 | 12 8 | Partick Thistle |
| Buchanan | Richard | Lawson | 16/11/76 | Dunfermline | 24/07/93 | 5 10.0 | 10 10 | Rosyth Recreation |
| Buist | Mark | | 13/09/75 | Kirkcaldy | 20/07/93 | 6 0.0 | 11 12 | Glenrothes Strollers |
| Cameron | Colin | | 23/10/72 | Kirkcaldy | 30/04/92 | 5 5.5 | 9 6 | Sligo Rovers |
| Cochrane | Matthew | | 06/04/77 | Bellshill | 20/08/94 | 5 11.0 | 11 4 | Bothkennar B.C. |
| Coyle | Ronald | | 04/08/64 | Glasgow | 08/01/88 | 5 11.0 | 12 9 | Rochdale |
| Crawford | Stephen | | 09/01/74 | Dunfermline | 13/08/92 | 5 10.0 | 10 7 | Rosyth Recreation |
| Dair | Jason | | 15/06/74 | Dunfermline | 03/07/91 | 5 11.0 | 10 8 | Castlebridge |
| Dalziel | Gordon | | 16/03/62 | Motherwell | 25/02/87 | 5 10.5 | 10 13 | East Stirlingshire |
| Dennis | Shaun | | 20/12/69 | Kirkcaldy | 03/08/88 | 6 1.0 | 13 7 | Lochgelly Albert |
| Drummond | John | George | 12/12/77 | Dunfermline | 21/07/94 | 5 10.0 | 9 8 | Inverkeithing Utd. U16 |
| Forrest | Gordon | Iain | 14/01/77 | Dunfermline | 21/07/93 | 5 6.0 | 8 2 | Rosyth Recreation |
| Graham | Alastair | | 11/08/66 | Glasgow | 23/09/93 | 6 3.0 | 12 7 | Motherwell |
| Kelly | Norman | | 10/10/70 | Belfast | 19/01/94 | 5 9.0 | 11 10 | Glenavon |
| Kirkwood | David | Stewart | 27/08/67 | St. Andrews | 10/08/94 | 5 10.0 | 11 7 | Airdrieonians |
| Lennon | Daniel | Joseph | 06/04/69 | Whitburn | 31/03/94 | 5 5.0 | 10 8 | Hibernian |
| Lothian | Christopher David | | 09/11/77 | Broxburn | 02/08/94 | 6 0.0 | 12 6 | Polbeth United U'16 |
| McAnespie | Stephen | | 01/02/72 | Kilmarnock | 25/01/94 | 5 9.0 | 10 7 | Vasterhaninge I.F. |
| McKinlay | Craig | | 19/10/76 | Edinburgh | 13/08/93 | 5 9.5 | 11 6 | I.C.I. Grangemouth |
| McMillan | Colin | | 24/10/77 | Irvine | 19/07/94 | 5 8.0 | 9 7 | Tass Thistle U'16s |
| McMillan | Ian | | 09/06/76 | Broxburn | 31/03/93 | 5 10.0 | 11 4 | Armadale Thistle |
| McPherson | Dean | | 07/06/78 | Aberdeen | 06/08/94 | 5 10.0 | 9 9 | Hutchison Vale B.C. |
| Morrell | Alistair | | 26/01/78 | W. Germany | 11/07/94 | 5 8.0 | 10 10 | Salveson B.C. U'16s |
| Nicholl | James | Michael | 20/12/56 | Hamilton, Canada | 27/11/90 | 5 10.0 | 11 10 | Dunfermline Athletic |
| Potter | Brian | | 26/01/77 | Dunfermline | 13/08/93 | 5 10.5 | 11 5 | Rosyth Recreation |
| Quinn | Mark | | 14/05/75 | Broxburn | 27/02/93 | 5 8.0 | 10 2 | Strathbrock U18's |
| Raeside | Robert | | 07/07/72 | South Africa | 13/09/90 | 6 0.0 | 11 10 | St. Andrews United |
| Redford | Ian | Petrie | 05/04/60 | Perth | 26/08/94 | 5 11.0 | 11 9 | Brechin City |
| Robertson | Graham | | 02/11/76 | Edinburgh | 03/08/93 | 5 11.0 | 10 10 | Balgonie Colts U16 |
| Rowbotham | Jason | | 03/01/69 | Cardiff | 31/07/93 | 5 10.0 | 11 7 | Plymouth Argyle |
| Sellars | Neil | Andrew | 09/05/77 | Kirkcaldy | 03/08/94 | 5 8.0 | 9 11 | Kirkcaldy Y.M. |
| Sinclair | David | | 06/10/69 | Dunfermline | 11/02/92 | 5 11.0 | 12 10 | Portadown |
| Thomson | Scott | Yuill | 08/11/66 | Edinburgh | 08/09/93 | 6 0.0 | 11 9 | Forfar Athletic |

## MILESTONES

**YEAR OF FORMATION:** 1883
**MOST CAPPED PLAYER:** David Morris
**NO. OF CAPS:** 6
**MOST LEAGUE POINTS IN A SEASON:** 65 (First Division – Season 1992/93)
**MOST LEAGUE GOALS SCORED BY A PLAYER IN A SEASON:** Norman Heywood (Season 1937/38)
**NO. OF GOALS SCORED:** 42
**RECORD ATTENDANCE:** 31,306 (-v- Heart of Midlothian – Scottish Cup 7.2.1953)
**RECORD VICTORY:** 10-1 (-v- Coldstream – Scottish Cup 13.2.1954)
**RECORD DEFEAT:** 2-11 (-v- Morton – Division 2. 18.3.1936)

## SEASON TICKET INFORMATION

**Seated**
| A & B Stands | Adult | £125 |
| | Juvenile/OAP | £75 |
| New Stand | Adult | £110 |
| | Juvenile/OAP | £60 |

**Standing**
| Enclosure | Adult | £105 |
| | Juvenile/OAP | £55 |
| Ground | Adult | £95 |
| | Juvenile/OAP | £45 |

## LEAGUE ADMISSION PRICES

**Seated**
| A & B Stands | Adult | £8 |
| | Juvenile/OAP | £5 |
| New Stand | Adult | £7 |
| | Juvenile/OAP | £4 |

**Standing**
| Enclosure | Adult | £6.50 |
| | Juvenile/OAP | £3.50 |
| Ground | Adult | £6 |
| | Juvenile/OAP | £3 |

REGISTERED STRIP: Shirt – Navy Blue with White Flashes, Shorts – White
Stockings – White with Navy Blue Tops
CHANGE STRIP: Shirt – White with Navy Blue Flashes
Shorts – Navy Blue, Stockings – Navy Blue with White Tops

# CLUB FACTFILE 1993/94 .. RESULTS .. APPEARANCES .. SCORERS

## The ROVERS

| Date | Venue | Opponents | Result | Carson T. | McStay J. | McLeod I. | Coyle R. | Dennis S. | McGeachie G. | Nicholl J. | Dalziel G. | Hetherston P. | Hawke W. | Cameron C. | Sinclair D. | Rowbotham J. | Broddle J. | Crawford S. | Arthur G. | Dair J. | Graham A. | Thomson S. | McAnespie S. | Kelly N. | Lennon D. | Potter B. |
|---|---|---|---|---|---|---|---|---|---|---|---|---|---|---|---|---|---|---|---|---|---|---|---|---|---|---|
| Aug 7 | H | St. Johnstone | 1-1 | 1 | 2 | 3 | 4 | $5^1$ | 6 | 7 | 8 | 9 | 10 | 11 | 12 | | | | | | | | | | | |
| 14 | A | Heart of Midlothian | 0-1 | 1 | 2 | 3 | 4 | 5 | | | 8 | 9 | | 14 | 10 | 6 | 7 | 11 | | | | | | | | |
| 21 | H | Partick Thistle | 2-2 | 1 | 2 | 3 | 4 | 5 | 6 | 7 | $8^1$ | 9 | | 11 | | | | | | 14 | 10 | | | | | |
| 28 | A | Motherwell | 1-4 | | 2 | | $4^1$ | 5 | 3 | 7 | 8 | 9 | | 11 | 6 | | 12 | 10 | 1 | | | | | | | |
| Sept 4 | H | Dundee United | 1-1 | 1 | 2 | | 4 | 5 | 6 | $7^1$ | | 9 | | 10 | | 3 | | 8 | | 11 | | | | | | |
| 11 | H | Celtic | 1-4 | 1 | 2 | | 4 | 5 | 6 | 7 | | 9 | | 8 | | 3 | | $10^1$ | | 11 | | | | | | |
| 18 | A | Dundee | 1-0 | 1 | 2 | | 4 | 5 | 6 | 7 | | $9^1$ | | 8 | 14 | 3 | | 10 | | 11 | | | | | | |
| 25 | A | Aberdeen | 1-4 | | 2 | | 4 | $5^1$ | 6 | 7 | | 9 | | 8 | | 3 | | 10 | | 11 | 12 | | | | | |
| Oct 2 | H | Rangers | 1-1 | | $2^1$ | | 4 | 5 | 6 | 7 | | 9 | | 12 | 14 | 3 | 10 | | | 11 | 8 | 1 | | | | |
| 5 | A | Hibernian | 2-3 | | 2 | | 4 | 5 | 6 | 7 | | 9 | | 12 | | $3^1$ | 10 | | | $11^1$ | 8 | 1 | | | | |
| 9 | H | Kilmarnock | 2-2 | | 2 | | 4 | 5 | 6 | 7 | 8 | 9 | | 12 | 14 | 3 | | | | $11^1$ | $10^1$ | 1 | | | | |
| 16 | H | Heart of Midlothian | 1-0 | | 2 | | 4 | 5 | 6 | 7 | 8 | $9^1$ | | 12 | 14 | 3 | | | | 11 | 10 | 1 | | | | |
| 23 | A | St. Johnstone | 1-1 | | 2 | | 4 | 5 | 6 | 7 | | 9 | | 8 | 12 | 3 | | 14 | | $11^1$ | 10 | 1 | | | | |
| 30 | A | Partick Thistle | 1-1 | | 2 | | 4 | 5 | | 7 | | 9 | | $10^1$ | 6 | 3 | | | | 11 | 8 | 1 | | | | |
| Nov 6 | H | Motherwell | 0-3 | | 2 | | 4 | 5 | | 7 | 12 | 9 | | 10 | 6 | 3 | 14 | | | 11 | 8 | 1 | | | | |
| 9 | A | Dundee United | 2-2 | | 2 | | 4 | | 12 | 7 | 8 | 9 | | 6 | 5 | 3 | | $14^1$ | | $11^1$ | 10 | 1 | | | | |
| 13 | A | Rangers | 2-2 | | 2 | | 4 | 5 | | 7 | $8^1$ | 9 | | 12 | 6 | 3 | 14 | | | 11 | $10^1$ | 1 | | | | |
| 27 | A | Celtic | 0-2 | | 2 | | 4 | 5 | | 7 | 8 | 9 | | 12 | 6 | 3 | | | | 11 | 10 | 1 | | | | |
| Dec 1 | H | Dundee | 2-1 | | 2 | | 4 | 5 | | 7 | $8^2$ | 9 | | 12 | 6 | 3 | | 14 | | 11 | 10 | 1 | | | | |
| 4 | H | Hibernian | 1-2 | | 2 | | 4 | 5 | 12 | 7 | 8 | 9 | | | 6 | 3 | | 14 | | 11 | $10^1$ | 1 | | | | |
| 7 | H | Aberdeen | 1-1 | | 2 | | 4 | 5 | 6 | | $8^1$ | 9 | | 7 | 14 | 3 | | | | 11 | 10 | 1 | | | | |
| 11 | A | Kilmarnock | 0-1 | | 2 | | 4 | 5 | 6 | | 8 | 12 | | 7 | 9 | 3 | | 14 | | 11 | 10 | 1 | | | | |
| 18 | A | Heart of Midlothian | 1-0 | | | | 4 | 5 | | 7 | 8 | | | 14 | $6^1$ | 2 | 3 | 9 | | 11 | 10 | 1 | | | | |
| Jan 12 | H | Partick Thistle | 0-1 | | | | 4 | 5 | | 7 | 8 | | | 14 | 6 | 2 | 3 | 9 | | 11 | 10 | 1 | | | | |
| 15 | H | Dundee United | 0-2 | | | | 4 | 5 | | 7 | 8 | | | 9 | 6 | 2 | 3 | 14 | | 11 | 10 | 1 | | | | |
| 19 | H | St. Johnstone | 1-1 | | 12 | | 4 | 5 | 6 | | $8^1$ | | | 7 | 9 | 2 | 3 | | | 11 | 10 | 1 | | | | |
| 22 | A | Dundee | † 2-2 | | 12 | | 4 | 5 | 6 | | $8^1$ | | | 7 | 9 | 2 | 3 | 14 | | 11 | 10 | 1 | | | | |
| 25 | A | Motherwell | 1-3 | | | | 4 | 5 | 6 | 7 | 8 | | | $11^1$ | 9 | 3 | | 12 | | | 10 | 1 | 2 | 14 | | |
| Feb 5 | H | Celtic | 0-0 | | 2 | | 4 | 5 | | 7 | | | | 10 | 6 | 3 | | 9 | | 11 | 8 | 1 | | | | |
| 12 | A | Aberdeen | 0-4 | | 2 | | 4 | 5 | | 7 | 12 | | | 10 | 6 | 3 | | 9 | | 11 | 8 | 1 | 14 | | | |
| 26 | H | Rangers | 1-2 | | 2 | | 4 | 5 | 14 | | 12 | 9 | | 7 | 6 | 3 | | $10^1$ | | 11 | 8 | 1 | | | | |
| Mar 5 | A | Hibernian | 0-3 | | 2 | | | 5 | | 7 | 12 | 9 | | 4 | 6 | 3 | | 10 | | 11 | 8 | 1 | | | | |
| 15 | H | Kilmarnock | 3-2 | | 2 | | | 5 | | 7 | | $9^1$ | | $4^1$ | 6 | 3 | | 10 | | 11 | $8^1$ | 1 | | | | |
| 19 | H | Heart of Midlothian | 2-2 | | $2^1$ | | | 5 | | 7 | | 9 | | $4^1$ | 6 | 3 | | 10 | | 11 | 8 | 1 | | | | |
| 26 | A | St. Johnstone | 0-2 | | 2 | | 4 | 5 | | 7 | 12 | 9 | | | 6 | 3 | | 10 | | 11 | 8 | 1 | | | | |
| 30 | A | Celtic | 1-2 | | 2 | | 4 | 5 | | 7 | 12 | 9 | | | 6 | 3 | | $10^1$ | | 11 | 8 | 1 | | | | |
| Apr 2 | H | Dundee | 1-1 | | 2 | | 4 | 5 | | 7 | | 9 | | | 6 | 3 | | $10^1$ | | 11 | | | | | 12 | 8 |
| 16 | A | Rangers | 0-4 | | 2 | | 4 | 5 | 6 | 7 | | 9 | | 14 | | 3 | | 10 | | 12 | 8 | 1 | | | 11 | |
| 23 | A | Kilmarnock | 0-0 | | 2 | | 4 | 5 | | | 9 | | | 7 | | 3 | | 10 | | 11 | 8 | 1 | | | | 6 |
| 26 | H | Hibernian | 1-1 | | 2 | | 4 | 5 | | | 9 | | | $7^1$ | 6 | | 12 | 3 | | 10 | | | | | 14 | |
| 30 | A | Partick Thistle | 2-2 | | | | 4 | 5 | | | $9^1$ | | | $10^1$ | 6 | 2 | 3 | 12 | 14 | | 8 | 1 | | | 7 | 11 |
| May 3 | H | Aberdeen | 0-2 | | | | 4 | 5 | | 7 | | 9 | | 11 | | 2 | 3 | 10 | 14 | | 8 | 1 | | | | 6 |
| 7 | H | Motherwell | 3-3 | 1 | | | 4 | 5 | | | $8^1$ | $9^1$ | | 12 | 7 | 3 | | 14 | | 11 | $10^1$ | | 2 | | | 6 |
| 14 | A | Dundee United | 3-2 | | 2 | | 4 | 5 | | | 12 | 9 | | $6^1$ | 14 | 3 | | 10 | | $11^2$ | 8 | | | | 7 | 1 |
| **TOTAL FULL APPEARANCES** | | | | 8 | 35 | 3 | 41 | 43 | 18 | 33 | 20 | 33 | 1 | 31 | 29 | 33 | 16 | 24 | 1 | 35 | 35 | 34 | 2 | 1 | 7 | 1 |
| **TOTAL SUB APPEARANCES** | | | | | | | | | (2) | | (2) | (1) | | (7) | | (1) | (11) | (7) | (3) | (2) | (12) | | (3) | (1) | (1) | (3) |
| **TOTAL GOALS SCORED** | | | | | 2 | | 1 | 3 | | 1 | 8 | 5 | | 6 | | 2 | | 1 | | 5 | 6 | 5 | | | | |

*Small bold figures denote goalscorers.  † denotes opponent's own goal.*

---

## STARK'S PARK

**CAPACITY**: 9,200; Seated 2,939, Standing 6,261

**PITCH DIMENSIONS**: 113 yds x 69 yds

**FACILITIES FOR DISABLED SUPPORTERS**: By prior arrangement with the Secretary.

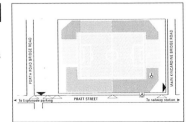

## HOW TO GET THERE

The following routes may be used to reach Stark's Park:

**TRAINS:** Kirkcaldy railway station is served by trains from Dundee, Edinburgh and Glasgow (via Edinburgh) and the ground is within walking distance of the station.

**BUSES:** The main bus station in Kirkcaldy is also within 15 minutes walking distance of the ground, but the Edinburgh, Dunfermline and Leven services pass close by the park.

**CARS:** Car parking is available in the Esplanade, which is on the south side of the ground, in Beveridge Park, which is on the north side of Stark's Road, and in ground adjacent to the railway station.

**YOUNGER'S TARTAN SPECIAL**

# ST. JOHNSTONE

McDiarmid Park, Crieff Road
Perth PH1 2SJ

**CHAIRMAN**
Geoffrey S. Brown

**DIRECTORS**
Douglas B. McIntyre
Henry S. Ritchie
David F. Sidey
A. Stewart M. Duff
Alexander Hay

**SECRETARY**
A. Stewart M. Duff

**MANAGER**
Paul Sturrock

**FIRST TEAM COACH**
John Blackley

**YOUTH COACH**
Alastair Stevenson

**CLUB DOCTOR**
Alastair McCracken

**PHYSIOTHERAPIST**
David Henderson

**S.F.A. COMMUNITY OFFICER**
Harry McKinlay

**STADIUM MANAGER**
Jimmy Hogg

**COMMERCIAL MANAGER**
Stuart Turnbull
(0738) 626961

**TELEPHONES:**
Ground/Ticket Office (0738) 626961
Fax (0738) 625771
Information Service (0891) 121559

**CLUB SHOP**
Mon-Fri Ticket Office at Ground
and Sat. Match days
Situated at South Stand

**OFFICIAL SUPPORTERS CLUB**
c/o McDiarmid Park,
Crieff Road Perth

**TEAM CAPTAIN**
Gary McGinnis

**SHIRT SPONSOR**
The Famous Grouse

## LIST OF PLAYERS 1994-95

| SURNAME | FIRST NAME | MIDDLE NAME | DATE OF BIRTH | PLACE OF BIRTH | DATE OF SIGNING | HEIGHT FT INS | WEIGHT ST LBS | PREVIOUS CLUB |
|---|---|---|---|---|---|---|---|---|
| Baillie | Robert | | 04/04/78 | Edinburgh | 15/06/94 | 5 10.0 | 10 8 | "S" Form |
| Cherry | Paul | Robert | 14/10/64 | Derby | 02/07/88 | 6 0.0 | 11 7 | Cowdenbeath |
| Curran | Henry | | 09/10/66 | Glasgow | 12/08/89 | 5 8.0 | 11 4 | Dundee United |
| Davenport | Peter | | 24/03/61 | Birkenhead | 16/08/94 | 5 11.0 | 11 3 | Airdrieonians |
| Davidson | Callum | Ian | 25/06/76 | Stirling | 08/06/94 | 5 10.0 | 11 0 | "S" Form |
| Davies | John | | 25/09/66 | Glasgow | 17/11/90 | 5 7.0 | 10 0 | Clydebank |
| Deas | Paul | Andrew | 22/02/72 | Perth | 24/01/90 | 5 11.0 | 10 2 | Kinnoull Juniors |
| Dempster | Ronald | | 01/10/76 | Govan | 06/05/94 | 5 8.0 | 10 3 | Possil Y.M. |
| Donegan | John | Francis Joseph | 19/05/71 | Cork | 26/03/93 | 6 1.0 | 12 8 | Millwall |
| Ferguson | Ian | | 05/08/68 | Dunfermline | 30/11/93 | 6 1.0 | 12 0 | Heart of Midlothian |
| Griffin | Daniel | Joseph | 10/08/77 | Belfast | 18/02/94 | 5 10.0 | 9 10 | St. Andrew's Belfast |
| Hamilton | Derek | | 09/08/76 | Bellshill | 22/09/93 | 6 0.0 | 12 1 | East Kilbride Thistle |
| Inglis | John | | 16/10/66 | Edinburgh | 23/06/90 | 5 11.0 | 12 7 | Meadowbank Thistle |
| Irons | David | John | 18/07/61 | Glasgow | 15/07/93 | 6 0.0 | 11 7 | Partick Thistle |
| Mathieson | David | James | 18/01/78 | Dumfries | 10/08/94 | 5 11.0 | 10 7 | Rangers |
| McAuley | Sean | | 23/06/72 | Sheffield | 22/04/92 | 6 0.0 | 11 7 | Manchester United |
| McCluskey | Stuart | Campbell | 29/10/77 | Bellshill | 07/07/94 | 5 11.0 | 10 12 | "S" Form |
| McGinnis | Gary | | 21/10/63 | Dundee | 09/02/90 | 5 11.0 | 10 13 | Dundee United |
| McGowne | Kevin | | 16/12/69 | Kilmarnock | 26/06/92 | 6 0.0 | 12 11 | St. Mirren |
| McGuinness | Allan | Kevin | 07/06/76 | Lanark | 22/09/93 | 6 0.0 | 12 4 | Scone Thistle |
| McMartin | Grant | Thomas | 31/12/70 | Linlithgow | 10/01/94 | 5 10.0 | 10 0 | Dundee |
| Miller | Colin | Fyfe | 04/10/64 | Lanark | 22/03/94 | 5 7.0 | 12 2 | Hamilton Academical |
| Morgan | Andrew | Alan | 10/12/74 | Glasgow | 19/11/91 | 5 10.0 | 10 9 | Hutchison Vale B.C. |
| Munro | Kenneth | Neil | 08/08/77 | Edinburgh | 06/05/94 | 5 10.0 | 10 4 | Possil Y.M. |
| O'Boyle | George | | 14/12/67 | Belfast | 24/07/94 | 5 8.0 | 11 6 | Dunfermline Athletic |
| O'Neil | John | | 06/07/71 | Bellshill | 04/08/94 | 5 7.0 | 10 9 | Dundee United |
| Preston | Allan | | 16/08/69 | Edinburgh | 26/03/94 | 5 10.0 | 11 7 | Dunfermline Athletic |
| Ramsey | Paul | Christopher | 03/09/62 | Derry | 08/10/93 | 5 11.0 | 12 10 | Cardiff City |
| Reynolds | Craig | Robert John | 03/10/77 | Dunfermline | 06/05/94 | 5 8.0 | 9 7 | Possilpark Y.M.C.A. |
| Rhodes | Andrew | Charles | 23/08/64 | Doncaster | 02/07/92 | 6 1.0 | 14 0 | Dunfermline Athletic |
| Rice | Paul | William | 25/08/77 | Glasgow | 18/02/94 | 5 9.0 | 11 4 | Possil Y.M. |
| Robertson | Stephen | | 16/03/77 | Glasgow | 22/09/93 | 5 10.0 | 10 5 | Scone Thistle |
| Scott | Philip | Campbell | 14/11/74 | Perth | 30/07/91 | 5 9.0 | 10 5 | Scone Thistle |
| Smith | Charles | Anthony | 30/04/76 | Glasgow | 17/08/94 | 5 10.0 | 11 6 | Newton Mearns B.C. |
| Sturrock | Paul | Whitehead | 10/10/56 | Ellon | 26/11/93 | 5 8.5 | 12 2 | Dundee United |
| Turner | Thomas | Gibson | 11/10/63 | Johnstone | 27/08/90 | 5 10.0 | 10 7 | Greenock Morton |
| Whiteford | Andrew | | 22/08/77 | Bellshill | 09/06/94 | 5 10.0 | 10 10 | Possil Y.M.C.A. |
| Winiarski | Stefan | Antoni | 08/09/77 | Dunfermline | 06/05/94 | 5 8.0 | 10 4 | Possilpark Y.M.C.A. |
| Wright | Paul | Hamilton | 17/08/67 | East Kilbride | 30/07/91 | 5 8.0 | 11 7 | Hibernian |
| Young | Scott | Robertson | 05/04/77 | Glasgow | 22/09/93 | 5 8.0 | 8 10 | West Park United |

## MILESTONES

YEAR OF FORMATION: 1884
MOST CAPPED PLAYER: Sandy McLaren
NO. OF CAPS: 5
MOST LEAGUE POINTS IN A SEASON: 59 (Second Division – Season 1987/88)
MOST LEAGUE GOALS SCORED BY A PLAYER IN A SEASON: Jimmy Benson (Season 1931/32)
NO. OF GOALS SCORED: 38
RECORD ATTENDANCE: 29,972 (-v- Dundee l0.2.1951)
RECORD VICTORY: 8-1 (-v- Partick Thistle – League Cup 16.8.1969)
RECORD DEFEAT: 0-12 (-v- Cowdenbeath – Scottish Cup 21.1.1928)

## SEASON TICKET INFORMATION

| | Seated | |
|---|---|---|
| West Stand | Adult | £162 |
| | Juvenile/OAP | £108 |
| East Stand | Adult | £126 |
| | Juvenile/OAP | £90 |
| South Stand | Adult | £108 |
| | Female/Juvenile/OAP | £50 |

## LEAGUE ADMISSION PRICES

| | Seated | |
|---|---|---|
| West Stand | Adult | £9 |
| | Juvenile/OAP | £6 |
| East Stand | Adult | £7 |
| | Juvenile/OAP | £5 |
| North Stand (Visitors) | Adult | £7 |
| | Juvenile/OAP | £5 |
| South Stand (Family Section) | Adult Male | £6 |
| | Female/Juvenile/OAP | £2 |

REGISTERED STRIP: Shirt – Royal Blue Broken Shadow Stripe, White Collar with Blue Trim
Shorts – White with Blue Trim, Stockings – Royal Blue with White Tops

CHANGE STRIP: Shirt – Gold with Royal Blue Stripes, Royal Blue Collar with Gold Trim
Shorts: Royal Blue with Gold Trim, Stockings: Gold with Royal Blue Tops

# CLUB FACTFILE 1993/94 .. RESULTS .. APPEARANCES .. SCORERS

## The SAINTS

| Date | Venue | Opponents | Result | Rhodes A. | Budden J. | Deas P. | McGinnis G. | Inglis J. | Curran H. | Ramsey P. | Turner T. | Wright P. | Torfason G. | Buglione M. | McCowne K. | Davies P. | Moore A. | Irons D. | McAuley S. | Morgan A. | Arkins V. | Scott P. | Cherry P. | Cole A. | McClelland J. | Ferguson I. | Dodds W. | McMartin G. | Miller C. | Preston A. | Maskrey S. |
|---|---|---|---|---|---|---|---|---|---|---|---|---|---|---|---|---|---|---|---|---|---|---|---|---|---|---|---|---|---|---|---|---|
| Aug 7 | A | Raith Rovers | 1-1 | 1 | 2 | 3 | 4 | 5 | 6 | 7 | 8 | $9^1$ | 10 | 11 | 12 | 14 | | | | | | | | | | | | | | | |
| 14 | H | Rangers | 1-2 | 1 | | 3 | 4 | 5 | 11 | 10 | 6 | $9^1$ | 8 | 12 | 2 | | | | | | 7 | | | | | | | | | | |
| 21 | H | Dundee United | 1-1 | 1 | | 3 | 10 | 5 | 8 | 6 | 14 | 9 | $11^1$ | | 2 | | | | 7 | 4 | | | | | | | | | | | |
| 28 | A | Aberdeen | 0-0 | 1 | | 3 | 4 | 5 | 11 | 10 | 6 | 9 | | | 2 | | | | 7 | | | | | 8 | 14 | | | | | | |
| Sept 4 | H | Motherwell | 3-0 | 1 | | 3 | 2 | 5 | $10^1$ | 8 | 4 | $9^2$ | | 11 | | | | | 7 | | | 6 | | 14 | | | | | | | |
| 11 | A | Kilmarnock | 0-0 | 1 | | 3 | 4 | 5 | 8 | 6 | | 9 | 10 | | | 2 | | | 7 | | 11 | | | | | | | | | | |
| 18 | H | Hibernian | 1-3 | 1 | 14 | 3 | 2 | 4 | 11 | 6 | | $9^1$ | 10 | 12 | | 5 | | | 7 | | 8 | | | | | | | | | | |
| 25 | H | Dundee | 2-1 | 1 | | 3 | 5 | | $8^1$ | 6 | 9 | 11 | 10 | 12 | | | | | $7^1$ | | 4 | | | 2 | | | | | | | |
| Oct 2 | A | Partick Thistle | 1-4 | 1 | | 3 | 2 | | 6 | 4 | 9 | 10 | 5 | | | | | | $7^1$ | 14 | 11 | | | 8 | 12 | | | | | | |
| 6 | H | Celtic | 2-1 | 1 | | 3 | 2 | 5 | 8 | 4 | 9 | 10 | | | | | | $7^2$ | | | 6 | | | 11 | | | | | | | |
| 9 | A | Heart of Midlothian | 1-1 | 1 | | 3 | 2 | 5 | 6 | 4 | | $9^1$ | 10 | | | 14 | | | 7 | | 11 | | | 8 | | | | | | | |
| 16 | A | Rangers | 0-2 | 1 | | 3 | 2 | 5 | 6 | 4 | | 9 | 10 | 12 | | | | | 7 | | 11 | | | 8 | | | | | | | |
| 23 | A | Raith Rovers | 1-1 | 1 | | 3 | 2 | 5 | 6 | | 8 | 9 | $10^1$ | | | | | | 7 | | 11 | 12 | | 4 | | | | | | | |
| 30 | A | Dundee United | 0-2 | 1 | | 3 | 2 | 5 | | 4 | 8 | 9 | 10 | 12 | | | | | 7 | | 11 | | 6 | | | | | | | | |
| Nov 6 | H | Aberdeen | 1-1 | 1 | | 3 | $6^1$ | 5 | | | 8 | 9 | 10 | | 2 | | | | 7 | 14 | 11 | | | 4 | | | | | | | |
| 9 | A | Motherwell | 0-1 | 1 | | 3 | 4 | 5 | 6 | | 8 | 9 | 10 | 12 | 2 | | | | 7 | | 11 | | | 14 | | | | | | | |
| 13 | H | Partick Thistle | 1-3 | 1 | | 2 | | 5 | $6^1$ | | | | 10 | 12 | | 14 | | | 7 | | 9 | | | 11 | | 8 | | | 3 | 4 | |
| 20 | A | Dundee | 1-0 | 1 | | | 4 | 5 | | 10 | 8 | 9 | 14 | | | 2 | | | | | $7^1$ | 3 | | 6 | 11 | | | | | | |
| 27 | H | Kilmarnock | 0-1 | 1 | 12 | | 4 | 5 | | 10 | 8 | 9 | 14 | | | 2 | | | | | 7 | 3 | | 6 | 11 | | | | | | |
| 30 | A | Hibernian | 0-0 | 1 | | | 4 | 5 | | 10 | 8 | 9 | | | | 2 | | | | | 7 | 3 | | 6 | 11 | | | | | | |
| Dec 4 | A | Celtic | 0-1 | 1 | | | 4 | 5 | | 10 | 8 | 9 | 14 | | | 2 | | | | | 7 | 3 | | 6 | 11 | | | | | | |
| 11 | H | Heart of Midlothian | 2-0 | 1 | | | 4 | 5 | | 10 | 8 | 9 | 7 | 14 | | 2 | | | | | $11^1$ | 3 | $6^1$ | | | | | | | | |
| 18 | H | Rangers | 0-4 | 1 | | | 4 | 5 | | 10 | 8 | 9 | 7 | | | 2 | | | | | 11 | 3 | | 12 | 6 | | | | | | |
| Jan 8 | A | Aberdeen | 1-1 | 1 | | | 4 | 5 | | 10 | 8 | $9^1$ | 7 | 14 | | 2 | | | | | 11 | 3 | | 12 | 6 | | | | | | |
| 19 | A | Raith Rovers | 1-1 | 1 | | | 4 | 5 | 6 | 10 | 8 | 9 | $14^1$ | | | 2 | | | 11 | | 7 | 3 | | | | 10 | | | | | |
| 22 | H | Hibernian | 2-2 | 1 | | | 4 | 5 | | | 8 | $9^1$ | | | | 2 | | | 11 | | 7 | 3 | | 6 | | $10^1$ | | | 12 | | |
| 25 | H | Dundee United | 1-1 | 1 | | | 4 | 5 | | | 8 | | $14^1$ | | | 2 | | | 11 | | 7 | 3 | | 6 | 9 | 10 | | 12 | | | |
| Feb 5 | A | Kilmarnock | 0-0 | 1 | | | 4 | 5 | 6 | | 8 | | | | | 2 | | | 11 | | 7 | 3 | | 4 | 9 | 10 | | | | | |
| 8 | H | Motherwell | 2-1 | 1 | | | 4 | 5 | 6 | | 8 | | | | | 2 | | | 11 | | 7 | 3 | | | $9^1$ | $10^1$ | | 12 | | | |
| 12 | H | Dundee | 1-1 | 1 | | | 4 | 5 | 6 | | 8 | 14 | | | | 2 | | | 11 | | 7 | 3 | | 8 | 9 | $10^1$ | | | | | |
| Mar 5 | H | Celtic | 0-1 | 1 | | 2 | 4 | 5 | | | 8 | 14 | | | 12 | | | | 11 | | 7 | 3 | | 6 | 9 | 10 | | | | | |
| 19 | A | Rangers | 0-4 | 1 | | | 4 | 5 | | | 8 | 9 | | | | 2 | | | 11 | | 7 | 3 | | 6 | | 10 | | 12 | | | |
| 22 | A | Partick Thistle | 0-0 | 1 | | | 4 | 5 | | | 8 | | | | | 2 | | | 11 | | 7 | 3 | | 6 | 9 | 10 | 12 | | | | |
| 26 | H | Raith Rovers | 2-0 | 1 | | | 4 | 5 | | | 8 | | | | | 2 | | | 11 | | | | 12 | 6 | 9 | $10^2$ | | | | 3 | 7 |
| 30 | H | Kilmarnock | 0-1 | 1 | | | 4 | 5 | | | 8 | 14 | | | | 2 | | | 11 | | | | 12 | 6 | 9 | 10 | | | | 3 | 7 |
| Apr 2 | A | Hibernian | 0-0 | 1 | | | | 5 | | | 11 | 4 | 8 | | | 2 | | | | | 7 | | 12 | 6 | 9 | 10 | | | | 3 | |
| 6 | H | Heart of Midlothian | 2-2 | 1 | | | | 5 | | | 11 | | 8 | | | 2 | | | | | 7 | | $4^1$ | 6 | $9^1$ | 10 | | | | 3 | 12 |
| 9 | A | Dundee | 1-0 | 1 | | | | 5 | | | 11 | | 8 | $9^1$ | | 2 | | | | | 7 | | 4 | 6 | | 10 | | | | 3 | 12 |
| 16 | H | Partick Thistle | 1-0 | 1 | | | | 5 | | | 11 | 14 | 8 | | | 2 | | | | | 7 | | $4^1$ | 6 | 9 | 10 | | | | 3 | 12 |
| 23 | H | Heart of Midlothian | 0-0 | 1 | | | | 5 | | | 11 | 9 | 8 | | | 2 | | | | | 7 | | 4 | 6 | | 10 | | | | 3 | 12 |
| 27 | A | Celtic | 1-1 | 1 | | | | 5 | | | 11 | | 8 | | | 2 | | | | | 7 | | 4 | 6 | 9 | $10^1$ | | | | 3 | 12 |
| 30 | A | Dundee United | 0-0 | 1 | | | 11 | 5 | | | 8 | 14 | | | | 2 | | | | | 7 | | 4 | 6 | 9 | 10 | | | | 3 | |
| May 7 | H | Aberdeen | 0-1 | 1 | | | 11 | 5 | | | 8 | | | | | 2 | | | | | 7 | | 4 | | 9 | 10 | 12 | | 6 | 3 | 14 |
| 14 | A | Motherwell | 1-0 | 1 | | | 11 | $5^1$ | | | 8 | | | | 12 | 2 | | | | | 7 | | 4 | 6 | 9 | 10 | | 14 | | 3 | |
| **TOTAL FULL APPEARANCES** | | | | 44 | 1 | 35 | 28 | 25 | 39 | 22 | 37 | 16 | 21 | 3 | 37 | 30 | 7 | 1 | 28 | | 19 | 31 | 1 | 1 | 22 | 20 | | 12 | 3 | 1 | |
| **TOTAL SUB APPEARANCES** | | | | | (1) | (1) | | | | (3) | (1) | (8) | (6) | (4) | (2) | (6) | | | (2) | | (1) | (5) | (2) | | | | | (6) | | (6) | (3) |
| **TOTAL GOALS SCORED** | | | | | | 1 | 1 | 3 | | | 7 | 5 | | | 5 | 1 | | | | | | 3 | | | | | | 3 | 6 | | |

*Small bold figures denote goalscorers.  † denotes opponent's own goal.*

---

## McDIARMID PARK

**CAPACITY:** 10,721 (All Seated)

**PITCH DIMENSIONS:** 115 yds x 75 yds

**FACILITIES FOR DISABLED SUPPORTERS:** Entrance via south end of West Stand and south end of East Stand. Visiting disabled fans should contact the club in advance.

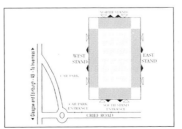

## HOW TO GET THERE

The following routes can be used to reach McDiarmid Park:

**TRAINS:** Perth Station is well served by trains from all parts of the country. The station is about 40 minutes walk from the park.

**BUSES:** Local services nos.1 and 2 pass near the ground. Both leave from Mill Street in the town centre.

**CARS:** The car park at the park holds 1,500 cars and 100 coaches. Vehicles should follow signs A9 to Inverness on Perth City by-pass, then follow "Football Stadium" signs at Inveralmond Roundabout South onto slip road adjacent to McDiarmid Park. Vehicle charges are £1.00 for cars and £5.00 for coaches.

# ST. MIRREN

St. Mirren Park, Love Street,
Paisley PA3 2EJ

**CHAIRMAN**
Allan W. Marshall, LL.B.

**VICE-CHAIRMAN**
William W. Waters, F.R.I.C.S.

**DIRECTORS**
Robert Earlie
J. Yule Craig, J.P., C.A.
Charles G. Palmer
George P. Campbell
John F. Paton

**CHIEF EXECUTIVE**
Robert Earlie

**SECRETARY**
A. Robin Craig LL.B.

**MANAGER**
James Bone

**GENERAL MANAGER**
Jack Copland
041-840 1337

**CLUB DOCTOR**
Stewart McCormack, M.B., Ch.B.

**PHYSIOTHERAPIST**
Andrew Binning B.Sc., M.C.S.P.

**S.F.A. COMMUNITY OFFICER**
Tony Fitzpatrick

**CHIEF SCOUT**
Joe Hughes

**GROUNDSMAN**
Tom Docherty

**COMMERCIAL MANAGER**
Bill Campbell
041-840 1337

**TELEPHONES**
Ground 041-889 2558/840 1337
Fax 041-848 6444
Sec. Bus. 041-221 5575

**CLUB SHOP**
Situated at Ground Open
10.30 a.m. – 2.30 p.m. Mon to Fri
and 10.00 a.m. – 3.00 p.m.
on Saturdays

**OFFICIAL SUPPORTERS CLUB**
St. Mirren Supporters Club,
11 Knox Street, Paisley

**TEAM CAPTAIN**
Norman McWhirter

**SHIRT SPONSOR**
Clanford Motors Ltd.

## LIST OF PLAYERS 1994-95

| SURNAME | FIRST NAME | MIDDLE NAME | DATE OF BIRTH | PLACE OF BIRTH | DATE OF SIGNING | HEIGHT FT INS | WEIGHT ST LBS | PREVIOUS CLUB |
|---|---|---|---|---|---|---|---|---|
| Archdeacon | Paul | | 11/10/76 | Greenock | 22/04/94 | 5 9.0 | 11 5 | St. Mirren B.C. |
| Baker | Martin | | 08/06/74 | Govan | 16/09/92 | 5 11.0 | 10 10 | St. Mirren B.C. |
| Bone | Alexander | Syme Frew | 26/02/71 | Stirling | 22/10/92 | 5 9.0 | 10 7 | Fallin |
| Combe | Alan | | 03/04/74 | Edinburgh | 07/08/93 | 5 11.0 | 10 13 | Cowdenbeath |
| Cummings | Paul | Robert | 23/03/74 | Greenock | 16/09/92 | 5 8.0 | 10 5 | St. Mirren B.C. |
| Dawson | Robert | McQuillan | 01/08/63 | Stirling | 05/06/87 | 5 9.0 | 10 10 | Stirling Albion |
| Dick | James | | 21/06/72 | Bellshill | 06/07/93 | 5 11.0 | 9 3 | Airdrieonians |
| Donaldson | Ross | | 27/06/77 | Bellshill | 26/03/94 | 5 9.0 | 10 6 | Camelon Juniors |
| Elliot | David | | 13/11/69 | Glasgow | 19/06/91 | 5 9.0 | 11 0 | Partick Thistle |
| Fullarton | James | | 20/07/74 | Bellshill | 13/06/91 | 5 10.0 | 10 6 | Motherwell B.C. |
| Gardner | James | | 27/09/67 | Dunfermline | 07/09/93 | 5 10.0 | 10 2 | Motherwell |
| Gillies | Kenneth | | 20/07/74 | Glasgow | 16/09/92 | 5 8.0 | 11 7 | St. Mirren B.C. |
| Gillies | Richard | Charles | 24/08/76 | Glasgow | 12/12/92 | 5 8.0 | 11 7 | St. Mirren B.C. |
| Harvie | Scott | Smith | 22/11/68 | Glasgow | 24/09/93 | 5 7.5 | 11 8 | Partick Thistle |
| Hetherston | Brian | | 23/11/76 | Bellshill | 26/03/94 | 6 0.0 | 9 12 | St. Mirren B.C. |
| Hewitt | John | | 09/02/63 | Aberdeen | 04/09/92 | 5 8.0 | 10 8 | Deveronvale |
| Hick | Martin | Allan | 16/05/74 | Paisley | 05/07/94 | 5 11.0 | 11 10 | Aberdeen |
| Lavety | Barry | | 21/08/74 | Johnstone | 10/08/91 | 6 0.0 | 12 12 | Gleniffer Thistle |
| McGrotty | Gary | | 26/09/76 | Glasgow | 28/04/94 | 5 5.0 | 8 7 | St. Mirren B.C. |
| McIntyre | Paul | | 18/01/67 | Girvan | 27/03/91 | 6 0.0 | 12 11 | Maybole Juniors |
| McLaughlin | Barry | John | 19/04/73 | Paisley | 01/08/91 | 5 10.0 | 11 2 | St. Mirren B.C. |
| McWhirter | Norman | | 04/09/69 | Johnstone | 16/09/85 | 5 9.0 | 9 6 | Linwood Rangers B.C. |
| Money | Israel | Campbell | 31/08/60 | Maybole | 08/06/78 | 5 11.0 | 12 3 | Dailly Amateurs |
| Orr | Neil | Ian | 13/05/59 | Greenock | 21/07/93 | 5 10.5 | 12 2 | Hibernian |
| Scrimgour | Derek | | 29/03/78 | Glasgow | 18/08/94 | 6 3.0 | 11 10 | Johnstone Burgh |
| Taylor | Stuart | | 26/11/74 | Glasgow | 16/09/92 | 6 1.0 | 10 10 | St. Mirren B.C. |
| Watson | Stephen | | 04/04/73 | Liverpool | 28/07/94 | 5 11.0 | 11 4 | Rangers |
| Watson | Derek | | 13/08/76 | Broxburn | 18/08/94 | 5 11.5 | 12 13 | Blackburn United |

## MILESTONES

**YEAR OF FORMATION:** 1877
**MOST CAPPED PLAYERS:** Iain Munro & Billy Thomson
**NO. OF CAPS:** 7
**MOST LEAGUE POINTS IN A SEASON:** 62 (Division 2 – Season 1967/68)
**MOST LEAGUE GOALS SCORED BY A PLAYER IN A SEASON:** Dunky Walker (Season 1921/22)
**NO. OF GOALS SCORED:** 45
**RECORD ATTENDANCE:** 47,438 (-v- Celtic 7.3.1925)
**RECORD VICTORY:** 15-0 (-v- Glasgow University – Scottish Cup 30.1.1960)
**RECORD DEFEAT:** 0-9 (-v- Rangers – Division 1, 4.12.1897)

## SEASON TICKET INFORMATION

**Seated**
Main Stand    Adult ........................................ £140
              Juvenile/OAP ............................ £82
North Stand   Adult ........................................ £125
              Juvenile/OAP ............................ £72
Enclosure     Adult ........................................ £125
              Juvenile/OAP ............................ £72

## LEAGUE ADMISSION PRICES

**Seated**
Main Stand       Adult .......................................... £8
                 Juvenile/OAP ......................... £4.50
Lower Enclosure  Adult ........................................... £7
                 Juvenile/OAP ............................... £4
North Stand      Adult ........................................... £7
                 Juvenile/OAP ............................... £4
                 1 Parent & 1 Juvenile ................ £8
Family Enclosure 1 Parent & 1 Juvenile ................ £7
                 Each additional Juvenile ............ £3

**Standing**
Adult ............................ £6    Juvenile/OAP ............... £3

**REGISTERED STRIP:** Shirt – Black and White Halves, Shorts: White with Black and Red Trim, Stockings: Black with White Trim

**CHANGE STRIP:** Shirt – Yellow with Black Shoulders and Sleeves, Shorts – Black with Yellow Trim, Stockings – White with Yellow and Black Trim

# CLUB FACTFILE 1993/94 . . RESULTS . . APPEARANCES . . SCORERS

## The BUDDIES

Players (columns): Combe A., Dawson R., Fullarton J., McWhirter N., Taylor S., Orr N., Bone A., Lambert P., Lavety B., Hewitt J., Elliot D., McIntyre P., Gallagher E., Baker M., Dick J., Money C., Gillies R., Gillies K., Paterson A., McCrotty G., Peacock J., McLaughlin B., Gardner J., Farrell S., Harvie S., Hetherston B., Archdeacon P., Smith Benjamin, Smith Brian

| Date | Venue | Opponents | Result | Combe A. | Dawson R. | Fullarton J. | McWhirter N. | Taylor S. | Orr N. | Bone A. | Lambert P. | Lavety B. | Hewitt J. | Elliot D. | McIntyre P. | Gallagher E. | Baker M. | Dick J. | Money C. | Gillies R. | Gillies K. | Paterson A. | McCrotty G. | Peacock J. | McLaughlin B. | Gardner J. | Farrell S. | Harvie S. | Hetherston B. | Archdeacon P. | Smith Benjamin | Smith Brian |
|---|---|---|---|---|---|---|---|---|---|---|---|---|---|---|---|---|---|---|---|---|---|---|---|---|---|---|---|---|---|---|---|---|
| Aug 7 | H | Airdrieonians | 0-1 | 1 | 2 | 3 | 4 | 5 | 6 | 7 | 8 | 9 | 10 | 11 | 12 | 14 | | | | | | | | | | | | | | | | |
| 14 | A | Hamilton Academical | 0-0 | 1 | 2 | 11 | | 4 | 5 | 6 | 14 | 9 | 10 | | 12 | 7 | 3 | 8 | | | | | | | | | | | | | | |
| 21 | H | Greenock Morton | 2-2 | | 5 | 4$^1$ | | 6 | | 8 | 9$^1$ | 10 | 14 | 11 | 7 | 3 | 2 | 1 | 12 | | | | | | | | | | | | | |
| 28 | H | Stirling Albion | 0-1 | | 5 | 4 | | 6 | 14 | 8 | 9 | 11 | 2 | 10 | 3 | 7 | 1 | 12 | | | | | | | | | | | | | | |
| Sept 4 | H | Ayr United | 0-1 | | 5 | 4 | | | | | 9 | 11 | 6 | 3 | 8 | 1 | 10 | | 2 | 7 | 12 | 14 | | | | | | | | | | |
| 11 | H | Dumbarton | 0-3 | 1 | | 5 | | 4 | | | 9 | 12 | 11 | 6 | 7 | 3 | 8 | 14 | 2 | | | 10 | | | | | | | | | | |
| 14 | A | Dunfermline Athletic | 4-3 | 1 | 2 | | 4 | | 6 | 12 | 14$^1$ | 10 | | 5 | 7$^1$ | 3$^1$ | 9 | | | | | 11$^1$ | 8 | | | | | | | | | |
| 18 | H | Clyde | 2-1 | 1 | 2 | 6 | 4$^1$ | | | 14 | 9 | 10 | | 5$^1$ | 7 | 3 | 12 | | | | | 11 | 8 | | | | | | | | | |
| 25 | H | Falkirk | 0-2 | 1 | 2 | 8 | 4 | | | | 6 | 14 | 10 | 9 | 5 | 7 | 3 | 12 | | | | 11 | | | | | | | | | | |
| 28 | H | Brechin City | 2-0 | | 2 | | 4 | | | 5 | 7 | 9 | 10 | 12$^1$ | 14 | 3 | 6$^1$ | 1 | 8 | | | 11 | | | | | | | | | | |
| Oct 2 | A | Clydebank | 1-1 | | 2 | 3 | 4 | | 6 | 7 | 9$^1$ | 12 | | 5 | | | 8 | 1 | | | | 14 | 11 | 10 | | | | | | | | |
| 9 | A | Airdrieonians | 1-1 | | 2 | 8 | 4 | | 6 | 7 | 9 | 12 | | | 14$^1$ | | 10 | 1 | | | | 5 | 11 | 3 | | | | | | | | |
| 16 | A | Dunfermline Athletic | 1-2 | | 2 | 4$^1$ | | 6 | 14 | | 9 | 10 | | 8 | | 5 | 7 | 1 | 12 | | | 11 | 3 | | | | | | | | | |
| 23 | A | Dumbarton | 3-3 | | 2 | 8 | | 6 | 14 | | 9 | 10 | | 5 | 7$^3$ | 3 | | 1 | | | | 11 | 12 | | | | | | | | | |
| 30 | A | Greenock Morton | 2-1 | | 2 | 11 | 4 | | 6$^1$ | | 9$^1$ | 10 | 14 | 5 | 7 | 3 | | 1 | | | | 8 | 12 | | | | | | | | | |
| Nov 6 | H | Stirling Albion | 0-1 | | | 4 | | 6 | 14 | | 9 | 10 | 11 | 5 | 7 | 3 | 12 | 1 | | | | 2 | 8 | | | | | | | | | |
| 9 | A | Ayr United | 1-0 | 1 | 2 | 8 | 4 | | 6 | | 9 | 10 | 11 | 5$^1$ | 7 | 3 | | | | | | 12 | 14 | | | | | | | | | |
| 13 | H | Clydebank | 1-0 | | 2 | 8 | 4$^1$ | | 6 | 7 | 9 | | 11 | 5 | | 3 | 1 | 12 | | | | 10 | 14 | | | | | | | | | |
| 20 | H | Brechin City | 4-1 | | 2$^1$ | 10 | 4 | | 6 | 7 | 9$^1$ | 14 | 11$^2$ | | 3 | 8 | 1 | 12 | | | | 5 | | | | | | | | | | |
| 30 | H | Hamilton Academical | 1-0 | | 2 | | 4$^1$ | | 6 | 7 | 9 | 10 | 11 | 5 | | 3 | 8 | 1 | | | | 12 | 14 | | | | | | | | | |
| Dec 4 | A | Clyde | 1-0 | | 2 | | 4 | | | 7 | 9$^1$ | 10 | 11 | 5 | | 3 | 8 | 1 | | | | 6 | | | | | | | | | | |
| 18 | A | Dunfermline Athletic | 2-4 | | 2 | 7 | 4 | | 6 | 14 | 9 | 10$^1$ | 11 | 5 | | 3 | 8 | 1 | | | | 12$^1$ | | | | | | | | | | |
| Jan 3 | H | Falkirk | 3-1 | | 2 | 8 | 4 | | 6 | 14 | 9 | 10$^1$ | 11 | 5$^2$ | | 3 | | 1 | | | | | 7 | | | | | | | | | |
| 8 | A | Stirling Albion | 0-3 | | 2 | 8 | 4 | | 6 | 7 | 9 | 10 | 11 | 5 | | 3 | | 1 | 14 | | | | | | | | | | | | | |
| 11 | H | Airdrieonians | 3-0 | 1 | 2$^1$ | 8 | 4$^1$ | 6 | | | 14 | 10 | 11$^1$ | 5 | | 3 | 7 | | 9 | | | | 12 | | | | | | | | | |
| 18 | H | Greenock Morton | 5-1 | 1 | 2$^1$ | 8 | 4 | 6 | | | 9$^1$ | 10 | 11$^1$ | 5$^1$ | | 3 | 7$^1$ | | 14 | | | | 12 | | | | | | | | | |
| 22 | A | Hamilton Academical | 0-0 | 1 | 2 | 8 | 4 | | 6 | 14 | 9 | 10 | 11 | 5 | | 3 | 7 | | 12 | | | | | | | | | | | | | |
| 25 | H | Ayr United | 3-1 | 1 | 2 | 8 | 4$^1$ | | | 14$^1$ | 9 | 10 | 11$^1$ | 5 | | 3 | 7 | | 12 | | | 6 | | | | | | | | | | |
| Feb 5 | H | Dumbarton | 0-3 | 1 | 2 | 8 | | 4 | | 14 | 9 | 10 | 11 | 5 | | 3 | 12 | | 7 | | | 6 | | | | | | | | | | |
| 12 | A | Clydebank | 3-0 | 1 | 2 | 6 | | 4 | | 8$^1$ | 9 | 10$^1$ | 11 | 5$^1$ | | 3 | 7 | | | | | | | 14 | 12 | | | | | | | |
| 26 | H | Brechin City | 1-1 | | 2 | 6 | | 4 | | 8$^1$ | 14 | 10 | 11 | 5 | | 3 | | 1 | | | | | 9 | 7 | 12 | | | | | | | |
| Mar 5 | H | Clyde | 0-0 | | 2 | 6 | | | 8 | | 9 | 10 | 11 | 5 | | 3 | 7 | 1 | 14 | 12 | | 4 | | | | | | | | | | |
| 12 | A | Falkirk | 0-4 | | 2 | 6 | 12 | | 8 | | 9 | | 11 | 5 | 14 | 3 | 7 | 1 | 10 | | | 4 | | | | | | | | | | |
| 19 | A | Dunfermline Athletic | 0-2 | | 2 | 10 | 4 | | 8 | | 9 | | 11 | 5 | 14 | 3 | | 1 | | 12 | | 7 | 6 | | | | | | | | | |
| 26 | A | Airdrieonians | 2-0 | 1 | 2 | 3 | | 4 | 9$^1$ | | | 10$^1$ | 11 | 5 | | | 7 | | 14 | | | 8 | 6 | | | | 12 | | | | | |
| 29 | H | Hamilton Academical | 0-2 | | 2 | 3 | | 4 | 9 | | 14 | 10 | 11 | 5 | | 12 | 7 | 1 | | | | 8 | 6 | | | | | | | | | |
| Apr 2 | A | Dumbarton | 3-2 | | 2 | 10 | | | 9$^1$ | | 14$^1$ | | 11$^1$ | 5 | | 3 | 7 | 1 | | | | 8 | 6 | 12 | | | | | | | | |
| 9 | H | Clydebank | 2-0 | | 2 | 10 | | 4 | 8 | | 9 | | 11 | 5 | | 3 | 7$^2$ | 1 | 14 | | | 6 | | | | | 12 | | | | | |
| 16 | A | Brechin City | 1-0 | | 2 | 10 | | 4 | 8 | | 9$^1$ | | 11 | 5 | | | 7 | 1 | 14 | | | 6 | | | | | 3 | 12 | | | | |
| 23 | A | Clyde | 0-3 | | 2 | 6 | | | 10 | | 9 | | 3 | 5 | | | 8 | 1 | 7 | 14 | | | 11 | | | 12 | 4 | | | | | |
| 26 | H | Falkirk | 0-3 | 1 | 2 | 6 | | 4 | | | 9 | 14 | 11 | 5 | | 3 | 8 | | 10 | 12 | | 7 | | | | | | | | | | |
| 30 | A | Greenock Morton | 2-1 | | 2 | 6 | | | | | 9$^1$ | 11 | 5 | | | 3 | 8 | 1 | 10$^1$ | 7 | | | 4 | 14 | | | | | | | | |
| May 7 | H | Stirling Albion | 4-0 | | 2 | 6 | | | | | 9 | 11$^2$ | 5 | | | 3 | 8 | 1 | 10$^1$ | 7 | | | 4 | 14 | | 12$^1$ | | | | | | |
| 14 | A | Ayr United | 1-0 | 1 | | | | 4 | | | | 11 | 5$^1$ | | | 3 | 8 | 10 | 7 | | | 2 | 9 | | | 6 | 14 | | | | 12 | |
| **TOTAL FULL APPEARANCES** | | | | 16 | 38 | 37 | 27 | 13 | 24 | 21 | 3 | 35 | 27 | 34 | 39 | 11 | 37 | 31 | 28 | 10 | 3 | 2 | 1 | 5 | 18 | 14 | 4 | 4 | | 2 | | |
| **TOTAL SUB APPEARANCES** | | | | | | (1) | | (12) | | (7) | (4) | (2) | (3) | (5) | (1) | (4) | | (12) | (6) | | | | (1) | (5) | (7) | (4) | (2) | (3) | (2) | | (2) | |
| **TOTAL GOALS SCORED** | | | | | 3 | | 1 | 5 | | 10 | 4 | 8 | 8 | 5 | 1 | 4 | | 2 | | | | | | 1 | 1 | | | | | | 1 | |

*Small bold figures denote goalscorers. † denotes opponent's own goal.*

## ST. MIRREN PARK

**CAPACITY:** 12,395; Seated 6,380, Standing 6,015

PLEASE NOTE: THAT IT IS ANTICIPATED THAT THE NEW STAND WILL BE OPEN IN DECEMBER, 1994 WITH A SEATED CAPACITY OF 3,000, INCREASING THE GROUND CAPACITY TO 15,395

**PITCH DIMENSIONS:** 112 yds x 73 yds

**FACILITIES FOR DISABLED SUPPORTERS:** For certain matches special arrangements can be made if prior notice is given.

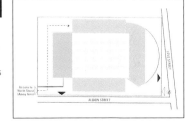

## HOW TO GET THERE

**St. Mirren Park can be reached by the following routes.**

**TRAINS:** There is a frequent train service from Glasgow Central Station and all coastal routes pass through Gilmour Street. The ground is about 400 yards from the station.

**BUSES:** All SMT coastal services, plus buses to Johnstone and Kilbarchan, pass within 300 yards of the ground.

**CARS:** The only facilities for car parking are in the streets surrounding the ground.

# STRANRAER

Stair Park, London Road,
Stranraer DG9 8BS

**CHAIRMAN**
George F. Compton

**VICE-CHAIRMAN**
R. A. Graham Rodgers

**COMMITTEE**
Andrew Hannah (Treasurer)
James Robertson
James Hannah
Robert J. Clanachan
Thomas Rice
James Bark
Leo R. Sprott
Alexander McKie
Nigel C. Redhead
Thomas L. Sutherland

**SECRETARY**
R. A. Graham Rodgers

**MANAGER**
Alex McAnespie

**COACH**
Derek McHarg

**CLUB DOCTOR**
Dr. Philip Martin

**PHYSIOTHERAPIST**
John Hart

**GROUNDSMAN**
Patrick Dowey

**KIT MAN**
William Milliken

**COMMERCIAL MANAGER**
Thomas L. Sutherland
(0776) 707070

**TELEPHONES**
Ground (0776) 703271
Sec. Home/Ticket Office/Information
Service (0776) 702194

**CLUB SHOP**
Situated at Ground
2.30 p.m. – 3.00 p.m. and
half-time on match days

**TEAM CAPTAIN**
Kenny Brannigan

**SHIRT SPONSOR**
Stena Sealink

## LIST OF PLAYERS 1994-95

| SURNAME | FIRST NAME | MIDDLE NAME | DATE OF BIRTH | PLACE OF BIRTH | DATE OF SIGNING | HEIGHT FT INS | WEIGHT ST LBS | PREVIOUS CLUB |
|---|---|---|---|---|---|---|---|---|
| Brannigan | Kenneth | | 08/06/65 | Glasgow | 22/11/91 | 6 0.0 | 12 4 | East Stirlingshire |
| Brown | Craig | | 23/09/71 | Greenock | 27/07/94 | 5 11.0 | 12 4 | Greenock Morton |
| Cody | Stephen | | 01/06/69 | Calderbank | 22/07/92 | 5 9.0 | 11 6 | Falkirk |
| Duffy | Bernard | John | 28/07/61 | Kilmarnock | 22/06/88 | 5 10.5 | 11 7 | Annbank United |
| Duncan | Graham | | 02/02/69 | Glasgow | 30/06/89 | 5 11.0 | 11 6 | Dumbarton |
| Farrell | Stephen | Edward | 08/03/73 | Kilwinning | 27/07/94 | 5 11.0 | 11 12 | St. Mirren |
| Ferguson | William | | 30/08/67 | Glasgow | 15/01/93 | 5 11.0 | 11 0 | Albion Rovers |
| Gallagher | Anthony | | 16/03/63 | Bellshill | 31/03/88 | 6 1.0 | 12 3 | Albion Rovers |
| Grant | Alexander | | 27/02/62 | Glasgow | 20/07/90 | 6 1.0 | 12 12 | Partick Thistle |
| Henderson | Darren | | 12/10/66 | Kilmarnock | 15/07/93 | 5 11.0 | 11 0 | Queen of the South |
| Howard | Nigel | | 06/10/70 | Morecambe | 27/06/94 | 6 0.0 | 13 8 | Ayr United |
| Hughes | James | Francis | 07/05/65 | Kilwinning | 29/03/91 | 5 10.0 | 11 5 | Ayr United |
| McCaffrey | John | Brendan | 17/10/72 | Glasgow | 11/03/94 | 6 1.0 | 12 0 | Albion Rovers |
| McCann | James | | 03/09/62 | Greenock | 23/03/91 | 5 10.0 | 11 7 | Ayr United |
| McIntyre | Stephen | | 15/05/66 | Ayr | 04/08/92 | 6 0.0 | 11 6 | Hereford United |
| McLean | Paul | | 25/07/64 | Johnstone | 24/10/92 | 5 10.0 | 12 0 | Ayr United |
| Millar | Graham | | 12/03/65 | Bellshill | 25/03/93 | 5 8.0 | 11 0 | Albion Rovers |
| Reilly | Robert | Piper | 23/09/59 | Kilmarnock | 05/08/94 | 5 10.0 | 11 1 | Stirling Albion |
| Ross | Stephen | | 27/01/65 | Glasgow | 22/09/92 | 5 9.0 | 10 10 | Clyde |
| Sloan | Thomas | | 24/08/64 | Irvine | 19/07/91 | 5 9.5 | 10 10 | Kilmarnock |
| Spittal | John | Ian | 14/02/65 | Glasgow | 10/03/89 | 6 1.0 | 12 0 | Partick Thistle |
| Treanor | Mark | | 01/04/62 | Glasgow | 09/08/94 | 6 0.0 | 11 0 | Clydebank |
| Walker | Thomas | | 23/12/64 | Glasgow | 26/02/94 | 5 7.5 | 10 10 | Dumbarton |

## MILESTONES

YEAR OF FORMATION: 1870
MOST LEAGUE POINTS IN A SEASON: 56 (Second Division – 1993/94)
MOST LEAGUE GOALS SCORED BY A PLAYER IN A SEASON: D. Frye (Season 1977/78)
NO. OF GOALS SCORED: 27
RECORD ATTENDANCE: 6,500 (-v- Rangers – 24.1.1948)
RECORD VICTORY: 7-0 (-v- Brechin City – Division 2, 6.2.1965)
RECORD DEFEAT: 1-11 (-v- Queen of the South – Scottish Cup 16.1.1932)

## SEASON TICKET INFORMATION

**Seated**
Adult ............................................................ £95
Juvenile/OAP .............................................. £55
**Standing**
Adult ............................................................ £80
Juvenile/OAP .............................................. £45

## LEAGUE ADMISSION PRICES

**Seated**
Adult ............................................................ £7.50
Juvenile/OAP .............................................. £4.50
**Standing**
Adult ............................................................ £6
Juvenile/OAP .............................................. £3

REGISTERED STRIP: Shirt – Royal Blue with White Trim
Shorts – White, Stockings – Royal Blue
CHANGE STRIP: Shirt – Red with 1" Black Stripes
Shorts – Black with Red Trim, Stockings – Black with Red Top

## CLUB FACTFILE 1993/94 .. RESULTS .. APPEARANCES .. SCORERS

### The BLUES

Player columns (left to right): Duffy B., McIntyre S., Hughes J., Millar G., Brannigan K., Gallagher A., Sloan T., Grant A., Duncan G., Cody S., Henderson D., Diver D., McLean P., Spittal J. I., Ferguson W., Brown J., Walker D., Johnston S., Ross S., Walker T., McCaffrey J., McCann J.

| Date | Venue | Opponents | Result | Du | Mc | Hu | Mi | Br | Ga | Sl | Gr | Dn | Co | He | Di | ML | Sp | Fe | Bn | WkD | Jo | Ro | WkT | McC | McCn |
|---|---|---|---|---|---|---|---|---|---|---|---|---|---|---|---|---|---|---|---|---|---|---|---|---|---|
| Aug 7 | H | Montrose | 2-4 | 1 | 2 | 3 | 4 | 5 | 6 | | 7 | 8 | 9 | 10 | 11¹ | 12¹ | 14 | | | | | | | | |
| 14 | A | Meadowbank Thistle | 3-1 | 1 | 2 | 3 | 6 | 5 | | 7¹ | 8 | 9 | 10 | 11 | 12² | 14 | 4 | | | | | | | | |
| 21 | A | Queen of the South | 1-0 | 1 | | 2 | 3 | 5 | | 7 | 8 | 6 | 10 | 11¹ | 9 | | 4 | | | | | | | | |
| 28 | H | Albion Rovers | 2-1 | 1 | 2 | 3 | 6 | 5 | | 7 | 8¹ | 9 | 10 | 11 | 12¹ | | 4 | 14 | | | | | | | |
| Sept 4 | H | Arbroath | 2-1 | 1 | 2 | 3 | 6 | 5 | | 7² | 8 | 9 | 10 | 11 | 12 | | 4 | | | | | | | | |
| 11 | A | Alloa | 0-1 | 1 | 2 | 3 | 6 | 5 | 9 | 7 | 8 | | 10 | 11 | | 14 | 4 | 12 | | | | | | | |
| 18 | A | Berwick Rangers | 0-1 | 1 | 2 | | | 5 | 6 | 7 | 8 | 9 | | 11 | | 10 | 4 | | 3 | 12 | | | | | |
| 25 | H | Cowdenbeath | 4-0 | 1 | | | 2 | 5 | | 7² | 8¹ | 9¹ | 10 | 11 | | 6 | 4 | 12 | 3 | 14 | | | | | |
| Oct 2 | A | Queen's Park | 0-0 | 1 | | | 2 | 5 | 14 | 7 | 8 | 9 | 10 | 11 | | 6 | 4 | | 3 | | | | | | |
| 9 | H | Stenhousemuir | 1-0 | 1 | | | 2 | 5¹ | 12 | 7 | 8 | 9 | 10 | 11 | | 6 | 4 | 14 | 3 | | | | | | |
| 16 | H | East Fife | 3-2 | 1 | 14 | | 2 | 5 | | 7¹ | 8¹ | 9 | 10 | 11¹ | | 6 | 4 | 12 | 3 | | | | | | |
| 23 | A | Arbroath | 1-0 | 1 | 14 | 3 | 2 | | 5 | 7 | 8¹ | 9 | 10 | 11 | | 6 | 4 | 12 | | | | | | | |
| 30 | A | East Stirlingshire | 2-2 | 1 | 14 | 3 | 2 | | 5 | 7¹ | 8 | 9 | 10¹ | 11 | | 6 | 4 | 12 | | | | | | | |
| Nov 6 | H | Meadowbank Thistle | 3-1 | 1 | 12 | | 2 | 5 | 10² | 7¹ | 8 | 3 | | 11 | | 6 | 4 | 9 | | | | | | | |
| 13 | H | Berwick Rangers | 3-0 | 1 | 3 | | 2 | 5 | 10 | 7² | 8 | 11¹ | | | | 6 | 4 | 9 | | | | | | | |
| 20 | A | Cowdenbeath | 2-1 | 1 | 3 | | 2 | 5 | 6¹ | | 8 | 10¹ | | 11 | | | 4 | 9 | 12 | | 7 | | | | |
| 30 | A | Stenhousemuir | 2-2 | 1 | 3¹ | | 2 | 5 | 6¹ | 7 | 8 | 9 | | 11 | | 10 | 4 | | | | | | | | |
| Dec 4 | H | Queen's Park | 2-0 | 1 | 3 | | 2 | 5 | 6 | 7¹ | 8¹ | 9 | | 11 | | | 4 | 12 | | 10 | | | | | |
| 27 | H | East Stirlingshire | 1-0 | | | 3 | 2 | | 5 | 7 | 8 | 6 | 10 | 11 | | | 4 | 9¹ | | | 1 | | | | |
| Jan 1 | H | Queen of the South | 1-2 | | | 14 | 3 | 2 | 5 | 6 | 7 | 8 | 9 | 10 | 11 | | 4 | 12¹ | | | 1 | | | | |
| 4 | A | Montrose | 2-0 | 15 | 4 | 3 | 2 | 5 | 6 | 7 | 8 | 9 | 10¹ | 11¹ | | | 12 | | | | 1 | | | | |
| 8 | A | Albion Rovers | 2-1 | 1 | 6¹ | 3 | 2 | 5 | | 7 | 8 | 9¹ | 10 | 11 | | 4 | | | | | | | | | |
| 25 | A | East Fife | 1-1 | 1 | | 3 | 2 | 5 | 6 | 7¹ | 8 | 9 | 10 | 11 | 4 | | | | | | | | | | |
| Feb 2 | H | Forfar Athletic | 2-0 | 1 | | 3 | 2 | 5 | 6 | 7² | 8 | 9 | | 11 | | 10 | 4 | 12 | | | | | | | |
| 5 | H | Alloa | 1-1 | 1 | | 3 | 2 | 5 | 6 | 7¹ | 8 | 9 | | 11 | | 10 | 4 | | | | | | | | |
| 12 | A | Arbroath | 0-0 | 1 | 8 | 3 | 2 | 5 | 6 | 7 | | 10 | | 11 | | 12 | 4 | 9 | | | | | | | |
| 22 | A | Berwick Rangers | 0-1 | 1 | 4 | | 2 | 5 | 6 | 7 | 8 | 9 | 10 | 11 | | 3 | | 12 | | | | | | | |
| 26 | H | Albion Rovers | 2-1 | | 3 | | 2 | 5 | 6 | 7 | | 8¹ | 10 | 11¹ | | | 4 | 12 | | | 1 | | 9 | | |
| Mar 5 | H | Queen of the South | 3-3 | | | 14 | 2 | 5 | 6 | 7 | | 3¹ | 10 | 11 | | 8¹ | 4 | 12 | | | 1 | | 9¹ | | |
| 12 | A | Meadowbank Thistle | 1-1 | 1 | 14 | | 2 | 5 | 6 | 7 | | 10 | 8 | 11¹ | | 3 | | 12 | | | | | 9 | 4 | |
| 19 | H | East Fife | 2-1 | 1 | 14 | 3 | 2 | 5 | 6 | 7 | | 10 | | | | 8 | 12 | 11² | | | | | 9 | 4 | |
| 26 | A | Alloa | 1-1 | 1 | 14 | 3 | 2 | 5 | 6 | 7 | | 10 | | | | 8 | | 11¹ | | | | | 9 | 4 | |
| Apr 2 | A | Queen's Park | 1-1 | 1 | | 3 | 2 | 5 | 6 | 7 | | 10 | 11 | | 14 | 12 | 8 | | | | | | 9¹ | 4 | |
| 13 | H | Montrose | 1-0 | 1 | | 3 | 2 | 5 | | 7 | 8 | 6 | 10¹ | 11 | | 12 | | | | | | | 9 | 4 | |
| 16 | H | Arbroath | 1-0 | 1 | | 3 | 2 | 5 | 14¹ | 7 | 8 | 6 | 10 | 11 | | 12 | | | | | | | 9 | 4 | |
| 23 | A | East Stirlingshire | 3-2 | | 3 | | | 5 | 6 | 7 | 8¹ | 12² | 10 | 11 | | 14 | 12 | | | | 1 | | 9 | 4 | |
| 30 | A | Forfar Athletic | 3-1 | | 3 | | | 5 | 6 | 7¹ | 8 | 2 | 10 | 11 | | 14 | 12 | | | | 1 | | 9² | 4 | |
| May 7 | H | Cowdenbeath | 2-0 | 15 | | 3 | 2 | 5 | | 7 | 8 | 6 | 10 | 11 | | | 12¹ | | | | 1 | | 9¹ | 4 | |
| 14 | H | Stenhousemuir | 0-1 | | | 3 | 2 | 5 | | 7 | 8 | 6 | 11 | | | 10 | 12 | | | | 1 | | 9 | 4 | 14 |
| **TOTAL FULL APPEARANCES** | | | | 30 | 16 | 24 | 36 | 36 | 26 | 38 | 32 | 35 | 29 | 35 | 1 | 20 | 25 | 8 | 5 | | 2 | | 9 | 12 | 10 |
| **TOTAL SUB APPEARANCES** | | | | | (2) | (8) | (1) | | (3) | | | | | | | (4) | (5) | (4)(21) | (1) | (2) | | | | (1) | |
| **TOTAL GOALS SCORED** | | | | | 2 | | | 1 | 5 | 16 | 6 | 8 | 3 | 6 | 4 | 1 | | 6 | | | | 5 | | |

*Small bold figures denote goalscorers. † denotes opponent's own goal.*

## STAIR PARK

**CAPACITY:** 5,000; Seated 700, Standing 4,300

**PITCH DIMENSIONS:** 110 yds x 70 yds

**FACILITIES FOR DISABLED SUPPORTERS:** By prior arrangement with Club Secretary.

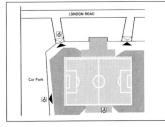

## HOW TO GET THERE

Stair Park can be reached by the following routes:

**TRAINS:** There is a regular service of trains from Ayr and the station is only 1 mile from the ground.

**BUSES:** Two services pass the park. These are the buses from Glenluce to Portroadie and the Dumfries-Stranraer service.

**CARS:** Car parking is available in the club car park at the ground, where there is space for approximately 50 vehicles and also in the side streets around the park. Signs for away supporters will be displayed and parking situated at Stranraer Academy, McMasters Road.

# Pressure for places

*Stranraer asserted their superiority at an early stage and throughout the season remained the driving force to win promotion for the first time in the history of the club.*

But the impending League reconstruction was a dominant force during the course of the 1993/94 season with clubs battling to be in the top six and remain outwith the new Third Division.

The increasing pressure was reflected in the play for at no stage throughout the long months was their a hint of an "easy" game as even one needlessly dropped point could prove crucial by the middle of May.

That pressure applied not only to the performances of the players on the field, but to the Managers, and was reflected in a rapid turnover. Indeed, for one reason or another, Arbroath, for example, began with former Celtic and Scotland defender Danny McGrain in charge, saw him leave to be replaced by the former Dunfermline manager Jocky Scott, and then he departed with Donald Park, who had earlier in the season left Meadowbank, moving in to take charge along with George Mackie as joint managers of

the Gayfield club. Ironically, Park had been superceded at Meadowbank by Mike Lawson, yet another former Arbroath manager.

But they were not the only clubs who saw a change in the occupant of their manager's chair! But more of that later!

Stranraer, however, dominated as they set the pace to win the League Championship and claim a place in the new First Division. Surely no-one could grudge them their moment of celebration after the heart-breaking events, a year previously, when they were first informed that they had been promoted, and then discovered that an incorrect scoreline had been flashed to them and they had been pipped on goal difference.

Manager, Alex McAnespie observed: "Following the bitter disappointment of a year ago, those associated with the club – players, officials and supporters – have shown resilience and character to battle through another long, hard season to achieve promotion.

"We have had to start from scratch at the beginning of the season, but I never doubted that we could achieve

our ambition.

"We have given an indication of the capabilities of the club not only in the League programme but when facing opposition from a higher division in cup matches, and we are looking forward to the challenge that lies ahead."

In any normal season there would have been only one other promotion place to play for with the majority of clubs idling until the end of the season. Not this time.

With Stranraer stepping into the new First Division, the next five clubs knew that they could find a place in the new Second Division leaving the others to remain in the new Third Division to meet the challenge of the Highland newcomers, Caledonian Thistle and Ross County.

The battle for these five places continued to the last minute of the final day. And, on that last day of the season, with only one place remaining to be settled, it would be either Alloa or East Fife who met at Recreation Park who would take it.

In the event it was the Methil club who earned the necessary one point under the astute leadership of experienced manager Alex Totten, who of course has now moved back into the big time as the new manager of Kilmarnock, while the Alloa manager, Billy Lamont, was left to bemoan the scoring chances missed throughout the season.

By then Berwick Rangers, who strengthened their backroom during the season with Jimmy Crease becoming general manager and Tom Hendrie taking over as team manager, had swept forward to clinch the second place in the division on 48 points, but that was eight points adrift of Stranraer.

Stenhousemuir were just a point behind, happy in the knowledge that manager Terry Christie had guided them out of the bottom division for the first time in their history.

The Larbert club just pipped Meadowbank, under manager Mike Lawson, for that place by goal difference for both were locked on 47 points. And it is an interesting sidelight that the Christie influence stretched over the three clubs for both Hendrie and Lawson had played under Christie during his previous lengthy tenure at Meadowbank.

Queen of the South, with the prolific scoring Andy Thomson correctly earning the award as the Second Division "Player of the Year", were also assured of a place in the top six before the end of the season. Despite the extra strain of changes at Boardroom level following an annual meeting of shareholders, the manager Billy McLaren, kept his players focussed firmly on what could be achieved on the field of play.

While these six had to be satisfied with their season's endeavours, there was disappointment for the remainder. Yet, even among those clubs, there were some notable performances.

Alloa lost out only on goal difference, East Stirlingshire were regenerated after the appointment of manager Billy Little, and both Forfar and Montrose failed narrowly.

Queen's Park, under their enthusiastic coach, Eddie Hunter, yet

*Stranraer skipper, Kenny Brannigan, holds aloft the Second Division trophy.*

again strived for perfection, and although they did not enjoy the amassing of a large points total, they had the quiet satisfaction of seeing one of their players, John O'Neill, move at the end of the season to Celtic with the opportunity of carving out a career in the game.

The three remaining clubs at the foot of the table were more noticeable for the change of managers than for their contribution on the field of play.

Arbroath had those switches already outlined, Albion Rovers said goodbye to Tommy Gemmell and welcomed their own player, Tom Spence, to the managerial chair.

Bottom club, Cowdenbeath, had a most peculiar season. Following the departure of manager, Andy Harrow, it was decided that the replacement would be John Reilly, then a player with neighbours East Fife. However, things did not go smoothly. Reilly had

to wait some weeks until his short-term contract at Methil had come to an end and even after that, the matter was the subject of a Compensation Tribunal when it was decided that the Methil club were not due financial compensation. But, after all those endeavours, there was to be no happy outcome. Reilly departed the scene before the end of the season to be replaced by the club's youth coach, Paddy Dolan.

All things considered, it was a very eventful and dramatic season, reflected by the increase in the number of fans watching Second Division matches last season and with two promotion places available from a ten club set-up in the new Third Division and Caledonian Thistle and Ross County bringing a fresh challenge from the Highlands, this season should witness a further rise in attendances in the bottom division.

**BILL MARWICK
(Freelance)**

*Stranraer's top goalscorer, Tommy Sloan, in action against Arbroath.*

# BERWICK RANGERS

Shielfield Park,
Shielfield Terrace, Tweedmouth,
Berwick Upon Tweed TD15 2EF

**CHAIRMAN**
Robert W. McDowell

**VICE-CHAIRMAN**
Thomas Davidson

**DIRECTORS**
John H. Hush
Peter McAskill
James M. S. Rose
Kenneth A. Rutherford
James G. Bell
Colin Walker F.C.C.A.
William M. McLaren
James Crease

**SECRETARY**
James Crease

**MANAGER**
Thomas Hendrie

**ASSISTANT MANAGER**
John Coughlin

**YOUTH COACH**
Warren Hawke

**HON. CLUB DOCTOR**
Dr. Frederick Wood
M.B.Ch.B., M.R.C.G.P.

**PHYSIOTHERAPIST**
Ian Oliver

**GROUNDSMAN**
Jim Simm

**COMMERCIAL MANAGER**
Conrad I. Turner
(0289) 307969

**TELEPHONES**
Ground/Ticket Office (0289) 307424
Sec. Home (0506) 843491
Sec. Bus. (0506) 36666
Information Service (0891) 800697

**CLUB SHOP**
Supporters Shop situated within
the ground. Open during first
team match days.

**OFFICIAL SUPPORTERS CLUB**
c/o Shielfield Park, Tweedmouth,
Berwick Upon Tweed TD15 2EF

**TEAM CAPTAIN**
Derek Bell

**SHIRT SPONSOR**
Allan Bros

## LIST OF PLAYERS 1994-95

| SURNAME | FIRST NAME | MIDDLE NAME | DATE OF BIRTH | PLACE OF BIRTH | DATE OF SIGNING | HEIGHT FT INS | WEIGHT ST LBS | PREVIOUS CLUB |
|---|---|---|---|---|---|---|---|---|
| Banks | Alan | | 25/02/70 | Edinburgh | 27/07/93 | 5 11.0 | 11 0 | Meadowbank Thistle |
| Bell | Derek | | 19/12/63 | Newcastle | 13/07/94 | 5 9.0 | 12 0 | Bishop Auckland |
| Clegg | Neil | | 03/01/77 | Berwick | 13/05/94 | 5 9.0 | 11 0 | Berwick H.S. |
| Cole | Anthony | Richard | 18/09/72 | Gateshead | 09/08/94 | 6 1.0 | 12 13 | Gateshead |
| Coughlin | John | Joseph | 11/04/63 | New York | 27/07/93 | 5 11.0 | 13 10 | Meadowbank Thistle |
| Cowan | Mark | | 16/01/71 | Edinburgh | 15/07/93 | 6 0.0 | 12 7 | Armadale Thistle |
| Cunningham | Craig | | 30/07/69 | Edinburgh | 03/08/92 | 6 0.0 | 11 10 | Newtongrange Star |
| Donaldson | Greig | William | 01/04/71 | Dunfermline | 30/03/94 | 5 10.0 | 12 0 | Rosyth Recreation |
| Forrester | Paul | | 03/11/72 | Edinburgh | 30/03/94 | 5 9.0 | 12 0 | Middlesbrough |
| Fraser | Graeme | William | 07/08/73 | Edinburgh | 31/03/94 | 5 11.0 | 11 8 | Dunfermline Athletic |
| Gallacher | John | Anthony | 26/01/69 | Glasgow | 26/08/94 | 5 9.0 | 10 12 | Falkirk |
| Graham | Thomas | Newlands | 25/08/65 | Edinburgh | 03/07/87 | 5 8.0 | 11 7 | Edina Hibs |
| Greenwood | Thomas | Paul | 22/05/75 | Newcastle | 13/07/94 | 6 0.0 | 11 7 | Seaham Red Star |
| Hall | Anthony | | 17/01/69 | Hartlepool | 05/08/92 | 6 1.0 | 12 4 | East Fife |
| Hawke | Warren | | 20/09/70 | Durham | 24/12/93 | 5 10.5 | 11 4 | Scarborough United |
| Irvine | William | | 28/12/63 | Stirling | 09/10/92 | 5 10.0 | 11 3 | Meadowbank Thistle |
| Kane | Kevin | | 30/12/69 | Edinburgh | 01/03/93 | 5 10.0 | 12 0 | Meadowbank Thistle |
| King | Thomas | Richard | 07/03/76 | St. Albans | 08/08/94 | 5 11.0 | 11 7 | "S" Form |
| Malone | Leslie | Andrew | 08/08/74 | Edinburgh | 30/03/94 | 5 8.0 | 9 6 | Rosyth Recreation |
| Neil | Martin | | 16/04/70 | Ashington | 31/03/93 | 5 8.0 | 11 7 | Dundee United |
| Osborne | Marc | Leslie | 05/08/72 | Broxburn | 23/03/94 | 6 3.0 | 11 10 | Pumpherston Juniors |
| Valentine | Craig | | 16/07/70 | Edinburgh | 03/08/92 | 5 8.0 | 11 0 | Easthouses B.C. |
| Watson | John | Martin | 13/02/59 | Edinburgh | 20/07/93 | 6 0.0 | 12 6 | Airdrieonians |
| Wilson | Mark | | 31/07/74 | Dechmont | 17/02/93 | 5 11.0 | 10 8 | Fauldhouse Utd B.C. |
| Young | Colin | | 09/08/76 | Berwick | 31/05/94 | 5 4.0 | 9 10 | Spittal Rovers |
| Young | Neil | Andrew | 14/10/67 | Beverley | 31/03/94 | 5 10.0 | 11 8 | Goole Town |

## MILESTONES

**YEAR OF FORMATION:** 1881
**MOST LEAGUE POINTS IN A SEASON:** 54 (Second Division – Season 1978/79)
**MOST LEAGUE GOALS SCORED BY A PLAYER IN A SEASON:** Ken Bowran (Season 1963/64)
**NO. OF GOALS SCORED:** 38
**RECORD ATTENDANCE:** 13,365 (-v- Rangers – 28.1.1967)
**RECORD VICTORY:** 8-1 (-v- Forfar Athletic – Division 2 25.12.1965)
**RECORD DEFEAT:** 1-9 (-v- Hamilton Academical – First Division 9.8.1980)

## SEASON TICKET INFORMATION

**Seated**
President's Box ............................................................ £200
Adult ................................................................................ £80
Youth/OAP ..................................................................... £40
(For Family Tickets add £20 per child under 14)
**Standing**
Adult ................................................................................ £60
Youth/O.A.P. ................................................................... £40

## LEAGUE ADMISSION PRICES

**Seated**
Adult .................................................................................. £5
Youth/Unemployed (with UB40) ........................... £2.50
Under 14 ............................................................................ £1
**Standing**
Adult .................................................................................. £4
Youth/Unemployed (with UB40) ........................... £2.50
Under 14 ............................................................................ £1

REGISTERED STRIP: Shirt – Gold with Black Collar and Shoulders
Shorts – Black with White Trim
Stockings – Black with White Hoops
CHANGE STRIP: Shirt – Red and White Vertical Stripes, Shorts – Red, Stockings – Red

## CLUB FACTFILE 1993/94 .. RESULTS .. APPEARANCES .. SCORERS

### The BORDERERS

Small bold figures denote goalscorers.  † denotes opponent's own goal.

| Date | Venue | Opponents | Result | O'Connor G. | Valentine C. | Banks A. | Hall A. | Cowan M. | Richardson S. | Wilson M. | Irvine W. | Cunningham C. | Scott D. | Graham T. | Kane K. | Tait A. | Gibson K. | Coughlin J. | Neil M. | Romaines S. | Gallacher S. | Sokoluk J. | Healer A. | King T. | Hawke W. | Boyle L. | Donaldson G. | Young K. | Kirkwood G. | Ceccarelli P. | Lawson O. | Osborne M. | Young N. | Forrester P. |
|---|---|---|---|---|---|---|---|---|---|---|---|---|---|---|---|---|---|---|---|---|---|---|---|---|---|---|---|---|---|---|---|---|---|---|
| Aug 7 | H | East Fife | 0-1 | 1 | 2 | 3 | 4 | 5 | 6 | 7 | 8 | 9 | 10 | 11 | 12 | | | | | | | | | | | | | | | | | | | | |
| 14 | A | East Stirlingshire | 1-2 | 6 | $3^1$ | 8 | 5 | | | 12 | 10 | 9 | 11 | 7 | 1 | 2 | 4 | | | | | | | | | | | | | | | | | | |
| 21 | A | Meadowbank Thistle | 1-1 | 1 | 2 | 3 | 8 | 5 | 6 | 14 | 10 | 12 | 9 | 7 | 11 | | | | $4^1$ | | | | | | | | | | | | | | | | |
| 28 | H | Arbroath | 2-0 | 1 | 2 | 3 | 8 | 5 | 6 | | | $10^1$ | 9 | 7 | $11^1$ | | | | 4 | | | | | | | | | | | | | | | | |
| Sep 4 | H | Albion Rovers | 1-1 | 1 | 2 | 3 | | 5 | 6 | 14 | 10 | 12 | 9 | 7 | 11 | | | | 4 | | | | | | | | | | | | | | | $8^1$ | |
| 11 | A | Cowdenbeath | 2-1 | 1 | 2 | 3 | | | 6 | 7 | $10^1$ | 14 | | $11^1$ | | | | 5 | 4 | | | | | | | | | | | | | | | 8 | 9 |
| 18 | H | Stranraer | 1-0 | 1 | 2 | 3 | | 5 | 6 | 10 | | $9^1$ | 12 | 11 | | | | 8 | 4 | | | | | | | | | | | | | | | 7 | |
| 25 | A | Forfar Athletic | 1-1 | 1 | 2 | 3 | | 5 | 6 | $10^1$ | | 9 | 14 | 11 | | | | 8 | 4 | | | | | | | | | | | | | | | 7 | |
| Oct 2 | A | Stenhousemuir | 1-2 | 1 | 2 | $3^1$ | 8 | 5 | 6 | | | 10 | | 9 | 11 | | | | 4 | | | | | 14 | 12 | | | | | | | | | 7 | |
| 9 | H | Queen's Park | †6-0 | 1 | 2 | 3 | 10 | $5^1$ | 6 | | 7 | $9^1$ | $12^1$ | $14$ | $11^2$ | | | | 4 | | | | | | | | | | | | | | | 8 | |
| 16 | H | Montrose | 3-3 | 1 | 2 | 3 | 8 | 5 | 6 | | 10 | 9 | 12 | $14^1$ | 11 | | | | 4 | | | | | | | | | | | | | | | $7^2$ | |
| 23 | A | Alloa | 0-1 | 1 | 2 | 3 | 10 | 5 | 6 | 11 | | 14 | 12 | | | 7 | 4 | 8 | 9 | | | | | | | | | | | | | | | | |
| 30 | A | Queen of the South | 5-2 | 1 | 2 | $3^1$ | $4^1$ | 5 | 6 | | | $10^1$ | | 9 | 7 | 11 | | $8^2$ | 12 | | | | | | | | | | | | | | | | |
| Nov 6 | H | East Stirlingshire | 2-2 | 1 | 2 | | 4 | 5 | 6 | $3^1$ | $10^1$ | 12 | 9 | 7 | 11 | | | | 8 | | | | | | | | | | | | | | | | |
| 13 | A | Stranraer | 0-3 | 1 | 2 | | 4 | 5 | 6 | 7 | 8 | 12 | 14 | 11 | 10 | | 3 | | 9 | | | | | | | | | | | | | | | | |
| 27 | A | Queen's Park | 0-0 | 1 | 3 | 14 | 4 | 5 | 6 | 12 | 7 | 9 | | 11 | 10 | | 2 | | 8 | | | | | | | | | | | | | | | | |
| 30 | A | Forfar Athletic | 0-2 | 1 | 4 | 3 | 8 | 5 | 6 | | 10 | | 9 | | | | 2 | 7 | | | | | | 14 | | | | | | | | | | | |
| Dec 4 | H | Stenhousemuir | 2-1 | 1 | 6 | 3 | 4 | 5 | | 10 | $7^2$ | 12 | 11 | | | | 2 | 8 | | | | | | 14 | 9 | | | | | | | | | | |
| 18 | A | East Fife | 1-1 | 1 | 4 | 3 | 6 | 5 | | 7 | | 9 | $12^1$ | 10 | 11 | | 2 | 8 | | | | | | 14 | | | | | | | | | | | |
| Jan 11 | H | Meadowbank Thistle | 2-2 | 1 | 4 | 3 | | 5 | | $6^1$ | | 7 | 11 | | 12 | | 8 | | | | | | | 14 | $9^1$ | 2 | 10 | | | | | | | | |
| 18 | H | Queen of the South | 1-2 | 1 | 4 | 3 | 8 | 5 | | 10 | | 14 | 11 | | 7 | | 6 | | | | | | | $9^1$ | 2 | 12 | | | | | | | | | |
| 22 | A | Montrose | 3-2 | 1 | 4 | $3^1$ | | 5 | 14 | 6 | $10^1$ | 11 | | 7 | | $8^1$ | | | | | | | | 9 | 2 | | | | | | | | | | * |
| 26 | A | Arbroath | 4-0 | 1 | 4 | 3 | | $5^1$ | 14 | 6 | 10 | $11^1$ | | 8 | | | | | | | | | | $9^2$ | 2 | | 7 | | | | | | | | |
| Feb 1 | H | Alloa | 1-1 | 1 | 4 | 3 | 14 | 5 | | 6 | 10 | 11 | 12 | 8 | | | | | | | | | | $9^1$ | 2 | | 7 | | | | | | | | |
| 5 | H | Cowdenbeath | 3-2 | 1 | 4 | 3 | 7 | $5^1$ | | 6 | $10^2$ | 14 | 11 | | 2 | 8 | | | | | | | | 9 | | | | | | | | 12 | | | |
| 12 | A | Albion Rovers | 2-0 | 1 | 4 | 3 | 7 | 5 | | $6^1$ | 10 | 14 | 11 | | 2 | 8 | | | | | | | | 9 | | | | | | | | $12^1$ | | | |
| 22 | A | Stranraer | 1-0 | 1 | 4 | 3 | 7 | 5 | | 6 | $9^1$ | 11 | | | | 10 | | | | | | | | | | | | | | | | | | | |
| Mar 1 | A | Queen's Park | 3-1 | | 4 | 3 | 7 | 5 | | 6 | 10 | 12 | $11^1$ | | 2 | 8 | | | | | | | | $9^2$ | | | 14 | | | | | 1 | | | |
| 5 | H | East Fife | 1-3 | | 4 | 3 | 7 | 5 | | 6 | 10 | 14 | 11 | | 2 | $8^1$ | | | | | | | | 9 | | | 12 | | | | | 1 | | | |
| 12 | A | Montrose | 1-3 | | 4 | 3 | | 5 | | 6 | 10 | 12 | $11^1$ | | 2 | 8 | | | | | | | | 9 | 14 | | 7 | | | | | 1 | | | |
| 19 | H | Alloa | 1-1 | | 4 | 3 | 12 | 5 | | 6 | 10 | 14 | 11 | | 7 | 8 | | | 2 | | | | | $9^1$ | | | | | | | | 1 | | | |
| 26 | A | Cowdenbeath | 5-1 | | 4 | 3 | 8 | 5 | | 6 | $10^3$ | $12^1$ | $11^1$ | | 2 | | | | | | | | | 9 | | | 7 | | | | | 1 | | | |
| Apr 2 | A | Queen of the South | 0-0 | | 4 | 3 | 12 | 5 | 14 | 6 | 10 | 11 | | | 2 | 8 | | | | | | | | 9 | | | 7 | | | | | 1 | | | |
| 9 | H | Forfar Athletic | 2-2 | | 4 | $3^1$ | 7 | 5 | | 6 | 10 | 11 | | | 2 | 8 | | | | | | | | $9^1$ | | | 12 | | | | | 1 | | | |
| 16 | H | Albion Rovers | 3-0 | | 4 | 3 | 8 | 5 | | 6 | 10 | $11^2$ | | | 2 | | | | | | | | | 9 | | | $7^1$ | | | | | 1 | | 14 | |
| 23 | A | Meadowbank Thistle | 2-1 | | 4 | 3 | 8 | 5 | | 6 | 10 | $11^1$ | | | 2 | | | | | | | | | 9 | | | 7 | | | | | 1 | | $14^1$ | |
| 30 | H | Stenhousemuir | 3-0 | | 4 | 3 | 8 | 5 | | 6 | 10 | 11 | | | 2 | | | | | | | | | $9^2$ | | | 7 | | | | | 1 | 15 | $14^1$ | |
| May 7 | A | East Stirlingshire | 3-1 | | 4 | $3^1$ | $8^1$ | 5 | 12 | 6 | 10 | 11 | | | 2 | | | | | | | | | 9 | | | 14 | | | | | 1 | | | $7^1$ |
| 14 | H | Arbroath | 5-0 | | 4 | 3 | 8 | | $5^1$ | 12 | 6 | $10^2$ | | 11 | | 2 | | | | | | | | | $9^2$ | | | 14 | | | | | 1 | | | 7 |
| **TOTAL FULL APPEARANCES** | | | | 26 | 39 | 36 | 28 | 37 | 17 | 23 | 37 | 7 | 11 | 14 | 34 | 1 | 22 | 11 | 28 | 4 | 2 | 1 | 1 | 20 | 6 | 1 | 9 | 1 | 1 | 1 | 6 | 3 | 2 | |
| **TOTAL SUB APPEARANCES** | | | | | (1) | (3) | | (5) | (3) | (1) | (6) | (7) | (11) | (2) | | | (1) | | | (2) | (1) | | (4) | | (1) | (1) | (7) | | | | (1) | (3) | | |
| **TOTAL GOALS SCORED** | | | | | 6 | 2 | 4 | | | 2 | 15 | 4 | 3 | 2 | 10 | | 1 | | 7 | | | | | 12 | | | 3 | | | | | | | 3 |

---

## SHIELFIELD PARK

**CAPACITY**: 4,131; Seated 2,765, Standing 1,366

**PITCH DIMENSIONS**: 112 yds x 76 yds

**FACILITIES FOR DISABLED SUPPORTERS**: Supporters should enter via gate adjacent to ground turnstiles (see ground plan).

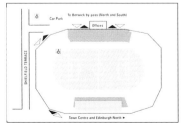

## HOW TO GET THERE

Shielfield Park can be reached by the following routes:

The ground is approximately 1.5 miles from the town centre (South) and is situated in Shielfield Terrace, Tweedmouth.

**BUSES:** The local bus route from the railway station is the Spittal/Highcliffe service and the nearest stop to the ground is Mountroad. The park is about a mile from this stop and is signposted. Buses bound for Prior Park also pass the ground (The latter service is from the town centre).

**TRAINS:** The only railway station is Berwick, which is situated on the East Coast line and a frequent service operates at various stages during the day. From just outside the station, fans can board the Spittal bus service which will then take them near the ground (see above).

**CARS:** There is a large car park at the rear of the ground. (Nominal charge).

# BRECHIN CITY

Glebe Park, Trinity Road,
Brechin, Angus DD9 6BJ

**CHAIRMAN**
Hugh A. Campbell Adamson

**VICE-CHAIRMAN**
David H. Birse

**HONORARY PRESIDENT**
Ricardo Gallaccio

**DIRECTORS**
David H. Will
George C. Johnston
William C. Robertson
Martin Smith
I. Michael Holland
Kenneth W. Ferguson

**SECRETARY**
George C. Johnston

**MANAGER**
John Young

**ASSISTANT MANAGER**

**CLUB DOCTOR**
Dr. R. W. Y. Martin

**PHYSIOTHERAPIST**
Tom Gilmartin

**CHIEF SCOUT**
Frank McGinnis

**GROUNDSMAN**
Alex Laing

**TELEPHONES**
Ground (0356) 622856
Sec. Home (0356) 622942
Sec. Bus. (0356) 624941
Sec. Bus. Fax (0356) 625371
Sec. Home Fax (0356) 622942

**CLUB SHOP**
Glebe Park, Brechin, Angus DD9 6BJ
Open during home match days

**OFFICIAL SUPPORTERS CLUB**
c/o Glebe Park, Brechin,
Angus DD9 6BJ

**TEAM CAPTAIN**
Bobby Brown

**SHIRT SPONSOR**
Ferguson Oliver

## LIST OF PLAYERS 1994-95

| SURNAME | FIRST NAME | MIDDLE NAME | DATE OF BIRTH | PLACE OF BIRTH | DATE OF SIGNING | HEIGHT FT INS | WEIGHT ST LBS | PREVIOUS CLUB |
|---------|-----------|-------------|---------------|----------------|-----------------|---------------|---------------|---------------|
| Baillie | Richard | Ketchen | 06/06/68 | Dunfermline | 24/11/89 | 5 5.5 | 10 0 | Cowdenbeath |
| Balfour | Derek | Alun | 16/02/72 | Arbroath | 15/03/94 | 6 0.0 | 12 2 | Arbroath Sporting Club |
| Bell | Stuart | Angus | 07/02/69 | Dundee | 04/08/93 | 5 9.0 | 10 5 | Dundee North End |
| Brand | Ralph | | 17/07/70 | Dundee | 10/08/91 | 5 9.0 | 10 3 | Lochee United |
| Brown | Robert | | 11/11/59 | Lincoln | 10/01/85 | 5 10.0 | 11 4 | Dundee North End |
| Cairney | Henry | | 01/09/61 | Holytown | 12/02/92 | 5 7.0 | 10 8 | Stenhousemuir |
| Christie | Graeme | | 01/01/71 | Dundee | 04/08/93 | 6 1.0 | 11 0 | Carnoustie Panmure |
| Conway | Francis | Joseph | 29/12/69 | Dundee | 25/11/89 | 5 11.0 | 11 4 | Lochee Harp |
| Feroz | Craig | | 24/10/77 | Aberdeen | 16/08/94 | 5 8.0 | 10 7 | Glentannar Kyle |
| Kemlo | Scott | Hall | 08/07/74 | Dundee | 31/03/94 | 5 10.0 | 11 0 | Dundee North End |
| Lawrie | David | Ernest | 09/04/65 | Aberdeen | 09/08/94 | 5 11.0 | 11 3 | Aberdeen |
| Marr | Sinclair | McLeod | 21/11/72 | Edinburgh | 05/07/94 | 5 8.0 | 10 10 | St. Andrews United |
| McKellar | James | Robert | 29/12/76 | Bellshill | 26/07/94 | 5 6.0 | 10 4 | Arbroath Lads Club |
| McNeill | William | John | 12/03/67 | Toronto | 05/03/93 | 5 9.0 | 11 0 | Meadowbank Thistle |
| Millar | Marc | | 10/04/69 | Dundee | 20/12/91 | 5 9.0 | 10 12 | Riverside Athletic |
| Nicolson | Keith | Derek | 16/07/68 | Perth | 03/08/91 | 6 1.0 | 12 9 | St. Johnstone |
| Petrie | Paul | Alexander B. | 19/08/76 | Salisbury | 26/07/94 | 5 6.0 | 10 4 | Douglas Lads Club |
| Scott | Walter | Douglas | 01/01/64 | Dundee | 25/05/94 | 5 9.0 | 10 7 | Dundee |
| Smith | Greig | Robert | 26/03/76 | Aberdeen | 26/07/94 | 5 9.0 | 10 12 | Aberdeen Lads Club |
| Vannett | Richard | Alexander | 20/01/73 | Dundee | 03/09/93 | 5 8.0 | 10 12 | Kinnoull |

## MILESTONES

**YEAR OF FORMATION:** 1906
**MOST LEAGUE POINTS IN A SEASON:** 55 (Second Division – Season 1982/83)
**MOST LEAGUE GOALS SCORED BY A PLAYER IN A SEASON:** W. McIntosh (Season 1959/60)
**NO. OF GOALS SCORED:** 26
**RECORD ATTENDANCE:** 8,122 (-v- Aberdeen – 3.2.1973)
**RECORD VICTORY:** 12-1 (-v- Thornhill – Scottish Cup 28.1.1926)
**RECORD DEFEAT:** 0-10 (Airdrieonians, Albion Rovers and Cowdenbeath – Division 2, 1937/38)

## SEASON TICKET INFORMATION

**Seated**
Adult .................................................................. £100
Parent/Juvenile (Under 12) (Family Section) ........... £110
OAP ..................................................................... £55
**Standing or Seated Enclosure**
Adult ................................................................... £90
Parent/Juvenile (Under 12) (Family Section) ........... £100
Juvenile ............................................................... £45

## LEAGUE ADMISSION PRICES

**Seated**
Adult ..................................................................... £7
Juvenile/OAP ....................................................... £4.50
**Enclosure**
Adult ...................................................................... £5
Juvenile/OAP ....................................................... £2.50
**Standing**
Adult ...................................................................... £5
Juvenile/OAP ....................................................... £2.50

**REGISTERED STRIP:** Shirt – Red with White Collar and Cuffs
Shorts – Red with White Stripe, Stockings – Red with Blue and White Stripe on Top
**CHANGE STRIP:** Shirt – White with Red and Blue Flash on Shoulder and Blue Collar
Shorts – White with Red Stripe, Stockings – White with Red and Blue Stripe at Top

## The CITY

Player columns (left to right): Allan R., Kopel S., Baillie R., Brown R., Conway F., Redford I., Lees G., Hutt G., Ross A., Miller M., Brand R., O'Brien P., Bell S., Cairney H., McNeill W., Scott W. D., McLaren P., Lorimer R., Alexander B., Vannett R., Greig L., Christie G., Nicolson K., Gray B., Balfour D., Fisher D., Kemlo S.

| Date | Venue | Opponents | Result | Allan | Kopel | Baillie | Brown | Conway | Redford | Lees | Hutt | Ross | Miller | Brand | O'Brien | Bell | Cairney | McNeill | Scott | McLaren | Lorimer | Alex. | Vannett | Greig | Christie | Nicolson | Gray | Balfour | Fisher | Kemlo |
|---|---|---|---|---|---|---|---|---|---|---|---|---|---|---|---|---|---|---|---|---|---|---|---|---|---|---|---|---|---|---|
| Aug 7 | H | Hamilton Academical | 1-2 | 1 | 2 | 3 | 4 | 5 | 6 | 7 | 8 | 9 | 10[1] | 11 | 12 | | 14 | | | | | | | | | | | | | |
| 14 | A | Airdrieonians | 0-1 | 1 | 2 | | 4 | 5 | 6 | 11 | 8 | 9 | 10 | | | | | 7 | 3 | 12 | | | | | | | | | | |
| 21 | H | Dunfermline Athletic | 1-0 | 1 | 2 | | 4 | 5 | 6 | | | 9 | 10[1] | 11 | 8 | | | | 12 | 3 | 7 | | | | | | | | | |
| 28 | A | Greenock Morton | 1-2 | 1 | 2 | | 4 | 5 | 6 | | 8 | 9 | 10[1] | 11 | 7 | | | | 12 | 3 | | | | | | | | | | |
| Sep 4 | H | Stirling Albion | 1-2 | 1 | | | 4 | 5 | 6 | 12 | | 9[1] | 10 | 11 | 8 | | 2 | | 3 | 7 | | | | | | | | | | |
| 11 | H | Ayr United | 0-2 | 1 | | | 4 | 5 | 6 | 14 | 3 | 9 | 10 | 11 | 8 | 7 | 2 | | | | | | | | | | | | | |
| 14 | A | Dumbarton | 0-1 | 1 | | | 4 | 5 | 6 | | 8 | 9 | 10 | 11 | 7 | 2 | 12 | 3 | | | | | | | | | | | | |
| 18 | H | Clydebank | 1-0 | 1 | | | 4 | 5 | 11[1] | 8 | 6 | 9 | 10 | | | | 2 | 14 | 3 | 7 | | | | | | | | | | |
| 25 | A | Clyde | 1-1 | 1 | | | 4 | 5 | 11[1] | 8 | | 9 | 10 | | | | 2 | 12 | 3 | 7 | 6 | | | | | | | | | |
| 28 | A | St. Mirren | 0-2 | 1 | | | 4 | 5 | 11 | | | 9 | 10 | 8 | | | 2 | 14 | 3 | 7 | 6 | 15 | | | | | | | | |
| Oct 2 | H | Falkirk | 0-0 | | | | 4 | 5 | 9 | 8 | 6 | | 10 | | | | 2 | 11 | 3 | 7 | 1 | | | | | | | | | |
| 9 | A | Hamilton Academical | 0-5 | | | | 4 | 5 | 11 | 8 | 6 | | 10 | 9 | | | 2 | 14 | 3 | | 1 | 7 | 12 | | | | | | | |
| 16 | A | Dumbarton | 0-3 | | | | 4 | 5 | 9 | 8 | 6 | | 10 | 14 | 2 | 11 | 3 | 1 | 7 | | | | | | | | | | | |
| 23 | A | Ayr United | 0-1 | | | | | 2 | 11 | | | | 10 | 6 | 8 | 3 | 1 | 7 | 9 | 4 | 5 | | | | | | | | | |
| 30 | A | Dunfermline Athletic | 0-4 | | | | 4 | 2 | 9 | 12 | 10 | 8 | | 6 | 1 | 7 | 11 | 3 | 5 | | | | | | | | | | | |
| Nov 6 | H | Greenock Morton | 0-3 | | | | 6 | 3 | 9 | 10 | 11 | 2 | | 7 | 1 | 8 | 4 | 5 | | | | | | | | | | | | |
| 9 | A | Stirling Albion | 1-2 | | | | 4[1] | 8 | 3 | 9 | | 11 | 2 | 10 | 7 | 1 | 6 | 5 | | | | | | | | | | | | |
| 13 | A | Falkirk | 0-2 | | | | 4 | 8 | 3 | 9 | | 11 | 2 | 10 | 7 | 1 | 6 | 5 | | | | | | | | | | | | |
| 20 | H | St. Mirren | 1-4 | | | | 4 | 8[1] | 12 | 9 | | 11 | 2 | 14 | 3 | 1 | 7 | 10 | 6 | 5 | | | | | | | | | | |
| 30 | A | Clyde | 4-2 | | | | 4 | 2 | 8 | 9 | 10 | 11[2] | 3[1] | 1 | 7 | 5[1] | 6 | | | | | | | | | | | | | |
| Dec 4 | H | Clydebank | 2-3 | | | | 4 | 8 | 9 | 10[1] | 2 | 11[1] | 3 | 1 | 7 | 6 | 5 | | | | | | | | | | | | | |
| 11 | H | Airdrieonians | 0-2 | | | | 4 | 6 | 8 | 9 | 10 | 12 | 2 | 11 | 3 | 1 | 7 | 5 | | | | | | | | | | | | |
| 18 | A | Dumbarton | 1-3 | 1 | | | 4 | 3 | 8 | 9 | 11 | 10[1] | 2 | 6 | 7 | 14 | 5 | | | | | | | | | | | | | |
| Jan 4 | H | Dunfermline Athletic | 0-1 | 1 | | | 4 | 2 | 8 | 9 | 10 | 11 | 12 | 6 | 7 | 3 | 5 | 14 | | | | | | | | | | | | |
| 8 | A | Greenock Morton | 1-1 | 1 | | | 4 | 2 | 8 | 12 | 10[1] | 9 | 11 | 6 | 7 | 3 | 5 | | | | | | | | | | | | | |
| 11 | H | Hamilton Academical | 0-0 | 1 | | | 4 | 2 | 8 | 9 | 10 | 11 | 7 | 6 | 14 | 3 | 5 | | | | | | | | | | | | | |
| 15 | H | Stirling Albion | 2-0 | 1 | | | 4 | 2 | 8 | 10[1] | 9 | 7[1] | 6 | 12 | 3 | 5 | 11 | | | | | | | | | | | | | |
| 22 | H | Airdrieonians | 1-0 | 1 | | | 4[1] | 2 | 8 | 10 | 9 | 11 | 6 | 7 | 3 | 5 | | | | | | | | | | | | | | |
| Feb 5 | A | Ayr United | 1-4 | 1 | | | 4 | 2 | 8 | 10[1] | 9 | 11 | 6 | 7 | 3 | 5 | | | | | | | | | | | | | | |
| 12 | H | Falkirk | 0-2 | 1 | | | 4 | 2 | 8 | 10 | 9 | 12 | 11 | 6 | 7 | 3 | 5 | | | | | | | | | | | | | |
| 26 | A | St. Mirren | 1-1 | 1 | | | 4 | 5 | 8[1] | 14 | 10 | 9 | 2 | 11 | 6 | 7 | 3 | | | | | | | | | | | | | |
| Mar 5 | H | Clydebank | 0-1 | | | | 4 | 5 | 8 | 10 | 9 | 2 | 11 | 6 | 7 | 1 | 12 | 3 | 14 | | | | | | | | | | | |
| 12 | A | Clyde | 0-1 | | | | 4 | 8 | 9 | 11 | 2 | 10 | 3 | 5 | 7 | 14 | 1 | 6 | | | | | | | | | | | | |
| 19 | A | Dumbarton | 0-0 | | | | 4 | 8 | 9 | 11 | 12 | 2 | 6 | 5 | 7 | 3 | 1 | 10 | | | | | | | | | | | | |
| 26 | A | Hamilton Academical | 1-9 | | | | 4 | 8 | 9 | 10[1] | 14 | 2 | 6 | 5 | 7 | 3 | 1 | 11 | 12 | | | | | | | | | | | |
| 29 | H | Airdrieonians | 0-2 | | | | 8 | 9 | 10 | 11 | 7 | 6 | 4 | 3 | 2 | 1 | 5 | | | | | | | | | | | | | |
| Apr 2 | A | Ayr United | 0-0 | | | | 4 | 6 | 9 | 10 | 11 | 2 | 5 | 8 | 7 | 3 | 1 | | | | | | | | | | | | | |
| 9 | A | Falkirk | 2-4 | | | | 4 | 2 | 6 | 9 | 10 | 11 | 7[1] | 3 | 8[1] | 1 | 5 | | | | | | | | | | | | | |
| 16 | H | St. Mirren | 0-1 | | | | 4 | 6 | 9 | 10 | 7 | 5 | 2 | 3 | 8 | 11 | 1 | | | | | | | | | | | | | |
| 23 | A | Clydebank | 1-2 | | | | 2 | 6 | 9 | 11 | 12 | 7 | 5 | 4 | 14 | 8 | 3[1] | 10 | 1 | | | | | | | | | | | |
| 26 | H | Clyde | 0-1 | | | | 14 | 2 | 12 | 9 | 10 | 7 | 4 | 6 | 5 | 8 | 3 | 11 | 1 | | | | | | | | | | | |
| 30 | A | Dunfermline Athletic | 1-2 | | | | 4[1] | 9 | 11 | 10 | 12 | 8 | 6 | 7 | 3 | 5 | 1 | 2 | | | | | | | | | | | | |
| May 7 | H | Greenock Morton | 1-2 | | | | 6 | 14 | 9[1] | 11 | 4 | 8 | 10 | 2 | 7 | 3 | 5 | 1 | | | | | | | | | | | | |
| 14 | A | Stirling Albion | 3-0 | | | | 4 | 8 | 14 | 10[2] | 9[1] | 2 | 11 | 6 | 7 | 12 | 5 | 1 | 3 | | | | | | | | | | | |
| **TOTAL FULL APPEARANCES** | | | | 19 | 4 | 1 | 38 | 35 | 40 | 7 | 10 | 31 | 39 | 25 | 10 | 7 | 28 | 19 | 33 | 24 | 4 | 13 | 24 | 3 | 26 | 24 | 1 | 12 | 3 | 4 |
| **TOTAL SUB APPEARANCES** | | | | | (1) | | (3) | (2) | | (4) | | (1) | (4) | (3) | | (11) | | (2) | (1) | (1) | (1) | (2) | | (3) | | (1) | | | | |
| **TOTAL GOALS SCORED** | | | | | | | 3 | 1 | 3 | | | 2 | 10 | 4 | | | | 2 | 1 | | | | | 1 | | 2 | 1 | | |

*Small bold figures denote goalscorers. † denotes opponent's own goal.*

---

## GLEBE PARK

**CAPACITY:** 3,960; Seated 1,519, Standing 2,441

**PITCH DIMENSIONS:** 110 yds x 67 yds

**FACILITIES FOR DISABLED SUPPORTERS:** Section of Terracing designated for disabled supporters.

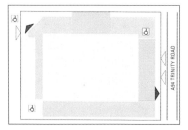

A94 TRINITY ROAD

## HOW TO GET THERE

The following routes may be used to reach Glebe Park:

**TRAINS:** The nearest railway station is Montrose, which is eight miles away. There is a regular Inter-City service from all parts of the country and fans alighting at Montrose can then catch a connecting bus service to Brechin.

**BUSES:** Brechin bus station is only a few hundred yards from the ground and buses on the Aberdeen-Dundee and Montrose-Edzell routes stop here.

**CARS:** Car parking is available in the Brechin City car park, which is capable of holding 50 vehicles. There are also a number of side streets which may be used for this purpose.

# CLYDE

Broadwood Stadium,
Cumbernauld G68 9NE

**CHAIRMAN**
John F. McBeth, F.R.I.C.S.

**VICE-CHAIRMAN**
William B. Carmichael

**DIRECTORS**
J. Sean Fallon
Robert B. Jack, M.A.,LL.B.
Harry McCall, B.A., C.Eng., M.I.C.E.
John D. Taylor, A.I.B
Gerard W. Dunn

**SECRETARY**
John D. Taylor, A.I.B.

**MANAGER**
Alexander N. Smith

**ASSISTANT MANAGER**
John Brownlie

**COACHES**
Gardner Speirs and Gordon Wylde

**CLUB DOCTOR**
John A. MacLean

**PHYSIOTHERAPIST**
John Watson

**S.F.A. COMMUNITY COACH**
Bill Munro

**CHIEF SCOUTS**
George Peebles & George Rankin

**COMMERCIAL MANAGER**
John Donnelly
(0236) 451511

**TELEPHONES**
Ground (0236) 451511
Fax (0236) 733490

**CLUB SHOP**
Situated at Ground

**OFFICIAL SUPPORTERS CLUB**
180 Main Street, Rutherglen

**TEAM CAPTAIN**
Keith Knox

**SHIRT SPONSOR**
OKI

## LIST OF PLAYERS 1994-95

| SURNAME | FIRST NAME | MIDDLE NAME | DATE OF BIRTH | PLACE OF BIRTH | DATE OF SIGNING | HEIGHT FT INS | WEIGHT ST LBS | PREVIOUS CLUB |
|---|---|---|---|---|---|---|---|---|
| Angus | Ian | Allan | 19/11/61 | Glasgow | 02/08/94 | 5 10.0 | 10 3 | Motherwell |
| Brown | James | | 21/10/74 | Bellshill | 09/07/93 | 6 0.0 | 10 0 | Rangers |
| Clark | Martin | John | 13/10/68 | Holytown | 22/01/94 | 5 9.0 | 11 4 | Partick Thistle |
| Dickson | John | | 23/12/69 | Glasgow | 07/08/92 | 5 5.0 | 9 7 | Clydebank |
| Falconer | Marc | | 04/11/72 | Glasgow | 27/06/94 | 5 10.0 | 11 2 | Campsie Black Watch |
| Frater | Alan | | 29/10/75 | Paisley | 24/06/94 | 5 7.0 | 10 8 | Gleniffer Thistle |
| Fridge | Leslie | Francis | 27/08/68 | Inverness | 11/08/93 | 5 11.0 | 11 10 | St. Mirren |
| Halpin | Michael | Christopher | 04/09/75 | East Kilbride | 19/07/94 | 6 0.0 | 11 3 | Oldham B.C. |
| Hillcoat | John | | 16/12/70 | East Kilbride | 31/03/94 | 5 11.0 | 10 10 | Dunfermline Athletic |
| Knox | Keith | | 06/08/64 | Stranraer | 16/03/88 | 5 10.0 | 12 2 | Stranraer |
| MacKenzie | Alan | | 08/08/66 | Edinburgh | 03/12/93 | 5 8.0 | 9 2 | Raith Rovers |
| McAulay | John | | 28/04/72 | Glasgow | 27/07/90 | 5 9.0 | 11 7 | Clyde B.C. |
| McCarron | James | | 31/01/71 | Glasgow | 29/07/92 | 5 6.0 | 9 12 | Aberdeen |
| McCheyne | Graeme | | 21/12/73 | Bellshill | 29/07/92 | 6 1.0 | 11 3 | Dundee United |
| McConnell | Ian | Paul | 06/01/75 | Glasgow | 04/10/93 | 6 1.0 | 12 8 | Derry City |
| McFarlane | Ross | | 06/12/61 | Glasgow | 30/06/83 | 5 8.0 | 12 0 | Queen's Park |
| McGill | Daniel | | 07/07/71 | Paisley | 26/02/93 | 5 8.0 | 10 9 | St. Mirren |
| McGregor | Allan | | 17/10/75 | Glasgow | 19/08/94 | 5 9.0 | 11 2 | Clydebank |
| Muir | Jack | | 08/02/75 | Hamilton | 14/10/93 | 5 10.0 | 10 10 | Dunipace Juniors |
| Neill | Alan | John | 13/12/70 | Baillieston | 15/02/93 | 6 1.0 | 12 7 | Bathgate Juniors |
| Nisbet | Iain | | 11/05/74 | Bellshill | 15/08/94 | 5 9.0 | 10 2 | Aberdeen |
| O'Neill | Martin | | 17/06/75 | Glasgow | 08/06/93 | 5 7.5 | 10 10 | Clyde B.C. |
| Parks | Gordon | John | 19/11/72 | Glasgow | 18/08/92 | 5 9.5 | 10 7 | Shettleston Juniors |
| Prunty | James | | 21/09/74 | Bellshill | 08/06/93 | 5 8.5 | 10 8 | Clyde B.C. |
| Ronald | Paul | | 19/07/71 | Glasgow | 24/07/91 | 6 1.0 | 11 12 | Campsie Black Watch |
| Smith | James | Richard | 13/07/73 | Stirling | 18/08/92 | 5 5.0 | 10 9 | St. Johnstone |
| Strain | Barry | | 04/08/71 | Glasgow | 18/08/92 | 5 11.0 | 12 7 | Greenock Morton |
| Tennant | Stephen | | 22/10/66 | Bellshill | 09/08/91 | 5 8.0 | 11 7 | Stirling Albion |
| Thomson | James | | 15/05/71 | Stirling | 09/08/91 | 6 1.0 | 12 7 | Campsie Black Watch |
| Tierney | Paul | | 08/09/72 | Bellshill | 06/09/91 | 5 7.0 | 10 7 | Anvil Amateurs |
| Watson | Graham | | 10/09/70 | St. Andrews | 03/06/94 | 5 9.5 | 11 6 | Aberdeen |
| Wright | Andrew | Matthew | 21/12/73 | Baillieston | 11/08/93 | 5 9.0 | 11 0 | Heart of Midlothian |
| Wylde | Gordon | Thomas | 12/11/64 | Glasgow | 17/08/94 | 5 9.0 | 12 12 | Queen of the South |

## MILESTONES

**YEAR OF FORMATION:** 1878
**MOST CAPPED PLAYER:** Tommy Ring
**NO. OF CAPS:** 12
**MOST LEAGUE POINTS IN A SEASON:** 64 (Division 2 – Season 1956/57)
**MOST LEAGUE GOALS SCORED BY A PLAYER IN A SEASON:** Bill Boyd (Season 1932/33)
**NO. OF GOALS SCORED:** 32
**RECORD ATTENDANCE:** 52,000 (-v- Rangers – 21.11.1908)
**RECORD VICTORY:** 11-1 (-v- Cowdenbeath – Division 2. 6.10.1951)
**RECORD DEFEAT:** 0-11 (-v- Dumbarton and Rangers – Scottish Cup)

## SEASON TICKET INFORMATION

Seated
Adult ........................................................... £100
Juvenile/OAP ............................................... £55

## LEAGUE ADMISSION PRICES

Seated
Adult ........................................................... £6
Juvenile/OAP ............................................... £3
Parent and Juvenile ..................................... £8

REGISTERED STRIP: Shirt – White with Black and Red Facings, with White, Black and Red Striped Sleeves
Shorts – Black with Red and Black Leg Band
Stockings – Black with Red and White Stripe
CHANGE STRIP: Shirt – Jade and Purple with Purple Collar
Shorts – Purple with White and Purple Leg Band, Stockings – Jade

## CLUB FACTFILE 1993/94 .. RESULTS .. APPEARANCES .. SCORERS

### The BULLY WEE

Player columns (left to right): Howie S., McFarlane R., Tennant S., Knox K., Thomson J., Neill A., Ronald P., Bell D., Sludden J., Clarke S., McCarron J., McAulay J., Quinn N., Fridge L., Morrison S., McCheyne G., Dickson J., McGill D., Strain B., Parks G., Wylde G., McConnell I., Mackenzie A., Brown J., Wright A., Clark M., O'Neill M., Tierney P., Hillcoat J.

| Date | Venue | Opponents | Result |
|---|---|---|---|
| Aug 7 | H | Greenock Morton | †2-1 |
| 14 | A | Dumbarton | 0-3 |
| 21 | H | Ayr United | 0-1 |
| 28 | A | Clydebank | 1-2 |
| Sep 4 | A | Dunfermline Athletic | 0-2 |
| 11 | H | Hamilton Academical | 2-0 |
| 14 | A | Airdrieonians | 1-2 |
| 18 | A | St. Mirren | 1-2 |
| 25 | A | Brechin City | 1-1 |
| 29 | H | Falkirk | 1-0 |
| Oct 2 | H | Stirling Albion | 3-0 |
| 9 | A | Greenock Morton | 1-1 |
| 16 | H | Airdrieonians | 0-2 |
| 23 | A | Hamilton Academical | 0-2 |
| 30 | A | Ayr United | 0-1 |
| Nov 6 | H | Clydebank | 1-1 |
| 9 | A | Dunfermline Athletic | 0-4 |
| 13 | A | Stirling Albion | 1-1 |
| 23 | H | Falkirk | 0-2 |
| 30 | A | Brechin City | 2-4 |
| Dec 4 | H | St. Mirren | 0-1 |
| 11 | H | Dumbarton | 2-1 |
| 18 | A | Airdrieonians | 2-3 |
| Jan 8 | A | Clydebank | 2-0 |
| 11 | A | Ayr United | 0-0 |
| 22 | A | Dumbarton | 1-1 |
| Feb 5 | H | Hamilton Academical | 0-2 |
| 12 | H | Stirling Albion | 0-0 |
| 19 | A | Dunfermline Athletic | 0-1 |
| 22 | H | Greenock Morton | 0-0 |
| Mar 1 | A | Falkirk | 0-2 |
| 5 | A | St. Mirren | 0-0 |
| 12 | H | Brechin City | 1-0 |
| 19 | H | Airdrieonians | 0-1 |
| 26 | A | Greenock Morton | 0-2 |
| 29 | H | Dumbarton | 1-2 |
| Apr 2 | A | Hamilton Academical | 1-2 |
| 9 | A | Stirling Albion | 1-0 |
| 16 | H | Falkirk | 1-1 |
| 23 | H | St. Mirren | 3-0 |
| 26 | A | Brechin City | 1-0 |
| 30 | A | Ayr United | 1-1 |
| May 7 | H | Clydebank | 1-1 |
| 14 | A | Dunfermline Athletic | 0-5 |

TOTAL FULL APPEARANCES: 1 34 30 44 35 36 9 13 16 16 26 21 3 42 13 23 8 4 19 19 6 23 18 1 2 12 8 1 1

TOTAL SUB APPEARANCES: (1) (3) (5) (5) (1) (5) (6)(10) (7) (1) (4)(12) (6) (9) (3) (3) (1) (1) (1) (1)

TOTAL GOALS SCORED: 2 1 3 4 2 2 1 1 1 2 3 5 5 1 1

*Small bold figures denote goalscorers. † denotes opponent's own goal.*

## BROADWOOD STADIUM

**CAPACITY:** 6,203 (All Seated)

**PITCH DIMENSIONS:** 112 yds x 76 yds

**FACILITIES FOR DISABLED SUPPORTERS:** Facilities available in both Home and Away Stands.

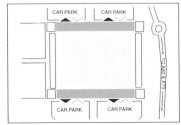

## HOW TO GET THERE

The Following routes may be used to reach Broadwood Stadium:

**BUSES:** From Buchanan Street Bus Station, Glasgow Bus No. 36A (Glasgow to Westfield).

**TRAINS:** From Queen Street Station, Glasgow to Croy Station. The Stadium is a 15 minute walk from here.

**CARS:** From Glasgow City Centre via Stepps By Pass joining A80 towards Stirling. Take Broadwood turn-off to Stadium.

# DUMBARTON

**LIST OF PLAYERS 1994-95**

| SURNAME | FIRST NAME | MIDDLE NAME | DATE OF BIRTH | PLACE OF BIRTH | DATE OF SIGNING | HEIGHT FT INS | WEIGHT ST LBS | PREVIOUS CLUB |
|---|---|---|---|---|---|---|---|---|
| Boyd | John | Robertson | 01/01/69 | Greenock | 14/11/89 | 6 0.0 | 11 2 | Greenock Juniors |
| Campbell | Calum | | 07/11/65 | Erskine | 11/02/94 | 6 1.0 | 12 0 | Kilmarnock |
| Fabiani | Roland | | 24/11/71 | Greenock | 20/08/93 | 5 11.0 | 10 2 | St. Mirren |
| Farrell | Gerard | | 14/06/75 | Glasgow | 17/12/93 | 5 8.0 | 10 10 | Unattached |
| Foster | Alan | | 10/03/71 | Glasgow | 20/02/91 | 5 8.0 | 10 8 | Kilsyth Rangers |
| Gibson | Charles | | 12/06/61 | Dumbarton | 09/06/89 | 5 10.0 | 10 10 | Stirling Albion |
| Gow | Stephen | | 06/12/68 | Dumbarton | 23/07/87 | 6 0.0 | 11 1 | Dumbarton United |
| MacFarlane | Ian | | 05/12/68 | Bellshill | 12/07/91 | 6 1.0 | 12 7 | Hamilton Academical |
| MacLeod | Murdo | Davidson | 24/09/58 | Glasgow | 07/07/93 | 5 9.0 | 12 4 | Hibernian |
| Marsland | James | | 28/08/68 | Dumbarton | 15/06/90 | 5 8.0 | 10 12 | Kilpatrick Juveniles |
| Martin | Paul | John | 08/03/65 | Bellshill | 30/01/91 | 5 11.5 | 11 0 | Hamilton Academical |
| McConville | Robert | | 22/08/64 | Bellshill | 07/09/91 | 5 8.5 | 10 8 | Stirling Albion |
| McGarvey | Martin | | 16/01/72 | Glasgow | 20/02/91 | 5 8.0 | 11 0 | Irvine Meadow |
| Meechan | James | | 14/10/63 | Alexandria | 05/10/90 | 5 9.0 | 11 7 | Irvine Meadow |
| Meechan | Kenneth | | 16/02/72 | Greenock | 31/03/94 | 6 0.0 | 12 8 | Greenock Juniors |
| Melvin | Martin | | 07/08/69 | Glasgow | 22/12/90 | 5 11.0 | 11 6 | Falkirk |
| Mooney | Martin | James | 25/09/70 | Alexandria | 24/09/92 | 5 7.5 | 9 11 | Falkirk |
| Ward | Hugh | | 09/03/70 | Dumbarton | 05/11/93 | 5 8.0 | 9 12 | Greenock Juniors |

## MILESTONES

**YEAR OF FORMATION:** 1872
**MOST CAPPED PLAYERS:** J. Lindsay and J. McAulay
**NO. OF CAPS:** 8 each
**MOST LEAGUE POINTS IN A SEASON:** 53 (First Division – Season 1986/87)
**MOST LEAGUE GOALS SCORED BY A PLAYER IN A SEASON:** Kenneth Wilson (Season 1971/72)
**NO. OF GOALS SCORED:** 38
**RECORD ATTENDANCE:** 18,001 (-v- Raith Rovers – 2.3.1957)
**RECORD VICTORY:** 13-2 (-v- Kirkintilloch – Scottish Cup)
**RECORD DEFEAT:** 1-11 (-v- Ayr United and Albion Rovers)

## SEASON TICKET INFORMATION

**Seated**
**President's Club**
Adult .................................................................£200
Juvenile/O.A.P. ...............................................£155
**Stand**
Adult .................................................................£105
Juvenile/O.A.P. .................................................£65
**Standing**
Adult ...................................................................£70
Juvenile/O.A.P. .................................................£30

## LEAGUE ADMISSION PRICES

**Seated**
Adult ...............................................................£6.50
Juvenile/OAP ......................................................£5
**Standing**
Adult ....................................................................£5
Juvenile/OAP ...................................................£2.50

REGISTERED STRIP: Shirt – Gold with Black Pattern and Cuffs
Shorts – Black, Stockings – Gold
CHANGE STRIP: Shirt – Navy Blue with White Pattern and Cuffs
Shorts – White, Stockings – White

# CLUB FACTFILE 1993/94 . . RESULTS . . APPEARANCES . . SCORERS

## The SONS

Players (left to right): MacFarlane I., Marsland J., Foster A., Melvin M., Meechan J., MacLeod M., Mooney M., McGarvey M., McQuade I., Gibson C., Boyd J., McAnenay M., Docherty R., Gow S., McConville R., Martin P., Fabiani R., MacDonald J., Nelson M., Walker T., Wilson T., Gilmour J., Campbell C., Cunnington E., Ward H., Meechan K., Farrell G.

| Date | Venue | Opponents | Result | Line-ups (shirt numbers, bold = goalscorers) |
|------|-------|-----------|--------|-----------------------------------------------|
| Aug 7 | A | Stirling Albion | 0-2 | 1 2 3 4 5 6 7 8 9 10 11 12 14 |
| 14 | H | Clyde | 3-0 | 1 _ 3 4 2 6 7 _ 9 10² 11¹ _ 5 8 |
| 21 | H | Clydebank | 2-4 | 1 _ 3 4 2¹ 6 7 14 9 10¹ 11 _ 5 8 |
| 28 | A | Ayr United | 1-0 | 1 2 3 4 7 6 9¹ 14 _ 10 12 _ 8 5 11 |
| Sep 4 | H | Hamilton Academical | 0-0 | 1 2 3 4 7 6 9 14 _ 10 11 _ 8 5 |
| 11 | A | St. Mirren | 3-0 | 1 2 14 4 7 6 9² _ 10¹ 3 _ 8 5 11 |
| 14 | H | Brechin City | 1-0 | 1 2 11 4 _ 6 9 7 _ 10 3 _ 8¹ 5 14 |
| 18 | H | Falkirk | 0-1 | 1 2 _ 4 7 6 9 14 _ 10 3 _ 8 5 11 12 |
| 25 | A | Greenock Morton | 1-3 | 1 2 6 4 7 _ 12 8¹ _ 10 3 _ 14 5 11 9 |
| 28 | H | Airdrieonians | 0-1 | 1 2 4 _ 14 6 7 8 _ 10 3 _ 5 11 9 12 |
| Oct 2 | A | Dunfermline Athletic | 1-4 | 1 2 8 4¹ _ 6 9 7 _ 10 3 _ 14 5 11 |
| 9 | H | Stirling Albion | 1-2 | 1 2 3¹ 4 14 6 7 10 _ 9 _ 8 5 12 _ 11 |
| 16 | A | Brechin City | 3-0 | 1 2 11¹ 4 _ 6 7¹ _ 9 _ 8 5 3 14¹ 10 |
| 23 | H | St. Mirren | 3-3 | 1 2 11 4 _ 6 7 12¹ 9 _ 8¹ 5 3 10¹ |
| 30 | A | Clydebank | 1-2 | 1 2 3 4 _ 6 7 11 _ 9 _ 8 5 12 10¹ |
| Nov 6 | H | Ayr United | 1-1 | 1 2 _ 4 _ 6 7 14 9¹ _ 8 11 5 3 10 |
| 10 | A | Hamilton Academical | 0-2 | 1 2 14 4 5 6 7 12 9 _ 8 11 3 10 |
| 13 | H | Dunfermline Athletic | 1-5 | 1 2 3 4 5 _ 7 6 9¹ _ 8 11 14 10 |
| 20 | A | Airdrieonians | 1-0 | 1 5¹ 11 4 _ 6 7 14 9 _ 8 3 12 2 |
| 27 | H | Greenock Morton | 2-0 | 1 5 11 4 _ 6 7 10¹ 9¹ _ 8 3 2 |
| Dec 4 | A | Falkirk | 1-1 | 1 5 11 4 12 6 7¹ 10 9 _ 8 3 14 2 |
| 11 | A | Clyde | 1-2 | 1 5 11 4 12 6 7¹ 10 9 _ 8 3 14 2 |
| 18 | H | Brechin City | 3-1 | 1 5 11 4¹ 8 6 7² 10 9 _ 3 2 12 |
| Jan 8 | A | Ayr United | 1-1 | 1 5 _ 4 11¹ 6 7 10 9 _ 8 3 2 14 |
| 11 | H | Stirling Albion | 0-0 | 1 5 _ 4 8 6 7 10 9 _ 3 14 2 11 |
| 15 | H | Hamilton Academical | 0-1 | 1 5 _ 4 12 6 7 10 9 11 8 3 2 14 |
| 18 | H | Clydebank | 2-2 | 1 5 _ 4¹ 8 6 7 10 9¹ _ 11 3 2 |
| 22 | H | Clyde | 1-1 | 1 12 _ 4 11 6 7 10 9¹ _ 5 8 3 2 14 |
| Feb 5 | A | St. Mirren | 3-0 | 1 5 11 4 8¹ 6 7 10 9¹ 14¹ 3 2 |
| 12 | A | Dunfermline Athletic | 2-3 | 1 5 11 4 8¹ 6 7 10 9¹ 14 3 2 12 |
| Mar 1 | H | Airdrieonians | 0-0 | 1 2 11 4 5 6 7 10 9 _ 3 8 |
| 5 | H | Falkirk | 0-1 | 1 14 12 4 5 6 7 10 9 _ 3 2 8 11 |
| 12 | A | Greenock Morton | 0-0 | 1 _ 12 4 5 6 7 10 9 _ 3 2 8 11 |
| 19 | A | Brechin City | 0-0 | 1 10 14 4 5 6 7 12 9 _ 3 2 8 11 |
| 26 | H | Stirling Albion | 0-0 | _ _ _ 4 5 6 7 _ 9 _ 10 3 2 8 11 14 |
| 29 | A | Clyde | 2-1 | 1 12 _ 4 5 6¹ 7 _ 9 _ 10 3 2 8 11 14¹ |
| Apr 2 | H | St. Mirren | 2-3 | 1 12 _ _ 5 6 7¹ _ 9¹ _ 4 3 2 8 11 10 |
| 12 | H | Dunfermline Athletic | 0-2 | 1 10 _ _ 4 5 6 7 _ 9 _ 14 3 2 8 11 12 |
| 16 | A | Airdrieonians | 1-1 | 1 _ 2 _ 4¹ 5 6 7 _ 9 _ 12 3 _ 14 8 10 11 1 |
| 23 | A | Falkirk | 0-4 | 1 _ 2 _ 4 5 6 7 _ 9 _ 12 14 3 _ 8 10 11 |
| 26 | H | Greenock Morton | 2-0 | 1 _ _ _ 4 5 6 _ 7 9¹ _ 2 3 _ 8 10¹ 11 |
| 30 | A | Clydebank | 0-2 | 1 _ _ _ 4 5 6 14 7 9 _ 2 3 _ 8 10 11 |
| May 7 | H | Ayr United | 1-1 | 1 _ _ _ 4 5 6 7 8 9 _ 2 3 _ 10¹ 11 |
| 14 | A | Hamilton Academical | 1-2 | 1 _ _ _ 4 5 6 7 8 _ 2 3 _ 14 10¹ 11 12 |

| | MacFarlane | Marsland | Foster | Melvin | Meechan J. | MacLeod | Mooney | McGarvey | McQuade | Gibson | Boyd | McAnenay | Docherty | Gow | McConville | Martin | Fabiani | MacDonald | Nelson | Walker | Wilson | Gilmour | Campbell | Cunnington | Ward | Meechan K. | Farrell |
|---|---|---|---|---|---|---|---|---|---|---|---|---|---|---|---|---|---|---|---|---|---|---|---|---|---|---|---|
| TOTAL FULL APPEARANCES | 43 | 32 | 22 | 42 | 31 | 42 | 41 | 27 | 3 | 44 | 11 | | 12 | 19 | 17 | 36 | 3 | | 6 | 19 | 1 | 12 | 13 | 7 | 1 | | |
| TOTAL SUB APPEARANCES | | (4) | (5) | | (5) | | (2) | (8) | | | (3) | (1) | (1) | (2) | (2) | (2) | (3) | (3) | (3) | (2) | | (5) | (2) | | (3) | | (1) |
| TOTAL GOALS SCORED | | 1 | 2 | 4 | 4 | | 1 | 9 | 3 | | 13 | 2 | | 1 | 1 | | | 2 | | 1 | | | 3 | 1 | | | |

*Small bold figures denote goalscorers. † denotes opponent's own goal.*

## BOGHEAD PARK

CAPACITY: 7,033; Seated 303, Standing 6,730

PITCH DIMENSIONS: 110 yds x 68 yds

FACILITIES FOR DISABLED SUPPORTERS: Wheelchairs are accommodated on the track.

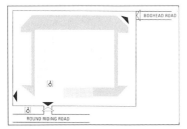

## HOW TO GET THERE

Boghead Park can be reached by the following routes:

TRAINS: The train service from Glasgow Queen Street and Glasgow Central Low Level both pass through Dumbarton East Station and Dumbarton Central Station both of which are situated just under a ten minute walk from the ground.

BUSES: There are two main services which pass close to the ground. These are bound for Helensburgh and Balloch from Glasgow.

CARS: Car Parking is available in side streets around the ground. Supporters buses should park on Dumbarton Common.

# EAST FIFE

**Bayview Park, Wellesley Road, Methil, Fife KY8 3AG**

**CHAIRMAN**
James W. Baxter

**VICE-CHAIRMAN**
Stephen Baxter

**DIRECTORS**
John Fleming
James Taylor
Julian S. Danskin

**SECRETARY**
William McPhee

**PLAYER/MANAGER**
Steven Archibald

**ASSISTANT MANAGER**

**COACH**
David Gorman

**CLUB DOCTOR**
Dr. William McCrossan

**PHYSIOTHERAPIST**
Ian Cardle

**CHIEF SCOUT**
Frank Donnelly

**GROUNDSMEN**
Alex Doig & James Hay

**COMMERCIAL DEPARTMENT**
(0333) 426323

**TELEPHONES**
Ground (0333) 426323/426376
Fax (0333) 426376

**CLUB SHOP**
A Supporters Club Shop is situated within the Ground

**OFFICIAL SUPPORTERS CLUB**
J. Tindal, 62 Harcourt Road, Kirkcaldy
Tel (0592) 642775

**TEAM CAPTAIN**
Alan Sneddon

**SHIRT SPONSOR**
Andrew Forrester, Leven

## LIST OF PLAYERS 1994-95

| SURNAME | FIRST NAME | MIDDLE NAME | DATE OF BIRTH | PLACE OF BIRTH | DATE OF SIGNING | HEIGHT FT INS | WEIGHT ST LBS | PREVIOUS CLUB |
|---|---|---|---|---|---|---|---|---|
| Allan | Gilbert | Chapman | 21/02/73 | St. Andrews | 16/11/93 | 6 0.0 | 9 7 | Anstruther Colts |
| Andrew | Benjamin | | 05/02/73 | Perth | 20/08/90 | 5 8.0 | 9 6 | Lochore Welfare |
| Archibald | Steven | | 27/09/56 | Glasgow | 24/08/94 | 5 10.5 | 11 7 | Clyde |
| Barron | Douglas | | 25/10/61 | Edinburgh | 31/03/93 | 5 11.0 | 10 0 | Clydebank |
| Beaton | David | Robert | 08/08/67 | Bridge of Allan | 24/11/90 | 5 11.0 | 11 4 | Falkirk |
| Bell | Graham | | 29/03/71 | St. Andrews | 12/08/87 | 5 10.0 | 11 0 | St. Andrews |
| Burns | William | | 10/12/69 | Motherwell | 07/08/91 | 5 10.0 | 11 7 | Rochdale |
| Charles | Raymond | | 17/06/61 | Leicester | 21/03/87 | 6 0.0 | 11 7 | Montrose |
| Cusick | John | James | 16/01/75 | Kirkcaldy | 18/03/94 | 5 8.0 | 10 0 | Dundonald Bluebell |
| Dow | Colin | John | 17/08/71 | Kirkcaldy | 09/02/94 | 5 9.0 | 10 7 | Hill of Beath Hawthorn |
| Gibb | Richard | | 22/04/65 | Bangour | 17/09/93 | 5 7.0 | 11 0 | Armadale Thistle |
| Hildersley | Ronald | | 06/04/65 | Kirkcaldy | 17/09/93 | 5 5.0 | 10 7 | Halifax Town |
| Hope | Douglas | | 14/06/71 | Edinburgh | 15/08/88 | 5 8.0 | 11 0 | Hutchison Vale B.C. |
| Hunter | Paul | | 30/08/68 | Kirkcaldy | 28/07/94 | 5 9.0 | 10 7 | Cowdenbeath |
| Irvine | Alan | James | 29/11/62 | Broxburn | 12/08/93 | 6 2.0 | 14 5 | Portadown |
| Logan | Paul | Michael | 13/06/76 | Sheffield | 29/07/94 | 5 11.0 | 11 4 | Bonnybridge Juniors |
| Long | Derek | | 20/08/74 | Broxburn | 31/03/93 | 5 10.0 | 12 0 | Newburgh Juniors |
| Scott | Robert | | 13/01/64 | Bathgate | 19/07/90 | 5 9.0 | 11 2 | Colchester United |
| Sneddon | Alan | | 12/03/58 | Baillieston | 27/07/93 | 5 11.0 | 12 3 | Motherwell |
| Taylor | Paul | Henry | 02/12/70 | Falkirk | 19/10/89 | 5 10.0 | 11 7 | Sauchie Juniors |
| Williamson | Andrew | | 04/09/69 | Kirkcaldy | 10/07/93 | 6 0.0 | 11 0 | Dunfermline Athletic |
| Wilson | Ewan | | 01/10/68 | Dunfermline | 15/04/93 | 6 2.0 | 12 0 | Strathmilgo United |

## MILESTONES

**YEAR OF FORMATION:** 1903
**MOST CAPPED PLAYER:** George Aitken
**NO. OF CAPS:** 5
**MOST LEAGUE POINTS IN A SEASON:** 57 (Division 2 – Season 1929/30)
**MOST LEAGUE GOALS SCORED BY A PLAYER IN A SEASON:** Henry Morris (Season 1947/48)
**NO. OF GOALS SCORED:** 41
**RECORD ATTENDANCE:** 22,515 (-v- Raith Rovers – 2.1.1950)
**RECORD VICTORY:** 13-2 (-v- Edinburgh City – Division 2, 11.12.1937)
**RECORD DEFEAT:** 0-9 (-v- Heart of Midlothian – Division 1, 5.10.1957)

## SEASON TICKET INFORMATION

**Seated**
Adult ..................................................... £95
Juvenile/OAP ........................................ £55
**Standing**
Adult ..................................................... £85
Juvenile/OAP ........................................ £45

## LEAGUE ADMISSION PRICES

**Seated**
Adult .......................................................... £6
Juvenile/OAP ......................................... £3.50
**Standing**
Adult .......................................................... £5
Juvenile/OAP ......................................... £2.50

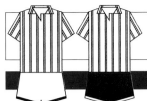

| | |
|---|---|
| **REGISTERED STRIP:** | Shirt – Amber with Black Vertical Stripe with White Pinstripe |
| | Shorts – Amber with Black Edgings |
| | Stockings – Amber with 3 Black Stripes on Top |
| **CHANGE STRIP:** | Shirt – White with Black Vertical Stripe with Amber Pinstripe, Shorts – Black with |
| | White Side Panel with Black/Amber Stripe, Stockings – Black with Amber Turnover |

## CLUB FACTFILE 1993/94 .. RESULTS .. APPEARANCES .. SCORERS

### The FIFERS

| Date | Venue | Opponents | Result | Wilson E. | Sneddon A. | Williamson A. | Barron D. | Beaton D. | Allan G. | Elliott D. | Beedie S. | Scott R. | Reilly J. | McBride J. | Taylor P. | Andrew B. | Irvine A. | Gowrie R. | Gibb R. | Hildersley R. | Charles R. | Bell G. | Burns W. | Yardley M. | Jackson S. | Hope D. | Logan P. | Dow C. | Cusick J. | Long D. |
|---|---|---|---|---|---|---|---|---|---|---|---|---|---|---|---|---|---|---|---|---|---|---|---|---|---|---|---|---|---|---|
| Aug 7 | A | Berwick Rangers | 1-0 | 1 | 2 | 3 | 4 | 5 | 6 | 7 | 8 | 9 | 10[1] | 11 | 12 | 14 | | | | | | | | | | | | | | |
| 14 | H | Stenhousemuir | †3-0 | 1 | 2 | 3 | 4 | 5 | | 7 | 8 | 9[1] | 10 | | 6 | | 11[1] | | | | | | | | | | | | | |
| 21 | A | Cowdenbeath | 2-1 | 1 | 2 | 3 | 4 | 5 | | 7 | 8 | 9[1] | 10[1] | | 6 | | 11 | 12 | | | | | | | | | | | | |
| 28 | H | Alloa | 4-1 | 1 | 2 | 3 | 4 | 5[1] | | 7 | 8 | 9[2] | 10[1] | 14 | 6 | | 11 | 12 | | | | | | | | | | | | |
| Sep 4 | H | Queen of the South | 0-2 | 1 | 2 | 3 | 4 | 5 | | 7 | 8 | 9 | 10 | 14 | 6 | | 11 | | | | | | | | | | | | | |
| 11 | A | Meadowbank Thistle | 0-1 | 1 | 2 | 3 | 4 | 5 | | 7 | 8 | 9 | 10 | 14 | 6 | 12 | 11 | | | | | | | | | | | | | |
| 18 | A | Queen's Park | 2-4 | 1 | 2 | 11[1] | 4 | 5 | | 7 | 6 | 9 | 14[1] | | 12 | | 10 | | | 3 | 8 | | | | | | | | | |
| 25 | H | East Stirlingshire | 0-1 | 1 | 2 | 3 | 4 | 5 | | | 8 | 14 | 10 | | 6 | | 9 | 11 | | 12 | 7 | | | | | | | | | |
| Oct 2 | H | Forfar Athletic | 3-2 | | 2 | 6[1] | 4 | 5 | | 7 | | 10 | 9[1] | | | | 11[1] | | | 3 | 8 | 1 | 12 | | | | | | | |
| 9 | A | Montrose | 1-0 | | | 6 | 4 | 5 | | 7 | | 10 | 9 | | | | 14[1] | 11 | | 3 | 12 | 1 | 2 | 8 | | | | | | |
| 16 | A | Stranraer | 2-3 | | 12 | 6[1] | 4 | 5 | | 7 | | 10 | 9 | | | | 11[1] | 14 | | 3 | | 1 | 2 | 8 | | | | | | |
| 23 | H | Albion Rovers | 1-1 | | 2 | 6 | | 5 | | 7 | | 10 | 12 | | | | 11 | 14 | | 3 | 8 | 1 | 4[1] | 9 | | | | | | |
| 30 | H | Arbroath | 1-0 | 15 | 2 | 3 | | 5 | | 7 | | 10 | 9[1] | | 12 | | 6 | 11 | | 8 | | 1 | 4 | | | | | | | |
| Nov 6 | A | Stenhousemuir | 1-0 | 1 | 2 | | | 5 | | 7 | | 10 | 9[1] | | 12 | 6 | 14 | 11 | | 3 | 8 | | 4 | | | | | | | |
| 13 | H | Queen's Park | 5-5 | 1 | 2 | 3 | 4 | 5 | | 7[1] | | 10 | 9[1] | | 14[1] | 6 | | 11[1] | | 8[1] | | | | | | | | | | |
| 20 | A | East Stirlingshire | 1-2 | 1 | 2[1] | 3 | | 5 | | 7 | | 6 | 9 | | 11 | 12 | 10 | 14 | | 8 | | | 4 | | | | | | | |
| 27 | A | Montrose | 5-2 | 1 | 2 | 3 | 12 | 5 | | | 10 | | 11 | | 6[1] | 7[2] | 9[2] | | | 8 | | | 4 | 14 | | | | | | |
| Dec 4 | A | Forfar Athletic | 0-1 | | 2 | 3 | | 5 | | 7 | | 10 | 14 | | 6 | 11 | 9 | | | 8 | | 1 | 4 | | | | | | | |
| 18 | H | Berwick Rangers | 1-1 | | 2 | 3 | | 5 | | 7 | | 6 | 9[1] | | 12 | 11 | 14 | | | 8 | | 1 | 4 | | | 10 | | | | |
| 29 | A | Arbroath | 2-3 | | 2 | 3 | 12 | 5[1] | | 7 | | 6 | 9 | | | 11 | 14[1] | | | 8 | | 1 | 4 | | | 10 | | | | |
| Jan 11 | H | Cowdenbeath | †2-0 | | 2 | 3 | 4 | 5[1] | | | 6 | | 11 | | | 9 | 10 | | | 1 | 7 | 8 | 12 | | | | | | | |
| 18 | A | Alloa | 2-2 | | | 3 | 4 | 5 | | 7 | 6 | | 11 | 14 | | 9[2] | 10 | 12 | | 1 | 2 | 8 | | | | | | | | |
| 25 | H | Stranraer | 1-1 | | | 3 | 4 | 5 | | 7 | 6 | | 11 | | | 9[1] | 10 | | | 1 | 2 | 8 | | | | 14 | | | | |
| 29 | A | Albion Rovers | 1-1 | | | 3 | 4 | 5 | | | 6 | | 11[1] | | 7 | 9 | 10 | | | 1 | 2 | 8 | | | 12 | 14 | | | | |
| Feb 5 | H | Meadowbank Thistle | 0-2 | | | 3 | 4 | 5 | | | 6 | 14 | 11 | | 7 | 9 | 10 | 12 | | 1 | 2 | 8 | | | | | | | | |
| 12 | H | Queen of the South | 0-0 | | 2 | 3 | | 5 | | 7 | | 14 | | | | 4 | 8 | 9 | | 10 | 1 | 12 | 6 | 11 | | | | | | |
| 19 | A | Montrose | 0-3 | | 2 | 3 | | 5 | | | | 9 | | | 7 | 10 | 12 | 8 | | 1 | 4 | 6 | 11 | | | 14 | | | | |
| 26 | H | Forfar Athletic | 1-1 | | 2 | 10 | | 5[1] | | 7 | | 9 | | | 4 | 14 | 3 | 8 | | 1 | 6 | | 12 | 11 | | | | | | |
| Mar 5 | A | Berwick Rangers | 3-1 | 1 | 2 | 3 | | 5 | | 7[1] | | 9 | | | | | | 8 | | 4 | 6 | | 10[1] | 11[1] | | | | | | |
| 12 | A | Queen's Park | 1-0 | 1 | 2 | 3 | | 5 | | 7 | | 9 | | | | 14[1] | | 8 | | 4 | 6 | | 10 | 11 | | | | | | |
| 19 | A | Stranraer | 1-2 | 1 | 2 | 3 | | 5 | | 7 | | | | | | 14 | 9 | 12 | | 8 | 4 | | 6[1] | 10 | | 11 | | | | |
| 26 | H | East Stirlingshire | 1-0 | 1 | 2 | 3 | | 5 | | 7 | | | | | | 11 | 14 | 12 | | 8 | 4[1] | | 10 | 9 | 6 | | | | | |
| Apr 2 | H | Albion Rovers | 3-1 | 1 | 2 | 3 | | 5 | 14[1] | | | 9[1] | | | | 11 | | 10 | | 4 | 6 | | 8[1] | 7 | | | | | | |
| 9 | A | Meadowbank Thistle | 2-2 | 1 | 2 | 3[1] | | 5 | | 7[1] | | 9 | | | | 11 | 14 | 10 | | 4 | 6 | | 8 | | | 12 | | | | |
| 16 | H | Queen of the South | 0-1 | 1 | 2 | 3 | | 5 | | 7 | | 9 | | | | 11 | 14 | 10 | 12 | 4 | 6 | | 8 | | | | | | | |
| 23 | A | Cowdenbeath | 2-1 | | 2 | | | 5 | 12 | | | 9 | | | | 3 | 8[1] | 1 | 4[1] | 6 | | 10 | 11 | 7 | | | | | | |
| 30 | H | Arbroath | 1-2 | | 2 | | 4 | 5 | 7 | | | 9 | | | | 14 | | 8 | 1 | 6 | | 10 | 11 | 3[1] | 12 | | | | | |
| May 7 | A | Stenhousemuir | 1-1 | | 2 | | 4 | 5[1] | 7 | | | 9 | | | | 14 | 10 | 3 | 1 | | 6 | | 11 | 8 | 12 | | | | | |
| 14 | A | Alloa | 1-1 | | 2[1] | | 4 | | 7 | | | 9 | | | | 14 | | 3 | 8 | 1 | 5 | 6 | | 11 | 10 | | | | | |
| **TOTAL FULL APPEARANCES** | | | | 19 | 33 | 34 | 20 | 38 | 31 | | 1 | 25 | 27 | 7 | 8 | 13 | 17 | 22 | | 19 | 21 | 20 | 16 | 29 | 1 | | 15 | | 8 | 5 |
| **TOTAL SUB APPEARANCES** | | | | (1) | (1) | | (2) | | (2) | | (3) | (2) | (7) | (6) | (7) | (8) | (2) | (6) | (4) | | (2) | | | | | (3) | (1) | (2) | (1) | (1) |
| **TOTAL GOALS SCORED** | | | | | 2 | 4 | | 5 | 4 | | | 10 | 5 | 2 | 1 | 4 | 9 | | | 2 | | | 1 | 3 | | 2 | | 1 | 1 | |

*Small bold figures denote goalscorers.   † denotes opponent's own goal.*

---

### BAYVIEW PARK

**CAPACITY:** 5,385; Seated 600, Standing 4,785

**PITCH DIMENSIONS:** 110 yds x 71 yds

**FACILITIES FOR DISABLED SUPPORTERS:** Area available at East End of Stand.

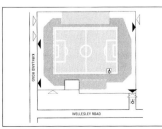

### HOW TO GET THERE

**Bayview Park can be reached by the following routes:**

**TRAINS:** The nearest railway station is Kirkcaldy (8 miles away), and fans will have to catch an inter-linking service from here to the ground.

**BUSES:** A regular service from Kirkcaldy to Leven passes outside the ground, as does the Leven to Dunfermline service.

**CARS:** There is a car park behind the ground, with entry through Kirkland Road.

# GREENOCK MORTON

**Cappielow Park, Sinclair Street, Greenock PA15 2TY**

**CHAIRMAN**
John Wilson

**DIRECTORS**
Duncan D. F. Rae
Kenneth Woods
Andrew Gemmell

**SECRETARY**
Mrs Jane W. Rankin

**MANAGER**
Allan McGraw

**ASSISTANT MANAGER**
Peter Cormack

**SENIOR COACH**
John McMaster

**CLUB DOCTOR**
Dr. R. Craig Speirs

**CROWD DOCTOR**
Dr. F. Gray

**PHYSIOTHERAPIST**
John Tierney

**S.F.A. COMMUNITY COACH**
David Provan

**GROUNDSMAN**
Ian Lyle

**SALES & MARKETING MANAGER**
Sandra Fisher

**TELEPHONES**
Ground/Ticket Office
(0475) 723571
Fax (0475) 781084

**CLUB SHOP**
Situated under Main Stand –
Open Home match days only

**OFFICIAL SUPPORTERS CLUB**
Greenock Morton Supporters Club,
Regent Street, Greenock

**TEAM CAPTAIN**
James Hunter

**SHIRT SPONSOR**
Buchanan's Toffees

## LIST OF PLAYERS 1994-95

| SURNAME | FIRST NAME | MIDDLE NAME | DATE OF BIRTH | PLACE OF BIRTH | DATE OF SIGNING | HEIGHT FT INS | WEIGHT ST LBS | PREVIOUS CLUB |
|---|---|---|---|---|---|---|---|---|
| Aitken | Stephen | Smith | 25/09/76 | Glasgow | 17/12/93 | 5 6.0 | 9 7 | Erskine B.C. |
| Alexander | Rowan | Samuel | 28/01/61 | Ayr | 09/08/86 | 5 7.0 | 11 10 | Brentford |
| Anderson | John | Patton | 02/10/72 | Greenock | 25/01/94 | 6 2.0 | 12 2 | Gourock Y.A.C. |
| Blair | Paul | | 05/07/76 | Greenock | 21/06/94 | 5 7.0 | 10 8 | Ferguslie United |
| Collins | Derek | J. | 15/04/69 | Glasgow | 23/07/87 | 5 8.0 | 10 7 | Renfrew Waverley |
| Cormack | Peter | Robert | 08/06/74 | Southport | 12/08/94 | 6 0.0 | 11 5 | Newcastle United |
| Flannery | Patrick | | 23/07/76 | Glasgow | 10/08/94 | 6 0.0 | 11 2 | Eadie Star U'18 |
| Fowler | John | James | 30/01/65 | Glasgow | 30/07/93 | 5 7.0 | 11 12 | Ashfield Juniors |
| Gibson | Lorn | | 06/07/76 | Paisley | 05/07/94 | 5 11.0 | 10 12 | Clydebank U'18 |
| Hunter | James | Addison | 20/12/64 | Johnstone | 18/09/85 | 5 9.0 | 10 10 | Glentyan Thistle |
| Johnstone | Douglas | Iain | 12/03/69 | Irvine | 31/08/91 | 6 2.0 | 12 8 | Glasgow University |
| Lilley | Derek | Symon | 09/02/74 | Paisley | 13/08/91 | 5 10.5 | 12 7 | Everton B.C. |
| Mahood | Alan | Scott | 26/03/73 | Kilwinning | 23/03/92 | 5 8.0 | 10 10 | Nottingham Forest |
| McArthur | Scott | | 28/02/68 | Johnstone | 26/12/92 | 5 11.0 | 11 10 | Heart of Midlothian |
| McCahill | Stephen | Joseph | 03/09/66 | Greenock | 02/10/92 | 6 2.0 | 12 0 | Celtic |
| McCann | Mark | | 26/01/76 | Kilwinning | 29/06/94 | 5 9.0 | 10 10 | Tass Thistle B.C. |
| McGhee | Dennis | | 01/04/75 | Greenock | 07/06/93 | 5 6.0 | 10 0 | Clyde Thistle |
| McInnes | Derek | John | 05/07/71 | Paisley | 13/08/88 | 5 7.0 | 11 4 | Gleniffer Thistle |
| McMillan | Allister | | 08/08/75 | Glasgow | 29/06/94 | 6 0.0 | 11 12 | Milngavie St. Mungos |
| Pickering | Mark | Fulton | 11/06/65 | Glasgow | 21/08/88 | 5 8.0 | 11 4 | Ardeer Thistle |
| Sexton | Brian | | 23/08/75 | Glasgow | 29/06/94 | 6 11.0 | 11 2 | Milngavie St. Mungos |
| Shearer | Neil | John | 06/01/75 | Paisley | 05/07/93 | 6 1.0 | 14 5 | St. Mungo's F.P. |
| Tolmie | James | | 21/11/60 | Glasgow | 20/12/91 | 5 8.0 | 10 4 | Markaryd |
| Wylie | David | | 04/04/66 | Johnstone | 01/08/85 | 6 0.0 | 13 0 | Ferguslie United |

## MILESTONES

**YEAR OF FORMATION:** 1874
**MOST CAPPED PLAYER:** Jimmy Cowan
**NO. OF CAPS:** 25
**MOST LEAGUE POINTS IN A SEASON:** 69 (Division 2 – Season 1966/67)
**MOST LEAGUE GOALS SCORED BY A PLAYER IN A SEASON:** Allan McGraw (Season 1963/64)
**NO. OF GOALS SCORED:** 58
**RECORD ATTENDANCE:** 23,500 (-v- Celtic – 1922)
**RECORD VICTORY:** 11-0 (-v- Carfin Shamrock – Scottish Cup 13.11.1886)
**RECORD DEFEAT:** 1-10 (-v- Port Glasgow Athletic – Division 2. 5.5.1884)

## SEASON TICKET INFORMATION

**Seated**
Adult .................................................................. £110
Juvenile/OAP ........................................................ £80
**Standing**
Adult ................................................................... £95
Juvenile/OAP ........................................................ £50

## LEAGUE ADMISSION PRICES

**Seated**
Adult ...................................................................... £7
Juvenile/OAP ...................................................... £3.50
**Standing**
Adult ...................................................................... £5
Juvenile/OAP ...................................................... £2.50

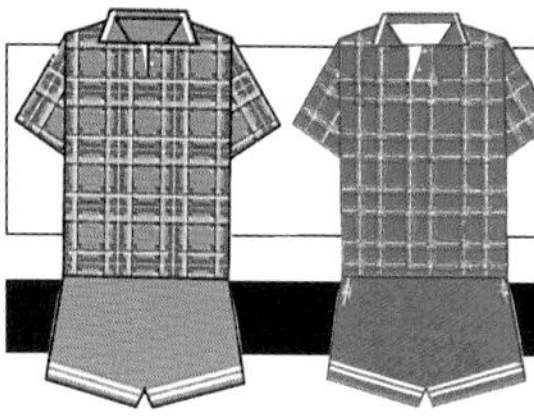

REGISTERED STRIP: Shirt – Royal Blue Tartan with Royal Blue Collar with White Stripe
Shorts – Royal Blue, Stockings – Royal Blue

CHANGE STRIP: Shirt – Red Tartan with Red Collar with White Stripe
Shorts – Red, Stockings – Red with White Stripe

## CLUB FACTFILE 1993/94 . . RESULTS . . APPEARANCES . . SCORERS

### The TON

| Date | Venue | Opponents | Result | Wylie D. | Collins D. | McArthur S. | Rafferty S. | Doak M. | Fowler J. | Lilley D. | Grace A. | Alexander R. | McInnes D. | Tolmie J. | Gahagan J. | Thomson R. | Pickering M. | Donaghy M. | McEwan A. | McCahill S. | Shearer N. | Aitken S. | McDonald I. | Johnstone D. | Beaton S. | Lothian D. | McCann M. | Hunter J. | Anderson J. | Brown C. | Sexton B. | Mahood A. | Blair P. |
|---|---|---|---|---|---|---|---|---|---|---|---|---|---|---|---|---|---|---|---|---|---|---|---|---|---|---|---|---|---|---|---|---|---|
| Aug 7 | A | Clyde | 1-2 | 1 | 2 | 3 | 4 | 5 | 6 | 7 | 8 | $9^1$ | 10 | 11 | 12 | 14 | | | | | | | | | | | | | | | | | |
| 14 | H | Falkirk | 1-5 | 1 | 2 | 6 | | $5^1$ | 4 | 7 | | 9 | 10 | 11 | | | 3 | 8 | | | | | | | | | | | | | | | |
| 21 | A | St. Mirren | 2-2 | 1 | 2 | 6 | | $5^1$ | 4 | 7 | | 9 | 10 | 11 | 12 | | 3 | $8^1$ | | | | | | | | | | | | | | | |
| 28 | H | Brechin City | 2-1 | 1 | 2 | 6 | 14 | 5 | 4 | $7^2$ | | 9 | 10 | 11 | 12 | | 3 | 8 | | | | | | | | | | | | | | | |
| Sept 4 | A | Airdrieonians | 0-2 | 1 | 2 | 6 | 14 | 5 | 4 | 7 | | 9 | 10 | 11 | 12 | | 3 | 8 | | | | | | | | | | | | | | | |
| 11 | A | Clydebank | 0-3 | 1 | 2 | 6 | 14 | 5 | 4 | 7 | | 9 | 10 | 11 | | | 3 | 8 | 12 | | | | | | | | | | | | | | |
| 14 | H | Stirling Albion | 2-2 | 1 | 2 | 6 | 7 | 5 | | | | 9 | 10 | $11^1$ | | | 3 | 8 | | $4^1$ | | | | | | | | | | | | | |
| 18 | A | Dunfermline Athletic | 0-4 | 1 | 2 | 3 | 6 | 5 | 12 | 8 | 14 | 9 | 10 | 11 | | | | 7 | | 4 | | | | | | | | | | | | | |
| 25 | H | Dumbarton | 3-1 | 1 | $2^1$ | 8 | 4 | $5^1$ | 14 | 7 | 11 | | 10 | | | | 3 | 12 | $9^1$ | | 6 | | | | | | | | | | | | |
| 28 | A | Ayr United | †2-2 | 1 | 2 | 8 | 4 | 5 | | 7 | | | 10 | 11 | | | 3 | | $9^1$ | | 6 | | | | | | | | | | | | |
| Oct 2 | H | Hamilton Academical | 1-2 | 1 | 2 | 8 | 4 | 5 | | 7 | | 12 | 10 | $11^1$ | | | 3 | 14 | 9 | | 6 | | | | | | | | | | | | |
| 9 | H | Clyde | 1-1 | 1 | 2 | 8 | 4 | 5 | | 14 | | 9 | 10 | 11 | | | 3 | 12 | $7^1$ | | 6 | | | | | | | | | | | | |
| 16 | A | Stirling Albion | 1-1 | 1 | 2 | 8 | 4 | | 5 | 12 | | 9 | $10^1$ | 11 | | | 3 | 7 | | | 6 | | | | | | | | | | | | |
| 23 | H | Clydebank | 0-0 | 1 | 2 | 6 | 4 | | 3 | | | 9 | 10 | 11 | 14 | | | 8 | 7 | | 5 | | | | | | | | | | | | |
| 30 | H | St. Mirren | †1-2 | 1 | 2 | 8 | 4 | | 14 | 12 | | 9 | 10 | 11 | | | 3 | | 7 | 5 | 6 | | | | | | | | | | | | |
| Nov 6 | A | Brechin City | 3-0 | 1 | 2 | 3 | | | 4 | 7 | | $9^3$ | 10 | 11 | 8 | 14 | | 12 | | 5 | 6 | | | | | | | | | | | | |
| 9 | H | Airdrieonians | 0-0 | 1 | 2 | 3 | | | 4 | | | 9 | | 11 | 7 | 14 | | 10 | | 5 | 6 | 8 | 12 | | | | | | | | | | |
| 13 | A | Hamilton Academical | 1-4 | 1 | 2 | 10 | | | 4 | | | $9^1$ | | 11 | | | 3 | 8 | | 5 | 6 | 7 | 14 | | | | | | | | | | |
| 20 | H | Ayr United | 0-1 | 1 | 2 | 10 | | | 4 | 7 | | 9 | | | 11 | 14 | 3 | 8 | | 5 | 6 | 12 | | | | | | | | | | | |
| 27 | A | Dumbarton | 0-2 | 1 | 2 | 10 | | | 4 | 7 | | | | | 11 | 14 | 3 | 12 | 9 | 5 | | | 8 | 6 | | | | | | | | | |
| Dec 4 | H | Dunfermline Athletic | 0-0 | 1 | 2 | | | | 4 | 7 | | | | | 11 | 10 | | 8 | 12 | | | | 6 | 5 | 3 | 9 | 14 | | | | | | |
| 18 | H | Stirling Albion | 0-1 | 1 | 2 | 3 | 12 | | 4 | 10 | | 9 | | 11 | 7 | 14 | | | | | 6 | | 8 | 5 | | | | | | | | | |
| Jan 8 | H | Brechin City | 1-1 | 1 | 2 | 10 | 4 | | 8 | 7 | | 9 | | 11 | 12 | | | 14 | | | 6 | | | 5 | | | | $3^1$ | | | | | |
| 11 | A | Falkirk | 1-5 | 1 | 2 | 3 | 4 | | 10 | 7 | | 9 | | | | $11^1$ | | 8 | | | | | | 5 | | | | 6 | | | | | |
| 18 | A | St. Mirren | 1-5 | 1 | 2 | 10 | 4 | | 8 | 7 | | | | 11 | | 12 | 3 | | $14^1$ | | 9 | | | 5 | | | | 6 | | | | | |
| 22 | H | Falkirk | 1-1 | 1 | 2 | | | $5^1$ | 12 | 7 | | | | 11 | | 14 | 3 | | 9 | | | | | | | | | 6 | 4 | 8 | 10 | | |
| Feb 1 | A | Airdrieonians | 2-2 | 1 | | | 4 | 5 | 10 | 7 | | | | 11 | | 14 | | | $9^2$ | | | | | 8 | | | | 6 | 2 | | 3 | | |
| 5 | A | Clydebank | 0-0 | 1 | | 12 | 4 | | 8 | | | | | 11 | | 7 | 3 | | 9 | | | | | 5 | | | | 6 | 2 | | 10 | | |
| 12 | H | Hamilton Academical | 2-2 | 1 | | 14 | 12 | 4 | | | | 9 | | 11 | | $8^1$ | 3 | | 7 | | | | | 5 | | | | 6 | $2^1$ | | 10 | | |
| 22 | A | Clyde | 0-0 | 1 | | 14 | 4 | | 8 | 12 | | 9 | | 11 | | 10 | 3 | | 7 | | | | | 5 | | | | 6 | 2 | | | | |
| Mar 1 | A | Ayr United | 1-2 | 1 | | 14 | | | 4 | 7 | | $9^1$ | | 11 | | 10 | 3 | | 12 | | 5 | | | | | | | 6 | 2 | 8 | | | |
| 5 | A | Dunfermline Athletic | 0-3 | 1 | | | 12 | | 4 | 7 | | 9 | | | | 11 | 3 | | | | 5 | | | | 10 | | | 6 | 2 | 8 | | | |
| 12 | H | Dumbarton | 0-0 | 1 | | 3 | 4 | | 8 | 7 | | 9 | | 11 | | | | 10 | 12 | | | | | 5 | | | | 6 | 2 | | | 14 | |
| 19 | A | Stirling Albion | 3-0 | 1 | 12 | $3^2$ | 4 | | 8 | $7^1$ | | 9 | | 11 | | | | | | | | | | 5 | | | | 6 | 2 | | | 10 | |
| 26 | H | Clyde | 2-0 | 1 | 12 | 3 | 4 | | 8 | 7 | | 9 | | 11 | | | | | 14 | | | | | 5 | | | | 6 | 2 | | | $10^2$ | |
| 29 | A | Falkirk | 0-1 | 1 | 8 | 3 | | | 4 | 7 | | 9 | | 11 | | 14 | | | | | | | | 5 | | | | 6 | 2 | | | 10 | |
| Apr 2 | H | Clydebank | 1-1 | 1 | 8 | 3 | | | 4 | 7 | | $9^1$ | | 11 | | 14 | | | | | | | | 5 | | | | 6 | 2 | | | 10 | |
| 13 | A | Hamilton Academical | 2-3 | 1 | 8 | 3 | | | 4 | 7 | | $9^1$ | | 11 | | 14 | | | | | | | | 5 | | | | 6 | 2 | | | $10^1$ | |
| 16 | H | Ayr United | 0-1 | 1 | 8 | 3 | | | 4 | 7 | | 9 | | 11 | | 14 | | | | | | | | 5 | | | | 6 | 2 | | | 10 | |
| 23 | H | Dunfermline Athletic | 2-2 | 1 | 8 | 3 | | | 4 | 7 | | $9^1$ | | 11 | | 14 | | | | | | | | 5 | | | | 6 | $2^1$ | | | 10 | |
| 26 | A | Dumbarton | 0-2 | 1 | 8 | 3 | | | 4 | 7 | | 9 | | 11 | | 14 | | | | | | | | 5 | | | | 6 | 2 | | | 10 | |
| 30 | H | St. Mirren | 1-2 | 1 | 8 | 11 | 14 | | 4 | $7^1$ | | 9 | | 12 | | | 3 | | | | | | | 5 | | | | 6 | 2 | | | 10 | |
| May 7 | A | Brechin City | 2-1 | 1 | 8 | 14 | | | 4 | $7^1$ | | $9^1$ | | | | | 3 | | | | | | | 5 | | | | 6 | 2 | 11 | | 10 | |
| 14 | H | Airdrieonians | 1-3 | 1 | 4 | 6 | | | | 7 | | $9^1$ | | | 11 | | 3 | | | | | 8 | | 5 | | | | | 2 | | | 10 | 12 |
| TOTAL FULL APPEARANCES | | | | 44 | 35 | 35 | 19 | 15 | 34 | 34 | 2 | 35 | 16 | 35 | 7 | 7 | 25 | 15 | 12 | 8 | 16 | 3 | 3 | 22 | 2 | 1 | | 21 | 19 | 4 | 4 | 11 | |
| TOTAL SUB APPEARANCES | | | | | (2) | (5) | (7) | | (4) | (4) | (1) | (1) | | (1) | (6) | (15) | | (6) | (6) | | | (1) | (2) | | | | (1) | | | | | (1) | (1) |
| TOTAL GOALS SCORED | | | | | 1 | 2 | | 4 | | 5 | | 11 | 1 | 2 | | 2 | | 1 | 6 | 1 | | | | | | | | 1 | 2 | | | 3 | |

*Small bold figures denote goalscorers. † denotes opponent's own goal.*

## CAPPIELOW PARK

**CAPACITY**: 14,267; Seating 5,257, Standing 9,010

**PITCH DIMENSIONS**: 110 yds x 71 yds

**FACILITIES FOR DISABLED SUPPORTERS**: Seating facilities below Grandstand.

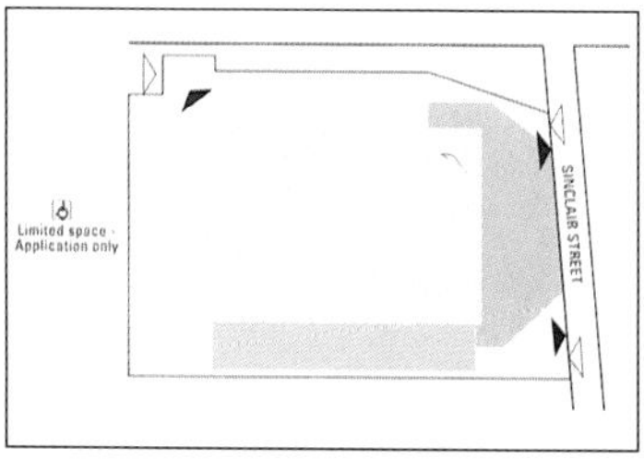

Limited space - Application only
SINCLAIR STREET


## HOW TO GET THERE

**Cappielow Park can be reached by the following routes:**

**BUSES:** Services from Glasgow stop just outside the park. There are also services from Port Glasgow and Gourock.

**TRAINS**: The nearest local station is Cartsdyke and it is a five minute walk from here to the ground. There are two to three trains every hour from Glasgow and from Gourock.

**CARS**: Car Parking is available in James Watt Dock which is on the A8 road just next to the ground.

# MEADOWBANK THISTLE

## LIST OF PLAYERS 1994-95

| SURNAME | FIRST NAME | MIDDLE NAME | DATE OF BIRTH | PLACE OF BIRTH | DATE OF SIGNING | HEIGHT FT INS | WEIGHT ST LBS | PREVIOUS CLUB |
|---|---|---|---|---|---|---|---|---|
| Bailey | Lee | | 10/07/72 | Edinburgh | 04/08/92 | 6 0.0 | 10 0 | Hibernian |
| Coyle | Malcolm | Arthur | 19/03/74 | Musselburgh | 18/07/92 | 6 2.0 | 11 0 | Hutchison Vale B.C. |
| Dallas | Andrew | Fraser | 26/08/73 | Edinburgh | 16/08/94 | 5 10.0 | 10 12 | Brechin City |
| Davidson | Graeme | | 18/01/68 | Edinburgh | 23/07/93 | 5 10.0 | 11 0 | Berwick Rangers |
| Douglas | Robert | James | 24/04/72 | Lanark | 26/10/93 | 6 3.0 | 14 12 | Forth Wanderers |
| Duthie | Mark | James | 19/08/72 | Edinburgh | 25/08/90 | 5 8.0 | 10 0 | Edina Hibs |
| Ellison | Steven | | 03/03/70 | Edinburgh | 25/08/90 | 6 1.0 | 12 3 | Lochend B.C. |
| Fergusson | Scott | Kenneth | 26/03/76 | Toronto | 26/10/93 | 5 7.0 | 10 10 | Celtic |
| Fleming | Derek | | 05/12/73 | Falkirk | 30/03/93 | 5 7.0 | 10 2 | Broxburn Athletic |
| Gardner | Robert | Lee | 11/07/70 | Ayr | 19/11/93 | 5 5.0 | 9 5 | Ayr United |
| Graham | Thomas | | 12/05/68 | Edinburgh | 18/06/90 | 6 0.0 | 13 0 | Cavalry Park B.C. |
| Hutchison | Mark | | 13/07/73 | Edinburgh | 22/06/91 | 5 10.0 | 10 7 | Links United |
| Ingram | Nicholas | Charles | 23/08/73 | Edinburgh | 08/11/93 | 5 8.5 | 10 9 | Hibernian |
| Little | Ian | James | 10/12/73 | Edinburgh | 25/08/90 | 5 6.0 | 8 12 | Tynecastle B.C. |
| MacLeod | Ian | Murdo | 19/11/59 | Glasgow | 01/11/93 | 5 11.0 | 11 6 | Raith Rovers |
| McCartney | Craig | | 18/11/71 | Edinburgh | 30/07/93 | 5 9.0 | 11 0 | Links United B.C. |
| McLeod | Gordon | Thomas | 02/09/67 | Edinburgh | 25/09/92 | 5 9.0 | 11 2 | Dundee |
| Martin | Craig | Richard S. | 16/04/71 | Haddington | 16/08/94 | 6 0.0 | 11 10 | Arbroath |
| Price | Gavin | Gilbert | 29/10/74 | Perth | 29/07/93 | 5 11.0 | 12 0 | Kinnoull |
| Rutherford | Paul | | 23/02/67 | Sunderland | 10/10/92 | 5 9.0 | 11 0 | Falkirk |
| Ryrie | Bryan | | 24/07/71 | Edinburgh | 13/09/91 | 5 6.0 | 10 0 | Penicuik Athletic |
| Sorbie | Stuart | Graham | 07/09/63 | Glasgow | 08/08/94 | 5 9.5 | 10 5 | Arbroath |
| Thorburn | Stuart | Halliday | 03/05/68 | Edinburgh | 10/03/94 | 5 10.0 | 12 7 | Whitehill Welfare |
| Williamson | Robert | | 12/01/75 | Edinburgh | 23/07/93 | 5 8.0 | 10 11 | Hutchison Vale B.C. |
| Williamson | Stewart | | 10/12/61 | Lasswade | 02/08/88 | 6 0.0 | 11 7 | Cowdenbeath |
| Wilson | Stuart | | 21/09/65 | Edinburgh | 09/08/94 | 5 10.0 | 12 0 | Bo'ness United |

## MILESTONES

YEAR OF FORMATION: 1974
MOST LEAGUE POINTS IN A SEASON: 55 (Second Division – Season 1986/87)
MOST LEAGUE GOALS SCORED BY A PLAYER IN A SEASON: John McGachie (Season 1986/87)
NO. OF GOALS SCORED: 21
RECORD ATTENDANCE: 4,000 (-v- Albion Rovers, 9.9.74)
RECORD VICTORY: 6-0 (-v- Raith Rovers – Second Division, 9.11.1985)
RECORD DEFEAT: 0-8 (-v- Hamilton Academical – Division 2, 14.12.1974)

## SEASON TICKET INFORMATION

Seated
Adult ............................................................. £65
Juvenile/OAP ............................................... £32
Parent & Juvenile ....................................... £85

## LEAGUE ADMISSION PRICES

Seated
Adult ................................................................ £4
Juvenile/OAP .............................................. £2.50
Parent & Juvenile ....................................... £5.50

REGISTERED STRIP:  Shirt – Amber with Black Trim
Shorts – Black, Stockings – Amber
CHANGE STRIP:  Shirt – White with Black Trim
Shorts – Blue, Stockings – White

# CLUB FACTFILE 1993/94 .. RESULTS .. APPEARANCES .. SCORERS

## The THISTLE

| Date | Venue | Opponents | Result | McQueen J. | Murray M. | Fleming D. | Williamson S. | Davidson G. | Little I. | Price G. | Wilson S. | Rutherford P. | McLeod G. | Hutchison M. | Bailey L. | Duthie M. | Elder S. | Williamson R. | Brock J. | Coulston D. | Ellison S. | MacLeod I. | Gardner L. | Douglas R. | Ingram N. | Graham T. | Scott S. | Coyle M. | McCartney C. | Thorburn S. |
|---|---|---|---|---|---|---|---|---|---|---|---|---|---|---|---|---|---|---|---|---|---|---|---|---|---|---|---|---|---|---|
| Aug 7 | A | Cowdenbeath | 2-1 | 1 | 2 | 3 | 4 | 5 | 6 | 7 | 8 | 9[1] | 10 | 11 | 12[1] | | | | | | | | | | | | | | | |
| 14 | H | Stranraer | 1-3 | 1 | 4 | 3 | 5 | 2 | 6 | 12 | 8 | 9 | 10[1] | 11 | 7 | | | | | | | | | | | | | | | |
| 21 | H | Berwick Rangers | 1-1 | 1 | 4 | 3 | 5 | 2 | 6 | 9[1] | 8 | | 10 | 11 | 7 | | | | | | | | | | | | | | | |
| 28 | A | East Stirlingshire | 1-0 | 1 | 4 | 3 | 5 | 2 | 6 | 9 | 8 | | 10 | 11 | 7 | 14[1] | | | | | | | | | | | | | | |
| Sep 4 | A | Forfar Athletic | 2-0 | 1 | 4 | 3 | 5 | 2 | 6[2] | 12 | 8 | 9 | 10 | 11 | 7 | | | | | | | | | | | | | | | |
| 11 | H | East Fife | 1-0 | 1 | 4 | 3 | 5 | 2 | 6[1] | 12 | 8 | 9 | 10 | 11 | 7 | 14 | | | | | | | | | | | | | | |
| 18 | A | Montrose | 3-0 | 1 | 4 | 3 | 5 | 2 | 6[1] | 12 | 8 | 9 | 10 | | 7[1] | 14[1] | | | | | | | | | | | | | | |
| 25 | H | Arbroath | 3-0 | 1 | 4 | 3 | 5 | 2 | 6[1] | | 8[1] | 9 | 10 | 11 | 7[1] | 12 | | | | | | | | | | | | | | |
| Oct 2 | A | Alloa | 0-1 | 1 | 4 | 3 | 5 | 2 | 6 | 14 | | 9 | 10 | 11 | 7 | | | | | 8 | 12 | | | | | | | | | |
| 9 | H | Queen of the South | 0-0 | 1 | 4 | 3 | 5 | | 6 | | 8 | 9 | 10 | 11 | 7 | 14 | | | | | 2 | 12 | | | | | | | | |
| 16 | A | Albion Rovers | 0-0 | 1 | 4 | 3 | 5 | | 6 | | 8 | 9 | 10 | 11 | 7 | 14 | | | | | 2 | 12 | | | | | | | | |
| 23 | H | Queen's Park | 1-1 | | 4 | 3 | 5 | | 6 | | 8 | 9 | 10[1] | 11 | 7 | 14 | | | | 1 | 2 | 12 | | | | | | | | |
| 30 | H | Stenhousemuir | 3-1 | | 4 | 3 | 5 | | 6[1] | | 8 | 9 | 10 | 11[1] | 7[1] | 14 | | | | 1 | 2 | | | | | | | | | |
| Nov 6 | A | Stranraer | 1-3 | | 4 | 3 | 5 | | 6 | 12 | | 9 | 10[1] | 11 | 7 | 14 | | | 8 | 1 | 2 | | | | | | | | | |
| 13 | H | Montrose | †5-3 | | 4 | 3 | 5 | | 6 | | 8 | 9[2] | 10 | 11[2] | 7 | | | | | 1 | 2 | | | | | | | | | |
| 20 | A | Arbroath | 2-3 | | 4 | 3 | 5 | | 6 | | 8[2] | 9 | 10 | 11 | 7 | 14 | | | | 1 | 2 | 12 | | | | | | | | |
| Dec 1 | A | Queen of the South | 1-5 | | 4[1] | 3 | 5 | | 6 | | 8 | 9 | 10 | | 7 | 14 | | | | 1 | 2 | 12 | | 11 | | | | | | |
| 4 | H | Alloa | 1-1 | | 4 | 3 | | | 6 | | 8 | 9 | 10[1] | | 7 | | | | | 1 | 2 | 12 | 5 | 11 | | | | | | |
| 18 | H | Cowdenbeath | 1-1 | | 4 | 3 | | | 6 | | 8 | 9[1] | 10 | | 7 | 14 | | 15 | | 1 | 2 | | 5 | 11 | | | | | | |
| Jan 11 | A | Berwick Rangers | 2-2 | | 4 | 3 | 5 | | 6 | | 8 | 9 | 10 | 11 | | 12 | 14[1] | | | 1 | | | | | 7 | | 2[1] | | | |
| 15 | H | East Stirlingshire | 1-1 | | 4 | 3 | 5 | | 6 | | 8 | 9 | 10 | 11 | | 12[1] | 14 | | | 1 | | | | | 7 | | 2 | | | |
| 22 | H | Albion Rovers | 4-2 | | 4 | 3[1] | 5 | | 6[1] | | 8 | 9 | 10[1] | 11 | 7[1] | 14 | | | | 1 | | 12 | | | | | 2 | | | |
| 25 | A | Stenhousemuir | 1-1 | | 4 | 3 | 5 | | 6 | | 8[1] | 9 | 10 | 11 | 7 | 12 | 14 | | | 1 | | | | | | | 2 | | | |
| 29 | A | Queen's Park | 2-3 | | 4[1] | 3 | 5 | | 6 | | 8 | 9[1] | 10 | 11 | 7 | 12 | | | | 1 | | | | | | | 2 | | | |
| Feb 5 | A | East Fife | 2-0 | | 4 | 3 | 5 | | 6 | | 8 | 9[2] | 10 | 11 | 7 | 12 | 14 | | | 1 | | | | | | | 2 | | | |
| 12 | H | Forfar Athletic | 4-2 | | 4[2] | 3 | 5 | | 6 | | 8 | 9[1] | 10[1] | 11 | 7 | 12 | 14 | | | 1 | | | | | | | 2 | | | |
| Mar 2 | H | Alloa | 3-2 | | 4 | 3 | 5 | | 6 | | 8[3] | 9 | 10 | 11 | 7 | 12 | 14 | | | 1 | | | | | | | 2 | | | |
| 5 | A | Cowdenbeath | 1-0 | | 4 | 3 | 5 | | 6 | | 8 | 9 | 10[1] | 11 | 7 | 12 | 14 | | | 1 | | | | | | | 2 | | | |
| 12 | H | Stranraer | 1-1 | | 4 | 3 | 5 | | 6 | | 8 | 9 | 10[1] | 11 | | 12 | 14 | | | 1 | | | | | 7 | | 2 | | | |
| 15 | A | East Stirlingshire | 0-1 | | 4 | 3 | 5 | | 6 | | 8 | 9 | 10 | 11 | 7 | 12 | 14 | | | 1 | | | | | | | 2 | | | |
| 19 | H | Stenhousemuir | 1-0 | | 4 | 3 | 5 | | 6 | | 8 | 9[1] | 10 | 11 | | 12 | 14 | | | 1 | | | | | 7 | | 2 | | | |
| 26 | H | Arbroath | 1-1 | | 4 | 3 | 5 | | 6 | | 8 | 9 | 10 | 11 | | 12 | 14 | | | 1 | | | | | 7 | | 2[1] | | | |
| Apr 2 | A | Forfar Athletic | 0-0 | | 4 | 3 | | | 6 | | 8 | 9 | 10 | 11 | | 12 | 14 | | | 1 | | | | | 7 | | 2 | | | |
| 9 | H | East Fife | 2-2 | | 4 | 3 | 5 | | 6 | | 8[1] | 9[1] | 10 | 11 | | 12 | 14 | | | 1 | | | | | 7 | | 2 | | | |
| 16 | A | Queen's Park | 3-1 | | 4 | 3[1] | 5 | | 6 | | 8 | 9 | 10[1] | 11 | | 12[1] | 14 | | | 1 | | | | | 7 | | 2 | | | |
| 23 | H | Berwick Rangers | 1-2 | | 4 | 3 | 5 | | 6 | | 8[1] | 9 | 10 | 11 | | 12 | 14 | | | 1 | | | | | 7 | | 2 | | | |
| 30 | A | Montrose | 0-2 | | 4 | 3 | 5 | | 6 | | 8 | 9 | 10 | 11 | | 12 | 14 | | | 1 | | | | | 7 | | 2 | | | |
| May 7 | H | Queen of the South | 2-1 | | 4 | 3 | 5 | | 6 | | 8[1] | 9 | 10 | 11 | | 12 | 14 | | | 1 | | | | | 7 | | 2[1] | | | |
| 14 | A | Albion Rovers | 2-0 | | 4 | 3 | 5 | | 6 | | 8[1] | 9 | 10 | 11[1] | | 12 | 14 | | | 1 | | | | | 7 | | 2 | | | |
| **TOTAL FULL APPEARANCES** | | | | 11 | 39 | 38 | 32 | 9 | 38 | 5 | 34 | 32 | 35 | 15 | 29 | 10 | 3 | 2 | 3 | 24 | 19 | 10 | 4 | 19 | 7 | 4 | 7 | | | |
| **TOTAL SUB APPEARANCES** | | | | | | | | | (1) | (7) | (1) | | | | (6) | (8) | (7) | (3) | | (6) | (2) | (1) | (2) | (6) | | (3) | (2) | (4) | (3) | (4) |
| **TOTAL GOALS SCORED** | | | | | | 4 | 2 | | 12 | 1 | 4 | 8 | 9 | | 2 | 11 | 3 | | | 1 | | | | | | | 2 | 1 | 1 | |

*Small bold figures denote goalscorers.*  † *denotes opponent's own goal.*

---

## MEADOWBANK STADIUM

**CAPACITY:** 16,000 (All Seated)
(Only 7,500 Capacity Main Stand Used)

**PITCH DIMENSIONS:** 105 yds x 72 yds

**FACILITIES FOR DISABLED SUPPORTERS:** By prior arrangement with Secretary.

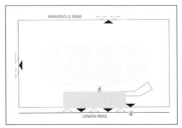

MARIONVILLE ROAD

LONDON ROAD

## HOW TO GET THERE

Meadowbank Stadium can be reached by the following routes:

**BUSES:** A frequent service of buses all pass close to the ground and any of the following can be boarded in Princes Street, St Andrew Square or Leith Street:

Eastern Scottish – C1, C5, C6, 34/35, 42/46, 104, 106, 107, 108, 112, 113, 124, 125, 129, 130 and 137.

Ian Glass – 7, 8 and 12.

Lothian Region Transport – 4, 5, 15, 26, 34/35, 42/46, 13, 44, 44A, 45, 51, 85 and 86.

Lowland Scottish – 104, 106, 124 and 125.

**TRAINS:** Trains from all over the country can be taken into Edinburgh Waverley Station and from there supporters can take any of the above buses to the Stadium. Please note that although a Station was opened at Meadowbank for the Commonwealth Games, it is no longer in use for public travel.

**CARS:** Meadowbank Stadium is located in London Road just 1 mile to the East of Princes Street and approximately half-a-mile away from Easter Road. Car parking facilities are good, with accommodation for 600 cars at Meadowbank Sports Centre. Visiting supporters coaches are advised to park in Lower London Road to the immediate South West of the Stadium.

# QUEEN OF THE SOUTH

Palmerston Park, Terregles Street,
Dumfries DG2 9BA

**CHAIRMAN**
Norman J. Blount

**VICE-CHAIRMAN**
Gordon R. McKerrow

**DIRECTORS**
William J. Harkness C.B.E.
Thomas G. Harkness
Keith M. Houliston

**CHIEF EXECUTIVE**
William J. Harkness C.B.E.

**SECRETARY**
Mrs. Doreen Alcorn

**MANAGER**
William McLaren

**ASSISTANT MANAGER**
Iain McChesney

**COACH**
Graham McLean

**YOUTH MANAGER**
Brian Oakes

**YOUTH COACH**
Scott Stirling

**CLUB DOCTORS**
Dr. Phil Clayton
Dr. Hennie

**PHYSIOTHERAPIST**
Derek Kelly

**CHIEF SCOUT**
Eddie McCulloch

**GROUNDSMAN**
Tom Kerr

**COMMERCIAL MANAGER**
Richard Shaw
(0387) 54853

**TELEPHONES**
Ground/Ticket Office/Information
Service (0387) 54853
Fax (0387) 54853

**CLUB SHOP**
Palmerston Park, Terregles Street,
Dumfries. Tel (0387) 54853.
Open 1.30 p.m. – 3.00 p.m.
on home match days

**OFFICIAL SUPPORTERS CLUB**
c/o Palmerston Park, Terregles Street,
Dumfries DG2 9BA

**TEAM CAPTAIN**
George Rowe

**SHIRT SPONSOR**
Fiat

## LIST OF PLAYERS 1994-95

| SURNAME | FIRST NAME | MIDDLE NAME | DATE OF BIRTH | PLACE OF BIRTH | DATE OF SIGNING | HEIGHT FT INS | WEIGHT ST LBS | PREVIOUS CLUB |
|---|---|---|---|---|---|---|---|---|
| Adams | Mark | James | 09/08/75 | Dumfries | 18/08/94 | 6 0.0 | 11 2 | Ayr United |
| Bell | Archie | McCallum | 12/04/66 | Kilmarnock | 01/05/91 | 6 0.0 | 12 4 | Annbank |
| Brown | James | William | 29/01/72 | Dumfries | 08/08/94 | 5 10.0 | 10 0 | Cumnock Juniors |
| Bryce | Thomas | Charles | 27/01/60 | Johnstone | 03/08/93 | 5 8.0 | 11 10 | Clydebank |
| Cochrane | Gary | | 20/02/76 | Castle Douglas | 29/06/94 | 5 10.0 | 11 0 | Ayr Boswell B.C. |
| Hetherington | Kevin | | 23/11/63 | Dumfries | 09/08/94 | 5 10.0 | 11 0 | Auchinleck Talbot |
| Jackson | David | | 06/12/68 | Motherwell | 15/06/93 | 5 7.0 | 10 6 | Queen's Park |
| Kelly | Patrick | | 04/02/68 | Paisley | 20/07/93 | 5 7.0 | 11 0 | Stranraer |
| Kennedy | David | | 07/10/66 | Ayr | 24/12/93 | 5 10.0 | 11 0 | Ayr United |
| Leslie | Stanley | | 30/11/71 | Dumfries | 25/03/94 | 5 9.0 | 11 7 | Annan Athletic |
| Mallan | Stephen | Patrick | 30/08/67 | Glasgow | 03/08/93 | 5 11.0 | 12 4 | Clyde |
| McColm | Robert | James | 25/08/74 | Dumfries | 03/08/93 | 5 10.0 | 12 0 | Annan Athletic |
| McFarlane | Andrew | | 22/02/70 | Glasgow | 30/10/90 | 5 7.0 | 10 7 | Arthurlie |
| McGuire | Douglas | John | 06/09/67 | Bathgate | 12/06/91 | 5 8.0 | 11 4 | Cumnock Juniors |
| McKeown | Brian | | 31/10/56 | Motherwell | 09/11/90 | 5 7.0 | 11 7 | Airdrieonians |
| McKeown | Desmond | Michael | 18/01/70 | Glasgow | 09/08/94 | 5 11.0 | 11 0 | Albion Rovers |
| McLaren | John | Stuart | 20/04/75 | Glasgow | 05/10/93 | 6 0.0 | 10 8 | Airdrieonians |
| Mills | Douglas | | 06/01/66 | Rutherglen | 27/03/86 | 6 2.0 | 13 0 | Albion Rovers |
| Proudfoot | Kevin | David | 20/01/76 | Dumfries | 11/10/93 | 6 2.0 | 12 7 | Dumfries H.F.P. |
| Purdie | David | Andrew | 15/04/66 | Dumfries | 09/12/93 | 6 2.0 | 14 2 | Ayr United |
| Rowe | John | George | 23/08/68 | Glasgow | 26/08/92 | 6 0.0 | 11 7 | Clydebank |
| Sermanni | Peter | Hugh | 09/09/71 | Glasgow | 27/08/92 | 5 9.0 | 10 0 | Clydebank |

## MILESTONES

YEAR OF FORMATION: 1919
MOST CAPPED PLAYER: William Houliston
NO. OF CAPS: 3
MOST LEAGUE POINTS IN A SEASON: 55 (Division 2 – Season 1985/86)
MOST LEAGUE GOALS SCORED BY A PLAYER IN A SEASON: J. Gray (Season 1927/28)
NO. OF GOALS SCORED: 33
RECORD ATTENDANCE: 24,500 (-v- Heart of Midlothian – Scottish Cup, 23.2.1952)
RECORD VICTORY: 11-1 (-v- Stranraer – Scottish Cup, 16.1.1932)
RECORD DEFEAT: 2-10 (-v- Dundee – Division 1, 1.12.1962)

## SEASON TICKET INFORMATION

**Seated**
Adult .................................................................. £100
Juvenile/OAP ....................................................... £60
**Standing**
Adult .................................................................... £80
OAP ..................................................................... £40
School Children ................................................... £15

## LEAGUE ADMISSION PRICES

**Seated**
Adult ...................................................................... £6
Juvenile/OAP/Unemployed ..................................... £4
**Standing**
Adult ...................................................................... £5
Unemployed/OAP ............................................... £2.50
School Children ...................................................... £1

REGISTERED STRIP: Shirt – White with Royal Blue Flashes, Royal Blue Collar and White Band
Shorts – Royal Blue with White and Royal Blue Leg Band, Stockings – White
CHANGE STRIP: Shirt – Yellow, Navy Blue and White Stripe with Navy Blue Collar with White Band
Shorts – Navy Blue with White, Navy Blue and White Leg Band
Stockings – Navy Blue

# CLUB FACTFILE 1993/94 .. RESULTS .. APPEARANCES .. SCORERS

## The DOONHAMERS

| Date | Venue | Opponents | Result | Davidson A. | Mills D. | McGhie W. | McKeown B. | Shanks D. | McFarlane A. | Jackson D. | Sermanni P. | Thomson A. | McGuire D. | Mallan S. | Bryce T. | Kelly P. | Bell A. | Rowe G. | McLaren J. | McColm R. | Proudfoot K. | Purdie D. | Kennedy D. | Leslie S. |
|---|---|---|---|---|---|---|---|---|---|---|---|---|---|---|---|---|---|---|---|---|---|---|---|---|
| Aug 7 | A | Arbroath | 5-2 | 1 | 2 | 3 | 4 | 5 | $6^1$ | 7 | 8 | $9^2$ | $10^1$ | $11^1$ | 12 | | | | | | | | | |
| 14 | H | Queen's Park | 5-2 | 1 | 2 | 3 | 4 | 5 | 6 | 7 | 8 | $9^1$ | $10^2$ | $11^1$ | 12 | | $14^1$ | | | | | | | |
| 21 | H | Stranraer | 0-1 | 1 | 5 | 2 | 4 | 8 | 6 | 7 | 14 | 9 | 10 | 11 | 12 | | | 3 | | | | | | |
| 28 | A | Forfar Athletic | 2-1 | 1 | 2 | | 3 | 5 | 7 | | 12 | 9 | 10 | $11^2$ | 8 | | 6 | 4 | | | | | | |
| Sep 4 | A | East Fife | 2-0 | 1 | 3 | | 4 | 5 | 6 | | | $9^2$ | 10 | 11 | 8 | | 7 | 2 | | | | | | |
| 11 | H | East Stirlingshire | 5-0 | 1 | 2 | | 4 | 5 | 8 | | 14 | $9^2$ | $7^1$ | $11^1$ | $6^1$ | 12 | 10 | 3 | | | | | | |
| 18 | H | Alloa | 0-1 | 1 | 2 | | 4 | 5 | 6 | | 14 | 9 | 7 | 11 | 10 | 12 | 8 | 3 | | | | | | |
| 25 | A | Albion Rovers | 1-1 | 1 | 3 | 14 | 2 | | 10 | 12 | | $9^1$ | 7 | 11 | 6 | 8 | 5 | 4 | | | | | | |
| Oct 2 | H | Montrose | 1-0 | 1 | 2 | | 4 | 5 | 8 | | 12 | $9^1$ | 7 | 11 | 6 | 10 | 3 | | | | | | | |
| 9 | A | Meadowbank Thistle | 0-0 | 1 | 2 | 3 | 4 | 5 | 8 | | | 9 | 12 | 11 | 6 | 7 | 10 | | | | | | | |
| 16 | A | Cowdenbeath | 3-3 | 1 | 3 | 2 | 4 | 5 | 7 | | 14 | 9 | | 11 | $8^1$ | 12 | $10^2$ | 6 | | | | | | |
| 23 | H | Stenhousemuir | 1-2 | 1 | $5^1$ | 2 | 4 | 6 | 8 | | | 9 | | 11 | 7 | 10 | 3 | 12 | | | | | | |
| 30 | H | Berwick Rangers | 2-5 | 1 | 5 | 2 | 4 | 8 | 14 | | | $9^1$ | $7^1$ | 11 | 10 | 12 | 6 | 3 | | | | | | |
| Nov 6 | A | Queen's Park | 1-3 | 1 | 2 | 5 | 8 | 10 | 14 | | | 9 | 12 | $11^1$ | 6 | 7 | 3 | 4 | | | | | | |
| 13 | A | Alloa | 0-1 | | | 4 | 5 | 8 | 14 | | | 9 | | 11 | 6 | 7 | 3 | 2 | | 12 | | 1 | 10 | |
| 20 | H | Albion Rovers | 1-2 | | 2 | 5 | 6 | | 12 | 14 | | $9^1$ | | 11 | 8 | 7 | 3 | 4 | | | | 1 | 10 | |
| Dec 1 | H | Meadowbank Thistle | 5-1 | | 3 | 2 | 4 | 8 | | | | $9^1$ | | $11^2$ | $6^1$ | $7^1$ | 10 | 5 | | | | 1 | | |
| 4 | A | Montrose | 1-2 | | 2 | 3 | 4 | 6 | 14 | | | $9^1$ | | 11 | 8 | 10 | 5 | | 12 | | | 1 | | |
| 18 | H | Arbroath | 6-0 | | 2 | | 4 | | 6 | 14 | 12 | $9^2$ | | 11 | $8^3$ | 7 | 5 | $10^1$ | 3 | | | 1 | | |
| Jan 1 | A | Stranraer | 2-1 | | 2 | | 4 | | 6 | | 7 | $9^1$ | | $11^1$ | 10 | 5 | 3 | | | | | 1 | | 8 |
| 15 | H | Forfar Athletic | 1-0 | | 2 | | 4 | | 6 | 7 | 12 | 9 | | 11 | 8 | 5 | 3 | | | | | 1 | $10^1$ | |
| 18 | A | Berwick Rangers | 2-1 | | 2 | 5 | 4 | 6 | 14 | 7 | 12 | $9^1$ | | $11^1$ | 10 | | 3 | 8 | | | | 1 | | |
| 22 | H | Cowdenbeath | 1-2 | | 2 | 5 | 4 | | | 7 | 12 | $9^1$ | | 11 | 6 | 10 | 3 | 8 | | | | 1 | | |
| Feb 5 | A | East Stirlingshire | 0-0 | | 2 | 5 | 4 | | | 7 | 12 | 9 | | 11 | 6 | 10 | 3 | 8 | | | | 1 | | |
| 8 | A | Stenhousemuir | 0-3 | | 2 | 5 | 4 | | | 7 | 12 | 9 | | 11 | 6 | 10 | 3 | 8 | | | | 1 | | |
| 12 | H | East Fife | 0-0 | | 2 | 5 | 4 | | | 7 | 14 | 9 | | 11 | 6 | 10 | 3 | 8 | | | | 1 | | |
| 19 | H | Queen's Park | 3-0 | | 2 | | 4 | | | 7 | $12^1$ | 9 | | $11^1$ | 6 | $10^1$ | 5 | 8 | 3 | | | 1 | | |
| Mar 5 | A | Stranraer | 3-3 | | 2 | | 4 | | | $7^1$ | $12^1$ | $9^1$ | 14 | 11 | 6 | 10 | 5 | 8 | 3 | | | 1 | | |
| 12 | H | Albion Rovers | 1-2 | | 2 | $5^1$ | 4 | 8 | | 7 | 12 | 9 | | 11 | 6 | 10 | 3 | | 14 | | | 1 | | |
| 15 | A | Alloa | 0-1 | | 2 | 5 | 4 | 8 | 14 | 7 | 12 | 9 | | 11 | 6 | 10 | 3 | | | | | 1 | | |
| 19 | A | Forfar Athletic | 4-4 | | 2 | 5 | 4 | | | 7 | 12 | $9^4$ | | 11 | 6 | 10 | 3 | 8 | | | | 1 | | |
| 26 | H | Montrose | 1-0 | | 2 | 5 | 4 | | | 7 | 12 | $9^1$ | | 11 | 6 | 10 | 3 | 8 | | | | 1 | | |
| Apr 2 | H | Berwick Rangers | 0-0 | | 2 | 5 | 4 | | 14 | 7 | 12 | 9 | | 11 | 6 | 10 | 3 | 8 | | | | 1 | | |
| 9 | A | Arbroath | 3-0 | | 2 | 5 | 4 | 8 | | 7 | 12 | $9^2$ | | $11^1$ | 6 | 10 | 3 | | | | | 1 | | |
| 16 | A | East Fife | 1-0 | | 2 | 5 | 4 | 8 | | 7 | | 9 | | 11 | 6 | 10 | 3 | | $14^1$ | 12 | | 1 | | |
| 23 | H | Stenhousemuir | 2-1 | | 2 | 5 | 4 | | | 7 | 12 | $9^2$ | | 11 | 6 | 10 | 3 | 8 | | | | 1 | | 14 |
| 30 | H | East Stirlingshire | 1-1 | | $2^1$ | 5 | 4 | | | 7 | 12 | 9 | | 11 | 6 | 10 | 3 | 5 | 14 | | | 1 | | |
| May 7 | A | Meadowbank Thistle | 1-2 | | 2 | $5^1$ | 4 | | 14 | 7 | 12 | 9 | | 11 | 6 | 10 | 3 | 8 | | | | 1 | | |
| 14 | A | Cowdenbeath | †2-0 | | 2 | 5 | 4 | | 14 | 7 | | 9 | | 11 | 6 | 10 | 3 | $8^1$ | | | | 1 | | |
| **TOTAL FULL APPEARANCES** | | | | 14 | 30 | 30 | 35 | 13 | 22 | 7 | 15 | 32 | 19 | 37 | 34 | 22 | 23 | 30 | 12 | 6 | 7 | 19 | 17 | 5 |
| **TOTAL SUB APPEARANCES** | | | | | (1) | | (1) | | | | (13) | (12) | (3) | (9) | | (3) | (7) | | | (7) | | | (1) | |
| **TOTAL GOALS SCORED** | | | | | | 1 | 2 | | 1 | | 2 | 29 | 6 | 11 | 7 | 3 | 2 | 2 | 2 | | | | | |

*Small bold figures denote goalscorers. † denotes opponent's own goal.*

## PALMERSTON PARK

**CAPACITY:** 6,750; Seated 1,357, Standing 5,393

**PITCH DIMENSIONS:** 112 yds x 73 yds

**FACILITIES FOR DISABLED SUPPORTERS:** On application to Club Secretary.

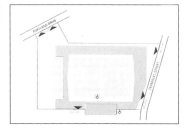

## HOW TO GET THERE

Palmerston Park can be reached by the following routes:

**TRAINS:** There is a reasonable service to Dumfries Station from Glasgow on Saturdays, but the service is more limited in midweek. The station is about ¾ mile from the ground.

**BUSES:** Buses from Glasgow, Edinburgh, Ayr and Stranraer all pass within a short distance of the park.

**CARS:** The car park may be reached from Portland Drive or King Street and has a capacity for approximately 174 cars.

# STENHOUSEMUIR

**Ochilview Park, Gladstone Road, Stenhousemuir FK5 4QL**

**CHAIRMAN**
A. Terry Bulloch

**VICE-CHAIRMAN**
Sidney S. Collumbine

**DIRECTORS**
David O. Reid
Gordon T. Cook (Treasurer)
James S. B. Gillespie
Alistair Jack
John G. Sharp
Alan J. McNeill
Greig H. C. Thomson

**SECRETARY**
David O. Reid

**MANAGER**
Terry Christie

**ASSISTANT MANAGER**
Graeme Armstrong

**COACH**
Gordon Buchanan

**CLUB DOCTOR**
Philip Lynch

**PHYSIOTHERAPIST**
Mrs. Lee Campbell

**COMMERCIAL MANAGER**
John G. Sharp
Bus. (0324) 562992

**TELEPHONES**
Ground (0324) 562992
Sec. Home (0324) 631895
Sec. Bus. 041-204 2511 Ext. 239

**CLUB SHOP**
Ochilview Park, Gladstone Road,
Stenhousemuir FK5 4QL.
Tel (0324) 562992. Open during
first team home match days between
2.00 p.m. until 5.00 p.m. & Tues
to Fri 9.00 a.m. till Noon

**OFFICIAL SUPPORTERS CLUB**
Ochilview Park, Gladstone Road,
Stenhousemuir FK5 4QL

**TEAM CAPTAIN**
Eddie Hallford

**SHIRT SPONSOR**
G & J Sports

## LIST OF PLAYERS 1994-95

| SURNAME | FIRST NAME | MIDDLE NAME | DATE OF BIRTH | PLACE OF BIRTH | DATE OF SIGNING | HEIGHT FT INS | WEIGHT ST LBS | PREVIOUS CLUB |
|---|---|---|---|---|---|---|---|---|
| Aitchison | James | | 10/10/76 | Edinburgh | 05/08/93 | 5 10.0 | 10 7 | Whitehill Welfare |
| Aitken | Neil | | 27/04/71 | Edinburgh | 26/01/90 | 6 1.0 | 11 7 | Penicuik Athletic |
| Armstrong | Graeme | John | 23/06/56 | Edinburgh | 31/10/92 | 5 9.0 | 10 12 | Meadowbank Thistle |
| Buchanan | Gordon | | 20/10/61 | Glasgow | 09/09/93 | 6 0.0 | 11 12 | Unattached |
| Christie | Martin | Peter | 07/11/71 | Edinburgh | 04/12/93 | 5 6.0 | 10 4 | Dundee |
| Clarke | John | | 23/11/70 | Glasgow | 04/05/92 | 5 11.0 | 11 10 | Milngavie Wanderers |
| Donaldson | Euan | Gordon | 20/08/75 | Falkirk | 18/05/93 | 5 10.0 | 10 7 | "S" Form |
| Farmer | Alan | | 15/05/76 | Falkirk | 16/10/93 | 5 10.5 | 10 7 | I.C.I. Juveniles |
| Fisher | James | | 14/10/67 | Bridge of Allan | 18/01/92 | 5 10.0 | 10 11 | Bo'ness United |
| Godfrey | Peter | James | 22/10/57 | Falkirk | 18/11/92 | 6 0.0 | 11 7 | Arbroath |
| Haddow | Lloyd | Simon | 21/01/71 | Lanark | 13/02/92 | 6 1.0 | 11 6 | Fauldhouse United |
| Hallford | Edward | | 04/10/67 | Shotts | 11/06/90 | 5 8.0 | 11 2 | Shotts Bon Accord |
| Harkness | Michael | | 24/08/68 | Edinburgh | 26/08/93 | 6 1.5 | 12 6 | Arbroath |
| Henderson | James | Charles | 18/10/76 | Falkirk | 23/07/94 | 6 1.0 | 11 0 | Bothkennar U'18 |
| Hutchison | Gareth | | 04/06/72 | Edinburgh | 26/07/94 | 5 10.0 | 11 7 | Tranent Juniors |
| Irvine | John | George | 22/07/63 | Musselburgh | 21/03/92 | 6 0.0 | 12 13 | Alloa |
| Mathieson | Miller | Stewart | 19/12/64 | Surrey | 14/11/91 | 5 11.0 | 11 12 | Edinburgh United |
| McGeachie | George | | 05/02/59 | Bothkennar | 26/07/94 | 5 11.5 | 11 12 | Raith Rovers |
| Roseburgh | David | | 30/06/59 | Loanhead | 26/08/93 | 5 10.5 | 9 9 | Meadowbank Thistle |
| Salton | Keith | | 07/08/77 | Edinburgh | 31/03/94 | 6 1.0 | 10 7 | Salveson B.C. |
| Sludden | John | | 29/12/64 | Falkirk | 24/01/94 | 5 10.0 | 10 10 | Clyde |
| Sprott | Adrian | | 23/03/62 | Edinburgh | 05/08/93 | 5 8.0 | 10 0 | Meadowbank Thistle |
| Steel | Thomas | Wright | 28/02/68 | Kilmarnock | 29/05/92 | 6 0.0 | 11 9 | Hurlford United |
| Swanson | Darren | | 12/02/76 | Stirling | 25/06/93 | 5 10.0 | 10 11 | "S" Form |
| Wilson | Christopher | Charles | 21/06/72 | Paisley | 25/06/93 | 6 3.0 | 13 12 | Campsie Black Watch |

## MILESTONES

**YEAR OF FORMATION:** 1884
**MOST LEAGUE POINTS IN A SEASON:** 50 (Division 2 – Season 1960/61)
**MOST LEAGUE GOALS SCORED BY A PLAYER IN A SEASON:** Evelyn Morrison (Season 1927/28) and Robert Murray (Season 1936/37)
**NO. OF GOALS SCORED:** 31
**RECORD ATTENDANCE:** 12,500 (-v- East Fife – 11.3.1950)
**RECORD VICTORY:** 9-2 (-v- Dundee United – Division 2, 16.4.1937)
**RECORD DEFEAT:** 2-11 (-v- Dunfermline Athletic – Division 2, 27.9.1930)

## SEASON TICKET INFORMATION

**Seated**
Adult ....................................................... £90
Juvenile/OAP ........................................... £45
Parent and Juvenile ................................. £110
**Standing**
Adult ....................................................... £70
Juvenile/OAP ........................................... £35
Parent and Juvenile ................................. £85

## LEAGUE ADMISSION PRICES

**Seated**
Adult ....................................................... £6.50
Juvenile/OAP ........................................... £4
**Standing**
Adult ....................................................... £5
Juvenile/OAP ........................................... £2.50

**REGISTERED STRIP:** Shirt – Maroon with Sky Blue Stripe, Shorts – White
Stockings – Maroon with Sky Blue Hoops on Top

**CHANGE STRIP:** Shirt – Black with Royal Blue/Yellow Trim, Shorts – Black
Stockings – Black with Royal Blue and Yellow Tops

# CLUB FACTFILE 1993/94 . . RESULTS . . APPEARANCES . . SCORERS

## The WARRIORS

Player columns (left to right): Robertson S., Aitken N., Haddow L., Armstrong G., Godfrey P., Logan S., Steel T., Clouston B., Mathieson M., Irvine J., Fisher J., Dickov S., Clarke J., O'Neill P., Sprott A., Harkness M., Roseburgh D., Hallford E., McConnell I., Christie M., Donaldson E., Swanson D., Gallacher J., Sludden J.

| Date | Venue | Opponents | Result | Robertson S. | Aitken N. | Haddow L. | Armstrong G. | Godfrey P. | Logan S. | Steel T. | Clouston B. | Mathieson M. | Irvine J. | Fisher J. | Dickov S. | Clarke J. | O'Neill P. | Sprott A. | Harkness M. | Roseburgh D. | Hallford E. | McConnell I. | Christie M. | Donaldson E. | Swanson D. | Gallacher J. | Sludden J. |
|---|---|---|---|---|---|---|---|---|---|---|---|---|---|---|---|---|---|---|---|---|---|---|---|---|---|---|---|
| Aug 7 | H | East Stirlingshire | 3-1 | 1 | 2 | 3 | 4 | 5 | 6 | 7¹ | 8 | 9² | 10 | 11 | 12 | | | | | | | | | | | | |
| 14 | A | East Fife | 0-3 | 1 | 2 | 3 | 4 | | 6 | 7 | 8 | 9 | 10 | 11 | 12 | 5 | 14 | | | | | | | | | | |
| 21 | A | Montrose | 0-2 | 1 | 2 | | 4 | | 6 | 7 | 8 | 9 | 10 | 11 | 14 | 5 | 12 | 3 | | | | | | | | | |
| 28 | H | Cowdenbeath | 1-1 | | 3 | 4 | | | 6 | 7 | | 9¹ | 8 | 11 | 12 | 5 | | 2 | 1 | 10 | | | | | | | |
| Sep 4 | H | Alloa | 1-1 | | 5 | 11 | 4 | | 6 | 12 | | 9 | 8¹ | 7 | | | | 2 | 1 | 10 | 3 | | | | | | |
| 11 | A | Albion Rovers | 2-1 | | 2 | 3 | 4 | | 6 | 7¹ | | 9 | 12 | 8 | 14 | 5 | | 11 | 1 | 10¹ | | | | | | | |
| 18 | A | Arbroath | 2-1 | | 2 | 3 | 4 | 5 | | 7¹ | | 9¹ | 8 | 6 | 12 | | | 11 | 1 | 10 | 14 | | | | | | |
| 25 | H | Queen's Park | 2-0 | | 2 | | 4 | 5 | 12 | 7² | | 9 | 8 | 6 | 14 | | | 11 | 1 | 10 | 3 | | | | | | |
| Oct 2 | H | Berwick Rangers | 2-1 | | 2 | | 4 | 5 | | 7 | | 9 | 8² | 6 | | | | 11 | 1 | 10 | 3 | | | | | | |
| 9 | A | Stranraer | 0-1 | | 2 | | 4 | 5 | 12 | 7 | | 9 | 8 | 6 | | 14 | | 11 | 1 | 10 | 3 | | | | | | |
| 16 | H | Forfar Athletic | 2-0 | | 2 | 3 | 4 | 5 | 10 | 7 | | 9¹ | 8¹ | 6 | | | | 11 | 1 | | | | | | | | |
| 23 | A | Queen of the South | 2-1 | | 2 | 3 | 4 | 5 | 7 | 12 | | 9 | 8¹ | 6 | | | | 11 | 1 | 10¹ | | | | | | | |
| 30 | A | Meadowbank Thistle | 1-3 | | 2 | 3 | 4 | 5 | | 7 | | 9 | 8 | 6 | 12 | 14 | | 11 | 1 | 10¹ | | | | | | | |
| Nov 6 | H | East Fife | 0-1 | | 2 | 3 | 4 | 5 | | 7 | | 9 | 8 | 6 | | 12 | | 11 | 1 | 10 | | | | | | | |
| 13 | H | Arbroath | 4-0 | | | 11 | 4 | 5 | | | | 9 | 8 | 6² | | 2 | | | 1 | 10² | 3 | | 7 | 12 | 14 | | |
| 20 | A | Queen's Park | 2-1 | | 2 | 3 | 4 | | | 7¹ | | 9¹ | 8 | 6 | | 5 | | 12 | 1 | 10 | | 11 | 14 | | | | |
| 30 | H | Stranraer | 2-2 | | 2 | 9 | 4 | 5¹ | | 7 | | | 8 | 6 | | | | 3 | 1 | 10¹ | | 11 | | | | | |
| Dec 4 | H | Berwick Rangers | 1-2 | | 2 | 9 | 4 | 5 | | 7¹ | | | 8 | 6 | | 12 | | 3 | 1 | 10 | | 11 | | | | | |
| 18 | A | East Stirlingshire | 2-0 | | 2 | 9 | 4 | 5 | | 7 | | 8¹ | | 10 | | | | 1 | | 3 | | | 14 | 6¹ | 11 | | |
| Jan 18 | H | Montrose | 3-4 | | 2 | 11¹ | 4 | 5 | | 7 | | 9 | 12 | | 8 | 6 | | 10² | 1 | | | | 3 | 14 | | | |
| 22 | A | Forfar Athletic | 1-1 | | 2 | 11 | 4 | 5 | | 7 | | 9 | | | 8 | 6 | | 10¹ | 1 | | 14 | | 3 | | | | |
| 25 | H | Meadowbank Thistle | 1-1 | | 2 | 3 | 4 | 5 | | 7 | | 9 | | | 8 | 6 | | 11 | 1 | | 14 | | 12 | | 10¹ | | |
| Feb 1 | A | Cowdenbeath | 3-1 | | 2 | 3 | 4 | | 6 | 7 | | 9¹ | | | 8 | 5 | | 11¹ | 1 | | 14 | | | | 10¹ | | |
| 5 | H | Albion Rovers | †5-1 | 12 | 3 | 4 | 5 | 6 | 7 | | | 9¹ | | | 14 | 2 | | 11¹ | 1 | 8¹ | | | | | 10¹ | | |
| 8 | H | Queen of the South | 3-0 | 7¹ | 3 | 4 | 5 | 6 | | | | 9² | | | 12 | 2 | | 11 | 1 | 8 | | | | | 10 | | |
| 12 | A | Alloa | 2-1 | 7 | | 4 | 5 | 6 | 3 | | | 9 | | | 2 | | | 11 | 1 | 8 | | | | 14 | 10² | | |
| 19 | H | Arbroath | 2-0 | | 2 | | 4 | 5 | 6 | 7¹ | | 9 | | | | | | 11 | 1 | 8 | 3 | | | | 10¹ | | |
| Mar 5 | A | Queen's Park | 4-2 | | 2 | | 4 | 5 | 6 | 12 | | 9¹ | 7¹ | | | | | 11 | 1 | 8 | 3 | | | | 10² | | |
| 12 | A | Forfar Athletic | 0-1 | | 2 | | 4 | 5 | 6 | 12 | | 9 | 7 | | | | | 11 | 1 | 8 | 3 | | | | 10 | | |
| 16 | A | Cowdenbeath | 1-1 | | 2 | | 4 | 5 | 6 | 7 | | 9 | 8 | | | | | 11 | 1 | 3 | | 14 | | | 10¹ | | |
| 19 | A | Meadowbank Thistle | 0-1 | | 2 | | 4 | 5 | 6 | 7 | | 9 | 8 | | | | | 11 | 1 | 3 | 14 | | | | 10 | | |
| 26 | H | Albion Rovers | 0-0 | | 2 | | 4 | | 6 | 12 | | 9 | 7 | 5 | | | | 11 | 1 | 3 | | 8 | 14 | | 10 | | |
| Apr 2 | H | Alloa | 1-0 | | 2 | | 4 | 5 | 12 | | | 9¹ | 7 | 6 | | | | 11 | 1 | 8 | 3 | | | | 10 | | |
| 9 | A | East Stirlingshire | 2-2 | | 2 | | 4 | 5 | 12 | | | 9 | 7 | 6 | | | | 11 | 1 | 8 | 3 | 14 | | | 10² | | |
| 16 | A | Montrose | 2-0 | | 2 | | 4 | 5 | 8 | | | 9² | 7 | 6 | | | | 12 | 1 | 3 | | 11 | | | 10 | | |
| 23 | A | Queen of the South | 1-2 | | 2 | | 4 | 5 | 8 | 14 | | 9 | 7 | 6 | | | | 12 | 1 | 3 | | 11 | | | 10¹ | | |
| 30 | A | Berwick Rangers | 0-3 | | 2 | | 4 | | 8 | 12 | | 9 | 7 | 14 | 5 | | | 11 | 1 | 3 | | 6 | | | 10 | | |
| May 7 | H | East Fife | 1-1 | | 2 | | 4 | 5 | 6 | | | 9 | 7 | | | | | 11¹ | 1 | 3 | | 8 | | | 10 | | |
| 14 | A | Stranraer | 1-0 | | 2 | 12 | 4 | | | 7 | | 9 | 6 | | 5 | | | 11 | 1 | 3 | | 8 | | | 10¹ | | |
| **TOTAL FULL APPEARANCES** | | | | 3 | 36 | 21 | 39 | 29 | 22 | 26 | 3 | 36 | 18 | 30 | 4 | 21 | | 32 | 36 | 28 | 10 | 13 | 1 | 2 | 1 | 18 | |
| **TOTAL SUB APPEARANCES** | | | | (1) | (1) | | (4) | (7) | | (2) | | | (11) | (4) | (2) | (3) | | (1) | (1) | (5) | (3) | (5) | | | | | |
| **TOTAL GOALS SCORED** | | | | 1 | 1 | | 1 | | | 8 | | 14 | 6 | 3 | | | | 6 | | 7 | | | | 1 | 13 | | |

*Small bold figures denote goalscorers.* † *denotes opponent's own goal.*

## OCHILVIEW PARK

**CAPACITY:** 3,520; Seated 340, Standing 3,180

**PITCH DIMENSIONS:** 113 yds x 74 yds

**FACILITIES FOR DISABLED SUPPORTERS:** Accommodation for disabled in front of Stand. Toilet facilities also provided.

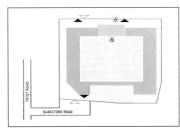

## HOW TO GET THERE

Ochilview Park can be reached by the following routes:

**TRAINS:** The nearest station is Larbert, which is about a mile away from the ground.

**BUSES:** Buses from Glasgow to Dunfermline, Leven, Dundee and Kirkcaldy pass through Stenhousemuir town centre and this is only a short distance from the park. There is also a regular bus service from Falkirk.

**CARS:** There is a large car park on the north side of the ground.

# STIRLING ALBION

**LIST OF PLAYERS 1994-95**

| SURNAME | FIRST NAME | MIDDLE NAME | DATE OF BIRTH | PLACE OF BIRTH | DATE OF SIGNING | HEIGHT FT INS | WEIGHT ST LBS | PREVIOUS CLUB |
|---------|-----------|-------------|---------------|----------------|-----------------|---------------|---------------|---------------|
| Armstrong | Paul | | 27/10/65 | Glasgow | 25/07/91 | 5 11.0 | 11 0 | Cork City |
| Callaghan | Thomas | | 28/08/69 | Glasgow | 13/08/93 | 5 10.0 | 11 4 | East Fife |
| Drinkell | Kevin | | 18/06/60 | Grimsby | 19/03/94 | 5 11.0 | 13 8 | Falkirk |
| Gibson | John | | 20/04/67 | Blantyre | 26/11/93 | 5 10.0 | 10 10 | Alloa |
| Hamilton | James | Michael | 09/12/66 | Duntocher | 03/12/93 | 5 9.0 | 11 0 | Arbroath |
| McAneny | Paul | James | 11/11/73 | Glasgow | 11/09/93 | 5 10.0 | 11 5 | Saltcoats Victoria |
| McGeown | Mark | | 10/05/70 | Paisley | 13/10/88 | 5 10.0 | 11 0 | Blantyre Victoria |
| McInnes | Ian | | 22/03/67 | Hamilton | 09/08/90 | 5 8.0 | 9 13 | Stranraer |
| McLeod | Joseph | | 30/12/67 | Edinburgh | 09/12/93 | 5 7.0 | 9 11 | Portadown |
| McQuilter | Ronald | | 24/12/70 | Glasgow | 24/12/93 | 6 1.0 | 12 7 | Ayr United |
| Mitchell | Colin | | 25/05/65 | Bellshill | 28/07/88 | 5 9.0 | 11 8 | Airdrieonians |
| Monaghan | Michael | Joseph | 28/06/63 | Glasgow | 22/02/94 | 6 0.0 | 12 2 | Dumbarton |
| Pew | David | John | 28/08/71 | Glasgow | 23/07/91 | 5 10.0 | 10 5 | Greenhills |
| Reid | William | Hamilton | 18/07/63 | Glasgow | 19/03/94 | 5 8.0 | 9 12 | Hamilton Academical |
| Roberts | Paul | | 24/03/70 | Glasgow | 12/11/93 | 6 0.0 | 12 0 | East Stirlingshire |
| Taggart | Craig | | 17/01/73 | Glasgow | 12/08/94 | 5 9.0 | 11 0 | Falkirk |
| Tait | Thomas | | 08/09/67 | Ayr | 12/09/92 | 5 10.0 | 11 7 | Kilmarnock |
| Watson | Paul | | 16/07/68 | Bellshill | 08/12/90 | 5 11.0 | 11 7 | Thorniewood United |
| Watters | William | Devlin | 05/06/64 | Bellshill | 23/08/91 | 5 9.5 | 11 1 | Queen of the South |

## MILESTONES

YEAR OF FORMATION: 1945
MOST LEAGUE POINTS IN A SEASON: 59 (Division 2 – Season 1964/65)
MOST LEAGUE GOALS SCORED BY A PLAYER IN A SEASON: Joe Hughes (Season 1969/70)
NO. OF GOALS SCORED: 26
RECORD ATTENDANCE: 26,400 (-v- Celtic – Scottish Cup 11.3.1959)
RECORD VICTORY: 20-0 (-v- Selkirk – Scottish Cup 8.12.1984)
RECORD DEFEAT: 0-9 (-v- Dundee United – League 30.12.1967)

## SEASON TICKET INFORMATION

**Seated**
Adult ........................................................................ £100
Juvenile/OAP ............................................................ £50

## LEAGUE ADMISSION PRICES

**Seated**
Adult .......................................................................... £6
Juvenile/OAP ............................................................ £3
**Standing**
Adult .......................................................................... £5
Juvenile/OAP ......................................................... £2.50

---

Forthbank Stadium, Springkerse, Stirling FK7 7UJ

**CHAIRMAN**
Peter McKenzie

**VICE-CHAIRMAN**
Peter Gardiner, C.A.

**DIRECTORS**
Duncan B. MacGregor
John L. Smith

**SECRETARY**
Mrs. Marlyn Hallam

**PLAYER/MANAGER**
Kevin Drinkell

**CLUB DOCTOR**
Dr. D. McGregor

**PHYSIOTHERAPIST**
George Cameron

**YOUTH DEVELOPMENT OFFICER**
Peter Caproni

**GROUND MAINTENANCE**
Souters of Stirling

**COMMERCIAL MANAGER**
Mrs. Marlyn Hallam
(0786) 450399

**TELEPHONES**
Ground (0786) 450399
Sec. Home (0786) 816274
Fax (0786) 448592
Ticket Office (0786) 450399

**CLUB SHOP**
Situated at Forthbank Stadium

**OFFICIAL SUPPORTERS CLUB**
Forthbank Stadium, Springkerse, Stirling FK7 7UJ

**TEAM CAPTAIN**
Colin Mitchell

**SHIRT SPONSOR**
McKenzie Trailers

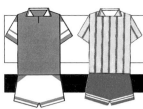

REGISTERED STRIP: Shirt – Red with White Sleeves with Two Red Bands, White Collar with Navy Band
Shorts – White with Red, Navy Blue, Red Leg Band
Stockings – Red, White Turnover with Red, White, Navy Blue Bands
CHANGE STRIP: Shirt – Sky Blue with Narrow Navy Blue Stripe with Sky Blue Collar and Navy Blue Tip
Shorts – Navy Blue with 2 White Bands, Stockings – Navy Blue with Sky Blue Turnover

# CLUB FACTFILE 1993/94 .. RESULTS .. APPEARANCES .. SCORERS

## The ALBION

| Date | Venue | Opponents | Result | McGeown M. | McCormack J. | Watson P. | Tait T. | Lawrie D. | Mitchell C. | Reilly R. | Moore V. | Watters W. | Armstrong P. | Flynn D. | Kinross S. | Pew D. | Callaghan T. | McCallum M. | Kerr J. | McKenna A. | Macdonald K. | Docherty A. | McInnes I. | McAneny P. | Roberts P. | Hamilton J. | Gibson J. | McQuilter R. | McLeod J. | Reid W. | Drinkell K. | Monaghan M. |
|---|---|---|---|---|---|---|---|---|---|---|---|---|---|---|---|---|---|---|---|---|---|---|---|---|---|---|---|---|---|---|---|
| Aug 7 | H | Dumbarton | 2-0 | 1 | 2 | 3 | 4 | 5 | 6 | 7¹ | 8 | 9¹ | 10 | 11 | 12 | 14 | | | | | | | | | | | | | | | | |
| 14 | A | Ayr United | 1-2 | 1 | 2 | 3 | 4 | 5 | 6 | 7 | 8 | 9 | 10 | 11 | | 14 | 12¹ | | | | | | | | | | | | | | | |
| 21 | A | Falkirk | 0-2 | 1 | | 3 | 4 | 5 | 6 | 7 | 8 | 9 | 10 | 11 | | 14 | 2 | 12 | | | | | | | | | | | | | | |
| 28 | H | St. Mirren | 1-0 | 1 | 2 | 3 | 4 | 5 | | | 8 | | | 11¹ | | 7 | 10 | 9 | | 6 | | 12 | 14 | | | | | | | | | |
| Sep 4 | A | Brechin City | 2-1 | 1 | 2 | 3 | 4 | 5 | 6 | | 8 | | | | | 10¹ | 11¹ | 9 | 7 | | | | 12 | | | | | | | | | |
| 11 | H | Dunfermline Athletic | 2-0 | 1 | 2 | 3 | 4 | 5 | 6 | | | 14² | 10 | 11 | | 7 | 8 | 9 | | | | | 12 | | | | | | | | | |
| 14 | A | Greenock Morton | 2-2 | 1 | 2 | 3 | 4¹ | 5 | 6 | | | 11 | 10¹ | | | 7 | 8 | 9 | | | | 14 | 12 | | | | | | | | | |
| 18 | A | Airdrieonians | 2-3 | 1 | | 3 | 4 | 5 | 2 | | | 14 | 10 | 11 | | 7 | 8¹ | 9 | 6¹ | | | | 12 | | | | | | | | | |
| 25 | H | Hamilton Academical | 3-1 | 1 | 2 | 3 | 4 | 5 | 6 | | | 14¹ | 10 | 11¹ | | 7 | 8 | 9¹ | | | | | | | | | | | | | | |
| 28 | H | Clydebank | 0-3 | 1 | 2 | 3 | 4 | 5 | 6 | 12 | | 14 | 10 | 11 | | 7 | 8 | 9 | | | | | | | | | | | | | | |
| Oct 2 | A | Clyde | 0-3 | 1 | | 3 | 4 | 5 | 2 | 12 | | 9 | 10 | 11 | | 7 | 8 | 14 | 6 | | | | | | | | | | | | | |
| 9 | A | Dumbarton | 2-1 | 1 | 2 | 3 | 4 | 5¹ | 6 | | | 14 | 10 | 11 | | 9¹ | 8 | | | | | 12 | 7 | | | | | | | | | |
| 16 | H | Greenock Morton | 1-1 | 1 | | 3 | 4 | 5¹ | 6 | 2 | | 14 | 10 | 11 | | 9 | 8 | | | | | 12 | 7 | | | | | | | | | |
| 23 | A | Dunfermline Athletic | 0-3 | 1 | | 3 | 4 | 5 | 6 | 9 | | 10 | 11 | | | 8 | | | | 2 | | | 7 | | | | | | | | | |
| 30 | H | Falkirk | 3-4 | 1 | 2 | 3 | 4 | 5 | 6 | 12 | | 9² | 10 | 11 | | 8 | 14 | | | | | | 7¹ | | | | | | | | | |
| Nov 6 | A | St. Mirren | 1-0 | 1 | | | 5 | 6 | 10 | | | 9 | 3 | 14 | | 8 | 11 | | 2¹ | | | 12 | 7 | 4 | | | | | | | | |
| 9 | H | Brechin City | 2-1 | 1 | | | 4 | 5 | 6 | 10 | | 9¹ | 3¹ | 14 | | 8 | 11 | | 2 | | | 12 | 7 | | | | | | | | | |
| 13 | H | Clyde | 1-1 | 1 | | | 4 | 5 | 6 | 10 | | 9 | 3 | 14 | | 8 | | | 2¹ | | | 12 | 7 | 11 | | | | | | | | |
| 20 | A | Clydebank | 1-2 | 1 | | | 4 | 5 | 6 | 3 | | 9¹ | | 11 | 14 | 8 | | | 2 | | | 10 | 7 | | | | | | | | | |
| Dec 4 | H | Airdrieonians | 0-4 | 1 | | 3 | 4 | 5 | 6 | 11 | | 9 | | 12 | | 8 | | | | 7 | | 14 | 2 | 10 | | | | | | | | |
| 11 | H | Ayr United | 0-0 | 1 | | 3 | 4 | | 6 | | | 9 | 10 | 14 | | 7 | | | | 11 | 2 | 12 | 5 | 8 | | | | | | | | |
| 18 | A | Greenock Morton | 1-0 | 1 | | 3 | 4 | | 6 | | | 9¹ | 10 | | | 7 | | | | 14 | 11 | 2 | 12 | 5 | 8 | | | | | | | |
| Jan 8 | A | St. Mirren | †3-0 | 1 | | 3 | 4 | | 6 | | | 9¹ | 10¹ | | | 7 | | | | 14 | 11 | 2 | 12 | 5 | 8 | | | | | | | |
| 11 | H | Dumbarton | 0-0 | 1 | | 3 | 4 | | 6 | | | 9 | 10 | | | 7 | | | | 14 | 11 | 2 | 12 | 5 | 8 | | | | | | | |
| 15 | A | Brechin City | 0-2 | 1 | | 3 | 4 | | 6 | | | 9 | 10 | | | 7 | 14 | | | 11 | 2 | 12 | 5 | 8 | | | | | | | | |
| 22 | A | Ayr United | 1-3 | 1 | | | 3 | 6¹ | 12 | | | 14 | 11 | | | 7 | 4 | | | 9 | 2 | 12 | 5 | 8 | | | | | | | | |
| Feb 2 | A | Hamilton Academical | 1-0 | 1 | | | 4 | | 6 | 14 | | 9¹ | 3 | | | 7 | 8 | | | | | 2 | 10 | 5 | 11 | | | | | | | | |
| 5 | H | Dunfermline Athletic | 1-0 | 1 | | | 4 | 6 | 7 | | | 9¹ | 3 | | | 8 | | | | 12 | | 2 | 10 | 5 | 11 | | | | | | | | |
| 12 | A | Clyde | 0-0 | 1 | | | 4 | 6 | 7 | | | 9 | 3 | | | 8 | | | | 14 | 2 | 10 | 5 | 11 | | | | | | | | |
| 15 | A | Falkirk | 1-3 | 1 | | | 4 | 6 | 7 | | | 9 | 3 | | | 8 | | | | 12 | | 2 | 10¹ | 5 | 11 | | | | | | | |
| 26 | H | Clydebank | 1-2 | 1 | | 3 | 4 | 6 | 7 | | | 9 | 8¹ | | | 12 | | | | 14 | 2 | 10 | 5 | 11 | | | | | | | | |
| Mar 5 | A | Airdrieonians | 0-3 | 1 | | 12 | 4 | 6 | | | | 14 | 3 | | | 7 | 8 | | | 9 | 2 | 10 | 5 | 11 | | | | | | | | |
| 12 | H | Hamilton Academical | 1-1 | 1 | | 3 | 4 | 6 | 8 | | | 14 | | | | 12 | | | | 7¹ | 9 | 2 | 10 | 5 | 11 | | | | | | | |
| 19 | H | Greenock Morton | 0-3 | 1 | | | 4 | 6 | | | | 14 | 3 | | | 12 | | | | 7 | | 2 | 10 | 5 | 11 | 8 | 9 | | | | | |
| 26 | H | Dumbarton | 0-0 | 1 | | | 5 | 4 | 6 | 7 | | | 3 | | | | | | | 10 | 2 | | 11 | 8 | 9 | | | | | | | |
| 29 | H | Ayr United | 1-3 | 1 | | | 5 | 4 | 6 | 7 | 12 | | 3 | | | | 14 | | | 10 | 2 | | 11 | 8 | 9¹ | | | | | | | |
| Apr 2 | A | Dunfermline Athletic | 1-2 | | | 3 | 8 | 4¹ | | | | 9 | 11 | | | 7 | 5 | 6 | | 14 | | 2 | | 10 | 12 | 1 | | | | | | |
| 9 | H | Clyde | 0-1 | 1 | | 3 | 4 | 6 | | | | 9 | 11 | | | 5 | | | | 14 | 7 | 2 | 12 | 8 | 10 | | | | | | | |
| 16 | A | Clydebank | 1-2 | 1 | | 3 | 4 | 6 | | | | 9¹ | 11 | 14 | 5 | | | | | 12 | 2 | 7 | 8 | 10 | | | | | | | | |
| 23 | A | Airdrieonians | 1-1 | 1 | | 3 | 6 | 4 | | | | 8 | 11¹ | 14 | 12 | | | | | 9 | 2 | 5 | 10 | 7 | | | | | | | | |
| 27 | H | Hamilton Academical | 1-0 | 1 | | | 6 | 4 | | | | 9 | 3 | 11 | 8 | | | | | 14¹ | 2 | 5 | 10 | 7 | | | | | | | | |
| 30 | H | Falkirk | 0-1 | 1 | | | 6 | 4 | | | | 8 | 3 | 14 | 11 | | | | | 9 | 12 | 2 | 5 | 10 | 7 | | | | | | | |
| May 7 | A | St. Mirren | 0-4 | 1 | | | 5 | 4 | | | | 8 | 3 | 11 | | | | | | 12 | 9 | 2 | 10 | 6 | 7 | | | | | | | |
| 14 | A | Brechin City | 0-3 | 1 | | | 6 | 4 | | | | 8 | 3 | 14 | | 11 | | | | 9 | 2 | 5 | 11 | 10 | 7 | 13 | | | | | | |
| **TOTAL FULL APPEARANCES** | | | | 43 | 10 | 29 | 42 | 21 | 43 | 17 | 5 | 29 | 39 | 16 | | 21 | 27 | 8 | 4 | 6 | | 1 | 12 | 1 | 16 | 21 | 16 | 18 | 17 | 11 | 10 | 1 |
| **TOTAL SUB APPEARANCES** | | | | | (1) | | | | (5) | | | (11) | | (4) | (1) | (10) | (5) | (3) | | (1) | (1) | (6) | (13) | (4) | (1) | (5) | | (1) | | | (1) | (1) |
| **TOTAL GOALS SCORED** | | | | | | 1 | 2 | 2 | 1 | | | 13 | 6 | 3 | | 1 | 2 | 1 | 1 | 2 | | | 3 | | | 1 | | | | | 1 |

*Small bold figures denote goalscorers.  † denotes opponent's own goal.*

---

## FORTHBANK STADIUM

**CAPACITY:** 3,808, Seated 2,508, Standing 1,300

**PITCH DIMENSIONS:** 110 yds x 74 yds

**FACILITIES FOR DISABLED SUPPORTERS:** Disabled access, toilets and spaces for 36.

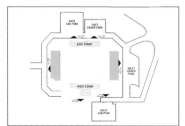

## HOW TO GET THERE

Forthbank Stadium can be reached by the following routes:

**TRAINS:** The nearest station is Stirling Railway Station, which is approximately 2 miles from the ground.

**BUSES:** To Goosecroft Bus Station, Stirling, and bus to stadium from Goosecroft Road (outside Bus Station) every 25 mins from 1.50 p.m. – 2.40 p.m. and return to town at 4.50 p.m.

**CARS:** Follow signs for A91 St Andrews/Alloa. Car Parking is available in the club car park. Home support in West Car Park and visiting support in East Car Park.

# ALBION ROVERS

## LIST OF PLAYERS 1994-95

Cliftonhill Stadium, Main Street,
Coatbridge ML5 9XX

**CHAIRMAN**
Robin W. Marwick J.P., R.I.B.A.

**VICE-CHAIRMAN**
David Lyttle

**DIRECTORS**
David Forrester, C.A.
Jack McGoogan LL.B., D.M.S., N.P.

**SECRETARY**
David Forrester, C.A.

**MANAGER**
Tom Spence

**PLAYER COACHES**
Sammy Conn & Joe McBride

**CLUB DOCTOR**
Dr. Alasdair Purdie,M.B.,Ch.B.

**PHYSIOTHERAPIST**
Michael McBride B.Sc., M.C.S.P.

**CHIEF SCOUT**
Robert Watt

**GROUNDSMAN**
Hugh McBride

**COMMERCIAL MANAGER**
Laurie Cameron
041-771 4585

**TELEPHONES**
Ground (0236) 432350
Sec. Home (0236) 421892
Sec. Bus. (0236) 433438

**CLUB SHOP**
Cliftonhill Stadium, Main Street,
Coatbridge ML5 3RB. Open one
hour prior to kick-off at first team
home matches.

**OFFICIAL SUPPORTERS CLUB**
Andy Morrison, 98 Dundyvan Road,
Coatbridge. Tel (0236) 420366

**TEAM CAPTAIN**
Derek Walker

**SHIRT SPONSOR**
John C. Dalziel (Airdrie) Limited

| SURNAME | FIRST NAME | MIDDLE NAME | DATE OF BIRTH | PLACE OF BIRTH | DATE OF SIGNING | HEIGHT FT INS | WEIGHT ST LBS | PREVIOUS CLUB |
|---|---|---|---|---|---|---|---|---|
| Beattie | James | | 16/02/73 | Glasgow | 27/11/93 | 5 11.0 | 13 2 | Ayr United |
| Collins | Lee | | 03/02/74 | Bellshill | 25/11/93 | 5 7.0 | 11 0 | Pollok |
| Conn | Samuel | Craig | 26/10/61 | Lanark | 01/10/93 | 5 11.0 | 12 0 | Airdrieonians |
| Davidson | Alan | | 17/04/60 | Airdrie | 10/08/94 | 5 10.0 | 11 0 | Ards |
| Deeley | Brian | | 10/11/72 | Alexandria | 14/07/94 | 6 0.0 | 12 0 | Kilpatrick Juveniles |
| Docherty | Anthony | Joseph | 24/01/71 | East Kilbride | 14/06/94 | 5 8.0 | 10 8 | East Stirlingshire |
| Gallagher | John | | 02/06/69 | Glasgow | 29/11/91 | 5 9.0 | 10 10 | Arbroath |
| Kelly | James | | 04/09/71 | Stirling | 19/12/91 | 5 10.0 | 11 0 | Airdrieonians |
| Malone | Paul | | 24/07/73 | Bellshill | 10/08/94 | 5 10.0 | 11 7 | Clyde |
| McBride | Joseph | | 17/08/60 | Glasgow | 25/03/94 | 5 8.5 | 11 2 | East Fife |
| McBride | Martin | Joseph | 22/03/71 | Glasgow | 22/07/92 | 5 9.0 | 10 7 | Campsie Black Watch |
| McDonald | David | | 21/01/69 | Glasgow | 11/03/94 | 5 8.0 | 11 3 | Fort William |
| Miller | David | John | 25/11/75 | Glasgow | 14/07/94 | 5 10.0 | 10 6 | Clyde B.C. |
| Parry | Kenneth | | 21/12/75 | Lanark | 14/07/94 | 5 8.0 | 10 10 | Clyde B.C. |
| Philliben | Robert | Devine | 19/03/68 | Stirling | 14/07/94 | 5 8.0 | 10 7 | Forfar Athletic |
| Quinn | Kenneth | | 19/12/71 | Glasgow | 14/07/94 | 5 9.0 | 9 12 | Clyde |
| Riley | Darren | Stephen | 02/10/71 | Glasgow | 22/07/92 | 5 10.0 | 12 7 | Campsie Black Watch |
| Ryan | Martin | | 16/03/73 | Glasgow | 14/06/94 | 6 1.0 | 12 6 | Kilpatrick Juveniles |
| Scott | Martin | | 27/04/71 | Bellshill | 31/07/92 | 5 10.0 | 10 0 | Clyde |
| Seggie | David | | 13/11/74 | Bellshill | 13/07/92 | 5 7.0 | 9 7 | Monklands Juveniles |
| Spence | Thomas | Agnew | 04/01/60 | Airdrie | 23/07/93 | 6 0.0 | 13 4 | East Fife |
| Thompson | David | Reid | 28/05/62 | Glasgow | 25/03/94 | 6 0.0 | 13 6 | Clyde |
| Walker | Derek | John | 03/07/66 | Bellshill | 10/03/94 | 5 5.0 | 9 1 | Stranraer |
| Wight | John | Campbell | 11/12/73 | Vale of Leven | 09/08/94 | 6 0.0 | 11 0 | Kilpatrick Juveniles |
| Young | Gordon | | 01/05/72 | Glasgow | 14/07/94 | 6 2.0 | 12 8 | Kilpatrick Juveniles |

## MILESTONES

YEAR OF FORMATION: 1882
MOST CAPPED PLAYER: John White
NO. OF CAPS: 1
MOST LEAGUE POINTS IN A SEASON: 54 (Division 2 – Season 1929/30)
MOST LEAGUE GOALS SCORED BY A PLAYER IN A SEASON: John Renwick (Season 1932/33)
NO. OF GOALS SCORED: 41
RECORD ATTENDANCE: 27,381 (-v- Rangers 8.2.1936)
RECORD VICTORY: 12-0 (-v- Airdriehill – Scottish Cup 3.9.1887)
RECORD DEFEAT: 1-11 (-v- Partick Thistle – League Cup, 11.8.1993)

## SEASON TICKET INFORMATION

Seated
Adult .................................................. £70
Juvenile/OAP ...................................... £45
Standing
Enclosure          Adult ......................... £60
                   Juvenile/OAP ............. £40

## LEAGUE ADMISSION PRICES

Seated
Adult ...................................................... £6
Juvenile/OAP ....................................... £3.50
Standing
Adult ...................................................... £5
Juvenile/OAP ....................................... £2.50

# REGISTERED STRIP / CHANGE STRIP

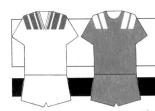

| REGISTERED STRIP: | Shirt – Yellow with Two Red Shoulder Flashes |
| --- | --- |
| | Shorts – Yellow, Stockings – Yellow |
| CHANGE STRIP: | Shirt – Purple with Two Yellow Shoulder Flashes |
| | Shorts – Purple, Stockings – Purple |

## CLUB FACTFILE 1993/94 .. RESULTS .. APPEARANCES .. SCORERS

### The WEE ROVERS

Player columns (left to right): McConnachie R., Kelly J., McKeown D., Spence T., Taylor G., Riley D., McBride M., Scott M., Kerrigan S., Fraser A., Gallagher J., Cadden S., Seggie D., Milner E., Watson E., McCaffrey T., Horne J., McCaffrey J., Burns R., Murray D., Conn S., McQuade A., Collins L., Friar P., Beattie J., Ryan M., Walker D., Lynch M., McDonald D., McBride J., Thompson D.

| Date | Venue | Opponents | Result | Appearances / Scorers |
| --- | --- | --- | --- | --- |
| Aug 7 | H | Alloa | 0-2 | 1 2 3 4 5 6 7 8 9 10 11 12 14 |
| 14 | A | Forfar Athletic | 0-3 | 1 4 3 6 5 2 7 10 9 11 8 14 12 |
| 21 | A | Queen's Park | 2-0 | 1 3 4 5 12 8 9²14 6 2 7 10 11 |
| 28 | A | Stranraer | 1-2 | 1 3 6 5 7 8 9¹14 10 2 12 11 4 |
| Sep 4 | A | Berwick Rangers | 1-1 | 1 3 6 4 7 8 9¹ 10 12 2 14 11 5 |
| 11 | H | Stenhousemuir | 1-2 | 1 10 3 2 11¹ 9 6 8 12 4 7 5 |
| 18 | A | Cowdenbeath | 1-0 | 2 10 3 7 8¹ 9 14 12 6 11 5 1 4 |
| 25 | H | Queen of the South | 1-1 | 2 6 3 7 10¹ 9 8 14 4 11 5 1 |
| Oct 2 | A | East Stirlingshire | 4-1 | 2 3 11 7 9⁴ 10 8 6 5 1 4 14 |
| 9 | H | Arbroath | 0-1 | 2 6 3 7 8 10 14 5 12 11 4 1 9 |
| 16 | A | Meadowbank Thistle | 0-0 | 2 6 3 5 7 11 10 14 8 12 4 1 9 |
| 23 | A | East Fife | 1-1 | 15 2 6 3 7 10 9 11 14 8¹ 4 1 5 |
| 30 | A | Montrose | 0-1 | 2 6 12 7 11 9 10 3 8 4 1 5 14 |
| Nov 6 | H | Forfar Athletic | 1-3 | 4 6 5 2 12 9 11¹ 3 8 1 10 7 14 |
| 13 | H | Cowdenbeath | 0-1 | 2 12 8 14 9 11 7 10 5 1 4 6 3 |
| 20 | A | Queen of the South | †2-1 | 3 2 11 10 4 8¹ 5 1 9 7 6 |
| 27 | A | Arbroath | †1-1 | 3 2 11 10 14 4 8 5 1 9 7 6 |
| Dec 4 | H | East Stirlingshire | 1-5 | 6 2 11¹10 12 4 8 5 1 9 7 6 |
| 18 | A | Alloa | 1-1 | 3 2 14 10 9 12 8 11 5 1 4¹ 7 6 |
| Jan 1 | A | Queen's Park | 0-2 | 6 7 10 9 12 14 8 11 5 1 4 2 3 |
| 8 | H | Stranraer | 1-2 | 6 7 10 9 12 8 11¹ 5 1 4 2 3 |
| 22 | A | Meadowbank Thistle | 2-4 | 2 11 14 10¹12 9 6 8 7¹ 5 1 4 3 |
| 25 | H | Montrose | 3-4 | 1 2 14 9¹12² 8 11 10 7 5 4 3 6 |
| 29 | H | East Fife | 1-1 | 1 2 11 10¹ 9 3 6 8 5 4 7 |
| Feb 5 | A | Stenhousemuir | 1-5 | 1 3 2 11 10 9 12 8¹ 6 7 5 4 |
| 12 | H | Berwick Rangers | 0-2 | 1 3 12 2 11 9 8 6 7 5 4 14 10 |
| 19 | A | East Stirlingshire | 3-1 | 1 2 3 5 11 9² 10 6 7 4 8 |
| 26 | A | Stranraer | 1-2 | 1 2 3 5 11 9¹ 10 8 7 4 6 14 |
| Mar 5 | H | Montrose | 0-1 | 1 5 2 11 9 10 6 7 4 12 8 3 14 |
| 12 | A | Queen of the South | 2-1 | 1 3 2 11¹ 9 7 6 4 14 10¹ 8 5 |
| 19 | H | Queen's Park | 1-1 | 1 3 2 11 10 7 6 4 14 8 9¹ 5 |
| 26 | A | Stenhousemuir | 0-0 | 1 3 2 11 10 14 6 12 4 8 9 5 7 |
| Apr 2 | A | East Fife | 1-3 | 1 3 2 11 9¹ 12 6 4 8 10 5 7 14 |
| 9 | H | Cowdenbeath | 1-0 | 1 3 2 11 9¹ 8 4 6 14 10 5 7 12 |
| 16 | A | Berwick Rangers | 0-3 | 1 2 3 7 12 9 14 4 8 6 10 5 11 |
| 23 | H | Forfar Athletic | 1-3 | 1 2¹ 5 14 9 12 3 8 4 6 10 11 7 |
| 30 | H | Alloa | 1-1 | 1 5 3 2 9¹ 14 8 4 6 10 11 7 |
| May 7 | A | Arbroath | 0-1 | 2 5 1 14 9 12 3 8 4 6 10 11 7 |
| 14 | H | Meadowbank Thistle | 0-2 | 1 4 5 2 9 14 12 7 6 8 3 10 11 |
| **TOTAL FULL APPEARANCES** | | | | 22 19 35 12 8 26 24 36 22 15 20 20 21 7 1 1 7 22 16 1 31 19 14 1 11 1 6 8 3 |
| **TOTAL SUB APPEARANCES** | | | | (1) (1) (2) (8) (1) (2)(13) (8) (1) (8) (2) (2) (5) (1) (1) (1) (2) (2) |
| **TOTAL GOALS SCORED** | | | | 1 2 17 6 1 1 1 3 1 2 |

*Small bold figures denote goalscorers. † denotes opponent's own goal.*

## CLIFTONHILL STADIUM

**CAPACITY**: 1,238; Seated 538, Standing 700

**PITCH DIMENSIONS**: 100 yds x 70 yds

**FACILITIES FOR DISABLED SUPPORTERS**: Access from East Stewart Street with toilet facilities and space for wheelchairs, cars etc. Advanced contact with club advised – this area is uncovered.

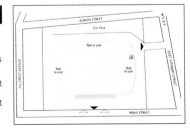

## HOW TO GET THERE

The following routes can be used to reach Cliftonhill Stadium:

**BUSES**: The ground is conveniently situated on the main Glasgow-Airdrie bus route and there is a stop near the ground. Local buses serving most areas of Coatbridge and Airdrie pass by the stadium every few minutes.

**TRAINS**: The nearest railway station is Coatdyke on the Glasgow-Airdrie line and the ground is a ten minute walk from there. The frequency of service is 15 minutes.

**CARS**: A large car park is situated behind the ground with access off Albion Street, and vehicles may also be parked in Hillcrest Avenue, Albion Street and East Stewart Street, which are all adjacent to the ground.

# ALLOA

**Recreation Park, Clackmannan Road, Alloa FK10 1RR**

**CHAIRMAN**
Robert F. Hopkins

**VICE-CHAIRMAN**
George Ormiston

**DIRECTORS**
Patrick Lawlor
Ronald J. Todd

**SECRETARY**
Ewen G. Cameron

**MANAGER**
William Lamont

**ASSISTANT MANAGER**
Billy Simpson

**RESERVE TEAM COACH**
James Dempsey

**CLUB DOCTOR**
Dr. Clarke Mullen

**PHYSIOTHERAPIST**
Alan Anderson

**GROUNDSMAN**
David Campbell

**COMMERCIAL MANAGER**
William McKie
Bus. Tel (0259) 722695
Home Tel (0259) 730572

**TELEPHONES**
Ground (0259) 722695
Sec. Bus. (0324) 612472
Sec. Home (0259) 750899

**OFFICIAL SUPPORTERS CLUB**
c/o Recreation Park,
Clackmannan Road, Alloa FK10 1RR

**TEAM CAPTAIN**
John McNiven

**SHIRT SPONSOR**
Campbell Homes

## LIST OF PLAYERS 1994-95

| SURNAME | FIRST NAME | MIDDLE NAME | DATE OF BIRTH | PLACE OF BIRTH | DATE OF SIGNING | HEIGHT FT INS | WEIGHT ST LBS | PREVIOUS CLUB |
|---|---|---|---|---|---|---|---|---|
| Bennett | John | Neil | 22/08/71 | Falkirk | 09/08/91 | 5 7.0 | 10 0 | St. Johnstone |
| Binnie | Neil | | 25/12/67 | Stirling | 28/03/91 | 6 2.0 | 12 4 | Bonnybridge Juniors |
| Bryan | Alan | | 26/09/76 | Alexandria | 19/08/94 | 5 9.0 | 11 0 | Unattached |
| Butter | James | Ross | 14/12/66 | Dundee | 27/08/90 | 6 1.0 | 12 2 | St. Johnstone |
| Cadden | Stephen | Joseph | 26/11/68 | Baillieston | 04/03/94 | 6 0.0 | 11 6 | Albion Rovers |
| Campbell | Colin | | 05/01/70 | Edinburgh | 15/05/91 | 5 11.0 | 12 0 | Armadale Thistle |
| Crombie | Lawrence | | 27/05/71 | Edinburgh | 12/12/92 | 5 11.0 | 12 0 | Lochend United |
| Diver | Daniel | | 15/11/66 | Paisley | 31/03/94 | 6 2.0 | 12 8 | Arbroath |
| Graham | Paul | Scott | 17/05/70 | Motherwell | 08/06/94 | 6 2.0 | 12 4 | Greenock Morton |
| Kemp | Brian | | 30/11/64 | Falkirk | 14/01/94 | 5 7.0 | 10 8 | East Stirlingshire |
| Lamont | Peter | Mitchell | 24/11/66 | Glasgow | 08/10/93 | 6 1.0 | 12 2 | Shettleston Juniors |
| Lawrie | Douglas | Gibb | 11/06/66 | Falkirk | 04/03/94 | 5 10.0 | 11 1 | Stirling Albion |
| McAnenay | Michael | Samuel P. | 16/09/66 | Glasgow | 09/10/93 | 5 10.0 | 10 7 | Dumbarton |
| McAvoy | Neil | | 29/07/72 | Stirling | 09/08/91 | 6 2.0 | 11 7 | Sauchie Juniors |
| McCormack | John | Thomas | 22/07/65 | Stirling | 26/11/93 | 5 9.0 | 10 0 | Stirling Albion |
| McCormick | Stephen | | 19/03/65 | Seafield | 21/03/92 | 5 10.0 | 11 4 | Stenhousemuir |
| McCulloch | Keith | George | 27/05/67 | Edinburgh | 28/08/87 | 5 10.0 | 12 0 | Cowdenbeath |
| McNiven | John | Martin | 23/12/62 | Glasgow | 01/08/92 | 5 11.0 | 10 7 | Stranraer |
| Moffat | Barrie | | 27/12/72 | Bangour | 09/10/90 | 5 8.0 | 10 4 | Gairdoch Colts U'18 |
| Morrison | Stephen | | 15/08/61 | St. Andrews | 10/08/94 | 6 0.0 | 13 3 | Clyde |
| Mulholland | Craig | | 19/12/77 | Alexandria | 19/08/94 | 5 10.0 | 10 4 | Unattached |
| Nelson | Mark | | 09/08/69 | Bellshill | 01/03/94 | 5 11.0 | 11 0 | Dumbarton |
| Newbigging | William | Matthew | 07/09/68 | Blairhall | 18/08/90 | 5 10.0 | 13 0 | Hill of Beath |
| Smith | Joseph | | 21/08/76 | Bellshill | 19/08/94 | 5 10.0 | 10 2 | Berwick Rangers |
| Willock | Andrew | | 13/01/64 | Southend on Sea | 09/10/93 | 5 6.0 | 9 12 | Dumbarton |

## MILESTONES

YEAR OF FORMATION: 1883
MOST CAPPED PLAYER: Jock Hepburn
NO. OF CAPS: 1
MOST LEAGUE POINTS IN A SEASON: 60 (Division 2 – Season 1921/22)
MOST LEAGUE GOALS SCORED BY A PLAYER IN A SEASON: William Crilley (Season 1921/22)
NO. OF GOALS SCORED: 49
RECORD ATTENDANCE: 13,000 (-v- Dunfermline Athletic – 26.2.1939)
RECORD VICTORY: 9-2 (-v- Forfar Athletic – Division 2, 18.3.1933)
RECORD DEFEAT: 0-10 (-v- Dundee – Division 2 and Third Lanark – League Cup)

## SEASON TICKET INFORMATION

**Seated**
Adult .......................................................................... £75
Juvenile/OAP ............................................................... £45
**Standing**
Adult .......................................................................... £60
Juvenile/OAP ............................................................... £30

## LEAGUE ADMISSION PRICES

**Seated**
Adult ............................................................................ £5
Juvenile/OAP ................................................................. £3
**Standing**
Adult ............................................................................ £4
Juvenile/OAP ................................................................. £2

REGISTERED STRIP: Shirt – Gold with Black Collar and Cuffs, Trimmed in White, Shorts – Black Stockings – Black with 1" Broad Gold Band at Turn-down

CHANGE STRIP: Shirt – Berry Red, Trimmed in Navy and White at Collar, Shorts – Berry Red Stockings – Navy with Berry Red Diamond Pattern at Turn-down

# CLUB FACTFILE 1993/94 .. RESULTS .. APPEARANCES .. SCORERS

## The WASPS

| Date | Venue | Opponents | Result | Butter J. | McNiven J. | Bennett N. | Campbell C. | McCulloch K. | Newbigging W. | Gibson J. | Ramsay S. | Hendry M. | Moffat B. | McAvoy N. | Herd W. | McCormick S. | Mackay J. | Dempsey J. | Russell G. | Tait G. | Lee R. | Crombie L. | McAnenay M. | Willock A. | Lamont P. | McCormack J. | Kemp B. | Craig N. | Nelson M. | Lawrie D. | Cadden S. | Diver D. |
|---|---|---|---|---|---|---|---|---|---|---|---|---|---|---|---|---|---|---|---|---|---|---|---|---|---|---|---|---|---|---|---|---|
| Aug 7 | A | Albion Rovers | 2-0 | 1 | 2 | 3 | 4 | 5 | $6^1$ | 7 | 8 | $9^1$ | 10 | 11 | 12 | 14 | | | | | | | | | | | | | | | | |
| 14 | H | Cowdenbeath | 0-1 | 1 | 2 | 3 | 4 | 5 | 6 | | 8 | 9 | 10 | 11 | | 7 | 12 | 14 | | | | | | | | | | | | | | |
| 21 | H | East Stirlingshire | 0-0 | 1 | | 3 | 4 | 5 | 6 | | 8 | 9 | 12 | 10 | 11 | | | | 2 | 7 | 14 | | | | | | | | | | | |
| 28 | A | East Fife | 1-4 | 1 | 12 | 14 | 2 | 5 | 6 | $7^1$ | 8 | | 10 | 11 | | 9 | | | 4 | | 3 | | | | | | | | | | | |
| Sep 4 | H | Stenhousemuir | 1-1 | 1 | 2 | | 4 | 5 | 6 | 11 | | 10 | $7^1$ | 8 | 14 | 9 | | | | 12 | 3 | | | | | | | | | | | |
| 11 | H | Stranraer | 1-0 | 1 | 2 | 8 | 4 | 5 | 6 | 12 | | 9 | 10 | $7^1$ | | | | | | 11 | 3 | 14 | | | | | | | | | | |
| 18 | A | Queen of the South | 1-0 | 1 | 2 | 8 | 4 | 5 | 6 | 12 | | $10^1$ | 11 | 7 | | | | | | 9 | 3 | 14 | | | | | | | | | | |
| 25 | H | Montrose | 0-1 | 1 | 2 | 10 | 4 | 5 | 6 | | | 8 | 9 | 7 | 14 | | | | 11 | | 3 | | | | | | | | | | | |
| Oct 2 | H | Meadowbank Thistle | 1-0 | 1 | 2 | 10 | 4 | 5 | $6^1$ | 7 | 8 | 9 | 11 | 14 | | | | | 12 | | 3 | | | | | | | | | | | |
| 9 | A | Forfar Athletic | 3-0 | 1 | | 2 | 4 | 5 | 6 | $14^1$ | 8 | $9^1$ | | | | | | | 10 | | 3 | $7^1$ | 11 | 12 | | | | | | | | |
| 16 | A | Arbroath | 3-2 | 1 | 2 | 10 | 4 | 5 | 6 | 12 | $8^2$ | 9 | | | | | | | 14 | | 3 | $7^1$ | 11 | | | | | | | | | |
| 23 | A | Berwick Rangers | 1-0 | 1 | 2 | 3 | 4 | 5 | $6^1$ | 10 | 9 | | | | | | | | 12 | | | 7 | 11 | 14 | | | | | | | | |
| 30 | H | Queen's Park | 1-1 | 1 | 2 | | 4 | 5 | $6^1$ | 10 | 3 | 8 | | | | | 14 | | 12 | | | 7 | 11 | 9 | | | | | | | | |
| Nov 6 | A | Cowdenbeath | 1-1 | 1 | 2 | 3 | 4 | 5 | 6 | 14 | $8^1$ | 12 | 10 | | | | | | | | | 7 | 11 | 9 | | | | | | | | |
| 13 | H | Queen of the South | 1-0 | 1 | 2 | 3 | 4 | 5 | 6 | 14 | $8^1$ | | | | 7 | | | | 12 | 10 | | | 11 | 9 | | | | | | | | |
| 20 | A | Montrose | 2-1 | | 2 | | 4 | 5 | $6^1$ | 7 | 8 | 9 | | | 12 | | | | | 14 | 3 | 10 | $11^1$ | | | | | | | | | |
| Dec 4 | H | Meadowbank Thistle | 1-1 | 1 | | 3 | 4 | 5 | 6 | | 8 | 9 | 11 | | | $14^1$ | | | | 7 | | | 10 | 12 | 2 | | | | | | | |
| 7 | H | Forfar Athletic | 1-1 | 1 | 2 | | 4 | 5 | 6 | | 8 | 14 | 12 | | | 9 | | | | 10 | | | 11 | | $7^1$ | 3 | | | | | | |
| 18 | H | Albion Rovers | 1-1 | 1 | 2 | | 4 | 5 | 6 | | 8 | 10 | | | | $14^1$ | | | 12 | | 3 | 7 | 11 | 9 | | | | | | | | |
| 27 | A | Queen's Park | 1-2 | 1 | 2 | | 4 | 5 | 6 | | 8 | 7 | | | | 12 | | | | 14 | 3 | 9 | $11^1$ | 10 | | | | | | | | |
| Jan 11 | A | East Stirlingshire | 1-0 | 1 | 2 | | 4 | 5 | 6 | | 8 | 12 | | | | $9^1$ | | | | | 3 | 14 | 11 | 10 | 7 | | | | | | | |
| 18 | H | East Fife | 2-2 | 1 | 2 | | 4 | $5^1$ | 6 | | 8 | 7 | | | | 9 | | | 12 | | | 14 | $11^1$ | 10 | | 3 | | | | | | |
| 22 | A | Arbroath | 1-2 | 1 | 2 | | 4 | 5 | 6 | | 8 | $12^1$ | | | 7 | 9 | | | | | | 14 | 10 | 11 | | 3 | | | | | | |
| Feb 1 | A | Berwick Rangers | 1-1 | 1 | 2 | | | 5 | | | 8 | 9 | $7^1$ | | | 12 | 4 | | 14 | | | 10 | 11 | | | 3 | 6 | | | | | |
| 5 | A | Stranraer | 1-1 | 1 | 2 | | | 5 | | | 8 | 11 | | | 10 | $9^1$ | | | 6 | 4 | | 12 | 14 | | 7 | 3 | | | | | | |
| 12 | H | Stenhousemuir | 1-2 | 1 | 2 | | 4 | 5 | $6^1$ | | 8 | 12 | | | 7 | 9 | | | | 10 | 3 | 14 | 11 | | | | | | | | | |
| Mar 2 | A | Meadowbank Thistle | 2-3 | 1 | 2 | | 4 | 5 | 6 | | | 12 | | | | $9^1$ | | | $14^1$ | 3 | | 8 | 11 | 10 | | | | | 7 | | | |
| 5 | H | East Stirlingshire | 0-1 | 1 | 2 | | 4 | 5 | 6 | | | 10 | | | | 9 | | | 12 | 14 | | 7 | 11 | | | | | | 3 | 8 | | |
| 12 | A | Arbroath | 0-0 | 1 | 2 | | 4 | 5 | | | | 10 | | | | 14 | | | 9 | 12 | 7 | | | | 3 | | | | 6 | 8 | | |
| 15 | H | Queen of the South | 1-0 | 1 | 2 | | $4^1$ | 5 | | | | 10 | 11 | 7 | | 9 | | | 14 | 12 | | | | | | 3 | | | 6 | 8 | | |
| 19 | A | Berwick Rangers | 1-1 | 1 | 2 | | 12 | 5 | 4 | 7 | | | | | | 14 | | | | | 8 | 11 | | $9^1$ | | 3 | | | 6 | 10 | | |
| 26 | H | Stranraer | 1-1 | 1 | 2 | | 4 | | | 5 | 8 | | | | 7 | | | | 6 | | | 14 | 11 | 9 | | 3 | | | | | $10^1$ | |
| Apr 2 | A | Stenhousemuir | 0-1 | 1 | 2 | | 5 | 4 | | | 8 | 12 | | | | | | | | 14 | | 11 | 7 | | | 3 | | | 6 | 10 | 9 | |
| 12 | H | Queen's Park | 0-0 | 1 | 2 | 3 | | 5 | | | 8 | | | | | 14 | | | 12 | 10 | | 11 | 7 | | | 6 | | | 4 | 9 | | |
| 16 | H | Cowdenbeath | 1-0 | 1 | 2 | | 4 | 6 | | | | 10 | | | 7 | | | | 14 | 12 | | 11 | | | | 3 | | | 5 | 8 | $9^1$ | |
| 23 | A | Montrose | 2-2 | 1 | 2 | | 4 | 5 | | | | 10 | 7 | | | $14^1$ | | | $12^1$ | 11 | | | 3 | | | | | | 6 | 8 | 9 | |
| 30 | A | Albion Rovers | 1-1 | 1 | 2 | | 4 | | 6 | | | 14 | 10 | | $7^1$ | 12 | | | | | 3 | 11 | | | | | | | 5 | 8 | 9 | |
| May 7 | H | Forfar Athletic | 1-3 | 1 | 2 | | 4 | | 6 | 10 | | | | | | | | | 11 | 7 | 14 | 12 | | | | 3 | | | 5 | 8 | $9^1$ | |
| 14 | H | East Fife | 1-1 | 1 | 2 | | 4 | 5 | 6 | | 8 | 10 | | | | 14 | | | 7 | 12 | | | | | | 3 | | | | $11^1$ | 9 | |
| **TOTAL FULL APPEARANCES** | | | | 39 | 34 | 14 | 34 | 36 | 33 | 8 | 30 | 5 | 20 | 23 | 4 | 13 | 3 | 3 | 3 | 9 | 13 | 19 | 20 | 17 | 7 | 12 | 1 | 2 | 10 | 10 | 7 | |
| **TOTAL SUB APPEARANCES** | | | | | (1) | (1) | (1) | | | (6) | | | (7) | (6) | (3) | (10) | | | (4) | (15) | | | (2) | (5) | | (6) | (6) | | | | | |
| **TOTAL GOALS SCORED** | | | | | | | 1 | | 7 | 2 | 4 | 1 | 4 | 2 | | 6 | | | 1 | | | 2 | 4 | 3 | 1 | | | 1 | | 2 | |

*Small bold figures denote goalscorers. † denotes opponent's own goal.*

---

## RECREATION PARK

**CAPACITY:** 4,111; Seated 424, Standing 3,687

**PITCH DIMENSIONS:** 110 yds x 75 yds

**FACILITIES FOR DISABLED SUPPORTERS:** Accommodation for wheelchairs and invalid carriages in front of Stand. Disabled toilets are also available.

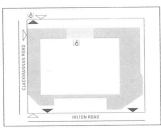

## HOW TO GET THERE

Recreation Park can be reached by the following routes.

**TRAINS:** The nearest railway station is Stirling, which is seven miles away. Fans would have to connect with an inter-linking bus service to reach the ground from here.

**BUSES:** There are three main services which stop outside the ground. These are the Dunfermline-Stirling, Stirling-Clackmannan and Falkirk-Alloa buses.

**CARS:** Car Parking is available in the car park adjacent to the ground and this can hold 175 vehicles.

# ARBROATH

**Gayfield Park,**
**Arbroath DD11 1QB**

**PRESIDENT**
John D. Christison

**VICE-PRESIDENT**
Charles Kinnear

**COMMITTEE**
R. Alan Ripley (Treasurer)
David Kean
Duncan Ferguson
Andrew J. Warrington
Ian S. C. Wyllie
William J. Thomson
George Johnson

**SECRETARY**
Andrew J. Warrington

**MANAGER**
George Mackie

**YOUTH COACH**
John Martin

**CLUB DOCTOR**
Dr. William Smith

**PHYSIOTHERAPIST**
William Shearer

**CHIEF SCOUT**
James Cant

**GROUNDSMAN**
William Nicoll

**COMMERCIAL MANAGER**
David Kean
(0382) 477783

**TELEPHONES**
Ground/Ticket Office/Club Shop
(0241) 872157
Sec. Home (0241) 852194
Sec. Bus. (0382) 303483

**CLUB SHOP**
Gayfield Park, Arbroath DD11 1QB
Open on match days and
weekday mornings

**OFFICIAL SUPPORTERS CLUB**
Brothock Bridge, Arbroath

**TEAM CAPTAIN**
Malcolm Murray

**SHIRT SPONSOR**
Windmill Hotel

## LIST OF PLAYERS 1994-95

| SURNAME | FIRST NAME | MIDDLE NAME | DATE OF BIRTH | PLACE OF BIRTH | DATE OF SIGNING | HEIGHT FT INS | WEIGHT ST LBS | PREVIOUS CLUB |
|---|---|---|---|---|---|---|---|---|
| Brock | John | Paul | 16/04/71 | Edinburgh | 05/05/94 | 6 3.0 | 12 0 | Meadowbank Thistle |
| Buick | Garry | Robert | 12/01/75 | Arbroath | 27/08/93 | 5 5.5 | 10 4 | Arbroath Sporting Club |
| Craib | Stephen | Thomas | 14/01/72 | Dundee | 09/08/94 | 5 10.0 | 10 7 | Montrose |
| Downie | Ian | | 16/11/72 | Dunfermline | 10/06/94 | 5 6.5 | 9 9 | Forfar Athletic |
| Duncan | Robert | Wallace | 15/11/68 | Dundee | 31/03/94 | 6 7.0 | 16 0 | Arbroath Victoria |
| Easton | Scott | Milne | 20/11/75 | Dundee | 31/03/93 | 6 0.0 | 12 0 | Arbroath Sporting Club |
| Elder | Stuart | Richard | 25/07/66 | Rinteln | 05/08/94 | 6 1.0 | 13 0 | Meadowbank Thistle |
| Elliot | David | Euan | 23/12/74 | Dundee | 30/03/94 | 5 9.5 | 10 3 | Arbroath Sporting Club |
| Farnan | Craig | | 07/04/71 | Dundee | 20/05/88 | 5 10.0 | 12 3 | Forfar West End |
| Finlay | Steven | | 31/05/72 | West Lothian | 19/07/94 | 5 11.0 | 11 0 | Whitburn J.F.C. |
| Florence | Steven | | 28/10/71 | Dundee | 20/05/88 | 5 6.0 | 10 5 | Arbroath Lads Club |
| Jackson | Derek | | 29/08/65 | Alloa | 02/08/93 | 6 1.0 | 13 7 | Sauchie |
| Kelly | Mark | Nicholas | 28/08/75 | Dundee | 18/11/93 | 6 1.0 | 12 0 | Carnoustie Panmure |
| King | Thomas | David | 23/01/70 | Dumbarton | 02/06/93 | 5 9.0 | 11 0 | Clydebank |
| Martin | Michael | David | 27/08/75 | Arbroath | 04/08/93 | 6 1.0 | 10 7 | Arbroath Victoria |
| McGovern | Justin | Patrick | 08/04/73 | Edinburgh | 08/07/94 | 5 7.0 | 11 0 | Easthouses B.C.A. |
| McGregor | Scott | Grant | 22/05/69 | Perth | 25/03/94 | 6 1.5 | 11 7 | Glenrothes Juniors |
| McKinnon | Colin | | 29/08/69 | Glasgow | 01/09/93 | 6 0.0 | 11 7 | East Stirlingshire |
| Mitchell | Brian | Charles | 29/02/68 | Arbroath | 27/07/84 | 5 8.0 | 13 0 | Arbroath Lads Club |
| Moffat | Paul | | 28/10/72 | Edinburgh | 08/07/94 | 6 3.0 | 13 10 | Easthouses B.C.A. |
| Murray | Malcolm | | 26/07/64 | Buckie | 02/08/94 | 5 11.0 | 11 4 | Meadowbank Thistle |
| Rae | James | | 08/07/69 | Edinburgh | 02/08/94 | 6 0.5 | 9 8 | Fauldhouse United |
| Reilly | John | Paul | 21/03/62 | Dundee | 09/08/94 | 5 7.5 | 10 10 | Cowdenbeath |
| Rennie | Steven | | 26/07/68 | Edinburgh | 16/06/94 | 6 1.0 | 11 8 | Craigroyston |
| Tosh | Steven | William | 27/04/73 | Kirkcaldy | 31/03/94 | 5 9.0 | 10 2 | Glenrothes Juniors |

## MILESTONES

**YEAR OF FORMATION:** 1878
**MOST CAPPED PLAYER:** Ned Doig
**NO. OF CAPS:** 2
**MOST LEAGUE POINTS IN A SEASON:** 57 (Division 2 – Season 1966/67)
**MOST LEAGUE GOALS SCORED BY A PLAYER IN A SEASON:** David Easson (Season 1958/59)
**NO. OF GOALS SCORED:** 45
**RECORD ATTENDANCE:** 13,510 (-v- Rangers – Scottish Cup. 23.2.1952)
**RECORD VICTORY:** 36-0 (-v- Bon Accord – Scottish Cup. 12.9.1885)
**RECORD DEFEAT:** 1-9 (-v- Celtic, League Cup, 25.8.1993)

## SEASON TICKET INFORMATION

**Seated**
Adult ........................................................ £80
Juvenile/OAP ............................................ £45
**Standing**
Adult ........................................................ £70
Juvenile/OAP ............................................ £45

## LEAGUE ADMISSION PRICES

**Seated**
Adult .......................................................... £5
Juvenile/OAP .......................................... £3.50
**Standing**
Adult .......................................................... £4
Juvenile/OAP/Unemployed (with UB40) ................ £2.50

| REGISTERED STRIP: | Shirt – Maroon with Sky Blue Trim |
| | Shorts – White, Stockings – Maroon with Sky Blue Hooped Tops |
| CHANGE STRIP: | Shirt – Black and White Striped Design |
| | Shorts – Black, Stockings – Black with White Hooped Tops |

# CLUB FACTFILE 1993/94 .. RESULTS .. APPEARANCES .. SCORERS

## The RED LICHTIES

Players (columns left to right): Harkness M., Hamilton J., Florence S., Mitchell B., Adam C., Martin C., Will B., King T., Russell R., Farnan C., Sorbie S., Hindson P., Tindal K., Jackson D., Elliot D., Strachan J., McKillop A., Clouston B., McKinnon C., Diver D., Buckley G., Scott D., McKeown J., McClelland J., Glennie R., Feeney P., McGregor S., Tosh S., Martin M., Duncan R.

| Date | Venue | Opponents | Result | Har | Ham | Flo | Mit | Adm | MarC | Wil | Kng | Rus | Far | Sor | Hin | Tin | Jak | Eli | Str | McK | Clo | McN | Div | Buc | Sco | Mcw | McC | Gle | Fee | McG | Tos | MarM | Dun |
|---|---|---|---|---|---|---|---|---|---|---|---|---|---|---|---|---|---|---|---|---|---|---|---|---|---|---|---|---|---|---|---|---|---|
| Aug 7 | H | Queen of the South | 2-5 | 1 | 2 | 3 | 4 | 5 | 6 | 7 | 8¹ | 9 | 10 | 11 | 12 | 14¹ | | | | | | | | | | | | | | | | | |
| 14 | A | Montrose | 0-0 | | 2 | 3 | 4 | 5 | 6 | 7 | 8 | | 10 | 11 | | 14 | | | 1 | | | 9 | | | | | | | | | | | |
| 21 | H | Forfar Athletic | 1-1 | | 2 | 3 | 4 | 5 | 6 | 7 | 8 | | 10 | 11 | | 14¹ | | | 1 | | | 9 | | | | | | | | | | | |
| 28 | A | Berwick Rangers | 0-2 | | 2 | 3 | | | 9 | 6 | 8 | | 4 | 11 | 12 | 14 | | | 1 | 10 | 5 | 7 | | | | | | | | | | | |
| Sep 4 | A | Stranraer | 1-2 | 12 | 3 | 4 | | | 6 | | 2 | | 10 | 11 | | 14 | | | 8 | 1 | 5 | 7 | 9¹ | | | | | | | | | | |
| 11 | H | Queen's Park | 2-0 | | 2 | 3 | 4 | 14 | | 12 | 8 | | | 11 | | | | | 1 | 6 | 5 | 7 | 10¹ | 9¹ | | | | | | | | | |
| 18 | H | Stenhousemuir | 1-2 | | 2 | 3 | 4 | 5 | 12 | | 8 | | | 11 | | | | | 1 | 6 | | 7 | 10¹ | 9 | | | | | | | | | |
| 25 | A | Meadowbank Thistle | 0-3 | | 2 | 3 | 4 | 5 | 6 | | 8 | | | 11 | 14 | | | | 1 | | 7 | 10 | 9 | | | | | | | | | | |
| Oct 2 | H | Cowdenbeath | 2-2 | | 2 | 3 | 4 | 5 | 6¹ | | 8 | | 12 | 11 | 14 | | | | 1 | 7 | | 10 | 9¹ | | | | | | | | | | |
| 9 | A | Albion Rovers | 1-0 | | 2 | 4 | | 5 | 3 | | 8 | | | | | | | | 7 | 1 | 6 | 10¹ | 9 | 11 | | | | | | | | | |
| 16 | A | Alloa | 2-3 | | 2 | 4 | | 5 | 3 | | 8 | 14 | 12 | | | | | | 7¹ | 1 | 6 | 10 | 9¹ | 11 | | | | | | | | | |
| 23 | A | East Stirlingshire | 4-2 | | 2 | 4 | | 5 | 3 | | 8 | | | 11¹ | | | | | 7 | 1 | 6 | 10 | 9³ | 12 | | | | | | | | | |
| 30 | A | East Fife | 0-1 | | 2 | | 4 | 5 | 6 | | 8 | | | 11 | | | | | 7 | 1 | 3 | 10 | 9 | 14 | 12 | | | | | | | | |
| Nov 6 | H | Montrose | 2-0 | | 2 | 3 | 4 | 5 | 6 | | 8 | | 14 | 11¹ | | | | | 7¹ | 1 | | 10 | 9 | 12 | | | | | | | | | |
| 13 | A | Stenhousemuir | 0-4 | | 2 | 4 | | 5 | 3 | | 8 | | 12 | 14 | | | | | 7 | | 6 | 9 | 11 | 10 | 1 | | | | | | | | |
| 20 | H | Meadowbank Thistle | 3-2 | | | 3 | | 5 | | 8¹ | 7 | | 4 | 11¹ | | | | | 1 | | | 2 | 10¹ | 9 | | | 6 | | | | | | |
| 27 | H | Albion Rovers | 1-1 | | | 3 | | 5 | | 8 | 7 | | 4 | 11¹ | | | | | 1 | 12 | 6 | 2 | 10 | 9 | 14 | | | | | | | | |
| Dec 4 | H | Cowdenbeath | 1-0 | | | 3 | | 5 | 6 | | 7 | | 4 | 11¹ | | | | | 1 | | | 2 | 10 | 9 | 8 | 14 | | | | | | | |
| 18 | A | Queen of the South | 0-6 | | | 3 | | 5 | 6 | | 7 | | 4 | 11 | | | | | 1 | 12 | 10 | 2 | 9 | | 8 | 14 | | | | | | | |
| 29 | H | East Fife | 3-2 | | | 3 | 4 | 5 | 6 | | 8¹ | | 2 | 11 | | | | | 1 | | | 7 | 10¹ | 9¹ | | | | | | | | | |
| Jan 11 | A | Forfar Athletic | 4-1 | | | 3 | 4 | 5¹ | | | 8 | | 2 | 11 | | | | | 1 | 6 | | 7 | 10¹ | 9²14 | | | | | | | | | |
| 22 | A | Alloa | 2-1 | | | 3 | 4 | 5 | 6¹ | | 8 | | 2 | 11 | | | | | 1 | | | 7¹ | 10 | 9 | 12 | 14 | | | | | | | |
| 26 | H | Berwick Rangers | 0-4 | | | 3 | 4 | 5 | 6 | | 8 | | 2 | | | | | | 1 | | | 7 | 10 | 9 | 11 | 14 | | | | | | | |
| Feb 2 | H | East Stirlingshire | 1-1 | | | 3 | 4 | 5 | 6 | | 8 | | 2 | 11 | | | | | 1 | | | 7 | 10 | 9¹14 | 12 | | | | | | | | |
| 5 | A | Queen's Park | 1-2 | | | 3 | 4 | 5 | 6 | | | | 2 | 11¹ | | | | | 1 | 12 | | 7 | 10 | 9 | 14 | 8 | | | | | | | |
| 12 | A | Stranraer | 0-0 | | | | 6 | 4 | 10 | | 8 | | 5 | 11 | | | | | 1 | | | 2 | 3 | 9 | 7 | 12 | | | | | | | |
| 19 | A | Stenhousemuir | 0-2 | | | 5 | | 4 | | | 10 | 8 | 6 | 11 | | | | | 1 | | | 2 | 3 | 9 | 7 | 12 | | | | | | | |
| 26 | H | Montrose | 0-0 | | | 3 | | | | 7 | | | 6 | 11 | | | | | 1 | | | 2 | 10 | 9 | 8 | | | | 4 | 5 | | | |
| Mar 5 | A | Forfar Athletic | 2-3 | | | 3 | 4 | | | | 8 | | 6 | 14 | | | | | 1 | 7 | 12 | 2 | 10 | 9 | | | | | 5 | 11² | | | |
| 12 | H | Alloa | 0-0 | | | 3 | 4 | | 7 | | | | 6 | 11 | | | | | 1 | | | 2 | 10 | 8 | 12 | | | | 5 | 9 | | | |
| 19 | A | East Stirlingshire | 0-2 | | | 3 | 4 | | 7 | | | | 6 | 11 | | | | | 1 | 14 | | 2 | | 8 | 10 | | | | 5 | 9 | | | |
| 26 | H | Meadowbank Thistle | 1-1 | | | 3 | 4 | | 7 | | | | 6 | 11¹ | | | | | 1 | 14 | | 2 | 12 | 8 | | | | | 5 | 9 | 10 | | |
| Apr 2 | A | Cowdenbeath | 0-1 | | | | 4 | | 7 | | | | 6 | | | | | | 1 | | | 2 | 11 | 14 | 8 | | | | 5 | 9 | 10 | 12 | 3 |
| 9 | H | Queen of the South | 0-3 | | | 8 | | | 4 | 2 | | | 6 | 11 | | | | | 1 | | | 5 | 12 | 14 | | | | | 9 | 10 | 7 | 3 | 1 |
| 16 | A | Stranraer | 0-1 | | | 3 | | | 4 | | | | 8 | 11 | | | | | 1 | | | 5 | 2 | | 7 | 14 | | | 6 | 12 | 10 | 9 | |
| 23 | H | Queen's Park | 2-1 | | | 3 | | | 4 | 2 | | | 12¹ | 11¹ | | | | | 1 | | | 5 | 9 | | 7 | | | | 6 | 14 | 10 | 8 | |
| 30 | A | East Fife | 2-1 | | | 3 | | | 4¹ | | | | 2 | 11 | | | | | 1 | | | 5 | 9 | | 8 | | | | 6 | 14 | 10¹ | 7 | |
| May 7 | H | Albion Rovers | 1-0 | | | 3 | | | 4¹ | | | | | 11 | | | | | 1 | | | 5 | 2 | 9 | 7 | 12 | | | 6 | 14 | 10 | 8 | |
| 14 | A | Berwick Rangers | 0-5 | | | 3 | | | 4 | | | | | 11 | | | | | 1 | | | 5 | 2 | 9 | 7 | | | | 6 | 12 | 14 | 10 | 8 |
| **TOTAL FULL APPEARANCES** | | | | 1 | 14 | 36 | 22 | 31 | 22 | 10 | 25 | 1 | 29 | 33 | | 7 | | | 36 | 7 | 8 | 11 | 25 | 29 | 21 | 18 | 6 | 1 | 2 | 11 | 6 | 3 | 6 |
| **TOTAL SUB APPEARANCES** | | | | | | | (3) | | (1) | | (5) | (3) | (1) | (6) | | | | | (7) | (1) | (1) | (2) | | (7) | (14) | | | | (2) | (4) | (1) | |
| **TOTAL GOALS SCORED** | | | | | | 3 | 4 | 2 | | | 1 | | 8 | | | 3 | | | | | | | 1 | 7 | 10 | | | | | 2 | 1 | |

*Small bold figures denote goalscorers.  † denotes opponent's own goal.*

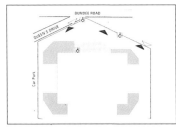

## GAYFIELD PARK

**CAPACITY**: 6,488; Seated 715, Standing 5,773

**PITCH DIMENSIONS:** 115 yds x 71 yds

**FACILITIES FOR DISABLED SUPPORTERS**: Enclosure at West end of Stand with wide steps to take a wheelchair. Toilet facilities are also available.

## HOW TO GET THERE

The following routes may be used to reach Gayfield Park:

**BUSES:** Arbroath is on the main route from both Glasgow and Edinburgh to Aberdeen. Buses from these three cities, plus Stirling, Dundee and Perth all stop at Arbroath Bus Station at hourly intervals. There is also a local service between Dundee-Arbroath and Montrose and this service is half hourly until 7.00 p.m. Between 7.00 p.m. and 10.45 p.m. the service is hourly. The bus station is 10 minutes walk from the ground.

**TRAINS:** Arbroath is on the Inter-City 125 route from London to Aberdeen and there are frequent local services between Arbroath, Dundee and Edinburgh. Trains also travel north from Glasgow, Stirling and Perth. The station is a 15 minute walk from the ground.

**CARS:** There is free parking for 500 cars just next to the ground in Queen's Drive.

# CALEDONIAN THISTLE

Telford Street Park,
Telford Street Inverness IV3 5LU

**CHAIRMAN**
John S. McDonald

**VICE-CHAIRMAN**
Norman H. Miller

**DIRECTORS**
Scott Byrnes
John Price
Alister I. MacKenzie
Craig R. MacLean
David MacDonald
Norman Cordiner
Dugald M. McGilvray
Kenneth A. Matheson
Ian Gordon

**SECRETARY**
Scott Byrnes

**MANAGER**
Sergei Baltacha

**COACHES**
Danny MacDonald
David Milroy
John Beaton
Jackie Sutherland
Alex Young

**CLUB DOCTOR**
Dr. John N. MacAskill

**PHYSIOTHERAPIST**
John King

**CHIEF SCOUTS**
Alan Smart (Snr.) & Alex Young

**GROUNDSMAN**
Donnie Gillies

**COMMERCIAL DEPARTMENT**
0463-233671

**TELEPHONES**
Ground (0463) 230274
Home/Sec. Bus. and
Information Service (0463) 233671

**OFFICIAL SUPPORTERS CLUB**
Scott Byrnes, 44 Midmills Road,
Inverness IV2 3NY

**TEAM CAPTAIN**
Alan Hercher

**SHIRT SPONSOR**
Scottish Citylink Coaches

## LIST OF PLAYERS 1994-95

| SURNAME | FIRST NAME | MIDDLE NAME | DATE OF BIRTH | PLACE OF BIRTH | DATE OF SIGNING | HEIGHT FT INS | WEIGHT ST LBS | PREVIOUS CLUB |
|---|---|---|---|---|---|---|---|---|
| Andrew | Ian | Michael R. | 19/04/59 | Lenzie | 08/08/94 | 6 0.0 | 12 10 | Caledonian |
| Baltacha | Sergei | Pavlovich | 17/02/58 | Kiev | 08/08/94 | 6 1.0 | 11 9 | Caledonian |
| Bennett | Graeme | Peter | 07/05/65 | Inverness | 08/08/94 | 5 10.0 | 12 7 | Clachnacuddin |
| Brennan | David | | 02/01/71 | Bellshill | 08/08/94 | 5 9.0 | 11 6 | Caledonian |
| Calder | James | Evan | 29/07/60 | Grantown-On-Spey | 29/06/94 | 5 11.0 | 13 4 | Inverness Thistle |
| Christie | Charles | | 30/03/66 | Inverness | 05/08/94 | 5 8.5 | 11 2 | Caledonian |
| Gray | Robin | Carr | 03/04/65 | Inverness | 29/06/94 | 6 0.0 | 12 7 | Caledonian |
| Hercher | Alan | Alexander | 11/08/65 | Dingwall | 29/06/94 | 6 1.0 | 14 3 | Caledonian |
| Lisle | Martin | Andrew | 09/01/63 | Inverness | 29/06/94 | 5 10.0 | 13 0 | Caledonian |
| MacDonald | Donald | | 29/08/66 | Inverness | 08/08/94 | 5 9.0 | 11 0 | Caledonian |
| MacDonald | Steven | | 07/12/75 | Inverness | 05/08/94 | 6 2.0 | 11 8 | Inverness Thistle |
| MacKenzie | Paul | | 04/10/69 | Aberdeen | 08/08/94 | 5 9.0 | 11 8 | Burnley |
| MacMillan | Norman | John | 09/12/74 | Portree | 22/08/94 | 6 1.0 | 12 2 | Nairn County |
| McAllister | Mark | | 13/02/71 | Inverness | 29/06/94 | 6 0.0 | 12 0 | Caledonian |
| McRitchie | Mark | Daniel | 07/07/70 | Clydebank | 08/08/94 | 6 2.0 | 12 7 | Caledonian |
| Mitchell | Colin | | 24/03/71 | Glasgow | 29/06/94 | 5 8.0 | 10 0 | Caledonian |
| Noble | Michael | | 18/05/66 | Inverness | 08/08/94 | 5 11.0 | 12 2 | Caledonian |
| Robertson | Wilson | | 27/01/63 | Aberdeen | 05/08/94 | 5 10.0 | 12 0 | Caledonian |
| Scott | John | Alan | 09/03/75 | Aberdeen | 08/08/94 | 5 8.0 | 11 2 | Liverpool |
| Sinclair | Colin | Morrison | 03/03/70 | Inverness | 22/08/94 | 6 3.0 | 13 0 | Caledonian |
| Smart | Allan | Andrew C. | 08/07/74 | Perth | 08/08/94 | 6 2.0 | 11 0 | Caledonian |

## TELFORD STREET PARK

**CAPACITY:** 5,498; Seated 498, Standing 5,000

**PITCH DIMENSIONS:** 110 yds x 70 yds

**FACILITIES FOR DISABLED SUPPORTERS:** By prior arrangement with Secretary.

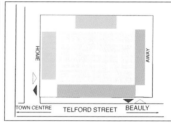

TOWN CENTRE — TELFORD STREET — BEAULY

## HOW TO GET THERE

The following routes can be used to reach Telford Street Park:

**TRAINS:** Nearest Railway Station is Inverness which is approximately 1 mile from ground.

**BUSES:** Local services available from Bus Station situated close to Inverness town centre.

**CARS:** The Ground is located to the West of Inverness on the old A9 Road. If approaching from North, South or East follow signs for town centre and Beauly. Car and bus parking is available within the Carsegate Industrial Estate area adjacent to the ground.

## SEASON TICKET INFORMATION

**Seated**
Adult ......................................................... £80
Juvenile/OAP ............................................. £40
**Standing**
Adult ......................................................... £50
Juvenile/OAP ............................................. £25
(Reduced Rates Available to Season Ticket Holders of Caledonian F.C. and Inverness Thistle F.C. during Season 1993/94)

## LEAGUE ADMISSION PRICES

**Seated**
Adult ........................................................... £5
Juvenile/OAP ............................................... £3
**Standing**
Adult ........................................................... £4
Juvenile/OAP ............................................... £2

| | |
|---|---|
| REGISTERED STRIP: | Shirt – Blue with White Flashes |
| | Shorts – White with Blue Flashes, Stockings – Blue |
| CHANGE STRIP: | Shirt – Red with White Stripes |
| | Shorts – Blue, Stockings – Red |

# INVERNESS THISTLE F.C. – A BRIEF HISTORY
## FORMED: 1885

HONOURS:

**Highland League**
1893/94, 1906/07, 1909/10, 1928/29, 1935/36,1971/72, 1972/73, 1986/87

**Highland League Cup**
1970/71, 1972/73, 1987/88

**Scottish Qualifying Cup**
1932/33, 1972/73, 1976/77, 1980/81, 1988/89

**North of Scotland Cup**
1892/93, 1893/94, 1912/13, 1930/31, 1934/35, 1938/39, 1945/46,
1952/53, 1959/60, 1977/78, 1984/85, 1987/88

**Inverness Cup**
1908/09, 1924/25, 1926/27, 1927/28, 1932/33, 1933/34, 1934/35,
1935/36, 1938/39, 1953/54, 1973/74, 1974/75, 1980/81, 1981/82,
1983/84, 1987/88, 1990/91, 1993/94

*The story of Inverness Thistle can be traced back to the late 1880s when they were but one of six Inverness sides. It was the coming together of Thistle with Citadel that gave the club its impetus and when Union added their weight to the new club the strength of Inverness Thistle was almost assured. In 1890 they moved to Kingsmills Park, having spent five years in the heady environs of Millburn Academy School, and early tests were tackled with a near academic rigour.*

The Jags became founder members of the North FA and they demonstrated their skill by winning the inaugural title in 1894. This did not, however, herald a period of domination and although the club won the 1907 and 1910 titles, there was a lull before taking the 1929 Championship. Red and Black ribbons did not bestow the bulk of early Highland trophies despite the best efforts of an enthusiastic Committee.

Such successes that were won were hard earned over a period of time. Not so their win over local rivals Citadel in 1895. The match was known throughout the North as the "two meenet geme" because Citadel left the field after a disputed Thistle goal in just 2 minutes!

1936 brought the title back to Kingsmills Park, but from then through to 1972 Thistle struggled to land the League flag. The only flag they consistently seemed to land was that belonging to enthusiastic Ross County supporters, and given its huge size, Thistle reluctantly banned it from the stadium for its distractive value. Ironically, such flags are now an accepted and colourful part of the Scottish football tradition and the new Inverness club are most unlikely to get into a flutter about flags in future.

It had been 36 years since the Championship had rested at Thistle's ground and Manager Willie Grant earned unprecedented acclaim for his 1972 success. When a few months later he steered the Jags to the Highland League Cup he assumed virtual Messiah status, and in unstoppable vein they added the Qualifying Cup to their burgeoning collection. Queen's Park were knocked out of the Scottish Cup and suddenly all in the Thistle garden was rosy.

It was therefore no surprise that Thistle retained the title. They ended the 1973 spring locked at the top of the League with Ross County on 47 points. A Championship decider was needed and a determined Thistle sent Inverness into raptures by winning 2-1.

Thistle, of course, have other claims to fame. Perhaps the most lasting is of the match that nearly never was. In 1979 the Jags were drawn to play Falkirk in the Scottish Cup at Kingsmills. However, such was the severity of the gripping winter that the tie was postponed a record 29 times before finally going ahead . It was another Scottish Cup tie that brought Thistle on-field fame. On 9th February, 1985 the Jags thrashed Killie 3-0 with goals from Milroy, Hay and Fraser sending the Ayrshire side home to think again. That win earned Thistle the right to play Celtic at Parkhead and young goalkeeper Les Fridge has gone on to carve out a career in The Scottish Football League after a brief spell in London with Chelsea.

In 1987 the Highland League title once more ended up at Kingsmills Park but only after a strong challenge from Caley had been seen off. Brian Black was the inspiration behind that win, a title achieved with just one League loss all season.

Now with the amalgamation of Thistle and Caley, Inverness has a strong club which could be capable of marching forward to challenging the best in Scottish football. There is a precedent for Thistle and Caledonian playing together. Back in the early 1920s, the two clubs tackled the FA Cup holders Tottenham Hotspur and the Highlanders recorded a famous 6-3 win. A similar level of achievement this time around would be most welcome in the capital of the Highlands.

by JIM JEFFREY

# CALEDONIAN F.C. – A BRIEF HISTORY
## FORMED: 1886

HONOURS:

**Highland League**
1895/96, 1910/11, 1913/14, 1925/26, 1930/31, 1950/51, 1951/52, 1963/64, 1970/71,
1976/77, 1977/78, 1981/82, 1982/83, 1983/84, 1987/88

**Highland League Cup**
1952/53, 1969/70, 1971/72, 1976/77, 1977/78

**Scottish Qualifying Cup**
1948/49, 1949/50, 1950/51, 1961/62, 1965/66, 1966/67, 1969/70,
1971/72, 1981/82, 1982/83, 1983/84, 1986/87, 1987/88, 1991/92

**North of Scotland Cup**
1889/90, 1891/92, 1896/97, 1901/02, 1910/11, 1911/12, 1913/14,
1921/22, 1924/25, 1925/26, 1927/28, 1933/34, 1950/51, 1951/52,
1973/74, 1974/75, 1976/77, 1981/82, 1983/84, 1985/86, 1993/94

**Inverness Cup**
1895/96, 1896/97, 1897/98, 1898/99, 1899/1900, 1901/02, 1907/08,
1910/11, 1911/12, 1912/13, 1913/14, 1920/21, 1922/23, 1925/26,
1963/64, 1977/78, 1982/83, 1984/85, 1986/87, 1988/89

*If any Highland League club owned a history which did not lend itself to a brief summary then it was surely Caledonian. Fifteen League titles, 14 Scottish Qualifying Cups and no fewer than 21 North of Scotland Cup triumphs marked the Blue and Whites out as a club of some standing. Furthermore, a host of Scottish League scalps taken in the Scottish Cup are equally indicative of an outstanding club.*

The Inverness club could trace their roots back to 1885 and their name derived from the proximity of the Caledonian Canal, thus like Scottish Football League members Clyde, they were named after a famous stretch of water. As with Ross County and Inverness Thistle, Caley were founder members of the North of Scotland FA and the Highland League, but in terms of honours and tradition, there were few that could equal Caley.

Yet in a sense their successes were modest before 1950 with only two titles between the 1920s and 1949. Eager to rectify this shortfall in silverware they landed both the 1951 and 1952 League titles with imperious style, but it was to be a further 12 years before they could celebrate a further Championship triumph.

The 1977 title win was celebrated more than most as it was won in a thriller, pipping Peterhead on goal difference, to secure a League and League Cup double. Caley were so buoyed by their epic triumph that under Alex Main's shrewd guidance they retained the title and the League Cup. Nevertheless, it was probably in the 1980s that the name Caley was most feared throughout Highland football. Their feat of taking three successive titles, between 1982 and 1984 was a remarkable achievement in what was a competitive environment. What was even more impressive was the club's ability to avoid defeat and they landed the 1983 title without losing a single League match; a hitherto unthinkable achievement.

The Telford Street club have given Scottish football some excellent players and in recent years the striking prowess of Billy Urquhart (Rangers) and the midfield orchestrations of Donald Park (Heart of Midlothian, Partick Thistle, Brechin City and Meadowbank Thistle) were ample evidence of the quality produced in Inverness. Urquhart may not have broken records at Ibrox but with the gallant Caley side he bagged a phenomenal 390 goals, a total that few will now be able to match. In appointing the former Soviet Internationalist Sergei Baltacha as boss Caledonian broke new ground, although he was not the first famous man to take charge at Telford Street Park. Amongst earlier Managers, the Inverness side could name the likes of Willie Hunter, former Ancell Babe at Motherwell and Scotland star.

Caledonian were arguably the strongest supported side in the Highlands, and graphic evidence of this was given in a Scottish Cup tie in 1991. Drawn against Premier Division St Johnstone, the Highland club held the Perth Saints in a thrilling 2-2 draw at Telford Street before over 5,000 spectators. The replay at McDiarmid Park was memorable in that hundreds of Caley fans were locked out of a match which with hindsight might have been deemed all-ticket. Of course, Caley's Cup tradition was well established before 1991. In 1955 they dumped Ayr United in a replayed cup tie at Somerset Park and in the 1990s saw off the likes of Clyde and Stenhousemuir. Thus for all associated with Caledonian, the prospect of the move into The Scottish Football League should not be too daunting.

by JIM JEFFREY

# COWDENBEATH

Central Park, High Street,
Cowdenbeath KY4 9QQ

**CHAIRMAN**
Gordon McDougall

**VICE-CHAIRMAN**
Eric Mitchell

**DIRECTORS**
Ian Fraser
Albert Tait
Paul McGlinchey

**SECRETARY**
Thomas Ogilvie

**MANAGER**
Patrick Dolan

**ASSISTANT MANAGER**
Alexander Hamill

**RESERVE TEAM COACH**
Tom Stevens

**YOUTH TEAM COACH**
William Aitchison

**CLUB DOCTOR**
Dr. Gordon Stewart

**GROUNDSMAN**
G. Chalmers

**COMMERCIAL MANAGER**
Ian Fraser
(0592) 780092

**TELEPHONES**
Ground/Ticket Office/Information
Service (0383) 610166
Sec. Home (0383) 513013
Fax (0383) 512132

**CLUB SHOP**
Situated at Stadium

**OFFICIAL SUPPORTERS CLUB**
Central Park,
Cowdenbeath KY4 9QQ

**TEAM CAPTAIN**
Gavin Tait

**SHIRT SPONSOR**
Racewall

## LIST OF PLAYERS 1994-95

| SURNAME | FIRST NAME | MIDDLE NAME | DATE OF BIRTH | PLACE OF BIRTH | DATE OF SIGNING | HEIGHT FT INS | WEIGHT ST LBS | PREVIOUS CLUB |
|---|---|---|---|---|---|---|---|---|
| Barclay | Alexander | Bruce | 28/11/74 | Edinburgh | 07/08/93 | 5 7.0 | 10 0 | Whitehill Welfare |
| Black | Ian | | 04/01/71 | Edinburgh | 04/04/94 | 5 10.0 | 10 12 | Bonnyrigg Rose |
| Bowmaker | Kevin | | 03/04/75 | Edinburgh | 05/07/93 | 5 11.0 | 11 13 | Links United |
| Callaghan | William | Thomas | 23/03/67 | Dunfermline | 17/09/92 | 5 10.5 | 12 7 | Montrose |
| Carr | Roger | | 13/09/74 | Edinburgh | 28/07/93 | 5 6.0 | 10 4 | Links United |
| Davidson | Ian | | 15/08/69 | Edinburgh | 05/07/93 | 5 8.0 | 9 8 | Musselburgh Athletic |
| Filshill | Stewart | | 04/10/74 | Kirkcaldy | 07/08/93 | 6 1.0 | 12 9 | Thornton Hibs |
| Halliday | Gavin | Watson | 21/07/70 | Edinburgh | 26/05/94 | 6 0.0 | 11 10 | Ormiston Primrose |
| Hamill | Alexander | | 30/10/61 | Coatbridge | 22/03/94 | 5 8.0 | 11 4 | Forfar Athletic |
| Hamilton | Alistair | Strathern | 12/11/75 | Irvine | 08/08/94 | 5 6.0 | 9 4 | Civil Service Colts |
| Humphreys | Martin | Jay | 16/03/76 | Dunfermline | 08/08/94 | 5 10.5 | 12 6 | Links United |
| Knowles | Alan | Francis | 22/01/75 | Falkirk | 02/09/93 | 5 6.0 | 10 9 | Musselburgh Athletic |
| Lynch | Jack | | 22/02/76 | Edinburgh | 08/08/94 | 5 9.0 | 10 5 | Links United |
| Malloy | Brian | John | 04/05/67 | Paisley | 26/05/94 | 5 11.0 | 12 0 | Bo'ness United |
| Maloney | James | John | 03/10/74 | Edinburgh | 09/08/93 | 5 11.0 | 15 10 | Lothian United |
| Maratea | Domenico | | 10/04/74 | Edinburgh | 22/09/92 | 5 9.0 | 12 4 | Kelty Hearts |
| McMahon | Barry | | 08/04/71 | Edinburgh | 23/11/92 | 6 1.0 | 12 2 | Kelty Hearts |
| Murdoch | Scott | | 10/10/68 | Edinburgh | 08/06/94 | 5 10.0 | 11 9 | Edinburgh United |
| Petrie | Edward | | 15/06/73 | Bathgate | 13/07/92 | 5 10.0 | 12 7 | Bathgate United U'21 |
| Russell | Neil | | 29/05/71 | Kirkcaldy | 31/05/94 | 6 3.0 | 13 9 | Forfar Athletic |
| Scott | Symon | Robert | 15/12/70 | Edinburgh | 14/07/94 | 5 10.0 | 10 2 | Meadowbank Thistle |
| Sim | Andrew | William D. | 07/03/76 | Glasgow | 07/07/94 | 5 11.0 | 12 3 | "S" Form |
| Soutar | Graeme | Douglas | 13/01/74 | Inverness | 09/08/94 | 5 7.0 | 11 0 | Newtongrange Star |
| Stout | Donald | McLauchlin | 14/04/72 | Johannesburg | 07/11/92 | 5 5.5 | 10 12 | Lochend United |
| Tait | Gavin | James | 28/07/61 | Edinburgh | 15/06/94 | 6 0.0 | 12 0 | Alloa |
| Thomson | James | | 31/07/69 | Edinburgh | 22/07/93 | 5 6.0 | 10 0 | Alloa |
| Winter | Craig | John | 30/06/76 | Dunfermline | 19/07/94 | 5 9.0 | 10 0 | Raith Rovers |
| Yardley | Mark | | 14/09/69 | Livingston | 04/07/94 | 6 2.0 | 13 1 | Livingston United |
| Young | Allan | John | 06/08/74 | Edinburgh | 24/09/93 | 5 11.0 | 10 13 | Dunbar United |

## MILESTONES

YEAR OF FORMATION: 1881
MOST CAPPED PLAYER: Jim Paterson
NO. OF CAPS: 3
MOST LEAGUE POINTS IN A SEASON: 60 (Division 2 – Season 1938/39)
MOST LEAGUE GOALS SCORED BY A PLAYER IN A SEASON: Willie Devlin (Season 1925/26)
NO. OF GOALS SCORED: 40
RECORD ATTENDANCE: 25,586 (-v- Rangers – 21.9.1949)
RECORD VICTORY: 12-0 (-v- St. Johnstone – Scottish Cup 21.1.1928)
RECORD DEFEAT: 1-11 (-v- Clyde – Division 2. 6.10.1951)

## SEASON TICKET INFORMATION

Seated
Adult .................................................... £80
Juvenile/OAP ........................................ £40
Standing
Adult .................................................... £80
Juvenile/OAP ........................................ £40

## LEAGUE ADMISSION PRICES

Seated
Adult ...................................................... £6
Juvenile/OAP .......................................... £3
Standing
Adult ...................................................... £5
Juvenile/OAP ....................................... £2.50

**REGISTERED STRIP:** Shirt – Royal Blue with White Vertical Chest Panel on Front, Royal Blue Random Design Horizontally across White Panel in two Places with White Random Design around Each Sleeve and White Trim with Red Pinstripe Edge, Shorts – Royal Blue with White Edge to Leg, Stockings – Royal Blue with White Vertical Stripes in Turnover

**CHANGE STRIP:** Shirt – Red with White Vertical Chest Panel on Front, Red Random Design Horizontally across White Panel in two Places with White Random Design around Each Sleeve and White Trim with Royal Blue Pinstripe Edge Shorts: Red with White Edge to Leg, Stockings: Red with White Vertical Stripes in Turnover

# CLUB FACTFILE 1993/94 . . RESULTS . . APPEARANCES . . SCORERS

## The BLUE BRAZIL

*Small bold figures denote goalscorers. † denotes opponent's own goal.*

Player columns (in order): Filshill S., Thomson J., Bowmaker K., Petrie E., McMahon B., Lee I., Henderson N., Scott C., Callaghan W., Young A., Harris C., Barclay A., Davidson I., Watt D., Maratea D., Hunter P., Herd W., Stout D., Carr R., Maloney J., Douglas H., Russell R., Law G., Reilly J., Moffat J., Burke P., Macdonald K., McMahon S., Hamill A., Sim A.

| Date | Venue | Opponents | Result | Fil | Tho | Bow | Pet | McMB | Lee | Hen | Sco | Cal | You | Har | Bar | Dav | Wat | Mar | Hun | Her | Sto | Car | Mal | Dou | Rus | Law | Rei | Mof | Bur | Mac | McMS | Ham | Sim |
|---|---|---|---|---|---|---|---|---|---|---|---|---|---|---|---|---|---|---|---|---|---|---|---|---|---|---|---|---|---|---|---|---|
| Aug 7 | H | Meadowbank Thistle | 1-2 | 1 | 2 | 3 | 4 | 5 | 6 | $7^{1}$ | 8 | 9 | 10 | 11 | 12 | 14 | | | | | | | | | | | | | | | | | |
| 14 | A | Alloa | 1-0 | 1 | | | 4 | 5 | 6 | $7^{1}$ | 8 | 9 | | 11 | | | 14 | 2 | 3 | 10 | | | | | | | | | | | | | |
| 21 | H | East Fife | 1-2 | 1 | | | 4 | 5 | 6 | $7^{1}$ | 8 | 9 | | 11 | | | | 2 | 3 | 10 | | | | | | | | | | | | | |
| 28 | A | Stenhousemuir | 1-1 | 1 | 12 | | 4 | 5 | 6 | $7^{1}$ | 8 | 9 | | 11 | | | | 2 | 3 | 10 | | 14 | | | | | | | | | | | |
| Sep 4 | A | Queen's Park | 3-1 | 1 | | | 4 | 5 | 6 | 7 | 8 | $9^{3}$ | | 11 | 12 | | | 2 | 3 | 10 | | | | | | | | | | | | | |
| 11 | H | Berwick Rangers | 1-2 | 1 | | | 4 | 5 | 6 | 7 | 8 | 9 | | 11 | 14 | | | 2 | 3 | $10^{1}$ | | | | | | | | | | | | | |
| 18 | H | Albion Rovers | 0-1 | 1 | | | 4 | 5 | 6 | 7 | 8 | 9 | 10 | 11 | 12 | | | 2 | 3 | | | | 14 | | | | | | | | | | |
| 25 | A | Stranraer | 0-4 | 1 | | | | 5 | 6 | 7 | 8 | 9 | | 11 | 12 | | 4 | 2 | 3 | 10 | | | | | | | | | | | | | |
| Oct 2 | A | Arbroath | 2-2 | 1 | | | 12 | 5 | $6^{1}$ | 7 | 8 | 9 | | 11 | | 14 | 4 | 2 | 3 | $10^{1}$ | | | | | | | | | | | | | |
| 9 | H | East Stirlingshire | 1-3 | 1 | | | 12 | 5 | 6 | 7 | 8 | 9 | | $11^{1}$ | | 14 | 4 | 2 | 3 | 10 | | | | | | | | | | | | | |
| 16 | H | Queen of the South | 3-3 | 1 | | | | 5 | $6^{1}$ | | | | | 11 | | 14 | 4 | 2 | 3 | $10^{1}$ | 8 | | $9^{1}$ | 7 | | | | | | | | | |
| 23 | A | Montrose | 2-1 | 1 | | | 12 | 5 | 6 | 7 | 8 | $9^{1}$ | | 11 | | | 4 | 2 | 3 | $10^{1}$ | | | | | | | | | | | | | |
| 30 | A | Forfar Athletic | 2-3 | 1 | | | | $5^{1}$ | 6 | 7 | 8 | 9 | | $11^{1}$ | | 14 | 4 | 2 | 3 | 10 | | | | | | | | | | | | | |
| Nov 6 | H | Alloa | 1-1 | 1 | | | | 5 | 6 | 7 | 8 | $9^{1}$ | 12 | 11 | | | 4 | 2 | 3 | 10 | | | 14 | | | | | | | | | | |
| 13 | A | Albion Rovers | 1-0 | 1 | | | | 5 | 6 | 7 | 8 | 9 | | 11 | | | 4 | 2 | 3 | $10^{1}$ | | | | | | | | | | | | | |
| 20 | A | Stranraer | 1-2 | 1 | | | | 5 | 6 | 7 | 8 | 9 | | 11 | | | 4 | 2 | 3 | 10 | | | | | | | 12 | | | | | | |
| 27 | A | East Stirlingshire | †2-3 | 1 | | | | 5 | 6 | 7 | 8 | 9 | | 11 | | 14 | $4^{1}$ | 2 | 3 | 10 | | | | | | | | | | | | | |
| Dec 4 | H | Arbroath | 0-1 | | | | | 5 | 6 | 7 | 8 | 9 | | 11 | | | 4 | 2 | 3 | 10 | | 1 | | | | | 12 | | | | | | |
| 18 | A | Meadowbank Thistle | 1-1 | | 2 | | | 5 | 6 | 7 | 8 | 9 | | 11 | | 14 | 4 | | 3 | $10^{1}$ | | 1 | | | | | | | | | | | |
| Jan 11 | A | East Fife | 0-2 | | 3 | | 6 | 5 | 8 | | | | 12 | | | | 4 | 2 | 7 | 10 | | 1 | | | | | 14 | 9 | | | | 11 | |
| 18 | H | Forfar Athletic | 1-2 | | 3 | 10 | 6 | 5 | $8^{1}$ | | | | | | | | 4 | 2 | 7 | | | 1 | | | | | 14 | 9 | | | | 11 | |
| 22 | A | Queen of the South | 2-1 | | 11 | 3 | 6 | 5 | 8 | | | | 12 | | | | $4^{1}$ | 2 | 7 | $10^{1}$ | | 1 | | | | | 14 | 9 | | | | | |
| Feb 1 | H | Stenhousemuir | 1-3 | | 3 | | 6 | 5 | $8^{1}$ | | | | 12 | | | | 4 | 2 | 7 | 10 | | 1 | | | | | | 9 | | | | 11 | |
| 5 | A | Berwick Rangers | 2-3 | | 3 | | 6 | 5 | 8 | | | | 12 | | | | 4 | 2 | 7 | $10^{1}$ | | 1 | | | | | 14 | 9 | | | | $11^{1}$ | |
| 12 | H | Queen's Park | 3-4 | | 3 | | 6 | 5 | | | | | 12 | | | | $4^{1}$ | 2 | $7^{1}$ | 10 | | 1 | | | | | | $9^{1}$ | | | | 11 | |
| Mar 2 | A | Forfar Athletic | 1-2 | | 3 | | $6^{1}$ | 5 | 8 | | | | 12 | | | | 4 | 2 | 7 | 10 | | 1 | | | | | 14 | 9 | | | | 11 | |
| 5 | H | Meadowbank Thistle | 0-1 | | 3 | | 6 | 5 | 8 | | | | 12 | | | | 4 | 2 | 7 | 10 | | | | | | | 14 | | 1 | 9 | | 11 | |
| 12 | A | East Stirlingshire | 0-4 | | 3 | | 6 | 5 | | | | | | | | | 4 | 2 | | 10 | | 1 | | | | 7 | 14 | 9 | | 8 | | 11 | |
| 16 | H | Stenhousemuir | 1-1 | | 3 | | 6 | | 8 | | | | 12 | | | | 4 | 2 | 7 | | | 1 | | | | | | 9 | | $10^{1}$ | 5 | 11 | |
| 19 | A | Montrose | 1-1 | | 3 | | 6 | 5 | 8 | | | | | | | | 4 | 2 | 7 | $10^{1}$ | | 1 | | | | | 14 | 9 | | 11 | | | |
| 22 | H | Montrose | 0-1 | | | | | 5 | 8 | | | | | | | | 4 | 2 | 7 | 10 | | 1 | | | | | 14 | 9 | | 11 | 6 | 3 | |
| 26 | H | Berwick Rangers | 1-5 | | | | 6 | 5 | 8 | | | | 12 | | | | 4 | 2 | 7 | | | 1 | | | | | | 9 | | 10 | 3 | $11^{1}$ | |
| Apr 2 | H | Arbroath | 1-0 | | 3 | | 6 | 5 | | | | | | | | | 4 | 2 | 7 | | | 1 | | | | | 14 | $9^{1}$ | | 10 | | 11 | 8 |
| 9 | A | Albion Rovers | 0-1 | | 3 | | 6 | 5 | | | | | | | | | 4 | 2 | 7 | | | 1 | | | | | 14 | 9 | | | | 11 | 8 |
| 16 | A | Alloa | 0-1 | | 3 | | 6 | 5 | | | | | 12 | | | | 4 | 2 | 7 | | | 1 | | | | | 14 | 9 | | 10 | | 11 | 8 |
| 23 | H | East Fife | 1-2 | | 3 | | 6 | $5^{1}$ | | | | | 12 | | | | 4 | 2 | 7 | | | 1 | | | | | | 9 | | 10 | | 11 | 8 |
| 30 | H | Queen's Park | 1-1 | 1 | 3 | | 6 | $5^{1}$ | 8 | | | | 12 | | | | 4 | 2 | 7 | | | | | | | | 14 | 9 | | | | 11 | 10 |
| May 7 | A | Stranraer | 0-2 | 1 | 3 | | 6 | 5 | | | | | 12 | | | | 4 | 2 | 7 | 10 | | | | | | | | 9 | | | | 11 | 8 |
| 14 | H | Queen of the South | 0-2 | | 3 | | 6 | 5 | | | | | 12 | | | | 4 | 2 | 7 | 10 | | | | | | | 14 | 9 | | | | 11 | 8 |
| **TOTAL FULL APPEARANCES** | | | | 18 | 17 | 4 | 26 | 32 | 24 | 22 | 17 | 33 | 7 | 9 | 7 | 21 | 35 | 17 | 23 | 33 | 5 | 17 | 4 | 1 | 2 | 1 | 10 | 17 | 1 | 10 | 2 | 9 | 5 |
| **TOTAL SUB APPEARANCES** | | | | | (2) | (2) | (3) | (2) | (1) | | (2) | (1) | (9) | (8) | | (3) | (2) | | | (5) | (3) | | | | | | (4) | (1) | (3) | | | | |
| **TOTAL GOALS SCORED** | | | | | | | | 2 | 1 | 9 | | 11 | 1 | 1 | | 1 | | | 6 | 4 | | | | | | | 1 | | | 1 | | | |

---

## CENTRAL PARK

**CAPACITY:** 5,258; Seated 1,552, Standing 3,706

**PITCH DIMENSIONS:** 107 yds x 66 yds

**FACILITIES FOR DISABLED SUPPORTERS:** Direct access from car park into designated area within ground. Toilet and catering facilities also provided.

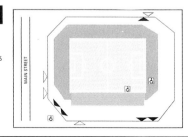

## HOW TO GET THERE

You can get to Central Park by the following routes:

**TRAINS:** There is a regular service of trains from Edinburgh and Glasgow (via Edinburgh) which call at Cowdenbeath and the station is only 400 yards from the ground.

**BUSES:** A limited Edinburgh-Cowdenbeath service stops just outside the ground on matchdays and a frequent service of Dunfermline-Ballingry buses also stop outside the ground, as does the Edinburgh-Glenrothes service.

**CARS:** Car parking facilities are available in the club car park for 300 cars. There are also another 300 spaces at the Stenhouse Street car park, which is 200 yards from the ground.

# EAST STIRLINGSHIRE

Firs Park, Firs Street,
Falkirk FK2 7AY

**CHAIRMAN**
William C. Whyte

**VICE-CHAIRMAN**
G. Marshall Paterson

**DIRECTORS**
William W. H. Lawless
Alexander S. H. Forsyth
Alexander C. Mitchell
G. Ross A. Strang
James Greenaway

**SECRETARY**
Alexander S. H. Forsyth

**MANAGER**
William Little

**ASSISTANT MANAGER/COACH**
Lenny Reid

**CLUB DOCTOR**
David A. Buchan

**PHYSIOTHERAPIST**
Sandra Lawlor

**COMMERCIAL MANAGER**
Thomas Kirk
Bus. (0786) 443434
Home (0324) 714686

**TELEPHONES**
Ground (0324) 623583
Sec. Bus (0324) 612965
Fax (0324) 637862

**CLUB SHOP**
At ground. Open Mon-Fri 10 a.m. –
2 p.m. (except Thursday)
and on all home match days

**TEAM CAPTAIN**
Brian Ross

**SHIRT SPONSOR**
Central F.M. Radio

## LIST OF PLAYERS 1994-95

| SURNAME | FIRST NAME | MIDDLE NAME | DATE OF BIRTH | PLACE OF BIRTH | DATE OF SIGNING | HEIGHT FT INS | WEIGHT ST LBS | PREVIOUS CLUB |
|---|---|---|---|---|---|---|---|---|
| Conroy | John | James | 03/11/70 | Glasgow | 04/08/93 | 5 7.0 | 10 2 | Alloa |
| Cuthbert | Lee | James | 28/02/70 | Edinburgh | 03/08/94 | 5 8.0 | 11 0 | Whitehill Welfare |
| Dempsey | Samuel | George | 15/10/74 | Bellshill | 02/08/94 | 6 0.0 | 12 0 | Airdrieonians |
| Dodds | John | Charles | 22/04/73 | Salsbury | 30/06/94 | 5 11.0 | 11 0 | Dunipace Juniors |
| Geraghty | Michael | John | 30/10/70 | Glasgow | 15/09/92 | 5 10.0 | 10 1 | Stranraer |
| Imrie | Paul | | 30/06/67 | Stirling | 05/08/94 | 5 11.0 | 12 0 | Plean Amateurs |
| Lee | Iain | Caird C. | 07/07/67 | Hamilton | 05/03/94 | 5 9.0 | 10 7 | Cowdebeath |
| Lee | Robert | | 19/05/66 | Broxburn | 14/01/94 | 5 10.0 | 11 0 | Alloa |
| Loney | James | | 29/08/75 | Stirling | 28/08/93 | 5 9.0 | 10 0 | Denny Hertbertshire |
| McCallum | Mungo | | 28/10/65 | Bellshill | 12/11/93 | 5 10.0 | 11 7 | Stirling Albion |
| McDougall | Gordon | | 17/02/71 | Bellshill | 16/07/93 | 6 2.0 | 12 3 | Falkirk |
| Millar | Glen | Archibald | 02/09/66 | Falkirk | 01/06/94 | 6 1.0 | 13 0 | Queen's Park |
| Moffat | James | | 27/01/60 | Dunfermline | 08/08/94 | 6 0.0 | 12 0 | Cowdenbeath |
| Robertson | Robert | Alexander | 27/07/66 | Lanark | 08/07/94 | 5 9.0 | 12 10 | Lesmahagow Juniors |
| Ross | Brian | | 15/08/67 | Stirling | 31/03/91 | 5 11.0 | 11 7 | Ayr United |
| Russell | Gordon | Alan | 03/03/68 | Falkirk | 04/08/86 | 5 9.5 | 10 0 | Gairdoch United |
| Scott | Colin | Andrew | 30/11/66 | Edinburgh | 08/08/94 | 5 8.0 | 13 0 | Cowdenbeath |
| Stirling | David | Park | 12/09/75 | Bellshill | 08/07/94 | 5 10.0 | 11 2 | Partick Thistle |
| Watt | David | | 05/03/67 | Edinburgh | 19/07/94 | 5 7.0 | 11 6 | Cowdenbeath |
| Yates | Derek | Alexander | 26/12/72 | Falkirk | 04/12/92 | 6 0.0 | 11 7 | Stenhousemuir |

## MILESTONES

**YEAR OF FORMATION**: 1881
**MOST CAPPED PLAYER**: Humphrey Jones
**NO. OF CAPS**: 5 (for Wales)
**MOST LEAGUE POINTS IN A SEASON**: 55 (Division 2 – Season 1931/32)
**MOST LEAGUE GOALS SCORED BY A PLAYER IN A SEASON**: Malcolm Morrison (Season 1938/39)
**NO. OF GOALS SCORED**: 36
**RECORD ATTENDANCE**: 11,500 (-v- Hibernian – 10.2.1969)
**RECORD VICTORY**: 10-1 (-v- Stenhousemuir – Scottish Cup, 1.9.1888)
**RECORD DEFEAT**: 1-12 (-v- Dundee United – Division 2 – 13.4.1936)

## SEASON TICKET INFORMATION

**Seated**
Adult .................................................................. £60
Juvenile/OAP ..................................................... £30
Family Ticket ..................................................... £60
**Standing**
Adult .................................................................. £50
Juvenile/OAP ..................................................... £25
Family Ticket ..................................................... £50

## LEAGUE ADMISSION PRICES

**Seated**
Adult .................................................................. £6
Juvenile/OAP ..................................................... £3
**Standing**
Adult .................................................................. £5
Juvenile/OAP ..................................................... £2.50

# CLUB FACTFILE 1993/94 . . RESULTS . . APPEARANCES . . SCORERS

## The SHIRE

Players (left to right): McDougall G., Russell G., Kemp B., Craig D., Yates D., McAulay I., Roberts P., McKinnon C., Geraghty M., Robertson S., Conroy J., Speirs W., McInally M., Ross B., Crews B., Millar G., Tierney S., Macdonald K., Loney J., Horne J., McCallum M., Conway M., Lee R., Docherty A., Lee I., Lee D., Teasdale J., Imrie P.

| Date | Venue | Opponents | Result | McDougall G. | Russell G. | Kemp B. | Craig D. | Yates D. | McAulay I. | Roberts P. | McKinnon C. | Geraghty M. | Robertson S. | Conroy J. | Speirs W. | McInally M. | Ross B. | Crews B. | Millar G. | Tierney S. | Macdonald K. | Loney J. | Horne J. | McCallum M. | Conway M. | Lee R. | Docherty A. | Lee I. | Lee D. | Teasdale J. | Imrie P. |
|---|---|---|---|---|---|---|---|---|---|---|---|---|---|---|---|---|---|---|---|---|---|---|---|---|---|---|---|---|---|---|---|
| Aug 7 | A | Stenhousemuir | 1-3 | 1 | 2 | 3 | 4¹ | 5 | 6 | 7 | 8 | 9 | 10 | 11 | 12 | 14 | | | | | | | | | | | | | | | |
| 14 | H | Berwick Rangers | 2-1 | 1 | 2¹ | 3 | 6 | 5 | 10 | 9 | 8 | 11¹ | 4 | 7 | | | | | | | | | | | | | | | | | |
| 21 | A | Alloa | 0-0 | 1 | 2 | 3 | 6 | 5 | 7 | 8 | 9 | 10 | 11 | 4 | | | | | | | | | | | | | | | | | |
| 28 | H | Meadowbank Thistle | 0-1 | 1 | 2 | 3 | 6 | 5 | 8 | 9 | 10 | 11 | 4 | 14 | 7 | 12 | | | | | | | | | | | | | | | |
| Sep 4 | A | Montrose | 2-3 | 1 | 2 | 3¹ | 6 | 5 | 8¹ | 9 | 11 | 12 | 4 | 10 | 7 | 14 | | | | | | | | | | | | | | | |
| 11 | A | Queen of the South | 0-5 | 1 | 2 | 3 | 6 | 5 | 12 | 7 | 11 | 10 | 4 | 14 | 8 | 9 | | | | | | | | | | | | | | | |
| 18 | H | Forfar Athletic | 1-2 | 1 | 2 | 3 | | 5 | 8 | 7 | | 10 | | 14 | 4 | 6 | 12¹ | | | | | 9 | 11 | | | | | | | | |
| 25 | A | East Fife | 1-0 | 1 | 2 | 3 | | 5 | 4 | 8 | 7 | 11 | | 12 | | 14 | 10 | | | | | 9¹ | 6 | | | | | | | | |
| Oct 2 | H | Albion Rovers | 1-4 | 1 | 2¹ | 3 | | 5 | 4 | | 7 | 11 | | 12 | | 8 | 10 | | | | | 9 | 6 | | | | | | | | |
| 9 | A | Cowdenbeath | †3-1 | 1 | 2 | 3 | | 5 | 6¹ | 12 | | 10¹ | | | | 4 | 7 | 8 | | | | 9 | 11 | | | | | | | | |
| 16 | A | Queen's Park | 1-1 | 1 | 2 | 3 | | 5 | 6 | 12 | | 10 | | | | 4 | 7 | 8 | | | | 9¹ | 11 | | | | | | | | |
| 23 | H | Arbroath | †2-4 | 1 | 2 | 3 | | 5 | 6 | 14 | | 10 | 4 | | | | 7 | 8 | | | | 9¹ | 11 | 12 | | | | | | | |
| 30 | H | Stranraer | 2-2 | 1 | 2 | 3 | | 5 | 6 | 4 | 12 | 10¹ | | | | | 7 | 8 | | | | 9¹ | 11 | | | | | | | | |
| Nov 6 | A | Berwick Rangers | 2-2 | 1 | 2 | 3¹ | | 5 | | 4 | 9 | 10 | | | | 6 | 7¹ | 8 | | | | | 11 | | | | | | | | |
| 13 | A | Forfar Athletic | 1-1 | 1 | 2 | 3 | | 5 | | 4 | | 10¹ | 12 | | | 14 | 6 | 7 | 8 | 9 | | | 11 | | | | | | | | |
| 20 | H | East Fife | 2-1 | 1 | 2 | 3¹ | | 5 | | 4 | | 10 | 12 | | | 6 | 7 | 8 | | | | 11 | | 9¹ | | | | | | | |
| 27 | A | Cowdenbeath | 3-2 | 1 | 2 | | | 5 | 12 | | | 10¹ | 7 | | | 6 | 3 | 8 | | | | 11 | | 9² | 4 | | | | | | |
| Dec 4 | H | Albion Rovers | 5-1 | 1 | 2 | | | 5 | 12 | | | 10³ | 7¹ | | | 6 | 3 | 8 | 14¹ | | | 11 | | 9 | 4 | | | | | | |
| 18 | H | Stenhousemuir | 0-2 | 1 | 2 | 3 | | 5 | | 4 | | 10 | | | | 6 | | 8 | | 12 | 11 | 9 | 7 | | | | | | | | |
| 27 | A | Stranraer | 0-1 | 1 | 2 | 3 | | 5 | | 4 | 14 | 10 | 7 | | | 6 | 12 | 8 | | | | 9 | 11 | | | | | | | | |
| Jan 11 | A | Alloa | 0-1 | 1 | 2 | 3 | | 5 | | 4 | | 10 | 14 | | | 6 | | 8 | | 12 | 11 | 9 | 7 | | | | | | | | |
| 15 | A | Meadowbank Thistle | 1-1 | 1 | 2 | | | 5 | 11 | 4 | | 10 | 7 | | | 6 | | 8 | | 12 | | 9¹ | 14 | 3 | | | | | | | |
| 22 | H | Queen's Park | 2-0 | 1 | 2 | | | 5¹ | | 4 | | 10 | 12 | 11 | | 6 | | 8 | | 14 | | 9¹ | 7 | 3 | | | | | | | |
| Feb 2 | A | Arbroath | 1-1 | 1 | 2 | | | 5¹ | | 4 | | 10 | 12 | 11 | | 6 | | 8 | | 9 | | | 7 | 3 | | | | | | | |
| 5 | H | Queen of the South | 0-0 | 1 | 2 | | | 5 | | 4 | | 12 | 10 | | | 6 | | 8 | | 9 | 11 | | 7 | 3 | | 14 | | | | | |
| 12 | A | Montrose | 2-2 | 1 | 2 | | | 5¹ | | | | 10 | 12 | 4¹ | | 6 | | 8 | | 11 | | 9 | 7 | 3 | | | | | | | |
| 19 | A | Albion Rovers | 1-3 | 1 | 2 | | | 5 | | | | 10 | | 11 | | 6 | 4 | 8 | | 9¹ | 12 | | 7 | 3 | | 14 | | | | | |
| Mar 5 | A | Alloa | 1-0 | 1 | 2 | | | 5 | | | | 10 | | 11 | | 6 | | 8 | | 9¹ | | | 7 | 3 | | 12 | 4 | 14 | | | |
| 12 | H | Cowdenbeath | 4-0 | 1 | 2 | | | 5 | | | | | | 11 | | 6 | 14¹ | 8¹ | | 12 | | 9¹ | 7 | 3 | | 10 | 4¹ | | | | |
| 15 | H | Meadowbank Thistle | 1-0 | 1 | 2 | | | 5 | | | | | | 11¹ | | 6 | 10 | 8 | | 12 | | 9 | 7 | 3 | | 4 | | | | | |
| 19 | A | Arbroath | 2-0 | 1 | | | | 5 | | | | | | 11 | | 6 | 2 | 8¹ | | 10 | | 9¹ | 7 | 3 | | 12 | 4 | | | | |
| 26 | A | East Fife | 0-1 | 1 | | | | 5 | 12 | | | | | 11 | | 6 | 2 | 8 | | 10 | | 9 | 7 | 3 | | 4 | | | | | |
| Apr 2 | A | Montrose | 2-0 | 1 | | | | 5 | 7¹ | | | | | | | 6 | 2 | 8 | | 14 | | 9¹ | | 3 | | 4 | 10 | 11 | | | |
| 9 | H | Stenhousemuir | 2-2 | 1 | 2 | | | 5 | 7 | | | | | 12 | | 6 | 4 | 8 | | 14 | | 9² | | 3 | | 10 | 11 | | | | |
| 16 | A | Forfar Athletic | 2-0 | 1 | 2 | | | 5 | | | | 10 | 11 | | | 6 | 4 | 8¹ | | 12 | | 9¹ | 7 | 3 | | 14 | | | | | |
| 23 | H | Stranraer | †2-3 | 1 | 2¹ | | | 5 | 14 | | | 10 | 9 | | | 6 | 7 | 8 | | 12 | | | | 3 | | 4 | 11 | | | | |
| 30 | A | Queen of the South | 1-1 | 1 | 2 | | | | 14 | | | 9 | 11 | | | 6 | 4 | 8 | | 12 | | | 7 | 3 | | 10¹ | 5 | | | | |
| May 7 | H | Berwick Rangers | 1-3 | 1 | 2 | | | 5 | | | | 10 | 9 | | | 6 | 4 | 8 | | 12 | | | 3 | 11¹ | | 7 | | | | | |
| 14 | A | Queen's Park | 0-2 | | 2 | | | 5 | | | | 10 | 12 | | | 6 | 4 | 8 | | 11 | | | 7 | 3 | | 9 | | | | | 1 |
| **TOTAL FULL APPEARANCES** | | | | 38 | 36 | 19 | 38 | 14 | 16 | 8 | 3 | 32 | 11 | 15 | 3 | 34 | 24 | 35 | 1 | 11 | 21 | 16 | 17 | 18 | 1 | 10 | 4 | 3 | 1 | | |
| **TOTAL SUB APPEARANCES** | | | | | | | (2) | (5) | (4) | | | (1) | | (7) | (1) | (4) | (3) | | | (5) | (1) | (3) | (3) | (10) | (1) | | (1) | | (4) | (3) | |
| **TOTAL GOALS SCORED** | | | | | | 3 | 3 | 4 | 1 | 2 | | 7 | | 1 | | 2 | 1 | 2 | | | | 4 | 1 | 5 | | 12 | | | 3 | |

*Small bold figures denote goalscorers. † denotes opponent's own goal.*

# FIRS PARK

**CAPACITY**: 1,880; Seated 280, Standing 1,600

**PITCH DIMENSIONS**: 106 yds x 73 yds

**FACILITIES FOR DISABLED SUPPORTERS:** By prior arrangement with Secretary.

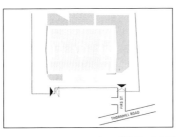

# HOW TO GET THERE

**The following routes may be used to reach Firs Park:**

**TRAINS:** Passengers should alight at Grahamston station and the ground is then ten minutes walk.

**BUSES:** All buses running from the city centre pass close by the ground. The Grangemouth via Burnbank Road and Tamfourhill via Kennard Street services both stop almost outside the ground.

**CARS:** Car parking is available in the adjacent side streets and in the car park adjacent to the Social Club. This can take 100 cars and there are also spaces available in the car park adjacent to the major stores around the ground.

YOUNGER'S
**TARTAN SPECIAL**

# FORFAR ATHLETIC

Station Park, Carseview Road,
Forfar DD8 3BT

**CHAIRMAN**
George A. Enston

**VICE-CHAIRMAN**
David McGregor

**DIRECTORS**
James Robertson
Ralph J. Stirton
William C. Taylor
Ian Stewart
Donald R. Cameron
James G. Robertson

**SECRETARY**
David McGregor

**MANAGER**
Tom Campbell

**ASSISTANT MANAGER**
Brian McLaughlin

**COACHING STAFF**
Tom McCallum, Stewart Kennedy
& Ian McPhee

**PHYSIOTHERAPIST**
Jim Peacock

**GROUNDSMAN**
Martin Gray

**COMMERCIAL DIRECTOR**
James G. Robertson

**TELEPHONES**
Ground (0307) 463576/462259
Sec. Home (0307) 464924
Sec. Bus. (0307) 462255
Fax (0307) 466956

**CLUB SHOP**
45 East High Street, Forfar.
Tel (0307) 465959. Open 9.00 a.m. –
5.00 p.m. Mon, Tue, Thur and Fri.

**OFFICIAL SUPPORTERS CLUB**
c/o Mrs. Yvonne Nicoll,
24 Turfbeg Drive, Forfar

**TEAM CAPTAIN**
Ian Heddle

**SHIRT SPONSOR**
Osnaburg Bar

## LIST OF PLAYERS 1994-95

| SURNAME | FIRST NAME | MIDDLE NAME | DATE OF BIRTH | PLACE OF BIRTH | DATE OF SIGNING | HEIGHT FT INS | WEIGHT ST LBS | PREVIOUS CLUB |
|---|---|---|---|---|---|---|---|---|
| Archibald | Eric | | 25/03/65 | Dunfermline | 23/10/93 | 5 11.0 | 13 4 | Cowdenbeath |
| Arthur | Gordon | | 30/05/58 | Kirkcaldy | 08/09/93 | 5 11.0 | 12 8 | Raith Rovers |
| Bingham | David | Thomas | 03/09/70 | Dunfermline | 08/12/92 | 5 10.0 | 10 6 | St. Johnstone |
| Buchan | Scott | Duncan | 22/12/75 | Aberdeen | 25/02/94 | 5 11.0 | 12 0 | Dundee United |
| Glennie | Stuart | Philip | 07/10/75 | Torphins | 14/09/93 | 5 10.0 | 11 8 | Banchory St. Ternan |
| Hall | Andrew | | 16/08/69 | Perth | 16/03/93 | 6 0.0 | 12 0 | Jeanfield Swifts |
| Heddle | Ian | Alexander | 21/03/63 | Dunfermline | 07/08/92 | 5 10.0 | 11 5 | St. Johnstone |
| Irvine | Neil | Donald | 13/10/65 | Edinburgh | 22/07/94 | 5 10.0 | 11 1 | Montrose |
| Kopel | Scott | Andrew | 25/02/70 | Blackburn | 11/10/93 | 5 8.0 | 12 9 | Brechin City |
| Leddie | Paul | | 11/10/74 | Dundee | 21/05/93 | 5 11.0 | 12 4 | St. Johnstone |
| Lees | Gordon | | 17/06/62 | Dundee | 23/12/93 | 5 9.0 | 10 7 | Brechin City |
| Mann | Robert | Alexander | 11/01/74 | Dundee | 21/07/92 | 6 2.0 | 14 2 | St. Johnstone |
| McKillop | Alan | Robert | 30/11/63 | Perth | 04/06/94 | 6 1.0 | 12 7 | Arbroath |
| McLaren | Paul | | 14/02/66 | Bellshill | 26/05/94 | 6 0.0 | 10 12 | Brechin City |
| McPhee | Ian | | 31/01/61 | Perth | 27/09/91 | 5 8.0 | 11 7 | Airdrieonians |
| Mearns | Gary | | 16/12/71 | Dundee | 11/08/90 | 5 8.0 | 10 2 | Dundee United |
| Morris | Robert | Martin | 07/03/57 | St. Andrews | 13/11/80 | 5 11.0 | 11 0 | Halbeath Juniors |
| O'Neill | Hugh | | 03/01/75 | Dunfermline | 21/07/94 | 6 1.0 | 11 3 | Dunfermline Athletic |
| Ross | Alexander | Robert | 01/08/63 | Bellshill | 26/05/94 | 6 0.0 | 9 7 | Brechin City |
| Smith | Raymond | | 01/04/72 | Airdrie | 13/10/92 | 5 8.0 | 12 0 | A.S.C. Perth |
| Stephen | Craig | | 10/07/73 | Torphins | 09/08/94 | 5 10.0 | 10 8 | Banchory St. Ternan |

## MILESTONES

**YEAR OF FORMATION:** 1885
**MOST LEAGUE POINTS IN A SEASON:** 63 (Second Division – Season 1983/84)
**MOST LEAGUE GOALS SCORED BY A PLAYER IN A SEASON:** Dave Kilgour (Season 1929/30)
**NO. OF GOALS SCORED:** 45
**RECORD ATTENDANCE:** 10,800 (-v- Rangers – 7.2.1970)
**RECORD VICTORY:** 14-1 (-v- Lindertis – Scottish Cup 1.9.1888)
**RECORD DEFEAT:** 2-12 (-v- King's Park – Division 2, 2.1.1930)

## SEASON TICKET INFORMATION

**Seated**
Adult ...................................................................£75
Juvenile/OAP .......................................................£37.50
**Standing**
Adult ...................................................................£65
Juvenile/OAP .......................................................£32.50

## LEAGUE ADMISSION PRICES

**Seated**
Adult ...................................................................£4.50
Juvenile/OAP .......................................................£2.50
**Standing**
Adult ...................................................................£4
Juvenile/OAP .......................................................£2

**REGISTERED STRIP:** Shirt – Sky Blue/Navy Blue Vertical Stripes, Shorts – Navy Blue
Stockings – Navy Blue with Three Sky Blue Bands on Turnover

**CHANGE STRIP:** Shirt – Red with Navy Blue Shoulder Flashes
Shorts – Red with Navy Blue Flash
Stockings – Red with Solid Navy Blue Turnover

## The LOONS

*Player columns (left to right):* Thomson S., Phillben R., McPhee I., Hamill A., Mann R., McIntyre S., Bingham D., Mearns G., Petrie S., Donaldson G., Heddle I., Smith R., Winter G., McCafferty A., Morris R., Leddie P., Arthur G., Downie I., Sheridan J., Kopel S., Archibald E., Gray B., Russell N., Lees G., Buchan S.

*Small bold figures (shown here in brackets, e.g. 9[3]) denote goalscorers. † denotes opponent's own goal.*

| Date | Venue | Opponents | Result | Tho | Phi | McP | Ham | Man | McI | Bin | Mea | Pet | Don | Hed | Smi | Win | McC | Mor | Led | Art | Dow | She | Kop | Arc | Gra | Rus | Lee | Buc |
|---|---|---|---|---|---|---|---|---|---|---|---|---|---|---|---|---|---|---|---|---|---|---|---|---|---|---|---|---|
| Aug 7 | A | Queen's Park | 3-0 | 1 | 2 | 3 | 4 | 5 | 6 | 7 | 8 | 9[3] | 10 | 11 | 12 | | | | | | | | | | | | | |
| 14 | H | Albion Rovers | 3-0 | 1 | 2 | 3 | 4 | 5 | 6 | 7[3] | 8 | 9 | 10 | 11 | 12 | | 14 | | | | | | | | | | | |
| 21 | A | Arbroath | 1-1 | 1 | 2 | 3 | 4 | 5 | 6 | 7 | 8 | 9 | 10[1] | 11 | | | 14 | | | | | | | | | | | |
| 28 | H | Queen of the South | 1-2 | 1 | 2 | 3 | | 5 | 6 | 7 | 8 | | 10[1] | 11 | 9 | 4 | 12 | | | | | | | | | | | |
| Sep 4 | A | Meadowbank Thistle | 0-2 | 1 | 2 | | 3 | 5 | | 7 | 8 | | 10 | 11 | 14 | 6 | 12 | 4 | 9 | | | | | | | | | |
| 11 | H | Montrose | 1-1 | | 2 | 3 | 4 | | 6 | 7[1] | 8 | | 10 | 11 | | 5 | | | 1 | | | | 9 | | | | | |
| 18 | A | East Stirlingshire | 2-1 | | 2 | 3 | 4 | | 6 | 7[1] | 8 | | 10 | 11 | | 14 | 5 | | 1 | | | | 9[1] | | | | | |
| 25 | H | Berwick Rangers | 1-1 | | 2 | 3 | 4 | | 6 | | | | 10 | 11 | | 8 | 5 | 14 | 1 | | | | 9[1] | | | | | |
| Oct 2 | A | East Fife | 2-3 | | 2 | 3 | 4 | 5 | 8 | 7 | | | 10[1] | 11 | 12 | 6 | | 14 | 1 | | | | 9[1] | | | | | |
| 9 | H | Alloa | 0-3 | | 2 | 6 | 3 | 5 | | 11 | | | 10 | 8 | 9 | 4 | | | 1 | | | | 7 | 14 | | | | |
| 16 | A | Stenhousemuir | 0-2 | | 2 | 3 | 6 | 4 | | 7 | | | 10 | 11 | 12 | 5 | | | 1 | | | | 9 | 8 | | | | |
| 23 | H | Stranraer | 0-1 | | 2 | | 3 | | | 7 | | | 11 | 9 | 6 | 12 | 8 | 1 | 10 | | | | 4 | 5 | 14 | | | |
| 30 | H | Cowdenbeath | 3-2 | | 2 | 3 | 8 | 4 | | 10 | | | 11[2] | | 6[1] | 14 | | 1 | 9 | | | | 7 | 5 | | | | |
| Nov 6 | A | Albion Rovers | †3-1 | | 2 | 3 | 8 | 4 | | 10[1] | | | 11 | | 6 | | | 1 | 9 | | | | 7 | 5[1] | | | | |
| 13 | H | East Stirlingshire | 1-1 | | 2 | 3 | 8 | 4 | | 10[1] | | | 11 | 12 | 6 | | | 1 | 9 | | | | 7 | 5 | | | | |
| 30 | A | Berwick Rangers | 2-0 | | 2 | 3 | 8[1] | 4 | | 10 | | | 11 | 12 | 6 | 14 | | | 9 | | | | 7[1] | 5 | 1 | | | |
| Dec 4 | A | East Fife | 1-0 | | 2 | 3[1] | 8 | 4 | | 10 | | | 11 | | 6 | | | 1 | 9 | | | | 7 | 5 | | | | |
| 7 | A | Alloa | 1-1 | | 2 | 3 | 8 | 4 | | 10[1] | | | 11 | | 6 | | | 1 | 9 | | | | 7 | 5 | | | | |
| 18 | H | Queen's Park | 4-0 | | 2 | 3 | 8 | 4 | | 10 | | | 11[1] | | 6[1] | 12 | | 1 | 9 | | | | 7[1] | 5 | | 14[1] | | |
| Jan 11 | A | Arbroath | 1-4 | | 2 | 3 | 8 | 4[1] | | 10 | 5 | | 11 | | 6 | | | 1 | 12 | | | | 7 | | 9 | | | |
| 15 | A | Queen of the South | 0-1 | | 2 | 3 | 8 | 4 | | 10 | 7 | | 11 | | 6 | | | 1 | 14 | | | | 12 | 5 | 9 | | | |
| 18 | A | Cowdenbeath | 2-1 | | 2 | 8 | 3 | 4 | | 10 | | | 11 | 12[2] | 6 | 14 | | 1 | 9 | | | | 5 | | 7 | | | |
| 22 | H | Stenhousemuir | 1-1 | | 2 | 8 | 3 | 4 | | | | | 11 | 10[1] | 6 | | | 5 | 1 | 9 | 14 | | | | 7 | | | |
| Feb 2 | A | Stranraer | 0-2 | | 2 | 3 | 8 | 4 | | 10 | | | 11 | | 6 | | | 5 | 1 | 9 | | | 14 | | 7 | | | |
| 5 | A | Montrose | | | 2 | | 3 | 4 | | 10 | 7 | | 8[1] | 9 | 6 | | | 5 | 1 | 14 | | | 12 | | 11 | | | |
| 12 | A | Meadowbank Thistle | 2-4 | | 2 | | 3 | 4 | | 10 | 8 | | 9[1] | 6 | | | 7 | 1 | | | | | 12[1] | 5 | 11 | | | |
| 26 | A | East Fife | 1-1 | | 2 | 7 | | 4[1] | | 10 | 8 | | 9 | | 6 | | | 12 | 14 | 5 | | 1 | 11 | | 3 | | | |
| Mar 2 | H | Cowdenbeath | 2-1 | | | 8 | | 4 | | 10[1] | 2 | | 11 | | 6 | | 14[1] | 7 | 5 | | 1 | | 9 | 3 | | | | |
| 5 | H | Arbroath | 3-2 | | | 8 | 14 | 4 | | 10[1] | 2 | | 11 | 12 | 6 | | | 9[1] | 7[1] | 5 | | 1 | | 3 | | | | |
| 12 | A | Stenhousemuir | 1-0 | | | 8 | 12 | 4 | | 10 | 2 | | 11 | 3 | 6 | | | 9[1] | 7 | 5 | | 1 | | | | | | |
| 19 | H | Queen of the South | 4-4 | | | 8[1] | | 4 | | 10 | | | 11[1] | 14 | 3[1] | | | 6[1] | 9 | 7 | | 5 | 1 | | 12 | 2 | | |
| 26 | A | Queen's Park | 2-3 | | 2 | 8 | | 4 | | 10 | | | 11[2] | 14 | 6 | | | 9 | 7 | 5 | | 1 | | | 12 | 3 | | |
| Apr 2 | H | Meadowbank Thistle | 0-0 | | 14 | 8 | | 4 | | 10 | 2 | | 11 | | | 3 | 6 | 12 | 7 | 5 | | 1 | | 9 | | | | |
| 9 | A | Berwick Rangers | 2-2 | | 3 | 8 | | 4 | | 10[1] | 2 | | 11 | | 12 | 6 | | 14 | 7 | 5 | | 1 | | 9[1] | | | | |
| 16 | A | East Stirlingshire | 0-2 | | 2 | 3 | | 4 | | 10 | 12 | | 11 | 14 | 6 | | | 9 | 7 | 5 | | 1 | | 8 | | | | |
| 23 | A | Albion Rovers | 3-1 | | 2 | 3 | | 4 | | 10 | | | 11 | 9[1] | 6 | | | 1 | 12 | 7[2] | 5 | | | 8 | | | | |
| 30 | H | Stranraer | 1-3 | | 2 | 3 | | 4 | | 10 | | | 11 | 9[1] | 6 | | | 1 | 12 | 7 | 5 | | | 8 | | | | |
| May 7 | A | Alloa | 3-1 | | 2 | 3 | | 4 | | 10[2] | 8 | | 11[1] | | | 12 | 6 | 1 | 14 | 7 | 5 | | | 9 | | | | |
| 14 | H | Montrose | 0-2 | | 2 | 3 | | 4 | | 10 | 8 | | 11 | 12 | 6 | | | 1 | 14 | 7 | 5 | | | 9 | | | | |
| **TOTAL FULL APPEARANCES** | | | | 5 | 34 | 35 | 25 | 37 | | 6 | 38 | 17 | | 3 | 11 | 39 | 9 | 21 | 1 | | 7 | 18 | 24 | 22 | | 22 | 24 | 10 | 16 | 5 |
| **TOTAL SUB APPEARANCES** | | | | | (1) | | (2) | | | (1) | | | | | (13) | (2) | (3) | (6) | (3) | | (11) | (2) | (5) | | (1) | | (3) |
| **TOTAL GOALS SCORED** | | | | | 2 | 1 | 2 | | | 13 | | | | | 3 | 3 | 8 | 6 | 3 | | 1 | | | 6 | | 6 | 1 | | 2 |

*Small bold figures denote goalscorers. † denotes opponent's own goal.*

---

## STATION PARK

**CAPACITY:** 8,732; Seated 800, Standing 7,932

**PITCH DIMENSIONS:** 115 yds x 69 yds

**FACILITIES FOR DISABLED SUPPORTERS:** Ramp entrance via Main Stand.

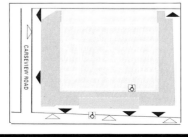

CARSEVIEW ROAD

## HOW TO GET THERE

Station Park can be reached by the following routes:

**BUSES:** There is a regular service of buses departing from Dundee City Centre into Forfar. The bus station in the town is about half a mile from the ground. There is also a local service.

**TRAINS:** The nearest railway station is Dundee (14 miles away) and fans who travel to here should then board a bus for Forfar from the city centre.

Arbroath station is also about 14 miles away.

**CARS:** There are car parking facilities in adjacent streets to the ground and also in the Market Muir car park.

# MONTROSE

**Links Park Stadium, Wellington Street, Montrose DD10 8QD**

**CHAIRMAN**
Bryan D. Keith

**DIRECTORS**
Malcolm J. Watters
Michael G. Craig
Ronald Clark

**HONORARY PRESIDENT**
William Johnston, M.B.E., J.P.

**SECRETARY**
Malcolm J. Watters

**MANAGER**
John W. Holt

**FIRST TEAM COACH**
Andy Dornan

**SECOND TEAM COACH**
Alan Lyons

**CLUB DOCTOR**
Dr. Francis W. Smith, M.D.

**PHYSIOTHERAPIST**
Neil Bryson

**COMMERCIAL DEPARTMENT**
Northern Promotions Ltd
(0592) 743205

**TELEPHONES**
Ground (0674) 673200
Sec. Home (0674) 830354
Sec. Bus. (0674) 674941
Fax (0674) 677311

**CLUB SHOP**
At Stadium Tel (0674) 674941.
Open 9.00 a.m. – 5.00 p.m. Fri.
and on match days

**OFFICIAL SUPPORTERS CLUB**
c/o Links Park, Wellington Street,
Montrose DD10 8QD

**TEAM CAPTAIN**
Ian Robertson

**SHIRT SPONSOR**
Bon Accord Glass

## LIST OF PLAYERS 1994-95

| SURNAME | FIRST NAME | MIDDLE NAME | DATE OF BIRTH | PLACE OF BIRTH | DATE OF SIGNING | HEIGHT FT INS | WEIGHT ST LBS | PREVIOUS CLUB |
|---|---|---|---|---|---|---|---|---|
| Beedie | Stuart | | 16/08/60 | Aberdeen | 11/02/94 | 5 10.5 | 11 0 | East Fife |
| Breen | Philip | | 10/09/74 | Aberdeen | 30/03/93 | 5 10.5 | 10 10 | Bon Accord Juniors |
| Brown | Michael | Derek | 26/10/75 | Aberdeen | 07/02/94 | 6 1.0 | 10 4 | Crombie Sports |
| Burnett | Clark | | 02/08/73 | Aberdeen | 11/01/94 | 5 9.0 | 10 3 | Bon Accord |
| Cooper | Craig | | 17/01/73 | Arbroath | 19/06/93 | 5 10.0 | 10 13 | Portcullis |
| Craib | Mark | | 08/02/70 | St. Andrews | 17/07/92 | 5 10.0 | 11 12 | Dundee |
| Dornan | Andrew | | 19/08/61 | Aberdeen | 29/01/90 | 5 8.5 | 10 13 | Worcester City |
| Fleming | John | Munro | 23/11/63 | Edinburgh | 07/09/90 | 5 9.0 | 11 8 | Arbroath |
| Garden | Mark | | 07/08/75 | Aberdeen | 02/08/93 | 5 11.0 | 11 8 | Middlefield United |
| Grant | Derek | | 19/05/66 | Edinburgh | 12/09/92 | 6 2.0 | 12 8 | Meadowbank Thistle |
| Haro | Mark | | 21/10/71 | Irvine | 12/07/93 | 6 2.0 | 11 7 | Dunfermline Athletic |
| Houghton | Grant | Paul | 04/04/74 | Dundee | 27/04/94 | 5 10.0 | 10 0 | Kinnoull Juniors |
| Kennedy | Allan | | 11/03/64 | Arbroath | 02/08/93 | 5 9.0 | 10 0 | Forfar West End |
| Larter | David | | 18/03/60 | Edinburgh | 27/07/87 | 5 10.5 | 11 4 | Dalkeith |
| Lavelle | Mark | | 26/04/74 | Hitchin | 20/03/93 | 5 11.0 | 11 5 | Bon Accord Juniors |
| MacRonald | Colin | William | 22/08/73 | Aberdeen | 12/08/94 | 5 7.5 | 10 0 | Aberdeen |
| Massie | Ronald | Wilson | 04/10/75 | Montrose | 28/08/93 | 5 11.0 | 11 5 | Montrose Roselea |
| Masson | Paul | Thomas | 07/12/74 | Aberdeen | 27/10/93 | 5 9.0 | 10 7 | Carnoustie Panmure |
| McGlashan | Colin | James | 17/03/64 | Perth | 12/07/94 | 5 7.0 | 10 12 | Ayr United |
| McKenna | Ian | Scott | 09/10/68 | Glasgow | 13/07/93 | 5 10.0 | 11 3 | Forfar Athletic |
| Milne | Colin | Richard | 23/10/74 | Aberdeen | 04/02/94 | 6 0.0 | 10 11 | Aberdeen |
| Mitchell | Craig | | 30/11/75 | Aberdeen | 07/02/94 | 5 11.0 | 11 7 | Crombie Sports |
| Robertson | Ian | William | 14/10/66 | Motherwell | 26/07/91 | 5 9.0 | 10 10 | Aberdeen |
| Stephen | Levi | | 19/03/74 | Hastings | 06/08/93 | 5 8.0 | 11 0 | Clydebank |
| Taylor | Darren | | 26/06/71 | Dundee | 20/11/93 | 5 11.0 | 11 0 | Lochee United |
| Tindal | Kevin | Douglas | 11/04/71 | Arbroath | 20/11/93 | 5 9.0 | 12 7 | Arbroath |
| Tosh | James | David | 12/09/74 | Arbroath | 19/06/93 | 6 0.0 | 10 11 | Arbroath Lads Club |
| Warman | David | William B. | 30/08/75 | Aberdeen | 10/11/93 | 5 11.0 | 10 5 | Culter |
| Wolecki | Edward | | 13/03/66 | Dundee | 05/08/93 | 5 10.0 | 10 7 | Deveronvale |

## MILESTONES

**YEAR OF FORMATION:** 1879
**MOST CAPPED PLAYER:** Sandy Keiller
**NO. OF CAPS:** 6 (2 whilst with Montrose)
**MOST LEAGUE POINTS IN A SEASON:** 53 (Division 2 – 1974/75 and Second Division 1984/85)
**RECORD ATTENDANCE:** 8,983 (-v- Dundee – 17.3.1973)
**RECORD VICTORY:** 12-0 (-v- Vale of Leithen – Scottish Cup 4.1.1975)
**RECORD DEFEAT:** 0-13 (-v- Aberdeen – 17.3.1951)

## SEASON TICKET INFORMATION

**Seated or Standing**
Adult ................................................................. £75
Juvenile/OAP ...................................................... £40
Family (1 Adult and 1 Juvenile) .............................. £85

## LEAGUE ADMISSION PRICES

**Seated or Standing**
Adult ..................................................................... £5
Juvenile/OAP ...................................................... £2.50

| | |
|---|---|
| REGISTERED STRIP: | Shirt – Royal Blue with White Sleeves and Royal Blue Cuffs, Shorts – White with Royal Blue and Red Trim, Stockings – White with Royal Blue and Red Tops |
| CHANGE STRIP: | Shirt – Tangerine with Royal Blue, White and Tangerine Sleeves, Shorts – Royal Blue with Tangerine and White Stripes, Stockings – Royal Blue with Tangerine and White Bands |

# CLUB FACTFILE 1993/94 .. RESULTS .. APPEARANCES .. SCORERS

## The GABLE ENDIES

| Date | Venue | Opponents | Result | Larter D. | Robertson I. | Craib M. | Haro M. | Smith J. | Irvine N. | Yeats C. | Craib S. | Grant D. | Kennedy A. | Stephen L. | Jack R. | McKenna I. | Tosh J. | Lavelle M. | Wolecki E. | Cooper C. | Houghton G. | Holt J. | Wilkins G. | Tindal K. | Taylor D. | Massie R. | Milne C. | Garden M. | Beedie S. | Masson P. |
|---|---|---|---|---|---|---|---|---|---|---|---|---|---|---|---|---|---|---|---|---|---|---|---|---|---|---|---|---|---|
| Aug 7 | A | Stranraer | 4-2 | 1 | 2 | 3 | 4 | 5 | 6 | $7^1$ | 8 | $9^3$ | 10 | 11 | 12 | 14 | | | | | | | | | | | | | | |
| 14 | H | Arbroath | 0-0 | 1 | 2 | 3 | 4 | 5 | 6 | 7 | 8 | 9 | 10 | 11 | 12 | 14 | | | | | | | | | | | | | | |
| 21 | H | Stenhousemuir | 2-0 | 1 | 2 | 3 | 4 | 5 | 6 | 7 | 8 | $9^1$ | 10 | 11 | | | $12^1$ | 14 | | | | | | | | | | | | |
| 28 | A | Queen's Park | 1-2 | 1 | 2 | $3^1$ | 4 | 5 | 6 | 7 | 8 | 9 | 10 | 11 | | | 12 | | | | | | | | | | | | | |
| Sep 4 | A | East Stirlingshire | 3-2 | 1 | | $3^1$ | 4 | | 6 | 7 | 8 | $10^2$ | | 11 | | 14 | 12 | 5 | 2 | 9 | | | | | | | | | | |
| 11 | A | Forfar Athletic | 1-1 | 1 | 2 | 3 | 4 | | | | 8 | | 10 | 11 | | | | 7 | 5 | 6 | $9^1$ | | | | | | | | | |
| 18 | H | Meadowbank Thistle | 0-3 | 1 | 2 | 3 | 4 | | | 12 | 8 | 10 | 14 | 11 | | | | 7 | 5 | 6 | 9 | | | | | | | | | |
| 25 | A | Alloa | 1-0 | 1 | 2 | 3 | | 5 | | $7^1$ | 8 | 9 | 10 | 11 | | | | 4 | 6 | | 14 | | | | | | | | | |
| Oct 2 | A | Queen of the South | 0-1 | 1 | 2 | 3 | | 5 | | 7 | 8 | 9 | 10 | 11 | | | | 4 | 6 | 14 | | 12 | | | | | | | | |
| 9 | H | East Fife | 0-1 | 1 | 2 | 3 | | 5 | | 7 | 8 | 9 | 10 | 11 | | | | 4 | 6 | 14 | | 11 | | | | | | | | |
| 16 | A | Berwick Rangers | 3-3 | 1 | 2 | 3 | | 5 | | 8 | 14 | $9^2$ | 10 | 11 | | | | 4 | 6 | | $7^1$ | | | | | | | | | |
| 23 | H | Cowdenbeath | 1-2 | 1 | 2 | 3 | | 5 | | | 8 | $9^1$ | 10 | 11 | | | 12 | | 6 | 14 | 7 | 4 | | | | | | | | |
| 30 | H | Albion Rovers | 1-0 | 1 | | 3 | 4 | 5 | 6 | 8 | 14 | 9 | $10^1$ | 11 | | | 12 | | | 7 | 2 | | | | | | | | | |
| Nov 6 | A | Arbroath | 0-2 | 1 | 2 | 3 | | 5 | | | 8 | | 10 | 11 | | | 9 | 4 | 6 | | 7 | | | 12 | 14 | | | | | |
| 13 | A | Meadowbank Thistle | 3-5 | 1 | 2 | $3^1$ | | 5 | | | 8 | | $10^1$ | 11 | | | $9^1$ | 4 | 6 | | 7 | | | 12 | | | 14 | | | |
| 20 | H | Alloa | 1-2 | 1 | | 3 | | 5 | | | | $9^1$ | 10 | 11 | | | 12 | 4 | 6 | | 7 | 2 | | | | 8 | 14 | | | |
| 27 | A | East Fife | 2-5 | 1 | | 3 | | 5 | 6 | $2^1$ | 8 | 9 | $10^1$ | 11 | | | | 4 | | | | | | 12 | 2 | 7 | | | | |
| Dec 4 | H | Queen of the South | 2-1 | 1 | | 3 | | 5 | 6 | 7 | 14 | $10^2$ | 12 | 11 | | | | | 4 | | | | | | | 8 | 9 | | | |
| Jan 4 | H | Stranraer | 0-2 | | 2 | 3 | | 5 | 6 | 7 | | | 10 | 11 | | | | | 4 | | | | | 14 | | 8 | 9 | 1 | | |
| 15 | H | Queen's Park | 1-2 | 1 | 2 | 3 | | 5 | 6 | 7 | 8 | 9 | $10^1$ | 11 | | | | | 4 | | | | | 12 | | | | | | |
| 18 | A | Stenhousemuir | 4-3 | | 2 | 3 | | 5 | 6 | | 8 | 4 | 10 | 11 | | | | | $9^2$ | $7^1$ | | | | 12 | $14^1$ | | | 1 | | |
| 22 | H | Berwick Rangers | 2-3 | 1 | 2 | 3 | | 5 | 6 | | | 4 | $10^1$ | 11 | | | | | 8 | 9 | 7 | | | 12 | $14^1$ | | | | | |
| 25 | A | Albion Rovers | 4-3 | 1 | | 3 | | 5 | 6 | | | 4 | 10 | $11^1$ | | | | | 12 | | | | | 7 | 2 | $8^1$ | $9^2$ | | | |
| Feb 5 | H | Forfar Athletic | 1-1 | 1 | | 3 | | 5 | | 12 | | 4 | 8 | $11^1$ | | | | 2 | 6 | | 7 | | | | | | 9 | 10 | 14 | |
| 12 | H | East Stirlingshire | 2-2 | 1 | | 3 | | 5 | | | 8 | 4 | $10^1$ | 11 | | | | 2 | 6 | | 7 | | | | | | $9^1$ | | | |
| 19 | H | East Fife | 3-0 | 1 | 2 | 3 | | 5 | | | | 4 | 10 | $8^1$ | | | 11 | | 6 | | 12 | | | 7 | $14^2$ | | 9 | | | |
| 26 | A | Arbroath | 0-0 | 1 | 2 | | | | | | | 4 | 10 | 8 | | | | 5 | 6 | | 12 | | | 3 | 7 | | 9 | 11 | | |
| Mar 5 | A | Albion Rovers | 1-0 | 1 | 2 | | | | | | | 4 | 10 | 7 | | | 14 | 5 | 6 | | 12 | | | 3 | 9 | | $8^1$ | 11 | | |
| 12 | H | Berwick Rangers | 3-1 | 1 | 2 | | | | 6 | | | $4^1$ | 10 | 11 | | | $12^1$ | 5 | $3^1$ | | 7 | | | 14 | | | 9 | 8 | | |
| 19 | H | Cowdenbeath | 1-1 | 1 | 2 | | | | 6 | | | 4 | 10 | 11 | | | | 5 | 3 | | 7 | | | 12 | | | $9^1$ | 14 | 8 | |
| 22 | H | Cowdenbeath | 1-0 | 1 | 2 | | | 5 | 6 | | | 4 | 10 | 11 | | | | 3 | 8 | 12 | 7 | | | | | | $9^1$ | 14 | | |
| 26 | A | Queen of the South | 0-1 | 1 | 2 | | | 5 | 6 | | | 4 | 14 | | | | 12 | 3 | 11 | 10 | 7 | | | | | | 9 | 8 | | |
| Apr 2 | A | East Stirlingshire | 0-2 | 1 | 2 | | 6 | 5 | 11 | | | 4 | 10 | | | | | | | | 7 | | | 14 | | | 9 | 8 | 3 | |
| 13 | A | Stranraer | 0-1 | 1 | 2 | | | 5 | 6 | | | 4 | 10 | | | | | 3 | 11 | 12 | 7 | | | | | | 9 | 8 | | |
| 16 | A | Stenhousemuir | 0-2 | 1 | 2 | | | 5 | 6 | | | 4 | 10 | 11 | | | | 3 | | 12 | 7 | | | | | | 9 | 14 | 8 | |
| 23 | H | Alloa | 2-2 | 1 | 2 | | | 5 | 6 | | | 4 | $10^1$ | | | | | 3 | 8 | | | | | 12 | | | 9 | $6^1$ | 11 | |
| 30 | H | Meadowbank Thistle | 2-0 | 1 | 2 | | | 5 | 6 | | | 4 | $10^1$ | | | | 14 | | 8 | | $7^1$ | | | 12 | | | 9 | 11 | 3 | |
| May 7 | H | Queen's Park | 2-3 | 1 | 2 | | | 5 | 6 | | | $4^1$ | $10^1$ | | | | 14 | | 8 | | 7 | | | 12 | | | 9 | 11 | 3 | |
| 14 | A | Forfar Athletic | 2-0 | 1 | 2 | | | | | | | 4 | 10 | 11 | | | | 5 | 8 | | 7 | | | 3 | 12 | | $9^2$ | | | 6 |
| **TOTAL FULL APPEARANCES** | | | | 37 | 35 | 23 | 8 | 31 | 22 | 16 | 15 | 35 | 35 | 28 | | | 9 | 26 | 27 | 6 | 22 | 5 | | 9 | 6 | 2 | 16 | 3 | 12 | 1 |
| **TOTAL SUB APPEARANCES** | | | | | | | | | (2) | (2) | (1) | | | | (2) | (5) | (3) | | (11) | | (1) | (9) | (6) | (3) | (1) | (1) | (2) | (10) | (4) |
| **TOTAL GOALS SCORED** | | | | | | 3 | | | 3 | | | 12 | 11 | 3 | | | | | 3 | 1 | 3 | 3 | | 1 | 6 | | 6 | 1 | | |

*Small bold figures denote goalscorers.  † denotes opponent's own goal.*

## LINKS PARK STADIUM

**CAPACITY:** 4,338; Seated 1,338, Standing 3,000

**PITCH DIMENSIONS:** 113 yds x 70 yds

**FACILITIES FOR DISABLED SUPPORTERS:** Area set aside for wheelchairs and designated area in new stand.

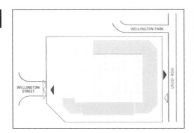

## HOW TO GET THERE

Links Park can be reached by the following routes:

**TRAINS:** Montrose is on the Inter-City 125 route from London to Aberdeen and also on the Glasgow-Aberdeen route. There is a regular service and the station is about 15 minutes walk from the ground.

**BUSES:** An hourly service of buses from Aberdeen and Dundee stop in the town centre and it is a 15 minute walk from here to the ground.

**CARS:** Car parking is available in the car park at the ground and there are numerous side streets all round the park which can be used if necessary.

# QUEEN'S PARK

Hampden Park, Letherby Drive,
Mount Florida, Glasgow G42 9BA

**PRESIDENT**
Malcolm Mackay

**COMMITTEE**
W. Lindsay Ross, M.A.,LL.B. (Treasurer)
Martin B. Smith, LL.B., N.P.
Peter G. Buchanan
John Campbell
Robert L. Cromar F.I.B.S.
Ian G. Harnett B.Sc.
William Omand
Austin Reilly
James Nicholson
H. Gordon Wilson

**SECRETARY**
James C. Rutherford

**COACH**
Edward Hunter

**ASSISTANT COACH**
Millar Hay

**CLUB DOCTOR**
Alan S. Hutchison

**PHYSIOTHERAPIST**
Robert C. Findlay

**CHIEF SCOUT**
William S. Burgess

**GROUNDSMAN**
Norman Henderson

**TELEPHONES**
Ground 041-632 1275
Fax 041-636 1612

**CLUB SHOP**
Home matches only – Hampden Park
(Police Building at end of West Stand)
2.15 p.m. – 3.00 p.m. and 4.45 p.m. –
5.00 p.m. on home match days

**OFFICIAL SUPPORTERS CLUB**
c/o Secretary, Keith McAllister,
58 Brunton Street,
Glasgow G44 3NQ

**TEAM CAPTAIN**
Graeme Elder

**SHIRT SPONSOR**
British Engine Insurance Ltd

## LIST OF PLAYERS 1994-95

| SURNAME | FIRST NAME | MIDDLE NAME | DATE OF BIRTH | PLACE OF BIRTH | DATE OF SIGNING | HEIGHT FT INS | WEIGHT ST LBS | PREVIOUS CLUB |
|---|---|---|---|---|---|---|---|---|
| Black | Simon | | 07/01/76 | Paisley | 12/06/93 | 5 9.0 | 10 7 | Unattached |
| Bradley | Robert | | 04/11/71 | Bellshill | 24/07/93 | 5 10.0 | 11 0 | Queen's Park Youth |
| Brodie | David | | 04/01/71 | Hardgate | 22/09/93 | 5 10.0 | 11 11 | Glenwood Amateurs |
| Campbell | Stephen | | 24/07/71 | Glasgow | 11/10/93 | 6 1.0 | 13 0 | Yoker Athletic U'21 |
| Cassidy | Martin | | 22/12/71 | Glasgow | 24/07/93 | 5 9.0 | 11 2 | Campsie Black Watch |
| Caven | Ross | | 04/08/65 | Glasgow | 12/06/93 | 6 0.0 | 12 0 | Possil Y.M.C.A. |
| Chalmers | James | | 03/02/70 | Glasgow | 12/06/93 | 6 0.0 | 11 4 | Yoker Athletic |
| Edgar | Scott | | 10/06/76 | Glasgow | 27/07/94 | 6 4.0 | 13 0 | Milngavie Wanderers |
| Elder | Graeme | | 21/11/61 | Glasgow | 12/06/93 | 6 1.0 | 13 0 | Drumchapel Y.M.C.A. |
| Ferguson | Paul | | 10/09/73 | Glasgow | 25/03/94 | 6 0.0 | 10 7 | Wolves B.C. |
| Fitzpatrick | Stephen | | 04/12/71 | Greenock | 03/08/93 | 6 2.0 | 11 10 | Port Glasgow H.S. |
| Graham | David | | 27/01/71 | Bellshill | 31/07/93 | 5 10.0 | 10 8 | Queen's Park Youth |
| Kavanagh | James | | 12/09/70 | East Kilbride | 12/06/93 | 6 1.0 | 11 0 | Muirend Amateurs |
| Kerr | Gary | | 24/02/74 | Paisley | 12/06/93 | 5 11.0 | 11 0 | Hamilton Academical |
| Lynch | Martin | James | 12/09/75 | Glasgow | 19/03/94 | 6 0.0 | 11 0 | Lenzie Y.C. |
| Maxwell | Ian | | 02/05/75 | Glasgow | 24/07/93 | 6 3.0 | 12 5 | Unattached |
| McCormick | Stephen | | 14/08/69 | Dumbarton | 12/06/93 | 6 4.0 | 11 4 | Yoker Athletic |
| McFadyen | Martin | | 21/01/77 | Glasgow | 09/08/94 | 5 11.0 | 10 8 | Ferguslie Juveniles |
| McPhee | Brian | | 23/10/70 | Glasgow | 26/08/93 | 5 10.0 | 11 4 | Rutherglen Amateurs |
| Moir | Alexander | | 20/03/68 | Glasgow | 03/08/93 | 6 3.0 | 13 0 | Barr & Stroud A.F.C. |
| Moonie | David | | 09/10/72 | Durban | 24/07/93 | 5 11.0 | 11 1 | Dunfermline Athletic |
| Orr | Garry | | 27/11/73 | Glasgow | 12/06/93 | 5 4.0 | 10 10 | Dundee United |
| Orr | James | P. | 01/02/72 | Blantyre | 24/07/93 | 5 9.0 | 11 2 | Queen's Park Youth |
| Rodden | James | | 13/08/65 | Glasgow | 12/06/93 | 5 9.0 | 11 0 | Pollok Juniors |
| Scott | George | | 02/08/75 | Vale of Leven | 27/07/94 | 5 11.0 | 11 10 | Milngavie Wanderers |
| Stevenson | Colin | | 28/08/72 | Glasgow | 12/06/93 | 5 9.0 | 10 7 | Unattached |

## MILESTONES

**YEAR OF FORMATION:** 1867
**MOST CAPPED PLAYER:** Walter Arnott
**NO. OF CAPS:** 14
**MOST LEAGUE POINTS IN A SEASON:** 57 (Division 2 – Season 1922/23)
**MOST LEAGUE GOALS SCORED BY A PLAYER IN A SEASON:** William Martin (Season 1937/38)
**NO. OF GOALS SCORED:** 30
**RECORD ATTENDANCE:** 149,547 (Scotland v England – 17.4.1937)
**RECORD VICTORY:** 16-0 (-v- St. Peters – Scottish Cup 29.8.1885)
**RECORD DEFEAT:** 0-9 (-v- Motherwell – Division 1, 29.4.1930)

## SEASON TICKET INFORMATION

Seated
Centre/West Stand Adult .......................................... £60
Juvenile/OAP ............................. £30

## LEAGUE ADMISSION PRICES

Seated
Adult ..................................................................... £4
Juvenile/OAP ............................................................. £2

**REGISTERED STRIP:** Shirt – 1" White and Black Hoops
Shorts – White with Black and White Leg Band,
Stockings – White with 2 Black Hoops
**CHANGE STRIP:** Strip – Red with Black Collar and Cuffs, Shorts: Red
Stockings: Red with 2 Black and White Hoops

# CLUB FACTFILE 1993/94 .. RESULTS .. APPEARANCES .. SCORERS

## The SPIDERS

Player columns: Chalmers J., Kerr G., Kavanagh J., Fitzpatrick S., Snedden S., Orr G., Elder G., O'Brien J., Black S., O'Neill J., McCormick S., Rodden J., Graham D., Caven R., Cassidy M., Orr J., McPhee B., Stevenson C., Maxwell I., MacKenzie K., Brodie D., Henrici G., Campbell S., Ferguson P., Moonie D., Moir A., Lynch M.

| Date | Venue | Opponents | Result | Appearances / Scorers |
|------|-------|-----------|--------|------------------------|
| Aug 7 | H | Forfar Athletic | 0-3 | 1 2 3 4 5 6 7 8 9 10 11 12 14 |
| 14 | A | Queen of the South | 2-5 | 1 2 3 4 6 5 9¹10 11¹12 8 7 14 |
| 21 | A | Albion Rovers | 0-2 | 1 4 3 6 8 5 11 10 9 12 7 2 14 |
| 28 | H | Montrose | 2-1 | 1 3 2 6 8¹ 5 10 9 12 7¹ 4 11 |
| Sep 4 | H | Cowdenbeath | 1-3 | 1 3 2 6 8 5 10¹11 12 7 4 9 |
| 11 | A | Arbroath | 0-2 | 1 14 6 10 5 12 11 7 8 4 9 2 3 |
| 18 | H | East Fife | 4-2 | 1 4 2 8 6 5 11 12¹ 9²10 3 7 14¹ |
| 25 | A | Stenhousemuir | 0-2 | 1 4 2 5 6 11 12 7 10 8 3 9 |
| Oct 2 | H | Stranraer | 0-0 | 1 4 12 10 11 9 7 3 8 2 6 5 14 |
| 9 | A | Berwick Rangers | 0-6 | 1 4 12 8 11 10 7 3 9 5 2 6 |
| 16 | H | East Stirlingshire | 1-1 | 1 4 6 10 5 9 11 7 2 8¹ 12 3 |
| 23 | A | Meadowbank Thistle | 1-1 | 1 4 5 6 12 11 7 10 8 9¹ 3 14 2 |
| 30 | A | Alloa | 1-1 | 1 5 6¹ 4 7 11 10 8 9 2 3 12 |
| Nov 6 | H | Queen of the South | 3-1 | 1 5 6 4 7 11 12¹ 10² 8 9 2 3 14 |
| 13 | A | East Fife | 5-5 | 1 5 6 4 11¹ 7 10 8 9⁴ 2 3 |
| 20 | H | Stenhousemuir | 1-2 | 1 5 6 4 11¹ 7 10 8 9 2 3 12 |
| 27 | A | Berwick Rangers | 0-0 | 1 2 5 6 4 11 14 10 8 9 12 3 7 |
| Dec 4 | A | Stranraer | 0-2 | 1 5 2 6 4 11 12 10 8 9 14 3 7 |
| 18 | A | Forfar Athletic | 0-4 | 1 14 2 6 4 11 12 7 10 8 9 5 3 |
| 27 | H | Alloa | 2-1 | 1 5 6 4 11¹ 9 7¹10 8 2 3 12 |
| Jan 1 | H | Albion Rovers | 2-0 | 1 5 6 4 11² 9 7 10 8 14 2 3 12 |
| 15 | A | Montrose | 2-1 | 1 14 5 6 4 11¹ 7 9 10 8¹ 2 3 12 |
| 22 | A | East Stirlingshire | 0-2 | 1 8 5 6 4 11 7 9 10 2 3 12 |
| 29 | H | Meadowbank Thistle | 3-2 | 1 5 6 4 9² 7 11 10 8 2 3¹ 14 |
| Feb 5 | A | Arbroath | 2-1 | 1 5 6 4 9¹11¹ 7 10 8 2 12 3 14 |
| 12 | A | Cowdenbeath | 4-3 | 1 5 6 4 9² 7¹11 10¹ 8 2 3 14 |
| 19 | A | Queen of the South | 0-3 | 1 5 6 4 9 7 11 10 8 2 14 3 12 |
| Mar 1 | H | Berwick Rangers | 1-3 | 1 4 6 12 11 10¹ 8 9 3 5 7 2 14 |
| 5 | H | Stenhousemuir | 2-4 | 1 5 6 4 9² 11 8 12 3 7 2 10 |
| 12 | A | East Fife | 0-1 | 1 4 8 6 5 9 7 10 11 2 12 3 |
| 19 | A | Albion Rovers | 1-1 | 1 4 5 6 9 7¹11 10 2 14 12 8 3 |
| 26 | H | Forfar Athletic | 3-2 | 1 4 5 6 9¹11² 10 2 7 8 3 |
| Apr 2 | A | Stranraer | 1-1 | 1 4 8 6 5 9 11 14 10¹ 2 7 3 |
| 12 | A | Alloa | 0-0 | 1 4 5 6 9 11 10 8 2 7 3 |
| 16 | H | Meadowbank Thistle | 1-3 | 1 4 5 6 9¹11 14 10 8 2 7 3 |
| 23 | A | Arbroath | 1-2 | 1 5 6 4 9 11 10¹ 8 2 3 7 |
| 30 | A | Cowdenbeath | 1-1 | 1 5 6 4 9 7 14 10 8¹ 2 3 11 12 |
| May 7 | H | Montrose | 3-2 | 6¹ 4 9¹11 12 10 8¹ 2 3 7 14 1 5 |
| 14 | H | East Stirlingshire | 2-0 | 1 6 4 9 11 14 8¹ 2 3 7¹ 10 5 12 |
| **TOTAL FULL APPEARANCES** | | | | 38 19 7 37 2 39 30 2 6 39 29 10 31 33 19 14 15 26 2 12 4 5 7 1 2 |
| **TOTAL SUB APPEARANCES** | | | | (2) (3) (1) (2) (7) (6) (4) (1) (5) (6) (13) (1) (2) (1) (1) |
| **TOTAL GOALS SCORED** | | | | 3 1 18 7 1 6 6 7 1 2 |

*Small bold figures denote goalscorers.  † denotes opponent's own goal.*

---

## HAMPDEN PARK

**CAPACITY:** 38,113 (All Seated)
**PITCH DIMENSIONS:** 115 yds x 75 yds
**FACILITIES FOR DISABLED SUPPORTERS:** Capacity 222 – Weelchair 54, Ambulant Seated 48, Ambulant Standing 120.

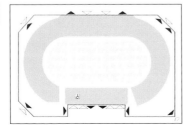

## HOW TO GET THERE

The following routes may be used to reach Hampden Park:

**TRAINS:** There are two stations within five minutes walk of the ground. Mount Florida Station, on the Cathcart Circle and King's Park Station. A 15 minute service runs from Glasgow Central.

**BUSES:** Services to approach Mount Florida end of Stadium: From City Centre: 5, 5A, 5B, M5, M14, 31, 37, 66, 66A, 66B, 66C; From Govan Cross: 34; From Drumchapel: 96,97; Circular Service: 89, 90; G.C.T. Service: 1; Services to approach King's Park end of Stadium; From City Centre: 12, 12A, 74; Circular Service: 89, 90; G.C.T. Service: 19.

**CARS:** Car parking facilities are available in the car park at the front of the Stadium, which is capable of holding 1,200 vehicles. Side streets can also be used on major occasions.

# ROSS COUNTY

Victoria Park, Jubilee Road,
Dingwall, Ross-shire IV15 9QW

CHAIRMAN
Hector MacLennan

VICE-CHAIRMAN
Donald MacBean

DIRECTORS
Kenneth Cameron
Douglas K. Harper
Roy MacGregor
Kenneth MacLeod
Ian Dingwall
Gordon Macrae
David Roan

SECRETARY
Donald MacBean

MANAGER
Robert Wilson

ASSISTANT MANAGER
Don Cowie

CLUB DOCTOR
Dr. G. Bruce

PHYSIOTHERAPIST
Dougie Sim

S.F.A. COMMUNITY COACH
Ross Jack

GROUND CONVENER AND
SAFETY OFFICER
J. Harper

COMMERCIAL MANAGER
Brian Campbell
(0349) 862253

TELEPHONES
Ground/Ticket Office (0349) 862253
Fax (0349) 866277

CLUB SHOP
Situated at Ground

OFFICIAL SUPPORTERS CLUB
G. Shiels, 4 Tulloch Place, Dingwall
Tel (0349) 865135

TEAM CAPTAIN
Cameron Robertson

SHIRT SPONSOR
MacGregor Group

## LIST OF PLAYERS 1994-95

| SURNAME | FIRST NAME | MIDDLE NAME | DATE OF BIRTH | PLACE OF BIRTH | DATE OF SIGNING | HEIGHT FT INS | WEIGHT ST LBS | PREVIOUS CLUB |
|---|---|---|---|---|---|---|---|---|
| Campbell | Gary | | 14/10/70 | Inverness | 08/08/94 | 5  9.0 | 10  6 | Invergordon |
| Cathcart | Ross | | 16/02/67 | Falkirk | 23/08/94 | 5 11.0 | 12  4 | Unattached |
| Connelly | Gordon | Paul | 20/09/67 | Stirling | 12/08/94 | 5  7.0 | 11  2 | Dunfermline Athletic |
| Duff | Alan | Smith | 02/05/63 | Tain | 08/08/94 | 5 10.0 | 11  0 | Tain |
| Ferries | Keith | | 16/08/65 | Inverness | 08/08/94 | 5  8.0 | 10 10 | Elgin City |
| Grant | Brian | | 13/12/68 | Inverness | 08/08/94 | 5 10.0 | 11  0 | Brechin City |
| Herd | William | David | 03/09/65 | Buckhaven | 08/08/94 | 5 11.0 | 12  0 | Cowdenbeath |
| Hutchison | Stephen | | 18/09/70 | Glasgow | 08/08/94 | 5 11.5 | 12 10 | Falkirk |
| MacLeod | Alexander | James | 01/02/68 | Inverness | 08/08/94 | 6  0.0 | 12  0 | Dingwall Thistle |
| MacLeod | Andrew | Donald | 14/08/69 | Glasgow | 08/08/94 | 5  8.0 | 10  2 | Fortuna Sittard |
| McMillan | Donald | | 12/12/73 | Helmsdale | 12/08/94 | 5 11.5 | 12  4 | Brora Rangers |
| MacPherson | Jamie | | 10/12/70 | Sydney | 08/08/94 | 6  0.0 | 11  6 | Inverness Clachnacuddin |
| Reid | Craig | | 16/02/74 | Aberdeen | 08/08/94 | 5 10.0 | 10 12 | Unattached |
| Robertson | Cameron | John | 03/02/61 | Luton | 08/08/94 | 5 11.0 | 12  0 | Invergordon |
| Somerville | Christopher Ian | | 08/12/67 | Larne | 08/08/94 | 5  5.0 | 10  0 | Brora Rangers |
| Williamson | Robert | | 25/04/69 | Inverness | 08/08/94 | 5 10.5 | 11  4 | Inverness Clachnacuddin |
| Wilson | Barry | John | 16/02/72 | Kirkcaldy | 08/08/94 | 5 11.0 | 12  4 | Southampton |

## MILESTONES

YEAR OF FORMATION: 1929
MOST LEAGUE POINTS IN A SEASON: 76 (Highland League – 3 Points for a Win)
MOST LEAGUE GOALS SCORED BY A PLAYER IN A SEASON: Brian Grant
NO. OF GOALS SCORED: 46 (Highland League)
RECORD ATTENDANCE: 8,000 (-v- Rangers – Scottish Cup 28.2.66)
RECORD VICTORY: 11-0 (-v- St. Cuthbert Wanderers – Scottish Cup 1994)
RECORD DEFEAT: 1-10 (-v- Inverness Thistle – Highland League)

## SEASON TICKET INFORMATION

**Seated**
Adult .................................................................. £65
Juvenile/OAP .......................................................... £40
**Standing**
Adult .................................................................. £50
Juvenile/OAP .......................................................... £25

## LEAGUE ADMISSION PRICES

**Seated**
Adult ................................................................... £5
Juvenile/OAP ........................................................... £3
**Standing**
Adult ................................................................... £4
Juvenile/OAP ........................................................... £2

| | |
|---|---|
| **REGISTERED:** | Shirt – Dark Blue with White Trim |
| | Shorts – White, Stockings – Red |
| **CHANGE STRIP:** | Shirt – White with Red Trim |
| | Shorts – Red, Stockings – White |

# ROSS COUNTY F.C. – A BRIEF HISTORY
## FORMED: 1929

**HONOURS:**

**Highland League**
1966/67, 1990/91, 1991/92

**Highland League Cup**
1949/50, 1968/69, 1978/79, 1991/92

**Scottish Qualifying Cup**
1973/74, 1993/94

**North of Scotland Cup**
1929/30, 1969/70, 1971/72, 1991/92

**Inverness Cup**
1930/31, 1959/60, 1964/65, 1966/67, 1978/79,
1979/80, 1991/92, 1992/93

*Although the record books say Ross County were founded in 1929, the story of senior football in Dingwall can be traced back a good deal further. Indeed, Ross County were founder members of the North of Scotland FA in 1888. Their tenure in the mainstream of Highland football was not complete however, for just three months into the inaugural Highland League, the Dingwall club became the first side to resign from the infant League.*

Ironically, the reason for their resignation was the inability, some would say unwillingness, to raise a team to meet Inverness Caley. Both sides are of course now embarking upon their first season in The Scottish Football League, albeit the Inverness club under a new formula. Doubtless when County meet the new amalgamated Inverness side they will be able to muster a side for the occasion!

It was 1929, when the football minded citizens of Dingwall reapplied for Highland League membership and Dingwall Victoria United were duly elected. Before the season could get under way the name of Ross County was adopted.

In August 1929, Victoria Park, Dingwall was opened and a Highland League select met Ross County to mark the occasion. One year later, Ross County annexed the North of Scotland Cup and a further year on they became the first non-Inverness side to win the Inverness Cup. Thus in the space of two years Ross County had made their presence in the Highland League game known.

A barren spell followed for County, and not until 1949/50

was the Dingwall trophy cabinet put to use again. The Highland League Cup had been set up shortly after the Second World War and the Victoria Park side won the 4th such tournament beating Buckie 4-1 in the Final. It is worth noting that for this 1949 triumph Ross were still resplendent in their original colours of red and blue hoops.

In 1965, County once again had a fine side to boast of and they gave notice of their growing strength by winning the Inverness Cup in some style. The Final against Nairn County turned into a veritable goal bonanza and in a 12 goal thriller Ross County scrambled home 7-5 at Telford Street Park, Inverness.

The nucleus of this side won the 1967 title, losing only two games and hammering in 107 goals. Such was their popularity that they were able to charter a special train to take supporters to the Ne'erday fixture with Brora Rangers. Six years later Inverness Thistle pipped County for a second title by winning a Championship Play-Off.

However, it was under the astute guidance of Bobby Wilson that this club really came to prominence and since 1990, have enjoyed unparralled success by winning all of the major trophies in the Highlands. In 1991 they lifted the League again, and this was the start of a run that brought the Highland League Cup and the retention of the League title in 1992. It was such consistency together with the completion of a £250,000 grandstand that convinced many League clubs to vote in favour of admitting Ross County to the League.

But Ross County's fame has spread far wider than the confines of the Highland League football scene. In the Scottish Cup they have enjoyed some memorable jousts. In 1965/66 they ousted both Forfar and Alloa en route to entertaining Rangers, who were delighted to exit from Dingwall clutching a 2-0 win. In 1991 they beat Alloa before thrashing Queen of the South 6-2 at Palmerston Park. Indeed, almost on the eve of the vote to decide who should join the expanded Scottish League, County beat St. Cuthbert's 11-0 and Forfar 4-0 in yet another memorable cup run.

With such a proud tradition, Ross County are certainly a welcome addition to The Scottish Football League.

*by JIM JEFFREY*

## VICTORIA PARK

**CAPACITY:** 8,322; Seated 322, Standing 8,000

**PITCH DIMENSIONS:** 110 yds x 75 yds

**FACILITIES FOR DISABLED SUPPORTERS:** Area in Main Stand and Terracing. Toilet facilities are also available.

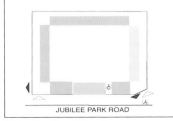

JUBILEE PARK ROAD

## HOW TO GET THERE

The following routes can be used to reach Victoria Park:

**TRAINS:** The nearest mainline station is Inverness and fans travelling from the South should alight and board a train that takes them direct to Dingwall Station.

**BUSES:** Regular buses on a daily basis from Glasgow, Edinburgh and Perth.

**CARS:** The major trunk roads, A9 and A96, connect Dingwall with the North, the South and the East.

## PREMIER DIVISION CHAMPIONSHIP

| | P | W | L | D | F | A | Pts |
|---|---|---|---|---|---|---|---|
| Rangers | 44 | 22 | 8 | 14 | 74 | 41 | 58 |
| Aberdeen | 44 | 17 | 6 | 21 | 58 | 36 | 55 |
| Motherwell | 44 | 20 | 10 | 14 | 58 | 43 | 54 |
| Celtic | 44 | 15 | 9 | 20 | 51 | 38 | 50 |
| Hibernian | 44 | 16 | 13 | 15 | 53 | 48 | 47 |
| Dundee United | 44 | 11 | 13 | 20 | 47 | 48 | 42 |
| Heart of Midlothian | 44 | 11 | 13 | 20 | 37 | 43 | 42 |
| Kilmarnock | 44 | 12 | 16 | 16 | 36 | 45 | 40 |
| Partick Thistle | 44 | 12 | 16 | 16 | 46 | 57 | 40 |
| St. Johnstone | 44 | 10 | 14 | 20 | 35 | 47 | 40 |
| Raith Rovers | 44 | 6 | 19 | 19 | 46 | 80 | 31 |
| Dundee | 44 | 8 | 23 | 13 | 42 | 57 | 29 |

## FIRST DIVISION CHAMPIONSHIP

| | P | W | L | D | F | A | Pts |
|---|---|---|---|---|---|---|---|
| Falkirk | 44 | 26 | 4 | 14 | 81 | 32 | 66 |
| Dunfermline Athletic | 44 | 29 | 8 | 7 | 93 | 35 | 65 |
| Airdrieonians | 44 | 20 | 10 | 14 | 58 | 38 | 54 |
| Hamilton Academical | 44 | 19 | 13 | 12 | 66 | 54 | 50 |
| Clydebank | 44 | 18 | 12 | 14 | 56 | 48 | 50 |
| St. Mirren | 44 | 21 | 15 | 8 | 61 | 55 | 50 |
| Ayr United | 44 | 14 | 16 | 14 | 42 | 52 | 42 |
| Dumbarton | 44 | 11 | 19 | 14 | 48 | 59 | 36 |
| Stirling Albion | 44 | 13 | 22 | 9 | 41 | 68 | 35 |
| Clyde | 44 | 10 | 22 | 12 | 35 | 58 | 32 |
| Greenock Morton | 44 | 6 | 21 | 17 | 44 | 75 | 29 |
| Brechin City | 44 | 6 | 31 | 7 | 30 | 81 | 19 |

## SECOND DIVISION CHAMPIONSHIP

| | P | W | L | D | F | A | Pts |
|---|---|---|---|---|---|---|---|
| Stranraer | 39 | 23 | 6 | 10 | 63 | 35 | 56 |
| Berwick Rangers | 39 | 18 | 9 | 12 | 75 | 46 | 48 |
| Stenhousemuir | 39 | 19 | 11 | 9 | 62 | 44 | 47 |
| Meadowbank Thistle | 39 | 17 | 9 | 13 | 62 | 48 | 47 |
| Queen of the South | 39 | 17 | 13 | 9 | 69 | 48 | 43 |
| East Fife | 39 | 15 | 13 | 11 | 58 | 52 | 41 |
| Alloa | 39 | 12 | 10 | 17 | 41 | 39 | 41 |
| Forfar Athletic | 39 | 14 | 14 | 11 | 58 | 58 | 39 |
| East Stirlingshire | 39 | 13 | 15 | 11 | 54 | 57 | 37 |
| Montrose | 39 | 14 | 17 | 8 | 56 | 61 | 36 |
| Queen's Park | 39 | 12 | 17 | 10 | 52 | 76 | 34 |
| Arbroath | 39 | 12 | 18 | 9 | 42 | 67 | 33 |
| Albion Rovers | 39 | 7 | 22 | 10 | 37 | 66 | 24 |
| Cowdenbeath | 39 | 6 | 25 | 8 | 40 | 72 | 20 |

## PREMIER RESERVE LEAGUE

| | P | W | L | D | F | A | Pts |
|---|---|---|---|---|---|---|---|
| Celtic | 28 | 17 | 6 | 5 | 60 | 32 | 39 |
| Rangers | 28 | 15 | 8 | 5 | 59 | 32 | 35 |
| Aberdeen | 28 | 14 | 7 | 7 | 62 | 36 | 35 |
| Dundee United | 28 | 14 | 8 | 6 | 54 | 30 | 34 |
| Hibernian | 28 | 13 | 12 | 3 | 49 | 48 | 29 |
| Heart of Midlothian | 28 | 11 | 13 | 4 | 33 | 34 | 26 |
| Dundee | 28 | 4 | 17 | 7 | 33 | 83 | 15 |
| Raith Rovers | 28 | 4 | 21 | 3 | 24 | 79 | 11 |

## RESERVE LEAGUE EAST

| | P | W | L | D | F | A | Pts |
|---|---|---|---|---|---|---|---|
| Falkirk | 22 | 16 | 1 | 5 | 72 | 24 | 37 |
| Hibernian | 22 | 16 | 2 | 4 | 53 | 18 | 36 |
| Dunfermline Athletic | 22 | 12 | 6 | 4 | 66 | 30 | 28 |
| St. Johnstone | 22 | 12 | 6 | 4 | 37 | 29 | 28 |
| East Fife | 22 | 10 | 9 | 3 | 35 | 49 | 23 |
| Montrose | 22 | 8 | 9 | 5 | 34 | 35 | 21 |
| Brechin City | 22 | 9 | 10 | 3 | 33 | 39 | 21 |
| Alloa | 22 | 6 | 10 | 6 | 26 | 31 | 18 |
| Meadowbank Thistle | 22 | 5 | 10 | 7 | 25 | 38 | 17 |
| Cowdenbeath | 22 | 6 | 13 | 3 | 20 | 44 | 15 |
| Forfar Athletic | 22 | 4 | 12 | 6 | 24 | 46 | 14 |
| Arbroath | 22 | 2 | 18 | 2 | 22 | 64 | 6 |

## RESERVE LEAGUE WEST "A" DIVISION

| | P | W | L | D | F | A | Pts |
|---|---|---|---|---|---|---|---|
| Celtic | 24 | 21 | 3 | 0 | 74 | 14 | 42 |
| Motherwell | 24 | 19 | 3 | 2 | 87 | 25 | 40 |
| Hamilton Academical | 24 | 14 | 6 | 4 | 52 | 35 | 32 |
| Clyde | 24 | 12 | 9 | 3 | 53 | 56 | 27 |
| Airdrieonians | 24 | 11 | 9 | 4 | 57 | 40 | 26 |
| Albion Rovers | 24 | 6 | 16 | 2 | 23 | 55 | 14 |
| Stirling Albion | 24 | 6 | 16 | 2 | 37 | 75 | 14 |
| Stenhousemuir | 24 | 6 | 17 | 1 | 24 | 58 | 13 |
| East Stirlingshire | 24 | 3 | 19 | 2 | 34 | 83 | 8 |

## RESERVE LEAGUE WEST "B" DIVISION

| | P | W | L | D | F | A | Pts |
|---|---|---|---|---|---|---|---|
| Rangers | 24 | 11 | 5 | 8 | 57 | 35 | 30 |
| St. Mirren | 24 | 11 | 6 | 7 | 53 | 38 | 29 |
| Partick Thistle | 24 | 13 | 8 | 3 | 45 | 31 | 29 |
| Kilmarnock | 24 | 11 | 9 | 4 | 41 | 29 | 26 |
| Clydebank | 24 | 8 | 9 | 7 | 33 | 34 | 23 |
| Ayr United | 24 | 9 | 10 | 5 | 49 | 52 | 23 |
| Dumbarton | 24 | 9 | 11 | 4 | 39 | 44 | 22 |
| Queen's Park | 24 | 7 | 14 | 3 | 30 | 52 | 17 |
| Greenock Morton | 24 | 4 | 11 | 9 | 37 | 69 | 17 |

*Please Note:* The play-off between the winners of Sections "A" and "B" was won by Rangers F.C. who defeated Celtic F.C. by three goals to nil at Celtic Park on Sunday, 15th May, 1994.

## YOUTH DIVISION

| | P | W | L | D | F | A | Pts |
|---|---|---|---|---|---|---|---|
| Aberdeen | 24 | 20 | 1 | 3 | 68 | 9 | 63 |
| Celtic | 24 | 13 | 4 | 7 | 44 | 10 | 46 |
| Heart of Midlothian | 24 | 13 | 6 | 5 | 51 | 17 | 44 |
| Dundee United | 24 | 12 | 10 | 2 | 52 | 29 | 38 |
| St. Johnstone | 24 | 10 | 8 | 6 | 36 | 37 | 36 |
| Dundee | 24 | 7 | 14 | 3 | 37 | 54 | 24 |
| *Greenock Morton | 23 | 7 | 15 | 1 | 27 | 55 | 22 |
| Cowdenbeath | 24 | 5 | 14 | 5 | 23 | 48 | 20 |
| *Berwick Rangers | 23 | 2 | 17 | 4 | 13 | 92 | 10 |

*Berwick Rangers F.C. and Greenock Morton F.C. were unable to fulfil their final fixture.

# Reserve League Cup – Season 1993/94

## FIRST ROUND

*18th August, 1993*
DUNFERMLINE ATHLETIC 2    CLYDEBANK 3
(AET – 2-2 after 90 minutes)

*23rd August, 1993*
ALLOA 2    HAMILTON ACADEMICAL 0

*24th August, 1993*
KILMARNOCK 5    STIRLING ALBION 1

*14th September, 1993*
MOTHERWELL 9    STENHOUSEMUIR 1

*22nd September, 1993*
ARBROATH 4    ALBION ROVERS 0

*23rd September, 1993*
AIRDRIEONIANS 1    EAST FIFE 3
PARTICK THISTLE 2    FALKIRK 0

*26th September, 1993*
CLYDE 1    ST. MIRREN 2

*27th September, 1993*
BRECHIN CITY 2    COWDENBEATH 1

*30th September, 1993*
DUMBARTON 0    ST. JOHNSTONE 2

*4th October, 1993*
FORFAR ATHLETIC 5    EAST STIRLINGSHIRE 0

## SECOND ROUND

*18th October, 1993*
MONTROSE 0    ALLOA 6
CLYDEBANK 1    ST. MIRREN 3

*20th October, 1993*
ARBROATH 3    QUEEN'S PARK 2

*25th October, 1993*
PARTICK THISTLE 2    MEADOWBANK THISTLE 1
FORFAR ATHLETIC 3    BRECHIN CITY 1

*1st November, 1993*
KILMARNOCK 2    ST. JOHNSTONE 3

*2nd November, 1993*
GREENOCK MORTON 0    EAST FIFE 2

*4th November, 1993*
MOTHERWELL 3    AYR UNITED 2

## THIRD ROUND

*17th November, 1993*
HIBERNIAN 1    DUNDEE 0
DUNDEE UNITED 3    ST. MIRREN 1

*22nd November, 1993*
PARTICK THISTLE 3    ALLOA 1

*26th November, 1993*
RANGERS 2    ST. JOHNSTONE 0

*29th November, 1993*
CELTIC 8    RAITH ROVERS 0

*1st December, 1993*
FORFAR ATHLETIC 2    ARBROATH 0

*8th December, 1993*
EAST FIFE 1    ABERDEEN 4

*17th January, 1994*
HEART OF MIDLOTHIAN 2    MOTHERWELL 2
(AET – 2-2 after 90 minutes)
Heart of Midlothian won 4-3 on Kicks from Penalty Mark

## FOURTH ROUND

*17th January, 1994*
PARTICK THISTLE 1    ABERDEEN 2

*18th January, 1994*
RANGERS 1    DUNDEE UNITED 2

*24th January, 1994*
CELTIC 2    FORFAR ATHLETIC 0

*9th February, 1994*
HIBERNIAN 0    HEART OF MIDLOTHIAN 1

## SEMI-FINALS

*2nd March, 1994*
DUNDEE UNITED 2    HEART OF MIDLOTHIAN 0

*21st March, 1994*
CELTIC 2    ABERDEEN 1
(AET – 1-1 after 90 minutes)

---

### FINAL

**Monday, 18th April, 1994**

**Tannadice Park, Dundee**

**DUNDEE UNITED 1    CELTIC 3**

**Dundee United:** A. Main, T. McMillan, F. Van Der Hoorn, C. Myers, M. Perry, G. Bollan (G. Benvie), J. Lindsay, P. Connolly, A. McLaren, C. Brewster, R. McBain

Substitutes not used: R. Hegarty, P. Shepherd (Goalkeeper)

**Celtic:** G. Marshall, B. Smith, J. McQuilken, M. Galloway, M. Mackay, R. McStay, P. Byrne, S. Gray, B. O'Neil, C. Nicholas, B. McLaughlin

Substitutes not used: C. Hay, J. Slavin, S. Given (Goalkeeper)

Scorers:  **Dundee United:** P. Connolly
**Celtic:** P. Byrne, B. O'Neil, C. Nicholas
Referee: J. Carlin (Linlithgow)
Attendance: 3,458

---

**Scottish Football League Champions 1890-1994**

| YEAR | DIVISION ONE | POINTS | DIVISION TWO | POINTS |
|---|---|---|---|---|
| 1890/91 | Dumbarton/Rangers | 29 | (No Competition) | |
| 1891/92 | Dumbarton | 37 | (No Competition) | |
| 1892/93 | Celtic | 29 | (No Competiton) | |
| 1893/94 | Celtic | 29 | Hibernian | 29 |
| 1894/95 | Heart of Midlothian | 31 | Hibernian | 30 |
| 1895/96 | Celtic | 30 | Abercorn | 27 |
| 1896/97 | Heart of Midlothian | 28 | Partick Thistle | 31 |
| 1897/98 | Celtic | 33 | Kilmarnock | 29 |
| 1898/99 | Rangers | 36 | Kilmarnock | 32 |
| 1899-1900 | Rangers | 32 | Partick Thistle | 29 |
| 1900/01 | Rangers | 35 | St. Bernards | 25 |
| 1901/02 | Rangers | 28 | Port Glasgow | 32 |
| 1902/03 | Hibernian | 37 | Airdrieonians | 35 |
| 1903/04 | Third Lanark | 43 | Hamilton Academical | 37 |
| 1904/05 | Celtic (after play-off) | 41 | Clyde | 32 |
| 1905/06 | Celtic | 49 | Leith Athletic | 34 |
| 1906/07 | Celtic | 55 | St. Bernards | 32 |
| 1907/08 | Celtic | 55 | Raith Rovers | 30 |
| 1908/09 | Celtic | 51 | Abercorn | 31 |
| 1909/10 | Celtic | 54 | Leith Athletic | 33 |
| 1910/11 | Rangers | 52 | Dumbarton | 31 |
| 1911/12 | Rangers | 51 | Ayr United | 35 |
| 1912/13 | Rangers | 53 | Ayr United | 34 |
| 1913/14 | Celtic | 65 | Cowdenbeath | 31 |
| 1914/15 | Celtic | 65 | Cowdenbeath | 37 |
| 1915/16 | Celtic | 67 | (No Competition) | |
| 1916/17 | Celtic | 64 | (No Competition) | |
| 1917/18 | Rangers | 56 | (No Competition) | |
| 1918/19 | Celtic | 58 | (No Competition) | |
| 1919/20 | Rangers | 71 | (No Competiton) | |
| 1920/21 | Rangers | 76 | (No Competition) | |
| 1921/22 | Celtic | 67 | Alloa | 60 |
| 1922/23 | Rangers | 55 | Queen's Park | 57 |
| 1923/24 | Rangers | 59 | St. Johnstone | 56 |
| 1924/25 | Rangers | 60 | Dundee United | 50 |
| 1925/26 | Celtic | 58 | Dunfermline Athletic | 59 |
| 1926/27 | Rangers | 56 | Bo'ness | 56 |
| 1927/28 | Rangers | 60 | Ayr United | 54 |
| 1928/29 | Rangers | 67 | Dundee United | 51 |
| 1929/30 | Rangers | 60 | Leith Athletic* | 57 |
| 1930/31 | Rangers | 60 | Third Lanark | 61 |
| 1931/32 | Motherwell | 66 | East Stirlingshire* | 55 |
| 1932/33 | Rangers | 62 | Hibernian | 54 |
| 1933/34 | Rangers | 66 | Albion Rovers | 45 |
| 1934/35 | Rangers | 55 | Third Lanark | 52 |
| 1935/36 | Celtic | 66 | Falkirk | 59 |
| 1936/37 | Rangers | 61 | Ayr United | 54 |
| 1937/38 | Celtic | 61 | Raith Rovers | 59 |
| 1938/39 | Rangers | 59 | Cowdenbeath | 60 |
| 1939/40 | (No Competition) | | (No Competition) | |
| 1940/41 | (No Competition) | | (No Competition) | |
| 1941/42 | (No Competition) | | (No Competition) | |
| 1942/43 | (No Competition) | | (No Competition) | |
| 1943/44 | (No Competition) | | (No Competition) | |
| 1944/45 | (No Competition) | | (No Competition) | |

# of the Scottish Football League in 1890

| YEAR | DIVISION ONE | POINTS | DIVISION TWO | POINTS |
|------|------|------|------|------|
| 1945/46 | (No Competition) | | (No Competition) | |
| 1946/47 | Rangers | 46 | Dundee | 45 |
| 1947/48 | Hibernian | 48 | East Fife | 53 |
| 1948/49 | Rangers | 46 | Raith Rovers* | 42 |
| 1949/50 | Rangers | 50 | Morton | 47 |
| 1950/51 | Hibernian | 48 | Queen of the South* | 45 |
| 1951/52 | Hibernian | 45 | Clyde | 44 |
| 1952/53 | Rangers* | 43 | Stirling Albion | 44 |
| 1953/54 | Celtic | 43 | Motherwell | 45 |
| 1954/55 | Aberdeen | 49 | Airdrieonians | 46 |
| 1955/56 | Rangers | 52 | Queen's Park | 54 |
| 1956/57 | Rangers | 55 | Clyde | 64 |
| 1957/58 | Heart of Midlothian | 62 | Stirling Albion | 55 |
| 1958/59 | Rangers | 50 | Ayr United | 60 |
| 1959/60 | Heart of Midlothian | 54 | St. Johnstone | 53 |
| 1960/61 | Rangers | 51 | Stirling Albion | 55 |
| 1961/62 | Dundee | 54 | Clyde | 54 |
| 1962/63 | Rangers | 57 | St. Johnstone | 55 |
| 1963/64 | Rangers | 55 | Morton | 67 |
| 1964/65 | Kilmarnock* | 50 | Stirling Albion | 59 |
| 1965/66 | Celtic | 57 | Ayr United | 53 |
| 1966/67 | Celtic | 58 | Morton | 69 |
| 1967/68 | Celtic | 63 | St. Mirren | 62 |
| 1968/69 | Celtic | 54 | Motherwell | 64 |
| 1969/70 | Celtic | 57 | Falkirk | 56 |
| 1970/71 | Celtic | 56 | Partick Thistle | 56 |
| 1971/72 | Celtic | 60 | Dumbarton¥ | 52 |
| 1972/73 | Celtic | 57 | Clyde | 56 |
| 1973/74 | Celtic | 53 | Airdrieonians | 60 |
| 1974/75 | Rangers | 56 | Falkirk | 54 |

| YEAR | PREMIER DIVISION | POINTS | FIRST DIVISION | POINTS | SECOND DIVISION | POINTS |
|------|------|------|------|------|------|------|
| 1975/76 | Rangers | 54 | Partick Thistle | 41 | Clydebank¥ | 40 |
| 1976/77 | Celtic | 55 | St. Mirren | 62 | Stirling Albion | 55 |
| 1977/78 | Rangers | 55 | Morton¥ | 58 | Clyde¥ | 53 |
| 1978/79 | Celtic | 48 | Dundee | 55 | Berwick Rangers | 54 |
| 1979/80 | Aberdeen | 48 | Heart of Midlothian | 53 | Falkirk | 50 |
| 1980/81 | Celtic | 56 | Hibernian | 57 | Queen's Park | 50 |
| 1981/82 | Celtic | 55 | Motherwell | 61 | Clyde | 59 |
| 1982/83 | Dundee United | 56 | St. Johnstone | 55 | Brechin City | 55 |
| 1983/84 | Aberdeen | 57 | Morton | 54 | Forfar Athletic | 63 |
| 1984/85 | Aberdeen | 59 | Motherwell | 50 | Montrose | 53 |
| 1985/86• | Celtic¥ | 50 | Hamilton Academical | 56 | Dunfermline Athletic | 57 |
| 1986/87• | Rangers | 69 | Morton | 57 | Meadowbank Thistle | 55 |
| 1987/88• | Celtic | 72 | Hamilton Academical | 56 | Ayr United | 61 |
| 1988/89# | Rangers | 56 | Dunfermline Athletic | 54 | Albion Rovers | 50 |
| 1989/90# | Rangers | 51 | St. Johnstone | 58 | Brechin City | 49 |
| 1990/91# | Rangers | 55 | Falkirk | 54 | Stirling Albion | 54 |
| 1991/92# | Rangers | 72 | Dundee | 58 | Dumbarton | 52 |
| 1992/93 | Rangers | 73 | Raith Rovers | 65 | Clyde | 54 |
| 1993/94 | Rangers | 58 | Falkirk | 66 | Stranraer | 56 |

*   Champions on goal average.     • Competition known as Fine Fare League.
¥   Champions on goal difference.   # Competition known as B & Q League.

# Ally's Cup of Joy

*Perhaps, in its one year between sponsors, the Skol Cup having been put to rest after a long life and the Coca-Cola Cup not yet conceived, it would have been an idea to rename the League Cup the Coisty Cup. Or maybe not. At any rate, the Rangers striker has a remarkable affinity with the tournament in which he holds a few records that seem unlikely to be beaten.*

For instance, as a consequence of his scoring exploits in the competition, he has won four holidays from Skol after being top scorer (or joint top) four times and has collected eight winners' medals, more than any other player.

Last season minus a sponsor, topping the scoring charts did not carry the holiday prize but we would not dare suggest that Ally tucked his shooting boots away as a consequence. In fact, the League Cup was to provide the major highlight of one of the most frustrating seasons the Ibrox and Scotland man has ever suffered. After having

broken his leg playing for Scotland in Portugal, Ally had a long, hard battle to recover and niggling injuries interrupted his climb back to match fitness. So much so that, by the time the League Cup Final came round on 24th October, he had started only two games for Rangers.

It was no big surprise then, that he was a substitute for the Final at Celtic Park (Hampden was unavailable because of reconstruction) against Hibernian, who were trying to win for the second time in three years. But McCoist was not to let such hindrances interfere with his sense of the dramatic.

However, we are ahead of ourselves. The League Cup is more than just a Final, more than just a chance for big clubs to win the first major trophy of the season and more than an early passport into Europe. It is an opportunity for the smaller clubs to get in among the big-time players and make a name for themselves.

First though, they have to take on their peers in the First Round. And so it was back on Tuesday, 3rd August, 1993, that Stenhousemuir, beat Forfar 3-1, Albion Rovers, travelled to Methil and overcame East Fife 2-1, Arbroath beat Queen's Park 1-0 and Alloa were winners by the same score over Berwick Rangers. The trail to Parkhead had begun.

The bigger names entered the fray a week later when the Second Round began, with Motherwell sinking Ayr United's ambitions with an embarrassingly easy 6-0 win at Somerset Park. Hamilton Academical, however, gave Dundee United a hard time before going down 1-0 at Douglas Park while Greenock Morton did even better, overcoming Kilmarnock at Rugby Park 2-1, and Falkirk needed extra time to beat

*Rangers goalscoring heroes, Ally McCoist and Ian Durrant celebrate.*

Stenhousemuir 2-1. Dundee had to go all the way to a penalty kick shoot-out before they put out Meadowbank Thistle.

The other Thistle, the one from Partick, had the biggest score of the tournament, thrashing Albion Rovers 11-1 at Fir Park, where the game was re-routed from Cliftonhill.

That was nearly rivalled in the next round by Celtic's 9-1 defeat of Arbroath but the real thriller of this stage came at Pittodrie where Aberdeen and Motherwell, who inevitably have titanic contests in cup matches, had to soldier on into extra time with the score at 2-2. By the time the final whistle blew Aberdeen had made it into the Quarter Finals by 5-2.

Greenock Morton's bold efforts came to an end but only after a narrow defeat by Partick Thistle at Cappielow while Rangers, by 2-0 at Dunfermline and Hibernian, by 2-1 at home against Dundee, made their progress towards that Final date.

Falkirk's talent for making life difficult for Hearts was demonstrated again when they knocked them out, thanks to a goal by Eddie May at Tynecastle, and the Brockville club were involved in a memorable Quarter Final with Dundee United at Tannadice when Richard Cadette scored three goals and still found himself on the losing side. The teams were locked at 3-3 after extra time and it was United who scraped through by dint of a 4-2 win in the penalty decider. Partick Thistle and Hibernian were involved in an equally thrilling confrontation at Firhill when, after a 1-1 full time score, the teams were still inseparable at 2-2, following extra time. Hibs made it into the Semi-Finals after a 3-2 success in the penalty shoot-out. The third tie played on the same evening saw Celtic manage to reach the last four without needing extra time to beat Airdrieonians but they made it with a single Frank McAvennie goal.

The third Quarter Final, out of four, to go into extra time took place at Ibrox the following evening where Rangers and perennial rivals,

*Ally McCoist scores the winning goal.*

*Captain, Richard Gough, with League Cup Trophy.*

Aberdeen, were level at 1-1 after 90 minutes. An Ian Ferguson goal proved just enough to get the home team through.

The drama did not end there, however, because the draw that took place immediately after the final whistle at Ibrox saw the Old Firm drawn together. With Hampden Park not available and with no other neutral venue sufficiently large enough to accommodate the respective supports of both clubs, it was agreed to toss a coin with the club calling correct hosting the Semi-Final. Celtic's assistant manager, Joe Jordan, called correctly and everyone thought that the fates had been kind enough to give Celtic a "home" tie. However, what many of the media had not realised was that Jordan and Rangers boss, Walter Smith, had agreed beforehand to initially toss the coin for the right to decide which club would call first for the venue and on the second toss, Jordan called heads, the coin landed tails giving Rangers the right to host the Semi-Final tie.

The other Semi-Final tie drawn that night paired Dundee United and Hibernian together and when this match was played at Tynecastle on Tuesday, 21st September, 1993 a solitary strike by Darren Jackson was enough to take the Hibees into their second League Cup Final in three years. The following night saw an unusual sight at Ibrox with Celtic fans occupying not only the Broomloan Road Stand, but also the Govan Stand, creating an incredible atmosphere inside the stadium. On the field of

play, the heat was equally as intense, with Rangers being reduced to ten men after Dutchman, Pieter Huistra, had been sent off. However, this seemed to inspire Rangers to greater efforts and a mistake by Celtic defender, Mike Galloway, allowed Ian Durrant to nip-in and cross for Mark Hateley to score the goal that took his team into their seventh Final in eight years.

And so to Sunday, 24th October at Celtic Park in front of 47,632 noisy spectators. An own goal by Dave McPherson gave Hibernian hope after Ian Durrant had put Rangers in front but as the tie roared towards its late stages the drama had yet to be completed. McCoist, itching to get a piece of the action, was called onto the park in place of Pieter Huistra in 67 minutes.

And with nine minutes left the script was given its inevitable denouement. The bold one sent in an overhead kick that left Jim Leighton with no chance and gave Rangers one of the most spectacular winning goals of the tournament.

"It was the best single moment of the season for me," says Ally, "but the League Cup has been a fantastic tournament for me through the years."

Stand by for his Coca-Cola turn.

**Ian Paul**
**(The Herald)**

# FIRST ROUND

*Tuesday, 3rd August, 1993*

**STENHOUSEMUIR 3**
B. Clouston, M. Mathieson,
J. Irvine

**FORFAR ATHLETIC 1**
A. Hamill

**Stenhousemuir:** S. Robertson, N. Aitken, L. Haddow, G. Armstrong,
P. Godfrey, S. Logan, T. Steel, B. Clouston, M. Mathieson, J. Irvine, J. Fisher
(J. Clarke)

Substitutes not used: S. Dickov, C. Kelly (Goalkeeper)

**Forfar Athletic:** S. Thomson, R. Philliben, I. McPhee, R. Morris (G. Mearns),
R. Mann, A. Hamill, D. Bingham, S. McIntyre, G. Donaldson, S. Petrie,
I. Heddle (A. McCafferty)

Substitute not used: N. Russell (Goalkeeper)

**EAST FIFE 1**
R. Scott

**ALBION ROVERS 2**
S. Kerrigan, A. Fraser

**East Fife:** E. Wilson, A. Sneddon, A. Williamson, D. Barron, D. Beaton,
W. Burns, D. Elliott, S. Beedie, R. Scott, J. Reilly, J. McBride

Substitutes not used: G. Allan, B. Andrew, R. Charles (Goalkeeper)

**Albion Rovers:** R. McConnachie, J. Kelly, T. Spence, D. Riley, G. Taylor,
D. McKeown, M. McBride, M. Scott, S. Kerrigan, A. Fraser, J. Gallagher
(S. Cadden)

Substitute not used: D. Seggie

**QUEEN'S PARK 0**

**ARBROATH 1**
J. Strachan

**Queen's Park:** J. Chalmers, G. Kerr, J. Kavanagh, S. Fitzpatrick, S. Sneddon,
G. Orr, G. Elder, J. O'Brien (D. Graham), S. Black, J. O'Neill, S. McCormick

Substitutes not used: J. Rodden, D. Moonie (Goalkeeper)

**Arbroath:** M. Harkness, J. Hamilton, S Florence, B. Mitchell, C. Adam,
C. Martin, B. Will (P. Hindson), T. King, J. Strachan, C. Farnan, S. Sorbie

Substitutes not used: M. Kelly, D. Jackson (Goalkeeper)

**ALLOA 1**
M. Hendry

**BERWICK RANGERS 0**

**Alloa:** J. Butter, J. McNiven, N. Bennett, C. Campbell, K. McCulloch,
W. Newbigging, W. Herd, S. Ramsay, M. Hendry, S. Smith (G. Russell),
N. McAvoy

Substitutes not used: B. Moffat, N. Binnie (Goalkeeper)

**Berwick Rangers:** G. O'Connor, K. Gibson, C. Valentine, A. Hall, M. Cowan,
S. Richardson, M. Neil (K. Kane), W. Irvine, C. Cunningham (D. Scott),
T. Graham, A. Banks

## Wednesday, 4th August, 1993

**QUEEN OF THE SOUTH 1**
D. Shanks

**STRANRAER 2**
D. Henderson (2)

**Queen of the South:** A. Davidson, D. Mills, W. McGhie, B. McKeown,
D. Shanks, A. McFarlane, D. Jackson, P. Sermanni (T. Bryce), A. Thomson,
D. McGuire (P. Kelly), S. Mallan

Substitute not used: R. McColm (Goalkeeper)

**Stranraer:** B. Duffy, S. McIntyre, J. Hughes, G. Millar, K. Brannigan,
A. Gallagher, T. Sloan, G. Duncan (P. McLean), D. Diver (A. Grant),
S. Cody, D. Henderson

Substitute not used: S. Ross (Goalkeeper)

**MONTROSE 0**

**EAST STIRLINGSHIRE 1**
J. Conroy

**Montrose:** D. Larter, I. Robertson, M. Craib, M. Haro, J. Smith, C. Yeats,
I. McKenna (N. Irvine), S. Craib, R. Jack (D. Grant), A. Kennedy, C. Maver

Substitute not used: R. Massie (Goalkeeper)

**East Stirlingshire:** G. McDougall, G. Russell, B. Kemp, I. McAulay, D. Craig,
A. Speirs (J. Loney), P. Roberts, C. McKinnon, M. Geraghty, S. Robertson,
J. Conroy

Substitutes not used: J. McMenanan, P. Imrie (Goalkeeper)

# SECOND ROUND

*Tuesday, 10th August, 1993*

**AYR UNITED 0**

**MOTHERWELL 6**
I. Ferguson, D. Arnott (2),
P. McGrillen (2), A. Graham

**Ayr United:** C. Duncan, G. Burley, G. Robertson, M. Shotton, J. Traynor,
D. George (D. Kennedy), T. Walker, S. Bryce, S. McGivern, N. McNab,
B. Scott

Substitutes not used: H. Burns, G. Grierson (Goalkeeper)

**Motherwell:** S. Dykstra, R. Shannon, R. McKinnon, M. Krivokapic,
B. Martin, C. McCart (J. Dolan), I. Ferguson, I. Angus, D. Arnott,
P. O'Donnell (A. Graham), P. McGrillen

Substitute not used: W. Thomson (Goalkeeper)

**AIRDRIEONIANS 2**
P. Davenport, D. Kirkwood

**COWDENBEATH 1**
N. Henderson

**Airdrieonians:** J. Martin, A. Stewart, D. Kirkwood, J. Sandison, G. Caesar,
W. Reid, J. Boyle, E. Balfour, P. Davenport, A. Lawrence (S. Conn),
Andrew Smith (M. Abercromby)

Substitute not used: W. McCulloch (Goalkeeper)

**Cowdenbeath:** S. Filshill, D. Watt, J. Thomson (A. Barclay), E. Petrie,
B. McMahon, I. Lee, N. Henderson, C. Scott (I. Davidson), W. Callaghan,
D. Maratea, C. Harris

Substitute not used: J. Maloney (Goalkeeper)

**HAMILTON ACADEMICAL 0**

**DUNDEE UNITED (A.E.T.) 1**
P. Connolly

**Hamilton Academical:** A. Ferguson, P. McKenzie, C. Napier, W. Reid,
J. Weir, S. McInulty, G. Clark, C. Baptie (S. McEntegart), P. Chalmers
(C. McLean), K. Ward, D. Lorimer

Substitute not used: C. Hendry (Goalkeeper)

**Dundee United:** A. Main, F. Van Der Hoorn, M. Malpas (G. Bollan),
A. Cleland, B. Welsh, D. Narey, D. Bowman, W. McKinlay, P. Connolly,
C. Dailly, C. Myers (A. McLaren)

Substitute not used: G. Van De Kamp (Goalkeeper)

**KILMARNOCK 1**
A. Mitchell

**GREENOCK MORTON 2**
D. Lilley, J. Tolmie

**Kilmarnock:** R. Geddes, A. MacPherson, T. Black, R. Montgomerie,
M. Skilling, A. Millen, A. Mitchell, M. Reilly, D. Crainie (M. Roberts),
G. McCluskey, S. McSkimming

Substitutes not used: I. Porteous, G. Matthews (Goalkeeper)

**Greenock Morton:** D. Wylie, D. Collins, M. Pickering, J. Fowler, M. Doak,
S. McArthur, D. Lilley, M. Donaghy, R. Alexander, D. McInnes, J. Tolmie
(S. Rafferty)

Substitutes not used: J. Gahagan, P. Graham (Goalkeeper)

**BRECHIN CITY 0**

**ST. MIRREN 1**
J. Dick

**Brechin City:** R. Allan, S. Kopel, G. Hutt, R. Brown, F. Conway, I. Redford,
S. Bell, P. O'Brien, S. Ross, M. Miller, G. Lees (W. McNeill)

Substitute not used: H. Cairney

**St. Mirren:** A. Combe, R. Dawson, M. Baker, N. McWhirter, S. Taylor,
N. Orr, A. Bone (B. Lavety), J. Dick, E. Gallagher (P. McIntyre), J. Hewitt,
J. Fullarton

Substitute not used: D. Watson (Goalkeeper)

**HIBERNIAN 2**
K. Wright, G. Donald

**ALLOA 0**

**Hibernian:** J. Leighton, W. Miller, J. Tortolano, T. McIntyre, S. Tweed,
G. Hunter, K. McAllister, B. Hamilton, K. Wright, D. Jackson, M. McGraw
(G. Donald)

Substitutes not used: D. Lennon, C. Reid (Goalkeeper)

**Alloa:** J. Butter, J. McNiven, N. Bennett, C. Campbell, K. McCulloch,
W. Newbigging, W. Herd, J. Gibson (B. Moffat), G. Russell (M. Hendry),
S. Ramsay, N. McAvoy

Substitute not used: N. Binnie (Goalkeeper)

**STENHOUSEMUIR 1**

J. Fisher

**FALKIRK 2 (A.E.T. –**
**1-1 after 90 minutes)**

C. Duffy, R. Cadette

**Stenhousemuir**: C. Kelly, N. Aitken, L. Haddow, G. Armstrong, P. Godfrey (J. Clarke), S. Logan, T. Steel, B. Clouston (S. Dickov), M. Mathieson, J. Irvine, J. Fisher

Substitute not used: C. Wilson (Goalkeeper)

**Falkirk**: A. Parks, N. Oliver, F. Johnston, D. Weir, J. Hughes, C. Duffy, E. May, S. Sloan (C. McDonald), R. Cadette, I. McCall, G. Shaw (T. McQueen)

Substitute not used: I. Westwater (Goalkeeper)

**STIRLING ALBION 0**

**CELTIC 2**

F. McAvennie, P. McGinlay

Match Played at Firhill Stadium, Glasgow

**Stirling Albion**: M. McGeown, J. McCormack, P. Watson, T. Tait, D. Lawrie, C. Mitchell, R. Reilly (S. Kinross), V. Moore, W. Watters, P. Armstrong, D. Flynn (D. Pew)

**Celtic**: P. Bonner, T. Boyd, D. Wdowczyk, P. Grant, M. McNally, M. Galloway, S. Slater (P. McGinlay), P. McStay, F. McAvennie, C. Nicholas, J. Collins

Substitutes not used: R. Vata, S. Kerr (Goalkeeper)

**ABERDEEN 5**

A. McLeish, L. Richardson, D. Shearer (3)

**CLYDEBANK 0**

**Aberdeen**: T. Snelders, S. Wright, R. Connor, P. Kane, A. McLeish, G. Smith, L. Richardson, J. Bett (J. Miller), S. Booth (E. Jess), D. Shearer, M-M. Paatelainen

Substitute not used: M. Watt (Goalkeeper)

**Clydebank**: S. Woods, M. Treanor, G. Hay, J. Maher, S. Sweeney, M. McIntosh (J. Crawford), P. Harvey, J. Henry, K. Eadie, C. Flannigan, A. Lansdowne (S. Jack)

Substitute not used: A. Monaghan (Goalkeeper)

**MEADOWBANK THISTLE 1**

I. Little

**DUNDEE 1 (A.E.T. –**
**1-1 after 90 minutes)**

G. Davidson (o.g.)

Dundee Won 3-1 on Kicks from the Penalty Mark

**Meadowbank Thistle**: J. McQueen, M. Murray, D. Fleming, G. Davidson, S. Williamson, I. Little, L. Bailey, S. Wilson (G. Price), P. Rutherford (R. Williamson), G. McLeod, M. Hutchison

Substitute not used: S. Ellison (Goalkeeper)

**Dundee**: P. Mathers, S. Frail (J. McQuillan), M. Christie, M. Weighorst, L. David (G. Paterson), J. McGowan, G. McMartin, D. Vrto, P. Ritchie, W. Dodds, P. Tosh

Substitute not used: B. Thompson (Goalkeeper)

*Wednesday, 11th August, 1993*

**ALBION ROVERS 1**

M. Scott

**PARTICK THISTLE 11**

R. Law, W. Jamieson, A. Craig (2), G. Britton, I. Cameron (4), I. English, R. Grant

Match Played at Fir Park, Motherwell

**Albion Rovers**: R. McConnachie, J. Kelly, T. Spence, E. Mirner, G. Taylor, D. McKeown, M. McBride (D. Seggie), S. Cadden, S. Kerrigan, M. Scott, A. Fraser (D. Riley)

**Partick Thistle**: C. Nelson, K. McKee, R. Law, W. Jamieson, G. Tierney (P. Kinnaird), M. Clark, D. Byrne, A. Craig, G. Britton (R. Grant), I. Cameron, I. English

Substitute not used: A. Murdoch (Goalkeeper)

**HEART OF MIDLOTHIAN 2**

J. Robertson (2)

**STRANRAER 0**

**Heart of Midlothian**: H. Smith, G. Locke, T. McKinlay, C. Levein, N. Berry, P. Van De Ven, J. Colquhoun (A. Johnston), G. Mackay, J. Fashanu, (K. Thomas), G. Wright, J. Robertson

Substitute not used: J. N. Walker (Goalkeeper)

**Stranraer**: B. Duffy, S. McIntyre, J. Hughes, G. Millar, I. Spittal, G. Duncan, T. Sloan, A. Grant, D. Diver (P. McLean), S. Cody (D. Walker), D. Henderson

Substitute not used: S. Ross (Goalkeeper)

**DUNFERMLINE ATHLETIC 2**

C. Robertson, H. French

**EAST STIRLINGSHIRE 0**
**(A.E.T.)**

**Dunfermline Athletic**: L. Hamilton, M. Bowes, E. Cunnington, N. McCathie, W. A. Baillie, W. Davies, I. Den Bieman (P. Smith), C. Robertson, H. French, G. O'Boyle (D. Laing), A. Preston

Substitute not used: J. Hillcoat (Goalkeeper)

**East Stirlingshire**: G. McDougall, G. Russell, B. Kemp, B. Ross, D. Yates, D. Craig, P. Roberts, C. McKinnon, M. Geraghty, S. Robertson, A. Speirs (J. Loney)

Substitutes not used: M. McInally, P. Imrie (Goalkeeper)

**CLYDE 1**

J. McAulay

**ST. JOHNSTONE 2**

P. Wright, A. Moore

**Clyde**: L. Fridge, R. McFarlane, S. Tennant, K. Knox, J. Thomson, A. Neill, P. Ronald (S. Morrison), J. McAulay, J. Sludden (D. McGill), S. Clarke, J. McCarron

**St. Johnstone**: A. Rhodes, J. Budden, P. Deas, G. McGinnis, J. Inglis, H. Curran, P. Ramsey, K. McGowne, P. Wright, G. Torfason, M. Buglione (A. Moore)

Substitutes not used: A. Cole, J. Donegan (Goalkeeper)

**RAITH ROVERS 1**

C. Cameron

**ARBROATH 2**

C. Martin, D. Elliot

**Raith Rovers**: T. Carson, J. McStay, I. MacLeod, R. Coyle, S. Dennis, G. McGeachie, J. Nicholl (D. Sinclair), G. Dalziel (J. Broddle), P. Hetherston, W. Hawke, C. Cameron

Substitute not used: G. Arthur (Goalkeeper)

**Arbroath**: D. Jackson, J. Hamilton, S. Florence, B. Mitchell, C. Adam, C. Martin, B. Will, T. King, D. Elliot (P. Hindson), C. Farnan, S. Sorbie

Substitutes not used: K. Tindal, M. Harkness (Goalkeeper)

**RANGERS 1**

I. Ferguson

**DUMBARTON 0**

**Rangers**: A. Maxwell, F. Wishart, C. Vinnicombe, R. Gough, S. Pressley, N. Murray, T. Steven, I. Ferguson, D. Hagen (P. Huistra), M. Hateley, I. Durrant

Substitutes not used: B. Reid, C. Scott (Goalkeeper)

**Dumbarton**: I. MacFarlane, J. Meechan, A. Foster, M. Melvin, S. Gow, M. MacLeod, M. McGarvey, R. McConville (J. Marsland), J. McQuade (M. McAnenay), C. Gibson, J. Boyd

Substitute not used: M. Monaghan (Goalkeeper)

# THIRD ROUND

*Tuesday, 24th August, 1993*

**ST. MIRREN 0**

**DUNDEE UNITED 1**

W. McKinlay

**St. Mirren**: C. Money, P. McIntyre, M. Baker, N. McWhirter, J. Fullarton, N. Orr, E. Gallagher, J. Dick (R. Gillies), B. Lavety, J. Hewitt (K. Gillies), D. Elliot

Substitute not used: D. Watson (Goalkeeper)

**Dundee United**: A. Main, J. Clark, G. Bollan, J. McInally, B. Welsh, D. Narey (F. Van Der Hoorn), D. Bowman, W. McKinlay, P. Connolly, C. Dailly, C. Myers (A. McLaren)

Substitute not used: G. Van De Kamp (Goalkeeper)

**ABERDEEN 5**

E. Jess, S. Booth (2), D. Shearer, J. Miller

**MOTHERWELL 2 (A.E.T. –**
**2-2 after 90 minutes)**

R. Shannon, D. Arnott

**Aberdeen**: T. Snelders, S. McKimmie, G. Smith, P. Kane, A. McLeish, B. Irvine, E. Jess, J. Bett (R. Connor), S. Booth, D. Shearer, T. Ten Caat (J. Miller)

Substitute not used: M. Watt (Goalkeeper)

**Motherwell**: S. Dykstra, R. Shannon, R. McKinnon, M. Krivokapic, B. Martin, C. McCart, J. Dolan, I. Angus, D. Arnott (P. McGrillen), P. O'Donnell, A. Burns (D. Cooper)

Substitute not used: W. Thomson (Goalkeeper)

| DUNFERMLINE ATHLETIC 0 | RANGERS 2 |
|---|---|
| | T. Steven, |
| | I. Ferguson |

**Dunfermline Athletic:** L. Hamilton, M. Bowes, C. Robertson, N. McCathie, W. A. Baillie, W. Davies, I. Den Bieman, P. Smith, H. French (E. Cunnington), G. O'Boyle (D. Laing), A. Preston

Substitute not used: J. Hillcoat (Goalkeeper)

**Rangers:** A. Maxwell, F. Wishart, D. Robertson, R. Gough, S. Pressley, I. Durrant, T. Steven, I. Ferguson, D. Ferguson, M. Hateley, A. Mikhailitchenko

Substitutes not used: N. Murray, J. Morrow, C. Scott (Goalkeeper)

| HIBERNIAN 2 | DUNDEE 1 |
|---|---|
| G. Hunter, K. Wright | H. Neilson |

**Hibernian:** J. Leighton, W. Miller, D. Beaumont, T. McIntyre, D. Farrell, G. Hunter, K. McAllister, W. Findlay, K. Wright, G. Evans, M. O'Neill (B. Hamilton)

Substitutes not used: G. Donald, C. Reid (Goalkeeper)

**Dundee:** P. Mathers, J. McQuillan, S. Pittman, M. Weighorst, G. Paterson, J. McGowan, D. Adamczuk, D. Vrto, P. Tosh (H. Neilson), W. Dodds, G. McKeown

Substitutes not used: S. Frail, B. Thompson (Goalkeeper)

| GREENOCK MORTON 0 | PARTICK THISTLE 1 |
|---|---|
| | A. Craig |

**Greenock Morton:** D. Wylie, D. Collins, M. Pickering (J. Gahagan), J. Fowler, M. Doak, S. McArthur, D. Lilley, M. Donaghy, R. Alexander, D. McInnes, J. Tolmie

Substitutes not used: S. Rafferty, P. Graham (Goalkeeper)

**Partick Thistle:** A. Murdoch, K. McKee, G. Watson (P. Kinnaird), A. Craig, W. Jamieson, D. Byrne, R. Grant, R. Farningham, G. Britton, I. Cameron, N. McKilligan

Substitutes not used: G. Shaw, C. Nelson (Goalkeeper)

## Wednesday, 25th August, 1993

| HEART OF MIDLOTHIAN 0 | FALKIRK 1 |
|---|---|
| | E. May |

**Heart of Midlothian:** H. Smith, G. Locke, T. McKinlay, C. Levein, G. Hogg, A. Mauchlen (A. Johnston), J. Colquhoun, G. Mackay, J. Fashanu (K. Thomas), G. Wright, J. Robertson

Substitute not used: J.N. Walker (Goalkeeper)

**Falkirk:** A. Parks, F. Johnston, T. McQueen, N. Oliver, D. Weir, C. Duffy, E. May, S. MacKenzie, R. Cadette, I. McCall, G. Shaw

Substitutes not used: C. McDonald, C. Taggart, I. Westwater (Goalkeeper)

| ST. JOHNSTONE 0 | AIRDRIEONIANS 2 |
|---|---|
| | E. Balfour, A. Lawrence |

**St. Johnstone:** A. Rhodes, J. Davies, P. Deas, T. Turner, J. Inglis, G. McGinnis (A. Cole), A. Moore (P. Scott), P. Ramsey, P. Wright, H. Curran, K. McGowne

Substitute not used: J. Donegan (Goalkeeper)

**Airdrieonians:** J. Martin, A. Stewart, C. Honor, J. Sandison, G. Caesar, K. Black, D. Kirkwood, E. Balfour, P. Davenport, Andrew Smith (W. Reid), A. Lawrence (J. Boyle)

Substitute not used: W. McCulloch (Goalkeeper)

| ARBROATH 1 | CELTIC 9 |
|---|---|
| K. Tindal | M. McNally, P. McGinlay, |
| | F. McAvennie (3), |
| | C. Nicholas, A. Payton (3) |

**Arbroath:** D. Jackson, J. Hamilton, S. Florence, B. Mitchell, C. Adam, C. Farnan, B. Will (K. Tindal), T. King, D. Elliot (P. Hindson), C. Martin, S. Sorbie

Substitute not used: M. Harkness (Goalkeeper)

**Celtic:** P. Bonner, T. Boyd, D. Wdowczyk, P. Grant, M. McNally, M. Galloway, P. McGinlay, P. McStay (B. O'Neil), F. McAvennie, C. Nicholas (A. Payton), J. Collins

Substitute not used: G. Marshall (Goalkeeper)

# FOURTH ROUND

## Tuesday, 31st August, 1993

| DUNDEE UNITED 3 | FALKIRK 3 (A.E.T. – 2-2 after 90 minutes) |
|---|---|
| J. Clark (2), A. McLaren | R. Cadette (3) |

**Dundee United Won 4-2 on Kicks from the Penalty Mark**

**Dundee United:** A. Main, J. Clark, G. Bollan, J. McInally, B. Welsh, F. Van Der Hoorn, D. Bowman (S. Crabbe), W. McKinlay, A. McLaren, C. Dailly, C. Myers (J. O'Neil)

Substitute not used: G. Van De Kamp (Goalkeeper)

**Falkirk:** A. Parks, F. Johnston, T. McQueen, N. Oliver, D. Weir, C. Duffy, E. May, S. MacKenzie, R. Cadette, I. McCall, G. Shaw

Substitutes not used: C. McDonald, C. Taggart, I. Westwater (Goalkeeper)

| PARTICK THISTLE 2 | HIBERNIAN 2 (A.E.T. – 1-1 after 90 minutes) |
|---|---|
| R. Grant, A. Craig | K. McAllister (2) |

**Hibernian Won 3-2 on Kicks from the Penalty Mark**

**Partick Thistle:** C. Nelson, K. McKee (P. Kinnaird), M. Clark, W. Jamieson, G. Tierney, A. Taylor, D. Byrne, A. Craig, R. Grant, I. English (G. Britton), I. Cameron

Substitute not used: A. Murdoch (Goalkeeper)

**Hibernian:** J. Leighton, W. Miller, S. Tweed (B. Hamilton), T. McIntyre, D. Farrell, G. Hunter, K. McAllister, W. Findlay, K. Wright, G. Evans (D. Jackson), M. O'Neill

Substitute not used: C. Reid (Goalkeeper)

| CELTIC 1 | AIRDRIEONIANS 0 |
|---|---|
| F. McAvennie | |

**Celtic:** P. Bonner, T. Boyd, D. Wdowczyk, P. Grant, M. McNally, M. Galloway, P. McGinlay, P. McStay, F. McAvennie (A. Payton), C. Nicholas, J. Collins

Substitutes not used: B. O'Neil, G. Marshall (Goalkeeper)

**Airdrieonians:** J. Martin, C. Honor, D. McVicar (J. Boyle), J. Sandison, G. Caesar, K. Black, D. Kirkwood, E. Balfour, P. Davenport, Andrew Smith, P. Jack (M. Abercromby)

Substitute not used: W. McCulloch (Goalkeeper)

## Wednesday, 1st September, 1993

| RANGERS 2 | ABERDEEN 1 (A.E.T. – 1-1 after 90 minutes) |
|---|---|
| M. Hateley, I. Ferguson | J. Miller |

**Rangers:** A. Maxwell, G. Stevens, D. Robertson, R. Gough, S. Pressley, N. Murray (D. Ferguson), T. Steven, I. Ferguson, I. Durrant, M. Hateley, P. Huistra (F. Wishart)

Substitute not used: C. Scott (Goalkeeper)

**Aberdeen:** T. Snelders, S. McKimmie, G. Smith (J. Miller), P. Kane, A. McLeish, B. Irvine, L. Richardson, J. Bett, S. Booth (D. Shearer), E. Jess, M-M. Paatelainen

Substitute not used: M. Watt (Goalkeeper)

# SEMI-FINALS

**TYNECASTLE PARK, EDINBURGH**

*Tuesday, 21st September, 1993*

**DUNDEE UNITED 0**  **HIBERNIAN 1**
D. Jackson

**Dundee United**: A. Main, F. Van Der Hoorn, G. Bollan (A. Cleland), M. Perry, B. Welsh, D. Narey, D. Bowman, W. McKinlay, A. McLaren, C. Dailly, I. G. Johnson (J. Clark)

Substitute not used: G. Van De Kamp (Goalkeeper)

**Hibernian**: J. Leighton, W. Miller, G. Mitchell, D. Farrell, S. Tweed, G. Hunter, K. McAllister, W. Findlay (B. Hamilton), K. Wright, D. Jackson (G. Evans), M. O'Neill

Substitute not used: C. Reid (Goalkeeper)

**IBROX STADIUM, GLASGOW**

*Wednesday, 22nd September, 1993*

**CELTIC 0**  **RANGERS 1**
M. Hateley

**Celtic**: P. Bonner, T. Boyd, D. Wdowczyk, P. Grant, M. McNally, M. Galloway, P. McGinlay, P. McStay, F. McAvennie (B. O'Neil), G. Creaney, S. Slater

Substitutes not used: A. Mowbray, G. Marshall (Goalkeeper)

**Rangers**: A. Maxwell, G. Stevens, D. Robertson, R. Gough, D. McPherson, S. McCall, T. Steven, I. Ferguson, I. Durrant (F. Wishart), M. Hateley, P. Huistra

Substitutes not used: J. Morrow, C. Scott (Goalkeeper)

*Ally McCoist celebrates his eighth League Cup Winners Medal.*

---

## LEAGUE CUP - SEASON 1993/94

### ROUND BY ROUND GOALS ANALYSIS

|  | No. of Goals Scored | Ties Played | Average per Game |
|---|---|---|---|
| FIRST ROUND | 13 | 6 | 2.2 |
| SECOND ROUND | 51 | 16 | 3.2 |
| THIRD ROUND | 27 | 8 | 3.4 |
| FOURTH ROUND | 14 | 4 | 3.5 |
| SEMI-FINALS | 2 | 2 | 1.0 |
| FINAL | 3 | 1 | 3 |

| | |
|---|---|
| Total No. of Goals Scored | 110 |
| Ties Played | 37 |
| Average Goals per Game | 3 |

---

# FINAL

*Sunday, 24th October, 1993*

## CELTIC PARK, GLASGOW

### Hibernian 1  Rangers 2
D. McPherson (o.g.)  I. Durrant, A. McCoist

**Hibernian**: J. Leighton, W. Miller, G. Mitchell, D. Farrell, S. Tweed, G. Hunter, K. McAllister, B. Hamilton, K. Wright, D. Jackson (G. Evans) M. O'Neill

Substitutes not used: D. Beaumont, C. Reid (Goalkeeper)

**Rangers**: A. Maxwell, G. Stevens, D. Robertson, R. Gough, D. McPherson, S. McCall, T. Steven, I. Ferguson, I. Durrant, M. Hateley, P. Huistra (A. McCoist)

Substitutes not used: A. Mikhailitchenko, C. Scott (Goalkeeper)

**Referee:** J. McCluskey (Stewarton)

**Attendance:** 47,632

*Ian Durrant and Willie Miller tussle for the ball.*

## SEASON 1946/47

*5th April, 1947 at Hampden Park;
Attendance 82,584;
Referee: Mr R. Calder (Rutherglen)*

**RANGERS 4**          **ABERDEEN 0**
Gillick, Williamson, Duncanson (2)

## SEASON 1947/48

*25th October, 1947 at Hampden Park;
Attendance 52,781; Referee: Mr P. Craigmyle (Aberdeen)*

**EAST FIFE 0**          **FALKIRK 0**
After Extra Time

**REPLAY**

*lst November, 1947 at Hampden Park;
Attendance 30,664; Referee: Mr P. Craigmyle (Aberdeen)*

**EAST FIFE 4**          **FALKIRK 1**
Duncan (3), Adams          Aikman

## SEASON 1948/49

*12th March, 1949 at Hampden Park; Attendance 53,359;
Referee: Mr W.G. Livingstone (Glasgow)*

**RANGERS 2**          **RAITH ROVERS 0**
Gillick, Paton

## SEASON 1949/50

*29th October, 1949 at Hampden Park;
Attendance 38,897; Referee: Mr W. Webb (Glasgow)*

**EAST FIFE 3**          **DUNFERMLINE ATHLETIC 0**
Fleming, Duncan, Morris

## SEASON 1950/5l

*28th October, 1950 at Hampden Park;
Attendance 63,074; Referee: Mr J. A. Mowat (Glasgow)*

**MOTHERWELL 3**          **HIBERNIAN 0**
Kelly, Forrest, Watters

## SEASON 195l/52

*27th October, 195l at Hampden Park; Attendance 91,075;
Referee: Mr J. A. Mowat (Glasgow)*

**DUNDEE 3**          **RANGERS 2**
Flavell, Pattillo, Boyd          Findlay, Thornton

## SEASON 1952/53

*25th October, 1952 at Hampden Park;
Attendance 51,830; Referee: Mr J. A. Mowat (Glasgow)*

**DUNDEE 2**          **KILMARNOCK 0**
Flavell (2)

## SEASON 1953/54

*24th October, 1953 at Hampden Park;
Attendance 88,529; Referee: Mr J. S. Cox (Rutherglen)*

**EAST FIFE 3**          **PARTICK THISTLE 2**
Gardiner, Fleming, Christie          Walker, McKenzie

## SEASON 1954/55

*23rd October, 1954 at Hampden Park;
Attendance 55,640; Referee: Mr J. A. Mowat (Glasgow)*

**HEART OF MIDLOTHIAN 4**          **MOTHERWELL 2**
Bauld (3), Wardhaugh          Redpath (Pen), Bain

## SEASON 1955/56

*22nd October, 1955 at Hampden Park;
Attendance 44,103; Referee: Mr H. Phillips (Wishaw)*

**ABERDEEN 2**          **ST. MIRREN 1**
Mallan (og), Leggat          Holmes

## SEASON 1956/57

*27th October, 1956 at Hampden Park;
Attendance 58,973; Referee: Mr J. A. Mowat (Glasgow)*

**CELTIC 0**          **PARTICK THISTLE 0**

**RFPLAY**

*31st October, 1956 at Hampden Park;
Attendance 31,126; Referee: Mr J. A. Mowat (Glasgow)*

**CELTIC 3**          **PARTICK THISTLE 0**
McPhail (2), Collins

## SEASON 1957/58

*19th October, 1957 at Hampden Park;
Attendance 82,293; Referee: Mr J. A. Mowat (Glasgow)*

**CELTIC 7**          **RANGERS 1**
Mochan (2), McPhail (3),          Simpson
Wilson, Fernie (pen)

## SEASON 1958/59

*25th October, 1958 at Hampden Park;
Attendance 59,960; Referee: Mr R. H. Davidson (Airdrie)*

**HEART OF MIDLOTHIAN 5**          **PARTICK THISTLE 1**
Murray (2), Bauld (2), Hamilton          Smith

## SEASON 1959/60

*24th October, 1959 at Hampden Park;
Attendance 57,974;
Referee Mr R. H. Davidson (Airdrie)*

**HEART OF MIDLOTHIAN 2**          **THIRD LANARK 1**
Hamilton, Young          Gray

## SEASON 1960/61

*29th October, 1960 at Hampden Park;
Attendance 82,063; Referee: Mr T. Wharton (Glasgow)*

**RANGERS 2**          **KILMARNOCK 0**
Brand, Scott

## SEASON 1961/62

*28th October, 1961 at Hampden Park; Attendance 88,635;
Referee: Mr R. H. Davidson (Airdrie)*

**RANGERS 1**          **HEART OF MIDLOTHIAN 1**
Millar          Cumming (pen)

**REPLAY**

*18th December, 1961 at Hampden Park;
Attendance 47,552; Referee: Mr R. H. Davidson (Airdrie)*

**RANGERS 3**          **HEART OF MIDLOTHIAN 1**
Millar, Brand, McMillan          Davidson

## SEASON 1962/63

*27th October, 1962 at Hampden Park;
Attendance 51,280; Referee: Mr T. Wharton (Glasgow)*

**HEART OF MIDLOTHIAN 1**          **KILMARNOCK 0**
Davidson

## SEASON 1963/64

*26th October, 1963 at Hampden Park; Attendance 105,907; Referee: Mr H. Phillips (Wishaw)*

| RANGERS 5 | MORTON 0 |
|---|---|
| Forrest (4), Willoughby | |

## SEASON 1964/65

*24th October, 1964 at Hampden Park; Attendance 91,000; Referee: Mr H. Phillips (Wishaw)*

| RANGERS 2 | CELTIC 1 |
|---|---|
| Forrest (2) | Johnstone |

## SEASON 1965/66

*23rd October, 1965 at Hampden Park; Attendance 107,609; Referee: Mr H. Phillips (Wishaw)*

| CELTIC 2 | RANGERS 1 |
|---|---|
| Hughes (2 (2 pen)) | Young (o.g.) |

## SEASON 1966/67

*29th October, 1966 at Hampden Park; Attendance 94,532; Referee: Mr T. Wharton (Glasgow)*

| CELTIC 1 | RANGERS 0 |
|---|---|
| Lennox | |

## SEASON 1967/68

*28th October, 1967 at Hampden Park; Attendance 66,660; Referee: Mr R. H. Davidson (Airdrie)*

| CELTIC 5 | DUNDEE 3 |
|---|---|
| Chalmers (2), Hughes, Wallace, Lennox | G. McLean (2), J. McLean |

## SEASON 1968/69

*5th April, 1969 at Hampden Park; Attendance 74,000; Referee: Mr W. M. M. Syme (Airdrie)*

| CELTIC 6 | HIBERNIAN 2 |
|---|---|
| Lennox (3), Wallace, Auld, Craig | O'Rourke, Stevenson |

## SEASON 1969/70

*25th October, 1969 at Hampden Park; Attendance 73,067; Referee: Mr J. W. Paterson (Bothwell)*

| CELTIC 1 | ST. JOHNSTONE 0 |
|---|---|
| Auld | |

## SEASON 1970/71

*24th October, 1970 at Hampden Park; Attendance 106,263; Referee: Mr T. Wharton (Glasgow)*

| RANGERS 1 | CELTIC 0 |
|---|---|
| Johnstone | |

## SEASON 1971/72

*23rd October, 1971 at Hampden Park; Attendance 62,740; Referee: Mr W. J. Mullan (Dalkeith)*

| PARTICK THISTLE 4 | CELTIC 1 |
|---|---|
| Rae, Lawrie, McQuade, Bone | Dalglish |

## SEASON 1972/73

*9th December, 1972 at Hampden Park; Attendance 71,696; Referee: Mr A. MacKenzie (Larbert)*

| HIBERNIAN 2 | CELTIC 1 |
|---|---|
| Stanton, O'Rourke | Dalglish |

## SEASON 1973/74

*15th December, 1973 at Hampden Park; Attendance 27,974; Referee: Mr R. H. Davidson (Airdrie)*

| DUNDEE 1 | CELTIC 0 |
|---|---|
| Wallace | |

## SEASON 1974/75

*26th October, 1974 at Hampden Park; Attendance 53,848; Referee: Mr J. R. P. Gordon (Newport on Tay)*

| CELTIC 6 | HIBERNIAN 3 |
|---|---|
| Johnstone, Deans (3), Wilson, Murray | Harper (3) |

## SEASON 1975/76

*25th October, 1975 at Hampden Park; Attendance 58,806; Referee: Mr W. Anderson (East Kilbride)*

| RANGERS 1 | CELTIC 0 |
|---|---|
| MacDonald | |

## SEASON 1976/77

*6th November, 1976 at Hampden Park; Attendance 69,268; Referee: Mr J.W. Paterson (Bothwell)*

| ABERDEEN 2 | CELTIC 1 |
|---|---|
| Jarvie, Robb | Dalglish (pen.) |
| After extra-time | |

## SEASON 1977/78

*18th March, 1978 at Hampden Park; Attendance 60,168; Referee: Mr D. F. T. Syme (Rutherglen)*

| RANGERS 2 | CELTIC 1 |
|---|---|
| Cooper, Smith | Edvaldsson |
| After extra-time | |

## SEASON 1978/79

*31st March, 1979 at Hampden Park; Attendance 54,000; Referee: Mr I. M. D. Foote (Glasgow)*

| RANGERS 2 | ABERDEEN 1 |
|---|---|
| McMaster (o.g), Jackson | Davidson |

## SEASON 1979/80 – BELL'S LEAGUE CUP

*8th December, 1979 at Hampden Park; Attendance 27,299; Referee: Mr B. R. McGinlay (Balfron)*

| DUNDEE UNITED 0 | ABERDEEN 0 |
|---|---|
| After extra time | |

### REPLAY

*12th December, 1979 at Dens Park; Attendance 28,984; Referee: Mr B.R. McGinlay (Balfron)*

| DUNDEE UNITED 3 | ABERDEEN 0 |
|---|---|
| Pettigrew (2), Sturrock | |

## SEASON 1980/81 –
## BELL'S LEAGUE CUP

*6th December, 1980 at Dens Park;*
*Attendance 24,466; Referee: Mr R. B. Valentine (Dundee)*

**DUNDEE UNITED 3**          **DUNDEE 0**
Dodds, Sturrock (2)

## SEASON 1981/82

*28th November, 1981 at Hampden Park;*
*Attendance 53,795; Referee: Mr E. H. Pringle (Edinburgh)*

**RANGERS 2**          **DUNDEE UNITED 1**
Cooper, Redford          Milne

## SEASON 1982/83

*4th December, 1982 at Hampden Park;*
*Attendance 55,372; Referee: Mr K. J. Hope (Clarkston)*

**CELTIC 2**          **RANGERS 1**
Nicholas, MacLeod          Bett

## SEASON 1983/84

*25th March, 1984 at Hampden Park;*
*Attendance 66,369; Referee: Mr R. B. Valentine (Dundee)*

**RANGERS 3**          **CELTIC 2**
McCoist 3 (2 pen)          McClair, Reid (pen)

## SEASON 1984/85 – SKOL CUP

*28th October, 1984 at Hampden Park;*
*Attendance 44,698; Referee: Mr B. R. McGinlay (Balfron)*

**RANGERS 1**          **DUNDEE UNITED 0**
Ferguson

## SEASON 1985/86 – SKOL CUP

*27th October, 1985 at Hampden Park;*
*Attendance 40,065; Referee: Mr R. B. Valentine (Dundee)*

**ABERDEEN 3**          **HIBERNIAN 0**
Black (2), Stark

## SEASON 1986/87 – SKOL CUP

*26th October, 1986 at Hampden Park;*
*Attendance 74,219; Referee: Mr D. F. T. Syme (Rutherglen)*

**RANGERS 2**          **CELTIC 1**
Durrant, Cooper (pen)          McClair

## SEASON 1987/88 – SKOL CUP

*25th October, 1987 at Hampden Park;*
*Attendance 71,961; Referee: Mr R. B. Valentine (Dundee)*

**RANGERS 3**          **ABERDEEN 3**
Cooper, Durrant, Fleck          Bett, Falconer, Hewitt
After extra-time
Rangers won 5-3 on Kicks from the Penalty Mark

## SEASON 1988/89 – SKOL CUP

*23rd October, 1988 at Hampden Park;*
*Attendance 72,122; Referee: Mr G. B. Smith (Edinburgh)*

**RANGERS 3**          **ABERDEEN 2**
McCoist (2), I. Ferguson          Dodds (2)

## SEASON 1989/90 – SKOL CUP

*22nd October, 1989 at Hampden Park; Attendance 61,190;*
*Referee: Mr G. B. Smith (Edinburgh)*

**ABERDEEN 2**          **RANGERS 1**
Mason (2)          Walters (pen)
After extra time – 1-1 after 90 minutes

## SEASON 1990/91 – SKOL CUP

*28th October, 1990 at Hampden Park;*
*Attendance 62,817; Referee: Mr J. McCluskey (Stewarton)*

**RANGERS 2**          **CELTIC 1**
Walters, Gough          Elliott

## SEASON 1991/92 – SKOL CUP

*27th October, 1991 at Hampden Park;*
*Attendance 40,377 Referee: B. R. McGinlay (Balfron)*

**HIBERNIAN 2**          **DUNFERMLINE ATHLETIC 0**
McIntyre (pen), Wright

## SEASON 1992/93 – SKOL CUP

*25th October, 1992 at Hampden Park;*
*Attendance 45,298; Referee: D. D. Hope (Erskine)*

**RANGERS 2**          **ABERDEEN 1**
McCall, Smith (o.g)          Shearer
After extra-time – 1-1 after 90 minutes

## SEASON 1993/94

*24th October, 1993 at Celtic Park;*
*Attendance 47,632; Referee: J. McCluskey (Stewarton)*

**RANGERS 2**          **HIBERNIAN 1**
Durrant, McCoist          McPherson

---

## WINNERS AT A GLANCE

| | |
|---|---|
| RANGERS | 19 |
| CELTIC | 9 |
| ABERDEEN | 4 |
| HEART OF MIDLOTHIAN | 4 |
| DUNDEE | 3 |
| EAST FIFE | 3 |
| DUNDEE UNITED | 2 |
| HIBERNIAN | 2 |
| MOTHERWELL | 1 |
| PARTICK THISTLE | 1 |

## APPEARANCES IN FINALS
### (Figures Do Not Include Replays)

| | | | |
|---|---|---|---|
| RANGERS | 25 | KILMARNOCK | 3 |
| CELTIC | 20 | DUNFERMLINE ATHLETIC | 2 |
| ABERDEEN | 10 | MOTHERWELL | 2 |
| HIBERNIAN | 7 | FALKIRK | 1 |
| DUNDEE | 5 | GREENOCK MORTON | 1 |
| HEART OF MIDLOTHIAN | 5 | RAITH ROVERS | 1 |
| DUNDEE UNITED | 4 | ST. JOHNSTONE | 1 |
| PARTICK THISTLE | 4 | ST. MIRREN | 1 |
| EAST FIFE | 3 | THIRD LANARK | 1 |

## Scottish Professional Footballers' Association

**1977/78**
Premier Division — Derek Johnstone *(Rangers)*
First Division — Billy Pirie *(Dundee)*
Second Division — Dave Smith *(Berwick Rangers)*
Young Player of the Year — Graeme Payne *(Dundee United)*

**1978/79**
Premier Division — Paul Hegarty *(Dundee United)*
First Division — Brian McLaughlin *(Ayr United)*
Second Division — Michael Leonard *(Dunfermline Athletic)*
Young Player of the Year — Raymond Stewart *(Dundee United)*

**1979/80**
Premier Division — Davie Provan *(Celtic)*
First Division — Sandy Clark *(Airdrieonians)*
Second Division — Paul Leetion *(Falkirk)*
Young Player of the Year — John MacDonald *(Rangers)*

**1980/81**
Premier Division — Mark McGhee *(Aberdeen)*
First Division — Eric Sinclair *(Dundee)*
Second Division — Jimmy Robertson *(Queen of the South)*
Young Player of the Year — Charlie Nicholas *(Celtic)*

**1981/82**
Premier Division — Sandy Clark *(Airdrieonians)*
First Division — Brian McLaughlin *(Motherwell)*
Second Division — Pat Nevin *(Clyde)*
Young Player of the Year — Frank McAvennie *(St Mirren)*

**1982/83**
Premier Division — Charlie Nicholas *(Celtic)*
First Division — Gerry McCabe *(Clydebank)*
Second Division — John Colquhoun *(Stirling Albion)*
Young Player of the Year — Paul McStay *(Celtic)*

**1983/84**
Premier Division — Willie Miller *(Aberdeen)*
First Division — Gerry McCabe *(Clydebank)*
Second Division — Jim Liddle *(Forfar Athletic)*
Young Player of the Year — John Robertson *(Heart of Midlothian)*

**1984/85**
Premier Division — Jim Duffy *(Morton)*
First Division — Gerry McCabe *(Clydebank)*
Second Division — Bernie Slaven *(Albion Rovers)*
Young Player of the Year — Craig Levein *(Heart of Midlothian)*

**1985/86**
Premier Division — Richard Gough *(Dundee United)*
First Division — John Brogan *(Hamilton Academical)*
Second Division — Mark Smith *(Queen's Park)*
Young Player of the Year — Craig Levein *(Heart of Midlothian)*

**1986/87**
Premier Division — Brian McClair *(Celtic)*
First Division — Jim Holmes *(Morton)*
Second Division — John Sludden *(Ayr United)*
Young Player of the Year — Robert Fleck *(Rangers)*

**1987/88**
Premier Division — Paul McStay *(Celtic)*
First Division — Alex Taylor *(Hamilton Academical)*
Second Division — Henry Templeton *(Ayr United)*
Young Player of the Year — John Collins *(Hibernian)*

**1988/89**
Premier Division — Theo Snelders *(Aberdeen)*
First Division — Ross Jack *(Dunfermline Athletic)*
Second Division — Paul Hunter *(East Fife)*
Young Player of the Year — Billy McKinlay *(Dundee United)*

**1989/90**
Premier Division — Jim Bett *(Aberdeen)*
First Division — Ken Eadie *(Clydebank)*
Second Division — Willie Watters *(Kilmarnock)*
Young Player of the Year — Scott Crabbe *(Heart of Midlothian)*

**1990/91**
Premier Division — Paul Elliott *(Celtic)*
First Division — Simon Stainrod *(Falkirk)*
Second Division — Kevin Todd *(Berwick Rangers)*
Young Player of the Year — Eoin Jess *(Aberdeen)*

**1991/92**
Premier Division — Alistair McCoist *(Rangers)*
First Division — Gordon Dalziel *(Raith Rovers)*
Second Division — Andrew Thomson *(Queen of the South)*
Young Player of the Year — Philip O'Donnell *(Motherwell)*

**1992/93**
Premier Division — Andy Goram *(Rangers)*
First Division — Gordon Dalziel *(Raith Rovers)*
Second Division — Alexander Ross *(Brechin City)*
Young Player of the Year — Eoin Jess *(Aberdeen)*

**1993/94**
Premier Division — Mark Hateley *(Rangers)*
First Division — Richard Cadette *(Falkirk)*
Second Division — Andy Thomson *(Queen of the South)*
Young Player of the Year — Phil O'Donnell *(Motherwell)*

## The Scottish Football Writers' Association

1965 — Billy McNeill *(Celtic)*
1966 — John Greig *(Rangers)*
1967 — Ronnie Simpson *(Celtic)*
1968 — Gordon Wallace *(Raith Rovers)*
1969 — Bobby Murdoch *(Celtic)*
1970 — Pat Stanton *(Hibernian)*
1971 — Martin Buchan *(Aberdeen)*
1972 — Dave Smith *(Rangers)*
1973 — George Connelly *(Celtic)*
1974 — World Cup Squad
1975 — Sandy Jardine *(Rangers)*
1976 — John Greig *(Rangers)*
1977 — Danny McGrain *(Celtic)*
1978 — Derek Johnstone *(Rangers)*
1979 — Andy Ritchie *(Morton)*
1980 — Gordon Strachan *(Aberdeen)*
1981 — Alan Rough *(Partick Thistle)*
1982 — Paul Sturrock *(Dundee United)*
1983 — Charlie Nicholas *(Celtic)*
1984 — Willie Miller *(Aberdeen)*
1985 — Hamish McAlpine *(Dundee United)*
1986 — Sandy Jardine *(Heart of Midlothian)*
1987 — Brian McClair *(Celtic)*
1988 — Paul McStay *(Celtic)*
1989 — Richard Gough *(Rangers)*
1990 — Alex McLeish *(Aberdeen)*
1991 — Maurice Malpas *(Dundee United)*
1992 — Alistair McCoist *(Rangers)*
1993 — Andy Goram *(Rangers)*
1994 — Mark Hateley *(Rangers)*

# Seventh time lucky!

*The last goal in the 1994 Tennents Scottish Cup may not have been the most spectacular in the competition, but it was certainly the most vital. For when bargain buy, Craig Brewster, pounced in the 47th minute at Hampden to push the ball into the gaping net, he at one and the same time destroyed a dream . . . and ended a nightmare.*

The Dundee United striker couldn't believe his luck as a low, lingering shot from team-mate, Christian Dailly, came bouncing back along the line after hitting the Rangers post. Rangers could not believe it either, particularly since the chance had come via a blootered clearance by goalkeeper, Ally Maxwell.

The keeper had been put under pressure by a slack pass back from colleague, Davie McPherson, and succeeded only in swiping the ball against young Dailly who then set up the chance for that man Brewster and the only goal of the game. Bizarre it may have been, but it was greeted with jubilation on

Tayside and United succeeded in winning the trophy after six previous Final failures.

"The best I have ever scored," joked Brewster. "Since it was the only one in the Final, it had to be."

Rangers had started as favourites, with their fans ready to celebrate unique back-to-back treble triumphs. But there is no doubt that Ivan Golac and his men were rightful winners before a 37,709 crowd.

Both Finalists had to go to replays to make it through. Indeed, United were just two minutes away from the exit door in the Semi-Final against Aberdeen. They were trailing all the

way to an early Duncan Shearer goal before big defender, Brian Welsh – one of the star players of the season in Scotland – rose to head a brilliant equaliser. That was on the Saturday.

A day later Rangers and Kilmarnock fought out a 0-0 draw and so it was back to Hampden in midweek for both lots . . . with Jim McInally edging United through on Tuesday, April 12th and two-goal Mark Hateley doing the business once again for Rangers 24 hours later.

That was the finale to the Cup. The curtain raiser came many months earlier . . . back in September, 1993 in fact when the minnows in the north and the south of the country set out to do battle in the Qualifying Cup, with eventually Ross County and Huntly from the north and Whitehill Welfare and St. Cuthbert's Wanderers in the south making it through to join the big boys, which is when sponsors Tennents come in to add the frothy bits to the competition.

The Ross County brigade came in with a Highland charge that fairly wandered St. Cuthbert's . . . 11-0 in fact, with Brian Grant scoring five of the goals. That performance was

*Ivan Golac, Dundee United Manager with the Scottish Cup.*

nearly matched by Tommy Sloan of Stranraer, who scored all four goals in his team's 4-0 replay win over Whitehill Welfare.

The bleak midwinter meant no fewer than ten postponements for the replay between Huntly and Albion Rovers, with the north side having their patience rewarded . . . eventually . . . with a 5-3 win.

Ross County defeated Forfar Athletic 4-0 to become the only non-League club in the Third Round of the competition. They went out 2-0 to Alloa in the Third Round – which meant they missed out on every wee club's dream draw . . . a trip to Ibrox.

But Ross County were not the only club to take a Third Round dive. Celtic crashed out to a Tommy Coyne goal against Motherwell, Falkirk went down 2-1 to Stranraer with the prolific Tommy Sloan scoring again. Alloa's reward for the Fourth Round was a 6-0 walloping from Rangers at Ibrox, with a certain A. McCoist netting a hat-trick, which delighted one punter who picked up £8,000 after investing a grand on Ally to do the trick on his comeback game after a broken leg. Alloa's pain was eased by their £100,000 share in a 37,804 gate at Ibrox.

Hearts eased through with a 2-1 win over Hibs at Easter Road, Wayne Foster nabbing the winner four minutes from the end. Big Brian Welsh was the Dundee United hero again, scoring the decisive goal in the 1-0 replay victory over Motherwell at Fir Park . . . the second game becoming necessary after big John Philliben had scored in injury time in the first match at Tannadice. Incidentally, there were two magnificent Craig Brewster goals in that first game which ended 2-2. However, that still didn't stop the volatile United boss Ivan Golac from lambasting his men as "amateurs".

Ex-Celt, Joe Miller, paid off a chunk of his transfer fee by nipping home the only goal of the game against Raith Rovers, at Pittodrie, nine minutes from time to put the Dons into the Quarter Final Draw.

Happy trio . . . Craig Brewster Ivan Golac Gordan Petric with trophy.

Craig Brewster shoots for goal.

In the Quarter Finals, Dundee United again needed two games to see off more Lanarkshire opposition . . . this time Airdrie, with Craig Brewster this time ordered off for two bookable offences in the first match at Broomfield, thereby denying the Tannadice club his goalscoring talents in the replay. However, goals by Andy McLaren and Billy McKinlay ensured United's place in the Semi-Finals.

At Ibrox, goals from John Brown and Mark Hateley took Rangers through against Hearts while another member of the Brown clan, Tom to be precise, got Kilmarnock through with the only goal against Dundee . . . collecting a black eye in the process as he collided with goalkeeper Paul Mathers.

Aberdeen overcame a very resilient St. Johnstone side, again in a replay, with goals from Duncan Shearer and

Lee Richardson setting up two intriguing Semis, Kilmarnock being paired with Rangers and Dundee United meeting Aberdeen, with both ties, as previously mentioned, being played at the refurbished National Stadium.

Finally, it came down to United and Rangers and nine months after it all started, the Cup was won and on its way to a new home on Tayside, for the first time. Maybe not the last, however, if the ebullient Yugoslav, Golac, has his way.

**Dixon Blackstock
(Sunday Mail)**

Dundee United fans celebrate the winning goal.

# FIRST ROUND

### 11th December, 1993

**ALBION ROVERS 0**  **HUNTLY 0**

**Albion Rovers:** Burns, Taylor (Gallagher), Beattie, Conn, McCaffrey, McKeown, Collins, Seggie, Kerrigan, Cadden, Scott (Fraser)

**Huntly:** Gardiner, McGinlay, Murphy, Walker, Rougvie, DeBarros, Stewart, Copland, Thomson, Whyte (Lennox), Selbie

Substitute not used: Dunsire

**STRANRAER 3**  **WHITEHILL WELFARE 3**
Sloan (2), Henderson  Thorburn (2 pens), Steel

**Stranraer:** Duffy, Millar, McIntyre, Spittal (Ferguson), Brannigan, Gallagher, Sloan, Grant, Duncan, Cody (Hughes), Henderson

**Whitehill Welfare:** Ramage, Smith D., Millar, Brown, Steel, Cuthbert, Thorburn, Samuel, Sneddon (Bird), McCulloch, Tulloch

Substitute not used: Richford

**COWDENBEATH 1**  **QUEEN'S PARK 1**
Callaghan  O'Neill

**Cowdenbeath:** Maloney, Watt, Davidson, Herd, McMahon B., Petrie, Lee, Scott, Callaghan, Reilly (Barclay), Henderson

Substitute not used: Maratea

**Queen's Park:** Chalmers, Sneddon, Maxwell, Elder, Fitzpatrick, Orr G., Stevenson (Kerr), Caven, McPhee, O'Neill, McCormick (Rodden)

**EAST FIFE 5**  **ROTHES 0**
Scott (3), Hope, Hildersley

**East Fife:** Charles, Sneddon, Williamson, Burns, Beaton, Beedie, Allan, Andrew, Scott, Hope (Hildersley), McBride (Irvine)

**Rothes:** Wallace, Madden, Winton, Esson, Henderson, Smith (Pilichos), Drews, Tulloch, Simpson, Thomson (Thain), Duncan

**ROSS COUNTY 11**  **ST. CUTHBERTS WANDERERS 0**
Grant (5), Williamson,
Duff (3), Ferries (2)

**Ross County:** Hutchison, Somerville, Reid, Williamson, Bellshaw, Alec MacLeod, Ferries, Grant, Duff (Drummond), Robertson (Ross), Wilson

**St. Cuthberts Wanderers:** McHendry, Kyle, Groves (Christie), McMillan, Morrison (McCreadie), Murray, Niven, Baker, Tweedie, Simpson, Adair

**FORFAR ATHLETIC 8**  **QUEEN OF THE SOUTH 3**
Downie (2), Heddle (2),  Mills, Thomson (2)
Bingham (3 (1 pen)), Kopel

**Forfar Athletic:** Arthur, Philliben (Morris), McPhee, Mann, Archibald, Winter, Kopel, Hamill, Downie, Bingham (Smith), Heddle

**Queen of the South:** Purdie, McGhie, Mills, Rowe, Shanks (Kelly), Bell, McLaren (McFarlane), McKeown, Thomson, Bryce, Mallan

## FIRST ROUND REPLAYS

### 14th December, 1993

**QUEEN'S PARK 2**  **COWDENBEATH 3**
McPhee, Rodden  Reilly, Henderson,
 Callaghan

**Queen's Park:** Chalmers, Stevenson (McCormick), Maxwell, Kerr, Elder, Orr G., Rodden, Fitzpatrick (Ferguson), McPhee, Graham, O'Neill

**Cowdenbeath:** Maloney, Petrie, Davidson, Herd, McMahon B., Maratea (Thomson), Lee, Scott, Reilly, Callaghan, Henderson

Substitute not used: Barclay

### 18th December, 1993

**WHITEHILL WELFARE 0**  **STRANRAER 4**
 Sloan (4)

**Whitehill Welfare:** Ramage, Smith D. (Richford), Millar, Brown, Steel, Cuthbert, Thorburn, Samuel, Sneddon (Smith R.), McCulloch, Tulloch

**Stranraer:** Ross, Millar, Hughes, Spittal, Gallagher, McCann (Cody), Sloan, Grant, Ferguson (McIntyre), Duncan, Henderson

### 15th January, 1994

**HUNTLY 5**  **ALBION ROVERS 3**
DeBarros, Stewart, Lennox,  Fraser, Scott, McCaffrey
Murphy, Thomson

**Huntly:** Gardiner, McGinlay, Murphy, Walker, Rougvie, DeBarros, Stewart, Copland (Dunsire), Thomson, Whyte (Selbie), Lennox

**Albion Rovers:** Burns, Riley, Beattie, Conn, McCaffrey, McKeown, Seggie, Cadden, Scott, Fraser, Gallagher

Substitutes not used: McBride, Kerrigan

# SECOND ROUND

### 8th January, 1994

**EAST STIRLINGSHIRE 4**  **COVE RANGERS 1**
McAulay, Geraghty (2),  Whyte
Robertson

**East Stirlingshire:** McDougall, Russell, Kemp, McAulay, Craig, Ross, Conway (Robertson), Millar, McCallum, Geraghty, Loney

Substitute not used: K. Macdonald

**Cove Rangers:** MacLean, Morrison, Whyte, Morland, Paterson, Baxter, Yule, Forbes, Stephen (Park), Murphy (Leslie), Megginson

**MEADOWBANK THISTLE 1**  **MONTROSE 2**
Rutherford  Kennedy, Bailey (o.g.)

**Meadowbank Thistle:** Ellison, Wilson, Scott, Murray, Graham, MacLeod I., Bailey, Little (Hutchison), Rutherford, McLeod G., Gardner (Brock)

**Montrose:** Larter, Robertson, Craib M., Tosh, Smith, Irvine, Tindal, Craib S., Grant (Wolecki), Kennedy, Stephen

Substitute not used: Yeats

**BERWICK RANGERS 1**  **EAST FIFE 0**
Kane

**Berwick Rangers:** Davidson, Boyle, Banks, Valentine, Cowan, Hall, Neil, Irvine, Hawke, Donaldson (Graham), Kane (Gibson)

**East Fife:** Charles, Sneddon, Williamson, Barron, Burns, Beedie, Allan (Taylor), Hildersley (McBride), Scott, Hope, Irvine

**FORFAR ATHLETIC 0**  **ROSS COUNTY 4**
 Grant (3), Wilson

**Forfar Athletic:** Arthur, Philliben, McPhee, Mann (Smith), Archibald, Winter, Kopel, Hamill, Downie (Lees), Bingham, Heddle

**Ross County:** Hutchison, Somerville, Reid (Ross), Williamson, Bellshaw, Alec MacLeod, Ferries, Grant (Robertson), Andrew MacLeod, Connelly, Wilson

### 15th January, 1994

**ALLOA 4**  **GALA FAIRYDEAN 0**
McCulloch, Wilson (o.g.),
McCormick, Lamont

**Alloa:** Butter, McNiven, McCormack J., Campbell, McCulloch, Newbigging, McAvoy, Ramsay, McCormick S., Moffat (McAnenay), Willock (Lamont)

**Gala Fairydean:** Cairns, Findlay, Henry, Wilson, Rae, Potts, Black, Campbell, McGovern (Simpson), Loughran (Lothian), Hunter

**COWDENBEATH 1**  **STENHOUSEMUIR 0**
Hunter

**Cowdenbeath:** Moffat, Watt, Scott, Herd, McMahon B., Petrie, Lee, Henderson (Thomson), Reilly, Callaghan, Hunter

Substitute not used: Barclay

**Stenhousemuir:** Harkness, Aitken, Donaldson, Armstrong, Godfrey, Clarke, Steel, Irvine (Swanson), Mathieson, Haddow, Dickov

Substitute not used: Gallacher

**SELKIRK 0**

**ARBROATH 3**
McKinnon, Adam,
Buckley

**Selkirk:** Massie, Brownlee M., Main, Scott (Ritchie), Brownlee P., Leckie, Kerr D. (Wilson), Kerr A., Whitehead, Cockburn, Smith

**Arbroath:** Jackson, Farnan, Florence, Mitchell, Adam, Buckley, Clouston, King, Diver, McKinnon, Sorbie

Substitutes not used: Scott, Elliot

## 22nd January, 1994

**HUNTLY 1**
DeBarros

**STRANRAER 2**
Duncan, Sloan

**Huntly:** Gardiner, McGinlay, Murphy, Walker, Rougvie, DeBarros, Stewart (Selbie), Copland, Thomson, Whyte, Lennox

Substitute not used: Dunsire

**Stranraer:** Duffy, Millar, Hughes, Spittal (Ferguson), Brannigan, Gallagher, Sloan, Grant, Duncan, Cody (McLean), Henderson

# THIRD ROUND

## 29th January, 1994

**GREENOCK MORTON 2**
McEwan, Lilley

**COWDENBEATH 2**
Henderson (2)

**Greenock Morton:** Wylie, Collins (McArthur), Pickering, Johnstone, Doak, Hunter, Lilley, Fowler (Thomson), McEwan, Sexton, Rafferty

**Cowdenbeath:** Moffat, Davidson, Scott (Carr), Herd, McMahon B., Petrie, Lee, Henderson, Reilly (Barclay), Hunter, Thomson

**AIRDRIEONIANS 1**
Kirkwood (pen)

**DUNFERMLINE ATHLETIC 1**
Tod

**Airdrieonians:** Martin, Stewart, McVicar, Sandison, Jack, Black, Kirkwood, Honor, Davenport, Ferguson (Andrew Smith), Lawrence

Substitute not used: Balfour

**Dunfermline Athletic:** Hamilton, McNamara, Sharp, McCathie, Baillie (Tod), Smith, Preston, Robertson, French, Laing (O'Boyle), McWilliams

**CLYDEBANK 1**
Henry

**DUNDEE 1**
Tosh

**Clydebank:** Monaghan, Ferguson, Crawford D., Harris (Jack), Sweeney, Currie, Cooper, Henry (Lansdowne), Crawford J., Flannigan, Thomson

**Dundee:** Mathers, Frail, Pittman, McQuillan, Blake, Duffy J. (Farningham), Shaw, Vrto, Ritchie (Tosh), Wieghorst, McCann

**STRANRAER 2**
Sloan, Ferguson

**FALKIRK 1**
Hughes

**Stranraer:** Duffy, Millar, Hughes, McLean, Brannigan, Gallagher, Sloan, Duncan, Ferguson (McIntyre), Cody (Spittal), Henderson

**Falkirk:** Westwater, Duffy, Johnston (Drinkell), Weir, McLaughlin, Hughes, May (McDonald), Sloan, Cadette, McCall, Rice

**HIBERNIAN 2**
O'Neill, McAllister

**CLYDE 1**
McCheyne

**Hibernian:** Leighton, Miller, Mitchell, Farrell, Tweed, Beaumont, McAllister, Tortolano (Evans), Wright, Jackson, O'Neill

Substitute not used: Findlay

**Clyde:** Fridge, McFarlane, McCheyne, Knox, Thomson, Neill, MacKenzie, McAulay, McConnell, McCarron (Ronald), Strain

Substitute not used: Parks

**STIRLING ALBION 1**
Pew

**BERWICK RANGERS 0**

**Stirling Albion:** McGeown, Hamilton, Watson, McAnenay (Armstrong), McQuilter, Mitchell, McInnes, Callaghan, Pew, Gibson, McLeod (Watters)

**Berwick Rangers:** O'Connor, Boyle, Banks, Valentine, Cowan, Wilson, Young (Hall), Neil (Kane), Hawke, Irvine, Graham

**ST. MIRREN 2**
Elliot, Bone

**MONTROSE 0**

**St. Mirren:** Combe, Dawson, Baker, Gillies R. (Gardner), McIntyre, McLaughlin, Dick, Fullarton, Bone, Hewitt (Harvie), Elliot

**Montrose:** Larter, Houghton (Yeats), Robertson, Grant, Smith, Irvine, Cooper, Tindal, Taylor, Kennedy, Stephen

Substitute not used: Wolecki

**KILMARNOCK 2**
McSkimming, Black (pen)

**AYR UNITED 1**
Bryce

**Kilmarnock:** Geddes, MacPherson, Black, Montgomerie, Brown, Millen, Mitchell, Reilly, Williamson, McCluskey, McSkimming

Substitutes not used: Paterson, Crainie

**Ayr United:** Spence, Burns, Mair, Shotton, Hood, George (Scott), Lennox (Moore), Traynor, Bryce, Jack, McGlashan

**ARBROATH 2**
Sorbie, McKinnon

**DUNDEE UNITED 3**
Crabbe, Brewster,
McKinlay (pen)

**Arbroath:** Jackson, Farnan, Florence, Mitchell, Adam, Martin (Scott), Clouston, King, Diver, McKinnon, Sorbie

Substitute not used: Buckley

**Dundee United:** Van De Kamp, Van Der Hoorn, Malpas, McInally, Petric, Cleland, Bowman, McKinlay, Connolly, Brewster, Crabbe

Substitutes not used: Nixon, Dailly

**PARTICK THISTLE 0**

**HEART OF MIDLOTHIAN 1**
Johnston M.

**Partick Thistle:** Nelson, Law, Milne, Watson, Jamieson, Cameron (Byrne), Gibson, Craig, Grant, English (Taylor), Charnley

**Heart of Midlothian:** Smith, McLaren, McKinlay, Levein, Berry, Locke, Colquhoun, Mackay, Leitch (Wright), Johnston M. (Foster), Robertson

**RANGERS 4**
Durie, Hateley (Pen), Steven,
Robertson D.

**DUMBARTON 1**
Mooney

**Rangers:** Maxwell, Stevens, Robertson D., Gough, Murray, Brown, Steven, McCall, Durie, Hateley, Mikhailitchenko (McCoist)

Substitute not used: Kouznetsov

**Dumbarton:** MacFarlane, Wilson, Fabiani, Melvin, Gow, MacLeod, Mooney, Meechan, Gibson, McGarvey, Foster (Boyd)

Substitute not used: Marsland

**RAITH ROVERS 2**
Dair, McStay

**BRECHIN CITY 0**

**Raith Rovers:** Thomson, McStay, McGeachie, Coyle, Dennis, Sinclair, Nicholl (Kelly), Dalziel, Cameron, Graham, Dair

Substitute not used: Crawford

**Brechin City:** Allan, Conway, Christie, Brown, Nicolson, Scott, McLaren, Redford, Brand (O'Brien), Miller, McNeill

Substitute not used: Vannett

**MOTHERWELL 1**
Coyne

**CELTIC 0**

**Motherwell:** Dykstra, Shannon, McKinnon, Krivokapic, Martin, McCart, Lambert (Kirk), Dolan, Arnott, O'Donnell, Coyne (McGrillen)

**Celtic:** Muggleton, Gillespie, Boyd, O'Neil, Mowbray, McNally, Byrne (Biggins), McStay, McAvennie, McGinlay, Collins

Substitute not used: Vata

**ST. JOHNSTONE 2**
Dodds, McMartin

**HAMILTON ACADEMICAL 0**

**St. Johnstone:** Rhodes, McGowne, McAuley, Ramsey, Deas, McGinnis, Scott, Turner (McMartin), Ferguson, Dodds (Torfason), Curran

**Hamilton Academical:** Ferguson, Napier, Miller, McEntegart, Baptie, McInulty, McQuade, Reid, Duffield (Campbell), Clark (McKenzie), McGill

## 8th February, 1994

**EAST STIRLINGSHIRE 1**          **ABERDEEN 3**
Geraghty                          Shearer (2), Craig (o.g.)

**East Stirlingshire**: McDougall, Russell, Lee R., McAulay (Conroy), Craig, Ross, Conway, Millar, McCallum, Geraghty, Loney

Substitute not used: Robertson

**Aberdeen**: Snelders, McKimmie, Wright, Grant, McLeish, Irvine, Jess (Booth), Bett, Winnie (Miller), Shearer, Paatelainen

**ALLOA 2**                       **ROSS COUNTY 0**
McAnenay, McAvoy

**Alloa**: Butter, McNiven, Tait, Campbell, McCulloch, Newbigging, McAnenay (Moffat), Ramsay (Mackay), McCormick, McAvoy, Willock

**Ross County**: Hutchison, Somerville, Reid (Robertson), Williamson, Bellshaw, Andrew MacLeod, Ferries (Duff), Grant, Alec MacLeod, Connelly, Wilson

## THIRD ROUND REPLAYS

### 8th February, 1994

**COWDENBEATH 1**                 **GREENOCK MORTON 2**
Callaghan                         Anderson, McEwan

**Cowdenbeath**: Moffat, Watt, Thomson (Reilly), Herd, Young, Petrie, Lee (Davidson), Henderson, Callaghan, Hunter, Carr

**Greenock Morton**: Wylie, Anderson, Pickering, Rafferty, Johnstone, Hunter, Thomson, Fowler, Alexander, Sexton (McArthur), McEwan

Substitute not used: Donaghy

**DUNFERMLINE ATHLETIC 1**        **AIRDRIEONIANS 3**
Tod                               Kirkwood (2 pens), Ferguson

**Dunfermline Athletic**: Hamilton, McNamara, Sharp, McCathie, Baillie, Smith, Den Bieman, Robertson, Petrie, O'Boyle (Tod), Preston (Laing)

**Airdrieonians**: Martin, Stewart, Jack (Sandison), Honor, Caesar, Black, Kirkwood, Balfour, Smith, Ferguson, Lawrence (Davenport)

### 9th February, 1994

**DUNDEE 2**                      **CLYDEBANK 1**
Britton, Shaw                     Sweeney

**Match Played at Forthbank Stadium, Stirling**

**Dundee**: Mathers, McQuillan, Pittman, Duffy J., Blake, Dinnie, Shaw, Vrto, Britton (Farningham), Wieghorst (Ristic), McCann

**Clydebank**: Monaghan, Ferguson (Lansdowne), Crawford D., Murdoch, Sweeney, Currie, Cooper, Henry, Harris, Flannigan (Smith), Thomson

## FOURTH ROUND

### 19th February, 1994

**AIRDRIEONIANS 1**               **STRANRAER 0**
Kirkwood (pen)

**Airdrieonians**: Martin, Stewart, Hay, Sandison, Caesar, Black, Kirkwood, Honor, Ferguson, Harvey (Andrew Smith), Lawrence (Davenport)

**Stranraer**: Duffy, Millar, McLean (Ferguson), McIntyre, Brannigan, Gallagher, Sloan, Grant, Duncan, Cody, Henderson

Substitute not used: Spittal

**RANGERS 6**                     **ALLOA 0**
Ferguson I., McPherson, McCoist
(3 (1 Pen)), Newbigging (o.g.)

**Rangers**: Goram, Stevens (Pressley), Robertson D., McCall, McPherson, Brown, Steven, Ferguson I., McCoist, Hateley, Mikhailitchenko

Substitute not used: Ferguson D.

**Alloa**: Butter, McNiven, Tait, Newbigging, McCulloch, McAvoy, McAnenay, Ramsay, McCormick, Lamont (Moffat), Willock (Mackay)

---

**GREENOCK MORTON 0**             **KILMARNOCK 1**
                                  Williamson

**Greenock Morton**: Wylie, Anderson, Pickering, Rafferty, Johnstone, Hunter, McEwan (Lilley), Fowler, Alexander, Thomson (Sexton), Tolmie

**Kilmarnock**: Geddes, MacPherson, Black, Montgomerie, Brown, Millen, Mitchell, Reilly, Williamson (Porteous), McInally, McSkimming (McCluskey)

**ABERDEEN 1**                    **RAITH ROVERS 0**
Miller

**Aberdeen**: Snelders, Smith, Wright, Grant, McLeish, Irvine, Jess (Booth), Bett (Miller), Kane, Shearer, Paatelainen

**Raith Rovers**: Thomson, McStay, Rowbotham, Coyle, Dennis, Sinclair, Nicholl, Cameron, Hetherston, Crawford (Graham), Dair

Substitute not used: McAnespie

**DUNDEE UNITED 2**               **MOTHERWELL 2**
Brewster (2)                      Kirk, Philliben

**Dundee United**: Van De Kamp, Van Der Hoorn, Malpas, McInally, Petric, Welsh, Dailly, McKinlay, Connolly, Brewster, Crabbe (Nixon)

Substitute not used: O'Neil

**Motherwell**: Dykstra, Shannon (Dolan), McKinnon, Krivokapic, Martin, McCart, Lambert (McGrillen), Philliben, Kirk, O'Donnell, Coyne

## 20th February, 1994

**DUNDEE 3**                      **ST. MIRREN 1**
Britton (2), Shaw                 Lavety

**Dundee**: Mathers, McQuillan, Pittman, Dinnie, Blake, Duffy, Shaw, Farningham (Frail), Britton (Tosh), Wieghorst, McCann

**St. Mirren**: Combe, Dawson, Baker, Taylor, McIntyre, Fullarton (Gardner), Dick (Farrell), Bone, Lavety, Hewitt, Elliot

**HIBERNIAN 1**                   **HEART OF MIDLOTHIAN 2**
Wright                            Robertson, Foster

**Hibernian**: Leighton, Miller, Beaumont, Farrell, Tweed, Lennon, McAllister, Hamilton, Wright, Jackson D. (Evans), O'Neill

Substitute not used: Findlay

**Heart of Midlothian**: Smith, McLaren, McKinlay, Levein, Berry, Millar, Colquhoun, Mackay, Robertson (Foster), Johnston M., Leitch (Weir)

## 28th February, 1994

**ST. JOHNSTONE 3**               **STIRLING ALBION 3**
Dodds (2), Ferguson               Roberts (2), Armstrong

**St. Johnstone**: Rhodes, Inglis, McAuley, Ramsey (McMartin), Deas, McGinnis, Scott, Moore (Torfason), Ferguson, Dodds, Curran

**Stirling Albion**: McGeown, Hamilton, Armstrong, Tait, McQuilter, Mitchell, Roberts (Reilly), Callaghan, Watters (Pew), Gibson, McLeod

## FOURTH ROUND REPLAYS

### 1st March, 1994

**MOTHERWELL 0**                  **DUNDEE UNITED 1**
                                  Welsh

**Motherwell**: Dykstra, Philliben, McKinnon, Krivokapic, Martin, McCart, Lambert (Dolan), Kirk (McGrillen), Arnott, O'Donnell, Coyne

**Dundee United**: Van De Kamp, Narey, Malpas, McInally, Petric, Welsh, Dailly, McKinlay, Nixon (Hannah), Brewster, Crabbe (Cleland)

*2nd March, 1994*

**STIRLING ALBION 0**                    **ST. JOHNSTONE 2**
                                         Scott, Ferguson

**Stirling Albion**: McGeown, Pew, Armstrong, Tait, McQuilter, Mitchell, Roberts (Reilly), Callaghan, Watters (Watson), Gibson, McLeod

**St. Johnstone**: Rhodes, Inglis, McAuley, Ramsey, Deas, Cherry, Scott, Turner, Ferguson, Dodds, Curran

Substitutes not used: McMartin, Torfason

# FIFTH ROUND

*12th March, 1994*

**KILMARNOCK 1**                         **DUNDEE 0**
Brown

**Kilmarnock**: Geddes, MacPherson, Black, Montgomerie, Burns, Millen, Mitchell, Reilly, Brown, McCluskey (Williamson), McSkimming

Substitute not used: McInally

**Dundee**: Mathers, McQuillan, Pittman, Dinnie (Tosh), Blake, Frail (Farningham), Shaw, Vrto, Britton, Wieghorst, McCann

**AIRDRIEONIANS 0**                      **DUNDEE UNITED 0**

**Airdrieonians**: Martin, Stewart, Honor, Sandison, Caesar, Hay, Boyle, Reid, Davenport (Andrew Smith), Harvey, Ferguson

Substitute not used: Wilson

**Dundee United**: Van De Kamp, Narey, Malpas, McInally, Petric, Welsh, Bowman, McKinlay (Hannah), Nixon (O'Neil), Brewster, Cleland

**RANGERS   2**                          **HEART OF MIDLOTHIAN 0**
Brown, Hateley

**Rangers**: Goram, McCall, Robertson D., Gough, McPherson, Brown, Steven, Ferguson I., McCoist (Mikhailitchenko), Hateley, Durie (Ferguson D)

**Heart of Midlothian**: Smith, Weir, McKinlay, Levein, Berry (Locke), McLaren, Colquhoun (Robertson), Leitch, Foster, Johnston M., Millar

**ST. JOHNSTONE  1**                     **ABERDEEN 1**
Dodds                                    Booth

**St. Johnstone**: Rhodes, McGowne, Inglis, Ramsey, Deas, Cherry (Torfason), Scott, Turner, Ferguson, Dodds, Curran

Substitute not used: McMartin

**Aberdeen**: Stillie, McKimmie, Wright, Smith, McLeish, Irvine, Jess (Miller), Richardson, Booth, Shearer, Kane

Substitute not used: Grant

## FIFTH ROUND REPLAYS

*15th March, 1994*

**DUNDEE UNITED 2**                      **AIRDRIEONIANS 0**
McLaren, McKinlay

**Dundee United**: Van De Kamp, Hannah, Malpas, McInally, Petric, Welsh, Bowman, McKinlay, Nixon (McLaren), Dailly, Cleland

Substitute not used: O'Neil

**Airdrieonians**: Martin, Stewart, Honor, Sandison, Caesar, Hay, Boyle, Reid, Davenport (Andrew Smith), Harvey (Jack), Ferguson

**ABERDEEN 2**                           **ST. JOHNSTONE 0**
Shearer, Richardson

**Aberdeen**: Stillie, McKimmie, Wright, Smith, McLeish, Irvine, Jess, Richardson, Booth (Miller), Shearer, Kane

Substitute not used: Grant

**St. Johnstone**: Rhodes, McGowne, Inglis, Ramsey (McMartin), Deas, Cherry, Scott, Turner, Ferguson, Dodds, Curran (Torfason)

# SEMI-FINALS

*9th April, 1994*

**HAMPDEN PARK, GLASGOW**

**DUNDEE UNITED 1**                      **ABERDEEN 1**
Welsh                                    Shearer

**Dundee United**: Van de Kamp, Cleland, Malpas, McInally, Petric, Welsh, Bowman, McKinlay, McLaren, Brewster, Nixon (Dailly)

Substitute not used: Bollan

**Aberdeen**: Burridge, McKimmie, Robertson (Miller), Kane, Smith, Irvine, Jess (Paatelainen), Richardson, McKinnon, Shearer, Grant

*10th April, 1994*

**HAMPDEN PARK, GLASGOW**

**KILMARNOCK 0**                         **RANGERS 0**

**Kilmarnock**: Geddes, MacPherson, Black, Montgomerie, Paterson, Millen, Mitchell (McCluskey), Reilly, Williamson, Brown (McInally), McSkimming

**Rangers**: Maxwell, Murray (McCoist), Robertson D., Gough, McPherson, Brown, McCall, Ferguson I., Durie, Hateley, Mikhailitchenko (Ferguson D.)

# SEMI-FINAL REPLAYS

*12th April, 1994*

**HAMPDEN PARK, GLASGOW**

**DUNDEE UNITED 1**                      **ABERDEEN 0**
McInally

**Dundee United**: Van De Kamp, Cleland, Malpas, McInally, Petric, Welsh, Bowman, McKinlay, McLaren (Nixon), Brewster (Dailly), Bollan

**Aberdeen**: Snelders, McKimmie, Robertson (Booth), Kane, Smith, Irvine, Jess, Richardson, McKinnon (Miller), Shearer, Grant

*13th April, 1994*

**HAMPDEN PARK, GLASGOW**

**KILMARNOCK 1**                         **RANGERS 2**
Black                                    Hateley (2)

**Kilmarnock**: Geddes, McPherson (McInally), Black, Montgomerie, Paterson, Millen, Mitchell, Reilly, Williamson, Brown (McCluskey), McSkimming

**Rangers**: Maxwell, McCall, Robertson D., Gough, McPherson, Pressley, Durie, Ferguson I., McCoist, Hateley, Durrant (Huistra)

Substitute not used: Ferguson D.

---

# FINAL

*Saturday, 21st May, 1994*

**HAMPDEN PARK, GLASGOW**

## RANGERS 0     DUNDEE UNITED 1

**Rangers**: Maxwell, Stevens (Mikhailitchenko), Robertson D., Gough, McPherson, McCall, Murray, Ferguson I., McCoist (Ferguson D.), Hateley, Durie

**Dundee United**: Van De Kamp, Cleland, Malpas, McInally, Petric, Welsh, Bowman, Hannah, McLaren (Nixon), Brewster, Dailly

Substitute not used: Bollan

**Scorer**: C. Brewster

**Referee**: D. D. Hope (Erskine)

**Attendance**: 37,709

## SEASON 1919/20

*17th April, 1920 at Hampden Park; Attendance 95,000; Referee: Mr W. Bell (Hamilton)*

**KILMARNOCK 3**
Culley, Shortt, J. Smith

**ALBION ROVERS 2**
Watson, Hillhouse

## SEASON 1920/21

*16th April, 1921 at Celtic Park; Attendance 28,294; Referee: Mr H. Humphreys (Greenock)*

**PARTICK THISTLE 1**
Blair

**RANGERS 0**

## SEASON 1921/22

*15th April, 1922 at Hampden Park; Attendance 75,000; Referee: Mr T. Dougray (Bellshill)*

**MORTON 1**
Gourlay

**RANGERS 0**

## SEASON 1922/23

*31st March, 1923 at Hampden Park; Attendance 80,100; Referee: Mr T. Dougray (Bellshill)*

**CELTIC 1**
Cassidy

**HIBERNIAN 0**

## SEASON 1923/24

*19th April, 1924 at Ibrox Stadium; Attendance 59,218; Referee: Mr T. Dougray (Bellshill)*

**AIRDRIEONIANS 2**
Russell (2)

**HIBERNIAN 0**

## SEASON 1924/25

*11th April, 1925 at Hampden Park; Attendance 75,137; Referee: Mr T. Dougray (Bellshill)*

**CELTIC 2**
Gallacher, McGrory

**DUNDEE 1**
McLean

## SEASON 1925/26

*10th April, 1926 at Hampden Park; Attendance 98,620; Referee: Mr P. Craigmyle (Aberdeen)*

**ST. MIRREN 2**
McCrae, Howieson

**CELTIC 0**

## SEASON 1926/27

*16th April, 1927 at Hampden Park; Attendance 79,500; Referee: Mr T. Dougray (Bellshill)*

**CELTIC 3**
Robertson (og), McLean, Connolly

**EAST FIFE 1**
Wood

## SEASON 1927/28

*14th April, 1928 at Hampden Park; Attendance 118,115; Referee: Mr W. Bell (Motherwell)*

**RANGERS 4**
Meiklejohn (pen), McPhail, Archibald (2)

**CELTIC 0**

## SEASON 1928/29

*6th April, 1929 at Hampden Park; Attendance 114,708; Referee: Mr T. Dougray (Bellshill)*

**KILMARNOCK**    2 v 0    **RANGERS**
Aitken, Williamson

## SEASON 1929/30

*12th April, 1930 at Hampden Park; Attendance 107,475; Referee: Mr W. Bell (Motherwell)*

**RANGERS 0**

**PARTICK THISTLE 0**

**REPLAY**

*16th April, 1930 at Hampden Park; Attendance 90,000; Referee: Mr W. Bell (Motherwell)*

**RANGERS 2**
Marshall, Craig

**PARTICK THISTLE 1**
Torbet

## SEASON 1930/31

*11th April, 1931 at Hampden Park; Attendance 104,803; Referee: Mr P. Craigmyle (Aberdeen)*

**CELTIC 2**
McGrory, Craig (o.g.)

**MOTHERWELL 2**
Stevenson, McMenemy

**REPLAY**

*15th April, 1931 at Hampden Park; Attendance 98,579; Referee: Mr P. Craigmyle (Aberdeen)*

**CELTIC 4**
R. Thomson (2), McGrory (2)

**MOTHERWELL 2**
Murdoch, Stevenson

## SEASON 1931/32

*16th April, 1932 at Hampden Park; Attendance 111,982; Referee: Mr P. Craigmyle (Aberdeen)*

**RANGERS 1**
McPhail

**KILMARNOCK 1**
Maxwell

**REPLAY**

*20th April, 1932 at Hampden Park; Attendance 110,695; Referee: Mr P. Craigmyle (Aberdeen)*

**RANGERS 3**
Fleming, McPhail, English

**KILMARNOCK 0**

## SEASON 1932/33

*15th April, 1933 at Hampden Park; Attendance 102,339; Referee: Mr T. Dougray (Bellshill)*

**CELTIC 1**
McGrory

**MOTHERWELL 0**

## SEASON 1933/34

*21st April, 1934 at Hampden Park; Attendance 113,430; Referee: Mr M. C. Hutton (Glasgow)*

**RANGERS 5**
Nicholson (2), McPhail, Main, Smith

**ST. MIRREN 0**

## SEASON 1934/35

*20th April, 1935 at Hampden Park; Attendance 87,286; Referee: Mr H. Watson (Glasgow)*

**RANGERS 2**
Smith (2)

**HAMILTON ACADEMICAL 1**
Harrison

## SEASON 1935/36

*18th April, 1936 at Hampden Park; Attendance 88,859; Referee: Mr J. M. Martin (Ladybank)*

**RANGERS 1**
McPhail

**THIRD LANARK 0**

## SEASON 1936/37

*24th April, 1937 at Hampden Park; Attendance 147,365; Referee: Mr M. C. Hutton (Glasgow)*

**CELTIC 2**
Crum, Buchan

**ABERDEEN 1**
Armstrong

## SEASON 1937/38

*23rd April, 1938 at Hampden Park; Attendance 80,091; Referee: Mr H. Watson (Glasgow)*

**EAST FIFE 1**
McLeod

**KILMARNOCK 1**
McAvoy

**REPLAY**

*27th April, 1938 at Hampden Park; Attendance 92,716;*
*Referee: Mr H. Watson (Glasgow)*

**EAST FIFE 4**                    **KILMARNOCK 2**
McKerrell (2), McLeod, Miller      Thomson (pen), McGrogan
After extra time

## SEASON 1938/39

*22nd April, 1939 at Hampden Park; Attendance 94,770;*
*Referee: Mr W. Webb (Glasgow)*

**CLYDE 4**                        **MOTHERWELL 0**
Wallace, Martin (2), Noble

## SEASON 1946/47

*19th April, 1947 at Hampden Park; Attendance 82,140;*
*Referee: Mr R. Calder (Glasgow)*

**ABERDEEN  2**                    **HIBERNIAN 1**
Hamilton, Williams                 Cuthbertson

## SEASON 1947/48

*17th April, 1948 at Hampden Park; Attendance 129,176;*
*Referee: Mr J. M. Martin (Blairgowrie)*

**RANGERS  1**                     **MORTON 1**
Gillick                            Whyte
After extra-time

**REPLAY**

*21st April, 1948 at Hampden Park; Attendance 131,975;*
*Referee: Mr J. M. Martin (Blairgowrie)*

**RANGERS 1**                      **MORTON 0**
Williamson
After extra-time

## SEASON 1948/49

*23rd April, 1949 at Hampden Park; Attendance 108,435;*
*Referee: Mr R. G. Benzie (Irvine)*

**RANGERS 4**                      **CLYDE 1**
Young (2 (2 pens)),                Galletly
Williamson, Duncanson

## SEASON 1949/50

*22nd April, 1950 at Hampden Park; Attendance 118,262;*
*Referee: Mr J. A. Mowat (Burnside)*

**RANGERS 3**                      **EAST FIFE 0**
Findlay, Thornton (2)

## SEASON 1950/51

*21st April, 1951 at Hampden Park; Attendance 131,943;*
*Referee: Mr J. A. Mowat (Burnside)*

**CELTIC 1**                       **MOTHERWELL 0**
McPhail

## SEASON 1951/52

*19th April, 1952 at Hampden Park; Attendance 136,304;*
*Referee: Mr J. A. Mowat (Burnside)*

**MOTHERWELL 4**                   **DUNDEE 0**
Watson, Redpath, Humphries, Kelly

## SEASON 1952/53

*25th April, 1953 at Hampden Park; Attendance 129,861;*
*Referee: Mr J. A. Mowat (Burnside)*

**RANGERS 1**                      **ABERDEEN 1**
Prentice                           Yorston

**REPLAY**

*29th April, 1953 at Hampden Park; Attendance 112,619;*
*Referee: Mr J. A. Mowat (Burnside)*

**RANGERS 1**                      **ABERDEEN 0**
Simpson

## SEASON 1953/54

*24th April, 1954 at Hampden Park; Attendance 129,926;*
*Referee: Mr C. E. Faultless (Giffnock)*

**CELTIC 2**                       **ABERDEEN 1**
Young (o.g.), Fallon               Buckley

## SEASON 1954/55

*23rd April, 1955 at Hampden Park; Attendance 106,111;*
*Referee: Mr C. E. Faultless (Giffnock)*

**CLYDE 1**                        **CELTIC 1**
Robertson                          Walsh

**REPLAY**

*27th April, 1955 at Hampden Park; Attendance 68,735;*
*Referee: Mr C. E. Faultless (Giffnock)*

**CLYDE 1**                        **CELTIC 0**
Ring

## SEASON 1955/56

*21st April, 1956 at Hampden Park; Attendance 133,399;*
*Referee: Mr R. H. Davidson (Airdrie)*

**HEART OF MIDLOTHIAN 3**          **CELTIC 1**
Crawford (2), Conn                 Haughney

## SEASON 1956/57

*20th April, 1957 at Hampden Park; Attendance 81,057;*
*Referee: Mr J. A. Mowat (Burnside)*

**FALKIRK 1**                      **KILMARNOCK 1**
Prentice (pen)                     Curlett

**REPLAY**

*24th April, 1957 at Hampden Park; Attendance 79,785;*
*Referee: Mr J. A. Mowat (Burnside)*

**FALKIRK  2**                     **KILMARNOCK 1**
Merchant, Moran                    Curlett
After extra-tim

## SEASON 1957/58

*26th April, 1958 at Hampden Park; Attendance 95,123;*
*Referee: Mr J. A. Mowat (Burnside)*

**CLYDE 1**                        **HIBERNIAN 0**
Coyle

## SEASON 1958/59

*25th April, 1959 at Hampden Park; Attendance 108,951;*
*Referee: Mr  J. A. Mowat (Burnside)*

**ST. MIRREN 3**                   **ABERDEEN 1**
Bryceland, Miller, Baker           Baird

## SEASON 1959/60

*23rd April, 1960 at Hampden Park; Attendance 108,017;*
*Referee: Mr R. H. Davidson (Airdrie)*

**RANGERS 2**                      **KILMARNOCK 0**
Millar (2)

## SEASON 1960/61

*22nd April, 1961 at Hampden Park; Attendance 113,618;*
*Referee: Mr H. Phillips (Wishaw)*

**DUNFERMLINE ATHLETIC 0**         **CELTIC 0**

**REPLAY**

*26th April, 1961 at Hampden Park; Attendance 87,866;*
*Referee: Mr H. Phillips (Wishaw)*

**DUNFERMLINE ATHLETIC 2**         **CELTIC 0**
Thomson, Dickson

## SEASON 1961/62

*21st April;, 1962 at Hampden Park; Attendance, 126,930;*
*Referee: Mr T. Wharton (Clarkston)*

**RANGERS 2**      **ST. MIRREN 0**
Brand, Wilson

## SEASON 1962/63

*4th May, 1963 at Hampden Park; Attendance 129,527;*
*Referee: Mr T. Wharton (Clarkston)*

**RANGERS 1**      **CELTIC 1**
Brand      Murdoch

**REPLAY**

*15th May, 1963 at Hampden Park; Attendance 120,263;*
*Referee: Mr T. Wharton (Clarkston)*

**RANGERS 3**      **CELTIC 0**
Brand (2), Wilson

## SEASON 1963/64

*25th April, 1964 at Hampden Park; Attendance 120,982;*
*Referee: Mr H. Phillips (Wishaw)*

**RANGERS 3**      **DUNDEE 1**
Millar (2), Brand      Cameron

## SEASON 1964/65

*24th April, 1965 at Hampden Park; Attendance 108,800;*
*Referee: Mr H. Phillips (Wishaw)*

**CELTIC 3**      **DUNFERMLINE ATHLETIC 2**
Auld (2), McNeill      Melrose, McLaughlin

## SEASON 1965/66

*23rd April, 1966 at Hampden Park; Attendance 126,559;*
*Referee: Mr T. Wharton (Clarkston)*

**RANGERS 0**      **CELTIC 0**

**REPLAY**

*27th April, 1966 at Hampden Park; Attendance 96,862;*
*Referee: Mr T. Wharton (Clarkston)*

**RANGERS 1**      **CELTIC 0**
Johansen

## SEASON 1966/67

*29th April, 1967 at Hampden Park; Attendance 127,117;*
*Referee: Mr W. M. M. Syme (Glasgow)*

**CELTIC 2**      **ABERDEEN 0**
Wallace (2)

## SEASON 1967/68

*27th April, 1968 at Hampden Park; Attendance 56,365;*
*Referee: Mr W. Anderson (East Kilbride)*

**DUNFERMLINE ATHLETIC 3**      **HEART OF MIDLOTHIAN 1**
Gardner (2), Lister (pen)      Lunn (o.g.)

## SEASON 1968/69

*26th April, 1969 at Hampden Park; Attendance 132,870;*
*Referee: Mr J. Callaghan (Glasgow)*

**CELTIC 4**      **RANGERS 0**
McNeill, Lennox, Connelly, Chalmers

## SEASON 1969/70

*11th April, 1970 at Hampden Park; Attendance 108,434;*
*Referee: Mr R. H. Davidson (Airdrie)*

**ABERDEEN 3**      **CELTIC 1**
Harper (pen), McKay (2)      Lennox

## SEASON 1970/71

*8th May, 1971 at Hampden Park; Attendance 120,092;*
*Referee: Mr T. Wharton (Glasgow)*

**CELTIC 1**      **RANGERS 1**
Lennox      D. Johnstone

**REPLAY**

*12th May, 1971 at Hampden Park; Attendance 103,332;*
*Referee: Mr T. Wharton (Glasgow)*

**CELTIC 2**      **RANGERS 1**
Macari, Hood (pen)      Callaghan (o.g.)

## SEASON 1971/72

*6th May, 1972 at Hampden Park; Attendance 106,102;*
*Referee: Mr A. MacKenzie (Larbert)*

**CELTIC 6**      **HIBERNIAN 1**
McNeill, Deans (3), Macari (2)      Gordon

## SEASON 1972/73

*5th May, 1973 at Hampden Park; Attendance 122,714;*
*Referee: Mr J. R. P. Gordon (Newport-on-Tay)*

**RANGERS 3**      **CELTIC 2**
Parlane, Conn, Forsyth      Dalglish, Connelly (pen)

## SEASON 1973/74

*4th May, 1974 at Hampden Park; Attendance 75,959;*
*Referee: Mr W. S. Black (Glasgow)*

**CELTIC 3**      **DUNDEE UNITED 0**
Hood, Murray, Deans

## SEASON 1974/75

*3rd May, 1975 at Hampden Park; Attendance 75,457;*
*Referee: Mr I. M. D. Foote (Glasgow)*

**CELTIC 3**      **AIRDRIEONIANS 1**
Wilson (2), McCluskey (pen)      McCann

## SEASON 1975/76

*1st May, 1976 at Hampden Park; Attendance 85,354;*
*Referee: Mr R. H. Davidson (Airdrie)*

**RANGERS 3**      **HEART OF MIDLOTHIAN 1**
Johnstone (2), MacDonald      Shaw

## SEASON 1976/77

*7th May, 1977 at Hampden Park; Attendance 54,252;*
*Referee: Mr R. B. Valentine (Dundee)*

**CELTIC 1**      **RANGERS 0**
Lynch (pen)

## SEASON 1977/78

*6th May, 1978 at Hampden Park; Attendance 61,563;*
*Referee: Mr B. R. McGinlay (Glasgow)*

**RANGERS 2**      **ABERDEEN 1**
MacDonald, Johnstone      Ritchie

## SEASON 1978/79

*12th May, 1979 at Hampden Park; Attendance 50,610;*
*Referee: Mr B. R. McGinlay (Glasgow)*

**RANGERS 0**      **HIBERNIAN 0**

**REPLAY**

*16th May, 1979 at Hampden Park; Attendance 33,504;*
*Referee: Mr B. R. McGinlay (Glasgow)*

**RANGERS  0**                        **HIBERNIAN 0**
After extra-time

**SECOND REPLAY**

*28th May, 1979 at Hampden Park; Attendance 30,602;*
*Referee: Mr I. M. D. Foote (Glasgow)*

**RANGERS 3**                        **HIBERNIAN 2**
Johnstone (2), Duncan (o.g.)         Higgins, MacLeod (pen)
After extra-time

## SEASON 1979/80

*10th May, 1980 at Hampden Park; Attendance 70,303;*
*Referee: Mr G. B. Smith (Edinburgh)*

**CELTIC 1**                         **RANGERS 0**
McCluskey
After extra-time

## SEASON 1980/81

*9th May, 1981 at Hampden Park; Attendance 53,000;*
*Referee: Mr I. M. D. Foote (Glasgow)*

**RANGERS 0**                        **DUNDEE UNITED 0**
After extra-time

**REPLAY**

*12th May, 1981 at Hampden Park; Attendance 43,099;*
*Referee: Mr I. M. D. Foote (Glasgow)*

**RANGERS 4**                        **DUNDEE UNITED 1**
Cooper, Russell, MacDonald (2)       Dodds

## SEASON 1981/82

*22nd May, 1982 at Hampden Park; Attendance 53,788;*
*Referee: Mr B. R. McGinlay (Balfron)*

**ABERDEEN 4**                       **RANGERS 1**
McLeish, McGhee, Strachan, Cooper    MacDonald
After extra-time – 1-1 after 90 minutes

## SEASON 1982/83

*21st May, 1983 at Hampden Park; Attendance 62,979;*
*Referee: Mr D. F. T. Syme (Rutherglen)*

**ABERDEEN 1**                       **RANGERS 0**
Black
After extra-time

## SEASON 1983/84

*19th May, 1984 at Hampden Park; Attendance 58,900;*
*Referee: Mr R. B. Valentine (Dundee)*

**ABERDEEN 2**                       **CELTIC 1**
Black, McGhee                        P. McStay
After extra-time – 1-1 after 90 minutes

## SEASON 1984/85

*18th May, 1985 at Hampden Park; Attendance 60,346;*
*Referee: Mr B. R. McGinlay (Balfron)*

**CELTIC 2**                         **DUNDEE UNITED 1**
Provan, McGarvey                     Beedie

## SEASON 1985/86

*10th May, 1986 at Hampden Park; Attendance 62,841;*
*Referee: Mr H. Alexander (Irvine)*

**ABERDEEN 3**                       **HEART OF MIDLOTHIAN 0**
Hewitt (2), Stark

## SEASON 1986/87

*16th May, 1987 at Hampden Park; Attendance 51,782;*
*Referee: Mr K. J. Hope (Clarkston)*

**ST. MIRREN 1**                     **DUNDEE UNITED 0**
Ferguson
After extra-time

## SEASON 1987/88

*14th May, 1988 at Hampden Park; Attendance 74,000;*
*Referee: Mr G. B. Smith (Edinburgh)*

**CELTIC 2**                         **DUNDEE UNITED 1**
McAvennie (2)                        Gallacher

## SEASON 1988/89

*20th May, 1989 at Hampden Park; Attendance 72,069;*
*Referee: Mr R. B. Valentine (Dundee)*

**CELTIC 1**                         **RANGERS 0**
Miller

## SEASON 1989/90

*12th May, 1990 at Hampden Park; Attendance 60,493;*
*Referee G. B. Smith (Edinburgh)*

**ABERDEEN 0**                       **CELTIC 0**
After extra-time
Aberdeen won 9-8 on Kicks from the Penalty Mark

## SEASON 1990/91

*18th May, l99l at Hampden Park; Attendance 57,319;*
*Referee: Mr D. F. T. Syme (Rutherglen)*

**MOTHERWELL 4**                     **DUNDEE UNITED 3**
Ferguson, O'Donnell, Angus, Kirk     Bowman, O'Neil, Jackson
After extra-time

## SEASON 1991/92

*9th May, 1992 at Hampden Park; Attendance 44,045;*
*Referee: D. D. Hope (Erskine)*

**RANGERS 2**                        **AIRDRIEONIANS 1**
Hateley, McCoist                     Smith

## SEASON 1992/93

*29th May, 1993 at Celtic Park; Attendance 50,715;*
*Referee: J. McCluskey (Stewarton)*

**RANGERS 2**                        **ABERDEEN 1**
Murray, Hateley                      Richardson

## SEASON 1993/94

*21st May, 1994 at Hampden Park; Attendance 37,709*
*Referee: D. D. Hope (Erskine)*

**DUNDEE UNITED  1**                 **RANGERS 0**
Brewster

# Bairns' B & Q Boost

*Driving rain, sleet and a howling wind. Hardly conditions you would choose to return to after a break in sunny Spain.*

But Falkirk battled the elements and a plucky St. Mirren side to lift the B & Q Cup at a packed Fir Park – and took the first step towards booking their place in the history books.

For, no sooner had Jim Jefferies' men emerged from a warm bath after the 3-0 victory over Saints than they were being reminded that no club had ever lifted the B & Q Cup and the First Division Championship in the same season.

A sunny day at Clydebank five months later saw that theory consigned to the "Says who?" bucket!

And, when the bubbly Bairns clinched the First Division title, they quickly reflected on the boost winning the B & Q Cup had provided during a long and difficult season.

Brockville keeper, Tony Parks, explained: "Coming out of the Premier Division last year, there was a lot of pressure put on us from our fans who expected us to win every game and get promoted without too much trouble.

"Winning the B & Q Cup mid-season took a bit of that pressure off us."

The players further eased the pressure on themselves by booking a short break in Spain.

In fact, it was a real "DIY" job – because the bonuses earned in the earlier rounds had been banked to fund the trip.

However, midway through their Semi-Final at home to Second Division Meadowbank, Falkirk's chance of a trip to the sun or the Final looked as likely as Londoner, Parks, developing a Scottish accent.

They trailed 2-0 until Richard Cadette hit the target, Eddie May knocked in the equaliser, and the tournament's top scorer Cadette popped up again with a late winner.

At the same time, across on the West coast, St. Mirren were staging a similar late smash-and-grab act to rob Ayr of their third Final appearance.

Sammy McGivern had put the Somerset Park men on their way to the December showpiece until Eddie Gallagher pounced with a knock-out one-two.

It was a final pairing which must have delighted the sponsors as much as it did the fans of Saints and the Bairns.

Falkirk's early round victory over Dunfermline marked them as favourites to take the trophy while

*Happy Bairns' Boss–Jim Jefferies.*

Saints could never be treated lightly after knocking out Airdrie at Broomfield.

With Final fever gripping both camps, not even Mother Nature could spoil the party. Tickets sold faster than umbrellas on the day. Just under 14,000 huddled together at Fir Park to create a party atmosphere which belied the foul conditions. And, fittingly, the fans were repaid for their suffering with a classic match.

Saints pummelled the Falkirk rearguard throughout the first half, only to find Parks in inspired form. And, after being "warmed" by boss Jim Jefferies' half-time blast, the Bairns re-emerged to turn up the heat. Neil Duffy opened the scoring two minutes after the restart. Cadette – frozen out in the first half by the Saints defence – grabbed the second two minutes later. And, fittingly, in 64 minutes, Bairns skipper, John Hughes, capped a great performance by heading in the third.

For Falkirk, the glory – and a handsome cheque from the sponsors. For Saints, thoughts of what might have been had they managed to find a way past Parks in that first period. For Parks, the restoration of the self-belief which had slowly ebbed away in

Brian Rice powers through the Saints defence.

John Hughes scores Falkirk's third goal.

recent seasons.

He reflected: "This was my first Cup Final since I'd helped Spurs win the UEFA Cup ten years earlier.

"I was only 21 then and thought I'd play in Finals every year.

"So, I was determined to enjoy the occasion at Fir Park. And I did.

"Saints deserved to be ahead on first half pressure. But everything they hit at me I managed to stop.

"I proved to myself in that game I was on the way back up after having watched my career go down the way for a few years."

Now, Parks has just one regret.

"I'd really like to be able to defend the trophy," he claimed.

"But, after being promoted, we're not eligible to enter.

"So I suppose I'll just have to be satisfied with knowing we made history.

"Rangers' achievements last season overshadowed us. But, the way I look at it, we won our own version of the League and Cup double."

**Ronnie Cully
(Evening Times)**

Bairns' goalscorers, John Hughes, Richard Cadette and Neil Duffy with the B & Q Cup Trophy.

# FIRST ROUND

*Tuesday, 5th October, 1993*

**DUMBARTON 1**      **STRANRAER 2**
A. Foster      T. Sloan, D. Henderson

**Dumbarton:** I. MacFarlane, J. Marsland, R. Fabiani, M. Melvin, P. Martin, S. Gow, M. Mooney, R. McConville, M. McAnenay, J. MacDonald, (A. Willock), A. Foster
Substitutes not used: M. Nelson, M. Monaghan (Goalkeeper)

**Stranraer:** B. Duffy, G. Millar, J. Brown, J. Spittal, K. Brannigan, P. McLean, T. Sloan, A. Grant, (W. Ferguson), G. Duncan, S. Cody, D. Henderson
Substitutes not used: A. Gallagher, S. Ross (Goalkeeper)

**AYR UNITED 3**      **EAST FIFE 1**
C. McGlashan, H. Burns,      G. Allan
S. Bryce

**Ayr United:** W. Spence, G. Robertson, G. Mair, (G. Hood), M. Shotton, J. Traynor, V. Moore, G. Lennox, C. McGlashan, S. McGivern, (B. Scott), H. Burns, S. Bryce
Substitute not used: C. Duncan (Goalkeeper)

**East Fife:** R. Charles, G. Bell, R. Gibb, D. Barron, W. Burns, A. Williamson, G. Allan, (P. Logan), R. Hildersley, R. Scott, (J. Reilly), P. Taylor, B. Andrew
Substitute not used: E. Wilson (Goalkeeper)

**STENHOUSEMUIR 0**      **CLYDEBANK 5**
     K. Lee, C. Flannigan (2),
     M. Nelson, N. Aitken (o.g.)

**Stenhousemuir:** M. Harkness, N. Aitken, E. Hallford, G. Armstrong, J. Clarke, S. Logan, T. Steel, S. Dickov, (J. Irvine), M. Mathieson, D. Roseburgh, (P. O'Neill), J. Fisher
Substitute not used: C. Wilson (Goalkeeper)

**Clydebank:** A. Monaghan, S. Jack, D. Crawford, S. Murdoch, T. Currie, J. Walker, (J. Crawford), K. Lee, A. Lansdowne, (J. Henry), S. Smith, C. Flannigan, M. Nelson

**ALBION ROVERS 2**      **COWDENBEATH 2** (AET –
     2-2 after 90 minutes)
M. McBride, M. Scott      W. Callaghan, I. Lee

**Cowdenbeath Won 3-2 on Kicks from the Penalty Mark**

**Albion Rovers:** R. Burns, J. Kelly, T. Spence, J. McCaffrey, S. Conn, E. Mirner, D. Seggie, (A. McQuade), M. McBride, M. Scott, S. Cadden, D. McKeown
Substitutes not used: J. Gallagher, R. McConnachie (Goalkeeper)

**Cowdenbeath:** S. Filshill, D. Watt, C. Scott, I. Davidson, B. McMahon, R. Carr, (N. Henderson), E. Petrie, (C. Harris), W. Herd, W. Callaghan, P. Hunter, I. Lee
Substitute not used: J. Maloney (Goalkeeper)

*Wednesday, 6th October, 1993*

**MONTROSE 5**      **EAST STIRLINGSHIRE 0**
M. Craib, C. Yeats,
A. Kennedy (2), E. Wolecki

**Montrose:** D. Larter, I. Robertson, M. Craib, J. Tosh, J. Smith, M. Lavelle, C. Yeats, S. Craib, (L. Stephen), D. Grant, (E. Wolecki), A. Kennedy, C. Cooper
Substitute not used: R. Massie (Goalkeeper)

**East Stirlingshire:** G. McDougall, G. Russell, B. Kemp, B. Ross, D. Craig, D. Yates, B. Crews, G. Millar, P. Roberts, M. Geraghty, J. Loney
Substitutes not used: M. McInally, J. Fitzpatrick, P. Imrie (Goalkeeper)

**QUEEN OF THE SOUTH 2**      **BERWICK RANGERS 1**
A. Thomson, P. Kelly      A. Banks

**Queen of the South:** A. Davidson, D. Mills, G. Rowe, B. McKeown, D. Shanks, (P. Kelly), T. Bryce, J. McLaren, (D. McGuire), A. McFarlane, A. Thomson, A. Bell, S. Mallan
Substitute not used: R. McColm (Goalkeeper)

**Berwick Rangers:** G. O'Connor, C. Valentine, A. Banks, J. Couglin, M. Cowan, S. Richardson, M. Wilson, (J. Sokoluk), S. Muir, S. Gallacher, (K. Kane), A. Hall, C. Cunningham

**FALKIRK 2**      **ALLOA 1**
E. May, S. Sloan      W. Newbigging

**Falkirk:** A. Parks, N. Oliver, T. McQueen, D. Weir, J. McLaughlin, B. Rice, E. May, (C. McDonald), C. Duffy, G. Shaw, (K. Young), S. Sloan, C. Taggart
Substitute not used: I. Westwater (Goalkeeper)

**Alloa:** J. Butter, N. Bennett, R. Lee, J. Mackay, K. McCulloch, W. Newbigging, W. Herd, (G. Russell), C. Campbell, S. McCormick, (G. Tait), B. Moffat, S. Ramsay
Substitute not used: N. Binnie (Goalkeeper)

**CLYDE 0**      **ST.MIRREN 1**
     B. Lavety

**Clyde:** L. Fridge, R. McFarlane, (K. Quinn), S. Tennant, D. Bell, J. Thomson, A. Neill, G. Parks, J. Prunty, (B. Strain), I. McConnelli, J. McAulay, J. McCarron

**St. Mirren:** C. Money, R. Dawson, S. Harvie, N. McWhirter, P. McIntyre, N. Orr, A. Bone, (G. McGrotty), J. Fullarton, B. Lavety, J. Hewitt, J. Gardner, (B. Hetherston)
Substitute not used: A. Combe (Goalkeeper)

**BRECHIN CITY 3**      **ARBROATH 1** (AET –
     1-1 after 90 minutes)
R. Brand (2), M. Miller      D. Diver

**Brechin City:** B. Alexander, H. Cairney, D. Fisher, F. Conway, G. Christie, G. Hutt, P. McLaren, (R. Vannett), W. McNeill, (I. Redford), R. Brand, M. Millar, L. Greig

**Arbroath:** D. Jackson, J. Hamilton, S. Florence, B. Mitchell, C. Adam, C. Martin, D. Elliot, (B. Will), K. Tindal, D. Diver, C. McKinnon, G. Buckley
Substitute not used: C. Farnan

**FORFAR ATHLETIC 2**      **MEADOWBANK THISTLE 3**
     (AET – 2-2 after 90 minutes)
R. Smith, D. Bingham      L. Bailey, J. Brock (2)

**Forfar Athletic:** G. Arthur, R. Philliben, A. Hamill, R. Morris, R. Mann, I. McPhee, I. Downie, I. Heddle, R. Smith, G. Donaldson, D. Bingham
Substitutes not used: S. McIntyre, J. Sheridan, N. Russell (Goalkeeper)

**Meadowbank Thistle:** J. McQueen, R. Williamson, D. Fleming, M. Murray, S. Williamson, M. Coyle, (G. Price), L. Bailey, S. Wilson, J. Brock, G. McLeod, M. Duthie, (C. McCartney)

# SECOND ROUND

*Tuesday, 19th October, 1993*

**AIRDRIEONIANS 3**      **HAMILTON ACADEMICAL 1**
K. Black, M. Abercromby,      C. Baptie
J. McIntyre

**Airdrieonians:** W. McCulloch, A. Stewart, C. Honor, P. Jack, J. Sandison, K. Black, J. Boyle, M. Wilson, M. Abercromby, A. Lawrence, J. McIntyre
Substitutes not used: G. Connelly, Anthony Smith

**Hamilton Academical:** A. Ferguson, C. Napier, C. Miller, P. Fitzpatrick, P. McKenzie, (C. McLean), S. McInulty, J. McQuade, (C. Baptie), W. Reid, P. Duffield, G. Clark, K. Ward

**QUEEN'S PARK 0**      **CLYDEBANK 1**
     A. Lansdowne

**Queen's Park:** J. Chalmers, C. Stevenson, I. Maxwell, G. Kerr, S. Fitzpatrick, G. Orr, S. McCormick, R. Caven, B. McPhee, D. Graham, G. Brodie, (D. Brodie)
Substitutes not used: S. Black, D. Mooney (Goalkeeper)

**Clydebank:** A. Monaghan, S. Jack, (J. Crawford), D. Crawford, S. Murdoch, T. Currie, A. Lansdowne, P. Harvey, J. Henry, K. Eadie, (J. Walker), S. Smith, M. Nelson

**AYR UNITED 2**      **BRECHIN CITY 1** (AET –
     1-1 after 90 minutes)
S. McGivern (2)      M. Millar

**Ayr United:** C. Duncan, G. Robertson, G. Mair, M. Shotton, J. Traynor, D. George, V. Moore, (D. Kennedy), C. McGlashan, S. McGivern, H. Burns, R. Jack, (B. Scott)
Substitute not used: G. Grierson (Goalkeeper)

**Brechin City:** B. Alexander, F. Conway, D. Scott, G. Christie, K. Nicolson, G. Hutt, (W. McNeill), R. Vannett, P. O'Brien, L. Greig, M. Millar, R. Brand
Substitute not used: S. Bell

*(left margin, vertical text)* **B & Q Cup Competition – Season 1993/94**

**FALKIRK 3**  COWDENBEATH 0
S. Sloan, C. McDonald (2)

Falkirk: A. Parks, N. Oliver, T. McQueen, D. Weir, J. McLaughlin, J. Hughes, S. Sloan, C. Duffy, (E. May), R. Cadette, (C. Taggart), I. McCall, C. McDonald

Cowdenbeath: S. Filshill, D. Watt, C. Scott, B. McMahon, I. Davidson, R. Russell, (D. Maratea), W. Herd, I. Lee, C. Harris, N. Henderson, W. Callaghan, (R. Carr)
Substitute not used: J. Maloney (Goalkeeper)

**GREENOCK MORTON 2**  ST. MIRREN 4
R. Alexander, J. Tolmie  E. Gallagher (2), B. Lavety, S. Harvie

Greenock Morton: D. Wylie, D. Collins, M. Pickering, S. Rafferty, N. Shearer, S. McArthur, A. McEwan, (D. Lilley), M. Donaghy, (J. Fowler), R. Alexander, D. McInnes, J. Tolmie
Substitute not used: P. Graham (Goalkeeper)

St. Mirren: C. Money, R. Dawson, M. Baker, (S. Harvie), N. McWhirter, P. McIntyre, N. Orr, E. Gallagher, J. Dick, B. Lavety, J. Hewitt, (A. Bone), J. Fullarton
Substitute not used: A. Combe (Goalkeeper)

## Wednesday, 20th October, 1993

**QUEEN OF THE SOUTH 0**  DUNFERMLINE ATHLETIC 6
I. Den Bieman, P. Smith, D. Laing (2), G. O'Boyle (2)

Queen of the South: A. Davidson, D. Mills, W. McGhie, B. McKeown, D. Shanks, A. Bell, P. Kelly, A. McFarlane, A. Thomson, K. Proudfoot, (D. Jackson), J. McLaren
Substitutes not used: D. McGuire, R. McColm (Goalkeeper)

Dunfermline Athletic: J. Hillcoat, J. McNamara, E. Cunnington, (R. Sharp), N. McCathie, (W. Davies), W. A. Baillie, C. Robertson, I. Den Bieman, P. Smith, D. Laing, G. O'Boyle, A. Preston
Substitute not used: L. Hamilton (Goalkeeper)

**MEADOWBANK THISTLE 2**  STIRLING ALBION 0
I. Little, P. Rutherford

Meadowbank Thistle: S. Ellison, R. Williamson, D. Fleming, M. Murray, S. Williamson, I. Little, L. Bailey, J. Brock, (G. Price), P. Rutherford, G. McLeod, D. Coulston, (S. Elder)

Stirling Albion: M. McGeown, A. McKenna, P. Watson, T. Tait, D. Lawrie, C. Mitchell, I. McInnes, (M. McCallum), T. Callaghan, W. Watters, P. Armstrong, D. Flynn, (R. Reilly)

**MONTROSE 0**  STRANRAER 0 (AET)

Montrose Won 6-5 on Kicks from the Penalty Mark

Montrose: D. Larter, I. Robertson, M. Craib,. J. Tosh, J. Smith, M. Lavelle, C. Cooper, (E. Wolecki), C. Yeats, D. Grant, A. Kennedy, L. Stephen
Substitute not used: G. Houghton

Stranraer: S. Ross, G. Millar, J. Hughes, J. Spittal, A. Gallagher, P. McLean, T. Sloan, A. Grant, G. Duncan, S. Cody, D. Henderson, (W. Ferguson)
Substitutes not used: J. Brown, B. Duffy (Goalkeeper)

## THIRD ROUND

## Tuesday, 26th October, 1993

**AIRDRIEONIANS 0**  ST. MIRREN 1 (AET)
P. McIntyre

Airdrieonians: W. McCulloch, A. Stewart, D. Kirkwood, P. Jack, C. Honor, K. Black, J. Boyle, M. Wilson, M. Abercromby, (W. Reid), A. Lawrence, J. McIntyre, (Anthony Smith)
Substitute not used: J. Martin (Goalkeeper)

St. Mirren: C. Money, R. Dawson, M. Baker, N. McWhirter, (B. McLaughlin), P. McIntyre, N. Orr, E. Gallagher, (A. Bone), J. Dick, B. Lavety, J. Hewitt, R. Gillies
Substitute not used: A. Combe (Goalkeepr)

**AYR UNITED 2**  CLYDEBANK 0
S. Murdoch (o.g.), H. Burns

Ayr United: C. Duncan, D. Kennedy, G. Robertson, M. Shotton, J. Traynor, (G. Hood), D. George, G. Lennox, C. McGlashan, S. McGivern, H. Burns, S. Bryce, (R. Jack)
Substitute not used: G. Grierson (Goalkeeper)

Clydebank: A. Monaghan, S. Jack, I. Thomson, S. Murdoch, S. Sweeney, T. Currie, A. Lansdowne, J. Henry, K. Lee, J. Walker, (J. Crawford), M. Nelson
Substitute not used: D. Crawford

## Wednesday, 27th October, 1993

**MEADOWBANK THISTLE 1**  MONTROSE 1
(AET – 1-1 after 90 minutes)
P. Rutherford  A. Kennedy

Meadowbank Thistle Won 3-1 on Kicks from the Penalty Mark

Meadowbank Thistle: S. Ellison, S. Elder, (M. Hutchison), D. Fleming, M. Murray, T. Graham, I. Little, L. Bailey, S. Wilson, P. Rutherford, G. McLeod, J. Brock, (M. Coyle)
Substitute not used: R. Douglas (Goalkeeper)

Montrose: D. Larter, G. Houghton, I. Robertson, M. Craib, D. Grant, N. Irvine, (M. Lavelle), C. Cooper, (S. Craib), C. Yeats, I. McKenna, A. Kennedy, L. Stephen
Substitute not used: R. Massie (Goalkeeper)

**FALKIRK 4**  DUNFERMLINE ATHLETIC 1
K. Drinkell,  R. Sharp
R. Cadette (3)

Falkirk: I. Westwater, N. Oliver, T. McQueen, D. Weir, J. McLaughlin, (S. Sloan), J. Hughes, E. May, K. Drinkell, R. Cadette, B. Rice, (C. McDonald), C. Duffy
Substitute not used: A. Parks (Goalkeeper)

Dunfermline Athletic: J. Hillcoat, J. McNamara, E. Cunnington, R. Sharp, W. A. Baillie, P. Smith, I. Den Bieman, (D. McWilliams), C. Robertson, H. French, D. Laing, (C. Sinclair), S. Petrie
Substitute not used: L. Hamilton (Goalkeeper)

## SEMI-FINALS

### Tuesday, 2nd November, 1993

**FALKIRK 3**  MEADOWBANK THISTLE 2
E. May, R. Cadette (2)  I. Little, G. MacLeod

Falkirk: A. Parks, C. Duffy, T. McQueen, D. Weir, J. Hughes, B. Rice, E. May, (G. Shaw), K. Drinkell, R. Cadette, S. Sloan, C. McDonald, (S. MacKenzie)
Substitute not used: I. Westwater (Goalkeeper)

Meadowbank Thistle: S. Ellison, I. MacLeod, D. Fleming, M. Murray, S. Williamson, I. Little, L. Bailey, S. Wilson, (D. Coulston), P. Rutherford, G. McLeod, J. Brock, (M. Coyle)
Substitute not used: R. Douglas (Goalkeeper)

**AYR UNITED 1**  ST. MIRREN 2
S. McGivern  E. Gallagher (2)

Ayr United: C. Duncan, D. Kennedy, G. Robertson, M. Shotton, G. Hood, D. George, G. Lennox, (J. Traynor), C. McGlashan, S. McGivern, H. Burns, S. Bryce, (R. Jack)
Substitute not used: G. Grierson (Goalkeeper)

St. Mirren: C. Money, R. Dawson, M. Baker, N. McWhirter, P. McIntyre, N. Orr, E. Gallagher, J. Dick, (B. McLaughlin), B. Lavety, J. Hewitt, D. Elliot
Substitutes not used: J. Gardner, A. Combe (Goalkeeper)

---

## FINAL

### Sunday, 12th December, 1993
### Fir Park, Motherwell
### FALKIRK 3  ST. MIRREN 0

Falkirk: A. Parks, C. Duffy, T. McQueen, D. Weir, J. McLaughlin, J. Hughes, E. May, K. Drinkell, (G. Shaw), R. Cadette, I. McCall (N. Oliver), B. Rice
Substitute not used: I. Westwater (Goalkeeper)

St. Mirren: C. Money, R. Dawson, M. Baker, N. McWhirter, B. McLaughlin, N. Orr, A. Bone, (R. Gillies), J. Dick, B. Lavety, J. Hewitt, (P. McIntyre), D. Elliot
Substitute not used: A. Combe (Goalkeeper)

Scorers: Falkirk – C. Duffy, J. Hughes, R. Cadette
Referee: D. D. Hope (Erskine)
Attendance: 13,763

---

## ROUND BY ROUND GOALS ANALYSIS

|  | No. of Goals Scored | Ties Played | Average Per Game |
|---|---|---|---|
| First Round | 37 | 10 | 3.7 |
| Second Round | 25 | 8 | 3.1 |
| Third Round | 10 | 4 | 2.5 |
| Semi-Finals | 8 | 2 | 4.0 |
| Final | 3 | 1 | 3.0 |
| Total No. of Goals Scored | 83 | | |
| Ties Played | 25 | | |
| Average Goals per Game | 3.3 | | |

## 1983/84

**Premier Division**
23 B. McClair (Celtic)
18 W. Irvine (Hibernian)
15 D. Dodds (Dundee United)
   J. Robertson (Heart of Midlothian)
13 M. McGhee (Aberdeen)
   G. Strachan (Aberdeen)
   W. McCall (Dundee)
   F. McDougall (St Mirren)
12 J. Hewitt (Aberdeen)
   I. Ferguson (Dundee)
   F. McAvennie (St Mirren)
   J. Scanlon (St Mirren)

**First Division**
19 I. M. Campbell (Brechin City)
17 J. F. Frye (Clyde)
   J. McNeil (Morton)
16 D. Robertson (Morton)
   J. Kerr (Raith Rovers)
15 A. McInally (Ayr United)
   J. Coyle (Dumbarton)
13 K. Ashwood (Dumbarton)
   J. Bourke (Dumbarton)
   K. McDowall (Partick Thistle)

**Second Division**
22 J. Liddle (Forfar Athletic)
18 J. Harley (Arbroath)
17 A. Grant (Queen's Park)
16 G. Durie (East Fife)
14 G. Forrest (Stenhousemuir)
13 C. Gibson (East Stirlingshire)
   K. Macdonald (Forfar Athletic)
   G. Murray (Stenhousemuir)
12 J. Clark (Forfar Athletic)
   W. Irvine (Stirling Albion)

## 1984/85

**Premier Division**
22 F. McDougall (Aberdeen)
19 B. McClair (Celtic)
17 E. Black (Aberdeen)
16 F. McAvennie (St Mirren)
15 W. Stark (Aberdeen)
   F. McGarvey (Celtic)
14 P. Sturrock (Dundee United)
   M. Johnston (Celtic)
12 A. McCoist (Rangers)
10 E. Bannon (Dundee United)

**First Division**
22 G. McCoy (Falkirk)
21 D. MacCabe (Airdrieonians)
19 J. F. Frye (Clyde)
17 J. Flood (Airdrieonians)
   K. Eadie (Brechin City)
14 K. Macdonald (Forfar Athletic)
   A. Sprott (Meadowbank Thistle)
12 G. Murray (East Fife)
   B. Millar (Kilmarnock)
   A. Logan (Partick Thistle)

**Second Division**
27 B. Slaven (Albion Rovers)
22 K. Wright (Raith Rovers)
21 W. Irvine (Stirling Albion)
19 P. Smith (Raith Rovers)
18 J. Nicholson (Queen's Park)
16 D. Lloyd (Alloa)
   K. Ward (Cowdenbeath)
15 J. Watson (Dunfermline Athletic)
12 I. Paterson (Cowdenbeath)
   S. Maskrey (East Stirlingshire)
   D. Somner (Montrose)

## 1985/86

**Premier Division**
24 A. McCoist (Rangers)
22 B. McClair (Celtic)
20 J. Robertson (Heart of Midlothian)
19 S. Cowan (Hibernian)
15 M. Johnston (Celtic)
14 F. McDougall (Aberdeen)
   R. Stephen (Dundee)
12 D. Dodds (Dundee United)
   A. Clark (Heart of Midlothian)
11 E. Bannon (Dundee United)
   J. Brown (Dundee)

**First Division**
23 J. Brogan (Hamilton Academical)
22 K. Eadie (Brechin City)
15 J. Gilmour (Falkirk)
14 S. Kirk (East Fife)
   I. Bryson (Kilmarnock)
   J. McNeil (Morton)
13 G. McCoy (Dumbarton)
12 J. F. Frye (Clyde)
11 J. Flood (Airdrieonians)
   M. Jamieson (Alloa)
   S. Sorbie (Alloa)
   J. McNaught (Hamilton Academical)
   S. McGivern (Kilmarnock)
   G. Smith (Partick Thistle)

**Second Division**
24 J. Watson (Dunfermline Athletic)
21 P. Smith (Raith Rovers)
   K. Wright (Raith Rovers)
17 D. Jackson (Meadowbank Thistle)
   A. Lawrence (Meadowbank Thistle)
   W. Irvine (Stirling Albion)
15 C. McGlashan (Cowdenbeath)
   I. M. Campbell (Dunfermline Athletic)
   T. Bryce (Queen of the South)
   S. Cochrane (Queen of the South)

## 1986/87

**Premier Division**
35 B. McClair (Celtic)
33 A. McCoist (Rangers)
23 M. Johnston (Celtic)
19 R. Fleck (Rangers)
16 J. Robertson (Heart of Midlothian)
   I. Ferguson (Dundee United)
15 A. McInally (Celtic)
13 J. Colquhoun (Heart of Midlothian)
12 G. Harvey (Dundee)
   W. Stark (Aberdeen)

**First Division**
23 R. Alexander (Morton)
21 G. McCoy (Dumbarton)
20 T. Bryce (Queen of the South)
18 D. Robertson (Morton)
17 O. Coyle (Dumbarton)
   K. Macdonald (Forfar Athletic)
15 B. McNaughton (East Fife)
13 D. MacCabe (Airdrieonians)
   J. Watson (Dunfermline Athletic)
12 C. Adam (Brechin City)
   J. Murphy (Clyde)
   S. Burgess (East Fife)

**Second Division**
26 J. Sludden (Ayr United)
25 W. Brown (St Johnstone)
22 C. Harris (Raith Rovers)
21 J. McGachie (Meadowbank Thistle)
14 S. Sorbie (Alloa)
   J. Fotheringham (Arbroath)
   W. Blackie (Cowdenbeath)
   R. Grant (Cowdenbeath)
13 R. Caven (Queen's Park)
   K. Wright (Raith Rovers)
   B. Cleland (Stranraer)

## 1987/88

**Premier Division**
33 T. Coyne (Dundee)
31 A. McCoist (Rangers)
26 J. Robertson (Heart of Midlothian)
   A. Walker (Celtic)
15 J. Colquhoun (Heart of Midlothian)
   F. McAvennie (Celtic)
   K. Wright (Dundee)
13 C. Robertson (Dunfermline Athletic)
11 I. Ferguson (Dundee United)
10 J. Bett (Aberdeen)
   P. Chalmers (St Mirren)
   I. Durrant (Rangers)
   P. Kane (Hibernian)

**First Division**
25 G. Dalziel (Raith Rovers)
20 D. MacCabe (Airdrieonians)
   K. Macdonald (Forfar Athletic)
17 J. Hughes (Queen of the South)
   P. Hunter (East Fife)
16 C. Harkness (Kilmarnock)
   C. McGlashan (Clyde)
   D. Walker (Clyde)
15 C. Campbell (Airdrieonians)
14 O. Coyle (Dumbarton)
   C. Harris (Raith Rovers)
   J. McGachie (Meadowbank Thistle)

**Second Division**
31 J. Sludden (Ayr United)
23 J. Brogan (Stirling Albion)
   H. Templeton (Ayr United)
19 T. Walker (Ayr United)
17 P. O'Brien (Queen's Park)
16 W. Watters (St Johnstone)
15 G. Buckley (Brechin City)
14 P. Rutherford (Alloa)
13 T. Coyle (St Johnstone)
   C. Gibson (Stirling Albion)

## 1988/89

**Premier Division**
16 M. McGhee (Celtic)
   C. Nicholas (Aberdeen)
14 S. Kirk (Motherwell)
13 S. Archibald (Hibernian)
12 K. Drinkell (Rangers)
   F. McAvennie (Celtic)
11 P. Chalmers (St Mirren)
10 M-M. Paatelainen (Dundee United)
9 T. Coyne (Dundee/Celtic)
   K. Gallacher (Dundee United)
   A. McCoist (Rangers)
   W. Stark (Celtic)

**First Division**
22 K. Macdonald (Airdrieonians)
21 K. Eadie (Clydebank)
19 G. McCoy (Partick Thistle)
18 R. Jack (Dunfermline Athletic)
17 H. Templeton (Ayr United)
16 T. Bryce (Clydebank)
   O. Coyle (Clydebank)
   C. McGlashan (Clyde)
15 J. Sludden (Ayr United)
14 C. Campbell (Airdrieonians)
   J. Watson (Dunfermline Athletic)

**Second Division**
23 C. Lytwyn (Alloa)
21 G. Murray (Montrose)
18 C. Gibson (Stirling Albion)
16 W. McNeill (East Stirlingshire)
15 C. Adam (Brechin City)
   J. Brogan (Stirling Albion)
   J. Chapman (Albion Rovers)
   A. Graham (Albion Rovers)
13 S. MacIver (Dumbarton)
11 J. Fotheringham (Arbroath)
   D. Lloyd (Stranraer)
   P. Teevan (Albion Rovers)

## 1989/90

**Premier Division**
17 J. Robertson (Heart of Midlothian)
16 R. Jack (Dunfermline Athletic)
15 M. Johnston (Rangers)
14 A. McCoist (Rangers)
13 W. Dodds (Dundee)
12 S. Crabbe (Heart of Midlothian)
   D. McWilliams (Falkirk)
11 N. Cusack (Motherwell)
   C. Nicholas (Aberdeen)
   K. Wright (Dundee)

**First Division**
27 O. Coyle (Airdrieonians/Clydebank)
21 K. Eadie (Clydebank)
20 G. Dalziel (Raith Rovers)
19 R. Grant (St Johnstone)
18 C. Campbell (Partick Thistle)
17 D. McWilliams (Falkirk)
15 K. Macdonald (Raith Rovers/Airdrieonians)
13 A. Moore (St Johnstone)
12 S. Maskrey (St Johnstone)
11 R. Alexander (Morton)
   J. Charnley (Partick Thistle)
   C. McGlashan (Clyde)

**Second Division**
23 W. Watters (Kilmarnock)
20 C. Gibson (Dumbarton)
19 S. MacIver (Dumbarton)
16 J. Reid (Stirling Albion)
   A. Ross (Cowdenbeath)
   S. Sloan (Berwick Rangers)
15 D. Lloyd (Stirling Albion)
   S. McCormick (Stenhousemuir)
14 P. Hunter (East Fife)
   V. Moore (Stirling Albion)

## 1990/91

**Premier Division**
18 T. Coyne (Celtic)
14 D. Arnott (Motherwell)
   H. Gillhaus (Aberdeen)
13 E. Jess (Aberdeen)
12 D. Jackson (Dundee United)
   J. Robertson (Heart of Midlothian)
   M. Walters (Rangers)
11 M. Johnston (Rangers)
   A. McCoist (Rangers)
10 M. Hateley (Rangers)

**First Division**
29 K. Eadie (Clydebank)
25 G. Dalziel (Raith Rovers)
21 D. MacCabe (Morton)
20 O. Coyle (Airdrieonians)
18 K. Wright (Dundee)
16 S. Stainrod (Dundee)
15 W. Dodds (Dundee)
   S. McGivern (Falkirk)
   D. Roseburgh (Meadowbank Thistle)
14 G. McCluskey (Hamilton Academical)
   P. Ritchie (Brechin City)
   R. Williamson (Kilmarnock)

**Second Division**
17 M. Hendry (Queen's Park)
   A. Speirs (Stenhousemuir)
16 A. Ross (Cowdenbeath/Berwick Rangers)
15 A. MacKenzie (Cowdenbeath)
14 C. Harkness (Stranraer)
   D. Lloyd (Stirling Albion)
   J. McQuade (Dumbarton)
   K. Todd (Berwick Rangers)
13 S. McCormick (Stenhousemuir)
   V. Moore (Stirling Albion)

## 1991/92

### Premier Division
34 A. McCoist (Rangers)
21 M. Hateley (Rangers)
    C. Nicholas (Celtic)
18 P. Wright (St Johnstone)
15 T. Coyne (Celtic)
    S. Crabbe (Heart of Midlothian)
    D. Ferguson (Dundee United)
14 G. Creaney (Celtic)
    J. Robertson (Heart of Midlothian)
12 E. Jess (Aberdeen)

### First Division
26 G. Dalziel (Raith Rovers)
22 K. Eadie (Clydebank)
19 W. Dodds (Dundee)
18 A. Mathie (Morton)
    C. McGlashan (Partick Thistle)
17 W. Watters (Stirling Albion)
14 G. Clark (Hamilton Academical)
    A. Graham (Ayr United)
13 T. Smith (Hamilton Academical)
12 C. Brewster (Raith Rovers)
    G. McCluskey (Hamilton Academical)

### Second Division
26 A. Thomson (Queen of the South)
21 G. Buckley (Cowdenbeath)
    J. Sludden (East Fife)
19 J. Gilmour (Dumbarton)
18 D. Diver (East Stirlingshire)
    P. Lamont (Cowdenbeath)
17 S. McCormick (Queen's Park)
16 R. Scott (East Fife)
    D. Thompson (Clyde)
14 T. Sloan (Stranraer)

## 1992/93

### Premier Division
34 A. McCoist (Rangers)
22 D. Shearer (Aberdeen)
19 M. Hateley (Rangers)
16 P. Connolly (Dundee United)
    W. Dodds (Dundee)
    M-M. Paatelainen (Aberdeen)
14 P. Wright (St Johnstone)
13 S. Booth (Aberdeen)
    D. Jackson (Hibernian)
    A. Payton (Celtic)

### First Division
32 G. Dalziel (Raith Rovers)
22 C. Brewster (Raith Rovers)
21 C. Flannigan (Clydebank)
20 K. Eadie (Clydebank)
18 B. Lavety (St Mirren)
15 J. McQuade (Dumbarton)
13 A. Mathie (Morton)
12 H. French (Dunfermline Athletic)
    E. Gallagher (St Mirren)
    J. Henry (Clydebank)
    M. Mooney (Dumbarton)

### Second Division
26 M. Mathieson (Stenhousemuir)
23 A. Ross (Brechin City)
21 S. Petrie (Forfar Athletic)
    A. Thomson (Queen of the South)
19 B. Moffat (Alloa)
    T. Sloan (Stranraer)
    S. Sorbie (Arbroath)
16 F. McGarvey (Clyde)
    M. Scott (Albion Rovers)
    R. Scott (East Fife)

## 1993/94

### Premier Division
22 M. Hateley (Rangers)
17 D. Shearer (Aberdeen)
16 C. Brewster (Dundee United)
    K. Wright (Hibernian)
14 A. Craig (Partick Thistle)
13 R. Grant (Partick Thistle)
12 T. Coyne (Motherwell)
    G. Durie (Rangers)
10 P. McGinlay (Celtic)
    J. Robertson (Heart of Midlothian)

### First Division
19 P. Duffield (Hamilton Academical)
18 R. Cadette (Falkirk)
17 G. O'Boyle (Dunfermline Athletic)
15 H. French (Dunfermline Athletic)
13 C. Gibson (Dumbarton)
    W. Watters (Stirling Albion)
12 S. McGivern (Ayr United)
11 R. Alexander (Greenock Morton)
    K. Eadie (Clydebank)
    C. Flannigan (Clydebank)
    A. Tod (Dunfermline Athletic)

### Second Division
29 A. Thomson (Queen of the South)
18 J. O'Neill (Queen's Park)
17 M. Scott (Albion Rovers)
16 D. Diver (2 for Alloa,
    10 for Arbroath, 4 for Stranraer)
    T. Sloan (Stranraer)
15 W. Irvine (Berwick Rangers)
14 M. Mathieson (Stenhousemuir)
13 D. Bingham (Forfar Athletic)
    J. Sludden (Stenhousemuir)
12 D. Grant (Montrose)
    W. Hawke (Berwick Rangers)
    I. Little (Meadowbank Thistle)
    M. McCallum (East Stirlingshire)

*Mark Hateley . . . last season's Premier Division top scorer.*

# Leading Goalscorers – Club By Club Since 1980/81

## ABERDEEN

| Season | Div | No.of Goals | Player |
|---|---|---|---|
| 1980-81 | P | 13 | M. McGhee |
| 1981-82 | P | 11 | J. Hewitt |
| 1982-83 | P | 16 | M. McGhee |
| 1983-84 | P | 13 | M. McGhee |
|  |  |  | G. Strachan |
| 1984-85 | P | 22 | F. McDougall |
| 1985-86 | P | 14 | F. McDougall |
| 1986-87 | P | 12 | W. Stark |
| 1987-88 | P | 10 | J. Bett |
| 1988-89 | P | 16 | C. Nicholas |
| 1989-90 | P | 11 | C. Nicholas |
| 1990-91 | P | 14 | H. Gillhaus |
| 1991-92 | P | 12 | E. Jess |
| 1992-93 | P | 22 | D. Shearer |
| 1993-94 | P | 17 | D. Shearer |

## AIRDRIEONIANS

| Season | Div | No.of Goals | Player |
|---|---|---|---|
| 1980-81 | P | 10 | A. Clark |
| 1981-82 | F | 15 | A. Clark |
| 1982-83 | F | 12 | B. Millar |
| 1983-84 | F | 11 | J. Flood |
| 1984-85 | F | 21 | D. MacCabe |
| 1985-86 | F | 11 | J. Flood |
| 1986-87 | F | 13 | D. MacCabe |
| 1987-88 | F | 20 | D. MacCabe |
| 1988-89 | F | 22 | K. Macdonald |
| 1989-90 | F | 10 | O. Coyle |
| 1990-91 | F | 20 | O. Coyle |
| 1991-92 | P | 11 | O. Coyle |
| 1992-93 | P | 9 | O. Coyle |
| 1993-94 | F | 10 | D. Kirkwood |

## ALBION ROVERS

| Season | Div | No.of Goals | Player |
|---|---|---|---|
| 1980-81 | S | 12 | I. Campbell |
| 1981-82 | S | 16 | S. Evans |
| 1982-83 | S | 13 | S. Evans |
| 1983-84 | S | 11 | T. McGorm |
| 1984-85 | S | 27 | B. Slaven |
| 1985-86 | S | 6 | S. Conn |
|  |  |  | V. Kasule |
|  |  |  | A. Rodgers |
| 1986-87 | S | 11 | C. Wilson |
| 1987-88 | S | 10 | A. Graham |
| 1988-89 | S | 15 | J. Chapman |
|  |  |  | A. Graham |
| 1989-90 | F | 10 | M. McAnenay |
| 1990-91 | S | 12 | M. McAnenay |
| 1991-92 | S | 11 | G. McCoy |
| 1992-93 | S | 16 | M. Scott |
| 1993-94 | S | 17 | M. Scott |

## ALLOA

| Season | Div | No.of Goals | Player |
|---|---|---|---|
| 1980-81 | S | 14 | A. Holt |
| 1981-82 | S | 14 | S. Murray |
| 1982-83 | F | 12 | L. McComb |
| 1983-84 | F | 10 | D. Lloyd |
| 1984-85 | S | 16 | D. Lloyd |
| 1985-86 | F | 11 | M. Jamieson |
|  |  |  | S. Sorbie |
| 1986-87 | S | 14 | S. Sorbie |
| 1987-88 | S | 14 | P. Rutherford |
| 1988-89 | S | 23 | C. Lytwyn |
| 1989-90 | F | 9 | P. Lamont |
| 1990-91 | S | 11 | J. Irvine |
| 1991-92 | S | 12 | M. Hendry |
| 1992-93 | S | 19 | B. Moffat |
| 1993-94 | S | 7 | W. Newbigging |

## ARBROATH

| Season | Div | No.of Goals | Player |
|---|---|---|---|
| 1980-81 | S | 15 | J. Harley |
| 1981-82 | S | 21 | D. Robb |
| 1982-83 | S | 15 | W. Gavine |
|  |  |  | W. Steele |
| 1983-84 | S | 18 | J. Harley |
| 1984-85 | S | 6 | R. Brown |
| 1985-86 | S | 14 | M. McWalter |
| 1986-87 | S | 14 | J. Fotheringham |
| 1987-88 | S | 13 | A. McKenna |
| 1988-89 | S | 11 | J. Fotheringham |
| 1989-90 | S | 12 | J. Marshall |
| 1990-91 | S | 10 | M. Bennett |
|  |  |  | S. Sorbie |
| 1991-92 | S | 12 | S. Sorbie |
| 1992-93 | S | 19 | S. Sorbie |
| 1993-94 | S | 10 | D. Diver |

## AYR UNITED

| Season | Div | No.of Goals | Player |
|---|---|---|---|
| 1980-81 | F | 10 | J. F. Frye |
|  |  |  | E. Morris |
| 1981-82 | F | 13 | J. F. Frye |
| 1982-83 | F | 7 | J. F. Frye |
|  |  |  | M. Larnach |
|  |  |  | A. McInally |
| 1983-84 | F | 15 | A. McInally |
| 1984-85 | F | 8 | G. Collins |
|  |  |  | J. McNiven |
| 1985-86 | F | 6 | D. Irons |
| 1986-87 | S | 26 | J. Sludden |
| 1987-88 | S | 31 | J. Sludden |
| 1988-89 | F | 17 | H. Templeton |
| 1989-90 | F | 10 | T. Bryce |
| 1990-91 | F | 11 | T. Bryce |
| 1991-92 | F | 14 | A. Graham |
| 1992-93 | F | 9 | A. Graham |
| 1993-94 | F | 12 | S. McGivern |

## BERWICK RANGERS

| Season | Div | No.of Goals | Player |
|---|---|---|---|
| 1980-81 | F | 8 | E. Tait |
| 1981-82 | S | 16 | M. Lawson |
| 1982-83 | S | 8 | I. Cashmore |
|  |  |  | S. Romaines |
| 1983-84 | S | 9 | P. Davidson |
|  |  |  | A. O'Hara |
| 1984-85 | S | 9 | P. Davidson |
| 1985-86 | S | 12 | J. Sokoluk |
| 1986-87 | S | 8 | E. Tait |
| 1987-88 | S | 3 | M. Cameron |
|  |  |  | H. Douglas |
|  |  |  | T. Graham |
|  |  |  | G. Leitch |
|  |  |  | C. Lytwyn |
|  |  |  | M. Thompson |
| 1988-89 | S | 10 | J. Hughes |
| 1989-90 | S | 16 | S. Sloan |
| 1990-91 | S | 14 | K. Todd |
| 1991-92 | S | 12 | S. Bickmore |
| 1992-93 | S | 11 | D. Scott |
| 1993-94 | S | 15 | W. Irvine |

## BRECHIN CITY

| Season | Div | No.of Goals | Player |
|---|---|---|---|
| 1980-81 | S | 11 | I. M. Campbell |
| 1981-82 | S | 16 | I. M. Campbell |
| 1982-83 | S | 23 | I. M. Campbell |
| 1983-84 | F | 19 | I. M. Campbell |
| 1984-85 | F | 17 | K. Eadie |
| 1985-86 | F | 22 | K. Eadie |
| 1986-87 | F | 12 | C. Adam |
| 1987-88 | S | 15 | G. Buckley |
| 1988-89 | S | 15 | C. Adam |
| 1989-90 | S | 12 | G. Lees |
| 1990-91 | F | 14 | P. Ritchie |
| 1991-92 | S | 12 | P. Ritchie |
| 1992-93 | S | 23 | A. Ross |
| 1993-94 | F | 10 | M. Miller |

## CELTIC

| Season | Div | No.of Goals | Player |
|---|---|---|---|
| 1980-81 | P | 23 | F. McGarvey |
| 1981-82 | P | 21 | G. McCluskey |
| 1982-83 | P | 29 | C. Nicholas |
| 1983-84 | P | 23 | B. McClair |
| 1984-85 | P | 19 | B. McClair |
| 1985-86 | P | 22 | B. McClair |
| 1986-87 | P | 35 | B. McClair |
| 1987-88 | P | 26 | A. Walker |
| 1988-89 | P | 16 | M. McGhee |
| 1989-90 | P | 8 | D. Dziekanowski |
| 1990-91 | P | 18 | T. Coyne |
| 1991-92 | P | 21 | C. Nicholas |
| 1992-93 | P | 13 | A. Payton |
| 1993-94 | P | 10 | P. McGinlay |

## CLYDE

| Season | Div | No.of Goals | Player |
|---|---|---|---|
| 1980-81 | S | 19 | D. Masterton |
| 1981-82 | S | 23 | D. Masterton |
| 1982-83 | F | 14 | D. Masterton |
| 1983-84 | F | 17 | J. F. Frye |
| 1984-85 | F | 19 | J. F. Frye |
| 1985-86 | F | 12 | J. F. Frye |
| 1986-87 | F | 12 | J. Murphy |
| 1987-88 | F | 16 | C. McGlashan |
| | | | D. Walker |
| 1988-89 | S | 16 | C. McGlashan |
| 1989-90 | S | 11 | C. McGlashan |
| 1990-91 | F | 8 | S. Mallan |
| 1991-92 | S | 16 | D. Thompson |
| 1992-93 | S | 16 | F. McGarvey |
| 1993-94 | F | 5 | I. McConnell |
| | | | G. Parks |

## CLYDEBANK

| Season | Div | No.of Goals | Player |
|---|---|---|---|
| 1980-81 | F | 18 | B. Millar |
| 1981-82 | F | 20 | B. Millar |
| 1982-83 | F | 21 | R. Williamson |
| 1983-84 | F | 10 | T. Coyne |
| 1984-85 | F | 11 | M. Conroy |
| 1985-86 | P | 7 | M. Conroy |
| | | | D. Lloyd |
| 1986-87 | P | 9 | M. Conroy |
| | | | S. Gordon |
| 1987-88 | F | 11 | M. Conroy |
| 1988-89 | F | 21 | K. Eadie |
| 1989-90 | F | 21 | K. Eadie |
| 1990-91 | F | 29 | K. Eadie |
| 1991-92 | F | 22 | K. Eadie |
| 1992-93 | F | 21 | C. Flannigan |
| 1993-94 | F | 11 | K. Eadie |
| | | | C. Flannigan |

## COWDENBEATH

| Season | Div | No.of Goals | Player |
|---|---|---|---|
| 1980-81 | S | 18 | J. Liddle |
| 1981-82 | S | 16 | G. Forrest |
| 1982-83 | S | 13 | W. Gibson |
| | | | C. McIntosh |
| 1983-84 | S | 7 | I. Paterson |
| 1984-85 | S | 16 | K. Ward |
| 1985-86 | S | 15 | C. McGlashan |
| 1986-87 | S | 14 | W. Blackie |
| | | | R. Grant |
| 1987-88 | S | 11 | R. Grant |
| 1988-89 | S | 8 | A. McGonigal |
| 1989-90 | S | 16 | A. Ross |
| 1990-91 | S | 15 | A. MacKenzie |
| 1991-92 | S | 26 | G. Buckley |
| 1992-93 | F | 9 | W. Callaghan |
| 1993-94 | S | 11 | W. Callaghan |

## DUMBARTON

| Season | Div | No.of Goals | Player |
|---|---|---|---|
| 1980-81 | F | 14 | B. Gallagher |
| 1981-82 | F | 9 | R. Blair |
| 1982-83 | F | 10 | R. Blair |
| 1983-84 | F | 15 | J. Coyle |
| 1984-85 | P | 7 | J. Coyle |
| 1985-86 | F | 13 | G. McCoy |
| 1986-87 | F | 21 | G. McCoy |
| 1987-88 | F | 14 | O. Coyle |
| 1988-89 | S | 13 | S. MacIver |
| 1989-90 | S | 20 | C. Gibson |
| 1990-91 | S | 14 | J. McQuade |
| 1991-92 | S | 19 | J. Gilmour |
| 1992-93 | F | 15 | J. McQuade |
| 1993-94 | F | 13 | C. Gibson |

## DUNDEE

| Season | Div | No.of Goals | Player |
|---|---|---|---|
| 1980-81 | F | 19 | E. Sinclair |
| 1981-82 | P | 12 | I. Ferguson |
| 1982-83 | P | 9 | I. Ferguson |
| 1983-84 | P | 13 | W. McCall |
| 1984-85 | P | 8 | R. Stephen |
| 1985-86 | P | 14 | R. Stephen |
| 1986-87 | P | 12 | G. Harvey |
| 1987-88 | P | 33 | T. Coyne |
| 1988-89 | P | 9 | T. Coyne |
| 1989-90 | P | 13 | W. Dodds |
| 1990-91 | F | 18 | K. Wright |
| 1991-92 | F | 19 | W. Dodds |
| 1992-93 | P | 16 | W. Dodds |
| 1993-94 | P | 6 | D. Ristic |

## DUNDEE UNITED

| Season | Div | No.of Goals | Player |
|---|---|---|---|
| 1980-81 | P | 14 | D. Dodds |
| 1981-82 | P | 15 | P. Sturrock |
| 1982-83 | P | 22 | D. Dodds |
| 1983-84 | P | 15 | D. Dodds |
| 1984-85 | P | 14 | P. Sturrock |
| 1985-86 | P | 12 | D. Dodds |
| 1986-87 | P | 16 | I. Ferguson |
| 1987-88 | P | 11 | I. Ferguson |
| 1988-89 | P | 10 | M-M. Paatelainen |
| 1989-90 | P | 7 | D. Jackson |
| | | | M-M. Paatelainen |
| 1990-91 | P | 12 | D. Jackson |
| 1991-92 | P | 17 | D. Ferguson |
| 1992-93 | P | 16 | P. Connolly |
| 1993-94 | P | 16 | C. Brewster |

## DUNFERMLINE ATHLETIC

| Season | Div | No.of Goals | Player |
|---|---|---|---|
| 1980-81 | F | 20 | A. McNaughton |
| 1981-82 | F | 13 | A. McNaughton |
| 1982-83 | F | 8 | R. Forrest |
| | | | S. Morrison |
| 1983-84 | S | 9 | S. Morrison |
| 1984-85 | S | 15 | J. Watson |
| 1985-86 | S | 24 | J. Watson |
| 1986-87 | F | 13 | J. Watson |
| 1987-88 | P | 13 | C. Robertson |
| 1988-89 | F | 18 | R. Jack |
| 1989-90 | P | 16 | R. Jack |
| 1990-91 | P | 8 | R. Jack |
| 1991-92 | P | 6 | D. Moyes |
| 1992-93 | F | 12 | H. French |
| 1993-94 | F | 17 | G. O'Boyle |

## EAST FIFE

| Season | Div | No.of Goals | Player |
|---|---|---|---|
| 1980-81 | S | 10 | R. Thomson |
| 1981-82 | S | 16 | G. Scott |
| 1982-83 | S | 14 | R. Thomson |
| 1983-84 | S | 16 | G. Durie |
| 1984-85 | F | 12 | G. Murray |
| 1985-86 | F | 14 | S. Kirk |
| 1986-87 | F | 15 | B. McNaughton |
| 1987-88 | F | 17 | P. Hunter |
| 1988-89 | S | 9 | P. Hunter |
| 1989-90 | S | 14 | P. Hunter |
| 1990-91 | S | 10 | W. Brown |
| | | | R. Scott |
| 1991-92 | S | 21 | J. Sludden |
| 1992-93 | S | 16 | R. Scott |
| 1993-94 | S | 10 | R. Scott |

## EAST STIRLINGSHIRE

| Season | Div | No.of Goals | Player |
|---|---|---|---|
| 1980-81 | F | 7 | P. Lamont |
| | | | D. McCaig |
| 1981-82 | F | 4 | J. Blair |
| | | | R. Edgar |
| | | | P. Lamont |
| 1982-83 | S | 6 | C. Gibson |
| 1983-84 | S | 13 | C. Gibson |
| 1984-85 | S | 12 | S. Maskrey |
| 1985-86 | S | 12 | S. Maskrey |
| 1986-87 | S | 5 | A. McGonigal |
| | | | J. Paisley |
| | | | D. Strange |
| 1987-88 | S | 9 | G. Murray |
| 1988-89 | S | 16 | W. McNeill |
| 1989-90 | S | 4 | W. McNeill |
| | | | D. Wilcox |
| | | | C. Wilson |
| 1990-91 | S | 10 | C. Lytwyn |
| | | | Dk. Walker |
| 1991-92 | S | 18 | D. Diver |
| 1992-93 | S | 9 | P. Roberts |
| 1993-94 | S | 12 | M. McCallum |

## FALKIRK

| Season | Div | No.of Goals | Player |
|---|---|---|---|
| 1980-81 | F | 5 | C. Spence |
| 1981-82 | F | 10 | W. Herd |
| 1982-83 | F | 8 | P. Houston |
| 1983-84 | F | 11 | K. McAllister |
| 1984-85 | F | 22 | G. McCoy |
| 1985-86 | F | 15 | J. Gilmour |
| 1986-87 | P | 6 | K. Eadie |
| 1987-88 | P | 9 | C. Baptie |
| 1988-89 | F | 12 | A. Rae |
| 1989-90 | F | 17 | D. McWilliams |
| 1990-91 | F | 16 | S. Stainrod |
| 1991-92 | P | 9 | K. McAllister |
| | | | E. May |
| 1992-93 | P | 8 | R. Cadette |
| 1993-94 | F | 18 | R. Cadette |

## FORFAR ATHLETIC

| Season | Div | No.of Goals | Player |
|---|---|---|---|
| 1980-81 | S | 13 | N. J. Watt |
| 1981-82 | S | 9 | J. Clark |
| | | | S. Hancock |
| 1982-83 | S | 16 | K. Macdonald |
| 1983-84 | S | 22 | J. Liddle |
| 1984-85 | F | 14 | K. Macdonald |
| 1985-86 | F | 10 | J. Clark |
| 1986-87 | F | 17 | K. Macdonald |
| 1987-88 | F | 20 | K. Macdonald |
| 1988-89 | F | 12 | K. Ward |
| 1989-90 | F | 8 | C. Brewster |
| 1990-91 | F | 12 | G. Whyte |
| 1991-92 | F | 8 | G. Winter |
| 1992-93 | S | 21 | S. Petrie |
| 1993-94 | S | 13 | D. Bingham |

## GREENOCK MORTON

| Season | Div | No.of Goals | Player |
|---|---|---|---|
| 1980-81 | P | 8 | A. Ritchie |
| 1981-82 | P | 6 | A. Ritchie |
| 1982-83 | P | 7 | J. Rooney |
| 1983-84 | F | 17 | J. McNeil |
| 1984-85 | P | 5 | J. Gillespie |
| 1985-86 | F | 14 | J. McNeil |
| 1986-87 | F | 23 | R. Alexander |
| 1987-88 | P | 8 | Jim Boag |
| 1988-89 | F | 11 | R. Alexander |
| 1989-90 | F | 11 | R. Alexander |
| 1990-91 | F | 21 | D. MacCabe |
| 1991-92 | F | 18 | A. Mathie |
| 1992-93 | F | 13 | A. Mathie |
| 1993-94 | F | 11 | R. Alexander |

## HAMILTON ACADEMICAL

| Season | Div | No.of Goals | Player |
|---|---|---|---|
| 1980-81 | F | 13 | J. Fairlie |
| 1981-82 | F | 10 | J. Fairlie |
| 1982-83 | F | 15 | J. Fairlie |
| 1983-84 | F | 9 | D. Somner |
| 1984-85 | F | 8 | J. Brogan |
| | | | J. McGachie |
| 1985-86 | F | 23 | J. Brogan |
| 1986-87 | P | 9 | J. Brogan |
| 1987-88 | F | 10 | M. Caughey |
| 1988-89 | P | 5 | S. Gordon |
| | | | C. Harris |
| 1989-90 | F | 9 | C. Harris |
| 1990-91 | F | 14 | G. McCluskey |
| 1991-92 | F | 14 | G. Clark |
| 1992-93 | F | 11 | P. McDonald |
| 1993-94 | F | 19 | P. Duffield |

## HEART OF MIDLOTHIAN

| Season | Div | No.of Goals | Player |
|---|---|---|---|
| 1980-81 | P | 4 | W. Gibson |
| | | | D. O'Connor |
| 1981-82 | F | 16 | W. Pettigrew |
| 1982-83 | F | 21 | J. Robertson |
| 1983-84 | P | 14 | J. Robertson |
| 1984-85 | P | 8 | A. Clark |
| | | | J. Robertson |
| 1985-86 | P | 20 | J. Robertson |
| 1986-87 | P | 16 | J. Robertson |
| 1987-88 | P | 26 | J. Robertson |
| 1988-89 | P | 5 | J. Colquhoun |
| | | | I. Ferguson |
| 1989-90 | P | 17 | J. Robertson |
| 1990-91 | P | 12 | J. Robertson |
| 1991-92 | P | 15 | S. Crabbe |
| 1992-93 | P | 11 | J. Robertson |
| 1993-94 | P | 10 | J. Robertson |

## HIBERNIAN

| Season | Div | No.of Goals | Player |
|---|---|---|---|
| 1980-81 | F | 15 | A. MacLeod |
| 1981-82 | P | 11 | G. Rae |
| 1982-83 | P | 6 | G. Murray |
| | | | G. Rae |
| | | | R. Thomson |
| 1983-84 | P | 18 | W. Irvine |
| 1984-85 | P | 8 | G. Durie |
| | | | P. Kane |
| 1985-86 | P | 19 | S. Cowan |
| 1986-87 | P | 9 | G. McCluskey |
| 1987-88 | P | 10 | P. Kane |
| 1988-89 | P | 13 | S. Archibald |
| 1989-90 | P | 8 | K. Houchen |
| 1990-91 | P | 6 | P. Wright |
| 1991-92 | P | 11 | M. Weir |
| 1992-93 | P | 13 | D. Jackson |
| 1993-94 | P | 16 | K. Wright |

## KILMARNOCK

| Season | Div | No.of Goals | Player |
|---|---|---|---|
| 1980-81 | P | 5 | J. Bourke |
| 1981-82 | F | 14 | J. Bourke |
| 1982-83 | P | 9 | B. Gallagher |
| 1983-84 | F | 11 | R. Clark |
| | | | B. Gallagher |
| 1984-85 | F | 12 | B. Millar |
| 1985-86 | F | 14 | I. Bryson |
| 1986-87 | F | 10 | I. Bryson |
| 1987-88 | F | 16 | C. Harkness |
| 1988-89 | F | 12 | W. Watters |
| 1989-90 | S | 23 | W. Watters |
| 1990-91 | F | 14 | R. Williamson |
| 1991-92 | F | 10 | C. Campbell |
| | | | A. Mitchell |
| 1992-93 | F | 11 | G. McCluskey |
| 1993-94 | P | 7 | R. Williamson |

## MEADOWBANK THISTLE

| Season | Div | No.of Goals | Player |
|---|---|---|---|
| 1980-81 | S | 12 | J. Jobson |
| 1981-82 | S | 15 | J. Jobson |
| 1982-83 | S | 13 | T. Hendrie |
| 1983-84 | F | 10 | C. Robertson |
| 1984-85 | F | 14 | A. Sprott |
| 1985-86 | S | 17 | D. Jackson |
| | | | A. Lawrence |
| 1986-87 | S | 21 | J. McGachie |
| 1987-88 | F | 14 | J. McGachie |
| 1988-89 | F | 6 | D. Roseburgh |
| 1989-90 | F | 8 | B. McNaughton |
| 1990-91 | S | 15 | D. Roseburgh |
| 1991-92 | F | 8 | D. Roseburgh |
| 1992-93 | F | 9 | P. Rutherford |
| 1993-94 | S | 12 | I. Little |

## MONTROSE

| Season | Div | No.of Goals | Player |
|---|---|---|---|
| 1980-81 | S | 12 | G. Murray |
| | | | D. Robb |
| 1981-82 | S | 9 | I. Campbell |
| 1982-83 | S | 12 | E. Copeland |
| 1983-84 | S | 7 | N. Burke |
| 1984-85 | S | 12 | D. Somner |
| 1985-86 | F | 6 | M. Allan |
| 1986-87 | F | 10 | I. Paterson |
| 1987-88 | S | 11 | H. Mackay |
| 1988-89 | S | 21 | G. S. Murray |
| 1989-90 | S | 11 | D. Powell |
| 1990-91 | S | 11 | G. Murray |
| 1991-92 | F | 9 | J. McGachie |
| 1992-93 | S | 10 | D. Grant |
| 1993-94 | S | 12 | D. Grant |

## MOTHERWELL

| Season | Div | No.of Goals | Player |
|---|---|---|---|
| 1980-81 | F | 13 | A. Kidd |
| 1981-82 | F | 20 | W. Irvine |
| 1982-83 | P | 11 | B. McClair |
| 1983-84 | P | 7 | J. Gahagan |
| 1984-85 | F | 9 | A. Harrow |
| | | | R. Stewart |
| 1985-86 | P | 9 | J. Reilly |
| 1986-87 | P | 10 | S. Kirk |
| | | | A. Walker |
| 1987-88 | P | 9 | S. Cowan |
| 1988-89 | P | 14 | S. Kirk |
| 1989-90 | P | 11 | N. Cusack |
| 1990-91 | P | 14 | D. Arnott |
| 1991-92 | P | 8 | D. Arnott |
| 1992-93 | P | 10 | S. Kirk |
| 1993-94 | P | 12 | T. Coyne |

## PARTICK THISTLE

| Season | Div | No.of Goals | Player |
|---|---|---|---|
| 1980-81 | P | 7 | A. Higgins |
| | | | A. O'Hara |
| 1981-82 | P | 9 | M. Johnston |
| 1982-83 | F | 22 | M. Johnston |
| 1983-84 | F | 13 | K. McDowall |
| 1984-85 | F | 12 | A. Logan |
| 1985-86 | F | 11 | G. Smith |
| 1986-87 | F | 10 | C. West |
| 1987-88 | F | 13 | E. Gallagher |
| 1988-89 | F | 19 | G. McCoy |
| 1989-90 | F | 18 | C. Campbell |
| 1990-91 | F | 13 | D. Elliot |
| 1991-92 | F | 18 | C. McGlashan |
| 1992-93 | P | 12 | G. Britton |
| 1993-94 | P | 14 | A. Craig |

## QUEEN OF THE SOUTH

| Season | Div | No.of Goals | Player |
|---|---|---|---|
| 1980-81 | S | 19 | J. Robertson |
| 1981-82 | F | 12 | G. Phillips |
| 1982-83 | S | 22 | R. Alexander |
| 1983-84 | S | 9 | J. Robertson |
| 1984-85 | S | 9 | G. Cloy |
| 1985-86 | S | 15 | T. Bryce |
| | | | S. Cochrane |
| 1986-87 | F | 20 | T. Bryce |
| 1987-88 | F | 17 | J. Hughes |
| 1988-89 | F | 7 | G. Fraser |
| 1989-90 | S | 8 | S. Gordon |
| 1990-91 | S | 11 | A. Thomson |
| 1991-92 | S | 26 | A. Thomson |
| 1992-93 | S | 21 | A. Thomson |
| 1993-94 | S | 29 | A. Thomson |

## QUEEN'S PARK

| Season | Div | No.of Goals | Player |
|---|---|---|---|
| 1980-81 | S | 17 | G. McCoy |
| 1981-82 | F | 10 | G. Crawley |
| 1982-83 | F | 10 | J. Gilmour |
| 1983-84 | S | 17 | A. Grant |
| 1984-85 | S | 18 | J. Nicholson |
| 1985-86 | S | 11 | G. Fraser |
| 1986-87 | S | 13 | R. Caven |
| 1987-88 | S | 17 | P. O'Brien |
| 1988-89 | S | 9 | M. Hendry |
| 1989-90 | S | 10 | M. Hendry |
| 1990-91 | S | 17 | M. Hendry |
| 1991-92 | S | 17 | S. McCormick |
| 1992-93 | S | 11 | R. Caven |
| 1993-94 | S | 18 | J. O'Neill |

## RAITH ROVERS

| Season | Div | No.of Goals | Player |
|---|---|---|---|
| 1980-81 | F | 12 | I. Ballantyne |
| 1981-82 | F | 12 | I. Ballantyne |
| 1982-83 | F | 18 | C. Harris |
| 1983-84 | F | 16 | J. Kerr |
| 1984-85 | S | 22 | K. Wright |
| 1985-86 | S | 21 | P. Smith |
| | | | K. Wright |
| 1986-87 | S | 22 | C. Harris |
| 1987-88 | F | 25 | G. Dalziel |
| 1988-89 | F | 11 | G. Dalziel |
| 1989-90 | F | 20 | G. Dalziel |
| 1990-91 | F | 25 | G. Dalziel |
| 1991-92 | F | 26 | G. Dalziel |
| 1992-93 | F | 32 | G. Dalziel |
| 1993-94 | P | 8 | G. Dalziel |

## RANGERS

| Season | Div | No.of Goals | Player |
|---|---|---|---|
| 1980-81 | P | 12 | C. McAdam |
| 1981-82 | P | 14 | J. MacDonald |
| 1982-83 | P | 10 | J. MacDonald |
| 1983-84 | P | 9 | A. Clark |
| | | | A. McCoist |
| 1984-85 | P | 12 | A. McCoist |
| 1985-86 | P | 24 | A. McCoist |
| 1986-87 | P | 33 | A. McCoist |
| 1987-88 | P | 31 | A. McCoist |
| 1988-89 | P | 12 | K. Drinkell |
| 1989-90 | P | 15 | M. Johnston |
| 1990-91 | P | 12 | M. Walters |
| 1991-92 | P | 34 | A. McCoist |
| 1992-93 | P | 34 | A. McCoist |
| 1993-94 | P | 22 | M. Hateley |

## ST. JOHNSTONE

| Season | Div | No.of Goals | Player |
|---|---|---|---|
| 1980-81 | F | 22 | A. McCoist |
| 1981-82 | F | 17 | J. Morton |
| 1982-83 | F | 26 | J. Brogan |
| 1983-84 | P | 9 | J. Brogan |
| 1984-85 | F | 9 | J. Reid |
| 1985-86 | S | 11 | W. Brown |
| 1986-87 | S | 25 | W. Brown |
| 1987-88 | S | 16 | W. Watters |
| 1988-89 | F | 12 | S. Maskrey |
| 1989-90 | F | 19 | R. Grant |
| 1990-91 | P | 9 | H. Curran |
| 1991-92 | P | 18 | P. Wright |
| 1992-93 | P | 14 | P. Wright |
| 1993-94 | P | 7 | P. Wright |

## ST. MIRREN

| Season | Div | No.of Goals | Player |
|---|---|---|---|
| 1980-81 | P | 13 | D. Somner |
| 1981-82 | P | 13 | F. McAvennie |
| 1982-83 | P | 9 | F. McAvennie |
| 1983-84 | P | 13 | F. McDougall |
| 1984-85 | P | 16 | F. McAvennie |
| 1985-86 | P | 7 | G. Speirs |
| 1986-87 | P | 10 | F. McGarvey |
| 1987-88 | P | 10 | P. Chalmers |
| 1988-89 | P | 11 | P. Chalmers |
| 1989-90 | P | 12 | G. Torfason |
| 1990-91 | P | 4 | P. Kinnaird |
| | | | K. McDowall |
| | | | G. Torfason |
| 1991-92 | P | 8 | G. Torfason |
| 1992-93 | F | 18 | B. Lavety |
| 1993-94 | F | 10 | B. Lavety |

## STENHOUSEMUIR

| Season | Div | No.of Goals | Player |
|---|---|---|---|
| 1980-81 | S | 20 | S. Hancock |
| 1981-82 | S | 8 | B. Jenkins |
| 1982-83 | S | 15 | G. Murray |
| 1983-84 | S | 14 | G. Forrest |
| 1984-85 | S | 6 | H. Erwin |
| | | | A. McNaughton |
| 1985-86 | S | 11 | J. Sinnet |
| 1986-87 | S | 5 | A. Bateman |
| | | | P. Russell |
| 1987-88 | S | 10 | T. Condie |
| 1988-89 | S | 9 | C. Walker |
| 1989-90 | S | 15 | S. McCormick |
| 1990-91 | S | 17 | A. Speirs |
| 1991-92 | S | 6 | M. Mathieson |
| 1992-93 | S | 26 | M. Mathieson |
| 1993-94 | S | 14 | M. Mathieson |

*Ally McCoist–top scorer at Ibrox for 7 of the last 11 seasons.* (Photo: courtesy of the Sun.)

## STIRLING ALBION

| Season | Div | No.of Goals | Player |
|---|---|---|---|
| 1980-81 | F | 4 | G. Armstrong |
| | | | W. B. Steele |
| 1981-82 | S | 13 | J. Colquhoun |
| 1982-83 | S | 21 | J. Colquhoun |
| 1983-84 | S | 12 | W. Irvine |
| 1984-85 | S | 21 | W. Irvine |
| 1985-86 | S | 17 | W. Irvine |
| 1986-87 | S | 7 | S. Gavin |
| | | | C. Gibson |
| 1987-88 | S | 23 | J. Brogan |
| 1988-89 | S | 18 | C. Gibson |
| 1989-90 | S | 16 | J. Reid |
| 1990-91 | S | 14 | D. Lloyd |
| 1991-92 | F | 17 | W. Watters |
| 1992-93 | F | 11 | W. Watters |
| 1993-94 | F | 13 | W. Watters |

## STRANRAER

| Season | Div | No.of Goals | Player |
|---|---|---|---|
| 1980-81 | S | 7 | H. Hay |
| 1981-82 | S | 11 | S. Sweeney |
| 1982-83 | S | 12 | S. Sweeney |
| 1983-84 | S | 11 | J. McGuire |
| 1984-85 | S | 10 | J. Sweeney |
| 1985-86 | S | 8 | J. McGuire |
| | | | S. Mauchlen |
| 1986-87 | S | 13 | B. Cleland |
| 1987-88 | S | 8 | B. Cleland |
| 1988-89 | S | 11 | D. Lloyd |
| 1989-90 | S | 13 | C. Harkness |
| 1990-91 | S | 14 | C. Harkness |
| 1991-92 | S | 14 | T. Sloan |
| 1992-93 | S | 19 | T. Sloan |
| 1993-94 | S | 16 | T. Sloan |

The following section details the League Championship careers, appearances and goals of all players currently registered with each Premier Division club for season 1994/95 as at 15th August, 1994. It should be noted that all appearances include both full League appearances and substitute League appearances made by players. All club names shown in italics are for League appearances made when a player moved to a club on a Temporary Transfer basis with the player's registration subsequently reverting back to his original club.

### AITKEN, Robert Sime
Born: Irvine 24/11/58

| SEASON | CLUB | LEAGUE APPEARANCES | GOALS |
|---|---|---|---|
| 1975-76 | Celtic | 12 | – |
| 1976-77 | Celtic | 33 | 5 |
| 1977-78 | Celtic | 33 | 2 |
| 1978-79 | Celtic | 36 | 5 |
| 1979-80 | Celtic | 35 | 3 |
| 1980-81 | Celtic | 33 | 4 |
| 1981-82 | Celtic | 33 | 3 |
| 1982-83 | Celtic | 33 | 6 |
| 1983-84 | Celtic | 31 | 5 |
| 1984-85 | Celtic | 33 | 3 |
| 1985-86 | Celtic | 36 | – |
| 1986-87 | Celtic | 42 | 1 |
| 1987-88 | Celtic | 43 | 1 |
| 1988-89 | Celtic | 32 | – |
| 1989-90 | Celtic | 18 | 2 |
| 1989-90 | Newcastle United | 22 | 1 |
| 1990-91 | Newcastle United | 32 | – |
| 1991-92 | St Mirren | 34 | 1 |
| 1992-93 | Aberdeen | 26 | 2 |
| 1993-94 | Aberdeen | 1 | – |

### ALLAN, Raymond George Kyle
Born: Cowdenbeath 05/05/55

| SEASON | CLUB | LEAGUE APPEARANCES | GOALS |
|---|---|---|---|
| 1978-79 | Cowdenbeath | 3 | – |
| 1979-80 | Cowdenbeath | 31 | – |
| 1980-81 | Cowdenbeath | 39 | – |
| 1981-82 | Cowdenbeath | 34 | – |
| 1982-83 | Cowdenbeath | 39 | – |
| 1983-84 | Cowdenbeath | 33 | – |
| 1984-85 | Cowdenbeath | 39 | – |
| 1985-86 | Cowdenbeath | 27 | – |
| 1986-87 | Cowdenbeath | 39 | – |
| 1987-88 | Cowdenbeath | 39 | – |
| 1988-89 | Cowdenbeath | 36 | – |
| 1989-90 | Cowdenbeath | 4 | – |
| 1989-90 | Forfar Athletic | 32 | – |
| 1990-91 | Forfar Athletic | 34 | – |
| 1991-92 | Brechin City | 26 | – |
| 1992-93 | Brechin City | 39 | – |
| 1993-94 | Brechin City | 19 | – |

### ARNOTT, Douglas
Born: Lanark 05/08/61

| SEASON | CLUB | LEAGUE APPEARANCES | GOALS |
|---|---|---|---|
| 1986-87 | Motherwell | 1 | – |
| 1987-88 | Motherwell | 2 | – |
| 1988-89 | Motherwell | 14 | 1 |
| 1989-90 | Motherwell | 30 | 5 |
| 1990-91 | Motherwell | 29 | 14 |
| 1991-92 | Motherwell | 26 | 8 |
| 1992-93 | Motherwell | 33 | 6 |
| 1993-94 | Motherwell | 29 | 8 |

### BEAUMONT, David
Born: Edinburgh 10/12/63

| SEASON | CLUB | LEAGUE APPEARANCES | GOALS |
|---|---|---|---|
| 1980-81 | Dundee United | – | – |
| 1981-82 | Dundee United | – | – |
| 1982-83 | Dundee United | – | – |
| 1983-84 | Dundee United | 2 | – |
| 1984-85 | Dundee United | 18 | 1 |
| 1985-86 | Dundee United | 13 | – |
| 1986-87 | Dundee United | 28 | – |
| 1987-88 | Dundee United | 10 | 1 |
| 1988-89 | Dundee United | 18 | 1 |
| 1988-89 | Luton Town | 15 | – |
| 1989-90 | Luton Town | 19 | – |
| 1990-91 | Luton Town | 33 | – |
| 1991-92 | Luton Town | 9 | – |
| 1991-92 | Hibernian | 21 | – |
| 1992-93 | Hibernian | 16 | – |
| 1993-94 | Hibernian | 26 | 2 |

### BERRY, Neil
Born: Edinburgh 06/04/63

| SEASON | CLUB | LEAGUE APPEARANCES | GOALS |
|---|---|---|---|
| 1980-81 | Bolton Wanderers | – | – |
| 1981-82 | Bolton Wanderers | 3 | – |
| 1982-83 | Bolton Wanderers | 9 | – |
| 1983-84 | Bolton Wanderers | 14 | – |
| 1984-85 | Bolton Wanderers | 6 | – |
| 1984-85 | Heart of Midlothian | 3 | – |
| 1985-86 | Heart of Midlothian | 32 | 2 |
| 1986-87 | Heart of Midlothian | 30 | 3 |
| 1987-88 | Heart of Midlothian | 35 | – |
| 1988-89 | Heart of Midlothian | 32 | 1 |
| 1989-90 | Heart of Midlothian | 10 | 1 |
| 1990-91 | Heart of Midlothian | 19 | 1 |
| 1991-92 | Heart of Midlothian | – | – |
| 1992-93 | Heart of Midlothian | 17 | 1 |
| 1993-94 | Heart of Midlothian | 30 | – |

### BLACK, Thomas
Born: Lanark 11/10/62

| SEASON | CLUB | LEAGUE APPEARANCES | GOALS |
|---|---|---|---|
| 1980-81 | Airdrieonians | – | – |
| 1981-82 | Airdrieonians | – | – |
| 1982-83 | Airdrieonians | 5 | – |
| 1983-84 | Airdrieonians | 32 | 4 |
| 1984-85 | Airdrieonians | 37 | 1 |
| 1985-86 | Airdrieonians | 12 | – |
| 1986-87 | Airdrieonians | 24 | 1 |
| 1987-88 | Airdrieonians | 29 | 1 |
| 1988-89 | Airdrieonians | 37 | 4 |
| 1989-90 | St Mirren | 31 | 1 |
| 1990-91 | St Mirren | 34 | 2 |
| 1991-92 | St Mirren | 9 | 1 |
| 1991-92 | Kilmarnock | 23 | 3 |
| 1992-93 | Kilmarnock | 10 | 1 |
| 1993-94 | Kilmarnock | 44 | 4 |

### BOLLAN, Gary
Born: Dundee 24/03/73

| SEASON | CLUB | LEAGUE APPEARANCES | GOALS |
|---|---|---|---|
| 1987-88 | Celtic | – | – |
| 1988-89 | Celtic | – | – |
| 1989-90 | Celtic | – | – |
| 1990-91 | Dundee United | 2 | – |
| 1991-92 | Dundee United | 10 | 1 |
| 1992-93 | Dundee United | 15 | 3 |
| 1993-94 | Dundee United | 12 | – |

### BONNER, Patrick Joseph
Born: Donegal 24/05/60

| SEASON | CLUB | LEAGUE APPEARANCES | GOALS |
|---|---|---|---|
| 1978-79 | Celtic | 2 | – |
| 1979-80 | Celtic | – | – |
| 1980-81 | Celtic | 36 | – |
| 1981-82 | Celtic | 36 | – |
| 1982-83 | Celtic | 36 | – |
| 1983-84 | Celtic | 33 | – |
| 1984-85 | Celtic | 34 | – |
| 1985-86 | Celtic | 30 | – |
| 1986-87 | Celtic | 43 | – |
| 1987-88 | Celtic | 32 | – |
| 1988-89 | Celtic | 26 | – |
| 1989-90 | Celtic | 36 | – |
| 1990-91 | Celtic | 36 | – |
| 1991-92 | Celtic | 19 | – |
| 1992-93 | Celtic | 33 | – |
| 1993-94 | Celtic | 31 | – |

### BOOTH, Scott
Born: Aberdeen 16/12/71

| SEASON | CLUB | LEAGUE APPEARANCES | GOALS |
|---|---|---|---|
| 1988-89 | Aberdeen | – | – |
| 1989-90 | Aberdeen | 2 | – |
| 1990-91 | Aberdeen | 19 | 6 |
| 1991-92 | Aberdeen | 33 | 5 |
| 1992-93 | Aberdeen | 29 | 13 |
| 1993-94 | Aberdeen | 25 | 4 |

### BOWMAN, David
Born: Turnbridge Wells 10/03/64

| SEASON | CLUB | LEAGUE APPEARANCES | GOALS |
|---|---|---|---|
| 1980-81 | Heart of Midlothian | 17 | 1 |
| 1981-82 | Heart of Midlothian | 16 | 1 |
| 1982-83 | Heart of Midlothian | 39 | 5 |
| 1983-84 | Heart of Midlothian | 33 | – |
| 1984-85 | Heart of Midlothian | 11 | 1 |
| 1984-85 | Coventry City | 10 | – |
| 1985-86 | Coventry City | 30 | 2 |
| 1986-87 | Dundee United | 29 | – |
| 1987-88 | Dundee United | 39 | 1 |
| 1988-89 | Dundee United | 29 | 1 |
| 1989-90 | Dundee United | 24 | 1 |
| 1990-91 | Dundee United | 20 | 1 |
| 1991-92 | Dundee United | 41 | 3 |
| 1992-93 | Dundee United | 24 | – |
| 1993-94 | Dundee United | 35 | 2 |

### BOYD, Thomas
Born: Glasgow 24/11/65

| SEASON | CLUB | LEAGUE APPEARANCES | GOALS |
|---|---|---|---|
| 1983-84 | Motherwell | 13 | – |
| 1984-85 | Motherwell | 36 | – |
| 1985-86 | Motherwell | 31 | – |
| 1986-87 | Motherwell | 31 | – |
| 1987-88 | Motherwell | 42 | 2 |
| 1988-89 | Motherwell | 36 | 1 |
| 1989-90 | Motherwell | 33 | 1 |
| 1990-91 | Motherwell | 30 | 2 |
| 1991-92 | Chelsea | 23 | – |
| 1991-92 | Celtic | 13 | 1 |
| 1992-93 | Celtic | 42 | – |
| 1993-94 | Celtic | 38 | – |

### BREWSTER, Craig James
Born: Dundee 13/12/66

| SEASON | CLUB | LEAGUE APPEARANCES | GOALS |
|---|---|---|---|
| 1985-86 | Forfar Athletic | 16 | 2 |
| 1986-87 | Forfar Athletic | 32 | 3 |
| 1987-88 | Forfar Athletic | 39 | 2 |
| 1988-89 | Forfar Athletic | 37 | 9 |
| 1989-90 | Forfar Athletic | 38 | 8 |
| 1990-91 | Forfar Athletic | 29 | 11 |
| 1991-92 | Raith Rovers | 42 | 12 |
| 1992-93 | Raith Rovers | 44 | 22 |
| 1993-94 | Dundee United | 33 | 16 |

### BROWN, John
Born: Stirling 26/01/62

| SEASON | CLUB | LEAGUE APPEARANCES | GOALS |
|---|---|---|---|
| 1979-80 | Hamilton Academical | 19 | – |
| 1980-81 | Hamilton Academical | 38 | 6 |
| 1981-82 | Hamilton Academical | 28 | 5 |
| 1982-83 | Hamilton Academical | 9 | – |
| 1983-84 | Hamilton Academical | 39 | – |
| 1984-85 | Dundee | 34 | 7 |
| 1985-86 | Dundee | 29 | 11 |
| 1986-87 | Dundee | 31 | 10 |
| 1987-88 | Dundee | 20 | 3 |
| 1987-88 | Rangers | 9 | 2 |
| 1988-89 | Rangers | 29 | 1 |
| 1989-90 | Rangers | 27 | 1 |
| 1990-91 | Rangers | 27 | 1 |
| 1991-92 | Rangers | 25 | 4 |
| 1992-93 | Rangers | 39 | 4 |
| 1993-94 | Rangers | 24 | – |

**BROWN, Thomas**
Born: Glasgow 01/04/68

| SEASON | CLUB | APP | GOALS |
|---|---|---|---|
| 1991-92 | Queen of the South | – | – |
| 1993-94 | Kilmarnock | 31 | 5 |

**BURNS, Alexander**
Born: Bellshill 04/08/73

| 1991-92 | Motherwell | – | – |
| 1992-93 | Motherwell | – | – |
| 1993-94 | Motherwell | 4 | 1 |

(Photo: courtesy of the Sun)

**BYRNE, David Stuart**
Born: London 05/03/61

| 1985-86 | Gillingham | 23 | 3 |
| 1986-87 | Millwall | 40 | 4 |
| 1987-88 | Millwall | 23 | 2 |
| 1988-89 | Millwall | – | – |
| 1988-89 | *Cambridge United* | 4 | – |
| 1988-89 | Blackburn | 4 | – |
| 1988-89 | Plymouth Argyle | 13 | 1 |
| 1989-90 | Plymouth Argyle | 2 | 1 |
| 1990-91 | *Bristol Rovers* | 2 | – |
| 1990-91 | Plymouth Argyle | 14 | – |
| 1990-91 | Watford | 17 | 2 |
| 1991-92 | Watford | – | – |
| 1991-92 | *Reading* | 7 | 2 |
| 1991-92 | *Fulham* | 5 | – |
| 1992-93 | St Johnstone | 12 | – |
| 1993-94 | Partick Thistle | 23 | – |
| 1993-94 | *Walsall* | 5 | – |

**BYRNE, Paul Peter**
Born: Dublin 13/06/72
From Bangor

| 1993-94 | Celtic | 22 | 2 |

**CADETTE, Richard Ray**
Born: Hammersmith 21/03/65

| 1984-85 | Orient | 21 | 4 |
| 1985-86 | Southend United | 44 | 24 |
| 1986-87 | Southend United | 46 | 24 |
| 1987-88 | Sheffield United | 28 | 7 |
| 1988-89 | Brentford | 32 | 12 |
| 1989-90 | Brentford | 16 | 1 |
| 1989-90 | *Bournemouth* | 8 | 1 |
| 1990-91 | Brentford | 28 | 6 |
| 1991-92 | Brentford | 11 | 1 |
| 1991-92 | Falkirk | 14 | 3 |
| 1992-93 | Falkirk | 31 | 8 |
| 1993-94 | Falkirk | 39 | 17 |

**CAMERON, Ian**
Born: Glasgow 24/08/66

| 1983-84 | St Mirren | 8 | – |
| 1984-85 | St Mirren | 9 | 1 |
| 1985-86 | St Mirren | 12 | – |
| 1986-87 | St Mirren | 31 | 6 |
| 1987-88 | St Mirren | 41 | 8 |
| 1988-89 | St Mirren | 26 | 2 |
| 1989-90 | Aberdeen | 11 | – |
| 1990-91 | Aberdeen | 10 | 1 |
| 1991-92 | Aberdeen | 6 | – |
| 1992-93 | Partick Thistle | 41 | 5 |
| 1993-94 | Partick Thistle | 41 | 1 |

**CHARNLEY, James Callaghan**
Born: Glasgow 11/06/63

| 1982-83 | St Mirren | 1 | - |
| 1983-84 | St Mirren | – | - |
| 1983-84 | Ayr United | 17 | 3 |
| 1984-85 | Ayr United | – | - |
| 1987-88 | Clydebank | 28 | 10 |
| 1988-89 | Clydebank | 3 | 1 |
| 1988-89 | Hamilton Academical | 14 | - |
| 1988-89 | Partick Thistle | 14 | 4 |
| 1989-90 | Partick Thistle | 29 | 11 |
| 1990-91 | Partick Thistle | 30 | 7 |
| 1991-92 | St Mirren | 26 | 4 |
| 1991-92 | *Bolton Wanderers* | 3 | - |
| 1992-93 | St Mirren | 14 | 1 |
| 1993-94 | Partick Thistle | 26 | 1 |

**CLELAND, Alexander**
Born: Glasgow 10/12/70

| 1987-88 | Dundee United | 1 | – |
| 1988-89 | Dundee United | 9 | – |
| 1989-90 | Dundee United | 15 | – |
| 1990-91 | Dundee United | 20 | 2 |
| 1991-92 | Dundee United | 31 | 4 |
| 1992-93 | Dundee United | 24 | – |
| 1993-94 | Dundee United | 33 | 1 |

**COLLINS, John Angus Paul**
Born: Galashiels 31/01/68

| 1984-85 | Hibernian | – | – |
| 1985-86 | Hibernian | 19 | – |
| 1986-87 | Hibernian | 30 | 1 |
| 1987-88 | Hibernian | 44 | 6 |
| 1988-89 | Hibernian | 35 | 2 |
| 1989-90 | Hibernian | 35 | 6 |
| 1990-91 | Celtic | 35 | 1 |
| 1991-92 | Celtic | 38 | 11 |
| 1992-93 | Celtic | 43 | 8 |
| 1993-94 | Celtic | 38 | 8 |

**COLQUHOUN, John Mark**
Born: Stirling 14/07/63

| 1980-81 | Stirling Albion | 13 | – |
| 1981-82 | Stirling Albion | 37 | 13 |
| 1982-83 | Stirling Albion | 39 | 21 |
| 1983-84 | Stirling Albion | 15 | 11 |
| 1983-84 | Celtic | 12 | 2 |
| 1984-85 | Celtic | 20 | 2 |
| 1985-86 | Heart of Midlothian | 36 | 8 |
| 1986-87 | Heart of Midlothian | 43 | 13 |
| 1987-88 | Heart of Midlothian | 44 | 15 |
| 1988-89 | Heart of Midlothian | 36 | 5 |
| 1989-90 | Heart of Midlothian | 36 | 6 |
| 1990-91 | Heart of Midlothian | 36 | 7 |
| 1991-92 | Millwall | 27 | 3 |
| 1992-93 | Sunderland | 20 | – |
| 1993-94 | Heart of Midlothian | 41 | 6 |

**CONNOLLY, Patrick**
Born: Glasgow 25/06/70

| 1986-87 | Dundee United | – | – |
| 1987-88 | Dundee United | – | – |
| 1988-89 | Dundee United | 2 | – |
| 1989-90 | Dundee United | 15 | 5 |
| 1990-91 | Dundee United | 10 | 2 |
| 1991-92 | Dundee United | 5 | – |
| 1992-93 | Dundee United | 42 | 16 |
| 1993-94 | Dundee United | 28 | 5 |

**CONNOR, Robert**
Born: Kilmarnock 04/08/60

| 1977-78 | Ayr United | 9 | – |
| 1978-79 | Ayr United | 29 | – |
| 1979-80 | Ayr United | 38 | 9 |
| 1980-81 | Ayr United | 39 | 8 |
| 1981-82 | Ayr United | 30 | – |
| 1982-83 | Ayr United | 39 | 4 |
| 1983-84 | Ayr United | 39 | 7 |
| 1984-85 | Dundee | 34 | 7 |
| 1985-86 | Dundee | 35 | 2 |
| 1986-87 | Dundee | 2 | – |
| 1986-87 | Aberdeen | 32 | 4 |
| 1987-88 | Aberdeen | 34 | 1 |
| 1988-89 | Aberdeen | 36 | 4 |
| 1989-90 | Aberdeen | 34 | 1 |
| 1990-91 | Aberdeen | 29 | 6 |
| 1991-92 | Aberdeen | 11 | – |
| 1992-93 | Aberdeen | 6 | – |
| 1993-94 | Aberdeen | 25 | 1 |

**COYNE, Thomas**
Born: Glasgow 14/11/62

| 1981-82 | Clydebank | 31 | 9 |
| 1982-83 | Clydebank | 38 | 18 |
| 1983-84 | Clydebank | 11 | 10 |
| 1983-84 | Dundee United | 18 | 3 |
| 1984-85 | Dundee United | 21 | 3 |
| 1985-86 | Dundee United | 13 | 2 |
| 1986-87 | Dundee | 20 | 9 |
| 1987-88 | Dundee | 43 | 33 |
| 1988-89 | Dundee | 26 | 9 |
| 1988-89 | Celtic | 7 | – |
| 1989-90 | Celtic | 23 | 7 |
| 1990-91 | Celtic | 26 | 18 |
| 1991-92 | Celtic | 39 | 15 |
| 1992-93 | Celtic | 10 | 3 |
| 1992-93 | Tranmere Rovers | 12 | 1 |
| 1993-94 | Tranmere Rovers | – | – |
| 1993-94 | Motherwell | 26 | 12 |

**CRABBE, Scott**
Born: Edinburgh 12/08/68

| 1986-87 | Heart of Midlothian | 5 | – |
| 1987-88 | Heart of Midlothian | 5 | – |
| 1988-89 | Heart of Midlothian | 1 | – |
| 1989-90 | Heart of Midlothian | 35 | 12 |
| 1990-91 | Heart of Midlothian | 21 | 3 |
| 1991-92 | Heart of Midlothian | 41 | 15 |
| 1992-93 | Heart of Midlothian | 8 | 1 |
| 1992-93 | Dundee United | 27 | 4 |
| 1993-94 | Dundee United | 21 | 2 |

**CRAIG, Albert Hughes**
Born: Glasgow 03/01/62

| 1981-82 | Dumbarton | 13 | 2 |
| 1982-83 | Dumbarton | 32 | 7 |
| 1983-84 | Dumbarton | 26 | 4 |
| 1984-85 | Dumbarton | 35 | 4 |
| 1985-86 | Dumbarton | 32 | 6 |
| 1986-87 | Hamilton Academical | 16 | 5 |

| SEASON | CLUB | LEAGUE APPEARANCES | GOALS |
|---|---|---|---|
| 1986-87 | Newcastle United | 6 | – |
| 1987-88 | Newcastle United | 3 | – |
| 1987-88 | *Hamilton Academical* | 6 | 1 |
| 1988-89 | Newcastle United | 1 | – |
| 1988-89 | Northampton Town | 2 | 1 |
| 1988-89 | Dundee | 6 | 2 |
| 1989-90 | Dundee | 20 | 2 |
| 1990-91 | Dundee | 12 | 3 |
| 1991-92 | Dundee | 25 | 7 |
| 1992-93 | Partick Thistle | 29 | 1 |
| 1993-94 | Partick Thistle | 38 | 14 |

**CRAIG, David William**
Born: Glasgow 11/06/69

| SEASON | CLUB | LEAGUE APPEARANCES | GOALS |
|---|---|---|---|
| 1989-90 | Partick Thistle | 9 | 1 |
| 1990-91 | Partick Thistle | 3 | – |
| 1991-92 | Partick Thistle | - | – |
| 1991-92 | East Stirlingshire | 34 | – |
| 1992-93 | East Stirlingshire | 16 | 2 |
| 1993-94 | East Stirlingshire | 38 | 4 |

**CRAINIE, Daniel**
Born: Kilsyth 24/05/62

| SEASON | CLUB | LEAGUE APPEARANCES | GOALS |
|---|---|---|---|
| 1979-80 | Celtic | – | – |
| 1980-81 | Celtic | – | – |
| 1981-82 | Celtic | 16 | 7 |
| 1982-83 | Celtic | 7 | – |
| 1983-84 | Celtic | 1 | – |
| 1983-84 | Wolverhampton Wanderers | 28 | 3 |
| 1984-85 | Wolverhampton Wanderers | 13 | – |
| 1984-85 | *Blackpool* | 6 | – |
| 1985-86 | Wolverhampton Wanderers | 23 | 1 |
| 1985-86 | Dundee | 3 | – |
| From Cork City, Wollongong City | | | |
| 1990-91 | Airdrieonians | 28 | 1 |
| 1991-92 | Airdrieonians | 3 | – |
| 1992-93 | Kilmarnock | 9 | 1 |
| 1993-94 | Kilmarnock | 14 | 1 |

**DAILLY, Christian Eduard**
Born: Dundee 23/10/73

| SEASON | CLUB | LEAGUE APPEARANCES | GOALS |
|---|---|---|---|
| 1990-91 | Dundee United | 18 | 5 |
| 1991-92 | Dundee United | 8 | – |
| 1992-93 | Dundee United | 18 | 4 |
| 1993-94 | Dundee United | 38 | 3 |

**DAVIES, William McIntosh**
Born: Glasgow 31/05/64

| SEASON | CLUB | LEAGUE APPEARANCES | GOALS |
|---|---|---|---|
| 1980-81 | Rangers | – | – |
| 1981-82 | Rangers | 4 | – |
| 1982-83 | Rangers | 4 | – |
| 1983-84 | Rangers | 3 | 1 |
| 1984-85 | Rangers | – | – |
| 1985-86 | Rangers | – | – |
| 1987-88 | St Mirren | 18 | – |
| 1988-89 | St Mirren | 27 | 4 |
| 1989-90 | St Mirren | 29 | 1 |
| 1990-91 | St Mirren | – | – |
| 1990-91 | Leicester City | 6 | – |
| 1990-91 | Dunfermline Athletic | 26 | – |
| 1991-92 | Dunfermline Athletic | 33 | – |
| 1992-93 | Dunfermline Athletic | 41 | 10 |
| 1993-94 | Dunfermline Athletic | 4 | – |
| 1993-94 | Motherwell | 10 | – |

**DOCHERTY, Stephen**
Born: Glasgow 18/02/76

| SEASON | CLUB | LEAGUE APPEARANCES | GOALS |
|---|---|---|---|
| 1992-93 | Partick Thistle | 1 | – |
| 1993-94 | Partick Thistle | – | – |

**DODDS, William**
Born: New Cumnock 05/02/69

| SEASON | CLUB | LEAGUE APPEARANCES | GOALS |
|---|---|---|---|
| 1986-87 | Chelsea | 1 | – |
| 1987-88 | Chelsea | – | – |
| 1987-88 | *Partick Thistle* | 30 | 9 |
| 1988-89 | Chelsea | 2 | – |
| 1989-90 | Dundee | 30 | 13 |
| 1990-91 | Dundee | 37 | 15 |
| 1991-92 | Dundee | 42 | 19 |
| 1992-93 | Dundee | 41 | 16 |
| 1993-94 | Dundee | 24 | 6 |
| 1993-94 | St. Johnstone | 20 | 6 |

**DOLAN, James**
Born: Salsburgh 22/02/69

| SEASON | CLUB | LEAGUE APPEARANCES | GOALS |
|---|---|---|---|
| 1987-88 | Motherwell | – | – |
| 1988-89 | Motherwell | 5 | – |
| 1989-90 | Motherwell | 12 | – |
| 1990-91 | Motherwell | 8 | 1 |
| 1991-92 | Motherwell | 32 | 2 |
| 1992-93 | Motherwell | 25 | 2 |
| 1993-94 | Motherwell | 36 | – |

**DONALD, Graeme Still**
Born: Stirling 14/04/74

| SEASON | CLUB | LEAGUE APPEARANCES | GOALS |
|---|---|---|---|
| 1991-92 | Hibernian | 5 | 3 |
| 1992-93 | Hibernian | 4 | – |
| 1993-94 | Hibernian | 6 | – |

**DONNELLY, Simon**
Born: Glasgow 01/12/74

| SEASON | CLUB | LEAGUE APPEARANCES | GOALS |
|---|---|---|---|
| 1993-94 | Celtic | 12 | 5 |

**DURIE, Gordon Scott**
Born: Paisley 06/12/65

| SEASON | CLUB | LEAGUE APPEARANCES | GOALS |
|---|---|---|---|
| 1981-82 | East Fife | 13 | 1 |
| 1982-83 | East Fife | 25 | 2 |
| 1983-84 | East Fife | 34 | 16 |
| 1984-85 | East Fife | 9 | 7 |
| 1984-85 | Hibernian | 22 | 8 |
| 1985-86 | Hibernian | 25 | 6 |
| 1985-86 | Chelsea | 1 | – |
| 1986-87 | Chelsea | 25 | 5 |
| 1987-88 | Chelsea | 26 | 12 |
| 1988-89 | Chelsea | 32 | 17 |
| 1989-90 | Chelsea | 15 | 5 |
| 1990-91 | Chelsea | 24 | 12 |
| 1991-92 | Tottenham Hotspur | 31 | 7 |
| 1992-93 | Tottenham Hotspur | 17 | 3 |
| 1993-94 | Tottenham Hotspur | 10 | 1 |
| 1993-94 | Rangers | 24 | 12 |

**DURRANT, Ian**
Born: Glasgow 29/10/66

| SEASON | CLUB | LEAGUE APPEARANCES | GOALS |
|---|---|---|---|
| 1984-85 | Rangers | 5 | – |
| 1985-86 | Rangers | 30 | 2 |
| 1986-87 | Rangers | 39 | 4 |
| 1987-88 | Rangers | 40 | 10 |
| 1988-89 | Rangers | 8 | 2 |
| 1989-90 | Rangers | – | – |
| 1990-91 | Rangers | 4 | 1 |
| 1991-92 | Rangers | 13 | – |
| 1992-93 | Rangers | 30 | 3 |
| 1993-94 | Rangers | 23 | – |

**ENGLISH, Isaac**
Born: Paisley 12/11/71

| SEASON | CLUB | LEAGUE APPEARANCES | GOALS |
|---|---|---|---|
| 1989-90 | St Mirren | – | – |
| 1989-90 | Partick Thistle | 6 | 2 |
| 1990-91 | Partick Thistle | 13 | 2 |
| 1991-92 | Partick Thistle | 26 | 5 |
| 1992-93 | Partick Thistle | 13 | – |
| 1993-94 | Partick Thistle | 36 | 4 |

**EVANS, Gareth John**
Born: Coventry 14/01/67

| SEASON | CLUB | LEAGUE APPEARANCES | GOALS |
|---|---|---|---|
| 1984-85 | Coventry City | – | – |
| 1985-86 | Coventry City | 6 | – |
| 1986-87 | Coventry City | 1 | – |
| 1986-87 | Rotherham United | 34 | 9 |
| 1987-88 | Rotherham United | 29 | 4 |
| 1987-88 | Hibernian | 12 | 2 |
| 1988-89 | Hibernian | 35 | 5 |
| 1989-90 | Hibernian | 28 | 3 |
| 1990-91 | Hibernian | 15 | 2 |
| 1990-91 | *Northampton Town* | 2 | – |
| 1990-91 | *Stoke City* | 5 | 1 |
| 1991-92 | Hibernian | 41 | 6 |
| 1992-93 | Hibernian | 39 | 6 |
| 1993-94 | Hibernian | 40 | 4 |

**FALCONER, William Henry**
Born: Aberdeen 05/04/66

| SEASON | CLUB | LEAGUE APPEARANCES | GOALS |
|---|---|---|---|
| 1982-83 | Aberdeen | 1 | – |
| 1983-84 | Aberdeen | 8 | 1 |
| 1984-85 | Aberdeen | 16 | 4 |
| 1985-86 | Aberdeen | 8 | – |
| 1986-87 | Aberdeen | 8 | – |
| 1987-88 | Aberdeen | 36 | 8 |
| 1988-89 | Watford | 33 | 5 |
| 1989-90 | Watford | 30 | 3 |
| 1990-91 | Watford | 35 | 4 |
| 1991-92 | Middlesbrough | 25 | 5 |
| 1992-93 | Middlesbrough | 28 | 5 |
| 1993-94 | Middlesbrough | – | – |
| 1993-94 | Celtic | 14 | 1 |

**FARRELL, David**
Born: Glasgow 29/10/69

| SEASON | CLUB | LEAGUE APPEARANCES | GOALS |
|---|---|---|---|
| 1988-89 | Hibernian | – | – |
| 1989-90 | Hibernian | – | – |
| 1990-91 | Hibernian | 2 | – |
| 1991-92 | Hibernian | 6 | – |
| 1992-93 | Hibernian | 12 | – |
| 1993-94 | Hibernian | 35 | 2 |

**FERGUSON, Duncan**
Born: Stirling 27/12/71

| SEASON | CLUB | LEAGUE APPEARANCES | GOALS |
|---|---|---|---|
| 1990-91 | Dundee United | 9 | 1 |
| 1991-92 | Dundee United | 38 | 15 |
| 1992-93 | Dundee United | 30 | 12 |
| 1993-94 | Rangers | 10 | 1 |

**FERGUSON, Ian**
Born: Glasgow 15/03/67

| SEASON | CLUB | LEAGUE APPEARANCES | GOALS |
|---|---|---|---|
| 1984-85 | Clyde | 2 | – |
| 1985-86 | Clyde | 19 | 4 |
| 1986-87 | Clyde | 5 | – |
| 1986-87 | St Mirren | 35 | 4 |
| 1987-88 | St Mirren | 22 | 6 |
| 1987-88 | Rangers | 8 | 1 |
| 1988-89 | Rangers | 30 | 6 |
| 1989-90 | Rangers | 24 | – |
| 1990-91 | Rangers | 11 | 1 |
| 1991-92 | Rangers | 16 | 1 |
| 1992-93 | Rangers | 30 | 4 |
| 1993-94 | Rangers | 35 | 5 |

**FINDLAY, William McCall**
Born: Kilmarnock 29/08/70

| SEASON | CLUB | LEAGUE APPEARANCES | GOALS |
|---|---|---|---|
| 1987-88 | Hibernian | – | – |
| 1988-89 | Hibernian | 3 | 1 |
| 1989-90 | Hibernian | 10 | – |
| 1990-91 | Hibernian | 26 | 2 |
| 1991-92 | Hibernian | 9 | – |
| 1992-93 | Hibernian | 7 | – |
| 1993-94 | Hibernian | 20 | 3 |

| SEASON | CLUB | LEAGUE APPEARANCES | GOALS |
|---|---|---|---|

**FOSTER, Wayne Paul**
Born: Tyldesley 11/09/63

| SEASON | CLUB | APPEARANCES | GOALS |
|---|---|---|---|
| 1981-82 | Bolton Wanderers | 23 | 2 |
| 1982-83 | Bolton Wanderers | 24 | 4 |
| 1983-84 | Bolton Wanderers | 30 | 3 |
| 1984-85 | Bolton Wanderers | 28 | 4 |
| 1985-86 | Preston North End | 31 | 3 |
| 1986-87 | Heart of Midlothian | 31 | 4 |
| 1987-88 | Heart of Midlothian | 39 | 4 |
| 1988-89 | Heart of Midlothian | 9 | 1 |
| 1989-90 | Heart of Midlothian | 17 | 1 |
| 1990-91 | Heart of Midlothian | 28 | 1 |
| 1991-92 | Heart of Midlothian | 7 | – |
| 1992-93 | Heart of Midlothian | 11 | – |
| 1993-94 | Heart of Midlothian | 18 | 1 |

**FRAIL, Stephen Charles**
Born: Glasgow 10/08/69

| SEASON | CLUB | APPEARANCES | GOALS |
|---|---|---|---|
| 1985-86 | Dundee | – | – |
| 1986-87 | Dundee | – | – |
| 1987-88 | Dundee | 4 | – |
| 1988-89 | Dundee | 23 | 1 |
| 1989-90 | Dundee | 6 | – |
| 1990-91 | Dundee | 26 | – |
| 1991-92 | Dundee | 3 | – |
| 1992-93 | Dundee | 7 | – |
| 1993-94 | Dundee | 32 | – |
| 1993-94 | Heart of Midlothian | 9 | 2 |

**FULTON, Stephen**
Born: Greenock 10/08/70

| SEASON | CLUB | APPEARANCES | GOALS |
|---|---|---|---|
| 1986-87 | Celtic | – | – |
| 1987-88 | Celtic | – | – |
| 1988-89 | Celtic | 3 | – |
| 1989-90 | Celtic | 16 | – |
| 1990-91 | Celtic | 21 | – |
| 1991-92 | Celtic | 30 | 2 |
| 1992-93 | Celtic | 6 | – |
| 1993-94 | Bolton Wanderers | 4 | – |

**GALLOWAY, Michael**
Born: Oswestry 30/05/65

| SEASON | CLUB | APPEARANCES | GOALS |
|---|---|---|---|
| 1983-84 | Mansfield Town | 17 | – |
| 1984-85 | Mansfield Town | 31 | 3 |
| 1985-86 | Mansfield Town | 6 | – |
| 1985-86 | Halifax Town | 19 | – |
| 1986-87 | Halifax Town | 43 | 3 |
| 1987-88 | Halifax Town | 17 | 2 |
| 1987-88 | Heart of Midlothian | 25 | 6 |
| 1988-89 | Heart of Midlothian | 31 | 2 |
| 1989-90 | Celtic | 33 | 2 |
| 1990-91 | Celtic | 6 | 1 |
| 1991-92 | Celtic | 34 | 2 |
| 1992-93 | Celtic | 30 | 3 |
| 1993-94 | Celtic | 22 | – |

**GEDDES, Alexander Robert**
Born: Inverness 12/08/60

| SEASON | CLUB | APPEARANCES | GOALS |
|---|---|---|---|
| 1977-78 | Dundee | – | – |
| 1978-79 | Dundee | – | – |
| 1979-80 | Dundee | – | – |
| 1980-81 | Dundee | 20 | – |
| 1981-82 | Dundee | 28 | – |
| 1982-83 | Dundee | 1 | – |
| 1983-84 | Dundee | 24 | – |
| 1984-85 | Dundee | 16 | – |
| 1985-86 | Dundee | 36 | – |
| 1986-87 | Dundee | 44 | – |
| 1987-88 | Dundee | 38 | – |
| 1988-89 | Dundee | 34 | – |
| 1989-90 | Dundee | 12 | – |
| 1990-91 | Kilmarnock | 38 | – |
| 1991-92 | Kilmarnock | 33 | – |
| 1992-93 | Kilmarnock | 44 | – |
| 1993-94 | Kilmarnock | 44 | – |

**GIBSON, Andrew**
Born: Dechmont, Broxburn 02/02/69

| SEASON | CLUB | APPEARANCES | GOALS |
|---|---|---|---|
| 1987-88 | Stirling Albion | 5 | – |
| 1988-89 | Stirling Albion | 12 | 1 |
| 1988-89 | Aberdeen | – | – |
| 1989-90 | Aberdeen | – | – |
| 1990-91 | Aberdeen | – | – |
| 1991-92 | Aberdeen | 5 | – |
| 1992-93 | Aberdeen | 1 | 1 |
| 1993-94 | Aberdeen | 2 | – |
| 1993-94 | Partick Thistle | 11 | – |

**GILLESPIE, Gary Thomson**
Born: Bonnybridge 05/07/60

| SEASON | CLUB | APPEARANCES | GOALS |
|---|---|---|---|
| 1977-78 | Falkirk | 22 | – |
| 1978-79 | Coventry City | 15 | – |
| 1979-80 | Coventry City | 38 | 1 |
| 1980-81 | Coventry City | 37 | 1 |
| 1981-82 | Coventry City | 40 | 2 |
| 1982-83 | Coventry City | 42 | 2 |
| 1983-84 | Liverpool | – | – |
| 1984-85 | Liverpool | 12 | 1 |
| 1985-86 | Liverpool | 14 | 3 |
| 1986-87 | Liverpool | 37 | – |
| 1987-88 | Liverpool | 35 | 4 |
| 1988-89 | Liverpool | 15 | 1 |
| 1989-90 | Liverpool | 13 | – |
| 1990-91 | Liverpool | 30 | 1 |
| 1991-92 | Celtic | 24 | 2 |
| 1992-93 | Celtic | 18 | – |
| 1993-94 | Celtic | 27 | – |

**GORAM, Andrew Lewis**
Born: Bury 13/04/64

| SEASON | CLUB | APPEARANCES | GOALS |
|---|---|---|---|
| 1981-82 | Oldham Athletic | 3 | – |
| 1982-83 | Oldham Athletic | 38 | – |
| 1983-84 | Oldham Athletic | 22 | – |
| 1984-85 | Oldham Athletic | 41 | – |
| 1985-86 | Oldham Athletic | 41 | – |
| 1986-87 | Oldham Athletic | 41 | – |
| 1987-88 | Oldham Athletic | 9 | – |
| 1987-88 | Hibernian | 33 | 1 |
| 1988-89 | Hibernian | 36 | – |
| 1989-90 | Hibernian | 34 | – |
| 1990-91 | Hibernian | 35 | – |
| 1991-92 | Rangers | 44 | – |
| 1992-93 | Rangers | 34 | – |
| 1993-94 | Rangers | 8 | – |

**GOUGH, Charles Richard**
Born: Stockholm 05/04/62

| SEASON | CLUB | APPEARANCES | GOALS |
|---|---|---|---|
| 1980-81 | Dundee United | 4 | – |
| 1981-82 | Dundee United | 30 | 1 |
| 1982-83 | Dundee United | 34 | 8 |
| 1983-84 | Dundee United | 33 | 3 |
| 1984-85 | Dundee United | 33 | 6 |
| 1985-86 | Dundee United | 31 | 5 |
| 1986-87 | Tottenham Hotspur | 40 | 7 |
| 1987-88 | Tottenham Hotspur | 9 | – |
| 1987-88 | Rangers | 31 | 5 |
| 1988-89 | Rangers | 35 | 4 |
| 1989-90 | Rangers | 26 | – |
| 1990-91 | Rangers | 26 | – |
| 1991-92 | Rangers | 33 | 2 |
| 1992-93 | Rangers | 25 | 2 |
| 1993-94 | Rangers | 37 | 3 |

**GRANT, Brian**
Born: Bannockburn 19/06/64

| SEASON | CLUB | APPEARANCES | GOALS |
|---|---|---|---|
| 1981-82 | Stirling Albion | 1 | – |
| 1982-83 | Stirling Albion | 1 | – |
| 1983-84 | Stirling Albion | 24 | 3 |
| 1984-85 | Aberdeen | – | – |
| 1985-86 | Aberdeen | – | – |
| 1986-87 | Aberdeen | 15 | 4 |
| 1987-88 | Aberdeen | 7 | 1 |
| 1988-89 | Aberdeen | 26 | 1 |
| 1989-90 | Aberdeen | 31 | 6 |
| 1990-91 | Aberdeen | 32 | 2 |
| 1991-92 | Aberdeen | 33 | 6 |
| 1992-93 | Aberdeen | 29 | 3 |
| 1993-94 | Aberdeen | 30 | 2 |

**GRANT, Peter**
Born: Bellshill 30/08/65

| SEASON | CLUB | APPEARANCES | GOALS |
|---|---|---|---|
| 1982-83 | Celtic | – | – |
| 1983-84 | Celtic | 3 | – |
| 1984-85 | Celtic | 20 | 4 |
| 1985-86 | Celtic | 30 | 1 |
| 1986-87 | Celtic | 37 | 1 |
| 1987-88 | Celtic | 37 | 2 |
| 1988-89 | Celtic | 21 | – |
| 1989-90 | Celtic | 26 | – |
| 1990-91 | Celtic | 27 | – |
| 1991-92 | Celtic | 22 | – |
| 1992-93 | Celtic | 31 | 2 |
| 1993-94 | Celtic | 28 | – |

**GRANT, Roderick John**
Born: Gloucester 16/09/66

| SEASON | CLUB | APPEARANCES | GOALS |
|---|---|---|---|
| 1986-87 | Cowdenbeath | 24 | 14 |
| 1987-88 | Cowdenbeath | 32 | 11 |
| 1988-89 | Cowdenbeath | 8 | 2 |
| 1988-89 | St Johnstone | 28 | 5 |
| 1989-90 | St Johnstone | 37 | 19 |
| 1990-91 | St Johnstone | 30 | 7 |
| 1991-92 | St Johnstone | 25 | 2 |
| 1992-93 | St Johnstone | – | – |
| 1993-94 | Partick Thistle | 37 | 13 |

**GRAY, Stuart**
Born: Harrogate 18/12/73

| SEASON | CLUB | APPEARANCES | GOALS |
|---|---|---|---|
| 1992-93 | Celtic | 1 | – |
| 1993-94 | Celtic | – | – |

**GRIFFIN, James**
Born: Hamilton 01/01/67

| SEASON | CLUB | APPEARANCES | GOALS |
|---|---|---|---|
| 1985-86 | Motherwell | 1 | – |
| 1986-87 | Motherwell | – | – |
| 1987-88 | Motherwell | 6 | – |
| 1988-89 | Motherwell | 1 | – |
| 1989-90 | Motherwell | 11 | – |
| 1990-91 | Motherwell | 23 | 4 |
| 1991-92 | Motherwell | 22 | 1 |
| 1992-93 | Motherwell | 25 | 1 |
| 1993-94 | Motherwell | 3 | – |

**HAGEN, David**
Born: Edinburgh 05/05/73

| SEASON | CLUB | APPEARANCES | GOALS |
|---|---|---|---|
| 1989-90 | Rangers | – | – |
| 1990-91 | Rangers | – | – |
| 1991-92 | Rangers | – | – |
| 1992-93 | Rangers | 8 | 2 |
| 1993-94 | Rangers | 6 | 1 |

**HAMILTON, Brian**
Born: Paisley 05/08/67

| SEASON | CLUB | APPEARANCES | GOALS |
|---|---|---|---|
| 1985-86 | St Mirren | 8 | – |
| 1986-87 | St Mirren | 28 | 3 |
| 1987-88 | St Mirren | 27 | – |
| 1988-89 | St Mirren | 23 | 1 |
| 1989-90 | Hibernian | 28 | 1 |
| 1990-91 | Hibernian | 26 | 2 |
| 1991-92 | Hibernian | 40 | 3 |
| 1992-93 | Hibernian | 41 | 1 |
| 1993-94 | Hibernian | 42 | 2 |

| CLUB | LEAGUE APPEARANCES | GOALS | SEASON | CLUB | LEAGUE APPEARANCES | GOALS | SEASON | CLUB | LEAGUE APPEARANCES | GOALS |
|---|---|---|---|---|---|---|---|---|---|---|

**HAMILTON, Graeme John**
Born: Stirling 22/01/74

| Season | Club | Apps | Goals |
|---|---|---|---|
| 1991-92 | Falkirk | 3 | – |
| 1992-93 | Falkirk | – | – |
| 1993-94 | Falkirk | 7 | – |

**HANNAH, David**
Born: Coatbridge 04/08/74

| Season | Club | Apps | Goals |
|---|---|---|---|
| 1991-92 | Dundee United | – | – |
| 1992-93 | Dundee United | 5 | – |
| 1993-94 | Dundee United | 10 | 2 |

**HARPER, Kevin Patrick**
Born: Oldham 15/01/76

| Season | Club | Apps | Goals |
|---|---|---|---|
| 1992-93 | Hibernian | – | – |
| 1993-94 | Hibernian | 2 | – |

**HARRISON, Thomas Edward**
Born: Edinburgh 22/01/74

| Season | Club | Apps | Goals |
|---|---|---|---|
| 1990-91 | Heart of Midlothian | 3 | – |
| 1991-92 | Heart of Midlothian | 1 | – |
| 1992-93 | Heart of Midlothian | 4 | 1 |
| 1993-94 | Heart of Midlothian | 1 | – |

**HATELEY, Mark**
Born: Wallasey 07/11/61

| Season | Club | Apps | Goals |
|---|---|---|---|
| 1978-79 | Coventry City | 1 | – |
| 1979-80 | Coventry City | 4 | – |
| 1980-81 | Coventry City | 19 | 3 |
| 1981-82 | Coventry City | 34 | 13 |
| 1982-83 | Coventry City | 35 | 9 |
| 1983-84 | Portsmouth | 38 | 22 |
| 1984-85 | AC Milan | 21 | 7 |
| 1985-86 | AC Milan | 22 | 8 |
| 1986-87 | AC Milan | 23 | 2 |
| From Monaco |  |  |  |
| 1990-91 | Rangers | 33 | 10 |
| 1991-92 | Rangers | 30 | 21 |
| 1992-93 | Rangers | 37 | 19 |
| 1993-94 | Rangers | 42 | 22 |

**HAY, Christopher Drummond**
Born: Glasgow 28/08/74

| Season | Club | Apps | Goals |
|---|---|---|---|
| 1993-94 | Celtic | 2 | – |

**HENDERSON, Nicholas Sinclair**
Born: Edinburgh 08/02/69

| Season | Club | Apps | Goals |
|---|---|---|---|
| 1990-91 | Raith Rovers | 1 | – |
| 1991-92 | Raith Rovers | – | – |
| 1992-93 | Raith Rovers | – | – |
| 1992-93 | Cowdenbeath | 32 | 5 |
| 1993-94 | Cowdenbeath | 22 | 9 |
| 1993-94 | Falkirk | 10 | 2 |

**HENRY, John**
Born: Vale of Leven 31/12/71

| Season | Club | Apps | Goals |
|---|---|---|---|
| 1990-91 | Clydebank | 3 | 1 |
| 1991-92 | Clydebank | 35 | 8 |
| 1992-93 | Clydebank | 32 | 12 |
| 1993-94 | Clydebank | 44 | 6 |

**HETHERSTON, Peter**
Born: Bellshill 06/11/64

| Season | Club | Apps | Goals |
|---|---|---|---|
| 1984-85 | Falkirk | 12 | 2 |
| 1985-86 | Falkirk | 22 | 2 |
| 1986-87 | Falkirk | 36 | 3 |
| 1987-88 | Watford | 5 | – |
| 1987-88 | Sheffield United | 11 | – |
| 1988-89 | Falkirk | 31 | 3 |
| 1989-90 | Falkirk | 22 | 2 |
| 1990-91 | Falkirk | 26 | 4 |
| 1991-92 | Raith Rovers | 31 | 1 |
| 1992-93 | Raith Rovers | 44 | 4 |
| 1993-94 | Raith Rovers | 33 | 5 |

**HOGG, Graeme James**
Born: Aberdeen 17/06/64

| Season | Club | Apps | Goals |
|---|---|---|---|
| 1982-83 | Manchester United | – | – |
| 1983-84 | Manchester United | 16 | 1 |
| 1984-85 | Manchester United | 29 | – |
| 1985-86 | Manchester United | 17 | – |
| 1986-87 | Manchester United | 11 | – |
| 1987-88 | Manchester United | 10 | – |
| 1987-88 | West Bromwich Albion | 7 | – |
| 1988-89 | Portsmouth | 41 | 1 |
| 1989-90 | Portsmouth | 39 | 1 |
| 1990-91 | Portsmouth | 20 | – |
| 1991-92 | Heart of Midlothian | 18 | 1 |
| 1992-93 | Heart of Midlothian | 22 | 2 |
| 1993-94 | Heart of Midlothian | 17 | – |

**HUGHES, John**
Born: Edinburgh 09/09/64

| Season | Club | Apps | Goals |
|---|---|---|---|
| 1988-89 | Berwick Rangers | 27 | 10 |
| 1989-90 | Berwick Rangers | 14 | 4 |
| 1989-90 | Swansea City | 24 | 4 |
| 1990-91 | Swansea City | – | – |
| 1990-91 | Falkirk | 32 | 2 |
| 1991-92 | Falkirk | 38 | 2 |
| 1992-93 | Falkirk | 15 | – |
| 1993-94 | Falkirk | 29 | 3 |

**HUISTRA, Pieter**
Born: Goenga 18/01/67

From F.C. Twente Enschede

| Season | Club | Apps | Goals |
|---|---|---|---|
| 1990-91 | Rangers | 27 | 4 |
| 1991-92 | Rangers | 32 | 5 |
| 1992-93 | Rangers | 30 | 4 |
| 1993-94 | Rangers | 21 | 6 |

**HUNTER, Gordon**
Born: Wallyford 03/05/67

| Season | Club | Apps | Goals |
|---|---|---|---|
| 1983-84 | Hibernian | 1 | – |
| 1984-85 | Hibernian | 6 | – |
| 1985-86 | Hibernian | 25 | – |
| 1986-87 | Hibernian | 29 | – |
| 1987-88 | Hibernian | 35 | – |
| 1988-89 | Hibernian | 33 | 1 |
| 1989-90 | Hibernian | 34 | – |
| 1990-91 | Hibernian | 20 | 1 |
| 1991-92 | Hibernian | 37 | 2 |
| 1992-93 | Hibernian | 23 | – |
| 1993-94 | Hibernian | 29 | 1 |

**IRVINE, Brian Alexander**
Born: Bellshill 24/05/65

| Season | Club | Apps | Goals |
|---|---|---|---|
| 1983-84 | Falkirk | 3 | – |
| 1984-85 | Falkirk | 35 | – |
| 1985-86 | Aberdeen | 1 | – |
| 1986-87 | Aberdeen | 20 | 1 |
| 1987-88 | Aberdeen | 16 | 1 |
| 1988-89 | Aberdeen | 27 | 2 |
| 1989-90 | Aberdeen | 31 | 1 |
| 1990-91 | Aberdeen | 29 | 2 |
| 1991-92 | Aberdeen | 41 | 4 |
| 1992-93 | Aberdeen | 39 | 5 |
| 1993-94 | Aberdeen | 42 | 7 |

**JACKSON, Christoper**
Born: Edinburgh 29/10/73

| Season | Club | Apps | Goals |
|---|---|---|---|
| 1992-93 | Hibernian | 1 | – |
| 1993-94 | Hibernian | 12 | – |

**JACKSON, Darren**
Born: Edinburgh 25/07/66

| Season | Club | Apps | Goals |
|---|---|---|---|
| 1985-86 | Meadowbank Thistle | 39 | 17 |
| 1986-87 | Meadowbank Thistle | 9 | 5 |
| 1986-87 | Newcastle United | 23 | 3 |
| 1987-88 | Newcastle United | 31 | 2 |
| 1988-89 | Newcastle United | 15 | 2 |

| Season | Club | Apps | Goals |
|---|---|---|---|
| 1988-89 | Dundee United | 1 | – |
| 1989-90 | Dundee United | 25 | 7 |
| 1990-91 | Dundee United | 33 | 12 |
| 1991-92 | Dundee United | 28 | 11 |
| 1992-93 | Hibernian | 36 | 13 |
| 1993-94 | Hibernian | 39 | 7 |

**JAMIESON, William George**
Born: Barnsley 27/04/63

| Season | Club | Apps | Goals |
|---|---|---|---|
| 1980-81 | Hibernian | 28 | 12 |
| 1981-82 | Hibernian | 12 | 5 |
| 1982-83 | Hibernian | 19 | 2 |
| 1983-84 | Hibernian | 33 | 4 |
| 1984-85 | Hibernian | 25 | 2 |
| 1985-86 | Hamilton Academical | 39 | 2 |
| 1986-87 | Hamilton Academical | 15 | – |
| 1987-88 | Hamilton Academical | 41 | 4 |
| 1988-89 | Hamilton Academical | 34 | 1 |
| 1989-90 | Dundee | 14 | – |
| 1990-91 | Dundee | 38 | 2 |
| 1991-92 | Dundee | 38 | 4 |
| 1992-93 | Partick Thistle | 28 | 3 |
| 1993-94 | Partick Thistle | 43 | 4 |

**JESS, Eoin**
Born: Aberdeen 13/12/70

| Season | Club | Apps | Goals |
|---|---|---|---|
| 1987-88 | Aberdeen | – | – |
| 1988-89 | Aberdeen | 2 | – |
| 1989-90 | Aberdeen | 11 | 3 |
| 1990-91 | Aberdeen | 27 | 13 |
| 1991-92 | Aberdeen | 39 | 12 |
| 1992-93 | Aberdeen | 31 | 17 |
| 1993-94 | Aberdeen | 41 | 6 |

**JOHNSON, Ian Grant**
Born: Dundee 24/03/72

| Season | Club | Apps | Goals |
|---|---|---|---|
| 1990-91 | Dundee United | – | – |
| 1991-92 | Dundee United | 10 | 1 |
| 1992-93 | Dundee United | 17 | 1 |
| 1993-94 | Dundee United | 10 | – |

**JOHNSTON, Allan**
Born: Glasgow 14/12/73

| Season | Club | Apps | Goals |
|---|---|---|---|
| 1991-92 | Heart of Midlothian | – | – |
| 1992-93 | Heart of Midlothian | 2 | 1 |
| 1993-94 | Heart of Midlothian | 28 | 1 |

**JOHNSTON, Forbes Duthie Stephen**
Born: Aberdeen 03/08/71

| Season | Club | Apps | Goals |
|---|---|---|---|
| 1990-91 | Falkirk | – | – |
| 1991-92 | Falkirk | 12 | – |
| 1992-93 | Falkirk | 22 | 1 |
| 1993-94 | Falkirk | 15 | 1 |

**JOHNSTON, Maurice Thomas**
Born: Glasgow 13/04/63

| Season | Club | Apps | Goals |
|---|---|---|---|
| 1980-81 | Partick Thistle | – | – |
| 1981-82 | Partick Thistle | 32 | 9 |
| 1982-83 | Partick Thistle | 39 | 22 |
| 1983-84 | Partick Thistle | 14 | 10 |
| 1983-84 | Watford | 29 | 20 |
| 1984-85 | Watford | 9 | 3 |
| 1984-85 | Celtic | 27 | 14 |
| 1985-86 | Celtic | 32 | 15 |
| 1986-87 | Celtic | 40 | 23 |
| 1987-88 | Nantes | 32 | 13 |
| 1988-89 | Nantes | 34 | 9 |
| 1989-90 | Rangers | 36 | 15 |
| 1990-91 | Rangers | 29 | 11 |
| 1991-92 | Rangers | 11 | 5 |
| 1991-92 | Everton | 21 | 7 |
| 1992-93 | Everton | 13 | 3 |
| 1993-94 | Everton | – | – |
| 1993-94 | Heart of Midlothian | 31 | 4 |

| SEASON | CLUB | LEAGUE APPEARANCES | GOALS |
|---|---|---|---|

**KANE, Paul James**
Born: Edinburgh 20/06/65

| SEASON | CLUB | APP | GOALS |
|---|---|---|---|
| 1982-83 | Hibernian | – | – |
| 1983-84 | Hibernian | 13 | 1 |
| 1984-85 | Hibernian | 34 | 8 |
| 1985-86 | Hibernian | 32 | 5 |
| 1986-87 | Hibernian | 37 | 1 |
| 1987-88 | Hibernian | 44 | 10 |
| 1988-89 | Hibernian | 35 | 5 |
| 1989-90 | Hibernian | 31 | 3 |
| 1990-91 | Hibernian | 21 | – |
| 1990-91 | Oldham Athletic | 17 | – |
| 1991-92 | Oldham Athletic | 4 | – |
| 1991-92 | Aberdeen | 25 | 2 |
| 1992-93 | Aberdeen | 27 | 4 |
| 1993-94 | Aberdeen | 39 | 3 |

**KIRK, Stephen David**
Born: Kirkcaldy 03/01/63

| 1979-80 | East Fife | 25 | 2 |
|---|---|---|---|
| 1980-81 | Stoke City | – | – |
| 1981-82 | Stoke City | 12 | – |
| 1982-83 | Partick Thistle | – | – |
| 1982-83 | East Fife | 25 | 8 |
| 1983-84 | East Fife | 33 | 5 |
| 1984-85 | East Fife | 38 | 8 |
| 1985-86 | East Fife | 39 | 14 |
| 1986-87 | Motherwell | 35 | 10 |
| 1987-88 | Motherwell | 38 | 4 |
| 1988-89 | Motherwell | 33 | 14 |
| 1989-90 | Motherwell | 34 | 8 |
| 1990-91 | Motherwell | 29 | 2 |
| 1991-92 | Motherwell | 38 | 6 |
| 1992-93 | Motherwell | 40 | 10 |
| 1993-94 | Motherwell | 36 | 7 |

**KRIVOKAPIC, Miodrag**
Born: Niksic Crna Gora 06/09/59

From Red Star Belgrade

| 1988-89 | Dundee United | 24 | 1 |
|---|---|---|---|
| 1989-90 | Dundee United | 26 | – |
| 1990-91 | Dundee United | 24 | – |
| 1991-92 | Dundee United | – | – |
| 1992-93 | Dundee United | 8 | – |
| 1993-94 | Motherwell | 42 | 1 |

**LAMBERT, Paul**
Born: Glasgow 07/08/69

| 1985-86 | St Mirren | 1 | – |
|---|---|---|---|
| 1986-87 | St Mirren | 36 | 2 |
| 1987-88 | St Mirren | 36 | 2 |
| 1988-89 | St Mirren | 16 | 2 |
| 1989-90 | St Mirren | 25 | 3 |
| 1990-91 | St Mirren | 31 | 2 |
| 1991-92 | St Mirren | 40 | 2 |
| 1992-93 | St Mirren | 39 | 1 |
| 1993-94 | St Mirren | 3 | – |
| 1993-94 | Motherwell | 32 | 3 |

**LAW, Robert Shearer**
Born: Bellshill 24/12/65

| 1984-85 | Partick Thistle | 1 | – |
|---|---|---|---|
| 1985-86 | Partick Thistle | 16 | 3 |
| 1986-87 | Partick Thistle | 31 | 2 |
| 1987-88 | Partick Thistle | 21 | 1 |
| 1988-89 | Partick Thistle | 33 | – |
| 1989-90 | Partick Thistle | 28 | 1 |
| 1990-91 | Partick Thistle | 27 | – |
| 1991-92 | Partick Thistle | 31 | 2 |
| 1992-93 | Partick Thistle | 34 | – |
| 1993-94 | Partick Thistle | 25 | – |

**LEIGHTON, James**
Born: Johnston 24/07/58

| 1978-79 | Aberdeen | 11 | – |
|---|---|---|---|
| 1979-80 | Aberdeen | 1 | – |
| 1980-81 | Aberdeen | 35 | – |
| 1981-82 | Aberdeen | 36 | – |
| 1982-83 | Aberdeen | 35 | – |
| 1983-84 | Aberdeen | 36 | – |
| 1984-85 | Aberdeen | 34 | – |
| 1985-86 | Aberdeen | 26 | – |
| 1986-87 | Aberdeen | 42 | – |
| 1987-88 | Aberdeen | 44 | – |
| 1988-89 | Manchester United | 38 | – |
| 1989-90 | Manchester United | 35 | – |
| 1990-91 | Manchester United | – | – |
| 1990-91 | *Arsenal* | – | – |
| 1991-92 | Manchester United | – | – |
| 1991-92 | *Reading* | 8 | – |
| 1991-92 | Dundee | 13 | – |
| 1992-93 | Dundee | 8 | – |
| 1993-94 | Hibernian | 44 | – |

**LEITCH, Donald Scott**
Born: Motherwell 06/10/69

| 1987-88 | Motherwell | – | – |
|---|---|---|---|
| 1989-90 | Dunfermline Athletic | – | – |
| 1990-91 | Dunfermline Athletic | 14 | 3 |
| 1991-92 | Dunfermline Athletic | 33 | 4 |
| 1992-93 | Dunfermline Athletic | 42 | 9 |
| 1993-94 | Heart of Midlothian | 28 | 2 |

**LEVEIN, Craig William**
Born: Dunfermline 22/10/64

| 1981-82 | Cowdenbeath | 15 | – |
|---|---|---|---|
| 1982-83 | Cowdenbeath | 30 | – |
| 1983-84 | Cowdenbeath | 15 | – |
| 1983-84 | Heart of Midlothian | 22 | – |
| 1984-85 | Heart of Midlothian | 36 | 1 |
| 1985-86 | Heart of Midlothian | 33 | 2 |
| 1986-87 | Heart of Midlothian | 12 | – |
| 1987-88 | Heart of Midlothian | 21 | – |
| 1988-89 | Heart of Midlothian | 9 | – |
| 1989-90 | Heart of Midlothian | 35 | – |
| 1990-91 | Heart of Midlothian | 33 | 4 |
| 1991-92 | Heart of Midlothian | 36 | 2 |
| 1992-93 | Heart of Midlothian | 37 | 3 |
| 1993-94 | Heart of Midlothian | 30 | 3 |

**LOCKE, Gary**
Born: Edinburgh 16/06/75

| 1992-93 | Heart of Midlothian | 1 | – |
|---|---|---|---|
| 1993-94 | Heart of Midlothian | 33 | – |

**LOVE, Graeme**
Born: Bathgate 07/12/73

| 1991-92 | Hibernian | 1 | – |
|---|---|---|---|
| 1992-93 | Hibernian | 1 | – |
| 1993-94 | Hibernian | 4 | – |

**MACKAY, Gary**
Born: Edinburgh 23/01/64

| 1980-81 | Heart of Midlothian | 12 | – |
|---|---|---|---|
| 1981-82 | Heart of Midlothian | 17 | 2 |
| 1982-83 | Heart of Midlothian | 34 | 6 |
| 1983-84 | Heart of Midlothian | 31 | 4 |
| 1984-85 | Heart of Midlothian | 17 | 2 |
| 1985-86 | Heart of Midlothian | 32 | 4 |
| 1986-87 | Heart of Midlothian | 37 | 7 |
| 1987-88 | Heart of Midlothian | 41 | 5 |
| 1988-89 | Heart of Midlothian | 29 | 2 |
| 1989-90 | Heart of Midlothian | 33 | 1 |
| 1990-91 | Heart of Midlothian | 30 | 3 |
| 1991-92 | Heart of Midlothian | 43 | 1 |
| 1992-93 | Heart of Midlothian | 37 | 2 |
| 1993-94 | Heart of Midlothian | 36 | 1 |

**MACKAY, Malcolm George**
Born: Bellshill 19/02/72

| 1989-90 | Queen's Park | – | – |
|---|---|---|---|
| 1990-91 | Queen's Park | 10 | – |
| 1991-92 | Queen's Park | 27 | 3 |
| 1992-93 | Queen's Park | 33 | 3 |
| 1993-94 | Celtic | – | – |

**MacKENZIE, Scott**
Born: Glasgow 07/07/70

| 1990-91 | Falkirk | – | – |
|---|---|---|---|
| 1991-92 | Falkirk | 2 | – |
| 1992-93 | Falkirk | 3 | – |
| 1993-94 | Falkirk | 19 | – |

**MacPHERSON, Angus Ian**
Born: Glasgow 11/10/68

| 1988-89 | Rangers | – | – |
|---|---|---|---|
| 1989-90 | Rangers | – | – |
| 1989-90 | *Exeter City* | 11 | 1 |
| 1990-91 | Kilmarnock | 11 | – |
| 1991-92 | Kilmarnock | 43 | 3 |
| 1992-93 | Kilmarnock | 40 | 5 |
| 1993-94 | Kilmarnock | 43 | 2 |

**MAIN, Alan David**
Born: Elgin 05/12/67

| 1986-87 | Dundee United | 2 | – |
|---|---|---|---|
| 1987-88 | Dundee United | 8 | – |
| 1988-89 | Dundee United | – | – |
| 1988-89 | *Cowdenbeath* | 3 | – |
| 1988-89 | *East Stirlingshire* | 2 | – |
| 1989-90 | Dundee United | 27 | – |
| 1990-91 | Dundee United | 31 | – |
| 1991-92 | Dundee United | 17 | – |
| 1992-93 | Dundee United | 43 | – |
| 1993-94 | Dundee United | 18 | – |

**MALPAS, Maurice Daniel Robert**
Born: Dunfermline 03/08/62

| 1979-80 | Dundee United | – | – |
|---|---|---|---|
| 1980-81 | Dundee United | – | – |
| 1981-82 | Dundee United | 19 | – |
| 1982-83 | Dundee United | 34 | 1 |
| 1983-84 | Dundee United | 34 | 2 |
| 1984-85 | Dundee United | 35 | 2 |
| 1985-86 | Dundee United | 36 | 2 |
| 1986-87 | Dundee United | 36 | – |
| 1987-88 | Dundee United | 44 | – |
| 1988-89 | Dundee United | 36 | 1 |
| 1989-90 | Dundee United | 30 | 2 |
| 1990-91 | Dundee United | 36 | 1 |
| 1991-92 | Dundee United | 44 | 3 |
| 1992-93 | Dundee United | 37 | – |
| 1993-94 | Dundee United | 35 | – |

**MARSHALL, Gordon George Banks**
Born: Edinburgh 19/04/64

| 1980-81 | Rangers | – | – |
|---|---|---|---|
| 1981-82 | Rangers | – | – |
| 1982-83 | Rangers | – | – |
| 1982-83 | *East Stirlingshire* | 15 | – |
| 1982-83 | East Fife | 10 | – |
| 1983-84 | East Fife | 34 | – |
| 1984-85 | East Fife | 39 | – |
| 1985-86 | East Fife | 39 | – |
| 1986-87 | East Fife | 36 | – |
| 1986-87 | Falkirk | 10 | – |
| 1987-88 | Falkirk | 44 | – |
| 1988-89 | Falkirk | 39 | – |
| 1989-90 | Falkirk | 39 | – |
| 1990-91 | Falkirk | – | – |
| 1991-92 | Celtic | 25 | – |
| 1992-93 | Celtic | 11 | – |
| 1993-94 | Celtic | 1 | – |
| 1993-94 | *Stoke City* | 10 | – |

## MARTIN, Brian
Born: Bellshill 24/02/63

| | CLUB | APP | GOALS |
|---|---|---|---|
| 1985-86 | Falkirk | 25 | 1 |
| 1986-87 | Falkirk | 34 | 1 |
| 1986-87 | Hamilton Academical | 7 | – |
| 1987-88 | Hamilton Academical | 23 | – |
| 1987-88 | St Mirren | 12 | 1 |
| 1988-89 | St Mirren | 34 | 2 |
| 1989-90 | St Mirren | 35 | 2 |
| 1990-91 | St Mirren | 31 | 2 |
| 1991-92 | St Mirren | 17 | 2 |
| 1991-92 | Motherwell | 25 | – |
| 1992-93 | Motherwell | 44 | 3 |
| 1993-94 | Motherwell | 43 | 2 |

## MARTIN, Lee Andrew
Born: Hyde, Manchester 05/02/68

| | | | |
|---|---|---|---|
| 1986-87 | Manchester United | – | – |
| 1987-88 | Manchester United | 1 | – |
| 1988-89 | Manchester United | 24 | 1 |
| 1989-90 | Manchester United | 32 | – |
| 1990-91 | Manchester United | 14 | – |
| 1991-92 | Manchester United | 1 | – |
| 1992-93 | Manchester United | – | – |
| 1993-94 | Manchester United | 1 | – |
| 1993-94 | Celtic | 15 | – |

## MAXWELL, Alastair Espie
Born: Hamilton 16/02/65

| | | | |
|---|---|---|---|
| 1981-82 | Motherwell | – | – |
| 1982-83 | Motherwell | – | – |
| 1983-84 | Motherwell | 4 | – |
| 1984-85 | Motherwell | 15 | – |
| 1985-86 | Motherwell | 4 | – |
| 1986-87 | Motherwell | 21 | – |
| 1987-88 | Motherwell | 1 | – |
| 1987-88 | Clydebank | 1 | – |
| 1988-89 | Motherwell | 17 | – |
| 1989-90 | Motherwell | 36 | – |
| 1990-91 | Motherwell | 36 | 1 |
| 1991-92 | Motherwell | – | – |
| 1991-92 | Liverpool | – | – |
| 1991-92 | Bolton Wanderers | 3 | – |
| 1992-93 | Rangers | 10 | – |
| 1993-94 | Rangers | 32 | – |

## MAY, Edward
Born: Edinburgh 30/08/67

| | | | |
|---|---|---|---|
| 1983-84 | Dundee United | – | – |
| 1984-85 | Dundee United | – | – |
| 1984-85 | Hibernian | – | – |
| 1985-86 | Hibernian | 19 | 1 |
| 1986-87 | Hibernian | 30 | 5 |
| 1987-88 | Hibernian | 35 | 2 |
| 1988-89 | Hibernian | 25 | 2 |
| 1989-90 | Brentford | 30 | 8 |
| 1990-91 | Brentford | 17 | 2 |
| 1990-91 | Falkirk | 13 | 6 |
| 1991-92 | Falkirk | 36 | 9 |
| 1992-93 | Falkirk | 42 | 6 |
| 1993-94 | Falkirk | 38 | 9 |

## McALLISTER, Kevin
Born: Falkirk 08/11/62

| | | | |
|---|---|---|---|
| 1983-84 | Falkirk | 35 | 11 |
| 1984-85 | Falkirk | 29 | 7 |
| 1985-86 | Chelsea | 20 | 1 |
| 1986-87 | Chelsea | 8 | – |
| 1987-88 | Chelsea | 5 | – |
| 1987-88 | Falkirk | 6 | 3 |
| 1988-89 | Chelsea | 36 | 6 |
| 1989-90 | Chelsea | 24 | 1 |
| 1990-91 | Chelsea | 13 | 1 |
| 1991-92 | Falkirk | 42 | 9 |
| 1992-93 | Falkirk | 41 | 3 |
| 1993-94 | Hibernian | 36 | 6 |

## McBAIN, Roy Adam
Born: Aberdeen 07/11/74

| SEASON | CLUB | APP | GOALS |
|---|---|---|---|
| 1991-92 | Dundee United | – | – |
| 1992-93 | Dundee United | – | – |
| 1993-94 | Dundee United | 1 | – |

## McCALL, Ian Holland
Born: Dumfries 30/09/65

| | | | |
|---|---|---|---|
| 1983-84 | Queen's Park | 3 | 1 |
| 1984-85 | Queen's Park | 28 | – |
| 1985-86 | Queen's Park | 35 | 8 |
| 1986-87 | Dunfermline Athletic | 43 | 8 |
| 1987-88 | Dunfermline Athletic | 4 | – |
| 1987-88 | Rangers | 12 | 1 |
| 1988-89 | Rangers | 5 | 1 |
| 1989-90 | Rangers | 4 | – |
| 1989-90 | Bradford City | 12 | 1 |
| 1990-91 | Dunfermline Athletic | 29 | 4 |
| 1991-92 | Dunfermline Athletic | 9 | 1 |
| 1991-92 | Dundee | 27 | 9 |
| 1992-93 | Falkirk | 35 | 6 |
| 1993-94 | Falkirk | 35 | 2 |

## McCALL, Stuart
Born: Leeds 10/06/64

| | | | |
|---|---|---|---|
| 1982-83 | Bradford City | 28 | 4 |
| 1983-84 | Bradford City | 46 | 5 |
| 1984-85 | Bradford City | 46 | 8 |
| 1985-86 | Bradford City | 38 | 4 |
| 1986-87 | Bradford City | 36 | 7 |
| 1987-88 | Bradford City | 44 | 9 |
| 1988-89 | Everton | 33 | – |
| 1989-90 | Everton | 37 | 3 |
| 1990-91 | Everton | 33 | 3 |
| 1991-92 | Rangers | 36 | 1 |
| 1992-93 | Rangers | 36 | 5 |
| 1993-94 | Rangers | 34 | 3 |

## McCARRISON, Dugald
Born: Lanark 22/12/69

| | | | |
|---|---|---|---|
| 1987-88 | Celtic | – | – |
| 1988-89 | Celtic | 1 | – |
| 1989-90 | Celtic | – | – |
| 1990-91 | Celtic | 1 | – |
| 1990-91 | Ipswich Town | – | – |
| 1991-92 | Celtic | – | – |
| 1991-92 | Darlington | 5 | 2 |
| 1992-93 | Celtic | 1 | – |
| 1992-93 | Kilmarnock | 8 | 1 |
| 1993-94 | Kilmarnock | – | – |

## McCART, Christopher
Born: Motherwell 17/04/67

| | | | |
|---|---|---|---|
| 1984-85 | Motherwell | – | – |
| 1985-86 | Motherwell | 13 | – |
| 1986-87 | Motherwell | – | – |
| 1987-88 | Motherwell | 1 | – |
| 1988-89 | Motherwell | 26 | – |
| 1989-90 | Motherwell | 34 | 1 |
| 1990-91 | Motherwell | 36 | – |
| 1991-92 | Motherwell | 22 | 2 |
| 1992-93 | Motherwell | 29 | 3 |
| 1993-94 | Motherwell | 36 | – |

## McCLOY, Steven
Born: Girvan 28/04/75

| | | | |
|---|---|---|---|
| 1993-94 | Kilmarnock | 6 | 1 |

## McCLUSKEY, George McKinlay Cassidy Joe
Born: Hamilton 19/09/57

| | | | |
|---|---|---|---|
| 1975-76 | Celtic | 4 | – |
| 1976-77 | Celtic | – | – |
| 1977-78 | Celtic | 15 | 6 |
| 1978-79 | Celtic | 21 | 5 |
| 1979-80 | Celtic | 23 | 10 |

| SEASON | CLUB | APP | GOALS |
|---|---|---|---|
| 1980-81 | Celtic | 22 | 10 |
| 1981-82 | Celtic | 35 | 21 |
| 1982-83 | Celtic | 10 | 2 |
| 1983-84 | Leeds United | 32 | 8 |
| 1984-85 | Leeds United | 19 | 5 |
| 1985-86 | Leeds United | 22 | 3 |
| 1986-87 | Hibernian | 35 | 9 |
| 1987-88 | Hibernian | 31 | 4 |
| 1988-89 | Hibernian | 16 | 3 |
| 1989-90 | Hamilton Academical | 28 | 8 |
| 1990-91 | Hamilton Academical | 35 | 14 |
| 1991-92 | Hamilton Academical | 32 | 12 |
| 1992-93 | Kilmarnock | 31 | 11 |
| 1993-94 | Kilmarnock | 23 | 2 |

## McCOIST, Alistair
Born: Bellshill 24/09/62

| | | | |
|---|---|---|---|
| 1978-79 | St Johnstone | 4 | – |
| 1979-80 | St Johnstone | 15 | – |
| 1980-81 | St Johnstone | 38 | 22 |
| 1981-82 | Sunderland | 28 | 2 |
| 1982-83 | Sunderland | 28 | 6 |
| 1983-84 | Rangers | 30 | 9 |
| 1984-85 | Rangers | 25 | 12 |
| 1985-86 | Rangers | 33 | 24 |
| 1986-87 | Rangers | 44 | 33 |
| 1987-88 | Rangers | 40 | 31 |
| 1988-89 | Rangers | 19 | 9 |
| 1989-90 | Rangers | 34 | 14 |
| 1990-91 | Rangers | 26 | 11 |
| 1991-92 | Rangers | 38 | 34 |
| 1992-93 | Rangers | 34 | 34 |
| 1993-94 | Rangers | 21 | 7 |

## McDONALD, Colin
Born: Edinburgh 10/04/74

| | | | |
|---|---|---|---|
| 1990-91 | Hibernian | – | – |
| 1991-92 | Hibernian | – | – |
| 1992-93 | Falkirk | – | – |
| 1993-94 | Falkirk | 17 | 1 |

## McGINLAY, Patrick David
Born: Glasgow 30/05/67

| | | | |
|---|---|---|---|
| 1985-86 | Blackpool | – | – |
| 1986-87 | Blackpool | 12 | 1 |
| 1987-88 | Hibernian | – | – |
| 1988-89 | Hibernian | 2 | – |
| 1989-90 | Hibernian | 28 | 3 |
| 1990-91 | Hibernian | 32 | 1 |
| 1991-92 | Hibernian | 43 | 9 |
| 1992-93 | Hibernian | 40 | 10 |
| 1993-94 | Celtic | 41 | 9 |

## McGOWAN, Jamie
Born: Morecambe 05/12/70

| | | | |
|---|---|---|---|
| 1992-93 | Dundee | 21 | 1 |
| 1993-94 | Dundee | 14 | – |
| 1993-94 | Falkirk | 9 | 2 |

## McGRAW, Mark Robertson
Born: Rutherglen 05/01/71

| | | | |
|---|---|---|---|
| 1988-89 | Morton | 1 | – |
| 1989-90 | Morton | 11 | 3 |
| 1990-91 | Hibernian | 13 | – |
| 1991-92 | Hibernian | 24 | 1 |
| 1992-93 | Hibernian | 2 | – |
| 1993-94 | Hibernian | 2 | – |

## McGRILLEN, Paul
Born: Glasgow 19/08/71

| | | | |
|---|---|---|---|
| 1990-91 | Motherwell | 2 | – |
| 1991-92 | Motherwell | 16 | – |
| 1992-93 | Motherwell | 22 | 6 |
| 1993-94 | Motherwell | 40 | 5 |

**McINALLY, James Edward**
Born: Glasgow 19/02/64

| Season | Club | Appearances | Goals |
|---|---|---|---|
| 1982-83 | Celtic | 1 | – |
| 1983-84 | Celtic | – | – |
| 1983-84 | Dundee | 11 | 2 |
| 1984-85 | Nottingham Forest | 24 | – |
| 1985-86 | Nottingham Forest | 12 | – |
| 1985-86 | Coventry City | 5 | – |
| 1986-87 | Dundee United | 32 | 1 |
| 1987-88 | Dundee United | 36 | 2 |
| 1988-89 | Dundee United | 29 | 1 |
| 1989-90 | Dundee United | 35 | 3 |
| 1990-91 | Dundee United | 33 | 1 |
| 1991-92 | Dundee United | 32 | 4 |
| 1992-93 | Dundee United | 32 | – |
| 1993-94 | Dundee United | 31 | – |

**McKIMMIE, Stewart**
Born: Aberdeen 27/10/62

| Season | Club | Appearances | Goals |
|---|---|---|---|
| 1980-81 | Dundee | 17 | – |
| 1981-82 | Dundee | 16 | – |
| 1982-83 | Dundee | 31 | – |
| 1983-84 | Dundee | 16 | – |
| 1983-84 | Aberdeen | 18 | 1 |
| 1984-85 | Aberdeen | 34 | 3 |
| 1985-86 | Aberdeen | 34 | 3 |
| 1986-87 | Aberdeen | 37 | – |
| 1987-88 | Aberdeen | 42 | – |
| 1988-89 | Aberdeen | 35 | – |
| 1989-90 | Aberdeen | 33 | – |
| 1990-91 | Aberdeen | 26 | 1 |
| 1991-92 | Aberdeen | 39 | – |
| 1992-93 | Aberdeen | 14 | – |
| 1993-94 | Aberdeen | 40 | – |

**McKINLAY, Thomas Valley**
Born: Glasgow 03/12/64

| Season | Club | Appearances | Goals |
|---|---|---|---|
| 1981-82 | Dundee | – | – |
| 1982-83 | Dundee | 1 | – |
| 1983-84 | Dundee | 36 | 3 |
| 1984-85 | Dundee | 34 | 3 |
| 1985-86 | Dundee | 22 | – |
| 1986-87 | Dundee | 32 | 2 |
| 1987-88 | Dundee | 19 | – |
| 1988-89 | Dundee | 18 | – |
| 1988-89 | Heart of Midlothian | 17 | 1 |
| 1989-90 | Heart of Midlothian | 29 | 1 |
| 1990-91 | Heart of Midlothian | 33 | 2 |
| 1991-92 | Heart of Midlothian | 39 | 2 |
| 1992-93 | Heart of Midlothian | 34 | – |
| 1993-94 | Heart of Midlothian | 43 | – |

**McKINLAY, William**
Born: Glasgow 22/04/69

| Season | Club | Appearances | Goals |
|---|---|---|---|
| 1986-87 | Dundee United | 3 | – |
| 1987-88 | Dundee United | 12 | 1 |
| 1988-89 | Dundee United | 30 | 1 |
| 1989-90 | Dundee United | 13 | – |
| 1990-91 | Dundee United | 34 | 2 |
| 1991-92 | Dundee United | 22 | 1 |
| 1992-93 | Dundee United | 37 | 1 |
| 1993-94 | Dundee United | 39 | 9 |

**McKINNON, Raymond**
Born: Dundee 05/08/70

| Season | Club | Appearances | Goals |
|---|---|---|---|
| 1987-88 | Dundee United | – | – |
| 1988-89 | Dundee United | 1 | – |
| 1989-90 | Dundee United | 10 | – |
| 1990-91 | Dundee United | 17 | 2 |
| 1991-92 | Dundee United | 25 | 4 |
| 1992-93 | Nottingham Forest | 6 | 1 |
| 1993-94 | Nottingham Forest | – | – |
| 1993-94 | Aberdeen | 5 | – |

**McKINNON, Robert**
Born: Glasgow 31/07/66

| Season | Club | Appearances | Goals |
|---|---|---|---|
| 1984-85 | Newcastle United | – | – |
| 1985-86 | Newcastle United | 1 | – |

**McLAREN, Alan James**
Born: Edinburgh 04/01/71

| Season | Club | Appearances | Goals |
|---|---|---|---|
| 1986-87 | Hartlepool United | 45 | – |
| 1987-88 | Hartlepool United | 42 | 2 |
| 1988-89 | Hartlepool United | 46 | 2 |
| 1989-90 | Hartlepool United | 46 | 1 |
| 1990-91 | Hartlepool United | 45 | 1 |
| 1990-91 | Manchester United | – | – |
| 1991-92 | Hartlepool United | 23 | 1 |
| 1991-92 | Motherwell | 16 | 1 |
| 1992-93 | Motherwell | 35 | – |
| 1993-94 | Motherwell | 42 | 4 |

**McLAREN, Alan James**
Born: Edinburgh 04/01/71

| Season | Club | Appearances | Goals |
|---|---|---|---|
| 1987-88 | Heart of Midlothian | 1 | – |
| 1988-89 | Heart of Midlothian | 12 | 1 |
| 1989-90 | Heart of Midlothian | 27 | 1 |
| 1990-91 | Heart of Midlothian | 23 | 1 |
| 1991-92 | Heart of Midlothian | 38 | 1 |
| 1992-93 | Heart of Midlothian | 34 | – |
| 1993-94 | Heart of Midlothian | 37 | 1 |

**McLAREN, Andrew**
Born: Glasgow 05/06/73

| Season | Club | Appearances | Goals |
|---|---|---|---|
| 1989-90 | Dundee United | – | – |
| 1990-91 | Dundee United | – | – |
| 1991-92 | Dundee United | 13 | – |
| 1992-93 | Dundee United | 5 | – |
| 1993-94 | Dundee United | 27 | 2 |

**McLAUGHLIN, Brian**
Born: Bellshill 14/05/74

| Season | Club | Appearances | Goals |
|---|---|---|---|
| 1992-93 | Celtic | – | – |
| 1993-94 | Celtic | 8 | – |

**McLAUGHLIN, Joseph**
Born: Greenock 02/06/60

| Season | Club | Appearances | Goals |
|---|---|---|---|
| 1977-78 | Morton | – | – |
| 1978-79 | Morton | – | – |
| 1979-80 | Morton | 30 | 2 |
| 1980-81 | Morton | 34 | 1 |
| 1981-82 | Morton | 36 | – |
| 1982-83 | Morton | 34 | – |
| 1983-84 | Chelsea | 41 | – |
| 1984-85 | Chelsea | 36 | 1 |
| 1985-86 | Chelsea | 40 | 1 |
| 1986-87 | Chelsea | 36 | 2 |
| 1987-88 | Chelsea | 36 | 1 |
| 1988-89 | Chelsea | 31 | – |
| 1989-90 | Charlton Athletic | 31 | – |
| 1990-91 | Watford | 24 | 1 |
| 1991-92 | Watford | 22 | 1 |
| 1992-93 | Watford | – | – |
| 1992-93 | Falkirk | 8 | 1 |
| 1993-94 | Falkirk | 37 | 2 |

**McLEISH, Alexander**
Born: Glasgow 21/01/59

| Season | Club | Appearances | Goals |
|---|---|---|---|
| 1977-78 | Aberdeen | 1 | – |
| 1978-79 | Aberdeen | 19 | 1 |
| 1979-80 | Aberdeen | 35 | 2 |
| 1980-81 | Aberdeen | 32 | 3 |
| 1981-82 | Aberdeen | 32 | 5 |
| 1982-83 | Aberdeen | 34 | 2 |
| 1983-84 | Aberdeen | 32 | 2 |
| 1984-85 | Aberdeen | 30 | 1 |
| 1985-86 | Aberdeen | 34 | 3 |
| 1986-87 | Aberdeen | 40 | 3 |
| 1987-88 | Aberdeen | 36 | 1 |
| 1988-89 | Aberdeen | 34 | – |
| 1989-90 | Aberdeen | 32 | 2 |
| 1990-91 | Aberdeen | 33 | – |
| 1991-92 | Aberdeen | 7 | – |
| 1992-93 | Aberdeen | 27 | – |
| 1993-94 | Aberdeen | 35 | – |

**McMillan, Stephen**
Born: Edinburgh 19/01/76

| Season | Club | Appearances | Goals |
|---|---|---|---|
| 1993-94 | Motherwell | 1 | – |

**McNALLY, Mark**
Born: Motherwell 10/03/71

| Season | Club | Appearances | Goals |
|---|---|---|---|
| 1987-88 | Celtic | – | – |
| 1988-89 | Celtic | – | – |
| 1989-90 | Celtic | – | – |
| 1990-91 | Celtic | 19 | – |
| 1991-92 | Celtic | 25 | 1 |
| 1992-93 | Celtic | 27 | – |
| 1993-94 | Celtic | 32 | 2 |

**McPHERSON, David**
Born: Paisley 28/01/64

| Season | Club | Appearances | Goals |
|---|---|---|---|
| 1980-81 | Rangers | – | – |
| 1981-82 | Rangers | – | – |
| 1982-83 | Rangers | 18 | 1 |
| 1983-84 | Rangers | 36 | 2 |
| 1984-85 | Rangers | 31 | – |
| 1985-86 | Rangers | 34 | 5 |
| 1986-87 | Rangers | 42 | 7 |
| 1987-88 | Rangers | 44 | 4 |
| 1988-89 | Heart of Midlothian | 32 | 4 |
| 1989-90 | Heart of Midlothian | 35 | 4 |
| 1990-91 | Heart of Midlothian | 34 | 2 |
| 1991-92 | Heart of Midlothian | 44 | 2 |
| 1992-93 | Rangers | 34 | 2 |
| 1993-94 | Rangers | 28 | 1 |

**McQUEEN, Thomas Feeney**
Born: Glasgow 01/04/63

| Season | Club | Appearances | Goals |
|---|---|---|---|
| 1981-82 | Clyde | 39 | – |
| 1982-83 | Clyde | 35 | – |
| 1983-84 | Clyde | 38 | 1 |
| 1984-85 | Aberdeen | 35 | 3 |
| 1985-86 | Aberdeen | 17 | 1 |
| 1986-87 | Aberdeen | 1 | – |
| 1986-87 | West Ham United | 9 | – |
| 1987-88 | West Ham United | 12 | – |
| 1988-89 | West Ham United | 2 | – |
| 1989-90 | West Ham United | 7 | – |
| 1990-91 | West Ham United | – | – |
| 1990-91 | Falkirk | 32 | 2 |
| 1991-92 | Falkirk | 26 | 1 |
| 1992-93 | Falkirk | 30 | 4 |
| 1993-94 | Falkirk | 26 | – |

**McQUILKEN, James**
Born: Glasgow 03/10/74

| Season | Club | Appearances | Goals |
|---|---|---|---|
| 1992-93 | Celtic | 1 | – |
| 1993-94 | Celtic | – | – |

**McSKIMMING, Shaun Peter**
Born: Stranraer 29/05/70

| Season | Club | Appearances | Goals |
|---|---|---|---|
| 1986-87 | Stranraer | – | – |
| 1987-88 | Dundee | – | – |
| 1988-89 | Dundee | – | – |
| 1989-90 | Dundee | 7 | – |
| 1990-91 | Dundee | 16 | 3 |
| 1991-92 | Kilmarnock | 30 | 1 |
| 1992-93 | Kilmarnock | 35 | 5 |
| 1993-94 | Kilmarnock | 40 | 3 |

**McSTAY, Paul Michael Lyons**
Born: Hamilton 22/10/64

| Season | Club | Appearances | Goals |
|---|---|---|---|
| 1981-82 | Celtic | 10 | 1 |
| 1982-83 | Celtic | 36 | 6 |
| 1983-84 | Celtic | 34 | 3 |
| 1984-85 | Celtic | 32 | 4 |
| 1985-86 | Celtic | 34 | 8 |
| 1986-87 | Celtic | 43 | 3 |

| CLUB | LEAGUE APPEARANCES | GOALS |
|---|---|---|
| 1987-88 Celtic | 44 | 5 |
| 1988-89 Celtic | 33 | 5 |
| 1989-90 Celtic | 35 | 3 |
| 1990-91 Celtic | 30 | 2 |
| 1991-92 Celtic | 31 | 7 |
| 1992-93 Celtic | 43 | 4 |
| 1993-94 Celtic | 35 | 2 |

**McWILLIAMS, Derek**
Born: Broxburn 16/01/66

| | LEAGUE APPEARANCES | GOALS |
|---|---|---|
| 1981-82 Hibernian | – | – |
| 1982-83 Hibernian | – | – |
| 1984-85 Dundee | 16 | 2 |
| 1985-86 Dundee | 11 | 1 |
| 1986-87 Dundee | 6 | – |
| 1986-87 *Stirling Albion* | 4 | – |
| 1987-88 Dundee | – | – |
| 1987-88 Falkirk | 31 | 4 |
| 1988-89 Falkirk | 28 | 11 |
| 1989-90 Falkirk | 32 | 16 |
| 1990-91 Falkirk | 29 | 10 |
| 1991-92 Dunfermline Athletic | 24 | 3 |
| 1992-93 Dunfermline Athletic | 25 | 3 |
| 1993-94 Dunfermline Athletic | 20 | 3 |

**MASKREY, Stephen William**
Born: Edinburgh 16/08/62

| | LEAGUE APPEARANCES | GOALS |
|---|---|---|
| 1983-84 Falkirk | – | – |
| 1984-85 East Stirlingshire | 37 | 12 |
| 1985-86 East Stirlingshire | 21 | 12 |
| 1985-86 Queen of the South | 12 | 2 |
| 1986-87 Queen of the South | 31 | 2 |
| 1987-88 St. Johnstone | 33 | 5 |
| 1988-89 St. Johnstone | 31 | 12 |
| 1989-90 St. Johnstone | 29 | 11 |
| 1990-91 St. Johnstone | 34 | 7 |
| 1991-92 St. Johnstone | 24 | 2 |
| 1992-93 St. Johnstone | 19 | 2 |
| 1993-94 St. Johnstone | 4 | – |

**MIKHAILITCHENKO, Alexei**
Born: Kiev 30/03/63
From Dynamo Kiev, UC Sampdoria SpA

| | LEAGUE APPEARANCES | GOALS |
|---|---|---|
| 1991-92 Rangers | 27 | 10 |
| 1992-93 Rangers | 29 | 5 |
| 1993-94 Rangers | 34 | 5 |

**MILLAR, John**
Born: Bellshill 08/12/66

| | LEAGUE APPEARANCES | GOALS |
|---|---|---|
| 1984-85 Chelsea | – | – |
| 1985-86 Chelsea | 7 | – |
| 1986-87 Chelsea | 4 | – |
| 1986-87 *Hamilton Academical* | 10 | – |
| 1986-87 *Northampton Town* | 1 | – |
| 1987-88 Blackburn Rovers | 15 | – |
| 1988-89 Blackburn Rovers | 38 | – |
| 1989-90 Blackburn Rovers | 39 | 1 |
| 1990-91 Blackburn Rovers | 34 | – |
| 1991-92 Heart of Midlothian | 41 | 7 |
| 1992-93 Heart of Midlothian | 24 | – |
| 1993-94 Heart of Midlothian | 20 | 4 |

**MILLEN, Andrew Frank**
Born: Glasgow 10/06/65

| | LEAGUE APPEARANCES | GOALS |
|---|---|---|
| 1983-84 St Johnstone | – | – |
| 1984-85 St Johnstone | 4 | – |
| 1985-86 St Johnstone | 36 | 1 |
| 1986-87 St Johnstone | 31 | 1 |
| 1987-88 St Johnstone | – | – |
| 1987-88 Alloa | 36 | 4 |
| 1988-89 Alloa | 38 | 3 |
| 1989-90 Alloa | 37 | 2 |
| 1990-91 Hamilton Academical | 39 | – |

| SEASON | CLUB | LEAGUE APPEARANCES | GOALS |
|---|---|---|---|
| 1991-92 | Hamilton Academical | 39 | 1 |
| 1992-93 | Hamilton Academical | 41 | 3 |
| 1993-94 | Kilmarnock | 44 | – |

**MILLER, Charles**
Born: Glasgow 18/03/76

| SEASON | CLUB | LEAGUE APPEARANCES | GOALS |
|---|---|---|---|
| 1992-93 | Rangers | – | – |
| 1993-94 | Rangers | 3 | – |

**MILLER, Graeme**
Born: Glasgow 21/02/73

| SEASON | CLUB | LEAGUE APPEARANCES | GOALS |
|---|---|---|---|
| 1992-93 | Hibernian | 1 | – |
| 1993-94 | Hibernian | 1 | – |

**MILLER, Joseph**
Born: Glasgow 08/12/67

| SEASON | CLUB | LEAGUE APPEARANCES | GOALS |
|---|---|---|---|
| 1984-85 | Aberdeen | 1 | – |
| 1985-86 | Aberdeen | 18 | 3 |
| 1986-87 | Aberdeen | 27 | 6 |
| 1987-88 | Aberdeen | 14 | 4 |
| 1987-88 | Celtic | 27 | 3 |
| 1988-89 | Celtic | 22 | 8 |
| 1989-90 | Celtic | 24 | 5 |
| 1990-91 | Celtic | 30 | 8 |
| 1991-92 | Celtic | 26 | 2 |
| 1992-93 | Celtic | 23 | 2 |
| 1993-94 | Aberdeen | 27 | 4 |

**MILLER, William**
Born: Edinburgh 01/11/69

| SEASON | CLUB | LEAGUE APPEARANCES | GOALS |
|---|---|---|---|
| 1989-90 | Hibernian | 11 | – |
| 1990-91 | Hibernian | 25 | 1 |
| 1991-92 | Hibernian | 30 | – |
| 1992-93 | Hibernian | 34 | – |
| 1993-94 | Hibernian | 37 | – |

**MILNE, Callum**
Born: Edinburgh 27/08/65

| SEASON | CLUB | LEAGUE APPEARANCES | GOALS |
|---|---|---|---|
| 1983-84 | Hibernian | – | – |
| 1984-85 | Hibernian | 1 | – |
| 1985-86 | Hibernian | 7 | – |
| 1986-87 | Hibernian | 2 | – |
| 1987-88 | Hibernian | 3 | – |
| 1988-89 | Hibernian | 19 | – |
| 1989-90 | Hibernian | 3 | – |
| 1990-91 | Hibernian | 21 | – |
| 1991-92 | Hibernian | 8 | – |
| 1992-93 | Hibernian | 15 | – |
| 1993-94 | Hibernian | – | – |
| 1993-94 | Partick Thistle | 31 | 1 |

**MITCHELL, Alistair Robert**
Born: Kirkcaldy 03/12/68

| SEASON | CLUB | LEAGUE APPEARANCES | GOALS |
|---|---|---|---|
| 1988-89 | East Fife | 18 | 4 |
| 1989-90 | East Fife | 35 | 12 |
| 1990-91 | East Fife | 34 | 7 |
| 1991-92 | Kilmarnock | 42 | 10 |
| 1992-93 | Kilmarnock | 32 | 6 |
| 1993-94 | Kilmarnock | 34 | 5 |

**MITCHELL, Graham**
Born: Glasgow 02/11/62

| SEASON | CLUB | LEAGUE APPEARANCES | GOALS |
|---|---|---|---|
| 1980-81 | Hamilton Academical | 4 | – |
| 1981-82 | Hamilton Academical | 37 | – |
| 1982-83 | Hamilton Academical | 32 | 1 |
| 1983-84 | Hamilton Academical | 21 | 1 |
| 1984-85 | Hamilton Academical | 30 | – |
| 1985-86 | Hamilton Academical | 32 | 6 |
| 1986-87 | Hamilton Academical | 23 | 1 |
| 1986-87 | Hibernian | 17 | 1 |
| 1987-88 | Hibernian | 41 | 1 |
| 1988-89 | Hibernian | 20 | – |
| 1989-90 | Hibernian | 31 | – |
| 1990-91 | Hibernian | 28 | – |
| 1991-92 | Hibernian | 27 | 1 |

| SEASON | CLUB | LEAGUE APPEARANCES | GOALS |
|---|---|---|---|
| 1992-93 | Hibernian | 41 | – |
| 1993-94 | Hibernian | 36 | 1 |

**MONTGOMERIE, Samuel Raymond**
Born: Irvine 17/04/61

| SEASON | CLUB | LEAGUE APPEARANCES | GOALS |
|---|---|---|---|
| 1980-81 | Newcastle United | – | – |
| 1981-82 | Dumbarton | 20 | 5 |
| 1982-83 | Dumbarton | 25 | 2 |
| 1983-84 | Dumbarton | 39 | 1 |
| 1984-85 | Dumbarton | 6 | – |
| 1985-86 | Dumbarton | 24 | – |
| 1986-87 | Dumbarton | 35 | – |
| 1987-88 | Dumbarton | 31 | – |
| 1988-89 | Kilmarnock | 31 | 2 |
| 1989-90 | Kilmarnock | 35 | 3 |
| 1990-91 | Kilmarnock | 37 | – |
| 1991-92 | Kilmarnock | 30 | 1 |
| 1992-93 | Kilmarnock | 42 | – |
| 1993-94 | Kilmarnock | 42 | – |

**MOORE, Craig Andrew**
Born: Canterbury, Australia 12/12/75

| SEASON | CLUB | LEAGUE APPEARANCES | GOALS |
|---|---|---|---|
| 1993-94 | Rangers | 1 | – |

**MORROW, John**
Born: Belfast 20/11/71
From Linfield

| SEASON | CLUB | LEAGUE APPEARANCES | GOALS |
|---|---|---|---|
| 1988-89 | Rangers | – | – |
| 1989-90 | Rangers | – | – |
| 1990-91 | Rangers | – | – |
| 1991-92 | Rangers | 3 | – |
| 1992-93 | Rangers | – | – |
| 1993-94 | Rangers | 2 | – |

**MOWBRAY, Anthony Mark**
Born: Saltburn 22/11/63

| SEASON | CLUB | LEAGUE APPEARANCES | GOALS |
|---|---|---|---|
| 1981-82 | Middlesbrough | – | – |
| 1982-83 | Middlesbrough | 26 | – |
| 1983-84 | Middlesbrough | 35 | 1 |
| 1984-85 | Middlesbrough | 40 | 2 |
| 1985-86 | Middlesbrough | 35 | 4 |
| 1986-87 | Middlesbrough | 46 | 7 |
| 1987-88 | Middlesbrough | 44 | 3 |
| 1988-89 | Middlesbrough | 37 | 3 |
| 1989-90 | Middlesbrough | 28 | 2 |
| 1990-91 | Middlesbrough | 40 | 3 |
| 1991-92 | Middlesbrough | 17 | – |
| 1991-92 | Celtic | 15 | 2 |
| 1992-93 | Celtic | 26 | 2 |
| 1993-94 | Celtic | 22 | 1 |

**MURDOCH, Andrew Gerard**
Born: Greenock 20/07/68

| SEASON | CLUB | LEAGUE APPEARANCES | GOALS |
|---|---|---|---|
| 1987-88 | Celtic | – | – |
| 1988-89 | Celtic | – | – |
| 1988-89 | *Partick Thistle* | 13 | – |
| 1989-90 | Celtic | – | – |
| 1989-90 | *Partick Thistle* | 13 | – |
| 1990-91 | Celtic | – | – |
| 1990-91 | Partick Thistle | 18 | – |
| 1991-92 | Partick Thistle | 32 | – |
| 1992-93 | Partick Thistle | 17 | – |
| 1993-94 | Partick Thistle | 6 | – |

**MURRAY, Neil**
Born: Bellshill 21/02/73

| SEASON | CLUB | LEAGUE APPEARANCES | GOALS |
|---|---|---|---|
| 1989-90 | Rangers | – | – |
| 1990-91 | Rangers | – | – |
| 1991-92 | Rangers | – | – |
| 1992-93 | Rangers | 16 | – |
| 1993-94 | Rangers | 22 | – |

| SEASON | CLUB | LEAGUE APPEARANCES | GOALS |
|---|---|---|---|
| **MYERS, Christoper** | | | |
| Born: Yeovil 01/04/69 | | | |
| 1986-87 | Torquay United | 9 | – |
| From local football | | | |
| 1990-91 | Torquay United | 29 | 2 |
| 1991-92 | Torquay United | 39 | 4 |
| 1992-93 | Torquay United | 28 | 1 |
| 1993-94 | Dundee United | 5 | – |
| 1993-94 | *Torquay United* | 6 | – |
| **NAPIER, Craig Cameron** | | | |
| Born: East Kilbride 14/11/65 | | | |
| 1984-85 | Clyde | 16 | – |
| 1985-86 | Clyde | 8 | – |
| 1986-87 | Clyde | 42 | – |
| 1987-88 | Clyde | 42 | 1 |
| 1988-89 | Clyde | 14 | – |
| 1988-89 | Hamilton Academical | 19 | 1 |
| 1989-90 | Hamilton Academical | 39 | 6 |
| 1990-91 | Hamilton Academical | 39 | 6 |
| 1991-92 | Hamilton Academical | 22 | 2 |
| 1992-93 | Hamilton Academical | 29 | 1 |
| 1993-94 | Hamilton Academical | 27 | 2 |
| 1993-94 | Kilmarnock | 15 | – |
| **NELSON, Craig Robert** | | | |
| Born: Coatbridge 28/05/71 | | | |
| 1990-91 | Partick Thistle | 1 | – |
| 1991-92 | Partick Thistle | 11 | – |
| 1992-93 | Partick Thistle | 27 | – |
| 1993-94 | Partick Thistle | 39 | – |
| **NICHOLAS, Charles** | | | |
| Born: Glasgow 30/12/61 | | | |
| 1980-81 | Celtic | 29 | 16 |
| 1981-82 | Celtic | 10 | 3 |
| 1982-83 | Celtic | 35 | 29 |
| 1983-84 | Arsenal | 41 | 11 |
| 1984-85 | Arsenal | 38 | 9 |
| 1985-86 | Arsenal | 41 | 10 |
| 1986-87 | Arsenal | 28 | 4 |
| 1987-88 | Arsenal | 3 | – |
| 1987-88 | Aberdeen | 16 | 3 |
| 1988-89 | Aberdeen | 29 | 16 |
| 1989-90 | Aberdeen | 33 | 11 |
| 1990-91 | Celtic | 14 | 6 |
| 1991-92 | Celtic | 37 | 21 |
| 1992-93 | Celtic | 16 | 2 |
| 1993-94 | Celtic | 35 | 8 |
| **NIXON, Jerren Kendall** | | | |
| Born: Trinidad 25/06/73 | | | |
| From ECM Motown | | | |
| 1993-94 | Dundee United | 15 | 1 |
| **O'CONNOR, Gary** | | | |
| Born: Newtongrange 07/04/74 | | | |
| 1991-92 | Heart of Midlothian | – | – |
| 1992-93 | Heart of Midlothian | – | – |
| 1992-93 | Berwick Rangers | 13 | – |
| 1993-94 | Berwick Rangers | 26 | – |
| 1993-94 | Heart of Midlothian | – | – |
| **O'DONNELL, Philip** | | | |
| Born: Bellshill 25/03/72 | | | |
| 1990-91 | Motherwell | 12 | – |
| 1991-92 | Motherwell | 42 | 4 |
| 1992-93 | Motherwell | 32 | 4 |
| 1993-94 | Motherwell | 35 | 7 |

| SEASON | CLUB | LEAGUE APPEARANCES | GOALS |
|---|---|---|---|
| **O'NEIL, Brian** | | | |
| Born: Paisley 06/09/72 | | | |
| 1991-92 | Celtic | 28 | 1 |
| 1992-93 | Celtic | 17 | 3 |
| 1993-94 | Celtic | 27 | 2 |
| **O'NEILL, John Joseph** | | | |
| Born: Glasgow 03/01/74 | | | |
| 1991-92 | Queen's Park | 25 | 6 |
| 1992-93 | Queen's Park | 27 | 6 |
| 1993-94 | Queen's Park | 39 | 18 |
| **O'NEILL, Michael Andrew Martin** | | | |
| Born: Portadown 05/07/69 | | | |
| 1987-88 | Newcastle United | 21 | 12 |
| 1988-89 | Newcastle United | 27 | 3 |
| 1989-90 | Dundee United | 18 | 5 |
| 1990-91 | Dundee United | 13 | – |
| 1991-92 | Dundee United | 8 | 4 |
| 1992-93 | Dundee United | 25 | 2 |
| 1993-94 | Dundee United | – | – |
| 1993-94 | Hibernian | 36 | 3 |
| **OLIVER, Neil** | | | |
| Born: Berwick-Upon-Tweed 11/04/67 | | | |
| 1985-86 | Berwick Rangers | 5 | – |
| 1986-87 | Berwick Rangers | 37 | – |
| 1987-88 | Berwick Rangers | 12 | – |
| 1988-89 | Berwick Rangers | 39 | – |
| 1989-90 | Blackburn Rovers | 3 | – |
| 1990-91 | Blackburn Rovers | 3 | – |
| 1991-92 | Falkirk | 35 | – |
| 1992-93 | Falkirk | 25 | – |
| 1993-94 | Falkirk | 33 | 2 |
| **PARKS, Anthony** | | | |
| Born: Hackney 28/01/63 | | | |
| 1980-81 | Tottenham Hotspur | – | – |
| 1981-82 | Tottenham Hotspur | 2 | – |
| 1982-83 | Tottenham Hotspur | 1 | – |
| 1983-84 | Tottenham Hotspur | 16 | – |
| 1984-85 | Tottenham Hotspur | – | – |
| 1985-86 | Tottenham Hotspur | – | – |
| 1986-87 | Tottenham Hotspur | 2 | – |
| 1986-87 | *Oxford United* | 5 | – |
| 1987-88 | Tottenham Hotspur | 16 | – |
| 1987-88 | *Gillingham* | 2 | – |
| 1988-89 | Brentford | 33 | – |
| 1989-90 | Brentford | 37 | – |
| 1990-91 | Brentford | 1 | – |
| 1990-91 | *Queens Park Rangers* | – | – |
| 1990-91 | Fulham | 2 | – |
| 1991-92 | West Ham United | 6 | – |
| 1992-93 | Stoke City | 2 | – |
| 1992-93 | Falkirk | 15 | – |
| 1993-94 | Falkirk | 41 | – |
| **PATERSON, Craig Stewart** | | | |
| Born: South Queensferry 02/10/59 | | | |
| 1978-79 | Hibernian | – | – |
| 1979-80 | Hibernian | 30 | – |
| 1980-81 | Hibernian | 38 | 3 |
| 1981-82 | Hibernian | 36 | 1 |
| 1982-83 | Rangers | 20 | – |
| 1983-84 | Rangers | 21 | 1 |
| 1984-85 | Rangers | 22 | 2 |
| 1985-86 | Rangers | 18 | 1 |
| 1986-87 | Rangers | 2 | – |
| 1986-87 | Motherwell | 16 | – |
| 1987-88 | Motherwell | 44 | 2 |
| 1988-89 | Motherwell | 33 | 1 |
| 1989-90 | Motherwell | 33 | 3 |
| 1990-91 | Motherwell | 32 | 2 |

| SEASON | CLUB | | |
|---|---|---|---|
| 1991-92 | Kilmarnock | 28 | – |
| 1992-93 | Kilmarnock | 21 | 1 |
| 1993-94 | Kilmarnock | 6 | – |
| **PETRIC, Gordan** | | | |
| Born: Belgrade 30/07/69 | | | |
| From Belgrade, FC Partizan Belgrade | | | |
| 1993-94 | Dundee United | 27 | 1 |
| **PERRY, Mark George** | | | |
| Born: Aberdeen 07/02/71 | | | |
| 1988-89 | Dundee United | – | – |
| 1989-90 | Dundee United | – | – |
| 1990-91 | Dundee United | – | – |
| 1991-92 | Dundee United | – | – |
| 1992-93 | Dundee United | 18 | 1 |
| 1993-94 | Dundee United | 9 | – |
| **PHILLIBEN, John** | | | |
| Born: Stirling 14/03/64 | | | |
| 1980-81 | Stirling Albion | 15 | – |
| 1981-82 | Stirling Albion | 37 | 1 |
| 1982-83 | Stirling Albion | 34 | – |
| 1983-84 | Stirling Albion | 23 | – |
| 1983-84 | Doncaster Rovers | 12 | – |
| 1984-85 | Doncaster Rovers | 36 | 1 |
| 1985-86 | Doncaster Rovers | 22 | – |
| 1985-86 | *Cambridge United* | 6 | – |
| 1986-87 | Doncaster Rovers | 1 | – |
| 1986-87 | Motherwell | 37 | – |
| 1987-88 | Motherwell | 35 | 2 |
| 1988-89 | Motherwell | 19 | – |
| 1989-90 | Motherwell | 24 | – |
| 1990-91 | Motherwell | 11 | 1 |
| 1991-92 | Motherwell | 32 | 1 |
| 1992-93 | Motherwell | 31 | – |
| 1993-94 | Motherwell | 28 | 2 |
| **PRESSLEY, Steven** | | | |
| Born: Elgin 11/10/73 | | | |
| 1991-92 | Rangers | 1 | – |
| 1992-93 | Rangers | 8 | – |
| 1993-94 | Rangers | 23 | 1 |
| **REID, Brian Robertson** | | | |
| Born: Paisley 15/06/70 | | | |
| 1988-89 | Morton | 2 | – |
| 1989-90 | Morton | 36 | 1 |
| 1990-91 | Morton | 19 | – |
| 1990-91 | Rangers | 3 | – |
| 1991-92 | Rangers | – | – |
| 1992-93 | Rangers | 2 | – |
| 1993-94 | Rangers | – | – |
| 1993-94 | *Newcastle United* | – | – |
| **REID, Christopher Thomas** | | | |
| Born: Edinburgh 04/11/71 | | | |
| 1989-90 | Hibernian | 2 | – |
| 1990-91 | Hibernian | 1 | – |
| 1991-92 | Hibernian | 9 | – |
| 1992-93 | Hibernian | 14 | – |
| 1993-94 | Hibernian | – | – |
| **REILLY, Mark** | | | |
| Born: Bellshill 30/03/69 | | | |
| 1988-89 | Motherwell | – | – |
| 1989-90 | Motherwell | 4 | – |
| 1990-91 | Motherwell | – | – |
| 1991-92 | Kilmarnock | 19 | – |
| 1992-93 | Kilmarnock | 19 | 3 |
| 1993-94 | Kilmarnock | 38 | – |

**RICE, Brian**
Born: Bellshill 11/10/63

| Season | Club | Apps | Goals |
|---|---|---|---|
| 1980-81 | Hibernian | 1 | – |
| 1981-82 | Hibernian | 1 | – |
| 1982-83 | Hibernian | 22 | 2 |
| 1983-84 | Hibernian | 25 | 5 |
| 1984-85 | Hibernian | 35 | 4 |
| 1985-86 | Nottingham Forest | 19 | 3 |
| 1986-87 | Nottingham Forest | 3 | 1 |
| 1986-87 | *Grimsby Town* | 4 | – |
| 1987-88 | Nottingham Forest | 30 | 2 |
| 1988-89 | Nottingham Forest | 20 | 1 |
| 1988-89 | *West Bromwich Albion* | 3 | – |
| 1989-90 | Nottingham Forest | 18 | 2 |
| 1990-91 | Nottingham Forest | 1 | – |
| 1990-91 | *Stoke City* | 18 | 1 |
| 1991-92 | Falkirk | 16 | 1 |
| 1992-93 | Falkirk | 17 | 2 |
| 1993-94 | Falkirk | 37 | 3 |

**RISTIC, Dragutin**
Born: Pula, Yugoslavia 05/08/64

From Benevento Sporting
| Season | Club | Apps | Goals |
|---|---|---|---|
| 1993-94 | Dundee | 18 | 6 |
| 1993-94 | Falkirk | 12 | 4 |

**ROBERTS, Mark Kingsley**
Born: Irvine 29/10/75

| Season | Club | Apps | Goals |
|---|---|---|---|
| 1991-92 | Kilmarnock | 1 | – |
| 1992-93 | Kilmarnock | 5 | – |
| 1993-94 | Kilmarnock | 13 | 2 |

**ROBERTSON, David**
Born: Aberdeen 17/10/68

| Season | Club | Apps | Goals |
|---|---|---|---|
| 1986-87 | Aberdeen | 34 | – |
| 1987-88 | Aberdeen | 23 | – |
| 1988-89 | Aberdeen | 23 | – |
| 1989-90 | Aberdeen | 20 | 1 |
| 1990-91 | Aberdeen | 35 | 1 |
| 1991-92 | Rangers | 42 | 1 |
| 1992-93 | Rangers | 39 | 3 |
| 1993-94 | Rangers | 32 | 1 |

**ROBERTSON, Hugh Scott**
Born: Aberdeen 19/03/75

| Season | Club | Apps | Goals |
|---|---|---|---|
| 1993-94 | Aberdeen | 8 | – |

**ROBERTSON, John Grant**
Born: Edinburgh 02/10/64

| Season | Club | Apps | Goals |
|---|---|---|---|
| 1980-81 | Heart of Midlothian | – | – |
| 1981-82 | Heart of Midlothian | 1 | – |
| 1982-83 | Heart of Midlothian | 23 | 19 |
| 1983-84 | Heart of Midlothian | 35 | 15 |
| 1984-85 | Heart of Midlothian | 33 | 8 |
| 1985-86 | Heart of Midlothian | 35 | 20 |
| 1986-87 | Heart of Midlothian | 37 | 16 |
| 1987-88 | Heart of Midlothian | 39 | 26 |
| 1987-88 | Newcastle United | – | – |
| 1988-89 | Newcastle United | 12 | – |
| 1988-89 | Heart of Midlothian | 15 | 4 |
| 1989-90 | Heart of Midlothian | 32 | 17 |
| 1990-91 | Heart of Midlothian | 31 | 12 |
| 1991-92 | Heart of Midlothian | 42 | 14 |
| 1992-93 | Heart of Midlothian | 42 | 11 |
| 1993-94 | Heart of Midlothian | 36 | 8 |

**ROBERTSON, Lee**
Born: Edinburgh 25/08/73

| Season | Club | Apps | Goals |
|---|---|---|---|
| 1990-91 | Rangers | – | – |
| 1991-92 | Rangers | 1 | – |
| 1992-93 | Rangers | 1 | – |
| 1993-94 | Rangers | – | – |

**RODDIE, Andrew Robert**
Born: Glasgow 04/11/71

| Season | Club | Apps | Goals |
|---|---|---|---|
| 1988-89 | Aberdeen | – | – |
| 1989-90 | Aberdeen | – | – |
| 1990-91 | Aberdeen | – | – |
| 1991-92 | Aberdeen | 10 | 2 |
| 1992-93 | Aberdeen | 11 | 2 |
| 1993-94 | Aberdeen | 6 | 1 |

**SCOTT, Colin**
Born: Glasgow 19/05/70

| Season | Club | Apps | Goals |
|---|---|---|---|
| 1987-88 | Rangers | – | – |
| 1988-89 | Rangers | – | – |
| 1989-90 | Rangers | – | – |
| 1989-90 | *Brentford* | 6 | – |
| 1990-91 | Rangers | – | – |
| 1990-91 | *Airdrieonians* | 1 | – |
| 1991-92 | Rangers | – | – |
| 1992-93 | Rangers | – | – |
| 1993-94 | Rangers | 6 | – |

**SHANNON, Robert**
Born: Bellshill 20/04/66

| Season | Club | Apps | Goals |
|---|---|---|---|
| 1982-83 | Dundee | – | – |
| 1983-84 | Dundee | 6 | – |
| 1984-85 | Dundee | 3 | – |
| 1985-86 | Dundee | 33 | – |
| 1986-87 | Dundee | 39 | 5 |
| 1987-88 | Dundee | 41 | – |
| 1988-89 | Dundee | 29 | 1 |
| 1989-90 | Dundee | 36 | 1 |
| 1990-91 | Dundee | 37 | 2 |
| 1991-92 | Dundee | 3 | – |
| 1991-92 | *Middlesbrough* | 1 | – |
| 1991-92 | Dunfermline Athletic | 27 | – |
| 1992-93 | Dunfermline Athletic | 42 | – |
| 1993-94 | Motherwell | 43 | – |

**SHAW, Gregory**
Born: Dumfries 15/02/70

| Season | Club | Apps | Goals |
|---|---|---|---|
| 1988-89 | Ayr United | 2 | – |
| 1989-90 | Ayr United | 3 | – |
| 1990-91 | Ayr United | 9 | – |
| 1991-92 | Ayr United | 39 | 10 |
| 1992-93 | Ayr United | 5 | – |
| 1992-93 | Falkirk | 6 | 2 |
| 1993-94 | Falkirk | 28 | 10 |

**SHEARER, Duncan**
Born: Fort William 28/08/62

| Season | Club | Apps | Goals |
|---|---|---|---|
| 1983-84 | Chelsea | – | – |
| 1984-85 | Chelsea | – | – |
| 1985-86 | Chelsea | 2 | 1 |
| 1985-86 | Huddersfield | 8 | 7 |
| 1986-87 | Huddersfield | 42 | 21 |
| 1987-88 | Huddersfield | 33 | 10 |
| 1988-89 | Swindon Town | 36 | 14 |
| 1989-90 | Swindon Town | 42 | 20 |
| 1990-91 | Swindon Town | 44 | 22 |
| 1991-92 | Swindon Town | 37 | 22 |
| 1991-92 | Blackburn Rovers | 6 | 1 |
| 1992-93 | Aberdeen | 34 | 22 |
| 1993-94 | Aberdeen | 43 | 17 |

**SKILLING, Mark James**
Born: Irvine 06/10/72

| Season | Club | Apps | Goals |
|---|---|---|---|
| 1992-93 | Kilmarnock | 40 | 4 |
| 1993-94 | Kilmarnock | 23 | 3 |

**SMITH, Barry Martin**
Born: Paisley 19/02/74

| Season | Club | Apps | Goals |
|---|---|---|---|
| 1991-92 | Celtic | 3 | – |
| 1992-93 | Celtic | 6 | – |
| 1993-94 | Celtic | 7 | – |

**SMITH, Gary**
Born: Glasgow 25/03/71

| Season | Club | Apps | Goals |
|---|---|---|---|
| 1988-89 | Falkirk | 3 | – |
| 1989-90 | Falkirk | 36 | – |
| 1990-91 | Falkirk | 31 | – |
| 1991-92 | Aberdeen | 16 | 1 |
| 1992-93 | Aberdeen | 40 | – |
| 1993-94 | Aberdeen | 21 | – |

**SMITH, Henry George**
Born: Lanark 10/03/56

| Season | Club | Apps | Goals |
|---|---|---|---|
| 1978-79 | Leeds United | – | – |
| 1979-80 | Leeds United | – | – |
| 1980-81 | Leeds United | – | – |
| 1981-82 | Heart of Midlothian | 33 | – |
| 1982-83 | Heart of Midlothian | 39 | – |
| 1983-84 | Heart of Midlothian | 36 | – |
| 1984-85 | Heart of Midlothian | 36 | – |
| 1985-86 | Heart of Midlothian | 36 | – |
| 1986-87 | Heart of Midlothian | 43 | – |
| 1987-88 | Heart of Midlothian | 44 | – |
| 1988-89 | Heart of Midlothian | 36 | – |
| 1989-90 | Heart of Midlothian | 36 | – |
| 1990-91 | Heart of Midlothian | 23 | – |
| 1991-92 | Heart of Midlothian | 44 | – |
| 1992-93 | Heart of Midlothian | 25 | – |
| 1993-94 | Heart of Midlothian | 27 | – |

**SMITH, Thomas William**
Born: Glasgow 12/10/73

| Season | Club | Apps | Goals |
|---|---|---|---|
| 1991-92 | Partick Thistle | – | – |
| 1992-93 | Partick Thistle | 2 | – |
| 1993-94 | Partick Thistle | 8 | 1 |

**SNELDERS, Theodorus G. A.**
Born: Westervoort 07/12/63

From FC Twente
| Season | Club | Apps | Goals |
|---|---|---|---|
| 1988-89 | Aberdeen | 36 | – |
| 1989-90 | Aberdeen | 23 | – |
| 1990-91 | Aberdeen | 21 | – |
| 1991-92 | Aberdeen | 42 | – |
| 1992-93 | Aberdeen | 41 | – |
| 1993-94 | Aberdeen | 33 | – |

**STEVEN, Trevor**
Born: Berwick Upon Tweed 21/09/63

| Season | Club | Apps | Goals |
|---|---|---|---|
| 1980-81 | Burnley | 1 | – |
| 1981-82 | Burnley | 36 | 3 |
| 1982-83 | Burnley | 39 | 8 |
| 1983-84 | Everton | 27 | 1 |
| 1984-85 | Everton | 40 | 12 |

| SEASON | CLUB | LEAGUE APPEARANCES | GOALS |
|---|---|---|---|
| 1985-86 | Everton | 41 | 9 |
| 1986-87 | Everton | 41 | 14 |
| 1987-88 | Everton | 36 | 6 |
| 1988-89 | Everton | 29 | 6 |
| 1989-90 | Rangers | 34 | 3 |
| 1990-91 | Rangers | 19 | 2 |
| 1991-92 | Rangers | 2 | 1 |
| 1991-92 | Marseille | 27 | 3 |
| 1992-93 | Rangers | 24 | 5 |
| 1993-94 | Rangers | 32 | 4 |

**STEVENS, Michael Gary**
Born: Barrow-In-Furness 27/03/63

| SEASON | CLUB | LEAGUE APPEARANCES | GOALS |
|---|---|---|---|
| 1980-81 | Everton | – | – |
| 1981-82 | Everton | 19 | 1 |
| 1982-83 | Everton | 28 | – |
| 1983-84 | Everton | 27 | 1 |
| 1984-85 | Everton | 37 | 3 |
| 1985-86 | Everton | 41 | 1 |
| 1986-87 | Everton | 25 | 2 |
| 1987-88 | Everton | 31 | – |
| 1988-89 | Rangers | 35 | 1 |
| 1989-90 | Rangers | 35 | 1 |
| 1990-91 | Rangers | 36 | 4 |
| 1991-92 | Rangers | 43 | 2 |
| 1992-93 | Rangers | 9 | – |
| 1993-94 | Rangers | 29 | – |

**STILLIE, Derek**
Born: Irvine 03/12/73

| SEASON | CLUB | LEAGUE APPEARANCES | GOALS |
|---|---|---|---|
| 1990-91 | Aberdeen | – | – |
| 1991-92 | Aberdeen | – | – |
| 1992-93 | Aberdeen | – | – |
| 1993-94 | Aberdeen | 5 | 1 |

**TAYLOR, Alexander**
Born: Baillieston 13/06/62

| SEASON | CLUB | LEAGUE APPEARANCES | GOALS |
|---|---|---|---|
| 1980-81 | Dundee United | – | – |
| 1981-82 | Dundee United | – | – |
| 1982-83 | Dundee United | 3 | – |
| 1983-84 | Dundee United | 9 | 1 |
| 1984-85 | Dundee United | 21 | 5 |
| 1986-87 | Hamilton Academical | 25 | 1 |
| 1987-88 | Hamilton Academical | 41 | 4 |
| 1988-89 | Walsall | 13 | 3 |
| 1989-90 | Walsall | 32 | 3 |
| 1990-91 | Walsall | – | – |
| 1990-91 | Falkirk | 29 | 2 |
| 1991-92 | Falkirk | 22 | 1 |
| 1992-93 | Falkirk | 8 | 1 |
| 1992-93 | Partick Thistle | 8 | 1 |
| 1993-94 | Partick Thistle | 32 | 4 |

**THOMAS, Kevin Roderick**
Born: Edinburgh 25/04/75

| SEASON | CLUB | LEAGUE APPEARANCES | GOALS |
|---|---|---|---|
| 1992-93 | Heart of Midlothian | 4 | 2 |
| 1993-94 | Heart of Midlothian | 12 | – |

**THOMSON, Scott Munro**
Born: Aberdeen 29/01/72

| SEASON | CLUB | LEAGUE APPEARANCES | GOALS |
|---|---|---|---|
| 1990-91 | Brechin City | 30 | 3 |
| 1991-92 | Brechin City | 11 | 3 |
| 1991-92 | Aberdeen | – | – |
| 1992-93 | Aberdeen | 2 | – |
| 1993-94 | Aberdeen | 3 | – |

**THOMSON, William Marshall**
Born: Linwood 10/02/58

| SEASON | CLUB | LEAGUE APPEARANCES | GOALS |
|---|---|---|---|
| 1975-76 | Partick Thistle | – | – |
| 1976-77 | Partick Thistle | – | – |
| 1977-78 | Partick Thistle | – | – |
| 1978-79 | St Mirren | 34 | – |
| 1979-80 | St Mirren | 36 | – |
| 1980-81 | St Mirren | 36 | – |
| 1981-82 | St Mirren | 35 | – |
| 1982-83 | St Mirren | 35 | – |
| 1983-84 | St Mirren | 30 | – |
| 1984-85 | Dundee United | 11 | – |
| 1985-86 | Dundee United | 28 | – |
| 1986-87 | Dundee United | 42 | – |
| 1987-88 | Dundee United | 36 | – |
| 1988-89 | Dundee United | 36 | – |
| 1989-90 | Dundee United | 7 | – |
| 1990-91 | Dundee United | 5 | – |
| 1991-92 | Motherwell | 43 | – |
| 1992-93 | Motherwell | 9 | – |
| 1993-94 | Motherwell | – | – |

**TIERNEY, Peter Grant**
Born: Falkirk 11/10/61

| SEASON | CLUB | LEAGUE APPEARANCES | GOALS |
|---|---|---|---|
| 1978-79 | Heart of Midlothian | – | – |
| 1979-80 | Heart of Midlothian | – | – |
| 1980-81 | Cowdenbeath | 32 | 1 |
| 1981-82 | Cowdenbeath | 32 | 2 |
| 1982-83 | Cowdenbeath | 32 | 2 |
| 1983-84 | Cowdenbeath | 35 | 1 |
| 1984-85 | Cowdenbeath | 25 | 1 |
| 1984-85 | Meadowbank Thistle | 8 | – |
| 1985-86 | Meadowbank Thistle | 35 | 4 |
| 1986-87 | Meadowbank Thistle | 36 | 4 |
| 1987-88 | Meadowbank Thistle | 36 | 2 |
| 1988-89 | Meadowbank Thistle | 18 | – |
| 1988-89 | Dunfermline Athletic | 18 | 1 |
| 1989-90 | Dunfermline Athletic | 33 | 2 |
| 1990-91 | Partick Thistle | 28 | 1 |
| 1991-92 | Partick Thistle | 13 | 1 |
| 1992-93 | Partick Thistle | 16 | 2 |
| 1993-94 | Partick Thistle | 22 | 1 |

**TORTOLANO, Joseph**
Born: Stirling 06/04/66

| SEASON | CLUB | LEAGUE APPEARANCES | GOALS |
|---|---|---|---|
| 1983-84 | West Bromich Albion | – | – |
| 1984-85 | West Bromich Albion | – | – |
| 1985-86 | Hibernian | 20 | 3 |
| 1986-87 | Hibernian | 33 | – |
| 1987-88 | Hibernian | 21 | 4 |
| 1988-89 | Hibernian | 25 | – |
| 1989-90 | Hibernian | 7 | – |
| 1990-91 | Hibernian | 18 | 1 |
| 1991-92 | Hibernian | 25 | 1 |
| 1992-93 | Hibernian | 21 | 3 |
| 1993-94 | Hibernian | 18 | 1 |

**TWEED, Steven**
Born: Edinburgh 08/08/72

| SEASON | CLUB | LEAGUE APPEARANCES | GOALS |
|---|---|---|---|
| 1991-92 | Hibernian | 1 | – |
| 1992-93 | Hibernian | 14 | – |
| 1993-94 | Hibernian | 29 | 3 |

**VAN DE KAMP, Guido**
Born: Den Bosch 08/02/64
From BVV Den Bosch

| SEASON | CLUB | LEAGUE APPEARANCES | GOALS |
|---|---|---|---|
| 1991-92 | Dundee United | 27 | – |
| 1992-93 | Dundee United | 1 | – |
| 1993-94 | Dundee United | 25 | – |

**VATA, Rudi**
Born: Schroder 13/02/69
From Dinamo Tirana

| SEASON | CLUB | LEAGUE APPEARANCES | GOALS |
|---|---|---|---|
| 1992-93 | Celtic | 22 | 2 |
| 1993-94 | Celtic | 10 | 1 |

**WALKER, Andrew**
Born: Glasgow 06/04/65

| SEASON | CLUB | LEAGUE APPEARANCES | GOALS |
|---|---|---|---|
| 1984-85 | Motherwell | 11 | 3 |
| 1985-86 | Motherwell | 22 | 4 |
| 1986-87 | Motherwell | 43 | 10 |
| 1987-88 | Celtic | 42 | 16 |
| 1988-89 | Celtic | 22 | 8 |
| 1989-90 | Celtic | 32 | 6 |
| 1990-91 | Celtic | 11 | – |
| 1991-92 | Celtic | 1 | – |
| 1991-92 | Newcastle United | 2 | – |
| 1991-92 | Bolton Wanderers | 24 | 15 |
| 1992-93 | Bolton Wanderers | 32 | 26 |
| 1993-94 | Bolton Wanderers | 11 | 3 |

**WALKER, Joseph Nicol**
Born: Aberdeen 29/09/62

| SEASON | CLUB | LEAGUE APPEARANCES | GOALS |
|---|---|---|---|
| 1980-81 | Leicester City | – | – |
| 1981-82 | Leicester City | 6 | – |
| 1982-83 | Motherwell | 16 | – |
| 1983-84 | Motherwell | 15 | – |
| 1983-84 | Rangers | 8 | – |
| 1984-85 | Rangers | 14 | – |
| 1985-86 | Rangers | 34 | – |
| 1986-87 | Rangers | 2 | – |
| 1986-87 | Falkirk | 8 | – |
| 1987-88 | Rangers | 5 | – |
| 1987-88 | Dunfermline Athletic | 1 | – |
| 1988-89 | Rangers | 12 | – |
| 1989-90 | Heart of Midlothian | – | – |
| 1990-91 | Heart of Midlothian | 13 | – |
| 1991-92 | Heart of Midlothian | – | – |
| 1991-92 | Burnley | 6 | – |
| 1992-93 | Heart of Midlothian | 18 | – |
| 1993-94 | Heart of Midlothian | 17 | – |

**WATSON, Gregg**
Born: Glasgow 21/09/70

| SEASON | CLUB | LEAGUE APPEARANCES | GOALS |
|---|---|---|---|
| 1986-87 | Aberdeen | – | – |
| 1987-88 | Aberdeen | – | – |
| 1988-89 | Aberdeen | 4 | – |
| 1989-90 | Aberdeen | 4 | – |
| 1990-91 | Aberdeen | 7 | – |
| 1991-92 | Aberdeen | 8 | – |
| 1992-93 | Aberdeen | – | – |
| 1993-94 | Aberdeen | – | – |
| 1993-94 | Partick Thistle | 37 | – |

**WATT, Michael**
Born: Aberdeen 27/11/70

| SEASON | CLUB | LEAGUE APPEARANCES | GOALS |
|---|---|---|---|
| 1989-90 | Aberdeen | 7 | – |
| 1990-91 | Aberdeen | 10 | – |
| 1991-92 | Aberdeen | 2 | – |
| 1992-93 | Aberdeen | 3 | – |
| 1993-94 | Aberdeen | 4 | – |

**WEIR, David Gillespie**
Born: Falkirk 10/05/70

| SEASON | CLUB | LEAGUE APPEARANCES | GOALS |
|---|---|---|---|
| 1992-93 | Falkirk | 30 | 1 |
| 1993-94 | Falkirk | 37 | 3 |

**WEIR, James McIntosh**
Born: Motherwell 15/06/69

| SEASON | CLUB | LEAGUE APPEARANCES | GOALS |
|---|---|---|---|
| 1986-87 | Hamilton Academical | 3 | – |
| 1987-88 | Hamilton Academical | 6 | – |
| 1988-89 | Hamilton Academical | 29 | – |
| 1989-90 | Hamilton Academical | 30 | 1 |
| 1990-91 | Hamilton Academical | 39 | 2 |
| 1991-92 | Hamilton Academical | 40 | 1 |
| 1992-93 | Hamilton Academical | 37 | 1 |
| 1993-94 | Hamilton Academical | 2 | – |
| 1993-94 | Heart of Midlothian | 26 | – |

**WEIR, Michael Graham**
Born: Edinburgh 16/01/66

| SEASON | CLUB | LEAGUE APPEARANCES | GOALS |
|---|---|---|---|
| 1982-83 | Hibernian | – | – |
| 1983-84 | Hibernian | – | – |
| 1984-85 | Hibernian | 12 | – |
| 1985-86 | Hibernian | 7 | – |
| 1986-87 | Hibernian | 24 | 4 |
| 1987-88 | Hibernian | 5 | 1 |
| 1987-88 | Luton Town | 8 | – |
| 1987-88 | Hibernian | 13 | 2 |

| CLUB | LEAGUE APPEARANCES | GOALS |
|---|---|---|
| 1988-89 Hibernian | 7 | – |
| 1989-90 Hibernian | 18 | 3 |
| 1990-91 Hibernian | 20 | 1 |
| 1991-92 Hibernian | 31 | 11 |
| 1992-93 Hibernian | 33 | 5 |
| 1993-94 Hibernian | – | – |

**WELSH, Brian**
Born: Edinburgh 23/02/69

| | CLUB | LEAGUE APPEARANCES | GOALS |
|---|---|---|---|
| 1986-87 | Dundee United | 1 | – |
| 1987-88 | Dundee United | 1 | 1 |
| 1988-89 | Dundee United | 1 | – |
| 1989-90 | Dundee United | 5 | – |
| 1990-91 | Dundee United | 17 | – |
| 1991-92 | Dundee United | 11 | 1 |
| 1992-93 | Dundee United | 15 | 1 |
| 1993-94 | Dundee United | 37 | 1 |

**WILLIAMSON, Robert**
Born: Glasgow 13/08/61

| | CLUB | LEAGUE APPEARANCES | GOALS |
|---|---|---|---|
| 1980-81 | Clydebank | 2 | – |
| 1981-82 | Clydebank | 12 | 1 |
| 1982-83 | Clydebank | 39 | 23 |
| 1983-84 | Clydebank | 17 | 4 |
| 1983-84 | Rangers | 17 | 6 |
| 1984-85 | Rangers | 1 | – |
| 1985-86 | Rangers | 23 | 6 |
| 1986-87 | West Bromwich Albion | 31 | 8 |
| 1987-88 | West Bromwich Albion | 22 | 3 |
| 1988-89 | Rotherham United | 42 | 27 |
| 1989-90 | Rotherham United | 42 | 19 |
| 1990-91 | Rotherham United | 9 | 3 |
| 1990-91 | Kilmarnock | 23 | 14 |
| 1991-92 | Kilmarnock | 36 | 9 |
| 1992-93 | Kilmarnock | 33 | 6 |
| 1993-94 | Kilmarnock | 38 | 7 |

**WINNIE, David**
Born: Glasgow 26/10/66

| | CLUB | LEAGUE APPEARANCES | GOALS |
|---|---|---|---|
| 1983-84 | St Mirren | 8 | – |
| 1984-85 | St Mirren | 30 | 3 |
| 1985-86 | St Mirren | 20 | 1 |
| 1986-87 | St Mirren | 14 | – |
| 1987-88 | St Mirren | 26 | 2 |
| 1988-89 | St Mirren | 30 | – |
| 1989-90 | St Mirren | 17 | – |
| 1990-91 | St Mirren | 1 | – |
| 1991-92 | Aberdeen | 28 | 1 |
| 1992-93 | Aberdeen | 21 | – |
| 1993-94 | Aberdeen | 6 | – |
| 1993-94 | *Middlesbrough* | 1 | – |

**WISHART, Fraser**
Born: Johnstone 01/03/65

| | CLUB | LEAGUE APPEARANCES | GOALS |
|---|---|---|---|
| 1983-84 | Motherwell | 6 | – |
| 1984-85 | Motherwell | – | – |
| 1985-86 | Motherwell | 26 | – |
| 1986-87 | Motherwell | 44 | 3 |
| 1987-88 | Motherwell | 43 | 1 |
| 1988-89 | Motherwell | 35 | 1 |
| 1989-90 | St Mirren | 20 | – |
| 1990-91 | St Mirren | 22 | – |
| 1991-92 | St Mirren | 9 | – |
| 1992-93 | Falkirk | 24 | 2 |
| 1993-94 | Rangers | 5 | – |

*Dundee United midfielder Jim McInally, who has made over 250 league appearances for the Tannadice club.*

▶

**WOODS, Stephen Gerard**
Born: Glasgow 23/02/70

| SEASON | CLUB | LEAGUE APPEARANCES | GOALS |
|---|---|---|---|
| 1989-90 | Hibernian | – | – |
| 1990-91 | Hibernian | – | – |
| 1991-92 | Hibernian | – | – |
| 1991-92 | Clydebank | 5 | – |
| 1992-93 | Clydebank | 42 | – |
| 1993-94 | Clydebank | 10 | – |
| 1993-94 | Preston North End | 20 | – |

**WOODTHORPE, Colin**
Born: Liverpool 13/01/69

| | CLUB | LEAGUE APPEARANCES | GOALS |
|---|---|---|---|
| 1986-87 | Chester City | 30 | 2 |
| 1987-88 | Chester City | 35 | – |
| 1988-89 | Chester City | 44 | 3 |
| 1989-90 | Chester City | 46 | 1 |
| 1990-91 | Norwich City | 1 | – |
| 1991-92 | Norwich City | 15 | 1 |
| 1992-93 | Norwich City | 7 | – |
| 1993-94 | Norwich City | 20 | – |

**WRIGHT, George**
Born: South Africa 23/12/69

| | CLUB | LEAGUE APPEARANCES | GOALS |
|---|---|---|---|
| 1987-88 | Heart of Midlothian | – | – |
| 1988-89 | Heart of Midlothian | – | – |
| 1989-90 | Heart of Midlothian | 1 | – |
| 1990-91 | Heart of Midlothian | 17 | 2 |
| 1991-92 | Heart of Midlothian | 24 | 1 |
| 1992-93 | Heart of Midlothian | 12 | – |
| 1993-94 | Heart of Midlothian | 12 | – |

**WRIGHT, Keith**
Born: Edinburgh 17/05/65

| | CLUB | LEAGUE APPEARANCES | GOALS |
|---|---|---|---|
| 1983-84 | Raith Rovers | 37 | 5 |
| 1984-85 | Raith Rovers | 38 | 22 |
| 1985-86 | Raith Rovers | 39 | 21 |
| 1986-87 | Raith Rovers | 17 | 13 |
| 1986-87 | Dundee | 20 | 10 |
| 1987-88 | Dundee | 42 | 15 |
| 1988-89 | Dundee | 35 | 8 |
| 1989-90 | Dundee | 34 | 11 |
| 1990-91 | Dundee | 36 | 18 |
| 1991-92 | Hibernian | 40 | 9 |
| 1992-93 | Hibernian | 42 | 11 |
| 1993-94 | Hibernian | 42 | 16 |

**WRIGHT, Stephen**
Born: Bellshill 27/08/71

| | CLUB | LEAGUE APPEARANCES | GOALS |
|---|---|---|---|
| 1987-88 | Aberdeen | – | – |
| 1988-89 | Aberdeen | – | – |
| 1989-90 | Aberdeen | 1 | – |
| 1990-91 | Aberdeen | 17 | 1 |
| 1991-92 | Aberdeen | 23 | – |
| 1992-93 | Aberdeen | 36 | – |
| 1993-94 | Aberdeen | 36 | – |

## TENNENTS SCOTTISH CUP 1994/95

First Round...........................................10th December, 1994
Second Round........................................... 7th January, 1995
Third Round...........................................28th January, 1995
Fourth Round...........................................18th February, 1995
Fifth Round...................................................11th March, 1995
Semi-Finals.......................................................8th April, 1995
Final..............................................................27th May, 1995

## EUROPEAN CHAMPIONSHIP QUALIFYING MATCHES

| | | | |
|---|---|---|---|
| Finland | -v- | Scotland | 7th September, 1994 |
| Scotland | -v- | Faroe Islands | 12th October, 1994 |
| Scotland | -v- | Russia | 16th November, 1994 |
| Greece | -v- | Scotland | 18th December, 1994 |
| Russia | -v- | Scotland | 29th March, 1995 |
| San Marino | -v- | Scotland | 26th April, 1995 |
| Faroe Islands | -v- | Scotland | 7th June, 1995 |

## EUROPEAN "UNDER 21" CHAMPIONSHIP 1994/96 (QUALIFYING MATCHES)

| | | | |
|---|---|---|---|
| Finland | -v- | Scotland | 6th September, 1994 |
| Scotland | -v- | Russia | 15th November, 1994 |
| Greece | -v- | Scotland | 17th December, 1994 |
| Russia | -v- | Scotland | 28th March, 1995 |
| San Marino | -v- | Scotland | 25th April, 1995 |

## 11TH EUROPEAN "UNDER 18" YOUTH CHAMPIONSHIP 1994/95
### Qualifying Round

Mini tournament - 30th September - 6th October, 1994
(involving Israel, (Kristiansand, Norway)
Norway & Scotland)

## FOUR NATIONS YOUTH TOURNAMENT FOR "UNDER 17" PLAYERS

Belgium, Denmark, - 12th - 18th September, 1994
The Netherlands & Scotland (Arlon, Belgium)

## 13TH EUROPEAN "UNDER 16" YOUTH CHAMPIONSHIP 1994/95

| | | | |
|---|---|---|---|
| Finland | -v- | Scotland | 6th September, 1994 |
| Iceland | -v- | Scotland | 19th September, 1994 |
| Scotland | -v- | Finland | 11th October, 1994 |
| Scotland | -v- | Iceland | 31st October, 1994 |

## EUROPEAN CLUB COMPETITION DATES

#### SUMMARY OF THE REFORMS IN THE THREE U.E.F.A. CLUB COMPETITIONS

As a result of decisions taken by U.E.F.A.'s Executive Committee in December, 1993, the format of the three club competitions has altered dramatically for the 1994/95 season. The biggest change has taken place in the Champion Clubs' Cup where the number of clubs authorised to enter has been reduced. Although each national association will still, in theory, have the opportunity to be represented by its domestic champion in the Champion Clubs' Cup, participation in the future will depend on the results of the club itself over a period of time or on those of its association. The new format guarantees that the champion clubs ranked in places 1-24 will play in the Champion Clubs' Cup with the champion clubs ranked between 25 and 48 playing in the U.E.F.A. Cup. The final phase of the Champion Clubs' Cup, which has been known as the U.E.F.A. Champions League for the past two seasons, will now feature 16 clubs with the cup holders and the first seven clubs in the list of co-efficients qualifying automatically for the flagship competition. The remaining 16 clubs will play a qualifying round on a home and away basis and the eight winners will join the clubs that have been seeded 1-8 and be divided into four groups of four to be played between September and December, 1994 with the top two clubs in each group thereafter qualifying for the Quarter-Finals. Both the Quarter-Finals and Semi-Final stages of the Champion Clubs' Cup will be played on a home and away basis with the Final being played on a one match basis at a neutral venue still to be decided on Wednesday, 24th May, 1994.

Accordingly, with the domestic champions ranked between places 25 and 48 now playing in the U.E.F.A. Cup, together with a substantial increase in the number of associations now in membership of U.E.F.A., 100 clubs will now participate in the U.E.F.A. Cup, necessitating a Preliminary Round to be played. 72 Clubs will participate in this Preliminary Round including the aforementioned domestic champions ranked between places 25 and 48 in the list

of co-efficients with only the 28 best placed clubs in the list of co-efficients being exempt from this round. The increase in the number of associations now in membership of U.E.F.A. also requires a Preliminary Round to be played in the Cup Winners' Cup and these matches will take place at the same time as the Qualifying matches in the Champion Clubs' Cup and the Preliminary Round of the U.E.F.A. Cup.

Another feature of the competition regulations stipulate that U.E.F.A. Cup matches will, in principle, be played on Tuesdays, Champion Clubs' Cup matches on Wednesdays, and Cup Winners' Cup matches on Thursdays. Any changes of dates will require the written consent of the two clubs concerned, as well as their respective national associations.

The complete list of dates for each of the three competitions is as follows:-

## EUROPEAN CHAMPION CLUBS' CUP

**Qualifying matches:**
Knock-out system in August 1994
First-leg matches: Wednesday, 10th August, 1994
Second-leg matches: Wednesday, 24th August, 1994

**Group Matches:**
Championship system between September, 1994 and December, 1994
1st match day: Wednesday, 14th September, 1994
2nd match day: Wednesday, 28th September, 1994
3rd match day: Wednesday, 19th October, 1994
4th match day: Wednesday, 2nd November, 1994
5th match day: Wednesday, 23rd November, 1994
6th match day: Wednesday, 7th December, 1994

**Quarter-Finals:**
Knock-out system in March 1995
First-leg matches: Wednesday, 1st March, 1995
Second-leg matches: Wednesday, 15th March, 1995
**Semi-Finals:**
Knock-out system in April 1995
First-leg matches: Wednesday, 5th April, 1995
Second-leg matches: Wednesday, 19th April, 1995
**Final:** Wednesday, 24th May, 1995

## U.E.F.A. CUP

**Preliminary Round:**
First-leg matches: Tuesday, 9th August, 1994
Second-leg matches: Tuesday, 23rd August, 1994
**First Round:**
First-leg matches: Tuesday, 13th September, 1994
Second-leg matches: Tuesday, 27th September, 1994
**Second Round:**
First-leg matches: Tuesday, 18th October, 1994
Second-leg matches: Tuesday, 1st November, 1994
**Third Round:**
First-leg matches: Tuesday, 22nd November, 1994
Second-leg matches: Tuesday, 6th December, 1994
**Quarter-Finals:**
First-leg matches: Tuesday, 28th February, 1995
Second-leg matches: Tuesday, 14th March, 1995
**Semi-Finals:**
First-leg matches: Tuesday, 4th April, 1995
Second-leg matches: Tuesday, 18th April, 1995
**Final:**
First-leg match: Wednesday, 3rd May, 1995
Second-leg match: Wednesday, 17th May, 1995

## EUROPEAN CUP WINNERS' CUP

**Preliminary Round:**
First-leg matches: Thursday, 11th August, 1994
Second-leg matches: Thursday, 25th August, 1994
**First Round:**
First-leg matches: Thursday, 15th September, 1994
Second-leg matches: Thursday, 29th September, 1994
**Second Round:**
First-leg matches: Thursday, 20th October, 1994
Second-leg matches: Thursday, 3rd November, 1994
**Quarter-Finals:**
First-leg matches: Thursday, 2nd March, 1995
Second-leg matches: Thursday, 16th March, 1995
**Semi-Finals:**
First-leg matches: Thursday, 6th April, 1995
Second-leg matches: Thursday, 20th April, 1995
**Final:** Wednesday, 10th May, 1995

# Coca-Cola Cup Draw

### 1st Round

| | | |
|---|---|---|
| East Fife | -v- | Forfar Athletic |
| East Stirlingshire | -v- | Caledonian Thistle |
| Stenhousemuir | -v- | Meadowbank This |
| Berwick Rangers | -v- | Montrose |

Above ties to be played on Tuesday, 9th August, 1994

| | | |
|---|---|---|
| Ross County | -v- | Queen's Park |
| Arbroath | -v- | Alloa |
| Queen of the South | -v- | Albion Rovers |
| Stranraer | -v- | Cowdenbeath |

Above ties to be played on Wednesday, 10th August, 1994

### 2nd Round

| | | |
|---|---|---|
| Motherwell | -v- | Clydebank |
| Dumbarton | -v- | Heart of Midlothian |
| Greenock Morton | -v- | Airdrieonians |
| Falkirk | -v- | Berwick Rangers or Montrose |
| Partick Thistle | -v- | Brechin City |
| Ayr United | -v- | Celtic |
| St. Mirren | -v- | Dundee United |

Above ties to be played on Tuesday, 16th August, 1994

| | | |
|---|---|---|
| * Queen of the South or Albion Rovers | -v- | Hibernian |
| Aberdeen | -v- | Stranraer or Cowdenbeath |
| Dundee | -v- | East Stirlingshire or Caledonian Thistle |
| Dunfermline Athletic | -v- | Stenhousemuir or Meadowbank Thistle |
| ^ Arbroath or Alloa or ** Ross County or Queen's Park | -v- | Rangers |
| | -v- | Raith Rovers |
| Kilmarnock | -v- | East Fife or Forfar Athletic |
| Stirling Albion | -v- | St. Johnstone |
| Hamilton Academical | -v- | Clyde |

Above ties to be played on Wednesday, 17th August, 1994

\* If Albion Rovers reach the Second Round, the above tie will be played on Tuesday, 16th August, 1994 at Stark's Park, Kirkcaldy.

^ If Alloa reach the Second Round, the above tie will be played at Brockville Park, Falkirk.

\** If Queen's Park F.C. reach the Second Round, the above tie will be played on Tuesday, 16th August, 1994.

### 3rd Round

........................ v ............................

........................ v ............................

........................ v ............................

........................ v ............................

........................ v ............................

........................ v ............................

........................ v ............................

........................ v ............................

Ties to be played on Tuesday, 30th or Wednesday, 31st August, 1994

### 4th Round

........................ v ............................

........................ v ............................

........................ v ............................

........................ v ............................

Ties to be played on Tuesday, 20th or Wednesday, 21st September, 1994

### Semi-Finals

........................ v ............................

........................ v ............................

Ties to be played on Tuesday, 25th or Wednesday, 26th October, 1994

### Coca-Cola Cup Final

........................ v ............................

To be played on Sunday, 27th November, 1994

**In the event of a draw after normal time in all rounds, extra time of 30 minutes (i.e. 15 minutes each way) will take place and thereafter, if necessary, kicks from the penalty mark in accordance with the rules laid down by the International Football Association Board will be taken.**

## SEASON 1994/95

### 1st Round

| | | |
|---|---|---|
| Queen's Park | -v- | Clydebank |
| East Fife | -v- | Ross County |
| Hamilton Academical | -v- | Stenhousemuir |
| Brechin City | -v- | Dunfermline Athletic |
| Stranraer | -v- | St. Mirren |
| Meadowbank Thistle | -v- | Montrose |
| Dundee | -v- | Arbroath |
| Stirling Albion | -v- | Albion Rovers |
| Cowdenbeath | -v- | Clyde |
| Forfar Athletic | -v- | Alloa |
| Dumbarton | -v- | St. Johnstone |
| Queen of the South | -v- | Raith Rovers |
| Airdrieonians | -v- | Berwick Rangers |
| *East Stirlingshire | -v- | Ayr United |

BYES: Greenock Morton and Caledonian Thistle

Above Ties will be played on Saturday, 17th September, 1994
* This tie will be played on Sunday, 18th September, 1994

### 2nd Round

........................... v ...........................

........................... v ...........................

........................... v ...........................

........................... v ...........................

........................... v ...........................

........................... v ...........................

........................... v ...........................

........................... v ...........................

Above ties to be played on Tuesday, 27th or Wednesday,
28th September, 1994

### 3rd Round

........................... v ...........................

........................... v ...........................

........................... v ...........................

........................... v ...........................

Above ties to be played on Tuesday, 4th or Wednesday,
5th October, 1994

### Semi-Finals

........................... v ...........................

........................... v ...........................

Above ties to be played on Tuesday, 18th or Wednesday,
19th October, 1994

### Final Tie

........................... v ...........................

Above tie to be played on Sunday, 6th November, 1994

In the event of a draw after normal time,
extra time of 30 minutes (i.e. 15 minutes each way)
will take place and thereafter, if necessary,
kicks from the penalty mark in accordance with
the Rules laid down by the International
Football Association Board will be taken.

---

# BREAKDOWN OF HOW ALL THE SPONSORSHIP MONIES WILL BE ALLOCATED DURING SEASON 1994/95

## DISTRIBUTION OF COCA-COLA CUP MONIES

| | |
|---|---|
| 8 First Round Losers will each receive | £ 5,000 |
| 16 Second Round Losers will each receive | £ 7,000 |
| 8 Third Round Losers will each receive | £11,000 |
| 4 Fourth Round Losers will each receive | £16,000 |
| 2 Semi-Final Losers will each receive | £22,000 |
| The Runner-Up will receive | £40,000 |
| The Winner will receive | £60,000 |

## DISTRIBUTION OF BELL'S LEAGUE CHAMPIONSHIP MONIES

| | |
|---|---|
| Each Premier Division Club will receive | £40,000 |
| Each First Division Club will receive | £17,000 |
| Each Second Division Club will receive | £10,000 |
| Each Third Division Club will receive | £ 8,500 |

## DISTRIBUTION OF B & Q CUP MONIES

| | |
|---|---|
| 14 First Round Losers will each receive | £ 2,125 |
| 8 Second Round Losers will each receive | £ 3,200 |
| 4 Third Round Losers will each receive | £ 4,400 |
| 2 Semi-Final Losers will each receive | £ 5,750 |
| The Runner-Up will receive | £10,000 |
| The Winner will receive | £14,000 |

**Saturday, August 13th, 1994**

Aberdeen v Heart of Midlothian
Falkirk v Celtic
Hibernian v Dundee United
Partick Thistle v Kilmarnock
Rangers v Motherwell

Airdrieonians v Dunfermline Athletic
Ayr United v Hamilton Academical
Clydebank v Stranraer
Dundee v St Mirren
Raith Rovers v St Johnstone

Brechin City v Meadowbank Thistle
Greenock Morton v Berwick Rangers
Queen of the South v Dumbarton
Stenhousemuir v Clyde
Stirling Albion v East Fife

Albion Rovers v Alloa
Caledonian Thistle v Arbroath
Cowdenbeath v Ross County
Montrose v East Stirlingshire
Queen's Park v Forfar Athletic

**Saturday, August 20th, 1994**

Aberdeen v Falkirk
Celtic v Dundee United
Hibernian v Kilmarnock
Motherwell v Heart of Midlothian
Partick Thistle v Rangers

Airdrieonians v St Johnstone
Ayr United v St Mirren
Clydebank v Dunfermline Athletic
Dundee v Stranraer
Raith Rovers v Hamilton Academical

Brechin City v Berwick Rangers
Greenock Morton v Meadowbank Thistle
Queen of the South v Clyde
Stenhousemuir v East Fife
Stirling Albion v Dumbarton

Albion Rovers v Montrose
Caledonian Thistle v Queen's Park
Cowdenbeath v Arbroath
East Stirlingshire v Ross County
Forfar Athletic v Alloa

**Saturday, August 27th, 1994**

Dundee United v Aberdeen
Falkirk v Partick Thistle
Heart of Midlothian v Hibernian
Kilmarnock v Motherwell
Rangers v Celtic

Dunfermline Athletic v Raith Rovers
Hamilton Academical v Airdrieonians
St Johnstone v Dundee
St Mirren v Clydebank
Stranraer v Ayr United

Berwick Rangers v Queen of the South
Clyde v Stirling Albion
Dumbarton v Greenock Morton
East Fife v Brechin City
Meadowbank Thistle v Stenhousemuir

Alloa v East Stirlingshire
Arbroath v Forfar Athletic
Montrose v Cowdenbeath
Queen's Park v Albion Rovers
Ross County v Caledonian Thistle

**Saturday, September 3rd, 1994**

Ayr United v St Johnstone
Dundee v Airdrieonians
Hamilton Academical v Stranraer
Raith Rovers v Clydebank
St Mirren v Dunfermline Athletic

Brechin City v Stenhousemuir
Clyde v Berwick Rangers
Dumbarton v Meadowbank Thistle
Queen of the South v East Fife
Stirling Albion v Greenock Morton

Albion Rovers v Caledonian Thistle
Arbroath v Queen's Park
Cowdenbeath v East Stirlingshire
Forfar Athletic v Montrose
Ross County v Alloa

**Saturday, September 10th, 1994**

Dundee United v Motherwell
Hibernian v Aberdeen
Kilmarnock v Falkirk
Partick Thistle v Celtic
Rangers v Heart of Midlothian

Airdrieonians v Ayr United
Clydebank v Dundee
Dunfermline Athletic v Hamilton Academical
St Johnstone v St Mirren
Stranraer v Raith Rovers

Berwick Rangers v Dumbarton
East Fife v Clyde
Greenock Morton v Brechin City
Meadowbank Thistle v Queen of the South
Stenhousemuir v Stirling Albion

Alloa v Arbroath
Caledonian Thistle v Forfar Athletic
East Stirlingshire v Albion Rovers
Montrose v Ross County
Queen's Park v Cowdenbeath

**Saturday, September 17th, 1994**

Aberdeen v Partick Thistle
Celtic v Kilmarnock
Falkirk v Rangers
Heart of Midlothian v Dundee United
Motherwell v Hibernian

**Saturday, September 24th, 1994**

Aberdeen v Rangers
Celtic v Hibernian
Dundee United v Falkirk
Heart of Midlothian v Kilmarnock
Partick Thistle v Motherwell

Airdrieonians v Clydebank
Ayr United v Dundee
Dunfermline Athletic v Stranraer
St Johnstone v Hamilton Academical
St Mirren v Raith Rovers

Dumbarton v Clyde
East Fife v Greenock Morton
Meadowbank Thistle v Stirling Albion
Queen of the South v Brechin City
Stenhousemuir v Berwick Rangers

Albion Rovers v Cowdenbeath
Alloa v Caledonian Thistle
East Stirlingshire v Forfar Athletic
Montrose v Queen's Park
Ross County v Arbroath

**Saturday, October 1st, 1994**

Falkirk v Heart of Midlothian
Hibernian v Partick Thistle
Kilmarnock v Aberdeen
Motherwell v Celtic
Rangers v Dundee United

Clydebank v St Johnstone
Dundee v Dunfermline Athletic
Hamilton Academical v St Mirren
Raith Rovers v Ayr United
Stranraer v Airdrieonians

Berwick Rangers v East Fife
Brechin City v Dumbarton
Clyde v Meadowbank Thistle
Greenock Morton v Stenhousemuir
Stirling Albion v Queen of the South

Arbroath v Montrose
Caledonian Thistle v East Stirlingshire
Cowdenbeath v Alloa
Forfar Athletic v Albion Rovers
Queen's Park v Ross County

**Saturday, October 8th, 1994**

Celtic v Aberdeen
Hibernian v Rangers
Kilmarnock v Dundee United
Motherwell v Falkirk
Partick Thistle v Heart of Midlothian

Airdrieonians v Raith Rovers
Clydebank v Ayr United
Dundee v Hamilton Academical
Dunfermline Athletic v St Johnstone
Stranraer v St Mirren

Berwick Rangers v Meadowbank Thistle
Brechin City v Stirling Albion
East Fife v Dumbarton
Greenock Morton v Clyde
Stenhousemuir v Queen of the South

Albion Rovers v Arbroath
Alloa v Montrose
Caledonian Thistle v Cowdenbeath
East Stirlingshire v Queen's Park
Forfar Athletic v Ross County

**Saturday, October 15th, 1994**

Aberdeen v Motherwell
Dundee United v Partick Thistle
Falkirk v Hibernian
Heart of Midlothian v Celtic
Rangers v Kilmarnock

Ayr United v Dunfermline Athletic
Hamilton Academical v Clydebank
Raith Rovers v Dundee
St Johnstone v Stranraer
St Mirren v Airdrieonians

Clyde v Brechin City
Dumbarton v Stenhousemuir
Meadowbank Thistle v East Fife
Queen of the South v Greenock Morton
Stirling Albion v Berwick Rangers

Arbroath v East Stirlingshire
Cowdenbeath v Forfar Athletic
Montrose v Caledonian Thistle
Queen's Park v Alloa
Ross County v Albion Rovers

**Saturday, October 22nd, 1994**

Celtic v Falkirk
Dundee United v Hibernian
Heart of Midlothian v Aberdeen
Kilmarnock v Partick Thistle
Motherwell v Rangers

Dunfermline Athletic v Airdrieonians
Hamilton Academical v Ayr United
St Johnstone v Raith Rovers
St Mirren v Dundee
Stranraer v Clydebank

Berwick Rangers v Greenock Morton
Clyde v Stenhousemuir
Dumbarton v Queen of the South
East Fife v Stirling Albion
Meadowbank Thistle v Brechin City

Alloa v Albion Rovers
Arbroath v Caledonian Thistle
East Stirlingshire v Montrose
Forfar Athletic v Queen's Park
Ross County v Cowdenbeath

## Saturday, October 29th, 1994

Aberdeen v Dundee United
Celtic v Rangers
Hibernian v Heart of Midlothian
Motherwell v Kilmarnock
Partick Thistle v Falkirk

Airdrieonians v Hamilton Academical
Ayr United v Stranraer
Clydebank v St Mirren
Dundee v St Johnstone
Raith Rovers v Dunfermline Athletic

Brechin City v East Fife
Greenock Morton v Dumbarton
Queen of the South v Berwick Rangers
Stenhousemuir v Meadowbank Thistle
Stirling Albion v Clyde

Albion Rovers v Queen's Park
Caledonian Thistle v Ross County
Cowdenbeath v Montrose
East Stirlingshire v Alloa
Forfar Athletic v Arbroath

## Saturday, November 5th, 1994

Dundee United v Celtic
Falkirk v Aberdeen
Heart of Midlothian v Motherwell
Kilmarnock v Hibernian
Rangers v Partick Thistle

Dunfermline Athletic v Clydebank
Hamilton Academical v Raith Rovers
St Johnstone v Airdrieonians
St Mirren v Ayr United
Stranraer v Dundee

Berwick Rangers v Brechin City
Clyde v Queen of the South
Dumbarton v Stirling Albion
East Fife v Stenhousemuir
Greenock Morton v Meadowbank Thistle

Alloa v Forfar Athletic
Arbroath v Cowdenbeath
Montrose v Albion Rovers
Queen's Park v Caledonian Thistle
Ross County v East Stirlingshire

## Tuesday, November 8th, 1994

Falkirk v Kilmarnock
Motherwell v Dundee United

## Wednesday, November 9th, 1994

Aberdeen v Hibernian
Celtic v Partick Thistle
Heart of Midlothian v Rangers

## Saturday, November 12th, 1994

Ayr United v Airdrieonians
Dundee v Clydebank
Hamilton Academical v Dunfermline Athletic
Raith Rovers v Stranraer
St Mirren v St Johnstone

Brechin City v Greenock Morton
Clyde v East Fife
Dumbarton v Berwick Rangers
Queen of the South v Meadowbank Thistle
Stirling Albion v Stenhousemuir

Albion Rovers v East Stirlingshire
Arbroath v Alloa
Cowdenbeath v Queen's Park
Forfar Athletic v Caledonian Thistle
Ross County v Montrose

## Saturday, November 19th, 1994

Dundee United v Heart of Midlothian
Hibernian v Motherwell
Kilmarnock v Celtic
Partick Thistle v Aberdeen
Rangers v Falkirk

Airdrieonians v Dundee
Clydebank v Raith Rovers
Dunfermline Athletic v St Mirren
St Johnstone v Ayr United
Stranraer v Hamilton Academical

Berwick Rangers v Clyde
East Fife v Queen of the South
Greenock Morton v Stirling Albion
Meadowbank Thistle v Dumbarton
Stenhousemuir v Brechin City

Alloa v Ross County
Caledonian Thistle v Albion Rovers
East Stirlingshire v Cowdenbeath
Montrose v Forfar Athletic
Queen's Park v Arbroath

## Saturday, November 26th, 1994

Falkirk v Dundee United
Hibernian v Celtic
Kilmarnock v Heart of Midlothian
Motherwell v Partick Thistle
Rangers v Aberdeen

Clydebank v Airdrieonians
Dundee v Ayr United
Hamilton Academical v St Johnstone
Raith Rovers v St Mirren
Stranraer v Dunfermline Athletic

Berwick Rangers v Stenhousemuir
Brechin City v Queen of the South
Clyde v Dumbarton
Greenock Morton v East Fife
Stirling Albion v Meadowbank Thistle

Arbroath v Ross County
Caledonian Thistle v Alloa
Cowdenbeath v Albion Rovers
Forfar Athletic v East Stirlingshire
Queen's Park v Montrose

## Saturday, December 3rd, 1994

Aberdeen v Kilmarnock
Celtic v Motherwell
Dundee United v Rangers
Heart of Midlothian v Falkirk
Partick Thistle v Hibernian

Airdrieonians v Stranraer
Ayr United v Raith Rovers
Dunfermline Athletic v Dundee
St Johnstone v Clydebank
St Mirren v Hamilton Academical

Dumbarton v Brechin City
East Fife v Berwick Rangers
Meadowbank Thistle v Clyde
Queen of the South v Stirling Albion
Stenhousemuir v Greenock Morton

Albion Rovers v Forfar Athletic
Alloa v Cowdenbeath
East Stirlingshire v Caledonian Thistle
Montrose v Arbroath
Ross County v Queen's Park

## Saturday, December 10th, 1994

Celtic v Heart of Midlothian
Hibernian v Falkirk
Kilmarnock v Rangers
Motherwell v Aberdeen
Partick Thistle v Dundee United

Airdrieonians v St Mirren
Clydebank v Hamilton Academical
Dundee v Raith Rovers
Dunfermline Athletic v Ayr United
Stranraer v St Johnstone

## Saturday, December 24th, 1994

Stirling Albion v Brechin City

## Monday, December 26th, 1994

Aberdeen v Celtic
Dundee United v Kilmarnock
Falkirk v Motherwell
Heart of Midlothian v Partick Thistle
Rangers v Hibernian

Ayr United v Clydebank
Hamilton Academical v Dundee
Raith Rovers v Airdrieonians
St Johnstone v Dunfermline Athletic
St Mirren v Stranraer

Clyde v Greenock Morton
Dumbarton v East Fife
Meadowbank Thistle v Berwick Rangers
Queen of the South v Stenhousemuir

Arbroath v Albion Rovers
Cowdenbeath v Caledonian Thistle
Montrose v Alloa
Queen's Park v East Stirlingshire
Ross County v Forfar Athletic

## Saturday, December 31st, 1994

Aberdeen v Heart of Midlothian
Celtic v Falkirk
Hibernian v Dundee United
Motherwell v Rangers
Partick Thistle v Kilmarnock

Airdrieonians v Dunfermline Athletic
Ayr United v Hamilton Academical
Clydebank v Stranraer
Dundee v St Mirren
Raith Rovers v St Johnstone

Berwick Rangers v Stirling Albion
Brechin City v Clyde
East Fife v Meadowbank Thistle
Greenock Morton v Queen of the South
Stenhousemuir v Dumbarton

Albion Rovers v Ross County
Alloa v Queen's Park
Caledonian Thistle v Montrose
East Stirlingshire v Arbroath
Forfar Athletic v Cowdenbeath

## Monday, January 2nd, 1995

Dundee United v Aberdeen
Falkirk v Partick Thistle
Heart of Midlothian v Hibernian
Kilmarnock v Motherwell
Rangers v Celtic

Dunfermline Athletic v Raith Rovers
Hamilton Academical v Airdrieonians
St Johnstone v Dundee
St Mirren v Clydebank
Stranraer v Ayr United

Berwick Rangers v Queen of the South
Clyde v Stirling Albion
Dumbarton v Greenock Morton
East Fife v Brechin City
Meadowbank Thistle v Stenhousemuir

Alloa v East Stirlingshire
Arbroath v Forfar Athletic
Montrose v Cowdenbeath
Queen's Park v Albion Rovers
Ross County v Caledonian Thistle

**Saturday, January 7th, 1995**

Aberdeen v Falkirk
Celtic v Dundee United
Hibernian v Kilmarnock
Motherwell v Heart of Midlothian
Partick Thistle v Rangers

Airdrieonians v St Johnstone
Ayr United v St Mirren
Clydebank v Dunfermline Athletic
Dundee v Stranraer
Raith Rovers v Hamilton Academical

**Saturday, January 14th, 1995**

Aberdeen v Partick Thistle
Celtic v Kilmarnock
Falkirk v Rangers
Heart of Midlothian v Dundee United
Motherwell v Hibernian

Ayr United v St Johnstone
Dundee v Airdrieonians
Hamilton Academical v Stranraer
Raith Rovers v Clydebank
St Mirren v Dunfermline Athletic

Brechin City v Meadowbank Thistle
Greenock Morton v Berwick Rangers
Queen of the South v Dumbarton
Stenhousemuir v Clyde
Stirling Albion v East Fife

Albion Rovers v Alloa
Caledonian Thistle v Arbroath
Cowdenbeath v Ross County
East Stirlingshire v Montrose
Forfar Athletic v Queen's Park

**Saturday, January 21st, 1995**

Dundee United v Motherwell
Hibernian v Aberdeen
Kilmarnock v Falkirk
Partick Thistle v Celtic
Rangers v Heart of Midlothian

Clydebank v Dundee
Dunfermline Athletic v Hamilton Academical
St Johnstone v St Mirren
Stranraer v Raith Rovers

Brechin City v Berwick Rangers
Clyde v Queen of the South
Dumbarton v Stirling Albion
East Fife v Stenhousemuir
Meadowbank Thistle v Greenock Morton

Albion Rovers v Montrose
Alloa v Forfar Athletic
Arbroath v Cowdenbeath
Queen's Park v Caledonian Thistle
Ross County v East Stirlingshire

**Wednesday, January 25th, 1995**

Airdrieonians v Ayr United

**Saturday, February 4th, 1995**

Falkirk v Heart of Midlothian
Hibernian v Partick Thistle
Kilmarnock v Aberdeen
Motherwell v Celtic
Rangers v Dundee United

Clydebank v St Johnstone
Dundee v Dunfermline Athletic
Hamilton Academical v St Mirren
Raith Rovers v Ayr United
Stranraer v Airdrieonians

Berwick Rangers v Dumbarton
East Fife v Clyde
Greenock Morton v Brechin City
Meadowbank Thistle v Queen of the South
Stenhousemuir v Stirling Albion

Alloa v Arbroath
Caledonian Thistle v Forfar Athletic
East Stirlingshire v Albion Rovers
Montrose v Ross County
Queen's Park v Cowdenbeath

**Wednesday, February 8th, 1995**

Airdrieonians v Clydebank

**Saturday, February 11th, 1995**

Aberdeen v Rangers
Celtic v Hibernian
Dundee United v Falkirk
Heart of Midlothian v Kilmarnock
Partick Thistle v Motherwell

Ayr United v Dundee
Dunfermline Athletic v Stranraer
St Johnstone v Hamilton Academical
St Mirren v Raith Rovers

Brechin City v Stenhousemuir
Clyde v Berwick Rangers
Dumbarton v Meadowbank Thistle
Queen of the South v East Fife
Stirling Albion v Greenock Morton

Albion Rovers v Caledonian Thistle
Arbroath v Queen's Park
Cowdenbeath v East Stirlingshire
Forfar Athletic v Montrose
Ross County v Alloa

**Saturday, February 18th, 1995**

Dumbarton v Clyde
East Fife v Greenock Morton
Meadowbank Thistle v Stirling Albion
Queen of the South v Brechin City
Stenhousemuir v Berwick Rangers

Albion Rovers v Cowdenbeath
Alloa v Caledonian Thistle
East Stirlingshire v Forfar Athletic
Montrose v Queen's Park
Ross County v Arbroath

**Saturday, February 25th, 1995**

Aberdeen v Motherwell
Dundee United v Partick Thistle
Falkirk v Hibernian
Heart of Midlothian v Celtic
Rangers v Kilmarnock

Ayr United v Dunfermline Athletic
Hamilton Academical v Clydebank
Raith Rovers v Dundee
St Johnstone v Stranraer
St Mirren v Airdrieonians

Berwick Rangers v East Fife
Brechin City v Dumbarton
Clyde v Meadowbank Thistle
Greenock Morton v Stenhousemuir
Stirling Albion v Queen of the South

Arbroath v Montrose
Caledonian Thistle v East Stirlingshire
Cowdenbeath v Alloa
Forfar Athletic v Albion Rovers
Queen's Park v Ross County

**Saturday, March 4th, 1995**

Celtic v Aberdeen
Hibernian v Rangers
Kilmarnock v Dundee United
Motherwell v Falkirk
Partick Thistle v Heart of Midlothian

Airdrieonians v Raith Rovers
Clydebank v Ayr United
Dundee v Hamilton Academical
Dunfermline Athletic v St Johnstone
Stranraer v St Mirren

Berwick Rangers v Meadowbank Thistle
Brechin City v Stirling Albion
East Fife v Dumbarton
Greenock Morton v Clyde
Stenhousemuir v Queen of the South

Albion Rovers v Arbroath
Alloa v Montrose
Caledonian Thistle v Cowdenbeath
East Stirlingshire v Queen's Park
Forfar Athletic v Ross County

**Saturday, March 11th, 1995**

Clyde v Brechin City
Dumbarton v Stenhousemuir
Meadowbank Thistle v East Fife
Queen of the South v Greenock Morton
Stirling Albion v Berwick Rangers

Arbroath v East Stirlingshire
Cowdenbeath v Forfar Athletic
Montrose v Caledonian Thistle
Queen's Park v Alloa
Ross County v Albion Rovers

**Saturday, March 18th, 1995**

Aberdeen v Hibernian
Celtic v Partick Thistle
Falkirk v Kilmarnock
Heart of Midlothian v Rangers
Motherwell v Dundee United

Ayr United v Airdrieonians
Dundee v Clydebank
Hamilton Academical v Dunfermline Athletic
Raith Rovers v Stranraer
St Mirren v St Johnstone

Brechin City v Greenock Morton
Clyde v East Fife
Dumbarton v Berwick Rangers
Queen of the South v Meadowbank Thistle
Stirling Albion v Stenhousemuir

Albion Rovers v East Stirlingshire
Arbroath v Alloa
Cowdenbeath v Queen's Park
Forfar Athletic v Caledonian Thistle
Ross County v Montrose

**Tuesday, March 21st, 1995**

Dundee United v Heart of Midlothian
Hibernian v Motherwell
Kilmarnock v Celtic
Rangers v Falkirk

**Wednesday, March 22nd, 1995**

Partick Thistle v Aberdeen

**Saturday, March 25th, 1995**

Airdrieonians v Dundee
Clydebank v Raith Rovers
Dunfermline Athletic v St Mirren
St Johnstone v Ayr United
Stranraer v Hamilton Academical

Berwick Rangers v Clyde
East Fife v Queen of the South
Greenock Morton v Stirling Albion
Meadowbank Thistle v Dumbarton
Stenhousemuir v Brechin City

Alloa v Ross County
Caledonian Thistle v Albion Rovers
East Stirlingshire v Cowdenbeath
Montrose v Forfar Athletic
Queen's Park v Arbroath

**Saturday, April 1st, 1995**

Aberdeen v Kilmarnock
Celtic v Motherwell
Dundee United v Rangers
Heart of Midlothian v Falkirk
Partick Thistle v Hibernian

Airdrieonians v Stranraer
Ayr United v Raith Rovers
Dunfermline Athletic v Dundee
St Johnstone v Clydebank
St Mirren v Hamilton Academical

Dumbarton v Brechin City
East Fife v Berwick Rangers
Meadowbank Thistle v Clyde
Queen of the South v Stirling Albion
Stenhousemuir v Greenock Morton

Albion Rovers v Forfar Athletic
Alloa v Cowdenbeath
East Stirlingshire v Caledonian Thistle
Montrose v Arbroath
Ross County v Queen's Park

**Saturday, April 8th, 1995**

Falkirk v Dundee United
Hibernian v Celtic
Kilmarnock v Heart of Midlothian
Motherwell v Partick Thistle
Rangers v Aberdeen

Clydebank v Airdrieonians
Dundee v Ayr United
Hamilton Academical v St Johnstone
Raith Rovers v St Mirren
Stranraer v Dunfermline Athletic

Berwick Rangers v Stenhousemuir
Brechin City v Queen of the South
Clyde v Dumbarton
Greenock Morton v East Fife
Stirling Albion v Meadowbank Thistle

Arbroath v Ross County
Caledonian Thistle v Alloa
Cowdenbeath v Albion Rovers
Forfar Athletic v East Stirlingshire
Queen's Park v Montrose

**Saturday, April 15th, 1995**

Aberdeen v Celtic
Dundee United v Kilmarnock
Falkirk v Motherwell
Heart of Midlothian v Partick Thistle
Rangers v Hibernian

Ayr United v Clydebank
Hamilton Academical v Dundee
Raith Rovers v Airdrieonians
St Johnstone v Dunfermline Athletic
St Mirren v Stranraer

Clyde v Greenock Morton
Dumbarton v East Fife
Meadowbank Thistle v Berwick Rangers
Queen of the South v Stenhousemuir
Stirling Albion v Brechin City

Arbroath v Albion Rovers
Cowdenbeath v Caledonian Thistle
Montrose v Alloa
Queen's Park v East Stirlingshire
Ross County v Forfar Athletic

**Tuesday, April 18th, 1995**

Hibernian v Falkirk
Kilmarnock v Rangers
Motherwell v Aberdeen
Partick Thistle v Dundee United

**Wednesday, April 19th, 1995**

Celtic v Heart of Midlothian

**Saturday, April 22nd, 1995**

Airdrieonians v St Mirren
Clydebank v Hamilton Academical
Dundee v Raith Rovers
Dunfermline Athletic v Ayr United
Stranraer v St Johnstone

Berwick Rangers v Stirling Albion
Brechin City v Clyde
East Fife v Meadowbank Thistle
Greenock Morton v Queen of the South
Stenhousemuir v Dumbarton

Albion Rovers v Ross County
Alloa v Queen's Park
Caledonian Thistle v Montrose
East Stirlingshire v Arbroath
Forfar Athletic v Cowdenbeath

**Saturday, April 29th, 1995**

Dundee United v Hibernian
Falkirk v Celtic
Heart of Midlothian v Aberdeen
Kilmarnock v Partick Thistle
Rangers v Motherwell

Dunfermline Athletic v Airdrieonians
Hamilton Academical v Ayr United
St Johnstone v Raith Rovers
St Mirren v Dundee
Stranraer v Clydebank

Berwick Rangers v Greenock Morton
Clyde v Stenhousemuir
Dumbarton v Queen of the South
East Fife v Stirling Albion
Meadowbank Thistle v Brechin City

Alloa v Albion Rovers
Arbroath v Caledonian Thistle
Montrose v East Stirlingshire
Queen's Park v Forfar Athletic
Ross County v Cowdenbeath

**Saturday, May 6th, 1995**

Aberdeen v Dundee United
Celtic v Rangers
Hibernian v Heart of Midlothian
Motherwell v Kilmarnock
Partick Thistle v Falkirk

Airdrieonians v Hamilton Academical
Ayr United v Stranraer
Clydebank v St Mirren
Dundee v St Johnstone
Raith Rovers v Dunfermline Athletic

Brechin City v East Fife
Greenock Morton v Dumbarton
Queen of the South v Berwick Rangers
Stenhousemuir v Meadowbank Thistle
Stirling Albion v Clyde

Albion Rovers v Queen's Park
Caledonian Thistle v Ross County
Cowdenbeath v Montrose
East Stirlingshire v Alloa
Forfar Athletic v Arbroath

**Saturday, May 13th, 1995**

Dundee United v Celtic
Falkirk v Aberdeen
Heart of Midlothian v Motherwell
Kilmarnock v Hibernian
Rangers v Partick Thistle

Dunfermline Athletic v Clydebank
Hamilton Academical v Raith Rovers
St Johnstone v Airdrieonians
St Mirren v Ayr United
Stranraer v Dundee

Berwick Rangers v Brechin City
Meadowbank Thistle v Greenock Morton
Queen of the South v Clyde
Stenhousemuir v East Fife
Stirling Albion v Dumbarton

Caledonian Thistle v Queen's Park
Cowdenbeath v Arbroath
East Stirlingshire v Ross County
Forfar Athletic v Alloa
Montrose v Albion Rovers

# Careers Of Scottish League Managers

## Premier Division

**■ ABERDEEN**
WILLIE MILLER, M.B.E.
*Player*: Aberdeen and Scotland
*Manager*: Aberdeen

**■ CELTIC**
TOMMY BURNS
*Player*: Celtic, Kilmarnock, Scotland
*Manager*: Kilmarnock, Celtic

**■ DUNDEE UNITED**
IVAN GOLAC
*Player*: Partizan Belgrade, Southampton, Bournemouth, Portsmouth, Manchester City, Yugoslavia
*Manager*: Macva, Partizan Belgrade (both Yugoslavia), Torquay, Macva, Dundee United

**■ FALKIRK**
JIM JEFFERIES
*Player*: Heart of Midlothian, Berwick Rangers
*Manager*: Berwick Rangers, Falkirk

**■ HEART OF MIDLOTHIAN**
TOMMY McLEAN
*Player*: Kilmarnock, Rangers, Scotland
*Manager*: Greenock Morton, Motherwell, Heart of Midlothian

**■ HIBERNIAN**
ALEX MILLER
*Player*: Rangers, Morton
*Manager*: Morton, St. Mirren, Hibernian

**■ KILMARNOCK**
Alex Totten
*Player*: Liverpool, Dundee, Dunfermline Athletic, Falkirk, Queen of the South, Alloa
*Manager*: Alloa, Falkirk, Dumbarton, St. Johnstone, East Fife, Kilmarnock

**■ MOTHERWELL**
ALEX McLEISH
*Player*: Aberdeen, Motherwell
*Manager*: Motherwell

**■ PARTICK THISTLE**
JOHN LAMBIE
*Player*: Falkirk, St. Johnstone
*Manager*: Hamilton Academical, Partick Thistle, Hamilton Academical, Partick Thistle

**■ RANGERS**
WALTER SMITH
*Player*: Dundee United, Dumbarton, Dundee United
*Manager*: Rangers

## First Division

**■ AIRDRIEONIANS**
ALEX MACDONALD
*Player*: St. Johnstone, Rangers, Heart of Midlothian, Scotland
*Manager*: Heart of Midlothian, Airdrieonians

**■ AYR UNITED**
SIMON STAINROD
*Player*: Sheffield United, Oldham Athletic, Queen's Park Rangers, Sheffield Wednesday, Aston Villa, Stoke City, Strasbourg, Rouen, Falkirk, Dundee
*Manager*: Dundee, Ayr United

**■ CLYDEBANK**
BRIAN WRIGHT
*Player*: Hamilton Academical, Motherwell, Clydebank, Partick Thistle, Clydebank, Queen of the South, Clydebank
*Coach*: Clydebank

**■ DUNDEE**
JAMES DUFFY
*Player*: Celtic, Greenock Morton, Dundee, Partick Thistle, Dundee
*Manager*: Falkirk, Dundee

**■ DUNFERMLINE ATHLETIC**
BERT PATON
*Player*: Leeds United, Dunfermline Athletic
*Manager*: Cowdenbeath, Raith Rovers, Dunfermline Athletic

**■ HAMILTON ACADEMICAL**
IAIN MUNRO
*Player*: St. Mirren, Hibernian, Rangers, St. Mirren, Stoke City, Sunderland, Dundee United, Hibernian, Scotland
*Manager*: Dunfermline Athletic, Dundee, Hamilton Academical

**■ RAITH ROVERS**
JIMMY NICHOLL
*Player*: Manchester United, Toronto Blizzards, Sunderland, West Bromwich Albion, Rangers (twice), Dunfermline Athletic, Raith Rovers, Northern Ireland
*Manager*: Raith Rovers

**■ ST. JOHNSTONE**
PAUL STURROCK
*Player*: Dundee United
*Manager*: St. Johnstone

**■ ST. MIRREN**
JIMMY BONE
*Player*: Partick Thistle, Norwich City, Sheffield United, Celtic, Arbroath, St. Mirren, Hong Kong Rangers, Heart of Midlothian, Arbroath, Scotland
*Manager*: Arbroath, Airdrieonians, Power Dynamos (Zambia), St. Mirren

**■ STRANRAER**
ALEX McANESPIE
*Player*: Ayr United
*Manager*: Stranraer

## Second Division

**■ BERWICK RANGERS**
THOMAS HENDRIE
*Player*: Meadowbank Thistle, Berwick Rangers
*Manager*: Berwick Rangers

**■ BRECHIN CITY**
JOHN YOUNG
*Player*: St. Mirren, Brechin City, Arbroath
*Manager*: Brechin City

**■ CLYDE**
ALEX SMITH
*Player*: Stirling Albion, East Stirlingshire, Albion Rovers, Stenhousemuir
*Manager*: Stenhousemuir, Stirling Albion, St. Mirren, Aberdeen, Clyde

**■ DUMBARTON**
MURDO MACLEOD
*Player*: Dumbarton, Celtic, Borussia Dortmund (Germany), Hibernian, Dumbarton, Scotland
*Manager*: Dumbarton

**■ EAST FIFE**
STEVEN ARCHIBALD
*Player*: East Stirlingshire, Clyde (twice), Aberdeen, Tottenham Hotspur, Barcelona, Blackburn Rovers, Hibernian, Espanol, St. Mirren, Reading, Fulham, Scotland.
*Manager*: East Fife

**■ GREENOCK MORTON**
ALLAN McGRAW
*Player*: Greenock Morton, Hibernian, Linfield (Northern Ireland)
*Manager*: Greenock Morton

**■ MEADOWBANK THISTLE**
MICHAEL LAWSON
*Player*: Stirling Albion, St. Johnstone, Raith Rovers, Berwick Rangers, Meadowbank Thistle
*Manager*: Arbroath, Meadowbank Thistle

**■ QUEEN OF THE SOUTH**
BILLY McLAREN
*Player*: Queen of the South (twice), Greenock Morton (twice), East Fife, Cowdenbeath, Dunfermline Athletic, Hibernian, Partick Thistle
*Manager*: Queen of the South, Hamilton Academical, Albion Rovers, Queen of the South

**■ STENHOUSEMUIR**
TERRY CHRISTIE
*Player*: Dundee, Raith Rovers, Stirling Albion
*Manager*: Meadowbank Thistle, Stenhousemuir

**■ STIRLING ALBION**
KEVIN DRINKELL
*Player*: Grimsby Town, Norwich City, Rangers, Coventry City, Falkirk, Stirling Albion
*Manager*: Stirling Albion

## Third Division

**■ ALBION ROVERS**
THOMAS SPENCE
*Player*: Stirling Albion, Clydebank, Clyde, Kilmarnock, East Fife, Albion Rovers
*Manager*: Albion Rovers

**■ ALLOA**
BILLY LAMONT
*Player*: Albion Rovers, Hamilton Academical
*Manager*: East Stirlingshire, Falkirk, Partick Thistle, Falkirk, Dumbarton, Alloa

**■ ARBROATH**
GEORGE MACKIE
*Player*: Dundee, Partick Thistle, Odense 1909 (Denmark), Dunfermline Athletic, Albion Rovers, Brechin City, Arbroath
*Manager*: Arbroath

**■ CALEDONIAN THISTLE**
SERGEI BALTACHA
*Player*: Dinamo Kiev (USSR), Ipswich Town, St. Johnstone, Caledonian, Caledonian Thistle, USSR
*Manager*: Caledonian, Caledonian Thistle

**■ COWDENBEATH**
PAT DOLAN
*Player*: Did Not Play at Senior Level
*Manager*: Cowdenbeath

**■ EAST STIRLINGSHIRE**
BILLY LITTLE
*Player*: Aberdeen, Falkirk, Stirling Albion, East Stirlingshire
*Manager*: Falkirk, Queen of the South, East Stirlingshire (twice)

**■ FORFAR ATHLETIC**
TOM CAMPBELL
*Player*: Did Not Play at Senior Level
*Manager*: Forfar Athletic

**■ MONTROSE**
JOHN HOLT
*Player*: Dundee United, Dunfermline Athletic, Dundee, Forfar Athletic, Montrose
*Manager*: Montrose

**■ QUEEN'S PARK**
EDDIE HUNTER
*Player*: Queen's Park
*Coach*: Queen's Park

**■ ROSS COUNTY**
BOBBY WILSON
*Player*: Dundee, Cowdenbeath
*Manager*: Keith, Raith Rovers, Ross County

*INFORMATION COMPILED BY*
JIM JEFFREY